UTOPIAS AND UTOPIANS

An Historical Dictionary

Richard C. S. Trahair

Greenwood Press
Westport, Connecticut

Library of Congress Cataloging-in-Publication Data

Trahair, R.C.S.
    Utopias and Utopians : an historical dictionary / Richard C. S.
Trahair.
        p.   cm.
    Includes bibliographical references and index.
    ISBN 0–313–29465–8 (alk. paper)
    1. Utopias—History—Dictionaries.   2. Utopian socialism—History—
Dictionaries.   3. Socialists—Biography—Dictionaries.   I. Title.
HX626.T73   1999
321'.07'09—dc21   98–28286

British Library Cataloguing in Publication Data is available.

Library of Congress Catalog Card Number: 98–28286
ISBN: 0–313–29465–8

First published in 1999

Greenwood Press, 88 Post Road West, Westport, CT 06881
An imprint of Greenwood Publishing Group, Inc.
www.greenwood.com

Printed in the United States of America

The paper used in this book complies with the
Permanent Paper Standard issued by the National
Information Standards Organization (Z39.48–1984).

10 9 8 7 6 5 4 3 2 1

CONTENTS

ACKNOWLEDGMENTS

Many people helped with this work. From the United States and Canada we had valuable advice from Jeff Gorbski, Hune Margulies, Steven Brown, Steve Burgess, George Lombard, Michael Gardner, and Alan Weisman. In Australia we are indebted to Isobel Mouthino for patiently translating European texts, and for valuable comments and contributions we thank Allan Kellehear, Peter Beilharz, Ken Dempsey, Marion Glanville, Rowan Ireland, and Tom Weber. In particular we thank Trevor Hogan for his help with the English material. At the Borchardt Library we were fortunate to have the guidance of Margot Hyslop, Eva Fisch, Val Forbes, Julie Marshall, and their helpers. Funds for the work came from La Trobe University's School of Social Sciences, 1995–1996. I am grateful to the office staff in the Department of Sociology and especially to Mrs. Heather Eather for typing much of the manuscript.

For several years Beatrice Meadowcroft worked with us on reference studies related to this dictionary. Her search for suitable utopias and utopians was outstanding, and we talked often about the limits that the work faced and the illusions that it engendered. Her advice and tireless efforts contributed enormously to this work. Also we thank Anitra Nelson, who helped find and decide on many cases for the book, and we regret we had to leave some out for lack of space. Finally, we are most grateful, indeed, to Alexandra Eather for her diligent and tenacious hunt for details that we had thought would be impossible to find.

Errors of interpretation and fact may emerge, and we would be pleased to know them and will acknowledge their source in the hope that the work can be improved.

INTRODUCTION

This dictionary and sourcebook provides illustrations of utopian ventures and the people who undertook them. Utopian venture is defined broadly and is not closely related to one academic discipline but to the field of utopian studies. Illustrations are taken from a range of human activities, policies, programs, and schemes; they include abodes of love, anarchy, anthropology, architecture, art colonies, brotherhoods, business, caravans, colonial schemes, communes, conservation and environmental groups, craft organizations, egalitarians, escapists, expositions, desert communities, fantastic entertainments, farms, health schemes, an island paradise, kingdoms of heaven, kindergartens, an ideal language, labor villages, management, national policies, novels, peace initiatives, personal havens and residences, political campaigns, psychological havens, racist settlements, religions, religious treatises, residential settlements, sects, self-help and self-sufficient economies, schools, spiritualism, suicide cults, sects, theories of utopian ideals, urban developments, welfare policies, worker's settlements, and wildly unrealizable schemes. The theme centers on a utopian venture, an activity aiming to make the world a better place.

The book has close to 620 entries; about half are short descriptions of utopian ventures, and the rest are brief biographical sketches of individuals who were involved. Each entry is followed by a list of sources that the reader can find in a good public library or with the guidance of a reference librarian. Many entries concern utopias long gone; others are recent; a few are on the Internet.

The entries were chosen for teachers and students in the humanities and social sciences, for scholars who are thinking of utopias and utopians as a subject of inquiry, and for readers who are curious about individuals who wanted to improve the world and what they did about it.

The choice of utopian ventures was based on their illustrative value and origin. The dictionary is not comprehensive or representative. It shows, first, that most human efforts have produced a utopian venture, and second, that utopian

ventures are found in many countries and nations. The United States has produced the best-documented research on its utopias.[1] In the following entries are
utopias in Africa, Alaska, Arabia, Australia, Bangladesh, Brazil, Canada, Colombia, England, France, Germany, India, Ireland, Israel, Japan, Malaysia, Mexico, the Netherlands, New Zealand, Paraguay, Scotland, the South Pacific, Spain,
Switzerland, Thailand, and Wales.

What are utopias and utopian ventures? Utopias begin with the hope that
world can be made a better place, largely because of the unhappiness of life in
a world that needs serious improvement. The term has two origins from the
Greek: "eu topia," meaning "good place," and "ou topia," meaning "no
place." The German is "Weisnichtwo," and the Scottish is "Kennaquhair."
The concept of utopia is attributed to Sir Thomas More (1478–1535), whose
Utopia (1516; trans. English, 1551) placed him among the great Renaissance
humanists. In his work the term refers to a nonexistent and happy or ideal place.

The task of defining utopia presents three orientations to a difficult problem.[2]
First, deciding on a final definition attracts so many problems for practicing
utopians that they are bound to argue that utopias should enjoy an infinity of
connotations and that in practice it is necessary merely to settle on a few features
of the future that matter to only the individuals involved. Another view on
defining utopias is that if we come to a single, lasting definition, as once we
did when the word came to mean a hare-brained scheme with impossible goals,
suited only to wool-gathering crackpots, then utopian thought will evaporate,
and utopian ventures will be, at worst, banned or, at best, considered bizarre
and replaced by a belief that we can make the world a better place with politically correct means. The third view assumes we need utopian thought and
reliable, empirical knowledge of utopian ventures and of the people who undertake them to take the next step in making the world a better place. This is
the viewpoint upheld by this book.

What are the characteristics of utopian ventures? The following assumptions
about social relations and work for individuals emerge from the illustrations in
this book: the aim of humankind is to realize what it is capable of; this is best
done in a society; humankind can realize its potential on collectively owned
property because it eliminates the distinction between individuals based on
wealth, power, and family; with these distinctions go the destructive and aggressive feelings of envy, jealousy, covetousness, and pride; all work for the
community should be done only by members of the community, and hired labor
should be banned so as to prevent exploitation of labor; all members should
reside and work on the communal property and cooperatively produce as much
as needed. Such characteristics seem necessary for a utopia to survive. The
realization of human potential through collective ownership, reduction in aggression, and commitment to communal residence and to work for the community are at the core of utopian ventures. Humans differ in their abilities,
interests, and needs; conflict arises between them over matters other than residence, work, and property. Values are sought to make sense of the conflict and

provide orderly conflict resolution. For this some people turn to religion, science, education, art, or lawmaking; others choose community expansion and engagements with the outside world. Illustrations in this book show utopian venturers turning inward to realize human potential or outward to enhance the community's potential.

What trends have there been in utopian ventures?[3] Utopian ventures have been studied more thoroughly in the United States than elsewhere, and many have set an example for the reorganization of society. This goal emerged from the thoughts of Robert Owen (1771–1858), Charles Fourier (1772–1837) and Étienne Cabet (1788–1856), who presented practical steps for starting a new society, a much better place to live than industrialized Britain or the political chaos of Europe in the early nineteenth century. In the United States the reorganization began in the mid-1820s, reached a peak fifteen years later, benefited from vigorous immigration in the 1850s, and failed after the American Civil War (1861–1865). The utopians began by following the principles of collective ownership and commitment to communal residence and work, but in time divisions among them emerged, the communities split, and great differences arose between leaders and followers. Nevertheless, utopia did not lose its principles of collective ownership and communal residence and work. Reasons for upholding the principles began to shift their locus of justification to new religions and governance systems: anarchism; spiritualism; free love or celibacy; destruction of machinery or advancement of technology; socialism; and nationalism. Also they shifted their activities and pattern of survival; while some utopias proselytized, others simply set a good example; while some grew to a point where they destroyed their original form, others expanded dynamically and thoughtfully and reproduced themselves with slight variations.

Before the search for utopias in the United States, utopian ventures were not so dynamic. For a thousand years before the French Revolution (1789–1799) many thinkers imagined a better place for humankind. In early utopian literature the most frequently mentioned are Plato's *The Republic* (c. 350 B.C.), Cicero's *De Republica* (51 B.C.), Aurelius Augustinus' *The City of God* (426), Dante's *De Monarchia* (c. 1309/1313), Thomas More's *Utopia* (1516), Tommaso Campanella's *The City of the Sun* (1602), Francis Bacon's *New Atlantis* (1627), and James Harrington's *Commonwealth of Oceana* (1656). Many more appear in Sargent's (1979, 1988) invaluable catalogs and in Cleay's (1994) research on the British Enlightenment and modern utopias.[4] From a psychodynamic viewpoint these literary works, foundations of utopian thought, offer a better world where all is calm and happiness. By contrast the nineteenth-century utopias in the United States offered a new society with a sincere commitment to different forms of Christianity and paternalistic socialism and, later, the early forms of modern social democracy.

The Enlightenment gave humanitarian optimism to thoughts on the future, an image of a national self, a superior race, and a short, clear path to heaven on earth through art, rational knowledge, and freedom. The preferred method was rapid, dramatic change, aided by new technology and a commitment to ethical associationism. The new society would be populated with vital, energetic, religious, practical men and women. In this new world dreary work would attract great rewards, toil would be accompanied by exciting intellectual exercises, sexual passions would be freed, and education for realizing human potential would be available to all.

Today utopian thought centers on philosophical and psychological states and issues; the relation between humankind and the physical environment; equal rights of women; rights of children; human rights generally; educational reform; psychological welfare; pursuit of human excellence; competition over cooperation, and vice versa; smashing capitalism or communism; and the eradication of war. The illustrations in this book reflect these stages of utopian action and thought.

One distressing modern feature of utopian thought and practice has been given close attention recently. Some large utopian ventures have had dreadful consequences: Nazi Germany (1933–1945) and Stalinist Russia (1924–1989). Both promised unlimited human potential and the expansion of community influence. Many leaders from other countries saw both as enemies of poverty, promising individual growth through noble social experiments, and as astounding advances on established Western society. They were false promises made by terrifying regimes. To these utopian ventures were given the term ''dystopia'': an ideal and evil place.

The term was coined in a humorous aside by John Stuart Mill (1806–1873) in a speech in the British House of Commons, 12 March 1868, during a debate on the problem of land-ownership in Ireland. Dystopia did not become a valuable idea in utopian thought until after World War II, when attention was riveted on the horrors of dictatorship and totalitarian corruption of power in Nazi Germany and Stalinist Russia. Earlier novels had drawn terrifying images of dystopia, for example, *We* and *Brave New World*, but in none so dramatically as George Orwell's *Nineteen Eighty-Four*.[5] Novels of Margaret Atwood (b. 1939), Aldous Leonard Huxley (1894–1963), Franz Kafka (1883–1924), George Orwell (1903–1950), and Evgeny Ivanovich Zamyatin (1884–1937) were chosen to illustrate the workings of the dystopian world.

The fact that utopian venturers can go wrong or last an unexpectedly short time raises the question, What makes for success in utopia? Several scholars have studied this question. They show, first, that we need to establish criteria for success. Has the utopia achieved its original goals, and have its goals changed for the good? How could we answer? Ask the members of the venture? What if many do not agree on the original goals and feel cheated as new goals emerge? Perhaps we should ask an outsider? If the venture assumes the Second Coming or Judgment Day, and it does not come on time, has the venture failed? Second, we could ask, How effective is the venture overall? This would require much professional study, comparison with other ventures, sophisticated and guarded detachment from the observer, and professional training in participant observation. Two illustrations appear in this book, one in England and the other in Spain. Third, how long did the utopia last? This criterion would not be relevant to utopias with a short-term goal. Other criteria that would also vary in relevance are popularity of the utopia, power, and capacity to accrue wealth. Fourth, to what extent do members feel they belong to a utopia of like-minded fellows? In a successful venture should we expect utopians to believe every member shared the community's goals, that the utopia worked well within its social and economic framework, and that formal and informal groupings within it would always enrich members? Some evidence shows large communities with a widely shared ideology that frequently reminds members that their own interests are second to the utopia's goals, tend to be larger, last longer, and exhibit a high social cohesiveness. Fifth, does the utopian venture influence life outside its boundaries? It is curious to note that some of the ventures in this book suffered for the influence they had. Finally, do the members experience personal growth and believe they are better for being part of the utopian venture? These questions are relevant to success in a utopian venture, but they are sometimes contradictory and cannot be put directly to every case.[6]

In a study of such contradictions Kesten (1993) turned to the feelings that members of utopian communities had recalled in daily life. The informants remembered both success and failure and the feeling that the past was both pleasant and happy. Some recalled how successfully their children had been given a moral and liberal education, while others compared life before they entered the community with experiences in the utopia. They concluded that the utopian experience provided a superior, contented life, a taste of the millennium, lasting friendships, and a feeling of personal unity. Also they felt that these benefits were won through sharing life with others and sacrificing personal interests to pursue otherwise worthwhile activities. On the other hand, some utopians emphasized the personal, instead of the communal, residue of their past. They enjoyed the exhilaration of a life with unique rewards, an Arcadian existence, a dreamy return to paradise, a personal history of poetry and deep, beautiful imagery; they loved to recall the utopian venture for its youthful vigor and freshness and, in one case, for being the romantic setting for finding their love.

Historical, sociological, and personal accounts of the conditions of success for utopian ventures are available, each with its own criteria for success. Harrison (1969) presents a professional historian's study of the circumstances under which Owenite communities emerged in England and rose and fell in nineteenth-century America[7]; in a sociological study Kanter (1973) discusses circumstances that contributed to the longevity of utopian ventures[8]; McCord (1989) provides an anthropological account of life in utopias, many of which are today offering to show visitors their way of life.[9] A more recent account of utopian ventures from the participants' viewpoint is available in Metcalf (1996).[10]

What is the value of utopias and utopians? Answer: to raise questions about the experience of making the world a better place, without being misled into dystopia.

The first question that the utopias and utopians raise in this collection of illustrations centers on equality, equity, fairness, justice, level playing fields, and related ideas. The utopian ventures show that people vary constantly. They differ from time to time, from one situation to another, and within and between themselves. Working for a better world draws attention to the problem of upholding justice when it is important to integrate individual differences with variations in the circumstances of life. In short, utopian ventures have the very useful purpose of reminding utopians of the problems of treating different people equally. In many of the Icarian communities where equality was highly valued, few, if any, women or children experienced it.

Second, utopias invite hopeful visions, imaginative thought, plans, plots, schemes, and blueprints for the future. To become real ventures they require careful thought,[11] but in the beginning they are dramas for players to feel, rehearse, and idealize. From the study of utopias and utopian ventures the reader begins to see the steps to take in moving from the vison to the blueprint, from the blueprint to responsible action, and finally to the irreversible decision to improve the world. On the way appear problems relating to sincerity and shallowness of character, to the truth and deceptions behind the justification for action, and to the unconscious and deliberate misplacement of hope behind the drama that enlivens the reality of a utopia. In short, utopian ventures show that when reality takes hold, God's blueprints can be seen for whose they are.[12]

Third, in everyday life utopias are not real. They are perfect. But the better world that utopians hope and plan for is a real place, not perfectly good but, instead, good enough. Because there are limits to choice in the pursuit of ideals, a utopian venture is useful to help the would-be utopian to decide what is ''good enough'' and to evaluate critically their ventures.[13]

Fourth, one peron's utopian's future may be another's dystopia. Illustrations in this book show this often where a utopian venture begins to split. The breakdown of utopian ventures draws attention to the importance of subjective experience, and illustrations show that patterns of understanding and the motives to be understood vary as the utopian venture dissolves. It appears that utopian venturers become very useful when they require a deep understanding among members as to what motivates them to change their lives.

Finally, utopian ventures and the company of utopians provide an ideal place to explore change, especially to rehabilitate the self, to review how the world has mistreated one, and to start life over. Utopia offers a chance to reconsider the ''if only'' and the ''as if'' features of the individual's life and to ask if ''this is as good as it gets.'' Utopian ventures offer a kind of therapy beyond professional limits and invite imaginative relearning, reforming of social and symbiotic relations with other individuals, groups, communities, and larger collectives. For example, the Civil Resettlement Units in England after World War II gave group therapy for rehabilitation of released prisoners of war under the Nazis. After the units had served their purpose, they closed and later reopened under another name to rehabilitate warriors from a more recent military action. On the California coast, in the late 1960s, similar therapeutic utopias emerged.

No dictionary, encyclopedia, or illustrative catalog can be entirely satisfactory; scholars and well-informed nonprofessionals will be disappointed in this effort for its omissions, eccentric choices, distressing emphases and disagreeable interpretations. This reminds us that until great support is given a board of knowledgeable advisers to employ experts in the field of utopian studies to commission a comprehensive account of attempts to make the world a better place, we shall continue to work with guides, lists, and companions to literature. This book offers support to utopian studies and demands their recognition. Also it intends to encourage, arouse, and inform curiosity about utopias and utopians; the entries illuminate utopias rather than focus on them sharply; they allude to a host of definitions, draw on scholarly and popular sources, and aim to seduce and otherwise persuade the untutored reader to explore them with hope for a better world.

Utopian studies is an interdisciplinary venture. The Society for Utopian Studies was founded in 1975 and is devoted to the study of utopias and utopians in all forms, especially literary and experimental. Members come from many learned specialties, including anthropology, architecture, economics, engineering, gender studies, history, humanities, philosophy, political science, psychology, and sociology. The society publishes *Utopian Studies*, edited by Professor Lyman Tower Sargent, Political Science, University of Missouri, St. Louis, and a newsletter and holds conferences and workshops. Society members subscribe to the "Utopian and utopianism" list on the Internet.[14]

NOTES

1. See, for example, Robert S. Fogarty, 1980, *Dictionary of American Communal History*, Westport, Conn.: Greenwood; Robert S. Fogarty, 1990, *All Things New: American Communes and Utopian Movements 1860–1914*, Chicago: University of Chicago Press; Timothy Miller, 1990, *American Communes 1860–1960*, New York: Garland; Yaacov Oved, 1987, *Two Hundred Years of American Communes*, New Brunswick, N.J.: Transaction Books.

2. Three orientations are not sufficient to examine the concept of utopia fully. For a critical and intelligent examination of the major definitions of utopia, see Ruth Levitas, 1991, *The Concept of Utopia*, Syracuse, N.Y.: Syracuse University Press.

3. For an account of trends in utopian ventures and literature see Krishan Kumar, 1987, *Utopia and Anti-utopia in Modern Times*, Oxford: Basil Blackwell.

4. Lyman Tower Sargent, 1979, *British and American Utopian Literature: 1516–1975*, Boston: G. K. Hall; Lyman Tower Sargent, 1988, *British and American Utopian Literature: 1516–1985: An Annotated Chronological Bibliography*, New York: Garland; Gregory Claeys, ed., 1994, *Utopias of the British Enlightenment*, New York: Cambridge University Press; Gregory Claeys, ed., 1997, *Modern British Utopias, 1700–1850*, 8 vols., London: Pickering and Chatto.

5. M. Keith Booker, 1994, *Dystopian Literature: A Theory and Research Guide*, Westport, Conn.: Greenwood.

6. Jon Wagner, 1995, "Success in Intentional Communities: The Problem of Evaluation," *Communal Studies* 5: 89–100.

7. John F. C. Harrison, 1969, *Robert Owen and the Owenites in Britain and America: Quest for the New Moral World*, New York: Charles Scribner's Sons.

8. Rosabeth Moss Kanter, 1973, *Communes: Creating and Managing the Collective Life*, New York: Harper and Row.

9. William McCord, 1989, *Voyages to Utopia: From Monastery to Commune, the Search for the Perfect Society in Modern times*, New York: W. W. Norton.

10. Bill Metcalf, ed., 1996, *Shared Visions, Shared Lives: Communal Living around the Globe*, Forres, Scotland: Findhorn Press.

11. Fred E. Emery, 1974, *Futures We Are In*, Canberra: Australian National University, Center for Continuing Education.

12. John McKelvie Whitworth, 1975, *God's Blueprints: A Sociological Study of Three Utopian Sects*, London: Routledge and Kegan Paul.

13. For a discussion of how one arrives at what is "good enough" see the writings of Donald W. Winnicott (1896–1971). On limited choice in the pursuit of ideals see Fred E. Emery, 1976, *In Pursuit of Ideals*, Australian National University, Canberra, ACT: Center for Continuing Education; Fred Emery. ed., 1978, *Limits to Choice*, Australian National University, Canberra, ACT: Center for Continuing Education.

14. For example, on the Internet, January 1999, Lyman Tower Sargent noted that he had found a seventeenth-century usage of "dystopia," thus indicating that the term was not coined, as widely believed, by John Stuart Mill in 1868.

UTOPIAS AND UTOPIANS

A

ABBOTT, LEONARD. Leonard Abbott (1878–1953) was born into a New England family and was raised in England, where he went to Uppingham, a noted private school. He returned to the United States in 1898 and was a magazine editor. Strongly influenced by the freethinking American revolutionary Thomas Paine (1737–1809), especially his *The Age of Reason* (1794, 1796), Abbott became a leader of an anarchist organization, the Ferrer Association (1910), in New York City. His upper-class manner and style made him well suited to being an effective public speaker for the organization. In 1915, with others, he moved to Stelton, New Jersey, to help establish a colony and a school. Their policy was to uphold education as the means to social change rather than political activism. Nevertheless, he left the movement. He joined the Works Progress Administration in Washington, D.C., in the 1930s. Shortly before he died, he had lost all hope for a better world. As he saw it, humankind had failed to accept humanitarian ideals and would continue on its way to greater wars and deeper poverty.

See Also Ferrer Colony

Sources:

Fogarty, Robert S. 1980. *Dictionary of American Communal History*. Westport, Conn.: Greenwood Press.
Oved, Yaacov. 1987. *Two Hundred Years of American Communes*. New Brunswick, N.J.: Transaction Books.
Veysey, Laurence. 1973. *The Communal Experience: Anarchist and Mystical Counter-cultures in America*. New York: Harper and Row.

ADDAMS, JANE. Jane Addams (1860–1935) was born in Cedarville, Illinois, graduated from Rockford College, and studied at Women's College, Philadelphia, until her health declined (1882). While recovering in Europe, she studied settlements for the underprivileged and in Chicago opened Hull House (1889). By 1905 she was noted for having financed and had built one of the best places for the education and recreational interests of the working class. She published her achievements in *Twenty Years at Hull House* (1910). She was strongly opposed to war and was a vigorous pacifist, 1915–1934.

See Also Settlement House of Henry Street, Hull House; Wald, Lillian

Source:

Starr, Harris E., ed. 1944. *Dictionary of American Biography.* Supplement 1. New York: Charles Scribner's Sons.

ADELAIDE. In the 1870s the prolific English novelist and travel writer Anthony Trollope (1815–1882) visited Adelaide in the colony of South Australia and described it as a "happy utopia" of free religious conscience, progress, and profit (Whitelock, 1977, p. 4). Adelaide was founded on the principles suggested by Edward Gibbon Wakefield (1796–1862) in his *Letter from Sydney* (London, 1929). Wakefield wanted societies where individuals could pursue their own interests in social harmony. He believed Britain's colonies did not achieve this and argued that because colonial land was too easily available, this destroyed the balance in the colony's economy. To solve this problem, he believed that government had to be sure that the land would sell at the correct price; the price was to be set such that it compelled workers to remain on the land until such time as their hard work and thrift could raise them to reasonable independence. The pioneers of South Australia were middle-class townsfolk, ambitious and radical in religion and politics. They were optimistic, enthusiastic, and greedy. As Pike (1957) concludes, they were motivated to achieve respectability in a social paradise, free of the constraints of the religious domination and aristocratic oppression that they had endured in Britain. Money was raised through a South Australian company that was dominated by a Baptist businessman and shipowner, George Fife Angas (1789–1879), who was the commissioner for the foundation of the colony of South Australia (1834) and emigrated himself to Adelaide (1851). To some observers Wakefield's doctrine appeared to be a rationalization of capitalist exploitation, and South Australia seemed as much a massive real estate gamble as a utopian venture. Between 1830 and 1836 Wakefield worked to have a colony established to illustrate the effectiveness of his theory. Land speculation and mismanagement in both Adelaide and London seriously affected the colony's early days, and it was not long before the British government had to provide financial assistance to the project.

See Also Wakefield, Edward Gibbon

Sources:

Pike, Douglas. 1957. *Paradise of Dissent: South Australia 1829–1857.* 2d ed. 1967. Melbourne: Melbourne University Press.
Roe, Michael. 1977. *A New History of Australia.* Melbourne: William Heinemann.
Trollope, Anthony. 1873. *Australia and New Zealand.* London: Chapman and Hall.

Abridged, edited, and introduced by P. D. Edwards and R. B. Joyce as *Australia*,
1967, Brisbane: Queensland University Press.
Whitelock, Derek. 1977. *Adelaide 1836–1976*. St. Lucia: University of Queensland Press.

AÏVANHOV, OMRAAM MIKHAËL. Omraam Mikhaël Aïvanhov (fl. 1900–
1981) was born in Bulgaria. Early he developed spiritual interests, read philosophy in his teens, and practiced controlled breathing as a meditative technique.
During these exercises he had a revelation that deeply affected the course of his
life. A year later he met and trained with the founder of a spiritual movement
who taught him the value of a community life wherein all people were one.
Such beliefs and teachings, anathema to established religions in Europe for centuries, impressed him. Aïvanhov adhered to them and trained at a university to
be an educator. Shortly before World War II he was chosen to teach his spiritual
beliefs in France. The teachings used "initiatic" knowledge as their claim to
authority. This knowledge emerges from changes to one's character due to meditative study of most religions. The main task is to put spiritual experiences into
action by helping others in collective living, which, in turn, will bring the collective in tune with the cosmos. Such collective synchronicity advances humankind's evolution. Consequently, materialism, self-gratification, and the narrow
selfishness taught in the nuclear family are rejected. Instead, the community
becomes one's family: one's family-based community becomes a member in the
universal community and embraces humankind. Aïvanhov uses a set of trinities
enunciated at three levels to make his ideas cohere. People live on three levels:
principles, laws, and actions. Each level equates, respectively, to the divine, the
spiritual, and the material world and to meaning, content, and form. He uses
three metaphors—one for each level—of Light (organization), Love (fruit), and
Life (observable human acts). He exhorts his followers to work through each
level. The general principle seems to be, first, that one must let the physical
world (Life) emerge, and then Love will be yours; then go through the world
of Light (organization) to see the origin of all life is the Sun. In everyday terms,
Light subsumes science, philosophy, knowledge, learning; Love incorporates
morality, ethics, and religion; Life is evident in movement, creation, and realization. Men and women find each other through love, tenderness, and affection:
sexual love, distinct from divine love, should be controlled and redirected toward
spiritual ends. In a suburb of Paris, Sèvres, he established a community of his
followers and later quit for a rural setting on sixty-five acres in southern France.
   See Also Bonfin, Le Domaine du

Sources:

Aïvanhov, Omraam Mikhaël. 1976. *The Great Universal White Brotherhood*. Fréjus,
      France: Prosveta.
Lejbowicz, Agnès. 1975. *Maître Omraam Mikhaël Aïvanhov and the Teaching of the
      Fraternité Blanche Universelle*. Lyons, France: Prosveta.
Popenoe, Cris, and Oliver Popenoe. 1984. *Seeds of Tomorrow*. San Francisco: Harper
      and Row.
Reynard, Pierre. 1979. *The Prophet*. Fréjus, France: Prosveta.

ALBERTSON, RALPH. Ralph Albertson (1866–1951) was born in Jamesport, New York, and educated at Greenport Academy (1880–1884), and Oberlin College and the college's seminary (1880–1891). He was ordained in 1890, appointed pastor at Penfield and later Springfield, Ohio (1889–1895), and worked in the Congregational Church to advance socialist ideas under the influence of such writers as Henry George (1839–1897), Edward Bellamy (1850–1898), and Leo Tolstoy (1828–1910). After a violent dispute over a local factory strike he resigned from the pulpit and joined a small colony of Christian socialists in North Carolina, the short-lived Willard Co-operative Colony, a temperance association. Although the failure of that venture affected him deeply, it did not deter his personal commitment to cooperative brotherhood in general. In 1896 he founded the Christian Commonwealth Colony, an experiment in nonsectarian Christian communism in Georgia (1896–1900). It closed in bankruptcy. He was the editor of the *Social Gospel* (1897–1900). In 1909 he acquired a farm outside Boston and opened a small community to those who sought to practice brotherly love. Albertson's "the Farm," a collective household, attracted more than thirty residents, who helped him enjoy, as he put it, "fellowship that grows out of many people living together, the yeast of many ideas and opinions, the fair division of what there is to share." But he did not enjoy the responsibilities of maintaining the Farm. It was not self-sufficient. He had to work daily in Boston and had only weekends in the community. Further financial responsibilities eroded his support for the venture, and he had to quit for other enterprises, leaving his wife to struggle with the Farm. He managed a department store in Boston (1910–1912), was the president of Twentieth Century Company, and published *Twentieth Century Magazine*. He published *Fighting without a War* (1920).

See Also Bellamy, Edward; Christian Commonwealth Colony; George, Henry; Tolstoy, Leo

Sources:

Fogarty, Robert S. 1980. *Dictionary of American Communal History*. Westport, Conn.: Greenwood Press.

Oved, Yaacov. 1987. *Two Hundred Years of American Communes*. New Brunswick, N.J.: Transaction Books.

Spann, Edward K. 1989. *Brotherly Tomorrows: Movements for a Cooperative Society in America 1820–1920*. New York: Columbia University Press.

Who Was Who in America. 1963. Vol. 3. Chicago: Marquis.

ALCOTT, AMOS BRONSON. Amos Bronson Alcott (1799–1888) was born near Wolcott, Connecticut. He was the son of Joseph Alcox and Anna Bronson and decided to adopt the name "Alcott" as his surname. Although he had a limited education and began work as a peddler, he became a brilliant, self-taught critic of educational practices, author, mystic, and transcendentalist. He held several teaching positions (1823–1833). He owed his views to Emmanuel Kant

(1724–1804), especially to Kant's *Critique of Reason* (1781). Although he was a capable teacher, often he was rejected when advancing his own educational and religious attitudes. In Boston he opened a small school in 1834, was rightly suspected of encouraging original thought in religious matters, and lost pupils, and his school closed. He moved to Concord in 1840. With Charles Lane (1800–1870) he founded Fruitlands, a short-lived utopian community that advocated vegetarianism and cooperative approaches to farming (1843). He was appointed superintendent of Concord schools in 1859 and introduced some of his finest educational innovations, singing, physiology, and calisthenics, and began parent-teacher meetings. His family's fortunes were salvaged when his daughter Louisa May Alcott (1832–1889) published her best-selling *Little Women* (1868), and in 1879 he established the Concord Summer School of Philosophy and Literature. He wrote poetry and prose and is remembered well for his associations at Brook Farm (1841–1847) with Nathaniel Hawthorne (1804–1864), Ralph Waldo Emerson (1803–1882), and Henry David Thoreau (1817–1862); and for his affirmation of the importance of any phenomenon that went beyond the immediate experience of the senses and relied on perception to form those experiences into an intelligible unity (extreme transcendental idealism).

See Also Alcott House or School and the First Concordium; Brook Farm Colony; Fruitlands Colony; Thoreau, Henry David

Sources:

Albanese, Catherine L. 1988. *The Spirituality of the American Transcendentalists: Selected Writings of Ralph Waldo Emerson, Amos Bronson Alcott, Theodore Parker, and Henry David Thoreau.* Macon, Ga.: Mercer University Press.

Herrnstadt, Richard L. 1969. *The Letters of A. Bronson Alcott.* Ames: Iowa State University Press.

Johnson, Allen. 1927; ed. 1927. *Dictionary of American Biography.* Vol. I. New York: Charles Scribner's Sons.

Oved, Yaacov. 1987. *Two Hundred Years of American Communes.* New Brunswick, N.J.: Transaction Books.

Sears, Clara Endicott, comp. 1975. *Bronson Alcott's Fruitlands with Transcendental Wild Oats by Louisa M. Alcott.* New pref. by William Henry Harrison. Philadelphia: Porcupine Press.

Shepard, Odell. 1937. *Pedlar's progress: The life of Bronson Alcott.* 1968 ed., Westport, Com.: Greenwood Press.

Snodgrass, Mary Ellen. 1995. *Encyclopedia of Utopian Literature.* Santa Barbara, Calif.: ABC-CLIO.

ALCOTT HOUSE OR SCHOOL AND THE FIRST CONCORDIUM. Alcott House was founded in 1838 at Ham Common and followed principles that had been developed for Amos Bronson Alcott's (1799–1888) Temple School, Boston. Boys and girls under twelve years attended the school, and the education was simple and natural. In July and September 1843 Alcott visited the school and its inspiring headmaster and chaired gala meetings at Alcott House on spiritual development, vegetarianism, and the question of the abolition of private property. That year the headmaster accompanied Alcott on his return to Massachusetts. Alcott House was then reorganized as the First Concordium; it was a residence for those who sought the Triune Universal Spirit. It was located two miles from Richmond Park and Hampden Court; its members, Concordists, united under a universal law, the Triune Law of Goodness, Wisdom, and Power. The law was expected to promote divine, human progress; it had originated with an idea from James Pierrepont Greaves (1777–1842), who lived at Alcott House toward the end of his life and whose guidelines for the good life were to put aside doctrines and creeds and seek pure air, exercise, and simple, good food. Tea, coffee, alcohol, and chocolate were banned. So Concordists would rise early, bathe, go for a run, return to a spartan and healthy breakfast and be at work by 9.00 A.M. At lunch the children and the members would have a reading and after the evening meal hear a lecture. The school taught primarily shoemaking, tailoring, carpentry, and gardening. Because simplicity was an important virtue, members wore a plain, brown, neat uniform and practiced vegetarianism. The aim of this school was to teach people to become proselytizers for the cause. To this end the founder toured the country giving lectures and left the impression that Concordists were unpretentious, considerate, and keen to have people know that they wanted to live simply from their printing, making clothes, and footwear. In 1848 the Concordium ended and under new management became an educational asylum for children orphaned by cholera. It was still run on vegetarian principles.

See Also Alcott, Amos Bronson; Greaves, James Pierrepont

Source:

Armytage, Walter H. Green. 1961. *Heavens Below: Utopian Experiments in England 1560–1950*. London: Routledge and Kegan Paul.

ALICE SPRINGS UTOPIA. In central Australia a group of Aboriginal artists live on or nearby 1,000 miles known as ''Utopia,'' 110 miles (270 km) northeast of Alice Springs. With few exceptions they speak Anmatyerre and Alyawarre. Most members are women. In the mid-1970s, after they responded enthusiastically to a series of workshops on batik, the artists began working in nontraditional media, and in the late 1980s they began using canvas and experimenting with nontraditional sculptural forms. Their art displays great freedom of expression when compared with other Aboriginal artists. White Australians, anthropologists, and art historians have only recently accepted evidence that Aboriginal art is the longest continuing art form on earth. It is at least twice as old as the cave paintings of Lascaux. Utopia is an area where the family clans are intent on leading as close to a traditional life as possible. Although missionaries visited their country, no mission stations were established, and the influence of mission work has been slight. The result has been a continuous thread of traditional life. In 1979 the Anmatyerre and Alyawarre made a successful claim for the freehold title of the Utopia Pastoral Lease, thus formally returning the land to its first owners. Utopia is recognized as being a very strong and cohesive community. Its Community Land Council consists of traditional elders who have the respect of the people nearby. This has been essential in coping with the incursion of modern white culture and technology. The council at Utopia forbids the consumption of alcohol in the region, and the people have moved decisively to stop liquor sellers.

Sources:

Boulter, Michael. 1993. *The Art of Utopia: A New Direction in Contemporary Aboriginal Art.* Tortula: Craftsman House.

Gault, Andres. 1990. *Health Survey, Urapunjata Health Service.* Alice Springs, N.T.: Institute for Aboriginal Development.

Schulz, Dennis. 1996. "Torn between Two Worlds." *The Bulletin* (3 December): 88–89.

Shaw, Ken, and Russell Grant. 1983. *Utopia Land Resources: Their Condition, Utilisation and Management.* Alice Springs, N.T.: Range Management Section, Department of Primary Production.

ALLEN, WILLIAM. William Allen (1770–1843) was a wealthy British Quaker chemist, deeply interested in providing education to the poor and in the abolition of slavery. He was much influenced by the Scottish philosopher James Mill (1773–1836) and was one of the original shareholders on Robert Owen's (1771–1858) venture at New Lanark, to which he gave much early praise (1813). He edited and published *The Philanthropist, a Repository of Hints and Suggestions Calculated to Promote the Comfort and Happiness of Man* (1811–1819) and publicized the community of Harmony (1815). After the Napoleonic Wars he traveled widely and, in his tall, dark Quaker hat, met most of Europe's dignitaries and worked to advance the Lancastrian method of education in France. Also he had a personal knowledge of the U.S. West and helped the Separatists to emigrate to the United States and establish themselves. He wrote "On Duty and Pleasure in Cultivating a Benevolent Disposition" in his *The Philanthropist* and was founder in July 1824 of a colony to alleviate the misery of poverty, cultivate wasteland, and build industrial cottages and schools in Lindfield, Sussex. On this work he published *Colonies at Home: Or, the Means for Rendering the Industrious Labourer Independent of Parish relief, and Providing the Poor Population of Ireland by the Cultivation of the Soil* (1826). He was at odds with Robert Owen on the use of schools for religious instruction. Following Allen's adverse report on New Lanark's administration, Owen declared that Allen was a pretentious Quaker, a busy, bustling character who professed friendship while undermining Owen's authority. The dispute centered on Allen's objection to Owen's attempts to curb the teaching of the Scriptures in the schools of Lanark. Allen also objected to the schoolchildren's wearing kilts and dancing. In 1838 Allen published *Analysis of Human Nature* and later wrote a three-volume autobiography, *Life of William Allen* (1846–1847).

See Also Allen's Colony; Harmony Society; Lancastrian school; Owen, Robert

Sources:

Armytage, Walter H. Green. 1961. *Heavens Below: Utopian Experiments in England 1560–1950.* London: Routledge and Kegan Paul.

Dunn, Henry. 1848. *Sketches: Part I Joseph Lancaster and His Contemporaries; Part II William Allen: His Life and Labours.* London: Houlston and Stoneman, Charles Gilpin.

Hall, Helena. 1953. *William Allen: 1770–1843, Member of the Society of Friends.* Sussex: Charles Clark (Haywards Heath).

Taylor, Anne. 1987. *Visions of Harmony: A Study in Nineteenth Century Millenarianism.* Oxford: Clarendon Press.

ALLEN'S COLONY. In July 1824, after observing the poverty in Lindfield Village near Brighton, England, William Allen (1770–1843) established a school for people of any religion. Located opposite the village common, the school had a farm, a printing office, and a workshop. Each family who sent children to the school paid for each child according to the number of children in the family and the regularity of their attendance. As a rule boys were three pennies, girls two pennies, and infants one penny a week. In 1825 John Smith (fl. 1825–1842) visited the village and was so impressed that he bought 100 acres for the colony. He built three-bedroom cottages—each with a kitchen and outhouses—and Allen even took one for himself. The colony was such a success that Allen published *Colonies at Home* (1827), an outline of his colony's organization. Every family had land to cultivate; he recommended that voluntary associations provide capital and inform farmers throughout England that in the home colonies the poor could work and provide for themselves, have their children educated, raise their moral standards and acquire a sense of independence. After nine years the colony was printing its own paper, the *Lindfield Reporter*. As well as a school the colony had cottages, its own bakery, piggeries, and washhouses. Other colonies included Lindfield Colony, John Cropper's Agricultural School and Samuel Gurney's Colony in West Ham; others experimented in Ireland and Devon and at Ballinderry near Lisburn and even in Germany. Allen argued that his "home colonies" were better schemes than Robert Owen's (1771–1858) settlements or utopian ventures overseas as remedies for poverty, because home colonies could be established without the costs of emigration. Also he argued that with a policy of emigration the best people leave the country, and the worst stay behind.

See Also Allen, William; Owen, Robert

Sources:

Armytage, Walter H. Green. 1961. *Heavens Below: Utopian Experiments in England 1560–1950.* London: Routledge and Kegan Paul.

Hall, Helena. 1953. *William Allen 1770–1843: Member of the Society of Friends.* Sussex: Charles Clark (Haywards Heath).

Harrison, John F. C. 1969. *Robert Owen and the Owenites in Britain and America: Quest for the New Moral World.* New York: Charles Scribner's Sons.

Holyoake, G. J. 1906. *A History of Co-operation.* London: T. Fisher Unwin.

ALPHADELPHIA. Alphadelphia Industrial Association was founded by Henry Schetterly (fl. 1844–1848). It was partly established on the ideas of Charles Fourier (1772–1837). It took the form of a joint-stock company in Comstock, Michigan (1844), and lasted until 1848. It was not strictly associationist or Fourierist. Although alcohol was not accepted, its purchase by members was minuted by the directors. It appeared to be organized by a petty bureaucracy that listed all its new members, their occupations, and their personal property in a legalistic and trivial manner. Property was offered by some members in place of buying shares in the company. Women were expected to do the traditional chores of women and work about 40 percent more hours than men; for example, women teachers were to work ten hours each day, while men teachers worked six. There were about 250 members listed, not all residential, about half being agricultural workers or low-skilled; about 30 percent were builders or mechanics. The community had no library, and members were not encouraged to take up artistic or intellectual activities but to work hard in traditional occupations. Nevertheless, their doctor, who worked an eight-hour day, could spend two hours in study. The community declined largely because its members seemed to lack confidence in each other, and its leadership seemed out of touch with the members' needs.

See Also Schetterly, Henry

Sources:

Kersten, Seymour R. 1993. *Utopian Episodes: Daily Life in Experimental Colonies Dedicated to Changing the World.* Syracuse, N.Y.: Syracuse University Press.

Oved, Yaacov. 1987. *Two Hundred Years of American Communes.* New Brunswick, N.J.: Transaction Books.

ALTNEULAND. *Altneuland* (1902) is a novel by Theodor Herzl (1860–1904) that tells of a Prussian nobleman and his Viennese Jewish lawyer, who spend twenty idyllic years on an island. On the way they visit Palestine and find it both decadent and ridden with disease. After twenty years they return to Palestine and find it has been transformed into a utopian land, peopled by many races, all living in harmony. The book attracted many Jews, not the bourgeois Western Jews but the Jewish communities of Eastern Europe that aimed to establish a Jewish state at Erez Israel. The work was part of Herzl's mission to establish Zionism on a practical footing. In 1904 on his death, the World Zionist Organization was established. It founded Jewish national policy, a bank, newspaper, relations with people of influence, and diplomatic connections. This was the beginning of a real Jewish state.

See Also Herzl, Theodor; Zionism

Sources:

Roth, Cecil E., ed. 1971. *Encyclopedia Judaica*. New York: Macmillan.
Stolow, Jeremy. 1997. "Utopia and Geopolitics in Herzl's *Altneuland*." *Utopian Studies*
     8: 55–76.

ALTRURIA. Altruria Colony was founded by Edward Biron Payne (1845–1923) in 1894 at Fountain Grove, Sonoma County, in California. Inspired by William Dean Howells' (1837–1920) novel *A Traveler from Altruria* (1894), the colony was organized by a group of Christian socialists from Berkeley who met in 1894 to plan a cooperative. It became the best known of the Altruist colonies. Most members came from Payne's Unitarian Church, and they chose to settle on 185 acres seven miles north of Santa Rosa. Democratic suffrage, complete equality of community goods, and a label check system were at the center of their constitution. In October 1894 about seven families and bachelors settled on the site. By 1895 they had seven cottages and had begun work on a hotel. They published a weekly paper, *The Altrurian*, in which their plans were outlined, and their progress described. There was an initiation fee of fifty dollars, which provided cash at the beginning, but their different domestic industries did not provide enough cash or working capital. By the summer of 1895 financial problems were evident, and support from Altruria Clubs in California was not enough to keep the colony going. In June that year the original colony closed its books; three smaller units emerged from the original settlement, but within a year all three closed.

See Also Howells, William Dean; Payne, Edward Biron

Sources:

Fogarty, Robert S. 1980. *Dictionary of American Communal History*. Westport, Conn.:
     Greenwood Press.
———. 1990. *All Things New: American Communes and Utopian Movements 1860–
     1914*. Chicago: University of Chicago Press.
Hine, Robert V. 1953. *California's Utopian Colonies*. 1983 ed. Berkeley: University of
     California Press.
Oved, Yaacov. 1987. *Two Hundred Years of American Communes*. New Brunswick, N.J.:
     Transaction Books.
Snodgrass, Mary Ellen. 1995. *Encyclopedia of Utopian Literature*. Santa Barbara, Calif.:
     ABC-CLIO.
Spann, Edward K. 1989. *Brotherly Tomorrows: Movements for a Cooperative Society in
     America 1820–1920*. New York: Columbia University Press.

AM OLAM. Am Olam is Hebrew for "Eternal People" and is the name of a Russian Jewish society formed to establish agricultural colonies in the United

States. Its name comes from a famous Hebrew essay. In Odessa, Russia (1881), Am Olam was founded by young utopian idealists who called for the settling of Jews in a socialist commune on farmland in the United States. Motivated by socialism and millennial vision, Am Olam aimed to make complementary its practical and idealistic elements. In the spring of 1881 the movement sent seventy Jewish refugees to the United States, and in 1882 groups of well over 100 emigrated. The migration was caused by a wave of anti-Semitism that followed the assassination of Alexander II (1818–1881) and the enthronement of Alexander III (1845–1894). The Am Olam attracted young intellectuals, university and high school students. They believed that farming was a noble occupation and were encouraged to seek help not through charity but cooperative work. In the 1880s the Am Olam movement saw the founding of twenty-six agricultural colonies in eight states, primarily in the West. The first colony was established on 1,000 acres at Sicily Island, Louisiana, with craftspeople, artisans, and students in the spring of 1881; they had to quit when the Mississippi River flooded. The second colony was founded at Crimeaux, South Dakota (1882), and lasted only until 1885 due largely to crop failure. The Am Olam colony that has lasted longest, as well as being the most communistic, was New Odessa, established by seventy members in Glendale, Douglas County, near Portland in Oregon (1882) under the leadership of William Frey (1839–1888), a non-Jewish disciple of the French social philosopher Auguste Comte (1798–1857) and his "religion of humanity." Members held land in common and agreed on a socialistic constitution. The settlement flourished until internal bickering, demoralization, economic problems, and Frey's unacceptable leadership brought its end in 1887.

See Also Frey, William; New Odessa Community; Rosenthal, Herman; Sicily Island Colony

Sources:

Eisenberg, Ellen. 1995. *Jewish Agricultural Colonies in New Jersey, 1882–1920*. Syracuse, N.Y.: Syracuse University Press.

Fogarty, Robert S. 1980. *Dictionary of American Communal History*. Westport, Conn.: Greenwood Press.

———. 1990. *All Things New: American Communes and Utopian Movements 1860–1914*. Chicago: University of Chicago Press.

Herscher, Uri D. 1981. *Jewish Agricultural Utopias in America 1880–1910*. Detroit: Wayne State University Press.

Miller, Timothy. 1990. *American Communes 1860–1960*. New York: Garland.

Oved, Yaacov. 1987. *Two Hundred Years of American Communes*. New Brunswick, N.J.: Transaction Books.

Roth, Cecil E., ed. 1971. *Encyclopedia Judaica*. New York: Macmillan.

AMANA COLONIES. In southern Germany during the eighteenth century Pietists gathered to discuss how they were being persecuted for their religious beliefs and their wish to live in simple piety, worship together, and share the religious philosophy of the Mennonites and other smaller, like-minded sects.

One group, enthused by reports of William Penn's (1644–1718) vision and plans for Pennsylvania, followed him and became one of the Amish settlements. Another group of 800 led by Christian Metz (1794–1867) emigrated to the United States in 1842 to escape persecution. Near Buffalo, New York, they purchased 5,000 acres, called the site "Ebenezer," and became known as the Ebenezer Society or Society of True Inspirationists, with a constitution written by Metz. The community throve until 1854 before moving to 18,000 acres in Iowa. For them, all property except personal and domestic goods was held by the community. This communism was necessary to amass enough capital for the purchase of land. The settlement of seven small villages in east-central Iowa clustered around the Iowa River northwest of Iowa City. It was named Amana, and Metz led the community until his death. Under Iowa law it was incorporated in 1859 as the Amana Church Society, had its own constitution, and was reorganized as a cooperative administration in 1932 with the separation of church and state. It developed a communal way of life that reached its peak in Iowa, where it had 24,000 acres of productive farmland. Amana is one of the most successful of such communities in the United States and is famous for the products of its woolen mills, especially blankets, and its farms and quaint villages, which attract many tourists.

See Also Metz, Christian; Penn, William

Sources:

Barthel, Diane L. 1984. *Amana*. Lincoln: University of Nebraska Press.

Fogarty, Robert S. 1990. *All Things New: American Communes and Utopian Movements 1860–1914*. Chicago: University of Chicago Press.

Harris, William, and Judith Levey, eds. 1979. *The New Illustrated Columbia Encyclopedia*. New York: Columbia University Press.

Oved, Yaacov. 1987. *Two Hundred Years of American Communes*. New Brunswick, N.J.: Transaction Books.

AMISH, AMISH MENNONITES. Amish and Amish Mennonites make up an eponymous schism of the Anabaptists, a strong and distinct cultural group in the United States for over two centuries and known as a people who have maintained a strong group identity. The Amish trace their religious heritage to the Swiss Anabaptists of sixteenth-century Europe. Unhappy with the practices and faith espoused by the Catholic Church in Europe, Martin Luther (1483–1546) led a protest in 1517, and his revolt inaugurated the Protestant Reformation, making Protestantism a permanent branch within the Christian Church. The religious renegades believed that baptism should be conferred only on adults who were willing to live a life of radical obedience to the teaching of Jesus. Adult baptism became the public symbol of the new movement. The young reformers were named "Anabaptists," meaning the "baptizers," as they had already been baptized as infants. Harsh persecution and missionary zeal of the Anabaptists scattered them through Northern Europe. In the Netherlands Menno

Simons (1496–1561) emerged as an influential proponent of Anabaptism. A powerful leader, writer, advocate, and preacher for the Anabaptist cause among his followers, Simons became so influential that many Anabaptists were eventually called Mennonists or Mennonites. The relentless persecution drove numerous Mennonites to remote mountain areas, where they turned to farming. The Amish take their name from a young Anabaptist who became a leader of a separatist group, Jacob Ammann (c. 1645–c. 1730). They believed foot washing should be part of the communion service. In 1710 Mennonite settlers purchased 10,000 acres in Pennsylvania. They were attacked by Indians, and plagued by uncertain weather conditions and crop failures and gradually dispersed and established themselves in comunities through the midwestern United States.

See Also Ammann, Jacob; Simons, Menno

Sources:

Dyck, Cornelius J. 1967. *An Introduction to Mennonite History.* 3d ed. 1993. Scotsdale, Pa.: Herald Press.

Hosteller, John A. 1963. *Amish Society.* 4th ed., 1993. Baltimore: Johns Hopkins University Press.

———, ed. 1989. *Amish Roots: A Treasury of History, Wisdom and Lore.* 1992 ed. Baltimore: Johns Hopkins University Press Paperbacks.

Kraybill, Donald B. 1989. *The Riddle of Amish Culture.* Baltimore: Johns Hopkins University Press.

———, ed. 1993. *The Amish and the State.* Baltimore: Johns Hopkins University Press.

Nolt, M. Steven. 1992. *A History of the Amish.* Intercourse, Pa.: Good Books.

AMMANN, JACOB. Jacob Ammann (c. 1645–c. 1730) was born in Switzerland, went to Alsace to care for Mennonite families, and later returned home. He sought to reform the Swiss Anabaptists by advocating a life of simplicity and separation from the everyday world, ceremonial foot washing, and day-to-day avoidance of excommunicated members. Disappointed at the Anabaptists in Switzerland for their failure to observe these reforms, he returned home to have pastors declare support for the proposals. Many refused on the grounds that avoidance of excommunicated members was not practiced by the Swiss and that excommunicated members should not take communion. Ammann excommunicated their leader and his immediate followers. The churches in Germany, Switzerland, and France were divided on these issues. Superficially, they identified themselves according to dress: the Amish or Häftler dressed using hooks and eyes to secure their clothing, and the other followers, or Knöpflers, favored the use of buttons.

See Also Amish, Amish Mennonites

Source:

Hosteller, John A. 1989. *Amish Roots: A Treasury of History, Wisdom and Lore.* Baltimore: Johns Hopkins University Press.

ANABAPTISTS IN ENGLAND. Originally, the English Anabaptists constituted a group in Munster who formed a community of Christians who believed
they were directly accountable to God and not in need of baptism to ensure
their religious survival. Some became communists, following *Acts.* 2:44–45,
which says, ''And all that believed were together and had all things in common
. . . and sold their possessions and goods and parted them to all *men*, as every
man had need.'' Many were put to death after being accused of both Anabaptism
and communism. This occurred before the trial and death of William Tyndale
(c. 1494–1536), who translated the Bible into English and had it published in
Europe (1525–1526). Anabaptists were driven from England between 1550 and
1575.

See Also Amish, Amish Mennonites

Source:

Armytage, Walter H. Green. 1961. *Heavens Below: Utopian Experiments in England
     1560–1950*. London: Routledge and Kegan Paul.

ANANDA CO-OPERATIVE VILLAGE. The Ananda Co-operative Village was
a spiritual community founded by Swami Kriyananda (b. 1926) in 1967 and
dedicated to the fulfillment of Paramahansa Yogananda's (1893–1952) vision.
He dreamed of spreading a spirit of brotherhood among all peoples and aimed
at establishing in many countries self-sustaining, world-brotherhood colonies for
plain living and high thinking. Ananda is a place where devotees, married or
unmarried, single or monastic, can live among influences of divine ideas and
feelings, where family and friends, environment and work are all conducive to
spiritual development. Paramahansa Yogananda's ideal world would be one in
which ''home, job and church are one place,'' and one has become fully ''self-
realized.'' Ananda is on 650 acres of forest and meadows 3,000 feet up in the
Sierra Nevada foothills near Nevada City, northern California. In 1977 the community had about 100 full-time residents; the community was organized like a
village, with individuals and families living in separate houses owned by the
community. The Ananda Community has two parts: the meditative retreat and
the farm. Members supported themselves with work in different Ananda businesses. A small dairy herd and large organic garden provided the milk and
vegetables for the community. A special goal was to provide the children with
a spiritual education. Preschool and elementary high school education derives
from Paramahansa Yogananda's principle of living harmoniously, growing in
harmony, in spirit, mind, and body.

See Also Paramahansa Yogananda; Swami Kriyananda

Sources:

Fogarty, Robert S. 1980. *Dictionary of American Communal History*. Westport, Conn.:
     Greenwood Press.
Popenoe, Cris, and Oliver Popenoe. 1984. *Seeds of Tomorrow*. San Francisco: Harper
     and Row.

Walters, Donald J. 1977. *The Path: Autobiography of a Western Yogi (Swami Kriyananda)*. Nevada City, California: Ananda.

ANARCHIST UTOPIAS. Anarchist utopias oppose all forms of coercive authority, especially that of the state; members are extremely optimistic about humankind's abilities and motives; they assume that if outside constraints are loosened, within everyone a true person will be released, and a fine voluntary commitment to a better world will emerge and surge forward on a never-ending wave of generous, kind, considerate human relationships. Thereby, society will flourish. While individual anarchists uphold private ownership and the freedom of self-expression, communal anarchists look to a self-sufficient commune that trades with its neighbors for essentials only and aims for sexual and racial equality, as well as freedom to express all deeply held feelings on the assumption that such expression can lead only to the benefit of all members. Prominent American anarchists were Stephen Pearl Andrews (1812–1886), William B. Greene (1819–1878), Ezra Heywood (1829–1893), Joshua K. Ingalls (fl. 1816–1890), Edward Kellogg (1790–1858), Henry Demarist Lloyd (1847–1943), Lysander Spooner (1808–1887), Benjamin Tucker (1854–1939), and Josiah Warren (1798–1874). Among British anarchists extreme social reformers were Edward Carpenter (1844–1929), Peter Kropotkin (1842–1921), and William Morris (1834–1896). More recent accounts of anarchists and their attempts at utopian settlements in Europe were advanced in Spain at the turn of the century and after the Spanish civil war (1936–1939), when rural and urban workers united. In France Pierre Joseph Proudhon (1809–1865) was a notable anarchist whose ideas were taken up at Saint Émilion.

See Also Andrews, Stephen Pearl; Carpenter, Edward; Equity Colony; Ferrer Colony; Lloyd, Henry Demarest; Modern Times; Morris, William; Norton Colony; Proudhon, Pierre Joseph; Saint Émilion; Unity House; Utopia; Warren, Josiah

Sources:

Armytage, Walter H. Green. 1961. *Heavens Below: Utopian Experiments in England 1560–1950*. London: Routledge and Kegan Paul.

Dolgoff, Sam, ed. and trans. 1990. *The Anarchist Collectives: Workers' Self-Management in the Spanish Revolution, 1936–1939*. New York and Montreal: Black Rose Books.

Fogarty, Robert S. 1980. *Dictionary of American Communal History*. Westport, Conn.: Greenwood Press.

Martin, James J. 1953. *Men against the State: The Exposition of Individual Anarchism in America: 1827–1908*. Dekalb, Ill.: Adrian Allen Associates.

Schor, Francis Robert. 1997. *Utopianism and Radicalism in a Reforming America, 1888–1918*. Westport, Conn.: Greenwood.

Snodgrass, Mary Ellen. 1995. *Encyclopedia of Utopian Literature*. Santa Barbara, Calif.: ABC-CLIO.

Veysey, Laurence. 1973. *The Communal Experience: Anarchist and Mystical Counter-cultures in America.* New York: Harper and Row.

ANDREWS, STEPHEN PEARL. Stephen Pearl Andrews (1812–1886) was born in Templeton, Massachusetts, and raised in Vermont by his father, a religious who had opposed the War of 1812. After graduating from Amherst (1829) Stephen taught in a seminary and a college in Louisiana, studied law (1831), and was admitted to the bar (1833); and practiced in Louisiana and Texas. His wife was a doctor and suffragette. Between 1835 and 1843 he was an active abolitionist and for his views was once forced by a mob to quit Houston. He took up phonography (1845), tried to establish a universal language, "Alwato," and, drawn to the social reforms and the economics of Josiah Warren (1798–1874), helped establish Modern Times in New York (1851). He was Warren's propagandist. Modern Times declined, partly due to prevailing attitudes to its policy of free love, and in 1854 Andrews went to New York City. In 1859 he set up Unity House, a cooperative household where he was the head of a spiritual order, and attracted a few followers. Using a pseudonym, Andrews published spiritualist ideas in *Constitution or Organic Basis of Pantarchy* (1860). After the Civil War (1861–1865) he turned to the woman's rights movement and, with support from Victoria Woodhull (1838–1827), attacked state intervention in marriage. Among those who supported his work were Elizabeth Rowell Thompson (1821–1899) and Marie Howland (1835–1921). He published esoteric philosophy and supported radical groups, for example, Manhattan Club in New York City.

See Also Howland, Marie Stevens; Modern Times; Thompson, Elizabeth Rowell; Unity House; Warren, Josiah

Sources:

Andrews, Stephen P. 1853. *Love, Marriage, Divorce, and the Sovereignty of the Individual.* 1972 ed. New York: Source Book Press.
Andrusius, Pantarch [Stephen Pearl Andrews]. 1860. *Constitution or Organic Basis of Pantarchy.* New York: Baker, Godwin.
Fogarty, Robert S. 1980. *Dictionary of American Communal History.* Westport, Conn.: Greenwood Press.
———. 1990. *All Things New: American Communes and Utopian Movements 1860–1914.* Chicago: University of Chicago Press.
Martin, James J. 1953. *Men against the State: The Expositors of Individual Anarchism in America, 1827–1908.* Dekalb, Ill.: The Adrian Allen Associates.
Oved, Yaacov. 1987. *Two Hundred Years of American Communes.* New Brunswick, N.J.: Transaction Books.

ANIMAL FARM. *Animal Farm* is a satirical fable describing how social change by revolution tends to dystopia. It is directed against Stalin's Russia, the totalitarian regime that emerged after the Bolshevik revolution. Mr. Jones, a farmer, exploits his animals. A boar, "Major," a Leninist character, incites a revolution, the animals get control, and Major dies, leaving authority in the hands of "Snowball" (Trotsky) and "Napoleon" (Stalin). With the expulsion of the human masters the farm is beset by external enemies and split by internal dissension. Egalitarian principles of domination give over to totalitarian practices, Snowball is expelled as a traitor, and his supporters are executed after their public "confessions." The carthorse, Boxer, is sent to his death at the knacker's yard, even though he was a pillar of strength in the revolution. In time power corrupts the pigs, privileges are taken that create a stratified and tyrannical social structure, and, under Napoleon, a new despotism secures itself. The ideas of the original revolution are undermined with deceptively persuasive propaganda, for example, "All animals are equal, but some animals are more equal than others." As the pigs learn to stand on two feet, drink alcohol, and gamble, they become indistinguishable from their oppressive human masters of the prerevolutionary days. In the end, the revolution is betrayed when the pigs arrange a deal with their original master, Mr. Jones. The work reflects George Orwell's deep conviction that those who work for social change must monitor its consequences for fear of the return of tyranny. It also suggests that power does not tend to corrupt, as Lord Acton (1834–1902) wrote, but that people tend to corrupt power when given the chance. The novel is used frequently to satirize the terrors of the Cold War; later, with his *Nineteen Eighty-Four* (1949), Orwell would bring home the same message in a realistic manner. Originally, *Animal Farm* was rejected for publication by T. S. Eliot (1888–1965), a pioneer of modern English poetry.

See Also Dystopia; *Nineteen Eighty-Four*; Orwell, George; Stalinist Russia

Sources:

Booker, M. Keith. 1994. *Dystopian Literature: A Theory and Research Guide*. Westport, Conn.: Greenwood Press.

Orwell, George. 1946. *Animal Farm*. 1961 ed. New York: New American Library.

Snodgrass, Mary Ellen. 1995. *Encyclopedia of Utopian Literature*. Santa Barbara, Calif.: ABC-CLIO.

Spencer, Luke. 1981. "Animal Farm and Nineteen Eighty Four." In J. A. Jowett and Richard K. S. Taylor, *George Orwell*, pp. 67–83. Bradford: University of Leeds.

ARIZMENDIARRIETA, JOSÉ MARIA. José Maria Arizmendiarrieta (1915–1976) was born into a farming family in Markina, near Mondragón, in the Basque region of Spain. An accident at the age of three deprived him of sight in one eye. He decided to study for the priesthood rather than follow Basque tradition and take up farming. In 1936, when civil war erupted, he joined the military but was ineligible for combat. He edited newspapers in Euskera (Basque language). Although faithful to Basque interests, he could see how the war would end. In June 1937 he turned himself in to the Franco authorities, was imprisoned for a month, faced military interrogation, and, classified as a prisoner of war, was released. He returned to studies for the priesthood, read widely on social problems, but failed to get permission to study sociology. He worked as a priest, but found he was a poor preacher and far more interested in group discussion than oration. He came to Mondragón in 1941 and acquired a reputation as a socialistic priest who believed work was for self-development rather than punishment. He helped establish a medical clinic and sporting facilities and gave religious instruction to apprentices in the company Unión Cerrajerra. Later he established a technical school and in 1943 from it developed the Mondragón Cooperative and the local community southeast of Bilboa in the valley of Guipuzcoa. His interest was not so much in ideals as realistic improvements in what people could do for themselves. The school was his first step in a new political economy for the region. He was an inspirational and practical teacher and did not formalize his power. He combined the ideas of Adam Smith (1723–1790) and Karl Marx (1818–1883) with the basic precepts of the Catholic Church on morals and the economy and used the experience of the nineteenth-century cooperative experiments in England. He preferred to be a teacher rather than administrator and occasionally took direct action; for example, he persuaded ULGOR, a Spanish business, to overcome its financial problems by creating its own bank. He espoused the view of combining a working technical cooperative with polytechnical education and used study groups and consultation rather than conventional bureaucratic controls. He learned to interpret Spanish laws and their government bureaucratic requirements; he did not use charismatic appeals to authority but based his influence on his ability to integrate ideas and practices in response to the requirements of the times.

See Also Mondragón cooperatives

Sources:

Hoover, Kenneth R. 1992. "Mondragón's Answers to Utopia's Problems." *Utopian Studies* 3, no. 2:1–20.
Larrañaga, Jesús. 1981. *Buscando un Camino: Don José Mariá Arizmendi-Arrieta y la Experiencia Cooperativa de Mondragóu*. Bilboa, Spain: R&F.
McCord, William. 1989. *Voyages to Utopia: From Monastery to Commune, the Search for the Perfect Society in Modern Times*. New York: W. W. Norton.

ARNOLD, EBERHARD. Eberhard Arnold (1883–1935) was born in Königsberg, East Prussia, into a Lutheran academic family. At sixteen, after a revelation, Eberhard decided to work for social reform in the service of God. He became a public speaker for the Salvation Army, radical Baptists, and Lutherans. Too unwell to serve in World War I, he directed publicity for the German Student Christian Union, published nationalist material for prisoners of war and the wounded, and became a vigorous pacifist. After the war, Arnold and his wife alienated the Student Christian Union and, with 200 followers, established a simple church at Sannerz, in preparation for God's new order on earth. Crafts, agriculture, and publicity supported them while they relieved distress among orphans and refugees. As God's instrument, Arnold upheld the organic com-

munity as an ideal; he advocated equality in poverty, joy in monogamous marriage, obedience of a wife to her husband, complete passivism and had total
reciprocity among members of the community, active evangelism, and internal
purity of membership. His enemies were egoism, factionalism, social stratification, privilege, and the pursuit of other worldly achievements. Experiments
like his had failed in Germany, but by July 1922 Sannerz had fifty members.
The community survived with difficulty until October, when it split, and most
members returned to the bourgeois life in Germany that they had been used to.
Arnold struggled to secure the welfare of the community for five years; financial
support came from some Dutch followers, and the group expanded and reestablished itself in the Rhone mountains as the Rhone Brüderhof (1927) with over
forty members. They lived in poverty. In 1933 Arnold fractured his leg, and it
would not heal. After the Rhone Brüderhof was relocated in Liechtenstein, he
went to England to raise funds for the establishment of communities there. In
1935 he had his damaged leg amputated and died. His main view of the world
had been that it was dominated by acquisitiveness, which had destroyed relationships between people and alienated humankind from God. Attracted to
Marxist economics, he rejected its approach to religion.

Sources:

Magnussen, Magnus, and Rosemary Goring, eds. 1990. *Chambers Biographical
    Dictionary*. 5th ed. Edinburgh: Chambers.
Oved, Yaacov. 1987. *Two Hundred Years of American Communes*. New Brunswick, N.J.:
    Transaction Books.
Whitworth, John McKelvie. 1975. *God's Blueprints: A Sociological Study of Three Uto-
    pian Sects*. London: Routledge and Kegan Paul.

ATWOOD, MARGARET. Margaret Atwood (b. 1939) was raised in Ontario,
Canada, and as a child began writing. She graduated from the University of
Toronto (B.A., 1961) and Radcliffe College (A.M., 1962) and studied in graduate school at Harvard (1962–1963; 1965–1967). She traveled widely and
worked at various jobs. Also she taught English at the University of British
Columbia (1964–1965), at Sir George Williams University (1967–1968) in Montreal, and at York University, Toronto (1971–1972). She was editor and a director of the House of Anansi Press in Toronto (1971–1972) and writer in
residence at the University of Toronto (1972–1973) and Macquarie University
(Australia) in 1987. In 1982 she won a literature prize from the Welsh Arts
Council. She published poetry beginning in 1966, short stories, and a controversial book on Kenladian literature, *Survival* (1972). She is one of Canada's
notable novelists, poets, and critics and has been translated into fifteen languages. Her novels are *The Edible Woman* (1969), *Surfacing* (1972), *Lady Oracle* (1976), *Life before Man* (1979), *Encounters with the Element Man* and
Bodily Harm (1982), and *Unearthing Suite* (1993). In 1986 her dystopian novel
The Handmaid's Tale (1985) won the Governor-General's Award in Canada

and was short-listed for the prestigious Booker Prize in Britain. The novel was made into a film (1990). In 1989 she published *Cat's Eye*.

See Also Dystopia; *Handmaid's Tale, The*

Sources:

Lesniak, James, ed. 1991. *Contemporary Authors*. Vol. 33. Detroit, Mich.: Gale Research.
Snodgrass, Mary Ellen. 1995. *Encyclopedia of Utopian Literature*. Santa Barbara, Calif.: ABC-CLIO.

AUGUSTINE, SAINT. Aurelius Augustinus—Saint Augustine—(354–430) was born in Tagaste, Algeria. His father was pagan; his mother a Christian. She raised him in Christianity. At age sixteen he went to Carthage to study humanities but became a promiscuous pleasure-seeker and followed Manichaeism, which assumes a primeval human conflict between dark and light. In 386, after hearing sermons by a bishop, Saint Ambrose, Augustine became a Christian and returned to Tagaste. He was so capable a speaker that he was soon appointed to assist the elderly bishop at Hippo Regius (now Bona) in 395. Augustine's *The Confession* is regarded as literature's first genuine self-analysis. He systematized the philosophy and dogma of Christianity and became known as the "Christian Aristotle." In his Christian philosophy of society he raised the political problems of church and state; he distinguished the secular and religious "spheres" or societies and the earthly or profane city of self-love from the heavenly city of love for God in *De Civitate Dei (The City of God)* (413–426). His doctrines argued that the Scriptures can guide all beings in their quest for knowledge; that God's principles, evident to all, should be established in philosophical science, for example, ethics and politics; that humankind need give no support to the earthly society but only to the divine order; and that holy laws and the example of Jesus are the true guides for all humankind. With the saints Ambrose, Gregory, and Jerome, Augustine is placed among the "Fathers of the Church."

See Also City of God, The

Sources:

Brown, Peter R. L. 1967. *Augustine of Hippo*. London: Faber and Faber.
Deane, Herbert A. 1963. *The Political and Social Ideas of St. Augustine*. New York: Columbia University Press.
McHenry, Robert ed. 1992. *The New Encyclopedia Britannica*. Chicago: Encyclopedia Britannica.
Oates, Whitney J. 1948. *Basic Writings of Saint Augustine*. 2 vols. New York: Random House.
Smith, Warren T. 1980. *Augustine: His Life and Work*. Atlanta: John Knox Press.
Snodgrass, Mary Ellen. 1995. *Encyclopedia of Utopian Literature*. Santa Barbara, Calif.: ABC-CLIO.
Zusne, Leonard. 1987. *Eponyms in Psychology: A Dictionary and Sourcebook*. Westport, Conn.: Greenwood Press.

B

BABEUF, FRANÇOIS NOËL (GRACCHUS). François Noël (Gracchus) Babeuf (1760–1797) was born in St. Quentin, France, son of a soldier—later, a tax collector—who was poor and gave his child little education. At about age fifteen the lad became a clerk and later an assistant to a surveyor (1772–1776). In 1778 he was apprenticed to a feudist—expert in seignorial law—and by twenty-five had become a feudist himself in Royce (1782–1789). He was thrown out of work by the abolition of feudalism early in the French Revolution and began to develop democratic and communistic views. After becoming acquainted with the Academy Arras and befriending its secretary, Babeuf developed increasingly hostile views on contemporary French society. In his *Manifesto of Equals* (1790) he assumed that individual ownership of property created inequalities and evil practices in society. In 1790 he was arrested after organizing a movement against the collection of indirect taxes. An extreme democrat, he began publishing *Le Tribun du peuple* clandestinely. Again he was arrested and, when released, had turned his thinking to true equality. He believed that property itself should be abolished and that the state should aim for common ownership and equal distribution of goods and, if necessary, pursue these aims in a campaign of terror. With his *Le Tribun du peuple* selling widely, he decided that power should be taken immediately in a coup d'état. He established an insurrectional committee to coordinate democrats and undermine both the police and the military and planned an uprising to unite all forces at once. An insurrectionare act was printed proclaiming, in the name of equality, liberty, and happiness, that conspirators in France had usurped power and must therefore be overthrown, judged, and given no mercy. Then the "Equals," as they were to be called, would rule and bring back the 1793 constitution—a radical political system based on communist theories—and distribute bread and land to all of France's needy patriots. The plan was betrayed, and Babeuf was arrested and tried, and some say he suicided, while others are sure he was guillotined in

1797. He was the first exponent of full-blooded communism. His opponents saw his ideas as a conspiracy of equals. During the French Revolution (1789–1797) he was known as "Gracchus Babeuf."

See Also Babouvistic communism

Sources:

Babeuf, François N. (Caius Gracchus). "A Society of Equals". Reprinted in Frank E. Manuel and Manuel Futzie P., eds., 1966, *French Utopias: An Anthology of Ideal Societies*, pp. 245–258. New York: Free Press.

Magnussen, Magnus, and Rosemary Goring, eds. 1990. *Chambers Biographical Dictionary*. 5th ed. Edinburgh: Chambers.

Miller, David, ed. 1987. *The Blackwell Encyclopedia of Political Thought*. Oxford: Blackwell.

Moncure, James A., ed. 1992. *European Historical Biography*. Vol. 1. Washington, D.C.: Beacham.

Scott, John A. 1972. *The Defense of Gracchus Babeuf before the High Court of Vendom*. With essay by Herbert Marcuse. New York: Schocken.

BABOUVISTIC COMMUNISM. A brochure from the French Revolutionary philosopher François Noël (Gracchus) Babeuf (1760–1797), *La Constitution de Corps-militare*, criticized the aristocratic caste system of the French army and sought the establishment of a people's assembly to which the king would be accountable. This assembly would act as a final court of appeal. Later, Babeuf advocated a policy of social equality, to be partly achieved through the communal ownership of lands and goods. To this extent his ideas and principles appealed to utopians. In his *Manifesto of Equals* (1790) he assumed that individual ownership of property created wicked inequalities and through revolution hoped for a better society that encouraged the view that all property was jointly owned and assumed, because all people had similar basic needs and capabilities, they should share the same diet and education. Also it was assumed that all people in an egalitarian world would work willingly, expend much the same effort, and through work live a happy, frugal life with sufficient means to satisfy basic needs and experience true social and personal joy. Babouvistic communism was the early foundation of nineteenth-century socialist utopias, particularly those espousing universal equality of incomes.

See Also Babeuf, François Noël (Gracchus)

Sources:

Bax, Ernest B. 1911. *The Last Episode of the French Revolution: Being a History of Gracchus Babeuf*. London: Grant Richards.

Doyle, William. 1989. *The Oxford History of the French Revolution*. New York: Oxford University Press.

Rose, R. B. 1978. *Gracchus Babeuf: The First Revolutionary Communist*. Stanford, Calif.: Stanford University Press.

Seligman, Edwin R. A., ed. 1930. *Encyclopedia of the Social Sciences*. New York: Macmillan.

BACON, FRANCIS. Francis Bacon (1561–1626) was born in London, the younger son of Sir Nicholas Bacon, and became a celebrated English philosopher, jurist, and statesman. He studied at Trinity College, Cambridge, and in Gray's Inn (1576), was called to the bar in 1582, and was elected to Parliament (1584–1614). He was knighted in 1603 after professing intense loyalty to the new king, James I, advocating the unification of Scotland and England, and lecturing Parliament on how royal and parliamentary interests could be integrated. Between 1614 and 1618 he wrote his utopian fantasy, *New Atlantis*, an allegorical romance about an imaginary island where members of a philosophical commonwealth cultivate the natural sciences. Successful political maneuvers achieved several posts for Bacon, and eventually he became lord chancellor and was made a peer. He was notable for abandoning deductive logic and high authorities as the basis of reliable knowledge, preferring careful observation and, where possible, experiment. He founded practical scientific induction. In 1620 his *Novum Organum* was published; its second book contains the principles of his inductive philosophy. Shortly afterward he was tried for bribery, condemned, fined, and removed from office. Thereafter he worked on his literary and philosophical writings. His *New Atlantis* contributed to founding the Royal Society (1662).

See Also New Atlantis

Sources:

Magnussen, Magnus, and Rosemary Goring, eds. 1990. *Chambers Biographical Dictionary*. 5th ed. Edinburgh: Chambers.

McHenry, Robert, ed. 1992. *The New Encyclopedia Britannica*. Chicago: Encyclopedia Britannica.

Overton-Fuller, Jean. 1981. *Francis Bacon: A Biography*. London: East-West.

Sills, David L., ed. 1968. *International Encyclopedia of the Social Sciences*. New York: Macmillan and Free Press.

Snodgrass, Mary Ellen. 1995. *Encyclopedia of Utopian Literature*. Santa Barbara, Calif.: ABC-CLIO.

Stephen, Leslie, and Sydney Lee, eds. 1917. *The Dictionary of National Biography*. London: Oxford University Press.

Zusne, Leonard. 1987. *Eponyms in Psychology: A Dictionary and Sourcebook*. Westport, Conn.: Greenwood Press.

BADER, ERNEST. Ernest Bader (1890–1982) was born in Switzerland, son of a Protestant farmer. Early, he became a vegetarian. At fourteen, as a clerk in a silk firm, he discovered something of business, but from his father's bitter experience with moneylenders Ernest learned to equate interest with usury. After completing military service, he went to England, married Dora Scott in 1915, and worked for a bank in London. In 1917 he and his wife moved to the countryside to join a community of conscientious objectors. In 1920 he established an importing agency, Scott Bader Ltd., which became a flourishing chemical, plastics, and resin manufacturer. In the London blitz, 1940, Bader moved to Wollaston Hall, where the firm expanded and prospered during World War II and afterward grew further with licenses from the United States to make chemicals. In 1945, as committed pacifists, he and his wife believed that society should be served by business, not the reverse, and established the Scott Bader Commonwealth, which upheld their belief. After self-government was established in the commonwealth, in 1970 Bader took on various humanitarian causes and toured the world with his wife in search of solutions to human distress and conflict. In 1978 he received an honorary doctor of social sciences. He died in 1982, leaving £10,000.

See Also Scott, Annie Eliza Dora; Scott Bader Commonwealth

Sources:

Hoe, Susanna. 1978. *The Man Who Gave His Company Away: A Biography of Ernest Scott Bader, Founder of Scott Bader Commonwealth*. London: Heinemann.
Jeremy, David J. 1984. ''Ernest Bader.'' In D. J. Jeremy and C. Shaw, eds., *Dictionary of Business Biography: A Biographical Dictionary of Business Leaders in Britain in the Period of 1860–1980*. London: Butterworths.

BAKUNIN, MIKHAIL. Mikhail Bakunin (1814–1876) was born into an aristocratic family in Moscow. He became an eccentric and an anarchist and once was condemned to die for his part in the German revolutionary movement of 1848. A forceful and inspiring speaker, he joined six disastrous revolutions and was jailed in Germany, Austria, and Russia in his struggle for liberty. In 1861, after being sent to prison in Siberia and escaping through Japan, he reached England and gained the support of Alexander Herzen (1812–1870), the revolutionary Russian exile and social propagandist. Nine years later Bakunin failed to incite an uprising in Lyon, but his reputation as the father of anarchism was well established in Italy, Spain, France, and Russia by late in the nineteenth century. In 1867 he was honored at the Congress for Peace and Freedom, was embraced by the Italian patriot Giuseppe Garibaldi (1807–1882), and was applauded by the English radical statesman John Bright (1811–1889). He became a member of the Communist International but was so attached to anarchist policy that he was expelled in 1872 at the Hague Congress. From his ideas many utopian ventures were established in Europe, for example, Saint Émilion in France, and many terrorists were inspired by his anarchist oratory. Finally, in 1874 after a failed insurrection in Bologna, his associates disguised him and secured his safety in Switzerland, where two years later he died in peace at Berne.

See Also Saint Émilion

Sources:

Magnussen, Magnus, and Rosemary Goring, eds. 1990. *Chambers Biographical Dictionary*. 5th ed. Edinburgh: Chambers.
McCord, William. 1989. *Voyages to Utopia: From Monastery to Commune, the Search for the Perfect Society in Modern Times*. New York: W. W. Norton.

Oved, Yaacov. 1987. *Two Hundred Years of American Communes*. New Brunswick, N.J.:
   Transaction Books.

BALLOU, ADIN. Adin Ballou (1803–1890), the seventh of eight children, was
descended in the sixth generation from a notable U.S. pioneer family who shared
in the proprietorship of Providence Plantations in 1646. Adin's elementary education was in Cumberland, Rhode Island, and nearby schools. At age twelve
he joined the Church of the Christian Connection in Cumberland and at eighteen,
pursuing what he believed to be a supernatural revelation, announced his intention to enter the ministry and to preach at the local church. In 1822 Ballou
married Abigail Sayles of Smithfield, who died in 1829. He married Lucy Hunt
of Milford in 1830 and had a daughter and a son. Ballou was noted for his
persuasive public speaking and prolific writing. The Universalists received him,
and with seven other clergymen, in 1841 he formed the Massachusetts Association of Universal Restorationists. He expounded their doctrine in the *Independent Messenger* (1831–1839) and had much influence on Unitarian thought.
He sought an outlet for his increasingly radical policy to eradicate the major
evils of his time, slavery and intemperance. His protest against them was the
formation of the Hopedale Community at Milford, the first of his utopian ventures (1840–1850). Some of his works include *Practical Christian Socialism*
(1854), *Primitive Christianity and Its Corruptions* (1870), *History of the Town
of Milford* (1882), *Autobiography* (1896), and *History of the Hopedale Community* (1897).
   See Also Hopedale Community

Sources:

Johnson, Allen, ed. 1927. *Dictionary of American Biography*. Vol. 1. New York: Charles
   Scribner's Sons.

BARMBY, JOHN GOODWYN. John Goodwyn Barmby (1820–1881) was born
at Yoxford, Suffolk. His father was a solicitor and died when Goodwyn was
fourteen. Refusing to be a solicitor, he became a political radical. At seventeen
he began four years' association with a revolutionary group in London; and in
1840, at age twenty, he went to Paris, lived in the students' quarters, studied
the city's social organization, and idealized the communitarianism of the Central
Communist Propaganda Society. He claimed to have coined the term ''communism'' when speaking with a French notable. In 1841 he helped establish a
social house—communitorium—to promote love, intelligence, and beauty, to
decry the acquisition of vast wealth in the name of Christ, and to uphold science
as the highest authority. The church of Jerusalem was his model for socialism,
and he revised orthodox Christianity with a variety of pantheism. People were
encouraged to establish agricultural communes and to give up their income for
the rewards of communal life; regions chosen for communes were London,
Cheltenham, Ipswich, and Merthyr Tydfil and Strabane in Ireland. Barmby the-

orized that humankind developed through four stages: paradization, barbariza-
tion, civilization, and communitarianism. His mission was to outline the fourth
phase, which itself had four stages, going from the imperfect community, to the
perfect community, to the city, and finally to the communist nation. Also he
was a health reformer and vegetarian, opposed alcohol and found his spiritual
and intellectual origins in Plato (c. 428–c. 348), Thomas More (1428–1535),
Daniel Defoe (1660–1731), Emanuel Swedenborg (1688–1772), and Immanuel
Kant (1724–1804). His first utopian experiment was at Moreville Communitorium, Hanwell, where he hoped to establish communism. To support his scheme,
he published tracts and journals and toured, giving lectures. In 1842 he met and
impressed Amos Bronson Alcott (1799–1888); in 1843 and again in 1845 he
supported communitarian efforts in Ireland; in 1845 he spoke at Bedworth,
where in 1847 a group established a communist church and honored him as its
head. In July 1847 he planned a communist immigration committee to support
Étienne Cabet's (1788–1856) Icarian plans. As a representative of the Communist Church he went to Paris in 1848 to speak at the Phalansterian Club.
Later that year, after attending a communist conference in London, he was much
influenced by William J. Fox, the Liberal member of Parliament (1786–1864),
and became a Unitarian, and thereafter his communitarian interests diminished
and were replaced with conventional religiosity. Nevertheless, he was a radical
to the last and in 1867 inspired the meeting at Wakefield in support of manhood
suffrage. In declining health he retired to Yoxford (1879).

   See Also Alcott, Amos Bronson; Cabet, Étienne; Moreville Communitorium

Sources:

Armytage, Walter H. Green. 1961. *Heavens Below: Utopian Experiments in England
    1560–1950.* London: Routledge and Kegan Paul.
Stephen, Leslie, and Sydney Lee, eds. 1917. *The Dictionary of National Biography.*
    London: Oxford University Press.

BARNETT, HENRIETTA. Henrietta Octavia Weston Barnett, née Rolland
(1851–1936), born at Clapham, was a keen horsewoman and fond of country
pursuits. An early interest in the poor and the needy became her guiding passion.
In 1873, at age twenty-one, she married Samuel Augustus Barnett (1844–1913),
a young curate in London. She was a member of many charity organizations
and a director and honorary manager and vice chair of the Hampstead Heath
Garden Suburb Trust. For her services to the community she was honored by
royalty (1917, 1924). A social reformer, she produced many publications, including *Canon Barnett: His Life, Work and Friends* (1918) and *Matters That
Matter* (1930), as well as several articles. For her support to the settlement idea
she was made the honorary president of the American Federation of Capitalists
Settlements. The contrast between living conditions in the impoverished East
End of London and the Barnetts' house on Hampstead Heath gave her the idea
of building a model suburb to make a bridge between poverty and privilege. It

was to be a residential suburb in pleasant surroundings. She chose architects Raymond Unwin (1863–1940) and Richard Barry Parker (1867–1947) to design the suburb and selected financial advisers of great commercial skill. She raised £43,000 to preserve 80 acres of heath for public enjoyment, and in 1903 she formed the Hampstead Garden Suburb Trust, which itself raised funds for the purchase of a further 240 acres. Work began in 1907. The new garden suburb was designed to provide homes for all classes of people, from low-rent cottages to grand houses. The model suburb integrated public transport and shopping facilities and churches of many denominations and greatly influenced town planning in Britain and elsewhere.

See Also Barnett, Samuel Augustus; Hampstead Garden Suburb; Parker, Richard Barry; Unwin, Raymond.

Sources:

Gill, Roger. 1984. "In England's Green and Pleasant Land." In Peter Alexander and Roger Gill, eds., *Utopias*, pp. 109–117. London: Duckworth.

Hayter, A., T. Crawford, et al., eds. 1983. *British Women*. London: Europa.

Legg, Leopold G. W., ed. 1949. *Dictionary of National Biography 1931–1940*. London: Oxford University Press.

Who Was Who (1929–1940). 1967. Vol. 3. London: Adam and Charles Black.

BARNETT, SAMUEL AUGUSTUS. Samuel Augustus Barnett (1844–1913) was born in Bristol and educated at Wadham College, Oxford. A curate, twenty-eight, he moved to a derelict church in the East End. His new parish was inhabited by criminals, and on arrival at St. Jude's he was knocked down and had his watch stolen. In 1873 he married Henrietta Octavia Rolland (1851–1936). Barnett's main community activities were to establish a local branch of the University Extension Society and spread higher education into the cities and to organize the Metropolitan Association for the Befriending of Young Servants; also he opened literary discussions and art exhibitions at St. Jude's, collected a Children's Country Holidays fund, and frequently took notables from government on tours of Whitechapel. As a result undergraduates would spend their vacation in the East End to see for themselves the poverty of London. Deeply committed to good works and much taken with Arnold Toynbee's (1852–1883) views on the duty of citizens to each other, Barnett suggested, on Toynbee's death, the establishment of a settlement in East London where graduates and undergraduates would live and work with the church and, as men of culture, see, as Toynbee had noted, that "the poorest class needs to be raised in the interest of all classes." A house was bought for £6,250, and an association was established to inquire into poverty, educate the poor, and promote their welfare. A salary would be paid to those who did this work, and every effort would be made to raise funds for it. Barnett was made the warden of Toynbee Hall (1884–1896). In 1895 he became Canon Barnett. Barnett saw himself as a "director of enthusiasm, disciplined for the service of East London" and believed that universities should be like their medieval counterparts, democratic, popular, and open to the poor. After the 1902 Education Act he saw education raising the general standard of living and leading to humane relationships in industry and the promotion of intelligent citizenship.

See Also Barnett, Henrietta; Toynbee, Arnold; Toynbee Hall

Sources:

Barnett, Henrietta O. 1918. *Canon Barnett: His Life, Work and Friends*. London: J. Murray.
Montague, Francis Charles. 1889. *Arnold Toynbee*. With an account of the work of Toynbee Hall in East London by Philip Lyttleton Gell. Baltimore: Publication agency of the Johns Hopkins University.
Pimlott, John Alfred Ralph. 1935. *Toynbee Hall: Fifty Years of Social Progress, 1883–1934*. London: J. M. Dent and Sons.

BEAVER ISLAND. Beaver Island was the United States' only kingdom (1851–1856). It was established in the Beaver archipelago of northern Lake Michigan and was ruled by James Jesse Strang (1813–1836), who pursued a variety of Mormonism. He practiced polygamy and ruled the kingdom autocratically. Fishing and trading were the bases of the economy, which flourished under Strang and boasted 2,608 permanent residents by 1854. The kingdom collapsed with the assassination of Strang in June 1856. Both Strang and his kingdom have attracted much academic interest and much scholarly work. Today visitors find a Mormon print shop and the township of St. James on Beaver Island.

See Also Strang, James Jesse

Sources:

Adams, James Truslow. 1963. *Dictionary of American History*. New York: Charles Scribner's Sons.
Beaver Island Historical Society. 1981. *The Journal of Beaver Island History*. 2 vols. St. James: Beaver Island Historical Society.
Gilbert, Bill. 1995. ''America's Only King Made Beaver Island His Promised Land.'' *Smithsonian* 26, no. 4: 85–92.
Quaife, Milo M. 1930. *The Kingdom of Saint James: A Narrative of the Mormons*. New Haven, Conn.: Yale University Press.

BEBEL, FERDINAND AUGUST. Ferdinand August Bebel (1840–1913) was born in Cologne, worked as a master turner, and, converted to socialism by Wilhelm Liebknecht (1826–1900), helped to found the League of German Workers' Clubs (1869). By 1871 Bebel had become leader of the German social democrat movement and was its most noted advocate in the Reichstag. Often he was jailed, and became ever more popular with each imprisonment. He published works on the Peasants' War and the standing of women and his autobiography, *My Life* (1912), and wrote exhaustively on socialism.

See Also Social democracy

Source:

Magnussen, Magnus, and Rosemary Goring, eds. 1990. *Chambers Biographical Dictionary*. 5th ed. Edinburgh: Chambers.

BEHMENISTS. The Behmenists espoused the ideas of Jakob Boehme (1575–1624) and as a community flourished in England between 1647 and 1662. Members of the community believed that Christians had scientific knowledge of Christ within themselves and did not acquire that knowledge from becoming a sect member. In the world's history Behmenists claimed to have attained stage seven, the advanced stage where all conflict between individuals ends, individuals are able to see their common origins, and the principle of light cast inwardly would make the outer world disappear. To achieve such an advanced mental state, all individuals had to do was to think it, set their mind to it, and believe in it, and on judgment day they would be counted among the angels. If not, then they were devils. At the time such ideas were condemned as carnal conceptions that originated from individuals rather than, as they should, from the prophets and the apostles. Jakob Boehme's work was translated into English (1647–1662), and some evidence indicates that his ideas influenced the poet John Milton (1608–1674) in his *Paradise Lost* (1667) and *Paradise Regained* (1671).

See Also Boehme, Jakob: Leade, Jane

Source:

Armytage, Walter H. Green. 1961. *Heavens Below: Utopian Experiments in England 1560–1950*. London: Routledge and Kegan Paul.

BEILHART, JACOB. Jacob Beilhart (1867–1908) was born into a family that struggled to realize the American Dream. His father, John Beilhart (1830–1872), emigrated from Würtemberg after the revolution of 1848 and married Barbara Schlotter, a native of Ohio and of Pennsylvania-Dutch heritage in 1852. The lad's parents worked the Schlotter family farm and were moderately prosperous. Jacob was the third youngest of ten children, five boys and five girls. When Jacob was six, his father died, leaving his mother with ten children, age twenty-one years to three months. They struggled to maintain the property, living a life dominated by work and passionately following strict Lutheran religious practices. Jacob's formal education was limited to a few years at Bonesville District School in Fairfield, and in 1884 he left the farm to work in southern Ohio and later moved to Kansas as a repairer of harnesses. He joined the Seventh-Day Adventists, and in 1887, aged twenty, he turned his energies totally to the church. Beilhart was a lecturer at the Roycrofters and a faith healer. In time he became interested in other religions and eventually formed the Spirit Fruit Society (c. 1889). The community was founded originally in Lisbon, Ohio, but later moved to Ingleside, Illinois, northwest of Chicago. They maintained their

Chicago branch at the same time. He died from peritonitis after having his appendix removed.

See Also Roycrofters; Spirit Fruit Society

Sources:

Fogarty, Robert S. 1980. *Dictionary of American Communal History*. Westport, Conn.: Greenwood Press.

———. 1990. *All Things New: American Communes and Utopian Movements 1860–1914*. Chicago: University of Chicago Press.

Grant, Roger H. 1988. *Spirit Fruit: A Gentle Utopia*. DeKalb: Northern Illinois University Press.

Murphy, James L. 1989. *The Reluctant Radicals: Jacob Beilhart and the Spirit Fruit Society*. Lanham, Md.: University Press of America.

BEISSEL, JOHANN CONRAD. Johann Conrad Beissel (1691–1768), an orphan in his hometown, Eberbach, Germany, had little education. He became a journeyman baker in Heidelberg. A Pietist, he was briefly associated with the Community of True Inspiration, some of whose members would later establish the Amana Colonies in Iowa. In 1720 Beissel sailed to Pennsylvania, where he was apprenticed to a minister of the German Baptist Brethren (Dunkers). He attached extra importance to personal revelations and worship on the Sabbath, and became a leader among the Brethren until 1728, when he left their company. In 1732 he founded the Solitary Brethren of the Community of the Seventh Day Baptists, or Ephrata Community, a semimonastic group, in Lancaster County. Beissel's reputation was based on excessively autocratic zeal, an imperious manner, and outstanding intellectual ability. When he died, his community declined.

See Also Amana Colonies; Ephratans

Sources:

Holloway, Mark. 1951. *Heavens on Earth: Utopian Communities in America: 1680–1880*. New York: Dover.

Oved, Yaacov. 1987. *Two Hundred Years of American Communes*. New Brunswick, N.J.: Transaction Books.

Pitzer, Donald E. 1984. "Collectivism, Community and Commitment: America's Religious Communal Utopias from the Shakers to Jonestown." In Peter Alexander and Roger Gill, eds., *Utopias*, pp. 119–135. London: Duckworth.

Reid, Daniel G. 1990. *Dictionary of Christianity in America*. Downers Grove, Ill.: InterVarsity Press.

BELL, ANDREW. Andrew Bell (1753–1832) was born at St. Andrew's, Scotland, the second son of a barber. When he was four, he entered the local school and recalled it mainly for its cruel disciplinary practices. In 1767 he entered St. Andrew's University, where he distinguished himself as a young mathematician and natural philosopher. In 1774 he sailed to Virginia to be a tutor in a planter's family. However, he made a fortune growing tobacco in Virginia. On his return to Britain he took orders in the Church of England (1781) and in 1787, after receiving the degree of doctor of divinity, sailed for India. He accepted the post of superintendent for Madras Male Orphan Asylum and introduced the idea of older students' teaching younger pupils. This became known as the Madras system of education, in which each student became a master and a scholar. Bell was convinced he had discovered a new method of teaching when he saw how rapidly the children learned. He published *An Experiment in Education Made at the Male Asylum of Madras* (1797). His ideas were taken over by Joseph Lancaster (1778–1838) at Southwark (1801) and by Robert Owen (1771–1858) at New Lanark. Bell was appointed rector at Swanage, Dorset (1801), and in 1811 became superintendent of the National Society for Promoting the Education of the Poor in the Principles of the Established Church. In 1819 he was made an honorary canon of Westminster Abbey, where he was buried. In his will he left £120,000 for schemes for better educational opportunities in Scotland.

See Also Lancaster, Joseph; Lancastrian school; Owen, Robert

Sources:

Aldrich, Richard, and Peter Gordon. 1987. *Dictionary of British Educationists*. London: Woburn Press.

Magnussen, Magnus, and Rosemary Goring, eds. 1990. *Chambers Biographical Dictionary*. 5th ed. Edinburgh: Chambers.

McHenry, Robert, ed. 1992. *The New Encyclopedia Britannica*. Chicago: Encyclopedia Britannica.

Preece, Warren E., ed. 1965. *Encyclopedia Britannica*. Chicago: Encyclopedia Britannica.

Stephen, Leslie, and Sydney Lee, eds. 1917. *The Dictionary of National Biography*. Vol. 11. London: Oxford University Press.

BELLAMY, EDWARD. Edward Bellamy (1850–1898) was born in Chicopee Falls near Springfield, Massachusetts. His father was a Baptist minister. Most of the boy's education was in the village school, although he spent a few months studying literature at Union College in Schenectady, New York. During 1868 he was abroad, mainly in Germany, where the sight of city slums in Dresden affected him deeply. On returning to the United States he studied law and was admitted to the bar (1871) but never practiced. After working briefly on the New York *Evening Post*, he was editor of the Springfield *Union* (1872–1877). He became ill and traveled to the Sandwich Islands for rest. In 1880, with his brother, he founded the *Springfield Daily News*. By 1889 he had secured a literary reputation; he published twenty-three stories and four novels, including the romances *Dr. Heidenhoff's Process* (1880) and *Miss Ludington's Sister* (1884). Now he is remembered for *Looking Backward: 2000–1887* (1888), which describes a utopia in Boston in 2000, where bureaucratic state capitalism ensures its citizens' welfare with equal wages, and culture is the main item of consumption. The book was the first to sell over 1 million copies. Bellamy Clubs were established, leading to the formation of a Nationalist Party. Bellamy's fame was immediate, and he entered politics as a Nationalist. In 1891 he founded the

New Nation in Boston to publish his views, but ill health forced him to give it up. In 1897 he published *Equality*, which set down in detail how a humane and rational nation could be achieved. A tuberculosis sufferer, he spent a brief, futile recovery in Denver and later went home to die in Chicopee Falls.

See Also Looking Backward: 2000–1887

Sources:

Bellamy, Edward. 1888. *Looking Backward: 2000–1887*. Boston. Ticknor (later, Houghton Mifflin.) Edited with introduction by Daniel H. Borus, 1995, Bedford Books of St. Martin's Press.

Bowman, Sylvia E. 1958. *The Year 2000: A Critical Biography of Edward Bellamy*. New York: Bookman Associates.

———. 1986. *Edward Bellamy*. Boston: Twayne.

Morgan, Arthur Ernest. 1944. *Edward Bellamy*. Reprinted 1974. Philadelphia: Porcupine Press.

Oved, Yaacov. 1987. *Two Hundred Years of American Communes*. New Brunswick, N.J.: Transaction Books.

Pollard, Arthur, ed. 1973. *Webster's New World Companion to English and American Literature*. New York: World, Times Mirror.

Snodgrass, Mary Ellen. 1995. *Encyclopedia of Utopian Literature*. Santa Barbara, Calif.: ABC-CLIO.

BENEDICT, SAINT. Saint Benedict (c. 480–c. 550) was born in Nursia, near Spoleto and was educated in Rome. Convinced that the only way to avoid evil was reclusive religious devotion, he went into a grotto near Subiaco for several years. For such notable piety he was made abbot of Vicovaro monastery, but he quit when he found how undisciplined the monks were. Benedict was sought by many for his pious wisdom, and he established twelve small monastic communities, all governed by his pious rules. From the information given to Pope Gregory I (c. 540–604) by four disciples of Saint Benedict, he became known as the "Patriarch of Western Monasticism" and compiler of a monastic rule, mainly employed at Monte Cassino, Italy. In Cassino he destroyed the remains of paganism and brought its people to full Christianity. It became one of the richest in Italy. His rule, *Regula Monachorum*, was composed in 515 and adds to the basic rules of monasticism the regulations that monks shall labor manually, give instruction to the young, and copy manuscripts for libraries. Probably he was not ordained and did not contemplate founding the order of Benedictines, which was established in Italy about 530. He was buried at Monte Cassino in the same grave as his sister, Saint Scholastica. The rules of Saint Benedict were gradually adopted by most Western monastic houses, though sometimes with modifications.

See Also Benedictines

Sources:

Magnussen, Magnus, and Rosemary Goring, eds. 1990. *Chambers Biographical Dictionary*. 5th ed. Edinburgh: Chambers.

Martin, John S., ed. 1981. *A Man with an Idea: St. Benedict of Nursia.* Melbourne: University of Melbourne.

McCann, Justin. 1937. *Saint Benedict.* 1979 ed. London: Sheed and Ward.

Oved, Yaacov. 1987. *Two Hundred Years of American Communes.* New Brunswick, N.J.: Transaction Books.

Peterson, Joan Margaret. 1983. *The Dialogues of Saint Gregory the Great in Their Late Antique Cultural Backgrounds.* Toronto: Pontifical Institute of Medieval Studies.

Richards, Jeffrey. 1980. *Consul of God: The Life and Times of Gregory the Great.* Boston: Routledge and Kegan Paul.

BENEDICTINES. Benedictines are communities of monks and nuns who follow the rule of Saint Benedict of Nursia. The first twelve Benedictine monasteries were communities founded early in the sixth century at Subiaco, near Rome, by Benedict, who later founded the famous abbey at Monte Cassino and established there a rule that organized and revitalized Western monasticism. The *Rule of St. Benedict* was drawn up, c. 540. For a monk it was a taut, inclusive directory of spiritual and administrative life, requiring obedience to a perfect following of Jesus Christ. The rule was administered by a patriarchal abbot who, chosen by his monks, had total authority over them and was allocated the task to care for, and counsel, each individual. It was an austere, prudent, and humane regimen. The community's major activities were work, private prayer, and spiritual reading. All members renounced private ownership, although the monastery itself could own property. By the standards of the time the Benedictine rule imposed no great austerity or aesthetic demands on members of the community. Depending on the season of the year and the festival celebrated, the monks each day devoted a period of four to eight hours to celebrating Divine Office and one period of seven to eight hours sleeping. The remainder of the day was divided equally between agricultural work and religious study. The abbot had full patriarchal authority over the community, but he himself was subjected to the rule, *Regula Monachorum*, and was required to consult members of the community on any important questions. During Benedict's lifetime his disciples spread the order through the countries of Central and Western Europe. It soon became the only important order in those lands. Pope Gregory I (c. 540–604) was the first of fifty Benedictines to occupy the papal throne. As early as 1354 the order had provided twenty-four popes, 200 cardinals, 7,000 archbishops, and 15,000 bishops.

See Also Benedict, Saint

Sources:

Cross, L. A., and E. A. Livingstone. 1997. *The Oxford Dictionary of the Christian Church.* 3d. ed. New York: Oxford University Press.

Douglas, James D., ed. 1974. *The New International Dictionary of the Christian Church.* Exeter: Paternoster Press.

BEREA. Berea was a major utopian experiment in race relations conducted in Berea, Kentucky (1866–1904). Berea College in Berea, Kentucky was originally founded in 1858 by an abolitionist missionary, Rev. John Gregg Fee (1816–1901). However, he, his family, and followers were driven out of Kentucky by an angry mob that would not tolerate a racially integrated school. Fee reopened the school in 1866 with the aim of creating a college with complete and genuine racial integration. Much of Berea was modeled on Oberlin, Ohio, the first northern college to welcome African Americans. Many of the teachers were alumni of Oberlin, although Fee was not. In 1869 an Oberlin graduate, Edward Henry Fairchild (1815–1889), was appointed the first president of the college. He remained president until his death, and the early success of the school was due largely to his leadership. The average proportion of black students was 61 percent, so genuine racial integration seems to have existed and been successful. In 1889, after Fairchild died, William Goodell Frost (1854–1938) replaced him. Although he, too, had an abolitionist background, he felt that the college finances needed improvement and worried that white enrollments were falling. He worked hard to increase enrollments and soon 80 percent of the students were white. This led to a deterioration of race relations and self-imposed segregation among students. Frost was accused of fostering a climate of racism, but by 1895 problems had resolved themselves, and all was well until public discussion of the Day Law of 1904. This was a bill introduced by Kentuckian Carl Day to prohibit biracial education. The bill was passed, and despite Frost's appeals all the way to the U.S. Supreme Court, it was upheld in 1908. In response Berea College had to pay for its black students to go to other schools, and it became a white college. Frost worked to raise the funds for an all-black college, the Lincoln Institute, which opened in 1910. In trying to overcome racial prejudice by making Berea College more attractive to whites, Frost appears to have compromised the early success of the college.

Sources:

McPherson, James M. 1975. *The Abolitionist Legacy: From Reconstruction to the NAACP*. Princeton: Princeton University Press.
Sears, Richard. 1996. *A Utopian Experiment in Kentucky Integration and Social Equality at Berea, 1886–1904*. Westport, Conn.: Greenwood Press.

BERRYMAN, MARGARET. Margaret Berryman (fl. 1971–1997) reports that in 1971 she heard from a local Australian artist about Bend of Islands, a rural area twenty-eight miles northeast of Melbourne, Victoria. At that time she joined a group that proposed to buy 80 acres of bushland that belonged to the family of a recently deceased Australian politician. The purchase aimed to preserve the flora and fauna of the bushland. Impressed by the town planner's vision for a residential cooperative in a "romantic environment," many like-minded people believed that by joining with each other they could flee the urban sprawl of Melbourne and conserve a valuable site of bushland. Despite their neighbors' cynicism, the group purchased 326 acres, and now eighteen of the thirty-two shareholders have built mud-brick homes and established transpiration beds to grow healthy vegetables and over the last twenty-six years have attracted researchers to study the community's effective techniques for preserving the bushland flora and fauna.

See Also Ealey, E. H. M.; Neale, Jeph; Round the Bend Conservation Cooperative

BETH EL COMMUNITY. A group of Germans who had been living in the United States for some time sought to establish an isolated commune in 1843. Most were too poor to buy their own land and, having put down no roots, had wandered all through Pennsylvania until, influenced by the revival meetings of the early 1840s, they began to seek salvation. The wandering colony was founded under the leadership of William Keil (1812–1877), an erstwhile associate of the Rappites. The community went to northeastern Missouri, settled, and called themselves Beth El. Although members shared property and labor, they were allowed private income. The Beth El society had no written agreement or constitution and remained unincorporated. For this reason the society was never legalized by state authorities and always remained a voluntary association. This was probably due to the views of Keil on the advantages of spontaneity in social groupings and the disadvantages of formalizing social beliefs. In the mid-1850s Keil led about half the community from Beth El, Missouri, away from crowds and external interference. About 250 members left in 1855 to travel 2,000 miles to a site in Oregon, near Portland, which they named after Keil's daughter, Aurora.

See Also Keil, Wilhelm

Sources:

Fogarty, Robert S. 1980. *Dictionary of American Communal History*. Westport, Conn.: Greenwood Press.

Nordhoff, Charles. 1875. *The Communistic Societies of the United States*. 1961 ed. New York: Hillare House.

Oved, Yaacov. 1987. *Two Hundred Years of American Communes*. New Brunswick, N.J.: Transaction Books.

BEVERIDGE, WILLIAM HENRY. William Henry Beveridge (1879–1963) was born in Rangpur, Bengal, son of a judge in the Indian civil service; he was educated at a boarding school in Worcester and later at Charterhouse (1882); he studied at Balliol and University Colleges, Oxford (1879–1902). A lawyer, he became subwarden at Toynbee Hall in East London and thereafter was an active social and economic reformer among progressive liberals and Fabians and associates of Sidney Webb (1859–1947) and Beatrice Webb (1858–1943). He wrote *Unemployment: A Problem of Industry* (1909) and established the London Unemployment Fund (1904–1905), turned to journalism with the *Morning Post*, and published over 1,000 articles on social and economic reforms. While serving the government during World War I, he came into conflict with trade unions over restrictions on their power to negotiate work conditions in the war industry and was later excluded from the Ministry of Labor and put in the Ministry for Food. In 1919 he was knighted. Thereafter, he helped raise funds to expand the London School of Economics and advance social sciences generally. In time his autocratic administrative style and his relations with the school's academic secretary limited his influence, and he took the mastership of University College at Oxford. In June 1941 he began his inquiry into poverty in Britain. To eradicate society's ignorance, idleness, disease, and squalor, he advanced a scheme— the Beveridge plan—of national health services, family allowances, a full employment, and subsistence-level social insurance. In 1944 he published *Full Employment and Free Society* to show ways to promote full employment. A member of Parliament briefly in 1945, he was made a baron and entered the House of Lords. He published his autobiography, *Power and Influence* (1953), a family history, *India Called Them* (1947), and *Voluntary Action* (1948). He always held that unemployment could be managed only by the state; his writings indicate that he did not make use of contemporary writings on welfare economics. His views on redistribution of wealth and income were largely pragmatic and made simple assumptions about human motives and behavior instead of using the more rigorous approach of marginal analysis. Universities in Britain, the United States, Canada, New Zealand, Australia, and Europe honored him.

See Also Beveridge Plan; Fabians; Peckham experiment; Toynbee Hall; Webb, Beatrice Martha; Webb, Sidney James

Sources:

Eatwell, John, Murray Milgate, and Peter Newman. 1987. *The New Palgrave: A Dictionary of Economics*. London: Macmillan.
Harris, José. 1977. *William Beveridge: A Biography*. Oxford: Clarendon Press.
Williams, E. T. and C. S. Nichols, eds. 1981. *Dictionary of National Biography 1961– 1970*. Oxford: Oxford University Press.

BEVERIDGE PLAN. The Beveridge Plan was a British welfare plan designed to provide a high standard of social security for people in Britain and replaced such community-based health systems as the Peckham experiment. Arguing that old age, ill health, and unemployment led to poverty, the *Social Insurance and Allied Services* (1942) report advanced the system to redistribute income and pay benefits to such disadvantaged people with national insurance contributions. Benefits were to vary according the family size, and they were to be paid without a time limit. The funds for the scheme were to come from contributions by employees and employers and from general taxes. Devised by William Beveridge (1879–1963) the system was broadly adopted in Britain after World War II, but unexpected income-related benefits became evident and produced the effect of a poverty tax, as rising incomes led to a loss of system benefits among those who needed them.

See Also Beveridge, William Henry; Peckham experiment

Sources:

Beveridge, Janet P. 1954. *Beveridge and His Plan*. London: Hodder and Stoughton.
Greenwald, Douglas, ed. 1982. *Encyclopedia of Economics*. New York: McGraw-Hill.
Hanson, J. L. 1974. *A Dictionary of Economics and Commerce*. Suffolk: Richard Clay.
McHenry, Robert, ed. 1992. *The New Encyclopedia Britannica*. Chicago: Encyclopedia
    Britannica.

BHAGWAN SHREE RAJNEESH. Bhagwan Shree Rajneesh (b. 1931) was
born in Kuchwada in Madhya Pradesh at his mother's parents' home. Until his
maternal grandfather died in 1938, he lived with his grandparents, then with his
parents in Gadarwara. The grandfather's death affected the boy deeply, and he
became a solitary figure. In 1940 he took an interest in politics and for ten years
moved against the British domination of India. He graduated from high school
in Gadarwara and later attended Hitkarini College in Jabalpur, where, aged
twenty-nine, he was a professor of philosophy at the university. He was a rebellious, original, and clever character. His first ten-day meditation camp was
held in 1964. He resigned from his university post two years later. In Bombay
he attracted a large following with his temporary meditation camps. Eighty miles
south of Bombay at Poona he opened a permanent camp. Friends established a
public trust, the Rajneesh Foundation, and bought six acres in luxurious surroundings on the outskirts of Poona. The group therapy received much attention
largely because it encouraged participants to shout, act out their suppressed
sexual and depressed feelings, fight, act violently, express their rage, indulge in
childish regression. Well-educated, middle-class, young travelers were drawn to
Poona from around the world. At any one time about 6,000 visitors would be
seen in Poona; some stayed months, others for weeks, and 2,000 were there in
permanent work. In June 1981, apparently in need of medical treatment, Bhagwan and his entourage flew to New Jersey. In truth they aimed to establish an
experiment in the United States, Rancho Rajneesh, a utopian experiment. It
flourished until 1985, when he was forced to leave the United States on a charge
of immigration fraud.
    See Also Rancho Rajneesh

Sources:

Keesing's Contemporary Archives. 1985: entry 34043A. London: Keesing.
Wright, Charles. 1985. *Oranges and Lemmings: The Story behind the Bhagwan Shree
    Rajneesh*. Richmond, Victoria: Greenhouse.

BIMELER, JOSEPH MICHAEL. Joseph Michael Bimeler—originally, Bäumler—(1778–1853) was born in Germany, probably in Würtemberg, where for
ten years he taught among a persecuted sect of Pietists and lived meekly, changing his residence from time to time to avoid government observers. He had been
a weaver and was lame and disfigured, with a large, protruding eye. Because of
his intelligence and considerable energy he appeared to have had a formal ed-

ucation, but, in fact, he had educated himself. Also he had a spiritual power, charisma, common among religious leaders. In 1817 he joined 300 Separatists from Würtemberg and Baden and sailed for the United States from Hamburg. Bimeler attended to the downhearted, provided religious and secular instruction, cared for the sick, and through his spiritual attractiveness offered them strong leadership. Bimeler led the main party of emigrants to establish a community, the Society of Separatists of Zoar (Zoarites) in Ohio. His benign autocracy over the colony helped establish it firmly and reach a high degree of prosperity. Despite some conflicts with dissatisfied members of the community Bimeler was venerated after his death as one of the saints, and written versions of his discourses became sacred; but without his intelligence and energy the society stagnated and finally disintegrated (1898).

See Also Zoarites

Sources:

Johnson, Allen, ed. 1927. *Dictionary of American Biography*. Vol. 1. New York: Charles
    Scribner's Sons.
Oved, Yaacov. 1987. *Two Hundred Years of American Communes*. New Brunswick, N.J.:
    Transaction Books.

BISHOP HILL COLONY. In 1846 Bishop Hill Colony was established in Henry County, Illinois, by Erik Jansson (1808–1850), an autocratic religious leader from Sweden. In 1845 he had to flee New York because he was about to be imprisoned for the second time. He had 1,200 followers, 700 of whom went to Bishop Hill Colony. During the first winter many died, and their problems in surviving forced them into a supportive communal life. The town of Bishop Hill had become prosperous by 1855, and the ''Big Brick,'' as it was known, was reputed to be the tallest building west of Chicago. The Bishop Hill Colony had 1,400 acres, on which it produced linen cloth; they also had cattle and an operating industrial works. Jansson was a strict leader, and in 1850 he was shot to death by the lover of a colonist whom he forbade to marry. After Jansson's death, the colony was controlled by a board of trustees, but its economy declined, and in 1862 it split into two religious factions and closed down.

See Also Jansson, Erik

Sources:

Fogarty, Robert S. 1990. *All Things New: American Communes and Utopian Movements
    1860–1914*. Chicago: University of Chicago Press.
Isaksson, Olov. 1969. *Bishop Hill: A Utopia on the Prairie*. Stockholm: L. T. Solna
    Seelig.
Oved, Yaacov. 1987. *Two Hundred Years of American Communes*. New Brunswick, N.J.:
    Transaction Books.

BLAVATSKY, HELENA PETROVNA HAHN. Helena Petrovna Hahn Blavatsky (1831–1891) was born into a prominent Russian family and is noted for having established the theosophical movement. Helena was a hysteric, often hallucinated, lived in a fantasy world, and frequently argued with her governesses. In 1844 her father took her to Paris and London, where she received music instruction and showed remarkable talent. She matured to become a reckless, self-willed, and erratic young woman. In 1848 she married General Nikifor Vasilevich Blavatsky, who at one time was the vice governor of Erivan. She said that he was seventy-three years old when they were married, although forty-five years later he was still alive. She deserted him and returned home. Later she wandered about the European capitals and gambling places in the Near East, visited Tibet, and returned home promoting the powers of occultism. She arrived in New York in 1873, claiming to have miraculous spiritualistic powers. In September 1875 she helped form what would become the Theosophical Society. She traveled to India and Ceylon (1879–1884) and in 1885 settled in Würzburg, Germany. Later she went to New York, where she wrote *Isis Unveiled* (1877) and *The Secret Doctrine* (1888). Also she edited the monthly theosophical magazine *Lucifer* (1887–1891) and wrote *Voice of Silence* (1889) and related works. Her psychic powers were widely accepted, and, even though they did not withstand scrutiny of the Society for Psychical Research, they never their lost extensive support. On her death she was recognized as the theosophical movement's leader.

See Also Point Loma; Tingley, Katherine Augusta Westcott

Sources:

Bowden, Henry W. 1977. *Dictionary of American Religious Biography*. Westport, Conn.: Greenwood Press.

Johnson, Allen, ed. 1927. *Dictionary of American Biography*. Vol. 1. New York: Charles Scribner's Sons.

Johnson, K. Paul. 1994. *The Masters Revealed: Madam Blavatsky and the Myth of the Great White Lodge*. Albany, N.Y.: State University of New York Press.

Meade, Marion. 1980. *Madame Blavatsky, the Woman behind the Myth*. New York: Putnam.

Purucker, Gottfried. 1974. *Fountain-Source of Occultism*. Edited by Grace F. Knoche. Pasadena, Calif.: Theosophical University Press.

Ryan, Charles J. 1975. *H. P. Blavatsky and the Theosophical Movement; A Brief Historical Sketch*. 2d ed. San Diego: Point Loma.

Washington, Peter. 1993. *Madam Blavatsky's Baboon: The History of Mystics, Mediums and Misfits Who Brought Spiritualism to America*. London: Secker and Warburg.

BOEHME, JAKOB. Jakob Boehme (or Böhme) (1575–1624) was born in Altseidenberg, Silesia, and had an elementary education. He was drawn to the Bible. He became an apprentice to a shoemaker and later opened his own shop in Gorlitz, Saxony. After having many visions, in 1600 he turned to meditation in the belief that he was divinely inspired. About 1612 he published *Aurora*, which recorded his visions and described the attributes of God and demonstrated a sound knowledge of alchemy and the Scriptures generally. Local religious and civil authorities condemned the manuscript as heretical. He sought asylum in Dresden, Saxony, where he was cleared of charges and returned to Gorlitz. In his *Der Weg zu Christo und Mysterium* (1623) he aimed to explain the origins of all things, especially evil. Fundamentally, he held that everything that exists is intelligible only through its opposites and that contradiction explains the great problems of philosophy. To Boehme God contained conflicting elements and was both everything and nothing. This made evil a necessary element in goodness; without evil the human will would become inert, and progress would become impossible. Boehme's religious attitudes influenced modern Western thought in philosophy and theology. He had many followers in Germany and Holland, and societies of Behmenites—the English term for his followers—were formed in England, many of them later being absorbed by the Quakers. In Britain he was known as a religious mystic from Germany. In the early nineteenth century notable thinkers like Johann Fichte (1762–1814), Georg Wilhelm Hegel (1770–1831) and Fredrich Schelling (1775–1854) returned philosophical interest to Boehme's ideas.

See Also Behmenists; Leade, Jane

Sources:

Harris, William H., and Judith S. Levey, eds. 1979. *New Illustrated Columbia Encyclopedia*. New York: Columbia University Press.

Magnussen, Magnus, and Rosemary Goring, eds. 1990. *Chambers Biographical Dictionary*. 5th ed. Edinburgh: Chambers.

McHenry, Robert, ed. 1992. *The New Encyclopedia Britannica*. Chicago: Encyclopedia Britannica.

Oved, Yaacov. 1987. *Two Hundred Years of American Communes*. New Brunswick, N.J.: Transaction Books.

Phillips, Robert S., ed. 1983. *Funk and Wagnall's New Encyclopedia*. New York: Funk and Wagnall.

Weekes, Andrew. 1991. *Boehme: An Intellectual Biography of the Seventeenth-Century Philosopher and Mystic*. Albany: State University of New York Press.

BOGDANOV, ALEKSANDR. Aleksandr Aleksandrovich Bogdanov (1873–1928) was born in Sokolka, Grodno Gouvt, and in 1899 graduated in medicine from Kharkov University. He became a Marxist revolutionary and was arrested and exiled in 1901. In 1903 he joined the Bolsheviks and was put on the Central Committee of the Bolshevik Party (1905–1907). He was a close associate of Anatoly Lunacharsky (1875–1933). In 1909 he was forced out of the Bolshevik Party by Vladimir Lenin (1870–1924) for deviating from the party line. After the October revolution (1917) he joined the communist Academy and was made a lecturer in economics at Moscow University. Always interested in medicine, especially blood transfusion, he became a minor figure in the movement to create a Bolshevik utopia. He became a science fiction writer and died while experimenting on himself with a blood transfusion from a malaria patient, one of his imaginative schemes vital to remaking the world. He published *Red Star* (1907), the first Bolshevik utopia; later, he published another utopia, *Engineer Menni: A Martian Stranded on Earth* (1912). The book included references to space rockets and a utopia populated by people who all voluntarily sought work. In his utopia people wear synthetic clothes, watch 3-D movies, and use a death ray. Today his science fiction is regarded as early Russian cybernetics.

See also Bolshevism; Lenin, Nikolai Vladimir; Lunacharsky, Anatoly Vasil'yevich

Sources:

Beilharz, Peter, ed. 1992. *Social Theory: A Guide to Central Thinkers*. Sydney: Allen and Unwin.

Jensen, K. N. 1978. *Beyond Marx and Mach: Alexander Bogdanov's Philosophy of Living Experience*. Dortrecht: Reidel.

Vronskaya, Jeanne, and Vladimir Chuguev. 1992. *The Biographical Dictionary of the Former Russian Soviet Union*. London: Bowker-Saur.

BOISSIERE, ERNEST VALETON DE. Ernest Valeton de Boissiere (1810–1894) was born in Chateau de Certes on the baronial estate of his family in the southwest of Bordeaux, France. After graduating from the Paris Polytechnique, he held a commission in the French Army Corps of Engineers before resigning to help administer the family estate. In 1848 he became a radical member of the Republican Party and opposed the policies of Louis Napoleon; when the 1848 revolution failed, de Boissiere went to the United States, returning to France regularly on business during the 1850s, and settled in New Orleans. After the U.S. Civil War (1861–1865) he drew attention to himself when he donated $10,000 to a school for orphaned black children being cared for by the Methodist Episcopal Church. In 1868 he met Albert Brisbane (1809–1890), and they decided to provide funds for a cooperative community. In Franklin County, Kansas, they bought 3,500 acres, and forty French people came to live there. It was guided by Fourierist principles (1870–1884). Most members were expert silk makers. De Boissiere planted 250 acres of mulberry trees (1869–1873), but because the silk production became unprofitable, it ceased in 1882, and two years later he returned to France. Originally, the colony he established was the Kansas Cooperative Farm, also called Silkville because it was established in Silkville, Kansas. The colony survived two more years, and afterward De Boissiere bequeathed the property for use as an orphanage to the Odd Fellows Lodge.

See Also Brisbane, Albert; Prairie Home Colony; Silkville

Sources:

Carpenter, Garret R. 1952. *Silkville; A Kansas Attempt in the History of Fourierism Utopias, 1869–1892*. Emporia: Graduate Division, Kansas State Teachers' College.

Fogarty, Robert S. 1980. *Dictionary of American Communal History*. Westport, Conn.: Greenwood Press.

————. 1990. *All Things New: American Communes and Utopian Movements 1860–1914*. Chicago: University of Chicago Press.

Nordhoff, Charles. 1961. *The Communistic Societies of the United States*. New York: Hillary House.

Oved, Yaacov. 1987. *Two Hundred Years of American Communes*. New Brunswick, N.J.: Transaction Books.

Veysey, Laurence. 1973. *The Communal Experience: Anarchist and Mystical Counter-cultures in America*. New York: Harper and Row.

BOLSHEVISM. Bolshevism is the political philosophy of the party that won power in the October revolution, 1917, in Russia and thereafter more generally of Marxist revolution following the Soviet pattern. The term ''Bolshevism'' is derived from the Russian word ''Bol'shinstuo,'' which means ''majority.'' It comprises a set of doctrines designed to provide guidance for a revolutionary party in an autocratic state that is collapsing in response to many challenges for control. The Bolshevik image of utopia offers a direct democracy where workers rule, organize, and produce goods and services on a large scale. They live in a one-class society where all citizens are employees and belong to a simply structured, nationwide state or syndicate under the dictatorship of an armed proletariat. In the development of the communist state in twentieth-century Russia and, later, the world, the Bolshevik state is the first stage, a turning point that must be reached in the progressive reduction in the need for any form of government. This utopia is Westernized and industrialized and reflects the Bolshevik ideal of government by all people. In the 1920s to this ideology were added an emphasis on cooperation among workers and the proletariat's overwhelming of the bourgeoisie. The major theoretician and tactician of Bolshevism was Nikolai Vladimir Ilyich Lenin (1870–1924). He insisted on the short-term value of a proletarian revolution and the essential part in it played by professional revolutionaries. Lenin provided the example of how a small minority, organized into a highly disciplined machine, could seize power, hold onto it, and transform society. His success in holding and maintaining power raised the USSR to the role of a leading country in world communism. The party dropped from its title the term ''Bolshevik'' in 1925. Lenin also showed that a socialist revolution could be started in an underdeveloped country by exploiting the grievances of peasants, ethnic groups, and other disaffected social groups. Other advocates for the Bolshevik utopia were Aleksandr Bogdanov (1873–1928), Nikolai Bukharin (1888–1928), Anatoly Lunacharsky (1875–1933), Leon Trotsky (1879–1940), and Evgenii Preobrazhebsky (1886–1937).

See Also Bogdanov, Aleksandr; Bukharin, Nikolai Ivanovich; Lenin, Nikolai Vladimir; Lunacharsky, Anatoly Vasil'yevich; Preobrazhebsky, Evgenii A.; Trotsky, Leon

Sources:

Beilharz, Peter. 1992. *Labour's Utopias: Bolshevism, Fabianism, Social Democracy*. London: Routledge.

Bogdanor, Vernon, ed. 1987. *The Blackwell Encyclopedia of Political Institutions.* Oxford: Blackwell.

BONFIN, LE DOMAINE DU. Le Domaine du Bonfin is a community near the resort town of Fréjus in France. Its name in English means "Estate of the Good Purpose." It is a large center of the Fraternité Blanche Universelle (the Universal White Brotherhood). The term "white" refers not to color but to uniformity of humankind. The community leader is Maître (Master) Omraam Mikhaël Aïvanhov (fl. 1900–1984), who espouses "initiatic" knowledge, a blend of religious beliefs. At sunrise the community begins the day with a special ceremony. The community established itself shortly after the end of World War II in Sèvres, a Paris suburb, and finding the place too small, bought sixty-five acres outside Fréjus, established full-time communal facilities, and founded a publishing and printing company, Prosveta (1977). The community members support the venture with their membership fees, pay board, and invite paying visitors. Surplus produce is sold. In 1981 the community split because some members felt that business activities of the community were taking precedence over spiritual matters. Some members quit the community, and the seventy who remained reoriented activities toward spirituality. The leader encourages communal living. Resident members, mainly eighteen–twenty-five years and a few retired people, are vegetarians and eat organic food, fish, eggs, and cheese. Nonresident members include professionals and some workers. Visitors come from Africa and Canada as well as some European countries. The community owns a company, Prosveta—Bulgarian for "teaching"—which employs ten members in publishing.

See Also Aïvanhov, Omraam Mikhaël

Source:

Popenoe, Cris, and Oliver Popenoe. 1984. *Seeds of Tomorrow.* San Francisco: Harper and Row.

BOURNVILLE EXPERIMENT. The Bournville experiment in housing and town planning was the work of George Cadbury (1839–1922), son of John Cadbury (1801–1889), founder of Cadbury's cocoa and chocolate business. In 1879, when the Cadbury brothers saw that their Birmingham factory was inadequate for the firm's needs, they undertook a social and economic experiment. They moved their works to the rural surroundings of Bournville four miles away. The employees remained where they were until 1895, when George Cadbury decided to build a model village close to the works. The experiment aimed to "alleviate the evils" that he wrote would arise from poor accommodations and unsanitary living conditions of the working classes. To avoid the growth of slums around factories between 1893 and 1900, Cadbury bought 300 acres of adjoining land and founded the Bournville Village Trust in December 1900. The village offered some healthy advantages of an outdoor life, because, it was assumed, if workers had healthy leisure activities, then the evils would not arise because workers would attend to their gardens rather what the bars had to offer. At Bournville 925 houses were built to be occupied by any applicants. In 1901 40 percent of the occupants worked at the Bournville factory, and about as many were at the Birmingham factory. In the village's open spaces were built a social center Ruskin Hall, and a school for 540 pupils. Classrooms were built especially for cookery, laundry, vegetable growing, and handicrafts. The cottages were compact, small, cheaply built, convenient, and not ornamented. Most had three bedrooms, a backyard, coal shed, and tool shed, outside lavatory, and laundry. At its inception Bournville was influenced by Cadbury's inspection of Bessboro in Ireland and was partly influenced by Owenism. In turn, the Bournville experiment influenced Ebenezer Howard's (1850–1928) Garden City. In 1906 it was noted that most residents attended to their gardens, and no liquor outlet could be found in the place. By 1931 the capital of the trust had increased from £170,000 to over £. 5 million, and the land to 1,000 acres.

See Also Cadbury, George; Howard, Ebenezer; Owenism

Sources:

Gill, Roger. 1984. "In England's Green and Pleasant Land." In Peter Alexander and Gill Roger, eds., *Utopias*, pp. 109–117. London: Duckworth.

Harvey, William Alexander. 1906. *The Model Village and Its Cottages*. London: B. T. Batesford.

Marsh, Jan. 1982. *Back to the Land: The Pastoral Impulse in England, from 1880 to 1914*. London: Quartet.

Williams, Iola A. 1931. *The Firm of Cadbury 1931–1931*. London: Constable.

BRACHER, SAMUEL V. Samuel Vale Bracher (fl. 1898–1923), a journalist from Gloucester argued with fellow writer John Coleman Kenworthy (1861–c. 1934) about the admission of tramps to Purleigh Colony in 1898. With support from those who agreed with him, Bracher founded his own colony. He and his followers discovered a stone-built house at Whiteway, near Stroud, Gloucestershire, on four acres. They bought it for £450, of which Bracher contributed £405 and established a community of nine men four women, and two children. Quarreling over land use began immediately. When Bracher married, he demanded half of the income of the community for himself and his wife. In time they took less and less interest in the community and lived in a house in the nearby village. Communal duties to work the land collapsed, and eventually it was decided that members would be responsible for their own land.

See Also Kenworthy, John Coleman; Purleigh Colony

Sources:

Armytage, Walter H. Green. 1961. *Heavens Below: Utopian Experiments in England 1560–1950*. London: Routledge and Kegan Paul.

Bracher, Samuel V. 1923. *The Herald Book of Labour Members*. London: Labour.

Marsh, Jan. 1982. *Back to the Land: The Pastoral Impulse in England, from 1880 to 1914*, pp. 107–108. London: Quartet.

BRANCH DAVIDIANS. Branch Davidians are a modern religious sect that claims to be an offshoot of the Seventh-Day Adventist Church. The church renounced any connection with the sect in the 1930s. The sect members believed David Koresh (1960–1993) to be the Lamb (Revelation 5), able to open the seven seals, loose catastrophe on humankind, and propel the group heavenward. Government forces beseiged sect headquarters at Waco, Texas, for fifty-one days after the sect murdered government investigators. The seige ended on 19 April 1993. David Koresh and seventy-four Branch Davidians were dead. This included twenty-one children under four years of age who were consumed by fire. Like Jonestown the Waco disaster is a modern example of a disastrous dystopian venture. Many authors have offered different explanations for the tragedy.

See Also Dystopia; Jonestown (Peoples Temple); Koresh, David

Sources:

Gibbs, Nancy. 1993. " 'Oh, My God' " Fire Storm in Waco. *Time* (Australia) (3 May): 22–44.

Keesing's Contemporary Archives. 1993. March 39358; April 39407; October 39677–39678. London: Keesing's.

"Six People Die in Sect Raid Shoot Out." 1993. *New York Times*, 1 March.

Tabar, James D., and Eugene V. Gallagher. 1995. *Why Waco: Cults and the Battle for Religious Freedom in America.* Berkeley: University of California Press.

BRAVE NEW WORLD. *Brave New World* (1932) is Aldous Huxley's (1894–1963) important dystopian novel on the misuse by totalitarian government of science and technology, that is, scientism. Central to the novel is the use of manipulation of motives to maintain social order. The society is dominated by the adoration of the image of a godlike figure, Henry Ford, who oversees an economy driven by a hectic linking of production and consumption. All human activities are pervaded by this unrelenting economic policy. It is a world of throwaway items that abhors maintenance and repair and lives by the slogan "Ending is better than mending." In consequence, advanced technology is valued highly, and applied not only to material goods like children's toys but also to genetic engineering. As a result, there emerges a class system based on hatching rather than birthing; intelligent citizens, Alphas, have high authority, while unintelligent and physically powerful citizens, Deltas and Epsilons, do heavy labor. This is the prime technique for maintaining social order. Second, advanced technology is used to condition people rather than teach them how to learn through problem solving. This helps eliminate frustrations in education and creates automatons who need not think deeply and thus have no access to the irritations that may drive them to change society. Third, contraceptives are readily available, and copulation abounds, thereby removing another source of tension that may contribute to political action. Where sex fails, drugs are available—particularly soma—to relieve feelings of anger and rage and are recommended over religion and liquor because side effects are minimal. As a result of these scientifically based techniques of social control, most individuals live a life of stunned delight, and the established order remains unthreatened. In this Fordian society intellectual development is stunted even further by the denial of history. Children are told that history is nonsense, the past is a chimera, and old facts are irrelevant to material progress. It is argued simply that the new, in the present, is better than the old, because it was ridden with conflict, for example, Tudor England, as evident in Shakespeare's irrelevant works. Set in the seventh century AF (After Ford), the novel concerns an unhappy Alpha-plus whose antenatal treatment was apparently flawed. On his return from a visit to a reservation in New Mexico he brings with him a savage. The brave new world fascinates the savage, but in time it repels him. He argues with the World Controller, and their conflict illustrates how incongruent are a problem-free scientific society and the needs of a free member of humankind. Countless debates may be made over Huxley's attack on scientism and how it raises the fears that emerge in conflicts over the old and new, past and present, conformity and nonconformity, natural and artificial, plans and unintended consequences, banality and notable achievement, fiction and reality, dreams and nightmares, progressives and conservatives, radicals and reactionaries, asceticism and pleasure, instinct and intellect, diminishing labor and expanding leisure, materialism and idealism, active production and passive consumerism.

See Also Dystopia; Huxley, Aldous

Sources:

Booker, M. Keith. 1994. *Dystopian Literature: A Theory and Research Guide*. Westport, Conn.: Greenwood Press.

Huxley, Aldous L. 1932. *Brave New World*. 1950 ed. with new foreword by author. London Chatto and Windus.

Kumar, Krishan. 1987. *Utopia and Anti-Utopia in Modern Times*. Oxford: Basil Blackwell.

Snodgrass, Mary Ellen. 1995. *Encyclopedia of Utopian Literature*. Santa Barbara, Calif.: ABC-CLIO.

BRISBANE, ALBERT. Albert Brisbane (1809–1890) was born in Batavia, New York, into a well-off, educated British family. Until he was fifteen, his mother educated him. He attended a Long Island boarding school and later went to school in New York City. At eighteen he sailed to Europe, lived in Paris, visited Berlin, Constantinople, and became familiar with social theorists in Europe. This grand tour of Europe introduced him to ideas of Saint-Simonians. In 1830 he returned to Paris and studied with Charles Fourier (1772–1837) and came back to the United States (1834), a strong advocate of Fourier's ideas, especially their sense of justice in the reorganization of society. He popularized Fourierism in the United States beginning in 1839. He published *Social Destiny of Man* (1840), which led to considerable interest and attracted the attention of Horace Greeley

(1811–1872), who gave Brisbane a column in the *New York Tribune*. Brisbane was helpful in the foundation of the Fourierist phalanxes in the 1840s and converted both Brook Farm in West Roxbury and Redbank in New Jersey. The societies flourished but later failed when people lost interest in associationism; for example, in 1844 Ripon Community was established in Wisconsin and disbanded in 1850. The failure of most other communal experiments was disastrous for the Fourierist cause, but Brisbane was always convinced of their value, as he showed in his *General Introduction to Social Science* (1876).

See Also Fourier, Charles; Greeley, Horace; Saint-Simonism

Sources:

Brisbane, Albert. 1840. *Social Destiny of Man*. Reprinted, 1868. Franklin, N.Y.: Burt.

Carlson, Oliver. 1937. *Brisbane: A Candid Biography*. New York: Stackpole Sons.

Fogarty, Robert S. 1990. *All Things New: American Communes and Utopian Movements 1860–1914*. Chicago: University of Chicago Press.

Johnson, Allen, and Dumas Malone, eds. 1929. *Dictionary of American Biography*. Vol. 2. New York: Charles Scribner's Sons.

Kanter, Rosabeth Moss. 1973. *Communes: Creating and Managing the Collective Life*. New York: Harper and Row.

McHenry, Robert, ed. 1992. *The New Encyclopedia Britannica*. Chicago: Encyclopedia Britannica.

Oved, Yaacov. 1987. *Two Hundred Years of American Communes*. New Brunswick, N.J.: Transaction Books.

BROOK FARM COLONY. Originally, this utopian venture was the Brook Farm Institute of Agriculture of Education (1841–1844), then Brook Farm Association for Industry and Education (1844–1845), and finally it was reorganized as Brook Farm Phalanx (1845–1847) when the association converted to Fourierism (1843–1847) in West Roxbury, Boston. Brook Farm was established by Rev. George Ripley (1802–1880) a Unitarian minister in Boston. It was a famous literary and economic utopia whose members shared equally in remuneration, benefits, and work. The members hoped to reform society and weekly published *The Harbinger* (1843–1849). Interested visitors included Ralph Waldo Emerson (1803–1882), Amos Bronson Alcott (1700–1888), Theodore Parker (1810–1860), Sarah Margaret Fuller (1810–1850), and other transcendentalists. Although Nathaniel Hawthorne's (1804–1864) *Blithedale Romance* (1852) depicts Brook Farm, he soon became disillusioned with the venture and left within its first year. It was disbanded in 1846 because it was unable to find a steady income, much less the funds needed to rebuild after a disastrous fire that year. The society dissolved in 1847. Years later Edward Bellamy (1850–1898) was much impressed by the venture and thought his utopia in *Looking Backward* (1888) to be a product of the spirit of socialism that had swept early nineteenth-century United States and led to Brook Farm Colony and other communistic experiments.

See Also Alcott, Amos Bronson; Bellamy, Edward; Dana, Charles Anderson; Orvis, John; Ripley, George

Sources:

Curtis, Edith Roelker. 1961. *A Season in Utopia: The Story of the Brook Farm.* New York: Nelson.
Fogarty, Robert S. 1980. *Dictionary of American Communal History.* Westport, Conn.: Greenwood Press.
Francis, Richard. 1997. *Trancendental Utopias: Individual and Community at Brook Farm, Fruitlands and Walden.* Ithaca, N.Y.: Cornell University Press.
Friebert, Lucy M. 1993. "Creative Women of Brook Farm." In Wendy E. Chmielewski, Louis J. Kern, and Marlyn Klee-Hartzell, eds. *Women in Spiritual and Communitarian Societies in the U.S.*, pp. 75–88. Syracuse, N.Y.: Syracuse University Press.
Kesten, Seymour. 1993. *Utopian Episodes: Daily Life in Experimental Colonies Dedicated to Changing the World.* Syracuse, N.Y.: Syracuse University Press.
Oved, Yaacov. 1987. *Two Hundred Years of American Communes.* New Brunswick, N.J.: Transaction Books.
Sams, Henry W., ed. 1958. *Autobiography of Brook Farm.* Englewood Cliffs, N.J.: Prentice-Hall.
Sears, John Van der Zee. 1975. *My Friends at Brook Farm.* New York: A.M.S. Press.

BROTHERHOOD OF THE NEW LIFE. The brotherhood established four spiritual communities under Thomas Lake Harris (1823–1906). The first was at Mountain Cove, Virginia, in 1851. It reputedly was the original Garden of Eden. The community developed internal conflicts and failed (1853). In 1861 Harris chose Wassiac, Dutchess County, New York, for the second attempt to found the community. It settled at nearby Amenia and prospered (1863–1867). With funds from Laurence Oliphant (1829–1888) and Oliphant's mother, the group moved to a large acreage at Brocton on Lake Erie, near Dunkirk, New York (1867). This was the third brotherhood community and was known as Brocton and as Salem-on-Erie. The Oliphants and others supported the community financially, saw it organized along semicommunistic lines, and established the growing of vines. A family partnership took over from the communistic scheme, and Harris became the fatherlike head of the community. In 1875 the community was divided by a split between Harris and the Oliphants. Some of Harris' followers went with him to a vineyard community, Fountain Grove, in Santa Rosa, California. This was the fourth community of the brotherhood.

See Also Fountain Grove; Harris, Thomas Lake

Sources:

Bailey, William S. 1935. "The Harris Community—Brotherhood of the New Life." *New York History*, 16: 278–285.
Fogarty, Robert S. 1990. *All Things New: American Communes and Utopian Movements 1860–1914.* Chicago: University of Chicago Press.

Hine, Robert V. 1953. *California's Utopian Colonies*. 1983 ed. Berkeley: University of
California Press.

BRUDERHOF. Bruderhof is known as the Society of Brothers, a modern utopian sect, established in Sannerz, Germany (1920); other communities established themselves later in Liechtenstein, Cotswold (1937–1940), and Wheathill
in England, also in Paraguay, Uruguay, and Woodcrest, New York.

See Also Arnold, Eberhard; Society of Brothers (Bruderhof)

Sources:

Arnold, Emmy. 1963. *Torches Together: The Beginning and Early Years of the Bruderhof Commune*. Rifton, N.Y.: Plough.
Bohlken-Zumpe, Elizabeth. 1993. *Torches Extinguished: Memories of Communal Bru-
derhof Childhood in Paraguay, Europe and the USA*. 2d ed. San Francisco: Carrier Pigeon.
Mow, Merrill. 1989. *Torches Rekindled; The Bruderhof's Struggle for Renewal*. 3d rev.
ed., 1991. Rifton, N.Y.: Plough.
Oved, Yaacov. 1987. *Two Hundred Years of American Communes*. New Brunswick, N.J.:
Transaction Books.
———. 1996. *The Witness of the Brothers: A History of the Bruderhof*. New Brunswick,
N.J.: Transaction Books.
Whitworth, John McKelvie. 1975. *God's Blueprints: A Sociological Study of Three Uto-
pian Sects*. London: Routledge and Kegan Paul.

BUCKINGHAM, JAMES SILK. James Silk Buckingham (1786–1855) was
born at Flushing, near Falmouth, and at age ten went to sea. On his return to
England he married Elizabeth Jennings (1806), who bore him several children.
In Calcutta he established a newspaper (1818), published politically disturbing
articles, and was promptly expelled by the governor-general of India, John Adam
(1779–1825), in 1823. He sailed home to England and established several newspapers that discussed politics, literature, and news about Britain's Oriental colonies and possessions. None were particularly successful. He was a member of
Parliament for the new borough of Sheffield (1832–1837) and displayed a deep
interest in social reform and the temperance movement. After leaving Parliament, he sailed to the United States, where he spent four years (1837–1841)
traveling and compiled two reports, concluding that the communal way of life
had much to offer. From 1843 to 1847 he was the resident director of the British
and Foreign Institute, Hanover Square, London. He traveled through Europe
(1847–1848) and wrote many books about his travels. In 1851 he received a
pension of £200 in recognition of his writing and another £200 as compensation
for the unfair treatment he had endured when his paper was closed in Calcutta.
By 1851 he had become president of the London Temperance League. Before
his death he developed a secure reputation as a public lecturer on diverse sub-

jects but is best remembered for his *National Evils and Practical Remedies* (1849), which set down his plan for a model town.

See Also Buckingham's Plan for a Model Town

Sources:

Buckingham, James Silk. 1849. *National Evils and Practical Remedies: With the Plan of a Model Town*. London: Peter Jackson. Reprinted, 1973. Clifton, N.J.: Augustus M. Kelley.
Oved, Yaacov. 1987. *Two Hundred Years of American Communes*. New Brunswick, N.J.: Transaction Books.
Stephen, Leslie, and Sydney Lee, eds. 1917. *The Dictionary of National Biography*. Vol. 3. London: Oxford University Press.

BUCKINGHAM'S PLAN FOR A MODEL TOWN. James Silk Buckingham's plan called for the formation of a company to be known as the Model Town Association. It was to be incorporated by royal charter or an act of Parliament so as to limit the responsibility of each individual to the shares held by him in its stock. The object of the company would be the building of an entirely new town—"Victoria"—which would contain "every improvement in its position, plan, drainage, ventilation, architecture, supply of water, light and every other elegance and convenience" that art and science had to offer. It would be one-mile-square and have 10,000 inhabitants. Around the town about 10,000 acres of land would be purchased or rented for the purpose of introducing varieties of agriculture, pasture, and horticulture. They would be worked under the most advanced methods. A suitable variety of manufactures and handicraft trade would be established nearest the outer edge of the town, thereby reserving the inner area for houses and offices free from the noises of industry. Liquor was prohibited, as were guns, pistols, bayonets, and other weapons. There was to be perfect freedom of all religious opinions and equality of all religious rites. The Sabbath was to be kept sacred to devotion, and no labor was to be permitted on that day. Women and children were never to be employed in any laborious occupations that may be injurious to their health, and no man should work more than eight hours each day. Individuals and families were to pay to the company a rent that would be regulated by a moderate interest on the actual cost of the premises they occupied. Child care for the young of working mothers and free education for older children would be provided by the company. It was proposed to raise £4 million in 200,000 shares of £20 each. The plan was never realized, but it influenced the ideas of Ebenezer Howard (1850–1928), founder of the Garden City.

See Also Buckingham, James Silk; Howard, Ebenezer

Sources:

Buckingham, James Silk. 1849. *National Evils and Practical Remedies: With the Plan of a Model Town*. London: Peter Jackson. Reprinted 1973. Clifton, N.J.: Augustus M. Kelley.

BUDDHIST CENTER IN LONDON. In London the Friends of the Western Buddhist Order, a small group, tried to practice generally many of the traditional Buddhist ideas. The founder was Dennis Philip Edward Lingwood, an Englishman who spent twenty years in India and who became the Venerable Sangharakshita. In 1967 he founded the order, which aimed to establish a new society whose members were free. The order has centers in Britain, Sweden, Finland, Australia and New Zealand, the United States, and India. They are residential centers, with educational areas and a business cooperative. At the London Buddhist Center are fifty members; members live in single-sex groups of up to twenty people, and they are housed in the center's Phoenix Housing cooperative. With them live another sixty friends of the order. In London the headquarters is an old, converted firehouse, with offices and teaching rooms and a natural food store. It has a vegetarian restaurant and accommodations for twenty visitors. One shop sells secondhand clothes, and another shop is a retail store. The leader's role is spiritual, not administrative. He studies, practices Buddhism, teaches, and provides spiritual inspiration to members.

Source:

Popenoe, Cris, and Oliver Popenoe. 1984. *Seeds of Tomorrow*. San Francisco: Harper and Row.

BUKHARIN, NIKOLAI IVANOVICH. Nikolai Ivanovich Bukharin (1888–1938), son of a teacher, was born in Moscow, graduated from high school, and studied at the Economics Department and Law Faculty, Moscow University (1907). In 1905 he joined a student revolutionary group and in 1908 became a member of the Russian Social-Democratic Workers' Party—Bolsheviks (RSDRP [B]). Twice he wrote articles for *Pravda*, and from 1912 to 1914 he worked among social democrats in Vienna. In 1914 he was arrested on espionage charges by the Austrian police shortly before the outbreak of World War I and deported to Switzerland after the leaders among the Austrian social democrats testified on his behalf. In July 1915 he went to Sweden under an alias—Dolgolevsky—and in 1916 was arrested for antiwar statements and deported to Norway. He left Norway in October 1916 and entered the United States illegally, where he edited a newspaper, *Nouy Mir*, in New York and made a propaganda tour of many U.S. cities. After the 1917 revolution he returned to Russia and was elected to the Executive Committee of the RSDRP (B) and was elected to the Central Committee and remained a member until 1934. He edited *Pravda* (1917–1918) and later undertook trips abroad for the Communist Party. He was a sociology professor at Moscow University and active in party congresses and conferences and delivered many speeches at workers' and party meetings. He drafted countless party documents and published pamphlets, popular books, articles, and several important theoretical works. He was expelled from the Communist Party in March 1937 and sentenced to death for espionage and counterrevolutionary activities at the trial of anti-Soviet rightist Trotskyite centers. He was shot by firing squad in 1938.

See Also Bolshevism

Sources:

McHenry, Robert, ed. 1992. *The New Encyclopedia Britannica*. Chicago: Encyclopedia Britannica.
Schulz, Heinrich E., Paul K. Urban, and Andrew I. Lebed, eds. 1972. *Who Was Who in the U.S.S.R.* Metuchen, N.J.: Scarecrow Press.

BURLEY COLONY. Burley Colony, also known as the Cooperative Brotherhood (1898–1908), was established in Burley, Washington, after a convention in June 1897 organized by the Colonization Commission of the Social Democracy of America. It was started after the leaders visited the Ruskin Colony in Tennessee. By 1901 there were 115 members, forty-five men, twenty-five women, and forty-five children. For several years membership was fairly stable and included nonresident members who, at one time, numbered over 1,000. The colony was reorganized (1904), and the original communal concept disappeared. The newly organized Burley Mercantile Rochdale Association continued until 1908. One of the founders, Cyrus Field Willard (1858–1935), later joined the theosophists at Point Loma. Members of Burley Colony frequently contacted members of the Equality and the Home Colonies.

See Also Equality Colony; Ruskin Colony; Willard, Cyrus Field

Sources:

Fogarty, Robert S. 1980. *Dictionary of American Communal History*. Westport, Conn.: Greenwood Press.
———. 1990. *All Things New: American Communes and Utopian Movements 1860–1914*. Chicago: University of Chicago Press.
LeWarne, Charles Pierce. 1975. *Utopias on Puget Sound, 1885–1915*. Seattle: University of Washington Press.
Oved, Yaacov. 1987. *Two Hundred Years of American Communes*. New Brunswick, N.J.: Transaction Books.

BURNETT, GEORGE. George Burnett (c. 1776–1811), son of a farmer, was born in Huntspill, Somersetshire. George was introduced to classical literature by the local clergyman and as a youth went to Balliol College, Oxford, to study theology. After two years at Oxford he became disillusioned with study and took part in planning a "pantisocracy" with Samuel Coleridge (1772–1834) at a site bought at the southern end of Otsego Lake near the Susquehanna River. The scheme fell through. The following year he studied in Manchester and for a short time became a pastor in Yarmouth. Later, he briefly studied medicine at Edinburgh University. With the help of friends he became a tutor for Lord Stanhope's sons. Shortly after this appointment the sons left home, and Burnett became an assistant surgeon in a militia regiment. He soon left this position and became an English tutor in Poland and on his return to England published a series of letters (1807), *View of the Present State of Poland*. Among his other published works were three volumes titled *Specimens of English Prose Writers, from the Earliest Times to the Close of the Seventeenth Century* (1807). His last publication was a selection of John Milton's prose works (1809), which he compiled at Huntspill and dedicated to Lord Erskine.

See Also Coleridge, Samuel Taylor; Pantisocracy; Southey, Robert

Source:

Stephen, Leslie, and Sydney Lee, eds. 1917. *The Dictionary of National Biography*. London: Oxford University Press.

BURNING BUSH. A group of dissatisfied Methodists formed the Metropolitan Church Association in Waukesha, Wisconsin, and in 1912 became known as the "the Society of the Burning Bush," or simply "Burning Bush." Their beliefs rejected predestination and favored salvation through grace, faith, and goodwill. They believed in humankind's moral freedom and even in apostasy. Also they believed in the gift of the Holy Ghost and the second blessing, after which a person lived without sin, had trances and visions, and could heal by faith. The church was intensely evangelistic. Members were deeply committed to prayer, praise, and music. They would sing and jump to musical accompaniment, and their neighbors in Bullard, Texas, would call them "Holy Jumpers" because of their exuberant religious rituals. Several other similar communal church settlements were established in Virginia, West Virginia, and New Orleans. The Burning Bush at Bullard, Texas, became the most prominent. The community purchased 1,500 acres in East Texas, was named Metropolitan Institute of Texas, and settled southeast of Bullard in Texas (1913). The community had 375 members, who varied from farm laborers to professionals. Their wealth was held in common, and all residents in the community would eat together. They built a tabernacle and a house each for married and single members. Every person had a task, and that was all that was expected. However, the finances of the settlement became strained in hard times, and some members were hired out to work in the local community. The community prospered until immediately after World War I (1919), when the financial backer of the colony lost his bond business in Chicago and could no longer support the community. The sheriff seized the land and sold it to the community's major creditor for $1,000. The colonists dispersed, their equipment sold cheaply, and some members went to similar colonies in Wisconsin, while others went home.

Sources:

Fogarty, Robert S. 1980. *Dictionary of American Communal History*. Westport, Conn.: Greenwood Press.
Miller, Timothy. 1990. *American Communes: 1860–1960*. New York: Garland.
Smyrl, Edwin. 1947. "Burning Bush." *Southwestern Historical Quarterly* 50: 335–343.

BUTLER, SAMUEL. Samuel Butler (1835–1902) was born near Bingham, Nottinghamshire, and educated at Cambridge. His father was in charge of Langar Rectory, and Samuel often argued with him and finally decided not to take orders but become a farmer in New Zealand, as far away from England and his father as possible. He liked to write and published *A First Year in Canterbury Settlement* (1863) about his New Zealand adventure. He returned to England in 1864 and studied painting, and one of his artistic works appears in the Tate Gallery. He was drawn to the ideas of Charles Darwin (1809–1882), accepted the theory of evolution, but rejected the principle of natural selection. His oppositon to the principle appeared in his *Luck or Cunning* (1886). He loved music, especially Handel's works, and composed two oratorios, fugues, minuets, and a cantata. Later, he turned to scholarly works and translated the *Iliad* (1898) and the *Odyssey* (1900). His autobiographical novel *The Way of All Flesh* (1903) was published after his death and earned the reputation of being a remarkable study of moral problems that arise between generations. The book greatly influenced George Bernard Shaw (1856–1950). Butler's publication on his New Zealand experiences reappeared in *Erewhon* (1872); it is interesting to note that the title of the book—an anagram of ''nowhere''—echoes the different meanings attaching to More's *Utopia*—''no place'' and ''ideal place''—and the satirical device of turning conventions on their head could find no better setting for a disaffected English writer than New Zealand, the antipodes, where, from England, it was commonly said, all people seemed to be on their heads!

See Also Erewhon; Shaw, George Bernard; *Utopia*

Sources:

Harris, John F. 1916. *Samuel Butler, Author of "Erewhon": The Man and His Work.* New York: Dodd, Mead.

Holt, Lee A. 1964. *Samuel Butler.* New York: Twayne.

Jones, Joseph. 1959. *The Cradle of Erewhon: Samuel Butler in New Zealand.* Austin: University of Texas Press.

Magnussen, Magnus, and Rosemary Goring, eds. 1990. *Chambers Biographical Dictionary.* 5th ed. Edinburgh: Chambers.

Raby, Peter. 1991. *Samuel Butler: A Biography.* Iowa City: University Press of Iowa.

Snodgrass, Mary Ellen. 1995. *Encyclopedia of Utopian Literature.* Santa Barbara, Calif.: ABC-CLIO.

C

CABET, ÉTIENNE. Étienne Cabet (1788–1856) was born in Dijon, France, son of a cooper. After a good education, the young man became a lycée instructor. In the 1830 revolution he was drawn to left-wing ideas and was elected to the Chamber of Deputies (1831). After making bitter attacks on the government, he was convicted of treason but escaped by exiling himself to Britain (1834–1839). He was influenced by Robert Owen (1771–1858), developed a theory of communism, and worked vigorously for the labor movement. After reading More's *Utopia* he wrote a novel, *Voyage en Icarie* (1840), about a society in which people are born essentially good but are often thrust into evil company and forced to face inequalities that tend to corrupt them. Like Robert Owen, Cabet believed that humankind can be perfected through universal education and that about fifty years would pass before a new social system could be achieved. In this new society equality would be the basic rule; every person would be productively employed and take turns at diverse occupations, rural and urban, and the slogan for distribution of the fruits of their labor would be "from each according to his ability, to each according to his needs." Everyone would have a vote. In his Icaria an elected government controls all economic and social affairs; the only other independent unit is the family. Because education and art are the paths to the peak of civilization, teachers and artists would rank high in Icaria. Cabet gained many adherents for his ideas in this popular book. In 1848 a group of Icarians attempted unsuccessfully to found an Icarian community on the Red River, Texas. In the following year Cabet established a temporary colony at an old Mormon town, Nauvoo in Illinois, but serious dissension arose. Later several Icarian communities established themselves in the United States and in time dispersed. He died soon after an Icarian community was established in St. Louis, where he went to live after the dissension in Nauvoo. Although equality was important to Cabet, it did not extend to women or children. He thought women should be only relatively equal to men; women could not vote or hold elected office. To attract young women to his utopian ventures he waived the 300-franc entry fee for unmarried women. At work he believed women should be employed according to their intelligence and ability: they were suited to washing, ironing, sewing, and teaching, and it was best for them to stay at home. Women were not accepted in the infirmary; only men could use the settlement's medical facilities. Only boys had music lessons. Girls had to learn to adorn themselves decently and modestly, and as women they were not to be interested in their attire. They should never hope ever to be materially independent because, if so, they might fail in their main duty, marriage. Although education was the path to perfection, schools were not built immediately in Icarian settlements, teachers were few, corporal punishment was employed, and children were not to contribute in making school rules. Also children and their parents were separated often as a matter of principle. In short, Cabet practiced his ideas imperfectly (Kesten, 1993, pp. 106–110, 116–122).

See Also Cheltenham; Corning; Icarian movement; Speranza; Texas-Nauvoo

Sources:

Cabet, Étienne. 1840. *Voyage en Icarie*. Paris: Bureau du Populaie.

———. 1966. "Work and Play in Icaria." Reprinted in Frank E. Manuel, and Futzie P. Manuel, eds. *French Utopias: An Anthology of Ideal Societies*, pp. 329–344. New York: Free Press.

Johnson, Allen, and Dumas Malone, eds. 1929. *Dictionary of American Biography*. Vol. 2. New York: Charles Scribner's Sons.

Kesten, Seymour. 1993. *Utopian Episodes: Daily Life in Experimental Colonies Dedicated to Changing the World*. Syracuse, N.Y.: Syracuse University Press.

Oved, Yaacov. 1987. *Two Hundred Years of American Communes*. New Brunswick, N.J.: Transaction Books.

Roberts, Leslie J. 1991. "Étienne Cabet and His *"Voyage en Icarie 1840."* *Utopian Studies* 2, nos. 1, 2: 77–94.

Ross, Marchand. 1976. *Child of Icaria*. Westport, Conn.: Hyperion Press.

Shaw, Albert. 1884. *Icaria: A Chapter in the History of Communism*. New York and London: G. P. Putnam and Sons.

Snodgrass, Mary Ellen. 1995. *Encyclopedia of Utopian Literature*. Santa Barbara, Calif.: ABC-CLIO.

CADBURY, GEORGE. George Cadbury (1839–1922) was born at Edgbaston, Birmingham, the third son and fourth child of John Cadbury (1801–1889) the tea and coffee dealer and founder of the cocoa and chocolate manufacturing firm Cadbury Bros. The Cadbury family had settled in Birmingham at the end of the eighteenth century, having been long associated with the Society of Friends (Quakers) since the days of George's great-great grandfather. George was educated at home and commuted to a Quaker school in Edgbaston. In 1855 his mother, a temperance worker, died, and his schooling ended shortly afterward. In April 1861 George and his elder brother Richard Cadbury (1835–1899) took full control of their late father's cocoa factory in Birmingham. The business expanded rapidly, mainly because of Cadbury's introduction in 1866 of the first unadulterated British cocoa. The Cadburys were also the first employers in Birmingham to introduce a weekly half-holiday for their employees and to take a great interest in their welfare. By 1879 their factory was inadequate, and the brothers decided to move to the rural surroundings four miles from Birmingham at Bournville. Although they were not the first to make a move of this kind, they were the first to associate it with welfare, education, and work in the factory and especially to introduce improvements of employee housing. To avoid the development of slums, he bought a large acreage of adjoining land, built 300 houses, and founded the Bournville Cadbury Village Trust in December 1900. In 1899, after Richard had died, the firm was turned into a company with George as chairman, and the Bournville experiment was largely due to him. He had been influenced by the ideas at another industrial town, Port Sunlight. In 1903 he handed over his home to the Society of Friends as a settlement for men and women engaged in religious and social work. He also led a campaign against sweat shops.

See Also Bournville Experiment; Port Sunlight

Sources:

Gardiner, A. G. 1923 *Life of George Cadbury*. London: Cassell.
Gill, Roger. 1984. "In England's Green and Pleasant Land." In Peter Alexander and Roger Gill, eds., *Utopias*, pp. 109–117. London: Duckworth.
Smith, Chris, John Child, and Michael Rowlinson. 1990. *Reshaping Work, the Cadbury Experience*. Cambridge: Cambridge University Press.
Weaver, John R. H., ed. 1937. *Dictionary of National Biography 1922–1930*. London: Oxford University Press.
Williams, Iona A. 1931. *The Firm of Cadbury 1831–1931*. London: Constable.

CADDY, EILEEN AND PETER. With Dorothy Maclean (b. 1920), a Canadian clairvoyant born in Guelph, Peter Caddy (1917–1994) an ex-Royal Air Force officer, and his wife, Eileen Caddy (b. 1917), ran the 150-bed Cluny Hill hotel in Forres, twenty-six miles east of Inverness in the far north of Scotland. Eileen was born in Alexandria, Egypt. She left her husband and children to be with Peter. Peter had been initiated into the Rosicrucian Order and already married twice before he met Eileen. For many years Eileen had been guided during meditations by instructions on how to run their hotel and in 1957 was told that they were to live in their small trailer at a nearby commercial trailer park in the village of Findhorn near the beach of Moray Firth. They were advised to tidy the area and put light into everything that they did and to establish positive energies in the place. They were told to cultivate a garden and to eat much homegrown food to raise their "vibrational level." Also they were told to tune in to an archetypal life force of each species of plant—the capital Devas. The Devas messages contained instructions about the treatment that different plants preferred. These instructions were followed, and the results were remarkable in view of the poor beach soil. Soil and garden experts were equally surprised to see the plants grow. The most notable success was the raising of a cabbage that weighed forty pounds. Word of these horticultural miracles spread, and members came to join the community (1957–1962). Peter used the advice of Eileen's voice as a directive in his business management and was convinced the voice was of divine origin. In 1979 Peter Caddy left the community.

See Also Findhorn Community

Sources:

Caddy, Eileen. 1993. *Flight into Freedom.* Findhorn, Scotland: Findhorn Press.

Caddy, Peter. 1996. *In Perfect Timing.* Findhorn, Scotland: Findhorn Press.

Inglis, Mary. 1996. "Findhorn Foundation: Nature Spirits and New Age Business." In Bill, Metcalf, ed., *Shared Visions, Shared Lives. Communal Living around the Globe*, Chapter 11. Findhorn, Scotland: Findhorn Press.

Popenoe, Cris, and Oliver Popenoe. 1984. *Seeds of Tomorrow.* San Francisco: Harper and Row.

Walker, Alex, ed. 1994. *The Kingdom Within; A Guide to the Spiritual Work of the Findhorn Community.* Forres, Scotland: Findhorn Foundation.

CAMISARDS. Camisards were Protestant millenarian peasants from the Cevennes region of France who wore their shirts outside their trousers, hence, their name. They came from a Huguenot sect known as French Prophets and escaped to England toward the end of the seventeenth century. They knew of four degrees of spirit: the first degree was knowing that the spirit would descend; the second was being inspired by the spirit; the third was the judgment of the spirit and its consequences; and the final state was being filled with the spirit. At this fourth state an individual could either perform miracles or indulge otherwise in unearthly activities. In their support for the authority of spiritual experiences Camisards opposed university learning. In 1702 they rebelled against persecutions that had followed the revocation in 1685 of the Edict of Nantes. They were identified probably because they were seen to be wearing shirts during their raids at night. They were lead by Durand Fage (fl. 1680–1708) and Elie Marion (fl. 1702). They held semisecret meetings in the British Isles, and among their few adherents were Jane and James Wardley (1747–1774), who were also adherents of the Friends until they developed their own form of Quakerism, that is, Shakers. By 1748 Camisards were evident as loosely organized groups in London.

See Also Fage, Durand; Marion, Elie; Wardley, Jane and James

Sources:

Armytage, Walter H. Green. 1961. *Heavens Below: Utopian Experiments in England 1560–1950.* London: Routledge and Kegan Paul.

Garret, Clarke. 1987. *Spirit Possession and Popular Religion.* Baltimore: Johns Hopkins University Press.

Tylor, Charles. 1893. *The Camisards.* London: Simpkin, Marshall, Hamilton, Kent.

CAMPANELLA, TOMMASO. Tommaso Campanella (1568–1639) was born in Stilo, Calabria, in southern Italy and baptized Giovanni Domenico. As a child he showed great intelligence and by thirteen years had mastered many Latin authors. He entered the Dominican order (1582), wrote poetry, studied philosophy, and his thinking turned against the orientation of Aristotle. In 1592 he was denounced and briefly imprisoned in the Dominican monastery, Naples. In 1593 he befriended Galileo (1564–1642) at the University of Padua shortly after the latter had become a professor of mathematics. Again he was denounced (1594), tried for heresy, and imprisoned. In 1599 he was again charged with heresy and cruelly tortured. When he feigned insanity he was spared and given life imprisonment (1599–1626), during which he composed sonnets, wrote philosophical, political, and theological works, including *La Città de Sole* (1602). An attempt at escape failed (1604), and he was transferred to a dungeon of Castel Sant'Élmo and lived under the most dreadful conditions for eight years before being sent to Castel Nuovo, a less severe prison. In 1626 he was released, and he fled Rome in 1634 to spend his last few years in Paris. He was one of the few early contributors to utopian thinking. His notable utopian work was *Civitas Solis Poetica: Idea Reipublicae Philosphiae* or *La Città de Sole* (published in 1637 as *The City of the Sun*). The work advocated a city in which illustrated walls ringed the classroom and proposed the ideas of modern eugenics and communism. His ideas contributed much to Lenin's (1870–1924) Monumental Propaganda Plan.

See Also City of the Sun, The

Sources:

Bonansea, Bernadino M. 1969. *Tommaso Campanella. Renaissance Pioneer of Modern Thought.* Washington, DC: Catholic University of America Press.

Campanella, Tommaso. 1602. *La Città del sole: diagelo Poetico. The City of the Sun; A Political Dialogue.* Trans. with introduction and notes by Daniel J. Donno. 1981. Berkeley: University of California Press.

Cross, L. A., and E. A. Livingstone. 1997. *The Oxford Dictionary of the Christian Church.* 3d. ed. New York: Oxford University Press.

Morely, Henry, ed. 1886. *Ideal Commonwealths: Plutarch's Lycurgus, More's Utopia, Bacon's New Atlantis, Campanella's City of the Sun, and a Fragment of Hall's Mundus Alter et Idem, with an Introduction by Henry Morely.* London: G. Routledge.

Oved, Yaacov. 1987. *Two Hundred Years of American Communes.* New Brunswick, N.J.: Transaction Books.

Snodgrass, Mary Ellen. 1995. *Encyclopedia of Utopian Literature.* Santa Barbara, Calif.: ABC-CLIO.

CAMPBELL, ALEXANDER. Alexander Campbell (1788–1866) was born near Ballymena in County Antrim, Ireland, and, like his father, Thomas Campbell (1763–1854), was educated at the University of Glasgow. Father and son were antiburgher Presbyterians, a division opposed to the discipline of the main church. In 1807 Thomas emigrated to the United States, was embraced by the Scotch-Irish community in southwestern Pennsylvania, and in 1809 formed the Christian Association of Washington in Pennsylvania. Alexander joined him that year and brought other family to the United States and was ordained (1812). Nominally, they were Baptists until 1827. Feeling that in important ways their views were not like those of most Baptists, Alexander, as the new leader of the group, advocated returning to a simple interpretation of the Scriptures and reorganizing the church to reflect that simplicity. His followers were called Reformers for the simplicity of their doctrine. In 1823 he established the *Christian Baptist* and, to promote widely his reformist views, traveled through the new western states addressing massive audiences in western Pennsylvania, West Virginia, and Ohio. To them he protested against the creeds that asserted the Bible to be the only authority on religious affairs and later published a translation of the New Testament in which "baptist" and "baptism" were replaced with "immerser" and "immersion" (1826). In 1840–1841 he founded Bethany College, West Virginia, and became its president. Meanwhile, many Reformers had quit or been pushed out by many Baptist churches; in response Campbell suggested that they form congregations and call themselves Disciples of Christ.

See Also Disciples of Christ

Source:

Harris, William H., and Judith Levy. 1978–1979. *The New Illustrated Columbia Encyclopedia.* New York: Rockville House.

CANNINGTON MANOR. Cannington Manor was situated in the Qu'Appelle valley of Saskatchewan, south of Moosomin (1882–c. 1900). Establishing the manor was the idea of an aristocratic, military gentleman, Captain Edward Mitchell Pierce, who had been bankrupted in London, England, and had four sons to support. He advertised in a British newspaper that he would train young bachelors of his class in rural pursuits for $500 to $1,000 per annum. He wanted to establish a feudal, self-sufficient community based on cooperation, bourgeois culture, and sporty male pleasures. At Cannington a village society was established with the Moose Mountain Trading Company at its center. The Moose Mountain Trading Company incorporated economic enterprises and social services; it provided a church, hall, school, and doctor and ran a cooperative cheese factory, post office, hotel, gristmill, blacksmith's, and woodworker's shop. The major factions in the community were workers and gentlemen of leisure. James Humphrey led the workers' faction; the leisured fellows were led by the Becker brothers, who lived on inherited wealth. Each leader built a spacious home. Humphrey's home had enough space to house twenty militia, should a rebellion rise up; Becker's home was a sumptuous manor of twenty rooms for bachelors and billiards players. The wealthy Becker brothers were at the center of the "drones" group, sailing, playing cricket and tennis, or discussing science, politics, and agriculture. They dressed for dinner, frolicked, and played cards. This social experiment broke with the mainstream of individualistic homestead farming and re-created traditional feudal structures. The bachelor society was eroded by marriage, patriotic desires to serve in the Boer War, and speculation in gold. The community's economic base was not sound and deteriorated badly once the Canadian Pacific Railway extended southward in 1900. The village store followed the railway, the bachelors wandered off, and the sporting culture was no more.

Source:

Rasporich, Anthony W. 1985. "Utopian Ideals and Community Settlements in Western Canada 1880–1914." In R. Francis, R. Douglas and Howard Palmer, eds., *The Prairie West: Historical Readings*, pp. 338–361. 2d ed. 1992. Edmonton, Alberta: Pica Pica Press.

CARDSTON COMPANY. Cardston Company is an example of a Mormon settlement in northern Alberta. This company got its charter from the Northwest Territories governor in 1890. The settlement practiced polygamy secretly on the assumption that every woman would secure a husband through polygamy, she would have a large number of men to choose from, and, according to the division of labor, this would ensure that the next generation was guaranteed better supervision and kinder personal treatment. John Taylor and Charles Ora Card planned a rural village with public buildings around a communal and business center. Supervised by church leaders, the company organized successful business ventures, and used a negotiable script, signed by Card, in the depression when dollars were scarce. By 1895 they managed to pay a dividend of 40 percent, half in cash, half in goods. Thereafter, the company declined, and 600,000 acres were sold to the Salt Lake City Church. In 1898 the Cardston *Record* and a branch of the Bank of Montreal were established, and in that year Salt Lake City invested in a canal and irrigation project. In 1901, a rich Utah businessman, Jesse Knight, overinvested in the company and the area. In 1904 John Taylor was excommunicated, the community was subject to more control from outside, and the communal experiment was overwhelmed by massive migration into the area of Cardston.

Sources:

Dawson, C. A. 1936. *Group Settlement: Ethnic Communities in Western Canada*, vol. 7, pp. 205–213. Toronto: Macmillan.

Rasporich, Anthony W. 1992. "Utopian Ideals and Community Settlements in Western Canada 1880–1914." In R. Douglas Francis and Howard Palmer, eds., *The Prairie West: Historical Readings*, 2d ed., pp. 338–361 Edmonton, Alberta: Pica Pica Press.

CARPENTER, EDWARD. Edward Carpenter (1844–1929) was born into a middle-class family in Brighton and became a mathematician. He also studied theology and was a rector as well as college tutor at Trinity Hall. Feeling that he wanted to quit the vacuous intellectual life of the university and enter the real world, he suddenly resigned his position (1874) to lecture through northern England for the University Extension program. After seven years he settled in Sheffield, and, a convinced egalitarian, he decided to keep close to nature. Drawn to outdoor life, he swam, sunbathed, worked with his hands, and became a vegetarian. He also wrote poems that reflected his passion for a life close to the earth and the experience of digging. He was much influenced by the early Hindu poem, sung by Krishna, about religious and philosophical values, *Bhagavad-Gita*, which he had read at the time of his mother's death. In 1882 he used his inheritance to buy land for a market garden and to live in the clean, open air. Although he had no political agenda, others saw him as a social reformer. On his Arcadian holding, south of Sheffield, he would dream, dig a garden and drains, and write. This combination of physical labor and writing made him content. In 1887 he published his *England's Ideal*, which outlines a simple, inexpensive life on a quarter acre. Two years later he published *Civilisation: Its Cause and Cure*, which claimed that a way to Eden lay in escaping into a primitive culture. Many noted British writers called on him, including the writer E. M. Forster (1879–1970) and the physician and sexologist Henry Havelock Ellis (1859–1939). Many homosexuals sought him after he published his most notable work, *Love's Coming of Age* (1896) and *The Indeterminate Sex* (1908). Carpenter felt that he had rid himself of life's complications and won a new life by dropping middle-class conventions, ridding himself of sexual conventions and restraints, and expounding on free love. He sought and lived a life of good health and joy; for others, he recommended new life dominated by manual labor, dreaming, fresh air, unpolluted streams, sunrises and sunsets, the passion of human touch, warm loving, and the values of working people.

See Also Norton Colony

Sources:

Armytage, Walter H. Green. 1961. *Heavens Below: Utopian Experiments in England 1560–1950*. London: Routledge and Kegan Paul.

Brown, Tony, ed. 1990. *Edward Carpenter and Late Victorian Radicalism*. London: Frank Cass.

Marsh, Jan. 1982. *Back to the Land: The Pastoral Impulse in England, from 1880 to 1914*. London: Quartet.

Rowbottom, Sheila, and Jeffrey Weeks. 1977. *Socialism and The New Life: The Personal and Sexual Practices of Edward Carpenter and Havelock Ellis*. London: Pluto Press.

Tsuzuki, Chushichi. 1980. *Edward Carpenter 1844–1929: Prophet of Human Fellowship*. Cambridge: Cambridge University Press.

Weaver, John R. H., ed. 1937. *Dictionary of National Biography 1922–1930*. London: Oxford University Press.

CASTLE, THE. The *Castle* (1926) is a novel of dystopian fiction by Franz Kafka (1883–1924) in which the protagonist, K, arrives at a village where he has been ordered to go to survey land for officials in the nearby castle. The Castle has a distant, but influential, political control over the villagers. At the Castle the officials deny having sent for K, and he feels this is because he has problems communicating with them. Powerful and bewildering forces appear to prevent him from doing what he knows he must do. He fails to get on with the work, a common theme in Kafka's writing. Several interpretations have been offered: the work is a modern-day *Pilgrim's Progress* that affords no progress for the protagonist; it centers on the individual's search for the meaning of existence; it reflects the overbearing significance of oedipal conflicts all men experience; it presents the world as in a shattered and meaningless condition in which rational organizations are madly conceived, follow unknowable policies, and are illogically administered. No matter what interpretation one chooses, in the story the individual struggles forever to understand. K finds many indicators to guide him, but all are unintelligible, in particular, the two letters he receives from Klamm, the head of the Castle, both of which are clear enough but have no definite meaning and offer no means to decipher them. The dystopian features of *The Castle* are its political control of village life and its personnel, who are respected but feared, known but not understood. All authority and power depend on this absence of definition among dominant figures, their elusiveness and their enigmatic qualities. They contribute to an aura surrounding the head of the Castle like that of the leader in a totalitarian state. The work has been regarded also as a political satire that illustrates the incongruity of spiritual and physical aspects of experience and depicts the great psychological distance between the leaders and the led, colonizers and those they colonize.

See Also Dystopia; Kafka, Franz; *Trial, The*

Sources:

Booker, M. Keith. 1994. *Dystopian Literature: A Theory and Research Guide*. Westport, Conn.: Greenwood Press.

Magnussen, Magnus, and Rosemary Goring, eds. 1990. *Chambers Biographical Dictionary*. 5th ed. Edinburgh: Chambers.

CEDAR VALE OR PROGRESSIVE COMMUNITY. In 1871 William Frey (1839–1888) established a community of three adults in Osage County, Kansas. It was named Cedar Vale or the Progressive Community. By 1872 the group comprised seven adults. They used no tobacco and abstained from pork, nor did they take tea or coffee. To help them with problems of interpersonal control, they practiced mutual criticism. In 1875, with another family, the Freys quit and formed the Investigating Community. They upheld communism and monogamy. Soon fifteen Russians joined them. They were God-men who followed a Quaker form of socialism. Unhappy with what they saw, the God-men quit the community and formed the Cedarville Community, four miles away. Interpersonal conflict among them led all to return to Frey's colony. Frey's disciplinary techniques were unacceptable to his followers, and by 1877 the colony broke down.

See Also Frey, William

Sources:

Fogarty, Robert S. 1980. *Dictionary of American Communal History*. Westport, Conn.:
    Greenwood Press.
———. 1990. *All Things New: American Communes and Utopian Movements 1860–
    1914*. Chicago: University of Chicago Press.

CELEBRATION. Celebration is a recent utopian venture of the Disney Company. An experimental community fifteen miles south of Orlando, it is to be completed in ten to fifteen years. Celebration will have five levels of accommodations: estate, village, cottage, town house, and apartment. The styles will be Classical, Victorian, Colonial Revival, Coastal, Mediterranean, or French. The community will house 15,000–20,000 people on 8,000 home sites. The cost will be $100 million, and sales will reap a minimum of $300+ million. Originally, the plans were for 'Disneyfield,' and came from Walt Disney (1901–1966). He planned that people would live under a dome with a monorail joining people to skyscrapers; no retirees or property owners would live there, only tenants. Disney died in 1966 and the plan was shelved. However when Disney Company found it had more property than it needed for theme parks, the plan was resurrected. In the plan commercial buildings will be owned by Disney Company and will be built in a Spanish style around a central parking lot. The architect was inspired by Pisa's main square, reflecting the Renaissance ideal city. The tallest building will be only three stories; people will use a model school from kindergarten through high school; teachers will be trained in an academy; a health campus with a hospital and gym will be available. For communication with shops, voting, mail, and school, houses will be wired with optical fiber. The cost of accommodations will vary from $100,000 to $125,000. There will be no municipal government, and central services will be provided by the county. Disney will control the public parks and other spaces. To some commentators, Celebration is the facade of utopia and will not be accepted as a place to live, merely a utopia to visit. To others it will be a model, a picture-perfect suburb, a model for the future suburban community, symbol of tradition, the perfect "hometown" in the United States, with its dependability and familiarity, designed for unity yet offering separate communities. In brief, it will be a piece of heaven in the bustle of a large tourist hub.

See Also Disney, Walt; Disneyland, Disney World

Sources:

Beardsley, J. 1997. "A Micky Mouse Utopia." *Landscape Architecture* 87: 76.
Dunlop, B. 1966. "Designs on the Future: Walt Disney Company's New Town, Cele-
    bration near Orlando." *Architectural Record* 184, no. 1 (January): 64–69.
Flower, Joe. 1996. "Downhome Technopia. Walt Disney's Dream Town, 'Celebra-
    tion.' " *New Scientist* 149, no. 20 (January): 32–36.
Rothchild, John. 1995. "A Mouse in the House. Disney Wants to Sell Americans the
    Ultimate Fantasy: A Utopian Community." *Time* (Australia) (4 December):
    58–59.

CELESTINES. Celestines were a congregation of hermits within the Benedictine Order. The congregation was founded by Pietro del Morrone, who later became Pope Celestine V (1215–1296). The congregation was established in 1259, and in 1263, Urban IV (c. 1200–1264), who had been pope from 1261, approved the Celestines' austere way of life, a combination of Cisterian severity and Franciscan poverty governed by an organization similar to that of other mendicant orders. Its constitution was based on the Rule of Saint Benedict but was eclectic. Its discipline was severe, and in Italy and France during the fifteenth century the Celestines had at least 150 houses. Under the suppression of anticlerical governments in France, Germany, and Italy during the late eighteenth and early nineteenth centuries the Celestines declined. The last house closed at Calavino, Trent (1785).

See Also Benedictines; Morrone, Pietro del

Sources:

Cross, L. A., and E. A. Livingstone. 1997. *The Oxford Dictionary of the Christian Church*. 3d. ed. New York: Oxford University Press.

McHenry, Robert, ed. 1992. *The New Encyclopedia Britannica*. Chicago: Encyclopedia Britannica.

Meagher, Paul K., Thomas C. O'Brien, and Marie Aherne, eds. 1979. *Encyclopedic Dictionary of Religion*. Washington, D.C.: Corpus.

CENNEDNYSS. In 1977 in Adelaide, South Australia, with other members of the Pilgrim Church, Estelle and Don Gobbett (fl. 1940–1995) established Cennednyss, Old English for "knowledge associated with birth." They define it as a post-Christian community. The Gobbetts, married in 1961, had lived in Rhodesia as Australian teacher missionaries (1964–1972) until they were deported for attempting nonviolent conflict-resolution techniques. In 1973 they were attracted to the Pilgrim Uniting Church, which had opposed the Vietnam War, and protested against sports tours by South African athletes to Australia. They studied feminism and patriarchy in the church organization and, unhappy with the Pilgrim Uniting Church's policies, decided to cut ties with it. In 1978 a group of twenty-two adults and five children acquired nine acres with two houses in the hills behind Adelaide. The community was established for many reasons: members felt they had been isolated in the city from their neighbors; they had found no support network in the suburbs; they felt personal needs to change their work and family roles; and they were unhappy with poor local schooling, consumerism, and degradation of suburban environments. Also, they had seen successful communities like the one they planned in Africa, New Zealand, France, and Scotland, and they felt a deep interest in communal sharing. Their community now has nineteen members sharing three to four households. Before the community started, individuals made gifts to the proposed community. Later, they organized a common financial fund, common meals, and common cars. They welcome visitors who wish to experience an alternative lifestyle.

The group shares interests in social justice and human rights issues, including racial and gender equality and nonviolence. The decision making at Cennednyss is by consensus. It is a well-resourced group, frequently learning new ways to consider communal and personal problems, which possibly explains their relative success at consensus decision making in matters of property, finances, and personal growth.

Source:

Gobbett, Estelle, and Don Gobbett. 1995. "From Mission Field to Potato Patch." In Bill Metcalf, ed., *From Utopian Dreaming to Communal Reality: Cooperative Life Styles in Australia*, pp. 84–98. Sydney: University of New South Wales Press.

CHANNING, WILLIAM H. William Henry Channing (1810–1884) was born in Boston, son of Francis Dana and Susan Higginson Channing. The year he was born, his father died, and he was brought up by his mother, a strong character who relied much on the advice of the boy's uncle, a noted Unitarian, William Ellery Channing (1780–1842). The boy studied at the Boston Latin School, graduated from Harvard (1829), and studied at Harvard Divinity School (1833). After working with several churches, he spent one year in Europe (1835–1836) and returned to New York City, where, supported by the Unitarians, he helped to establish a free church among workers in industry. The project was abandoned in 1837, and he was appointed pastor of the Unitarian Church in Cincinnati, ordained in 1839 but resigned in 1841. He led an independent society in New York (1843–1845) whose members were "fellow-seekers after a higher holiness, wisdom and humanity." This group dispersed when Channing was drawn to Brook Farm, where he remained for only a few months. He never joined the colony as such. In Boston he led the Religious Union of Associationists. Brook Farm, with its several origins, had developed to some degree from William Ellery Channing's Transcendental Club of reformers and writers for *The Dial*. At Brook Farm William Henry Channing urged members to follow religion, and whenever he visited, he conducted services. He published *The Present*, a New England periodical, which spread Fourierist ideas and greatly influenced people at Brook Farm. Later, he lived in England and took charge of the Renshaw Street Chapel in Liverpool. He wrote many articles for periodicals and published sermons and addresses, and his most important literary work was the biography of his uncle, *Life of William Ellery Channing* (1848).

See Also Brook Farm Colony

Sources:

Delano, Sterling F. 1983. *The Harbinger and New England Transcendentalism: A Portrait of Associationism in America*. London: Associated University Presses.

Johnson, Allen, and Dumas Malone, eds. 1929. *Dictionary of American Biography*. Vol. 2. New York: Charles Scribner's Sons.

Kesten, Seymour. 1993. *Utopian Episodes: Daily Life in Experimental Colonies Dedicated to Changing the World*. Syracuse, N.Y.: Syracuse University Press.

Manuel, Frank Edward, ed. 1966. *Utopias and Utopian Thought*. Boston: Houghton Mifflin. (Daedalus Library, vol. 5, pp. 183–200.)

Myerson, Joel. 1978. *Brook Farm*. New York: Garland.

Oved, Yaacov. 1987. *Two Hundred Years of American Communes*. New Brunswick, N.J.: Transaction Books.

CHARLES, PRINCE OF WALES. Charles Philip Arthur George (b. 1948), Prince of Wales, son of Queen Elizabeth and Prince Philip, duke of Edinburgh, is heir apparent to Britain's throne. In 1958 he was given the title of Prince of Wales. He was educated with tutors at Buckingham Palace, Mill House (1956), Cheam School (1957–1962), Gordonstoun School, Scotland (1962–1967) and attended Timbertop, Australia (1966). He studied at Trinity College, Cambridge (B.A., 1971). After further studies at the Royal Air Force College and the Royal Naval College he served with the Royal Navy (1971–1976). In 1981 he married Lady Diana Frances Spencer (1961–1997) and had two boys. He is noted for his concern for social and environmental issues, has led many self-help schemes for the young and underprivileged, and is a leading critic of unsympathetic features of modern architecture. He put great effort into the establishment of Poundberry, a model urban village in rural Dorset.

See Also Poundberry

Sources:

Magnussen, Magnus, and Rosemary Goring, eds. 1990. *Chambers Biographical Dictionary*. 5th ed. Edinburgh: Chambers.

McHenry, Robert, ed. 1992. *The New Encyclopedia Britannica*. Chicago: Encyclopedia Britannica.

CHARTIST LAND COLONIES. Chartist Land Colonies were six attempts by Feargus O'Connor (1794–1855) to establish self-sufficient agricultural colonies in Britain. The first was O'Connorville, which was established on 103 acres near Watford in March 1846. Subscriptions were raised, and thirty-five people settled. The houses cost £100, and O'Connor worked there to build the colony. In August 1846 many visitors came to the opening, in May 1847 more settlers gathered, and by August many were celebrating the success of the experiment. It failed due to financial and agricultural mismanagement and was auctioned, with only three settlers in residence. The second colony, Lowbands, was established in August 1847, and it failed also. The third colony was called Minster Lovell, a colony of eighty-five houses with a school on 197 acres in Oxfordshire. It was renamed Charterville and survived a scandal in 1851. By 1914 the original eighty-five holdings fell to sixty-nine, and the residents were farm laborers. The fourth chartist land colony was Snig's End, established in 1848 on a 268 acres in Gloucestershire. It also failed. The fifth colony was called Mathon and was to be established in Worcestershire, but it hardly got started. The sixth scheme was to take place at Dodford, and it, too, did not become firmly established.

See Also O'Connor, Feargus

Sources:

Armytage, Walter H. Green. 1961. *Heavens Below: Utopian Experiments in England 1560–1950.* London: Routledge and Kegan Paul.
British Parliamentary Papers, Agriculture No. 13. National Land Company; 1st–6th Reports of the Select Committee on the National Land Session, in company with Minutes of Evidence, Appendices and Index. 1847–1848. 1969. Vol. 13. Shannon, Ireland: Irish University Press.
Ward, S. T. 1973. *Chartism.* London: Batsford.

CHEESEBOARD. Cheeseboard is a worker's cooperative in San Francisco that specializes in fine imported and domestic cheese. The shop began as a privately owned business in 1967. In 1971, after years of much success, it became a collective of eight members, including the original husband-and-wife owners and their six employees. It was a fully owned and managed worker cooperative in two years. By 1983 the cooperative had twenty-one members; eighteen worked regularly and averaged twenty-six hours per week. Cheeseboard is noted for its successful resolution of conflicts created by the freedom in its organizational structure. All decisions are made in group discussion. Working hours are agreed on collectively and depend on the individual member's influence within the group. Such influence is based on the commitment of the individual to the collective. This may be a source of conflict in itself, and members can perceive commitment differently. Nevertheless, the cooperative has enjoyed considerable success in resolving its conflicts and maintaining the financial viability of the business.

Source: Jackall, Robert, and Henry M. Levin. 1984. *Worker Cooperatives in America.* Berkeley: University of California Press.

CHELTENHAM. Cheltenham, a short-lived Icarian community, was established in 1856 in a suburb of St. Louis, Missouri, by 180 Icarians loyal to the French socialist Étienne Cabet (1788–1856). The original Icarians had settled only four months in Red River Valley, Texas, and moved to Nauvoo, an old Mormon town in Illinois. There the Icarians split. One group was loyal to Cabet, but the other did not accept his autocratic rule. With Cabet the loyalists purchased twenty-eight acres in the suburbs of St. Louis and called their settlement Cheltenham. Cabet died shortly afterward. After 1859, forty-two members withdrew from the community because of a constitutional dispute. Only fifteen adults and a few children were left when Cheltenham finally abandoned its community (1864).

See Also Cabet, Étienne; Corning; Icarian movement; Speranza; Texas-Nauvoo

Sources:

Fogarty, Robert S. 1980. *Dictionary of American Communal History.* Westport, Conn.: Greenwood Press.

Oved, Yaacov. 1987. *Two Hundred Years of American Communes*. New Brunswick, N.J.: Transaction Books.

Sutton, Robert P. 1994. *Les Icariens: The Utopian Dream in Europe and America*. Urbana: University of Illinois Press.

CHESHIRE, JEFFREY LEONARD. Jeffrey Leonard Cheshire (1917–1992) was born in Chester, England, the son of an Oxford law lecturer, and educated at Dragon and Stowe and Merton College at Oxford. He studied law, played tennis, and was a racing driver and pilot. In World War II he commanded No. 617, "Dam Busters" Royal Air Force (RAF) Bomber Squadron, which dropped the bouncing bombs used to destroy dams. He became Britain's most decorated pilot and in 1943, at age twenty-four, was the youngest captain in the RAF. In 1944 he was awarded the Victoria Cross. He was the only British military observer at the bombing of Nagasaki (1945). After the war in Hampshire, he established a commune on a farm. It was intended for disabled war veterans, and it failed. After suffering mental illness, Cheshire considered becoming a religious, went to British Columbia as a lumberjack, and eventually returned to a solitary life on his farm in England. There a friend who was dying from cancer lived with him, and he helped his friend to die. In the early 1950s, seeking money for the disabled and ill, he toured England to see if he could open homes for the welfare of disabled people. In 1959 he married Sue Ryder (b. 1923), an English philanthropist with similar humanitarian interests, raised two children, and helped establish the Cheshire Foundation Homes. It gained much support from many prominent public figures. His wife established the Sue Ryder Foundation, a philanthropic organization that works to relieve suffering due to World War II. In some countries her work is linked with her husband's work under the auspices of the Ryder-Cheshire Foundation. In 1991 he was made a life peer in the House of Lords. He wrote several books; *Bomber Pilot* (1943), *Pilgrimage to the Shroud* (1956), *The Face of Victory* (1961), *The Hidden World* (1981), and *The Light of Many Suns; The Meaning of the Bomb* (1985). To carry his work forward, he traveled to Moscow and the Middle East. He published an autobiography, *Where Is God in All This?* (1990).

See Also Cheshire Foundation Homes

Sources:

Barker, Dennis. 1992. "Obituary: Lord Cheshire, a Struggle to Selflessness." *Guardian Weekly*, 8 August: 23.

Braddon, Russell. 1954. *Cheshire, V. C.: The Story of War and Peace*. London: Evans Brothers.

Cheshire, Jeffrey L. 1961. *The Face of Victory*. London: Hutchinson.

Graham, Judith, ed. 1992. *Current Biography Yearbook 1992*. New York: H. W. Wilson.

The International Who's Who. 1992–1993. London: Europa.

Who's Who. 1993. London: A. & C. Black.

CHESHIRE FOUNDATION HOMES. Cheshire Foundation Homes is an international organization of homes to care for the sick and disabled. It originated with the attempt by Jeffrey Leonard Cheshire (1917–1992) to raise interest in caring for people who were dying or gravely ill. The need for such care became evident to him when he nursed a friend to his death by cancer after World War II. In the early 1950s Group Captain Cheshire, V. C., held a public meeting to raise money for the disabled and ill. Lionel Curtis (1872–1955), once a promoter of the British Commonwealth through Round Table Groups, was the president at the meeting, a community was established near Market Harborough at Gumley, and a country house of forty-five bedrooms was lent free of rent to the community. A second home for the incurably sick was established at Le Court, Liss, in Hampshire. Cheshire toured England to see if he could open more homes; many were established in association with Royal Air Force stations in Kent, Sussex, Bedfordshire, and Leicestershire. Support grew, and Cheshire Homes were administered through a trust. By the early 1990s there were 267 homes flourishing in forty-nine countries.

See Also Cheshire, Jeffrey Leonard

Sources:

Armytage, Walter H. Green. 1961. *Heavens Below: Utopian Experiments in England 1560–1950*. London: Routledge and Kegan Paul.
Cheshire, Leonard. 1961. *The Face of Victory*. London: Hutchinson.

CHILDREN OF GOD. The Children of God Community emerged in the Jesus movement—a gush of conservative, evangelical groups of the 1960s and 1970s—in California in 1968. The founder was David Berg (1919–1994). The community became known as "the Family of Love" and, later, "the Family." The movement derived from Evangelical Christianity. It rejects the world as it is, upholds a totalitarian patriarchalism, and makes religion a full-time commitment. It is critical of the established church and advocates godly socialism, which appears in the "Mo" letters issued by Berg and covers many topics, including predictions of doom and instructions on good living. Members attach much importance to women and motherhood because to them children are vital to increasing their numbers. Sex is regarded as a gift from God; reproduction is a duty and a means to attract new followers. Members are young adults who, since they have put aside careerism and material possessions, tend to live in colonies and direct most of their efforts to selling literature about the movement and proselytizing. At any one time the membership is about 6,000 throughout North America and Europe. The beliefs of the movement appear in 100 volumes, primarily drawn on the Bible and Berg's "Mo" letters to members, tracts illustrated with cartoons about prophecies, likely disasters, and instructions on good health, child care, and sexual practices. Much antagonism developed toward the "Mo" letters because, to some critics, they seemed both blasphemous and pornographic. Others criticized the Children of God for using sex to lure its converts.

Sources:

Eliade, Mircea, ed. 1987. *Encyclopedia of Religion.* New York: Macmillan.

Hinnels, John R. 1984. *The Penguin Dictionary of Religions.* London: Allen Lane Penguin Books.

Pitzer, Donald E. 1984. "Collectivism, Community and Commitment: America's Religious Communal Utopias from the Shakers to Jonestown." In P. Alexander and R. Gill, eds., *Utopias,* pp. 119–135. London: Duckworth.

Pritchett, W. Douglas. 1985. *The Children of God/Family of Love: An Annotated Bibliography.* New York: Garland.

Van Zandt, David E. 1991. *Living in the Children of God.* Princeton.: Princeton University Press.

Wangerin, Ruth Elizabeth. 1984. "Women in the Children of God: 'Revolutionary Women' or 'Mountain Maids'?" In Ruby Rohrlich and Elaine Hoffman Baruch, eds., *Women in Search of Utopia: Mavericks and Mythmakers,* pp. 130–139. New York: Schocken Books.

CHRISTENSEN, JOHN B. John B. Christensen (fl. ?1874–1930) was born of Danish descent in Kansas City and graduated from the University of Missouri School of Law, Columbia (1895), youngest in his class. In Missouri he practiced law for a railroad company in southwest Missouri. In 1914, after moving to Dallas, Texas, he bought and reorganized short-line railroads. Later, when living near Glen Rose, he became interested in a Scandinavian settlement, Danevang (Danish Meadow), whose members fared well on a few acres. This led him to decide to establish a similar colony, Kristenstaet, in Hood County, southwest of Fort Worth. No down payment was required, and an applicant was allowed to buy at forty dollars per acre only as much land as he and his family could work. Notes were issued for twenty years at 6 percent interest. The community prospered until the end of the 1930s depression. It throve on self-help and mutual assistance. Christensen believed that the community had little to offer that had not been already done by others who worked with the same philosophy as Kristenstaet. Large-scale corporation farming and water conservation projects contributed finally to the community's decline.

See Also Kristenstaet

Source:

Fischer, Ernest G. 1980. *Marxists and Utopias in Texas.* Burnet, Tex.: Eakin Press.

CHRISTIAN COMMONWEALTH COLONY. The Christian Commonwealth Colony was established in west-central Georgia (1896) by Ralph Albertson (1866–1951). It had twenty-five families of Christian socialists who intended to create an unrestricted, communitarian society on almost 1,000 acres of an old plantation. Albertson took a leading role in the organization and management of the Christian Commonwealth Colony (1895–1900). He had been greatly distressed by the plight of manual workers in Chicago, associated himself with socialist leaders, was greatly influenced by their beliefs, and wrote articles about socialism. The colonists were much drawn to Albertson's articles in *The Kingdom* (1895–1906). They discussed socialism, property, and Christianity and raised many social issues. Some of the members had come from the Willard Cooperative Colony and the Christian Corporation. There were twenty-three unmarried men and ten unmarried women among the sixty-four adult members. The commonwealth lasted four years and was beset by financial problems— many members came empty-handed, and only a few had money—and illegal practices. *The Social Gospel* was its periodical, and with a circulation of 2,000 it became the accepted name for social Christianity. After the commonwealth disbanded in 1900, seventeen members joined the Southern Cooperative Association in Florida.

See Also Albertson, Ralph

Sources:

Fogarty, Robert S. 1980. *Dictionary of American Communal History*. Westport, Conn.: Greenwood Press.

Ovid, Yaacov. 1988. *Two Hundred Years of American Communes*. New Brunswick, N.J.: Transaction Books.

Spann, Edward K. 1989. *Brotherly Tomorrows: Movements for a Cooperative Society in America 1820–1920*. New York: Columbia University Press.

CICERO. Marcus Tullius Cicero (106–43 B.C.) was born in Apinium, became an advocate in Rome, studied oratory for three years in Greece, and, when the Roman dictator Sulla (138–78 B.C.) died, became a notable figure in Rome for his support of the people's interests. He was exiled when the First Triumvirate formed, and he turned to literary interests. During the civil war (49–48 B.C.) he took Pompey's (106–48 B.C.) side, and, after being pardoned by Caesar (102–44 B.C.) returned to Rome, where, on Caesar's assassination he gave support to Octavian (63 B.C.–A.D.14), who would become the emperor. In speeches known as the "Philippics," Cicero denounced Anthony (83–30 B.C.). When Octavian and Anthony developed mutual interests, one of the latter's agents executed Cicero because he was a threat to state security. Cicero was a noted intellectual whose works *On the Republic, On the Laws, On the Nature of the Gods*, and *On the Orator* tell much about life in his day.

See Also De Republica

Sources:

Powell, J. G. F., ed. 1995. *Cicero the Philosopher*. New York: Oxford University Press.

Rawson, Elizabeth. 1975. *Cicero: A Portrait*. 1983 ed. London: Allen Lane.

Stockton, David L. 1971. *Cicero: Political Biography*. New York: Oxford University Press.

Upshall, Michael, ed. 1992. *Webster's Dictionary of Famous People*. Edinburgh: Random Century Group.

CITY OF GOD, THE. *The City of God* (426), a work of twenty volumes, depicts a Christian commonwealth, a heavenly, eternal city. *The City of God* was written in response to the chaos in the period following the Goths' sacking of Rome (410), when a growing fear and sense of defeatism arose as the Roman empire declined. When Rome, the city that would last forever, fell, great moral and intellectual confusion followed. Using historical proof, brilliant argument, and persuasive rhetoric, Aurelius Augustinus—Saint Augustine—(354–430), a man of broad learning, took the opportunity to instruct intelligent pagans that humankind's welfare lay in Christianity. The first four books of the work consider the idea that polytheism is necessary for happiness; the next examines the belief that the worship of the gods benefits life after death; the remaining books construct a worldview to replace paganism. Saint Augustine saw the city of the world as a wretched place; but the City of God was a place of splendor, because it was ruled by truth and controlled by love.

See Also Augustine, Saint

Sources:

Augustine, Saint Bishop of Hippo. 1981–1990. *The City of God*. Translated by Demetrius B. Zema. Reprinted from the 1950–1954 ed. Washington, D.C.: Catholic University of America Press.

Sills, David L., ed. 1968. *International Encyclopedia of the Social Sciences*. New York: Macmillan and Free Press.

Snodgrass, Mary Ellen. 1995. *Encyclopedia of Utopian Literature*. Santa Barbara, Calif.: ABC-CLIO.

CITY OF THE SUN, THE. In *The City of the Sun*, a treatise on the ideal republic by Tommaso Campanella (1568–1639), a sea captain from Genoa, gives details of an ideal society that presumably he has seen. The treatise is similar to More's *Utopia* (1516) and Plato's *Republic* (c. 428–c. 348). Also it values humanistic principles and scientific knowledge and combines imaginative ideas with rational explanations of unusual social practices. In this respect the treatise reflects the author's intellect and understanding. In the ideal republic individuals are in second place to the community and the state. The state is well advanced technically; astrology has a scientific base, and there are flying machines. Property is held in common, and marriage is completed for reproduction, not love, in the interests of the state. The young are watched as they exercise so it is clear who should mate with whom. No young woman may decorate herself in any way for fear of making herself more attractive than any other. The Ministry of Love requires that the young copulate between the ages of nineteen and twenty-one, and, with permission of the First Master of Reproduction, young men may copulate with older, younger, or pregnant women, since they are unlikely to bear unexpected children. Sodomy is frowned upon, and if repeated often, the sodomist might be executed. For two years infants are breast-fed, then promptly weaned and placed in a state-controlled education system. The work was originally written in Italian in 1602 but was not printed until the twentieth century. Campanella completed a Latin translation, *Civitas solis*, in 1613, and it was published in Frankfurt in 1623 and in Paris in 1637.

See Also Campanella, Tommaso

Sources:

Campanella, Tommaso. 1602. *La Città del sole: diagelo Poetico. The City of the Sun; A Political Dialogue*. Translated with introduction and notes by Daniel J. Donno, 1981. Berkeley: University of California Press.

Morely, Henry, ed. 1886. *Ideal Commonwealths: Plutarch's Lycurgus, More's Utopia, Bacon's New Atlantis, Campanella's City of the Sun, and a Fragment of Hall's Mundus Alter et Idem, with an Introduction by Henry Morely*. London: G. Routledge. Abridged and reprinted, 1968. Port Washington, N.Y.: Kennikat Press.

Mumford, Lewis. 1922. *The Story of Utopias*. 1962 ed. New York: Viking.

Negley, Glenn, and J. Max. Patrick, eds. 1952. *The Quest for Utopia: An Anthology of Imaginary Societies*. New York: Henry Schuman.

Snodgrass, Mary Ellen. 1995. *Encyclopedia of Utopian Literature*. Santa Barbara, Calif.: ABC-CLIO.

CLOU(W)SDEN HILL. Clou(w)sden Hill was an anarchist colony, known as the Clou(w)sden Hill (Free) Communist and Co-operative Colony, established in 1895. The community was based on ideas of Leo Tolstoy (1828–1910) and Peter Kropotkin (1842–1921), the Russian exile. In opposition to the social Darwinism of the day, they advanced the establishment of self-sufficient communities, the end of globalized trading, and the massive growth of the industrial system. These proposals were published in Kropotkin's essays "The Breakdown of the Industrial System" and "The Industrial Village of the Future" and brought together in his book *Fields, Factories and Workshops* (1896). Such ideas lay behind the founding of Clou(w)sden Hill, when two single men and two married men gave money to a common fund to lease twenty acres at Forest Hall near Newcastle in England. Work was voluntary, authority was informal, and meals were eaten communally. By 1896 many people wanted to join the community and enjoyed support from the local labor movement. Its economy flourished on poultry and fresh vegetables. They made their own bread, had their own entertainments, and worked to undermine injustices, inequality, and the war between the social classes in Britain. Membership reached twenty-four, they affiliated with the Home Colonisation Society of Glasgow, and many visitors came from Continental Europe and Scandinavia. They built greenhouses and sold their produce to cooperatives to show the superiority of free communist association over competitive capitalism. Such colonies aimed to develop character, deepen experience, and exhibit to members a new pattern for life. The colony broke up, the men who took over the management could not agree, and by 1900 it had disbanded.

See Also Tolstoy, Leo; Tolstoyan communities

Sources:

Armytage, Walter H. Green. 1961. *Heavens Below: Utopian Experiments in England 1560–1950.* London: Routledge and Kegan Paul.
Marsh, Jan. 1982. *Back to the Land: The Pastoral Impulse in England, from 1880 to 1914.* London: Quartet.

CLUB OF ROME. In 1967 Aurelio Peccei (1900–1983), noted Italian industrialist and economist, met with the head of the Organization for Economic Cooperation and Development in Paris, and they agreed, first, that the world was being poorly managed because population was increasing too rapidly, resources were being depleted too fast, and pollution and poverty were rampant; and, second, that national institutions could not cope with the many complex, interrelated global problems raised by these conditions. Thirty notables from ten countries met at the Accademia dei Lincei in Rome in April 1968, and the Club of Rome was formed. It was to have only 100 members, all scientists, industrialists, educationists, statesmen, and economists. It would be informal, not political. Peccei believed the world already had too many formal organizations. The club's first mission was to support the Project on the Predicament of Mankind. The project was organized at the Massachusetts Institute of Technology, Boston, where a computer model of the world was developed with variables relating to population, industrialization, food supply, depleting natural resources, and pollution. From the data used in the model, the scholars predicted that catastrophes would occur over the next 100 years. The work appeared in *The Limits to Growth* (1972), which sold 3 million copies in over thirty languages and attracted much criticism for both its gloomy predictions and its methodology. The authors' reply was that the work was experimental and that the model was a mere approximation to reality. Emerging from the debate were scholars (Kahn, 1976) who argued that rapidly advancing technology would ensure the means were available to offset the anticipated catastrophes like starvation and pollution. But others predicted even more dire consequences (Miles, 1976) A second model was offered that pointed to two major problems facing the world. First, the gap between rich and poor nations was widening; second, human civilization was growing away from its natural environment. Members agreed that only differentiated and selective growth rates would curb population increases, create employment, lower alienation, and guarantee minimum standards of living. The club also supported another project that stressed the value of human dignity and recommended it could be raised and maintained by establishing an international monetary system, arms reduction, and more improved research institutes in the Third World. Also the club's attention was drawn to the wisdom of socioeconomic, rather than the merely physical, curtailment of growth. After competition had heightened pursuit of the world's diminishing natural resources, it was argued that intense self-defeating conflict would emerge for what was called "positional goals," for example, privacy for individuals, open and clear space, work that was personally fulfilling. Two conditions were needed to prevent these conflicts: a new social ethic combined with large-scale public intervention and massive public regulation. If these needs were not met, then oppressive governments would flourish, and individuals would lose their civil rights (Hirsch, 1977). Today the traces of the Club of Rome's futuristic and utopian ideas are put forward to curb the greenhouse effect, which presumably has arisen due to the excessive use of fossil fuels and which involves the excessive warming of the earth by producing greenhouse gases in the atmosphere, for example, water vapor, carbon dioxide, methane, chloroflourocarbons, nitrous oxide, and ozone. These gases trap energy given off by the globe, thereby warming earth. The cause is human; the following human actions would make the world a better place to live: free access to birth control; equal educational opportunities for men and women; better health care services to those in poverty; making cities more livable; protection of indigenous people; phasing out nuclear fission and fusion; encouraging efficient use of energy; improving transport systems; redesigning buildings and communities; funding superconductivity; using solar and wind power; using renewable energy sources; cooperating to establish worldwide goals for control of greenhouse effects; changing subsidies for agriculture and international aid; promoting sustainable agriculture; cutting back livestock production; supporting small family farms; taxing military expenditure; reforesting available land; reducing overconsumption.

Sources:

Cornish, Edward. 1977. *The Study of the Future.* Washington, D.C.: World Future Society.

Ehrlich, Ann, and Paul Ehrlich. 1990. *The Population Explosion.* New York: Simon and Schuster.

Harman, Willis. 1977. "The Coming Transformation." *The Futurist* (February): 5–11.

Hirsch, Fred. 1976. *Social Limits to Growth.* Cambridge: Harvard University Press. Rev. ed., 1995. London: Routledge.

Kahn, Herman. 1976. *The Next 200 Years: A Scenario for America and the World.* London: Associated Business Program.

King, Alexander. 1980. *The State of the Planet.* New York: Pergamon Press.

King, Alexander, and Bertrand. Schneider. 1991. *The First Global Revolution.* London: Simon and Schuster.

Lazlo, Ervin, et al. 1977. *Goals for Mankind.* New York: E. P. Dutton.

Meadows, Donella H., et al. 1972. *The Limits to Growth: A Report for the Club of Rome's Project on the Predicament of Mankind.* London: Potomac Associates.

Miles, Rufus E., Jr. 1976. *Awakening from the American Dream: The Social and Political Limits to Growth.* New York: Universe Books.

Tinbergen, Jan. 1976. *Reshaping the International Order.* New York: E. P. Dutton.

Van Dieran, Wouter, ed. 1995. *Taking Nature into Account: A Report to the Club of Rome.* New York: Copernicus.

COALSAMAO. Coalsamao was the name given to a cooperative commonwealth for Canada that emerged from the ideas of Edward Partridge (1862–1931) in his *A War on Poverty* (1926). The commonwealth was so named from the first two letters of the western provinces of Canada, plus the *o* of Ontario. The establishment of the commonwealth required the secession of the Canadian west from Lake Superior to the Pacific Ocean. Many of Partridge's ideas were drawn from the writings of British socialists and Fabians. In the commonwealth all production would be used for members, not for profit; everyone had to work or starve; all members would work in the interest of the community, which valued human rights over property; the state would own all natural resources, and past owners would be recompensed for property taken from them by the state; monetary-based contracts would no longer exist; lawyers, landlords, and businessmen would vanish; there would be no need for railways, shipping, marketing, or gambling on grains prices; there would be no class conflict, poverty, or lack of capital. In time members would develop an immutable, humane ego, and some of them would be reincarnated. The basic social unit of the commonwealth would be an encampment of 3,500–7,000 residents. The commonwealth would be governed by a board of twenty-five administrators elected annually, one each from twenty-five regions. Ten administrative departments would handle day-to-day matters. Living standards would be established; for example, houses would be similar, all homes would have the same domestic equipment (phone, sewage, heating, etc.), and all residents would have the same educational, social, and sporting facilities. Transportation would be the same for all, as would be clothing, and there would be a standard phonetic language. Education would be practical and tied to agriculture and use of machinery. Civil services, teaching, and administration would be in the hands of intellectuals. Teachers would espouse goodwill, cooperation, justice, collectivization, morality, and human kindness. The sexes would be separated and taught to appreciate each other through social interaction like conversation, not dancing. Many of the political ideas were evident in the establishment of the Canadian League for Social Reconstruction and the Commonwealth Cooperation Foundation.

See Also Fabians

Sources:

Berger, Carl. 1970. "A Canadian Utopia: The Cooperative Commonwealth of Edward Partridge." In Stephen, Clarkson, ed., *Visions 2020: Fifty Canadians in Search of a Future*, pp. 257–262. Edmonton: M. G. Hurtig.

Horn, Michael. 1970. "Visionaries of the 1930s: The League for Social Reconstruction." In Stephen, Clarkson, ed., *Visions 2020: Fifty Canadians in Search of a Future*, pp. 263–267. Edmonton: M. G. Hurtig.

COHEN, JOSEPH. Joseph Cohen (1881–1953) was born in Russia and studied to be a rabbi. In 1898 he served in the czar's army and from this experience developed a libertarian philosophy. He sailed to Philadelphia in 1903 and ten years later went to New York, where he joined the Ferrer center, and in 1915 moved with others to Stelton, where a colony and school were established. He stayed with the colony until 1925. He edited *Freie Arbeiter Stimme*, a Yiddish newspaper, until 1932. In 1933 he joined a group of Jewish anarchists, and they bought a 10,000-acre farm in Michigan and established the Sunrise Community (1933–1939). He published an account of the Sunrise Community in *The Quest of Heaven: The Story of the Sunrise Cooperative Farm Community* (1935). After World War II he returned to magazine editing and went to France and Mexico to edit *Der Freier Gedank*, a Yiddish anarchist magazine. He returned to New York in 1952.

See Also Abbott, Leonard; Ferrer Colony; Kelly, Harry

Sources:

Fogarty, Robert S. 1980. *Dictionary of American Communal History.* Westport, Conn.: Greenwood Press.

Oved, Yaacov. 1987. *Two Hundred Years of American Communes.* New Brunswick, N.J.: Transaction Books.

Veysey, Laurence. 1973. *The Communal Experience: Anarchist and Mystical Counter-cultures in America.* New York: Harper and Row.

COLE, GEORGE DOUGLAS HOWARD. George Douglas Howard Cole (1889–1959) was born in Cambridge, son of a jeweler, and was educated at St. Paul's School and Balliol College, Oxford. He was prizewinning scholar and a keen student of socialism, which he accepted as a way of life by 1906. He joined the Oxford Fabian Society (1908). With a sharp mind and a passionate belief in social democracy he became a prominent member of the intellectuals in what was known as "the movement." He was rebellious and independent in his approach to the business of the Fabian Society, to whose executive he was elected in 1914. He did not support the bureaucratic approach of Sidney Webb (1859–1947) and Beatrice Webb (1858–1943), nor did he seek the company of politicians or civil servants. To him "the movement" got its energy from below, not from the forces of domination from above. His views led him to quit the Fabian Society (1915), but he remained with its research group. Between 1915 and 1924 he researched labor problems for unions and was appointed the first secretary for research in the British Labour Party (1919). He published *Trade Unions and Munitions* (1923), *Self-Government in Industry* (1918), *Guild Socialism Restated* (1920), and *Workshop Organisation*, all showing his keen interest in participative democracy as the utopian solution to industrial conflict. Guild socialism faded with the onset of the Russian revolution (1917), but Cole did not want to join the communist cause. He preferred to integrate different kinds of socialism rather than support only one variety. He refused to accept rigid principles in social organization, so the Bolsheviks were not for him. He resigned from the Labor Research Department when it was dominated by communist thinkers (1924). He taught at the University of London (1921) and in 1924 was made a reader in economics at Oxford. His differences with the Webbs evaporated, and in 1928 he rejoined the Fabian Society, worked closely with socialist politicians, founded the Society for Socialist Enquiry and Propaganda

(1930), and was secretary of the New Fabian Research Bureau until 1935 and later its chairman (1937–1939). He was chairman of the reorganized Fabian Society (1939–1946; 1948–1950) and wrote many books on socialism, a biography of William Cobbett (1925), a life of Robert Owen (1925) and a history of the British working-class movements, 1789–1947 (1948). These works made him a noted British historian and economist. In 1944, after serving the government in wartime, he accepted a professorship of political and social theory at Oxford. He and his wife, Margaret, also wrote detective stories.

See Also: Fabians; Social democracy

Sources:

Cole, George D. H. 1918. *Self-Government in Industry*. London: Bell.
———. 1920. *Guild Socialism Restated*. London: L. Parsons.
Williams, E. T., and Helen M. Palmer, eds. 1971. *Dictionary of National Biography 1951–1960*. London: Oxford University Press.
Wright, A. 1979. *G.D.H. Cole and Socialist Democracy*. Oxford: Oxford University Press.

COLERIDGE, SAMUEL TAYLOR. Samuel Taylor Coleridge (1772–1834), son of a vicar, was born in Devonshire, England, had an unhappy childhood, and was educated at Christ's Hospital, London, 1782–1790. In 1791 he moved to Jesus College, Cambridge, where, a restless student, he adopted extreme religious and political views. On his return to London in 1793 he enlisted in the 15th Dragoons under a pseudonym, was bought out of the military by family, and in 1794 returned to Cambridge. He befriended the poet Robert Southey (1774–1843), and they traveled together to Wales. With others they planned to escape to a "pantisocracy," a romantic utopia, and lead a communistic life on the Susquehanna River in Pennsylvania. The scheme was started but became an illusion and was finally thwarted when its major supporters married. Coleridge married a friend of Southey's, Sara Fricker, and Southey married her sister, Edith (1895). Coleridge became a journalist, public lecturer, and wandering preacher. At this time he began taking laudanum and, later, opium. His first book of poetry, *Poems on Various Subjects*, appeared in 1796, and that year he met William Wordsworth (1770–1850), with whom he worked closely. Coleridge's poetry was outstanding, and he attracted an annuity from Josiah Wedgwood (1730–1795) and his family, lived near Southey with the Wordsworths, and envisaged a great literary career, but he suffered from the misery of an opium addiction. His relations with Wordsworth deteriorated, and he went to Malta as secretary to its governor (1804–1806). He published a weekly, *The Friend* (1809), broke finally with Wordsworth (1810), and lectured, notably, on Shakespeare. His creative period gone, Coleridge turned to philosophic speculation, published an autobiography and reflective writing, edited his notebooks, and visited Germany and brought home some of its better writing to England's intellectuals.

See Also Pantisocracy; Southey, Robert

Sources:

Ashton, Rosemary. 1996. *The Life of Samuel Taylor Coleridge*. Oxford: Blackwells.
Colmer, John. 1959. *Coleridge: Critic of Society*. Oxford: Clarendon Press.
Hansen, Lawrence. 1962. *The Life of Samuel Taylor Coleridge: The Early Years*. New
     York: Russell and Russell.
Holmes, Richard. 1982. *Coleridge*. Oxford: Oxford University Press.
Snodgrass, Mary Ellen. 1995. *Encyclopedia of Utopian Literature*. Santa Barbara, Calif.:
     ABC-CLIO.
Stephen, Leslie, and Sydney Lee, eds. 1917. *The Dictionary of National Biography*.
     London: Oxford University Press.

COLFAX COLONY. In 1869 Karl Wulston (fl. 1869–1870), editor at Chicago's
Stats Zeitung and a veteran of the Union army during the Civil War (1861–
1865) proposed establishing a colony of poor Germans from Chicago. He
wanted to ameliorate the dreadful employment and living conditions of German
workers in the factories of Chicago. He organized a band of about 100 into a
colony at El Juda. Called "pioneers of civilization" by the *Chicago Tribune*,
they began their journey in a blaze of publicity. The railhead was festooned
with a banner, "Westward the star of empire takes its course—the German
colonization of Colfax Freemon County Colorado Territory." The site they selected was south Canon City in West Mountain Valley, which had agricultural
and mining potential. To secure a land grant, they petitioned Congress to modify
the Homestead Act so that they would be allowed to develop cooperative ownership of the land. The colony town was to be called Colfax after Schuyler
Colfax, their vice president. The Germans arrived March 1870: ninety-two families, 337 members in all. Dissatisfaction with Wulston's leadership caused some
families to leave by July. The colonists were not experienced in farming, and
they delayed getting in the crop, and an early crop failure spoiled their work.
They had to petition the governor for rations when the colony's store burned
down. Always an optimist, Wulston saw their work as successful, and encouraged those who stayed in the area to develop the land in their own way without
recourse to a utopian, cooperative organization.

Sources:

Fogarty, Robert S. 1980. *Dictionary of American Communal History*. Westport, Conn.:
     Greenwood Press.

COLLINS, JOHN ANDERSON. John Anderson Collins (c. 1810–1880) was an
abolitionist, perfectionist, and founder of the Skaneateles Community. He was
born in Vermont, attended Middlebury College, and graduated from Andover
Theological Seminary. As a general agent for the American Anti-Slavery Society, Collins organized the One Hundred Convention in 1843 at Syracuse,
where the abolitionists hoped to increase their membership in the western states.
Although he was paid to promote the abolitionist cause, his first interest was in
other reforms, which he used the slavery issue to promote. During the spring of

1843 a group discussed their interest in founding a colony at Skaneateles, Mottville, Onandaga County, New York. From this convention emerged the Skaneateles Community, and Collins was its leader. In January 1844 practical operations began on a full scale, but Collins so alienated some of the ninety residents with his radical views on property, religion, and marriage that by 1846 he had to resign, even though the economic future of the community was sound. In 1849 he moved to California to search for gold. While there he organized the National Cooperative Homestead Society to reform the industrial system through using production and distribution cooperatives. He also practiced spiritualism and served as president of the Society of Progressive Spiritualists shortly before he died.

See Also Skaneateles Community

Sources:

Fogarty, Robert S. 1980. *Dictionary of American Communal History.* Westport, Conn.: Greenwood Press.
Oved, Yaacov. 1987. *Two Hundred Years of American Communes.* New Brunswick, N.J.: Transaction Books.

COLORADO COOPERATIVE COMPANY. The Colorado Cooperative Company was founded in Montrose County, Colorado (1894), to reclaim, by irrigation, 20,000 acres of desert in southwest Colorado. However, the founders hoped for more than an acreage of arable land and declared principles that aimed to have an advanced social and intellectual community at the project. Community members were to pay $100 for a share and receive water rights and a vote. The land was to be privately owned, with a limit of forty acres per owner. At Pinon fifty buildings were erected, and the community had 200 members by 1897. But the community began to split over future policy and inadequate consultation on the technical construction of the irrigation ditch. Nevertheless, the project was half completed by 1903, and in 1904 water was available to some acreage. In 1910 the project was finished, and the company was renamed Nucla Town Improvement Company. Members who sought a more communal life went to Louisiana to join the Newllano Cooperative Colony. At one point the community was hoping to use Henry George's (1839–1897) single tax scheme, but it seems this did not happen. Some socialist members thought the community should be more cooperative, and a few did take up joint farming. In 1899 Pinon was likened to Brook Farm. Otherwise, the communal spirit was limited to working cooperatively for an agreed-upon goal, sharing much the same interests, and upholding the community goals rather than advocating individualism when the splitting arose. The cooperative spirit was encouraged by a leading member of the community who spent five years working on the project, E. L. Gallatin (fl. 1828–1900).

See Also Brook Farm Colony; Gallatin, E. L.; Topolobampo Colony

Source:

Fogarty, Robert S. 1980. *Dictionary of American Communal History*. Westport, Conn.:
    Greenwood Press.

COMBE, ABRAM. Abram Combe (1785–1827) was born in Edinburgh and from his father, a brewer, learned Calvinist principles for a proper life. Abram became a tanner, had his own business in Edinburgh by 1807, and worked hard himself while admonishing those who did not, in the belief that if each man pursued his interest, all humankind would benefit. In 1820, with his brother, George, the Scottish phrenologist (1788–1858), Abram met Robert Owen (1771–1858) at New Lanark. Abram was quickly converted to Owen's ideas and changed his views on humankind, evinced compassion for the weak, turned to vegetarianism and temperance, and quit attending the theater. Upholding justice and benevolence, he became a noted philanthropist. He was practical and determined and, after a few failures, established a cooperative venture, the Orbiston experiment. It was called the First Society of Adherents to Divine Revelation, which Combe explained by referring to Divine Revelation as facts and truths of the great power of the universe that individuals grasp through their senses and understanding. Such understanding is guided by reason, the means by which man and nature relate in harmony. Others thought Combe was outlining a new natural religion. In fact, he was defending Owen's ideas against charges of atheism. Owenism became Combe's religion, and he believed great social changes were imminent, all issues could be made into simple alternatives, and logical problems could be solved through divine absolutes. He sought a secular utopia at Orbiston and to advance education, which to him meant simply the acquisition of ideas and permission to form judgments from which action follows. For four years Combe collaborated with others in the Orbiston community experiment nine miles east of Glasgow on the banks of the Calder, Scotland. In 1827 Combe fell ill while spade-digging at Orbiston, had to retire from the work, and soon died. The community went into a rapid decline, and the land was sold.

See Also Orbiston; Owen, Robert; Owenism

Sources:

Armytage, Walter Henry Green. 1961. *Heavens Below: Utopian Experiments in England
    1560–1950*. London: Routledge and Kegan Paul.
Campbell, Alexander, ed. 1844. *Life and Dying Testimony of Abram Combe*. London:
    A. Campbell.
Combe, Abram. 1823. *Metaphysical Sketches of the Old and the New Systems with
    Opinions on Interesting Subjects*. Edinburgh: N.p.
———. 1824. ''A Proposal for Commencing the Experiment of Mr. Owen's System in
    a Way Which Is Not Altogether Opposed to the Prevailing Prejudices of Mankind.'' *Edinburgh Observer*, 31 January.
Jones, Benjamin. 1894. *Co-operative Production*. Oxford: Clarendon Press.

Harrison, John F. C. 1969. *Robert Owen and the Owenites in Britain and America: Quest for the New Moral World*. New York: Charles Scribner's Sons.

COMMON GROUND COOPERATIVE. Common Ground Cooperative developed during the early 1980s from a communal household of social workers on fifty-five hectares north of Melbourne in rural Victoria, Australia. Members began to build a large retreat and workshop to accommodate groups up to forty and offer their skills in a productive setting. Common Ground advised and otherwise supported groups working for social change and self-empowerment, for example, Community Aid Abroad, government agencies, and environmental groups. Ochre (1996) writes that "we named feminism, anarchy, non-violence and environmental sustainability as our major philosophical underpinnings." Common Ground trains people in consensus decision making, nonviolent direct action, and facilitation of financial management. Although having the smallest membership of all the alternative communities, it is considered by Metcalf (1996) to be one of the most radical and dramatic in Australia.

Source:

Ochre, Glen. 1995. "From a Circle of Stones to Common Ground Dreaming." In Bill Metcalf, ed., *From Utopian Dreaming to Communal Reality: Cooperative Life Styles in Australia*, pp. 140–153. Sydney: University of New South Wales Press.

COMMUNIST CHINA AS UTOPIA. In China after Deng Xiaoping (1904–1997) came to power in September 1978, the nation's policy moved from centralized planning of a communist state to the utopian practice of partly decentralized decision making in production and a growing acceptance of some features of capitalism, particularly the recognition of market forces. The policy was generally referred to as "socialism with Chinese characteristics." China's policies were changed in this way further when Deng achieved control of Beijing in 1979 and got rid of the last of the Maoists. He was the final authority in all things political and military in China, but he kept out of the public eye. Peasants were allowed private plots and to sell surplus crops and invest in village factories. People were fed, and a few could build their own houses and have modern domestic appliances. Although public dissent was permitted, Deng feared it most. By 1984 cosmetics and discotheques were present in China. In 1985 a play, *WM*—showing the Chinese Communist Party's control over society as being merely curtailed, not removed—was banned. By the late 1980s more student demonstrations were in progress, and Deng was much concerned. Nevertheless, China prospered, and corruption and inflation spread. In 1989 public protests became intense, and Deng used the military to quell the Tiananmen Square protests. Afterward Deng became self-critical and silent. He noted the conservative authorities were being used to curb protests, and he saw a chance in them to rid himself of his opponents. Quickly, he used various means to exhibit China as a free-market economy with vast opportunities. This utopian policy was taken up and followed by local Chinese and outsiders and was followed by an explosion of economic growth. China thereafter became more like a capitalist nation than ever before. But the change was based not so much on a reappraisal of economic theory as on pragmatism.

See Also Deng, Chairman

Source:

Goodman, David S. G., et al. 1986. *The China Challenge*. London: Cardinal.

COMMUNITY OF THE ARK. Community of the Ark was established in 1948 by Lanza del Vasto (1901–1981), his wife, and another couple. In 1963 it moved to la Borie Noble (''noble borough'') on 1,200 acres in southern France. The property was too poor to farm easily, and its buildings required much restoration. The community is founded on the principles of Mahatma Gandhi (1869–1948). It has three residential, self-governing communities; la Borie Noble, the largest, is its organizational center and has a bakery and a primary school for all members. The members aim to be self-sufficient. The vegetarian commune grows its own vegetables and wheat for the bakery and makes its own cheese, and the women spin and weave wool. They vow poverty, share all possessions, and appear to live comfortably. Most members are in families, few are single, and children abound. Children begin school at three years, attend the local village school for annual examinations, and work for their money to pay for books by growing produce, raising chickens, and printing a newspaper and greeting cards. To become a full member of the community, individuals go through several stages: live for two years in the community; become novice for one year; and afterward take seven vows to become a full member. The vows are to give service to others; assume responsibility for one's own acts; accept and right one's wrongs; cleanse oneself from acrimony, gain, domination, and prejudice; live simply, soberly, and in poverty and charity; serve truth; do no harm, defend justice, and resolve all conflict without violence. The order is headed by a patriarch who guards the rules and upholds order; decisions are made by a council; admission requires unanimity; members have no right to exact punishment; leadership is by consensus and rotated from one to another. They protest and fast against military action, torture, and nuclear power. Discussion camps are held to spread their communal ideology. Since its foundation, the Community of the Ark has worked with nonviolent methods for peace in many conflicted countries, including Morocco and France, opened communities in Spain and Italy, and protested with Greenpeace at Tahiti (1995) over French nuclear tests.

See Also Gandhi, Mohandas K.; Vasto, Lanza del

Sources:

Parodi, Thérèse. 1997. ''In Search of Non-violence—Communauté de l'Arche (France).'' In Bill Metcalf, ed., *Shared Visions, Shared Lives. Communal Living around the Globe*. Chapter 3. Findhorn, Scotland: Findhorn Press.

Popenoe, Cris, and Oliver Popenoe. 1984. *Seeds of Tomorrow*. San Francisco: Harper
    and Row.
Shepard, Mark. 1990. *The Community of the Ark*. Arcata, Calif.: Simple Productions.

COMMUNITY OF THE SON OF MAN. In 1849, the Community of the Son
of Man was established at Spaxton, near Bridgewater in Somerset, England.
About sixty men and women constituted the community. It followed the ideas
of Henry James Prince (1811–1899). The project was supported at first by a
wealthy engineer and paper manufacturer whose three daughters married strong
adherents to the religious views of Henry Prince. Prince's followers believed
that the Holy Ghost was about to come and that when he did, they would live
a heavenly existence. They also believed that they were free of sin, saved entirely—in body as well as soul—and could live and love without restraint, like
the angels in heaven, unrestrained by the laws of marriage. The community was
known as "Agapemone"—from the Greek for "love" and "dwelling"—as an
abode of love, a title that at the time elicited lewd connotations among the
neighborhood. The community entered fiction in Aubrey Menen's *The Abode
of Love* in 1957.
See Also Prince, Henry James

Source:

Armytage, Walter H. Green. 1961. *Heavens Below: Utopian Experiments in England
    1560–1950*. London: Routledge and Kegan Paul.

COMMUNITY OF UNITED FRIENDS. The Community of United Friends
was established in 1840 in Liverpool to provide members with constant work,
adequate food and accommodations, welfare for the aged and ill, and an education for members' children. Eight directors sat on the governing body; members paid between £5 and £12 annual subscription and sixpence a week. They
leased 1,000 acres at Pant Glas, Merionethshire, with a farmhouse, outbuildings,
and cottages. At first they seemed short of capital but believed the market would
demand enough of their produce to meet the annual rent of £140. The members
hoped to buy the property in two years. By April 1840 members included a
carpenter and agriculturalists, but they needed a blacksmith, a tailor, a shoemaker, and a stone mason. All would need to be self-denying and tolerate un-
comfortable accommodations. In July 1840 the community was flourishing, even
though one member was suggesting the community move to another site. In
August he attacked the agricultural management of the community and declared
that he did not any longer support its president. Further reports in September
declared the estate quite unsuited to agriculture and revealed its secret history
of failure with previous tenants who could never make it pay. The problem was
exacerbated when a local landowner ejected the community's cattle from common land. The community promptly failed.

Source:

Armytage, Walter H. Green. 1961. *Heavens Below: Utopian Experiments in England 1560–1950*. London: Routledge and Kegan Paul.

CONDER, CHARLES EDWARD. Charles Edward Conder (1868–1909) was born in London, and his father sent the lad to Australia in the hope that he would not become an artist. In the evenings, however, Charles studied at the Royal Art Society School in Sydney and later at the National Gallery School (1888–1889). In 1888 he went south to Victoria to join Tom Roberts (1856–1931), Arthur Streeton (1867–1943), and Frederick McCubbin (1855–1917) at the artists' camp at Box Hill outside Melbourne, later to be named the Heidelberg School. He went to Paris (1890) and London (1893). In London he joined the New English Art Club and became noted for his paintings on silk fans. Through these works and others, he became identified with art nouveau. He married Stella Belford in 1901, and they lived in London, where Conder exhibited regularly until he became ill in 1906.

See Also Heidelberg School; McCubbin, Frederick; Roberts, Thomas William; Streeton, Arthur Ernest

Sources:

Robb, Gwenda, and Elaine Smith. 1993. *Concise Dictionary of Australian Art*. Edited by Robert Smith. Melbourne: Melbourne University Press.
Splatt, William, and Dugald McLellan. 1986. *The Heidelberg School: The Golden Summer of Australian Painting*. Melbourne: Lloyd O'Neil.

CONSIDÉRANT, VICTOR PROSPER. Victor Prosper Considérant (1808–1893) was born at Salins, France, and died in Paris. He was educated at École Polytechnique Paris and Ecole de Metz and quickly became a captain in the French army's engineering division and fought in the war against Algiers in 1830. He gave up his promising military career and helped Charles Fourier (1772–1837) to found *La Phalange* and continued to publish it after Fourier's death in 1837. He became recognized as a leader of Fourierism and a noted social philosopher. His ideas were published in three volumes, *Destinee Sociale* (1835–1844). With funds from Arthur Young, an Englishman, Considérant founded a short-lived socialist colony at Condé-Sur-Vesgres. He also founded a daily paper, *La Democratie Pacifique* (1843), in which he presented his social philosophy. He believed humankind to be basically good, and if the appropriate socioeconomic environment could be created, and cooperation upheld, then humankind could be made so much better. He was the practical utopian, while Fourier remained a theorist. He published *Le socialism devant le vieux monde* (1848). After the 1848 revolution he was a representative of the Department of the Loire in the Constitutional Capital Assembly, but in 1849 he was accused of treason and forced to flee France. He had a widespread following in the United States and in 1855 established La Réunion, a Fourierist colony near San

Antonio, Texas. It was not a successful venture financially. It was affected by serious drought, and few settlers were skilled in agriculture. But it was a forerunner of several similar communities in the United States. He moved to San Antonio. He became a U.S. citizen and returned to France in 1859 to live in poverty until death.

See Also Fourier, Charles; Fourierist communities or phalanxes; Reunion Colony

Sources:

Fogarty, Robert S. 1980. *Dictionary of American Communal History.* Westport, Conn.: Greenwood Press.

Johnson, Allen, and Dumas Malone, eds. 1931. *Dictionary of American Biography.* Vol. 4. New York: Charles Scribner's Sons.

Kesten, Seymour. 1993. *Utopian Episodes: Daily Life in Experimental Colonies Dedicated to Changing the World.* Syracuse, N.Y. Syracuse University Press.

Magnussen, Magnus, and Rosemary Goring, eds. 1990. *Chambers Biographical Dictionary.* 5th ed. Edinburgh: Chambers.

Oved, Yaacov. 1987. *Two Hundred Years of American Communes.* New Brunswick, N.J.: Transaction Books.

Wheeler, Preston, ed. 1974. *American Biographies.* New York: Harper and Brothers.

COPELAND, WILBUR F. Wilbur F. Copeland (fl. 1869–1899?) graduated from Ohio Wesleyan University in 1889. To work in rescue houses, he went to New York City and in 1899 formed the Straight Edge Society, a practical experiment in Christianity. He was much influenced by Edward Bellamy (1850–1898), Laurence Gronlund (1846–1899), and Leo Tolstoy (1828–1910). Copeland was a Christian socialist but did not believe that his community should separate from the rest of society. The settlement of the Straight Edge Industrial Settlement in New York City was originally a cooperative business venture but later established itself as a workers' residence at Alpine, New Jersey.

See Also Bellamy, Edward; Gronlund, Laurence; Straight Edge Industrial Settlement; Tolstoy, Leo

Sources:

Fogarty, Robert S. 1980. *Dictionary of American Communal History.* Westport, Conn.: Greenwood Press.

———. 1990. *All Things New: American Communes and Utopian Movements 1860–1914.* Chicago: University of Chicago Press.

CORNING. After supporters of Étienne Cabet (1788–1856) left Nauvoo, 221 Icarians remained but had financial difficulties, which they planned to resolve by selling all assets in Illinois and removing to Corning in Iowa. The decision was taken in April 1857. But not until September 1860 was the Iowa community of Icarians recognized by the state. A small settlement had started in Corning by 1853, and as people from Nauvoo joined them by April 1857, numbers rose to about sixty. Their men did not join in the Civil War (1861–1865), so their financial problems were lightened, and by June 1867 they had almost paid for their 1,729 acres and dealt fully with their creditors. They were prospering by 1870. Their president had power to manage the leadership problems endured earlier with Cabet. Notwithstanding, the women's lot was poor; food was better, but they still had to wear uniforms. Unlike residents at Nauvoo and Cheltenham, Corning members lived privately in small homes, ate communally, and pursued common recreations. They had a school, enjoyed cultural pastimes, went on picnics, and lived in unity, democracy, and equality—a true brotherhood. That was so until the mid-1870s, when the communistic, progressive members split from conservatives. The conservatives all resolved to divide their settlement, but their differences ended them in court. In 1878 the court gave the progressives the eastern half to develop and the conservatives the western half. The progressives created Young Icaria. By 1880 they had seventy-two residents, although by 1881 most had gone. They were ruled more by Fourierist and Saint-Simonist principles of organization. One leader of the Socialist Labor Party suggested they quit and go to Cloverdale, eighty miles south of San Francisco, and call the place Speranza. In August 1886 they were dissolved. The conservatives became an association called the New Icarian Community of Adams County in Iowa (1879). They enjoyed a communal spirit, worked hard, and by 1883 had thirty-four members. However, by the end of the 1880s the community comprised only nine elderly men. In 1898 Corning was dissolved.

See Also Cabet, Étienne; Cheltenham; Icarian movement; Speranza; Texas-Nauvoo

Sources:

Fogarty, Robert S. 1980. *Dictionary of American Communal History*. Westport, Conn.: Greenwood Press.
Hine, Robert V. 1953. *California's Utopian Colonies*. 1983 ed. Berkeley: University of California Press.
Oved, Yaacov. 1987. *Two Hundred Years of American Communes*. New Brunswick, N.J.: Transaction Books.
Sutton, Robert P. 1994. *Les Icariens: The Utopian Dream in Europe and America*. Urbana: University of Illinois Press.

COSME. Cosme was a group that broke away in 1894 from New Australia, a utopian community in Paraguay, and settled at Cosme, forty-five miles distant. The split in the utopian venture was provoked by many factors, not the least of which was the autocratic leadership of the founder, William Lane (1861–1917). In 1899, tired and depressed, he left the community. At one time Cosme's membership reached 130. Today a few descendants of New Australia and Cosme live there.

See Also Lane, William; New Australia

Sources:

Souter, Gavin. 1968. *A Peculiar People: The Australians in Paraguay.* Sydney: Angus and Robertson.
Whitehead, Anne. 1997. *Paradise Mislaid: In Search of the Australian Tribe of Paraguay.* St. Lucia, Queensland: University of Queensland Press and Penguin.

CRAIG, EDWARD THOMAS. Edward Thomas Craig (1804–1894) became a member of the Manchester Mechanic Institute at the age of eleven years and later edited the *Lancashire and Yorkshire Cooperator.* In 1828 he visited Ireland and again in 1831, when he went to visit Ralahine on the banks of the Shannon, where he agreed with John Scott Vandeleur (fl. 1828–1831) to reorganize Vandeleur's estates to curb outbursts of agrarian terrorism, responses to Vandeleur's autocratic control of the estates. At first the peasants saw Craig as a spy and his plan as foolish, while Vandeleur's family thought the whole scheme a joke. After mingling with the peasants, Craig had their trust and, with money from Vandeleur, provided new accommodations for the peasants. Craig ensured that married couples had a house of their own, that youths lived in dormitories, that sanitation was effective, and that advanced technology and industrial training among residents were promoted vigorously. His wife ran the Ralahine school. Among their distinguished visitors were Robert Owen (1771–1858) and William Thompson (1785–1833), the political economist who supported Owen's system of cooperation and expounded principles of scientific socialism and the theory that unearned income and private property were fundamentally unjust. Another visitor was William Pare (1805–1873), who was a founder of the first Birmingham Cooperative Society (1828), and was interested in the promotion of cooperation, and eventually became the acting governor of Robert Owen's community at Queenwood, Hampshire, in the early 1840s. He wrote on the "Ralahine experiment." The experiment collapsed, and Craig and his wife went to England, where in 1844 he organized an industrial school at Ealing in London. Craig became known as a pioneer in the cooperative movement in England, and Ralahine was celebrated as a success. Between 1858 and 1893 he published many books on the cooperative movement and edited such papers as the *Leamington Advertiser, Brighton Times*, and the *Oxford University Herald.* He wrote on phrenology, Shakespeare, the blood, and advanced technology and published a book of his own verse.

See Also Owen, Robert; Ralahine

Sources:

Armytage, Walter H. Green. 1961. *Heavens Below: Utopian Experiments in England 1560–1950.* London: Routledge and Kegan Paul.
Garnett, R. G. 1963. "E. T. Craig: Communitarian, Educator, Phrenologist." *The Vocational Aspect* (Summer): 135–150.

CRAM, RALPH ADAMS. Ralph Adams Cram (1863–1942) was born in Hampton Falls, New Hampshire. During the Civil War (1861–1865) his father was a conscientious objector, became a Unitarian cleric, and returned to the family farm in Hampton Falls in 1876 to care for his elderly parent. Ralph was educated in Augusta and Westford. He finished high school (1880), but his family had no money for his college education. Following the ideas of British architects, Ralph began to construct models of cities and houses; his father suggested the boy take up architecture. For five years the lad worked in an architect's office in Boston and in 1890 became a partner with an architectural firm that specialized in church design. Also at the Mission Church of St. John he began his religious education. In 1909 he was made supervising architect of Princeton University. For twenty-two years he occupied that position and developed a strong Gothic style that was not often seen in U.S. universities. In 1914 he was appointed a professor of architecture at Massachusetts Institute of Technology and chaired the Boston City Planning Board. He wrote several essays advocating both Gothic and Christian ideas for management of the world's problems and was always held in high regard for his contribution to U.S. church architecture. In 1919 he published *Walled Towns*, a book that much impressed a writer on utopias, Lewis Mumford (1895–1990) and led him to declare it a scholarly, utopian text that upheld the values and sanctions of the Christian Church.

Sources:

Cram, Ralph A. 1919. *Walled Towns*. Boston: Marshal Jones.
James, Edward T. 1973. *Dictionary of American Biography*. Supplement 3. New York: Charles Scribner's Sons.
Mumford, Lewis. 1922. *The Story of Utopias*. 1962 ed. New York: Viking.

CRYSTAL WATERS. Crystal Waters, originally a community settlement cooperative, was reorganized at Malene in Queensland, Australia, by Barry Goodman (fl. 1930–1996). It began in 1986 after a National Permaculture Conference at Offord, New South Wales. A group of would-be communal settlers decided to redevelop Crystal Waters. The project was originally organized by four designers, including Barry Goodman, who became its site manager. It became the first community designed according to permaculture principles. It has 500 acres of forested, arable land and operates on a group title development. Crystal Waters is a residential cluster housing of 150 residences where the houses are freely bought and sold, but the members belong to a cooperative and a body corporate and share the management of the community and its property. The main principles follow permaculture ideals and emphasize natural use of the landscape, minimal environmental impact by humans and their dwellings, and the use of renewable energy. Other communal activities involve establishing a commercial kitchen. It is the oldest, largest permaculture village in the world and is widely known for supporting many alternative communities. It is located above Nambor, Queensland, north of Brisbane and regularly has visitors tour its settlement to learn more of how it came into being and what it has to offer.

See Also Goodman, Barry; Mollison, Bill; Permaculture

Source:

Goodman, Barry. 1995. "From Grey-Suited Engineer to Birthday-Suited Hippie." In Bill Metcalf, ed., *From Utopian Dreaming to Communal Reality: Cooperative Life Styles in Australia*, pp. 127–139. Sydney: University of New South Wales Press.

D

DAHARMANANDA. Daharmananda is an Australian community established in 1972 near Lismore, New South Wales, on 260 acres that had once been so thoroughly cleared that it was unsuitable for conventional agriculture. In June 1979 Leigh and Ellen Davidson (fl. 1950–1996) joined the community. The community is based on Buddhist meditation and sound biodynamic-environmental management and has a policy of slow growth. Two members are nonresident, and no members have quit. Cohesion among members is strong; it is based on shared values and mutual respect for one another and the environment. Each member must give a day's work to the community and give Saturday morning to work in the garden; often members are expected to eat together. All members are directors; administrative positions are rotated among members. One member has become a skilled negotiator and conflict resolution expert. No one gossips, cliques do not form, members share a strong work ethic, and all oppose depending on the government dole. No one can sell his or her holding unless to a person other members accept. Residents share their meals, resources, and work in regenerating the bush. The members are skilled in the development of advanced technology that is environmentally sustainable.

See Also Davidson, Leigh

Source:

Davidson, Leigh. 1995. ''From Barbecues at Bondi to Biodynamic Bananas.'' In Bill Metcalf, ed., *From Utopian Dreaming to Communal Reality: Cooperative Life Styles in Australia*, pp. 41–56. Sydney: University of New South Wales Press.

DANA, CHARLES ANDERSON. Charles Anderson Dana (1819–1897) was born in Hinsdale, New Hampshire. When he was nine, his mother died, and he was sent to Buffalo, New York, to become a clerk in his uncle's general store. The business was bankrupt in 1837, and at age eighteen, Dana was alone. He had taught himself Latin and Greek and read the classics, so he joined a literary society to develop his interests in these areas. He went on to matriculate at Harvard (1839), but eyestrain forced him to give up study before completing his college degree. Twenty years later he received an honorary A.B. from Harvard. After leaving college, Dana joined Brook Farm, where he taught for five years. In 1846 he became the assistant editor at Boston's *Daily Chronotype*. After a year he was appointed editor of the *New York Tribune*, where he remained for fifteen years. His opinions were primarily liberal. While he did not support the abolitionists, he opposed the expansion of slavery. He was in favor of high tariffs and against striking labor unions. Due to increasing differences of opinion with his employer, Horace Greeley (1811–1872), Dana resigned from the *Tribune* in 1862. He began work for the War Department and became assistant secretary of war (1863–1865). He resigned in 1865. At the end of 1867, Dana purchased the *New York Sun* and became editor in January 1868. He challenged standards of newsworthiness, giving importance to human interest crime and the use of catchy headlines. The paper aimed to be enjoyable, witty, and bright and attracted some outstanding writers. Dana had many interests, including learning languages, Chinese porcelain, wine, and gardening. He married in 1846 and had several children. He collaborated on a biography of Ulysses Grant (1868) and with George Ripley edited the *New American Cyclopaedia* (1873–1876).

See Also Brook Farm Colony

Sources:

Johnson, Allen, and Dumas Malone, eds. 1930. *Dictionary of American Biography.* Vol. 3. New York: Charles Scribner's Sons.

Lockwood, Maren. 1966. "The Experimental Utopia in America." In Frank Edward Manuel, ed., *Utopias and Utopian Thought*, pp. 183–200. Boston: Houghton Mifflin. (Daedalus Library, vol. 5.)

Magnussen, Magnus, and Rosemary Goring, eds. 1990. *Chambers Biographical Dictionary.* 5th ed. Edinburgh: Chambers.

Oved, Yaacov. 1987. *Two Hundred Years of American Communes.* New Brunswick, N.J.: Transaction Books.

DANTE. Dante Alighieri (1265–1321) was born into a noble Guelph family of Florence and early in his youth turned to the study and writing of poetry. In c. 1292 he married Gemma Donati, had four children, and entered Florence's politics as a member of the People's Council (White Guelphs). By 1300 he was concerned about internal conflicts in Italy and especially the territorial ambitions of the pope. The papacy's intentions raised in Dante the general question about the proper relation between the powers of the state and the church. When he went on a political mission to Rome, unexpectedly he found himself exiled from his hometown of Florence (1302). In his absence the opposing and previously exiled Black Guelphs had taken over Florence and exiled him for speaking out fervently against the policy of the pope. In response Dante began to write as an imperialist instead of a papal supporter to the divided Italians and their princes, welcoming the advance of Henry VII of Germany (c. 1269/1274–1313) into the conflicted Italy. To Dante Henry was Italy's savior, peacemaker, divinely appointed ruler (1310). Two more epistles a year later attacked the Florentines for not accepting Henry as chosen by God and upbraided Henry for not moving quickly enough into Tuscany (1311). The letters were revised as *De Monarchia* (c. 1313) and written in Latin. His early notable work included lyrics and a sensitive, fine analysis of youth and love, *Vita Nuova* (New Life), which is based on his early passion for a young woman. Later works were completed in exile and include *Divina Commedia* (Divine Comedy), written between 1306 and 1320. He never returned to Florence and died in Ravenna.

See Also De Monarchia

Sources:

Bloom, Harold, ed. 1986. *Dante*. New York: Chelsea House.
Boyde, Patrick. 1981. *Dante, Philomythes and Philosopher: Man in the Cosmos.* Cambridge: Cambridge University Press.
Chubb, Thomas Caldecot. 1966. *Dante and His World*. Boston: Little, Brown.
Collins, James. 1984. *Pilgrim in Love: An Introduction to Dante and His Spirituality*. Chicago: Loyola University Press.
Mazzotta, Guiseppe. 1993. *Dante's Vision and the Circle of Knowledge*. Princeton: Princeton University Press.
McHenry, Robert, ed. 1992. *The New Encyclopedia Britannica*. Chicago: Encyclopedia Britannica.
Snodgrass, Mary Ellen. 1995. *Encyclopedia of Utopian Literature*. Santa Barbara, Calif.: ABC-CLIO.

DARTINGTON HALL. Dartington Hall, a progressive school, was established in 1925 at a Tudor manor on 800 acres in South Devon, England, by Leonard Elmhirst (1893–1874) and his wife, Dorothy Whitney Straight (1887–1968). This experimental educational community was based on four principles: mankind can be liberated through education; the arts can change a society that has been impoverished by secularization and industry; a community can be built that draws upon the best of town and country life; the efficient operation of industrial and agricultural activities on a small scale can be reconciled with a lasting interest in individuals. The Elmhirsts used educational consultants from Denmark, Norway, Bengal, and Cornell University. Around the hall were clustered villages with stone cottages, a church, a small store that was used as a post office, a midwife, a hand pump. The locals looked with suspicion as Dartington Hall was restored. School began in 1926 with fourteen waifs and teachers from Leonard Elmhirst's Cambridge days. Manual work was emphasized, each student had a room, and permissiveness guided most activities. Education was a life, not a preparation for life or a means to acquire certificates. Classes were voluntary, and the curriculum followed the interests of teachers and the students, not the entry requirements for a university. Learning was by doing, and students participated in decisions, while teachers were used as counselors and friends. There was to be no punishment, rules and regulations were to be kept to a minimum, and members of the school were to be guided by self-discipline. The school met great resistance from other private schools. It was pacifist, nudist, anticurriculum and anti-authoritarian, with a philosophy that combined ideas of Jean-Jacques Rousseau (1712–1778) with the attitude toward activities outdoors of Lord Baden-Powell (1857–1941). To the school came many European Jewish immigrants fleeing Nazi persecution in the 1930s. In 1931 Dartington Hall Trust was formed to manage the venture. Many distinguished artists and scientists visited Dartington Hall. Among the distinguished visitors were Walter Adolph Gropius (1883–1969), founder of the Bauhaus school of architecture, and notable artists, particularly women. Among Dartington's parents were the English biologist Julian Huxley (1887–1975), the English philosopher and mathematician Bertrand Russell (1872–1970), and the left-wing writer and publisher Victor Gollancz (1893–1967). While earlier English British progressive schools, such as Abbotsholme (1889) and Bedales (1893), emphasized handicrafts and British middle-class values, Dartington was transatlantic and centered attention on the value of new technology. Dartington summer school is the main remnant of the Dartington ideal, and today it attracts tourists with its music, farm food of local cider and berry products, renowned fine glassware, Scandinavian-style tableware, and a restaurant. Recently, Dartington has been the location of New Age conferences, for example, on Zen Buddhism, and simple organic farming.

See Also Elmhirst, Leonard Knight; Straight, Dorothy Whitney

Sources:

Armytage, Walter H. Green. 1961. *Heavens Below: Utopian Experiments in England 1560–1950*. London: Routledge and Kegan Paul.

Bonham-Carter, Victor. 1958. *Dartington Hall: The History of an Experiment*. London: Phoenix House.

Braham, Mark. 1982. *Aspects of Education: Selected Papers from the Dartington Conference*. Chichester, England; New York: Wiley.

Kidel, Mark. 1982. *Dartington*. Exeter, England: Webb and Bower.

———. 1990. *Beyond the Classroom: Dartington's Experiments in Education*. Bideford, Devon, England: Green Books.

Popenoe, Cris, and Oliver Popenoe. 1984. *Seeds of Tomorrow*. San Francisco: Harper and Row.

Straight, Michael. 1983. *After Long Silence*. New York: Norton.

Young, Michael D. 1982. *The Elmhirsts of Dartington: The Creation of a Utopian Community*. London: Routledge and Kegan Paul.

DAVIDSON, LEIGH. Leigh Davidson (fl. 1950–1995) was born in Australia and raised in a middle-class, suburban family. He studied mathematics and engineering at the University of New South Wales, became a research student, and felt his life had become typical of many Australian youths, that is, an overweight sports lover and surfer caught in the trap of suburban life. To escape, he went to England (1968) but on the way was much taken by ideas he discovered in Southeast Asia. He meditated, studied yoga, learned much from the *Bhagavad-Gita*, and questioned the ambivalence of being a pacifist while researching under a navy-funded contract and of emphasizing competition in sport and attendant boozing and camaraderie, while being told this was the model for healthy interpersonal relations. He returned home, a slim vegetarian. He enrolled to do a Ph.D. and afterward traveled to Canada, met Ellen, his wife-to-be, and together they decided to live on the land. In 1979 he and Ellen came to Daharmananda. His motives were to live a simple life, work the land, about which he knew little, and improve the planet. In time he became obsessed by the idea of agricultural sustainability. They had no money; he believed he had few social skills, felt shy of people, and was relatively ignorant of agricultural matters. He and his wife worked hard for less money than they would have received on the dole; they put in dams and irrigation schemes and became devoted to the work that would help the planet to live. He became committed to people, not to career, and aimed to make a permaculture paradise. To do so, he has combined his academic work with his utopian practices at Daharmananda. He is best known for originating a composting toilet that has been approved by health authorities and can be built easily and cheaply.

See Also Daharmananda; Permaculture

Source:

Davidson, Leigh. 1995. ''From Barbecues at Bondi to Biodynamic Bananas.'' In Bill Metcalf, ed. *From Utopian Dreaming to Communal Reality: Cooperative Life Styles in Australia*, pp. 41–56. Sydney: University of New South Wales Press.

DAVIES, WILLIAM W. William W. Davies (1833–1906) was born in Denbigh, Wales. At sixteen he converted to Mormonism and became a preacher at eighteen. He was a mystic, a deeply spiritual character. In 1855 he and his wife sailed to the United States, settled in Willard, Utah, and took up with the Mormon leader Joseph Morris (fl. 1848–1862), who had separated from the original church in 1861 and upheld a devout belief in the Second Coming and reincarnation. After Morris was murdered in 1862, Davies quit the Morrisites and fled first to Idaho and later to Montana. Persuaded by his own visions and directed by imaginary forces, Davies led about forty followers to Walla Walla, Washington, and settled on a 480-acre property, naming it the Kingdom of Heaven colony. Arthur Davies, William's son, was born in 1868. Immediately, William declared that his son was the incarnation of Jesus Christ ''Walla Jesus'' at the Kingdom of Heaven Colony. Next year the second son was announced to be the spirit of God the Father. In 1880 both boys died of diphtheria, and the colony dissolved.

See also Kingdom of Heaven Colony; Morris, Joseph

Sources:

Fogarty, Robert S. 1980. *Dictionary of American Communal History*. Westport, Conn.: Greenwood Press.

———. 1990. *All Things New: American Communes and Utopian Movements 1860–1914*. Chicago: University of Chicago Press.
Miller, Timothy. 1990. *American Communes: 1860–1960*. New York: Garland.

DAWN VALCOUR COMMUNITY. Dawn Valcour was a spiritualist community founded at Colchester, Vermont, and Valcour Island, New York. John Wilcox (fl. 1874–1875) and Oren (or Orrin) Shippman (fl. 1874–1875) were its founders. Wilcox distributed a prospectus that described the colony as ''[t]he head centre of advanced spiritualism and free love.'' The colony was to flourish on his 800-acre farm on Valcour Island as well as a farm on the mainland. Shippman offered 800 acres on Dawn Valcour Island and a nursery on the Vermont side of the lake in repayment for his debts of $9,000 and $26,000 for land supposedly valued at $100,000. In August 1874 a dozen people visited the island; some left immediately, while the remainder stayed in the face of a hostile reception from locals. The community called a public meeting to explain their philosophy, and their group's free love ideology was made clear. The colony became unstable largely because Shippman had deceived the emigrants about his debts and evidence that the land did not have clear title. In March 1875 Wilcox sued Shippman; by November the last of the emigrants had left for New York, and the experimental colony failed.

Sources:

Fogarty, Robert S. 1980. *Dictionary of American Communal History*. Westport, Conn.: Greenwood Press.
———. 1990. *All Things New: American Communes and Utopian Movements 1860–1914*. Chicago: University of Chicago Press.

DE MONARCHIA. *De Monarchia* (c. 1309/1313) is a treatise by Dante (1265–1321) that outlines his position on the proper division between the powers of church and state. In 1312 King and Emperor Henry VII (c. 1269/1274–1313) of Germany aimed to place conflicted Italy within his empire. Dante wrote letters to the Italians and to Henry in support of Henry's move on Italy. Afterward the letters were included in *De Monarchia*, which asserts that true justice can occur only under a single ruling monarch, conforming to divine intention, and argues for the separation of church and state powers. So Italy should have two rulers, pope and emperor, both divinely appointed. From this belief Dante envisaged an ideal world or utopia ruled by truth, law, and grace, subject to the planned efforts of the university, the emperor, and the pope. This would recapture the combined greatness of Rome, Athens, and Jerusalem; and the ideal world would enjoy advanced civilization, high culture, and a deeply spiritual religion.

See Also Dante

Sources:

Avery, Catherine B., ed. 1972. *The New Century Italian Renaissance Encyclopedia*. New York: Appleton-Century-Crofts, Meredith Corporation.

McHenry, Robert, ed. 1992. *The New Encyclopedia Britannica*. Chicago: Encyclopedia Britannica.
Snodgrass, Mary Ellen. 1995. *Encyclopedia of Utopian Literature*. Santa Barbara, Calif.: ABC-CLIO.

DE REPUBLICA. *De Republica* (On the State, or Republic) is a six-volume, philosophical dialogue about the state begun by Cicero (106–43 B.C.) in 54 B.C. and published in 51 B.C. Only a fragment of the dialogue exists. It comprises most of the first three books and parts of the last three. It follows the form of Plato's *Republic* and covers a three-day discussion held in the garden of Scipio Aemilianus (c. 185–129 B.C. The discussion is between Scipio and Laelius, who in 140 B.C. was a Roman consul. The work opens with Cicero's views on patriotism and statesmanship, and then the two discussants center attention on how much better an active life is than one of contemplation and reflection. The concept of a republic is taken up, and its monarchic, aristocratic, and democratic forms are carefully examined. The best form integrates each with the others. The Roman Republic is accepted as the best example. Book 2 outlines the history of the Roman Republic and takes up the values of justice and harmony in state affairs and their ideal forms. Arguments by Carneades (213–129 B.C.) are in the third book, which is a fragment of the original and asserts that to promote welfare, humankind must be unjust. Because it is necessary to promote one's own welfare with a little injustice, Laelius and Scipio argue that the state cannot establish or continue itself without supporting justice to a limited degree, and this becomes the main proposal in the ensuing discussions. Only fragments exist of the last three books.

See Also Cicero

Sources:

Feder, Lillian. 1964. *Crowell's Handbook of Classical Literature*. New York: Thomas Y. Crowell and Co.
Howatson, M. C., ed. 1989. *The Oxford Companion to Classical Literature*. Oxford: Oxford University Press.
Snodgrass, Mary Ellen. 1995. *Encyclopedia of Utopian Literature*. Santa Barbara, Calif.: ABC-CLIO.

DENG, CHAIRMAN. Deng Xiaoping, Teng Hsiao-p'ing (1904–1997), was born in Szechwan Province in China. At age sixteen he went to Shanghai to learn French, where he won a scholarship to a work-study program in France (1921–1924). During the program he did menial jobs to support himself, and he joined the Communist Youth League, which had been established by ex-patriot Chinese in France. In 1926 he studied Marxist-Leninist ideas in Moscow. On returning to China, he began to serve communist ideals with great difficulty; nevertheless, he met a lifelong supporter in Mao Zedong (1893–1976). Against prevailing Soviet policy, he and Mao chose guerrilla warfare over conventional tactics for their political mission. They established the Red Army in Jiangxi (1931–1935).

When Mao was denounced for his military efforts, Deng was removed from power at the same time. Nevertheless, in 1934, together they joined the Red Army on its "Long March" 6,000 miles into northwest China, with the loss of 92,000 lives. They were made heroes, and Mao was made the great leader. After the civil war in China and the Japanese invasion and eventual defeat in 1945, Deng helped divide China militarily, forced the Nationalist opposition to withdraw, and helped Mao become China's leader in October 1949. By 1956 Deng had risen in the Communist Party ranks to the level of deputy premier. He supported Mao's policy, the Great Leap Forward (1958–1960), to match the industrial productivity of Britain within fifteen years. The famine that ensued was devastating. When Chou En-lai (1898–1976) changed the direction of China's economic policy, Deng moved with him, and together they evaded following Mao's agricultural schemes. Mao took revenge in 1966 with the Great Proletarian Cultural Revolution. Deng was well supported by Mao even during the Cultural Revolution (1966–1970). He harassed and persecuted intellectual rivals in support of Mao. Deng and others were expelled from power. Deng was tried for capitalist crimes. Mao intervened cautiously, Deng and his wife were put under house arrest, and eventually Deng returned to Jiangxi to work in disgrace at manual labor. He suffered tragedies in his family and spent his time reading in peace. In 1973, after the Red Guard's influence had waned, Deng was brought back to Beijing. Although he became deputy premier again, conflict within the party led to his being purged and escaping to Guangzhon. Shortly after Mao's death, September 1976, Deng was returned to influence and came to power in September 1978. By 1979 he was in control of Beijing. Between 1979 and 1997 Deng introduced pragmatic forms of capitalism to China. His final effort was followed by sudden economic growth. Thereafter, while he ruled and purged the military leadership, a new China emerged, and he drifted into senescence.

See Also Communist China as Utopia

Sources:

Goodman, David S. G. 1990. *Deng Xiaoping*. London: Cardinal.

Goodman, David S. G. et al. 1986. *The China Challenge*. London: Cardinal.

McHenry, Robert, ed. 1992. *The New Encyclopedia Britannica*. Chicago: Encyclopedia Britannica.

Uli Franz. 1988. *Deng Xiaoping*. Translated by Tom Artin. Boston: Harcourt Brace Jovanovich.

DENMARK AS A SOCIAL-DEMOCRATIC, CAPITALIST UTOPIA. In a 1984 study that compared 124 countries for quality of life, Denmark was rated highest. In a second study of the physical quality of life—infant mortality, life expectancy, literacy—Denmark again scored very high, with other Scandinavian nations. In Denmark about 90% of production is privately owned. Denmark encourages political dissent, and tolerates different lifestyles, and offers advantages of capital accumulation to all citizens. Medical costs are low, education at all levels is free, and the government cares for the aged in pleasant cottages. Long ago Denmark led in the application of a humanitarian philosophy to national issues. Denmark abolished slavery in 1798; in 1814 it provided free education; in the 1870s it began health insurance for workers, and by 1930 Danes enjoyed great employment benefits. Its capital has few, if any, slums, its countryside comprises small villages and viable farms, and its factories are often hidden by forest. Denmark upholds free trade and has few import tariffs. Despite this utopian form of capitalism, some social critics in Denmark suggest that government policies have promoted too much egalitarianism, and eroded a personal sense of responsibility and many traditional controls; family influence is weak, and alienation and social conflict are high. The number of marriages has declined, divorce rates have risen, and solitary life is on the rise. The suicide rate is high. Some observers complain cultural creativity is absent, while others allege that Danish social policies have eroded or dissolved the social networks of the country. Although Denmark has had troubles, it maintains an image of a capitalist paradise, a nation that supports a humanitarian policy toward those who suffer great social disadvantages.

Source:

McCord, William. 1989. *Voyages to Utopia: From Monastery to Commune, the Search for the Perfect Society in Modern Times*. New York: W. W. Norton.

DISCIPLES OF CHRIST. Disciples of Christ, or Churches of Christ, were founded in the U.S. frontier in the early nineteenth century. They were once called "Campbellites," after Thomas Campbell (1763–1854) and his son Alexander Campbell (1788–1866). Barton W. Stone (1772–1844) was also a founder of the church. Much influenced by John Glas (1695–1773), the Disciples aimed to restore the authority of the New Testament and by 1832 had established themselves as a separate religious identity. They organized in congregations, held the basis of faith to be the Scriptures, practiced baptism, and regarded the Lord's Supper as their major act of worship. Missionaries established the sect around the world. By 1881 the sect had 5,100 churches and over a half a million members. In the United States three varieties developed by 1906: Disciples of Christ; Christian Church of Christ, and Church of Christ. Major differences rested on biblical interpretation and the use of instrumental music during mass.
    See Also Campbell, Alexander

Sources:

Cross, L. A., and E. A. Livingstone. 1997. *The Oxford Dictionary of the Christian Church*. 3d ed. New York: Oxford University Press.
McDonald, William, ed. 1967. *New Catholic Encyclopedia*. New York: McGraw-Hill.
McHenry, Robert, ed. 1992. *The New Encyclopedia Britannica*. Chicago: Encyclopedia Britannica.

DISNEY, WALT. Walter Elias Disney (1901–1966), born in Chicago, was ten when taken to Kansas. Later he returned to Chicago to study at McKinley High School, where his drawing talent was clear. During World War I he served in the Voluntary Ambulance Unit in France (1918) and then returned to Kansas to work in the Pesman-Rubin art studio as a commercial artist. He became a cartoonist in 1920. He and Ubbe Iwerks (1901–1971) joined forces to begin a film animation company in Disney's garage. In 1920 Disney-Iwerks Studio was founded and produced Laugh-O-Gram cartoons (1922). Disney went to Hollywood, established himself as a cartoonist, and in 1928, with help from Iwerks, invented Mickey Mouse, the cartoon character in *Plane Crazy*, which secured Disney's career. He is noted for bringing the animated cartoon to perfection. During World War II he made training films and, later, True-Life Adventure films. In the early 1950s, funded by television companies, Disney had built the amusement park Disneyland at Anaheim, California, a utopian entertainment world of fantasy based on cartoon characters. In 1955 the Mickey Mouse Club began its television career. Disney won thirty-nine awards from the Academy of Motion Picture Arts and Sciences, four Emmy Awards, and over 800 other awards and decorations for his work. Among his most noted animated motion pictures were his *Snow White and the Seven Dwarfs* (1938), *Bambi* (1942), *Fantasia* (1940), *Dumbo* (1941), *Pinocchio* (1940), and *Cinderella* (1950). Disney planned a utopian community, Celebration. Residents would live under a dome; a monorail would lead them into skyscrapers; no retirees or property owners would live there, only tenants. The plan was shelved when Disney died. On his death his empire was taken over by his brother, Roy.

See Also Celebration; Disneyland, Disney World

Sources:

Echikson, Bill. 1992. "Disney's Rough Ride in France." *Fortune* 125: 14–16.
Holliss, Richard, and Brian Sibley. 1988. *The Disney Studio Story*. New York: Crown.
Leebron, Elizabeth, and Lynn Gartley. 1979. *Walt Disney: A Guide to References and Resources*. Boston: G. K. Hall.
Mosley, Leonard. 1986. *The Real Walt Disney: A biography*. London: Grafton.
Sterling, John. 1994. "The World according to Disney." *Earth Island Journal* 9:32–34.
Toy, Stewart. 1994. "Disney Headed for the Euro Trash Heap?" *Business Week* 3355 (24 January): 52.

DISNEYLAND, DISNEY WORLD. Disneyland (California) and Disney World (Florida) are U.S. fantasylands based largely on the cartoons and children's films made by the Disney movie studios. Both promote an ideal, middle-class utopia where everyone's dreams come true, all adventurers are heroic, all young people are clean and well behaved and respect their parents, and life is free from disease, filth, and the bitterness of class conflict. The first Disneyland was built at Anaheim outside Los Angeles. The second was constructed at Orlando, Florida. Many others are planned for nations outside the United States. Since 1956 over 310 million visitors have seen Disneyland; 300 million have been attracted to

Florida's Disney World; in ten years 100 million people visited Japan's Disney-Nippon. Disney pioneers are searching Kiev, Warsaw, Stockholm, and Moscow for sites for Disney-Mir and other theme parks, and by 2000 the growth rate in attendance at such places will exceed the growth rate of the human race. Notwithstanding, between 1992 and 1994 attempts to establish a Disneyland in France met with considerable resistance. It was claimed that EuroDisney Park would harm the environment by filling open spaces with hotels, shopping malls, and golf courses. In September 1994 its losses were U.S.$900 million. In the spring of 1998 Disneyland's new "Tomorrowland" opened its futuristic theme park with its rides through outer space, 3-D movies, and a pavilion devoted to the latest technology for the future, using interactive displays. In 2001 at Anaheim is planned Disney's Californian "Adventureland," another theme park with a public plaza and five-star hotel and television and film displays.

See Also Celebration; Disney, Walt

Sources:

Echikson, Bill. 1992. "Disney's Rough Ride in France." *Fortune* 125: 14–16.

Holliss, Richard, and Brian Sibley. 1988. *The Disney Studio Story*. New York: Crown.

Leebron, Elizabeth, and Lynn Gartley. 1979. *Walt Disney: A Guide to References and Resources*. Boston: G. K. Hall.

Mosley, Leonard. 1986. *The Real Walt Disney: A biography*. London: Grafton.

Sterling, John. 1994. "The World according to Disney." *Earth Island Journal* 9: 32–34.

Toy, Stewart. 1994. "Disney Headed for the Euro Trash Heap?" *Business Week* 3355 (24 January): 52.

DODWELL, HENRY. Henry Dodwell (1641–1711) was born in Dublin of English parents. His parents moved to York, England, in 1648, and by 1650 both had died. Dodwell was raised by his uncle. In 1656 he went to Trinity College, Dublin. He became a fellow but had to resign his fellowship in 1666 because he would not take holy orders as was required. He went to London, 1674; in 1688 he was appointed Camden Professor of History at Oxford. He lost his professorship in 1691 because he refused to take an oath of allegiance to King William III (1650–1702) and Queen Mary II (1662–1694). In 1694 he married and had ten children. He became a classical scholar and controversialist. Between Dodwell and a colleague, Francis Lee (1661–1719), argument rose because of Lee's adherence to the Philadelphian Society. This conflict continued until 1701. Dodwell's arguments and those of others in 1702 probably led to the demise of the Philadelphian Society in 1703. Dodwell died after catching a cold on a walk from Shottesbrooke to London.

See Also Leade, Jane; Lee, Francis; Philadelphians

Sources:

Smith, Benjamin. 1903. *The Century Cyclopaedia of Names*. London: Times.

Stephen, Leslie, and Sydney Lee, eds. 1917. *The Dictionary of National Biography*. London: Oxford University Press.

DONNER, GEORGE. George Donner (c. 1785–1847) was born of German parents in North Carolina. He was in Kentucky in 1818 and Illinois in 1828. At the time of the Donner Party (1846–1847) he was an elderly and prosperous farmer near Springfield, Illinois. A gentle and amiable character of sixty-two, "Uncle George," as he was called, was the father of fifteen children and husband to three wives. He was an experienced ox-team traveler. He decided to emigrate to California and was chosen to be party leader. In April 1846 he left Springfield, Illinois, with his third wife, Tamsen (c. 1801–1847), and five daughters. Eventually, the caravan included ninety emigrants with 200–300 wagons. Within the wagon train, the Donner group had about forty wagons. In July George Donner was elected train captain, and the whole caravan became known as the Donner Party. When the group reached Fort Bridger, they decided against the traditional route to California and decided to go by way of the Hastings cutoff. This was expected to cut the journey by 300 miles. The group did not know that the originator of this route, Lansford W. Hastings (c. 1818–c. 1868), was about to try the route himself for the first time. The new route was a disaster, adding time instead of reducing it. There followed a difficult crossing of the Salt Lake desert; some animals died of thirst, while others were stolen by the Native Americans. By late October snow had trapped them. Some died of starvation; others were thought to have been murdered and eaten by survivors. George Donner died from starvation and gangrene from a wound in his hand; his wife died two weeks later. All five of the daughters were rescued and survived the ordeal.

See also Donner Party

Source:

Thrapp, Dan L. 1988. *Encyclopaedia of Frontier Biography*. Lincoln: University of Nebraska Press.

DONNER PARTY. The Donner Party, a caravan of affluent midwestern farmers and merchants, emigrated to California during the expansion of the West in the United States. The party—also known as the Donner-Reed Party—arrived late in the Sierra Nevada mountains and were stranded in the winter snows of 1846–1847. The delay had been caused by problems encountered while crossing the Wasatch Mountains and the Great Salt Lake desert, Utah. Also they had to cut a new trail through Emigration Canyon east of Salt Lake City. They lost four wagons and many oxen in the mud of the desert west of the Great Salt Lake. They began the journey overladen, in outside wagons, and decided to take an untested route, a shortcut of hundreds of miles, with the wagons across the Wasatch mountains and the Great Salt Lake. Many oxen died when crossing the desert. Food became short, tempers flared, fights began, and time ran out as the snow came. They were trapped near the summit, where almost half the party died from starvation and exposure to the cruel cold. Rumors were that food was so scarce that members were murdered and cannibalized. Starr (1985) notes that the community, in striving for a better life, illustrated life in a dystopia.

See Also Donner, George; Dystopia

Sources:

Hawkins, Bruce R., David B. Madsen, Ann Hanniball, et al. 1990. *Excavation of the Donner-Reed Wagons: Historic Archaeology along the Hastings Cut-Off.* Salt Lake City: University of Utah Press.

McGlashan, C. F. 1947. *History of the Donner Party.* Stanford, Calif.: Stanford University Press.

Starr, Kevin. 1985. *Inventing the Dream: California through the Progressive Era.* New York: Oxford University Press.

Stewart, George R. 1936. *Ordeal by Hunger: The Story of the Donner Party.* 1960 ed. Lincoln: University of Nebraska Press.

DOUKHOBORS. The Doukhobors, or "Dukhobors" (Russian for "spirit wrestlers"), was a religious sect prominent in Russia in the eighteenth and nineteenth centuries. The name was coined by the orthodox opponents of the Doukhobors, who eventually called themselves "Christians of the Universal Brotherhood." They were like Quakers, rejecting completely the priesthood, sacraments, military service, and other outward symbols of Christianity. The members came from the lower level of society, primarily farmers. The Doukhobors promoted a communal, democratic attitude and preached equality. Because they rejected the authority of both church and state, they were persecuted under Catherine II (1729–1796). Alexander I (1777–1825) persuaded them to settle near the Sea of Azov, where they built a flourishing agricultural community. When they did not agree to military conscription and stated it was sinful, the government in 1840 ejected them from their lands and pushed them farther east, where they again built thriving communities. In 1887 military conscription was again extended to them, and their resistance brought severe persecution. Leo Tolstoy (1828–1910) befriended the Doukhobors and helped them escape oppression by migrating to Canada. Over 7,000 moved to Swan River, now Saskatchewan (1898–1899). Again they produced flourishing communities, and after 1908 they had spread to British Columbia. The sect became a small, but important, group in the development west Canada; however, there were internal divisions, primarily over the question of communal ownership of land. Later, they had much trouble with the government and their non-Doukhobor neighbors; occasionally, they were violent but usually expressed hostility with passive resistance. In 1945 the group divided and formed the Union of Doukhobors of Canada and the Sons of Freedom. Most have integrated fully into modern Canadian society.

See Also Tolstoy, Leo; Verigin, Peter Vasil'evich

Sources:

Armytage, Walter Henry Green. 1961. *Heavens Below: Utopian Experiments in England 1560–1950.* London: Routledge and Kegan Paul.

Harris, William H., and Judith S. Levy, eds. 1977. *The New Illustrated Columbia Encyclopedia*. New York: Rockville House and Columbia University Press.

Janzen, William. 1992. ''Limits on Liberty: The Experience of Mennonite, Hutterite and Doukhobor Communities in Canada.'' *University of Toronto Law Journal* 42: 239–246.

Woodcock, George, and Ivan Avakumovic. 1968. *The Doukhobors*. London: Faber and Faber.

DOWIE, JOHN ALEXANDER. John Alexander Dowie (1847–1907) was born in Edinburgh, Scotland. His mother was illiterate, and his father worked as a tailor and became a community preacher. After being raised in poverty and illness, John, age six, took the pledge of temperance and became a lifelong enemy to alcohol and a deep believer in God's care. In 1860 his family took him to Adelaide, South Australia, where he was put to work with a wholesale dry goods firm of which he eventually became a junior partner. At age twenty he gave up business for study, later attended the University of Edinburgh, and on returning to Australia in 1870 became a religious. Between 1873 and 1878 he was a noted eccentric in Adelaide, Sydney, and Melbourne. He entered a variety of disputes in Melbourne over the ownership of property and became an outstanding authoritarian religious figure. He was jailed for not paying his debts, following the belief that he was answerable only to God. He changed from the Congregational Church to become an Evangelist, and in 1882 in Melbourne, Victoria, he built an independent tabernacle. Six years later he went to San Francisco and then to Chicago and began faith healing. In January 1896 he led a meeting outside Chicago to establish the Christian Apostolic Catholic Church in Zion. As its general overseer he was in charge of its property. On Lake Michigan, forty-two miles from Chicago, he built his town, Zion City, which comprised 5,000 of his chosen followers. Zion had no theaters, no dance halls, no drugstores or physicians' rooms, no smoking or eating pork, and no secret lodge. Dowie controlled all the town's industry, banking and colleges, general store, factories, and fresh fruit supply; he had whistles blown to call the members to public prayers. In 1904 he tried to convert New York to his thoughts but failed; then he went on a worldwide evangelical mission. He went to Dublin, and his visit was recorded later in James Joyce's *Ulysses* (1922), where riots followed his meeting. His kingdom revolted against him in 1906, and he fell from power largely because its finances had become insecure. He may have been a charlatan or a borderline personality, but he was certainly a pugnacious, self-opinionated, autocratic man who had a luxurious way of life. In Mexico he had a stroke (1905) and went to Jamaica. Meanwhile, he was deposed as leader of Zion City (1906), entered litigation, and died at Zion City a year later.

See Also Zion City

Sources:

Johnson, Allen, and Dumas Malone, eds. 1930. *Dictionary of American Biography*. Vol. 3. New York: Charles Scribner's Sons.

Kiek, Edward S. 1927. *An Apostle in Australia*. London: Independent Press.

Pike, Douglas, et al., eds. 1966–1990. *Australian Dictionary of Biography*. Carlton, Victoria: University of Melbourne Press.

DRYSDALE, GEORGE RUSSELL. George Russell Drysdale (1912–1981) was born in Sussex, England, and was taken to settle in Melbourne in 1923. He planned to go into farming but instead took up art. He participated in the 1939 exhibition of the Contemporary Art Society of Australia and settled in Sydney to begin painting full-time (1942). In 1950, prominent British art historian Kenneth Clark (1903–1983) encouraged him to exhibit in Britain, and in 1954 he represented Australia at the Venice Biennale. His paintings emphasize the drought and erosion of the Australian outback in an abstract and often surrealist form. He and Donald Friend (1915–1989) established Hill End, an artist's colony in Australia based on a community that believed life and art coexist. It was established when the two young artists explored New South Wales and stopped at an old gold-mining town forty-five miles north of Bathurst. They found Hill End, a small township living on the memory of 50,000 inhabitants and fabulous tales of gold strikes, with a handful of residents searching for gold and hunting rabbits.

See Also Friend, Donald; Hill End

Sources:

Magnussen, Magnus, and Rosemary Goring, eds. 1990. *Chambers Biographical Dictionary*. 5th ed. Edinburgh: Chambers.

Robb, Gwenda, and Elaine Smith. 1993. *Concise Dictionary of Australian Artists*. Edited by Robert Smith. Melbourne: Melbourne University Press.

Van Nunen, Linda. 1995. "Golden Summers: In a Harsh Environment, the Artists of Hill End Forged a New Vision of the Australian Landscape." *Time (Australia)* (2 August): 71–72.

DUMAS, ALEXANDRE. Alexandre Dumas (1802–1870), known as "Dumas père," was born in Villers-Cotterets. Four years later his father died, and the child grew up feeling he was a social outcast. He went to Paris and worked as a copyist for the duc d'Orleans and began writing. He became acquainted with French romanticists Victor Hugo (1802–1895) and George Sand (1804–1876) and in four years became himself a noted playwright of historical drama. His *Henry III and His Court* (1829), *Antony* (1831), and *La Tour de Nesle* (1832) made him famous. Onto the stage he brought much of the action that had for many years been left in the wings, for example, brutality, and he would end his play at a high point of suspense. When newspapers began to serialize novels, Dumas' writing of stories developed apace. In time he became a prodigious storyteller and worked to put the history of France into novels. Two novels are well known: *The Count of Monte Cristo* and *The Three Musketeers*. Both have been filmed over fifty times. His novel about the French Revolution, *Ingénue* (1853), gives a distressing account of the slave trade and reflected Dumas' pursuit of social justice, loathing of inequity, and democratic political interests in France and abroad. Dumas was a workaholic who used writing to distract him from personal illness. To find peace for writing, he built a private utopia, Monte-Cristo. When it was built, so many visitors appeared that Dumas quit the building to write in a pavilion surrounded by a moat and left the many strangers at his Monte-Cristo to roam with his children, mistresses, friends, and pet vulture. Monte-Cristo was so costly that it threw him into bankruptcy. Thereafter, he produced his memoirs and novels of French history, lived in exile in Belgium (1855–1857), and ran guns for the Italian republican Guiseppe Garibaldi (1807–1882) between 1860 and 1864. He died at his son's villa in Dieppe, with little of the wealth he had earned as a writer.

See Also Monte-Cristo

Sources:

Clouard, Henri. 1955. *Alexandre Dumas*. Paris: A. Michel.
Hemmings, Frederick W. J. 1979. *The King of Romance: A Portrait of Alexandre Dumas*. London: Hamish Hamilton.
Maurois, Andre. 1955. *Alexandre Dumas; A Great Life in Brief*. New York: Knopf.
Ross, Michael. 1981. *Alexandre Dumas*. Newton Abbot, Devon, and North Pomfret, Vt.: David and Charles.
Stowe, Richard S. 1976. *Alexandre Dumas Père*. Boston: Twayne.

DUNCAN, WILLIAM. William Duncan (1832–1918) was born at Bishop Burton in England and was trained to be a schoolmaster by the Church Missionary Society. In the fall of 1857 he went to Fort Simpson in British Columbia, Canada. Quickly, he established good working relations with Paul Legaic (c. 1799–1869 or 1894), the Indian chief at Fort Simpson. Duncan moved his mission to Metlakatla, the location of an ancestral Tsimshian village, and began building a church and homes. It became known as Mission Point. Some months later Legaic came with 200 followers, probably because of a smallpox and probably because he wanted to secure his authority by keeping Duncan an ally in a conflict he had with Tsimshian clans. Duncan adopted the policy of the Christian Church Mission Society as laid down by its secretary and helped establish with the Indians a utopian Christian settlement. He and Legaic became highly influential, but, although they had many common goals, often conflict arose between them. The Indian chief would challenge Duncan in an effort to shore up his own authority. In time Duncan became the dominant figure, and in 1879 the village became the seat of the new Anglican diocese of Caledonia. Indians on the northwest coast were attracted to the settlement for its remarkable prosperity, and Duncan received international recognition for his leadership. However, when a new bishop was appointed at Victoria, Duncan's practices were questioned, and his authority was challenged. In response he led a group of villagers to establish New Metlakatla on Annette Island, Alaska (1887).

See Also Metlakatla Pass

Sources:

Arctander, John William. 1909. *The Apostle of Alaska: The Story of William Duncan of Metlakatla*. New York: Fleming H. Revell.
Halpenny, Frances G., ed. 1990. *Dictionary of Canadian Biography*. Toronto: University of Toronto Press and Les Presses de L'Université Laval.
Usher, Jean. 1976. *William Duncan of Metlakatla*. Ottawa: National Museums of Canada.

DYSTOPIA. Dystopia was first used probably by John Stuart Mill (1806–1873) in a speech in the British House of Commons, 12 March 1868. He was debating the Conservative government's policy on the Irish question. For thirty-nine years England had ruled Ireland, Mill said, as he attacked the government on the question of land-ownership and religious equality in Ireland. Earlier, the government had indicated it might consider the principle of religious equality in Ireland; but this was not possible, Mill continued, as long as the national property administered by the Episcopal Church of Ireland was not divested from its present purpose. The cost involved would be far too high for the English and Scottish people to accept, he claimed, and the Roman Catholic clergy were never to be bribed. In a humorous way Mill then said that he and his betters had sometimes been called Utopians (largely because they had espoused impractical schemes) and now suggested that the Conservative government seemed to have joined "such goodly company." Suddenly, Mill changed his mind. He said: "It is perhaps too complimentary to call them Utopians, they ought rather to be called dys-topians, or caco-topians. What is commonly called Utopian is something too good to be practicable; but what they appear to favour is too bad to be practicable." "Dys" meant diseased, abnormal, faulty, difficult, painful, unfavorable, bad, from the Greek "dus"; "caco" meant bad, unpleasant, incorrect, from the Greek "kakos." Negley and Patrick (1952) used the term to mean the opposite of eutopia, "the idea that society is a dystopia, if it is permissible to coin a term." Walsh (1962, p. 12) used the term to mean an "inverted utopia," and in 1967 in an article in the *Listener* it was stated that "the modern classics, Aldous Huxley's *Brave New World* and George Orwell's *Nineteen Eighty-Four* are dystopias." Booker (1994) suggests Kafka's *The Castle* and *The Trial* are bureaucratic dystopias; also Golding's *Lord of the Flies* is a dystopia because it shows the breakdown of civilized life and firstlings of totalitarian rule, as does Margaret Atwood's *The Handmaid's Tale*. Actual dystopias were the Donner Party, a tragic adventure that may have led to murder and cannibalism; Nazi Germany, which was probably the model for Orwell's *Nineteen Eighty-Four*; Stalin's Russia, the model for Orwell's *Animal Farm*. Valuable critical discussion of Booker (1994) can be found in *Utopian Studies* 6, no. 2: 134–139, 147–150.

See Also Animal Farm; Brave New World; Castle, The; Donner Party; *Handmaid's Tale, The*; Jonestown (Peoples Temple); *Lord of the Flies; Nineteen Eighty-Four*; Russia as Utopia; *Trial, The*

Sources:

Booker, M. Keith. 1994. *Dystopian Literature: A Theory and Research Guide*. Westport, Conn.: Greenwood Press.

Negley, Glenn, and J. Max Patrick. 1952. *The Quest for Utopia: An Anthology of Imaginary Societies*, pp. xvii, 298. New York: Schuman.

Robson, John M., and Bruce L. Kinzer. 1988. *Public and Parliamentary Speeches by John Stuart Mill. November 1850–November 1868*, pp. 247–261. Toronto: Toronto University Press and Routledge.

Simpson, J. A., and E.S.C. Weiner. 1989. *The Oxford English Dictionary*. Oxford: Oxford University Press.

Snodgrass, Mary Ellen. 1995. *Encyclopedia of Utopian Literature*. Santa Barbara, Calif.: ABC-CLIO.

Walsh, Chad. 1962. *From Utopia to Nightmare*, pp. 11–12. London: Geoffrey Bles.

E

EALEY, E.H.M. E.H.M. (Tim) Ealey (fl. 1922–1997), an Australian scholar, studied biology and Antarctic oceanography and completed a Ph.D. on the ecology of desert kangaroos (1963) in Western Australia. He taught zoology at Monash University (Melbourne) in Victoria and was foundation director of the Graduate School of Environmental Sciences. In 1950s he and a colleague planned to preserve an untouched bushland site near Bend of Islands, about twenty-eight miles northeast of Melbourne in Victoria. With the support of government officials, artists and colleagues they organized a conservation co-operative. It began with twelve shareholders, was enlarged by twenty, and bought eighty acres from the family of a prominent deceased politician who had long supported their ideas. The formation of the cooperative saved the site from becoming an extension of Melbourne's urban sprawl. By making tough rules for members to follow, Ealey believed that the cooperative survived, while others like it in Australia failed.

See Also Berryman, Margaret; Neale, Jeph; Round the Bend Conservation Co-operative

EBERT, FRIEDRICH. Friedrich Ebert (1871–1925), born in Heidelberg, was the son of a tailor. He became a saddler and an innkeeper and later took up journalism and the cause of the German social democrats. In 1912 he entered the Reichstag and in the following year was made chairman of his party. In the revolution of 1918, when the kaiser abdicated and fled Germany, Ebert was a majority socialist leader. He favored a constitutional monarchy like that in Britain and abhorred the social revolution that the Spartacists, led by Germany's leading political agitators, Karl Liebknecht (1871–1919) and Rosa Luxemburg (1871–1919), were advocating, and did not want to be supplanted by the Bolsheviks, as Alexander Kerensky (1881–1970) had been in Russia. He hoped to save the Hohenzollern monarchy and believed the Treaty of Versailles was both unrealizable and unbearable for Germany. It had been made public in Berlin on 7 May 1919 and signed in the Hall of Mirrors in the Palace of Versailles, on 28 June. Ebert, who had been elected the head of the Council of People's Representatives, was to govern Germany as if it were a republic, for the time being. He led the well-meaning trade unionist party of social democrats and secretly agreed to keep Field Marshal Paul von Hindenberg (1847–1934) in command of the German army. Early in January 1919 the Spartacists were crushed, their two leaders murdered, and the German National Assembly elections put Ebert in authority. Its constitution, framed in Weimar, was passed 31 July 1919 and for Germany promised a democracy with the best parts taken from experience in the most advanced democracies. Government by a cabinet came from France and Britain; a strong and popular president came from the United States; the use of referenda came from Switzerland; proportional representation would give minorities a say and adequate representation in Parliament. As president of the German Reich (1919–1925), he endured the Kapp Putsch in March 1920 and, on the anniversary of the German Republic, 9 November 1923, the attempt by Adolf Hitler (1889–1945) and Erich von Ludendorff (1865–1937) to establish a dictatorship in Munich, Bavaria. He died at the end of February 1925, a few months before Hitler's *Mein Kampf* appeared, and was succeeded by the elderly Paul von Hindenburg.

See Also Hindenburg, Paul von: Weimar Republic

Sources:

Dudley, Lavinia P. 1963. *The Encyclopedia Americana*. International ed. New York: Americana Corporation.
Heuss, Theodor. 1971. *Friedrich Ebert, 1871/1971*. Bonn: Inter Nations.
Magnussen, Magnus, and Rosemary Goring, eds. 1990. *Chambers Biographical Dictionary*. 5th ed. Edinburgh: Chambers.
Snyder, Louis Leo. 1996. *The Weimar Republic: A History of Germany from Ebert to Hitler*. Princeton: Van Nostrand.

ECONOMY. Economy was the third settlement of the Rappite Harmony Society, established in 1824, and situated at the Harmony township (now Ambridge), Beaver County, Pennsylvania. It flourished later due to its Economy Oil Company, which employed many from outside the settlement. In 1905 Economy was dissolved by the last of its three members.

See Also Harmony Society; Rapp, George

Sources:

Fogarty, Robert S. 1980. *Dictionary of American Communal History*. Westport, Conn.: Greenwood Press.
Oved, Yaacov. 1987. *Two Hundred Years of American Communes*. New Brunswick, N.J.: Transaction Books.

EIN-HOD. Ein-Hod is an artists' utopian village that was established in May 1953 in the hills of Mount Carmel, Israel, by Marcel Janco (1895–1984), a

Dadaist painter. It emerged from the ruins of an old town near Mount Carmel, Israel. Janco became its first mayor, and as residents settled, a gallery was erected, and tourists came to see the efforts of the village's artists. At the village is the Ein-Hod Art Gallery, the Janco-Dada Museum, the Artists' House, and the Artists' Studios. At the Gertrude Krause House are lectures twice a week and chamber music concerts and lectures. In summer there are music and other entertainments in the outdoor amphitheater, and in the village center is a restaurant. The Ein-Hod Gallery is the largest in Israel. Also Ein-Hod hosts a biennial sculpture exhibition; the most recent was in November 1997. Many visitors seek membership in Ein-Hod. To become a member one has to be an artist or married to one; to rent a space for a period as a visiting artist; to wait a year for the committee's decision about one's suitability. Successful applicants can then buy a sixty-four-year lease of government-owned land and build a home and studio. Communal studios are available for those who have insufficient funds to build their own. The General Council manages life at Ein-Hod through an administrative committee elected every two years.

See Also Janco, Marcel

Sources:

Popenoe, Cris, and Oliver Popenoe. 1984. *Seeds of Tomorrow*. San Francisco: Harper and Row.
Roth, Cecil E., ed. 1971. *Encyclopedia Judaica*. New York: Macmillan.

ELIOT, JOHN. John Eliot (1604–1690) was born in Widford, Hertfordshire. He studied at Cambridge and in 1622 was an usher at the school of Rev. Thomas Hooker (c. 1586–1647) near Chelmsford. Because his religious opinions were opposed to those in England, he sailed to Boston in 1631 and became pastor of the church at Boston. In 1634, after criticizing the colonial government's treatment of Indians, he was asked to retract his public censure. Eliot learned the Indian language and after two years made his first pastoral visit to Indians, October 1646, at Nonantum, Massachusetts. He gave a sermon in the native dialect but prayed in English. This was one of his first attempts toward the "civilizing" of his converts. He then established settlements that provided Indians with industrial occupations, homes and clothing, and some form of self-government, allowing them the comfort and security that white men had. Eliot sought the approval of fellow ministers in his attempt to integrate his Indian civilization with his religion. In July 1649 in New England was passed a law to found "a corporation for the promoting and propagating of the gospel among the Indians of New England," and in 1651 the first township was established at Natick, a township of "praying indians." Fourteen settlements were founded altogether under Eliot's auspices. The first Indian church was founded at Natick (1660) and continued until the last pastor died (1716). Eliot translated the Bible into the Algonquian language, and it was long recognized for its linguistic value. Eliot's two sons, both Harvard graduates, helped him put the dialect of the

Indians into a grammatical form in *Indian Primer* (1669) and *Logick Primer* (1672). By 1674 the number of "praying indians" was close to 3,500. Eliot continued translating, and he left a legacy of twenty books in the Algonquian language; he was preaching to native Indians well into his final years.

See Also Praying villages

Sources:

Bowden, Henry W., and James P. Ronda, eds. 1980. *John E. Eliot: Indian Dialogues.* Westport, Conn.: Greenwood Press.

Fogarty, Robert S. 1990. *All Things New: American Communes and Utopian Movements 1860–1914.* Chicago: University of Chicago Press.

Lee, Sidney, ed. 1920. *Dictionary of National Biography: Supplement 1901–1911.* London: Oxford University Press.

Tinkler, George E. 1993. *Missionary Conquest: The Gospel and Native American Genocide.* Minneapolis: Fortress Press.

Winslow, Ola Elizabeth. 1968. *John Eliot: Apostle to the Indians.* Boston: Houghton Mifflin.

ELMHIRST, LEONARD KNIGHT. Leonard Knight Elmhirst (1893–1974) was born at the vicarage, Laxton in Yorkshire; both his parents came from families of parsons. At eight Leonard was sent to boarding school, St. Anselm's, Bakewell in Derbyshire, where he wrote home about the sadistic, mindless brutality characteristic of English education. At fourteen he attended his father's old school, Repton, then studied at Cambridge for the cloth. Two of his brothers died in World War I; Leonard was unfit for military duties. After graduation he went to India (1915) as private secretary to the head of the Young Men's Christian Association and later was temporary secretary to Lionel Curtis (1872–1955), a fellow of All Souls, who promoted the idea of a British Commonwealth as opposed to a British empire through his Round Table Groups and the *Round Table*. Leonard's thinking was much influenced by Curtis and by Rabindranath Tagore (1861–1941), the promoter of agrarian reforms at his International University, Santiniketan. Shortly after returning to England, Leonard went to study at Cornell University in the United States, where he graduated in agricultural science (1921). In 1925 he married Dorothy Whitney Straight (1887–1968), widow of Willard Dickerman Straight (1880–1918), founder of the U.S. liberal weekly *New Republic*. He and Dorothy founded a progressive school, Dartington Hall, near Totnes in Devonshire, England; and much of its utopian educational philosophy may be traced to Leonard's early educational experiences and to his wife's liberalism and belief in education for life, not certification. In 1930 he helped found the International Conference of Agricultural Economists, was president until 1958 and on the Board of Trade mission to the United States (1944–1945), was agricultural adviser to Bengal's governor (1954–1955), and consulted with the Indian government's committee on higher education in rural regions. After Dorothy's death in 1968 he married a daughter of a noted music publisher and died in Beverly Hills.

See Also Dartington Hall; Straight, Dorothy Whitney

Sources:

Armytage, Walter H. Green. 1961. *Heavens Below: Utopian Experiments in England 1560–1950*. London: Routledge and Kegan Paul.

Blake, (Lord), and C. S. Nicholls, eds. 1986. *Dictionary of National Biography 1971– 1980*. Oxford: Oxford University Press.

Young, Michael D. 1982. The *Elmhirsts of Dartington: The Creation of a Utopian Community*. London: Routledge and Kegan Paul.

EMERY, FREDERICK E. Frederick Edmund Emery (1925–1997) was born in Narrogin, Western Australia, and died in Canberra 1997. His father was cattle drover and sheep shearer in Western Australia. Frederick was top of his class Fremantle Boys' High School (1939), studied science in the Psychology Department at the University of Western Australia, and completed a Ph.D. at the University of Melbourne (1953). In the 1960s at the Tavistock Institute, London, using action research in organizations in the United Kingdom and Scandinavia, he established the value of self-managing work teams and a brilliant theory of self-management of open social systems, a cornerstone of modern organizational theory. He returned to Australia in 1969, where after a few years in academe he became an effective, independent scholar of administrative alternatives to bureaucracy. These alternatives—both practical and theoretical—were established on the basis of scientific action research. His home office in Canberra became an international center of open-systems thinkers and workplace reformers. Emery withstood many attacks from those who assumed bureaucracy was the most suitable form of domination. With Eric L. Trist (1909–1993) he devised the Search Conference in 1959–1960. With his wife, Merrelyn, Emery developed participative design workshops to help ordinary people choose realizable, realistic futures and organize themselves in self-managed work groups. As well as helping individuals, he contributed to a worldwide trend of organizations to rebuild themselves around self-management teams of multiskilled workers. Emery secured a reputation as a outstanding social scientist in systems thinking, organizational theory, communications, penology, education, political science, strategic thinking, policy sciences, marketing, defense studies, military strategy, addiction, learning, and perception. Except for the degree of doctor of science honoris causa (1992) from Macquarie University, Emery received little formal recognition within Australian academic circles.

See Also Search Conference; Trist, Eric Lansdown

Source:

Gloster, Michael 1997. "Obituary: A Pioneer in Self-Management." *The Age*, 2 June: C2.

ENFANTIN, BARTHÈLEMY PROSPER. Barthèlemy Prosper Enfantin (1796– 1864) was born in Paris and became a leader of a movement started by Saint-Simon (1760–1825). Under his guidance the Saint-Simonian school of thought emphasized religious and moral regeneration and political reform. In 1832 Enfantin established a monastic settlement in Ménilmontant. He was known as Pére Enfantin and would call himself "the supreme father" of the church of Saint-Simonians. The settlement disintegrated with the imprisonment of Enfantin for a year on charges of incitement to immorality and financial fraud. When he was released, he undertook business enterprises. His writings include *Religion Saint Simonienne* (1831) and *Life Eternal* (1861), which was translated into English in 1920. His complete works were published in sixteen volumes, 1868–1878.

See also Ménilmontant; Saint-Simon, Claude Henri de Rouvroy, Comte de

Sources:

Kanter, Rosabeth Moss. 1973. *Communes: Creating and Managing the Collective Life.* New York: Harper and Row.
Smith, Benjamin. 1903. *The Century Cyclopedia of Names.* London: Times.

EPHRATANS. The Ephrata Society, a Pietist community, also known as the Solitary Brethren of the Community of Seventh-Day Baptists, or the Ephrata Colony, was founded in Pennsylvania (1732) by Johann Conrad Beissel (1691-1768). The community comprised "sisters" and "brothers" who led celibate lives and "householders" who were married and practiced continence. Like the Dunkers (German Baptist Brethren), the Ephratans upheld threefold immersion at baptism, love feasts at which feet were washed, and nonresistance. An important cultural community in Pennsylvania, the Ephratans became noted for their architecture, philanthropy, agricultural successes, choral work, devotional and mystical music, academic studies, and publication of illuminated manuscripts. Their printing press, founded in 1745, issued the largest book ever produced at that time in the U.S. colonies. It was a German-language account of the Mennonite martyrs (1748). With more than 300 members at its most influential period, the community was celebrated for its erudition, asceticism, and outstanding discipline. After Beissel's death the Ephratans declined in influence, and in 1814 its celibate order was abandoned, but a small, nonmonastic community, the German Seventh-Day Baptist Church, survived, Snow Hill Nunnery. In 1845 when the Ephratan Cloister became too prosperous, the leader closed down the mills, canceled contracts, fired employees, tore up the orchards, and rid the community of its capable businessmen.

See Also Beissel, Johann Conrad; Snow Hill Nunnery

Sources:

'Holloway, Mark. 1951. *Heavens on Earth: Utopian Communities in America: 1680–1880.* London: Turnstile Press.
Oved, Yaacov. 1987. *Two Hundred Years of American Communes.* New Brunswick, N.J.: Transaction Books.
Pitzer, Donald E. 1984. "Collectivism, Community and Commitment: America's Reli-

gious Communal Utopias from the Shakers to Jonestown.'' In P. Alexander and R. Gill, eds., pp. 119–135. *Utopias*. London: Duckworth.

EPIC PLAN. The EPIC plan aimed to ''End Poverty in California'' between July and November 1934. Upton Sinclair (1878–1968) was the Democratic nominee for state governor and represented the Socialist Army for EPIC against the Republican incumbent, Frank Merriam (1865–1955). Sinclair advocated ''Sinclairism,'' that is, production for use, not profit. His strategy was to end poverty by employing those out of work in industrial colonies owned by the state; the industries would be financed from confiscatory taxes put on banks, shares, and high-income earners as well as the use of inheritance taxes. Small bonds would be issued to provide capital. The policy was too radical for the U.S. president, Franklin Delano Roosevelt (1882–1945), who was working toward a social security system and a health insurance plan for all Americans. A movie about poverty was made, *Our Daily Bread*, depicting cooperatives and unions meeting the threat of hunger. A general, four-day strike in California, 15–19 July 1934, was accompanied by imagined threats of civil war and had a serious effect on businesses along the Pacific Coast. Troops were in the streets, slogans like ''Round up the Reds!'' were bandied about, and a ''nest of communists'' was identified. The strikers' strategy committee ordered the strikers to go back to work immediately, after winning a narrow vote, 194 to 174. In August 1934 membership of EPIC clubs had reached the thousands. But the utopia was never to be realized. Louis B. Mayer (1885–1957) of Metro-Goldwyn-Mayer (MGM) was thought to have threatened unemployed actors who were cooperating to make their own films; farm holders did not want land cooperatives; newspapermen advocated staunch support for Merriam. He won by only about 200,000 votes, which, given the corruption involved in the campaign, was a remarkable success for Sinclair and his EPIC plan.

See Also Sinclair, Upton

Sources:

Bloodworth, William A. 1977. *Upton Sinclair*. Boston: Twayne.
Garraty, John A., ed. 1977. *Dictionary of American Biography*. Supplement 5. New York: Charles Scribner's Sons.
''San Francisco—General Strike Ended.'' 19 July 1934. *Keesings Contemporary Archives* 1301G. London: Keesing.

EQUALITY, SOCIETY OF. In 1843 twenty-one people—the Society of Equality—purchased 263 acres at Spring Lake, Waukesha County, Wisconsin. They were British Owenites who aimed to form a community of united interests. In England the management of Owenite communities, Manea Fen and Queenwood, had been disappointing, so Owenites turned to the United States. The people at Equality found that the task of clearing the land, building, and raising crops was enormous. Many left the community. In 1845 sixteen arrived and settled at the edge of the acreage on the south. By the summer of 1846 the end of the community was imminent, and in 1847 the land was sold, and funds were distributed to shareholders. The community dissolved for many reasons; the members were not prepared for the new life they would have to lead; many departed and bought a farm for themselves as individuals or went to Milwaukee to follow their trade. The principles of Owenism and variations on them were neither understood nor discussed. Between members personal conflicts emerged, and many thought that opportunities for a better life lay outside, not inside, the community. The early efforts that were necessary for the community to establish a niche in the difficult frontier environs took away time needed to consider communitarian principles for building the venture.

See Also Manea Fen; Owen, Robert; Owenism

Sources:

Harrison, John F. C. 1969. *Robert Owen and the Owenites in Britain and America: Quest for the New Moral World.* New York: Charles Scribner's Sons.

Kesten, Seymour. 1993. *Utopian Episodes: Daily Life in Experimental Colonies Dedicated to Changing the World.* Syracuse, N.Y.: Syracuse University Press.

EQUALITY COLONY. Equality Colony was established in 1897 by the Brotherhood of the Cooperative Commonwealth in Skagit County, Washington. It was to be a socialist colony within the state that would establish for itself a socialist government and later convert the whole nation to socialism. The main founder was Wallace Lermond (1862–1944). With an associate he arranged to purchase 280 acres in Skagit County, and by June 1898 Equality Colony had 600 acres. The colony was named after Edward Bellamy's (1850–1898) novel *Equality* (1894). By 1899 the brotherhood had moved its headquarters to Equality, and Lermond had resigned. With a lack of capital, an insufficient number of dedicated workers, and an adverse marketing environment, the colony began to decline. In 1904, Alexander Horr (1871–1947), an anarchist from New York, arrived at Equality, reorganized it into small, competitive groups largely influenced by ideas in the novel *Freeland* by the Austrian economist Theodor Hertzka (1845–1924). Despite Horr's invigoration of the community, it began to split, and its decline hastened. The structure of the community changed from being cooperative to competitive, and conflict emerged between the socialists and the anarchists. In 1907 the colony was dissolved by court order.

See Also Bellamy, Edward; Hertzka, Theodor; Horr, Alexander

Sources:

Fogarty, Robert S. 1980. *Dictionary of American Communal History.* Westport, Conn.: Greenwood Press.

Le Warne, Charles Pierce. 1975. *Utopias on Puget Sound, 1885–1915.* Seattle: University of Washington Press.

Oved, Yaacov. 1987. *Two Hundred Years of American Communes.* New Brunswick, N.J.: Transaction Books.

EQUITY COLONY. Equity Colony, also known as Tuscarawas, was established in Tuscarawas County, Ohio (fl. 1833–1837). It was founded by Josiah Warren (1798–1874), an Owenite. The venture was not strictly an Owenite community largely because the Owenite movement to establish communities in the United States had waned after 1829. It was the first U.S. anarchist community. The land was puchased in 1831, and there were a few inhabitants there in 1837.

See Also Tuscarawas; Warren, Josiah

Sources:

Fogarty, Robert S. 1980. *Dictionary of American Communal History*. Westport, Conn.: Greenwood Press.

Oved, Yaacov. 1987. *Two Hundred Years of American Communes*. New Brunswick, N.J.: Transaction Books.

EREWHON. *Erewhon* (1872) is a novel—its title an anagram of "nowhere"—in the form of a utopian satire by British writer Samuel Butler (1835–1902). The novel turns many conventions on their head; for example, crime is an illness, and illness a crime; machines are banned for fear of their gaining mastery over humankind's mind; fraud and theft are thought to need medical attention. Absurd at first, these unusual conventions begin to make some sense to the narrator, Higgs, who discovered Erewhon on the distant side of a mountain range in a remote land. Higgs' description is a criticism of the hypocrisy, moral vacuum, and intellectual poverty of modern society and centers attention on child raising and religion as well as crime, mental illness, and work. A central theme in the novel concerns the role of machines. On one hand, machines are forbidden because they might evolve a human consciousness and become, in time, more intelligent than people. The opposing argument suggests that machines need not be the source of anxiety because humankind is of the same species as the machines it has produced. The second argument asserts that all machines have helped humans to extend their activities, not lose control of them. This debate captures the ambivalence toward technological progress that was emerging in Butler's Victorian England. Ambivalence and ambiguity are two strands that run through the book consistently. Higgs falls in love, makes a balloon, and flees the colony with the woman he adores. Butler's sequel, *Erewhon Revisited* (1901), tells how Higgs returns to Erewhon after twenty years and notes that his ascent in the balloon triggered the development of a religion in his absence, Sunchildism. The people of Erewhon are about to dedicate a temple to Higgs. He is appalled at how gullible the residents of the colony are and how easily Professors Hanky and Panky have exploited them. *Erewhon* is often compared with *Gulliver's Travels* (1726) as an amusing revelation of human folly; it may also be seen as a critical discussion of the ambiguities surrounding the emerging machine age; finally, it seems to be a provocative description of a society with both utopian and dystopian features.

See Also Butler, Samuel

Sources:

Booker, M. Keith. 1994. *Dystopian Literature: A Theory and Research Guide.* Westport, Conn.: Greenwood Press.
Kumar, Krishan. 1987. *Utopia and Anti-Utopia in Modern Times.* Oxford: Basil Blackwell.
Snodgrass, Mary Ellen. 1995. *Encyclopedia of Utopian Literature.* Santa Barbara, Calif.: ABC-CLIO.
Walsh, Chad. 1972. *From Utopia to Nightmare.* Westport, Conn.: Greenwood Press.

ESALEN. Esalen is a semi-intellectual retreat founded by graduates of Stanford University, Michael Murphy (b. 1930) and Richard Price (d. 1985) in 1962. It advocated unusual methods of psychotherapy, for example, hypnosis, group psychotherapy, sex, and psychedelic drugs. In the 1970s it became less experimental and was criticized by the Human Potential movement, it was plagued by management problems in the 1980s, its programs and finances were reorganized, and Murphy began the Esalen Soviet-American Exchange Program. Today it appeals to teachers, counselors, doctors, and other professional groups, including corporations that send Esalen its employees to learn social skills. Its early aim was to enhance individuals' sensitivity and to train them in interpersonal competence. The intellectual interests centered on the self and countless ideas and theories of the day drawn from astrology, psychiatry, psychology, self-realization theories, Sufism, the occult, natural foods programs, recent yoga philosophies, vegetarianism, varieties of group encounter and therapy, meditation in many forms, and feminist theories. These ideas were combined with drug taking in a effort to explore unconscious mental states. Most people who attended Esalen were young, educated, middle-class, and white. To visit or reside at Esalen is regarded as a privilege, and some people are more or less permanent residents. Esalen became known as a commune of flower people, counterculture activists, and an outlaw university. Many notables have visited, including Soviet cosmonauts. Many expert therapists would visit and subsidize their short periods at the institute by giving lectures. Their quest seems to be for a simple life, and the membership is itinerant and transitory, more like a utopian center of attention for the self than a permanent community of like-minded followers.

See Also Murphy, Michael

Sources:

Leonard, George. 1992. "How to Have an Extraordinary Life." *Psychology Today* 25, no. 3: 42ff.
McCord, William 1989. *Voyages to Utopia: From Monastery to Commune, the Search for the Perfect Society in Modern Times.* New York: W. W. Norton.
Morris, Bob. 1994. "Mind Games." *Vogue* 184: 136.

ESCAPIST COMMUNITIES. The Cabin was one of twenty-seven escapist communal groups that were studied firsthand by John Hall (1978). In the summer of 1970 a small group, the Cabin, gathered in the mountains of Colorado and, sharing an ideology and similar visions, sought an alternative to everyday life. Although visitors differed in their opinion of what the group was aiming for, the members enjoyed common charismatic attributes and spiritual experiences. The group had an unstable economy and declined due largely to incompatible social relations and unattainable career goals. Only one household from the group maintained itself for long. Among other communal ventures in Hall's personal study were New Vrindaban, a Krishna temple, whose members lived on ancient forms of technology, social organization, and culture; the Brotherhood of the Spirit, a haven for dropouts and street people, founded by a charismatic rock star; Country Collapse Farm, a group of disillusioned academics who used some grant money to study communal life (1972) and established a wavering economy based on cottage industries; the Farm in Tennessee; Karmu in Cambridge, Massachusetts, where an old black shaman nightly uttered his wisdom; Leaping Star Ranch, Colorado, a failed attempt to marry a hippie lifestyle with escapist, gypsylike adventures of students; Love Family, a primitive, Christian, self-supporting group in houses and on farms in Washington, Alaska, and Hawaii who barter and are led by a patriarch, Israel Love; Uroneath Farm, an anarchist, leaderless family that was supported by any means its members could find; the Lyman family or Fort Hall Community, Boston, where, thriving on the charisma of Mel Lyman, who claimed to be Christ, the group established a dubious reputation for theft and assault.

See Also Farm Eco-Village, The; Symbionese Liberation Army

Sources:

Hall, John R. 1978. *The Ways Out: Utopian Communal Groups in an Age of Babylon.* London: Routledge and Kegan Paul.
Snodgrass, Mary Ellen. 1995. *Encyclopedia of Utopian Literature.* Santa Barbara, Calif.: ABC-CLIO.

ESPERANTO. Esperanto is the most successful of the artificial, universal languages devised in the late nineteenth century and has the utopian aim of bringing international harmony through a common tongue. The system is based on common words in most tongues that have a basis in Latin grammar. It is easy to learn and master quickly. It was published first in 1887 in that part of Poland under oppressive rule by czarist Russia. Although Esperanto spread first into Russia and later to Germany and the United States, its Russian supporters attracted much hostile attention, and attempts to advance its use were subject to strong censorship. Accepted in 1924 as a clear language for telegraphy, it was also used at international conferences, in commerce, and on radio. Over 30,000 items of original or translated literature are in the language as well as some scientific journals. It has over 8 million supporters. The original publication of 1887 is today known as ''Unua Libro'' and appeared in Russian, French, German, and Polish. The author's name—Dr. Lazarus Ludwig Zamenhof (1859–1917)—did not appear on the book. The title was *Lingvo Internacia de la*

Doktoro Esperanto; "Doktoro Esperanto" meaning "Doctor Hopeful," the pseudonym of its inventor, reflects his feeling for its future. "Esperanto" is the present participle in the noun form of the verb "esperi," meaning "to hope." Through this usage the term entered other languages. Esperanto was accepted in Europe, but only by literate, educated people. A survey of the role of Esperanto in the reduction of tensions among nations shows, first, that although Esperanto could provide a partial solution to some difficulties, most of them are not so great as to require a radical adoption of Esperanto worldwide; second, that Esperanto's supporters are, in some way, deviant characters; third, that Esperanto has many different meanings and purposes; and fourth, that it is taken up as a hobby, sometimes linked with family interests, and other times given subversive overtones and an aura of not being politically correct. Consequently, Esperanto has yet to be adopted officially by any major nation, state, group, or organization.

See Also Zamenhof, Lazarus Ludwig

Sources:

Barnhardt, Robert, ed. 1988. *The Barnhardt Dictionary of Etymology.* New York: H. Wilson.

Boulton, Marjorie. 1960. *Zamenhof, Creator of Esperanto.* London: Routledge and Kegan Paul.

Connor, George A., Doris T. Connor, William Solzbacher, and J. B. Se-Tsien Kao, eds. 1959. *Esperanto, the World Language.* New York: Thomas Yoseloff.

Forster, Peter. 1982. *The Esperanto Movement.* The Hague, Paris, and New York: Mouton.

ESSENES. Essenes were a Jewish, semimonastic sect active during the Second Temple era (second century B.C.–first century A.D.) in different parts of Israel. They lived primarily along the western coast of the Dead Sea. Their name appears to mean both piety and healing; their origins are obscure and may be traced to the period before the Maccabean uprising (167 B.C.), when Jews were persecuted by Antiochus IV (d. 163 B.C.), who aimed to eradicate Judaism. By the first century A.D. the Essenes had 4,000 adherents, and their community was structured in a strict, communitarian order. Members swore total obedience to their superiors; candidates for membership underwent a three-year probationary period; all potential members had to swear a vow of frankness to their fellow brethren and one of total secrecy about the community's teaching. Only unmarried adult men could be admitted because women were considered by nature to be both wanton and unfaithful. Men worked at different crafts and agriculture, held all property in common, had no slaves, upheld temperance, thought pleasure was a vice, ate all meals—largely, a sacred event—in common, suffered expulsion for many minor crimes, and were executed if they spoke badly of Moses. The Essenes supported a revolt against Roman domination of the Middle East. So the Roman emperor, Nero (37–68), sent Vespasian (9–79) and his son, Titus (39–81), in A.D. 70 to destroy the temple, the center of Jewish worship, in

Jerusalem. Consequently, the Essenes' monastic community evaporated from recorded Jewish history. But recently (1947–1956) scholars, noting the discovery of the Dead Sea Scrolls, which date mainly from 150 B.C. to A.D. 68, suggested they were evidence of Essenes' library and that John the Baptist could well have been a member of the Essenes.

Sources:

Meurois-Givaudan, Anne, and Daniel Meurois-Givaudan. 1993. *The Way of the Essenes: Christ's Hidden Life Remembered*. English trans. Originally in French, 1989. Rochester, V.: Destiny.

Oved, Yaacov. 1987. *Two Hundred Years of American Communes*. New Brunswick, N.J.: Transaction Books.

Pitzer, Donald E. 1984. "Collectivism, Community and Commitment: America's Religious Communal Utopias from the Shakers to Jonestown." In Peter Alexander and Roger Gill, eds., *Utopias*, pp. 119–135. London: Dickworth.

Rexroth, Kenneth. 1974. *Communalism: From Its Origins to the Twentieth Century*. New York: Seabury Press.

Wigoder, Geoffrey. 1989. *The Encyclopedia of Judaism*. New York: Macmillan.

EUPSYCHIA. Eupsychia is an imagined culture of 1,000 self-actualizing people devised by Abraham Maslow (1908–1970) that could answer the question, How good a society does human nature allow? It was based on knowledge of the heights attainable by human nature and developed as an extrapolation of the higher forms of interpersonal and social organization. "Eupsychian" implies real possibilities that could be improved, rather than the usual psychosocial values of certainty, prophecy, inevitability of progress, perfect ability, and confidence in future predictions. Maslow believed his utopia was psychological and empirical, not a wish-fulfillment or a dream. The limits on admission to Eupsychia were based on Maslow's belief that people who actively sought community life probably needed it in the sense that they were deficient in that need, that is, clearly neurotic. Consequently, they were unable to function in a community, and the community would fail. Therefore, in setting rules for membership, it is important to differentiate the neurotic need for love in people from the healthy pleasure in loving and separate the neurotic need for company and togetherness from healthy pleasure of friendship. The rule for a successful Eupsychian community would be to exclude radicals, hippies, all revolutionaries, most neurotics, all narcissists, immature, self-indulgent characters, in short, all people who could not tolerate boredom or work willingly at routine chores. When these people are excluded, the need for privacy can be met together with the need for pleasure from the company of others. The reason many modern alternative attempts at utopia fail—hippie communities, groups of draft resisters, member of drop-in coffeehouses—is that they attract only a few workers, and remaining members become parasites who shift responsibilities to the few genuine workers. Those few workers, in time, realize that they have been manipulated, feel hurt and disillusioned, see a great discrepancy between words and actions, and after slogging through the long haul and seeing failure, feel deeply betrayed and give up in disgust. Maslow also warns to beware the enthusiasm at the beginning of a utopian venture, especially from those who avow a willingness to die for the revolution but not to peel potatoes for it. Maslow believed he should write on community, especially his Eupsychia—a planned culture— because he had been through community experiences that succeeded with decent, solid, reliable people.

See Also Maslow, Abraham H.

Sources:

Garraty, John A., and Mark C. Carnes, eds. 1988. *Dictionary of American Biography.* Supplement 8. New York: Charles Scribner's Sons and Collier Macmillan.

Lowry, Richard J., and Jonathan Freedman, eds. and abridgers. 1982. *The Journals of Abraham Maslow.* Lexington, Mass.: Lewis.

Maslow, Abraham H. 1961. "Eupsychia—the Good Society." *Journal of Humanistic Psychology* 1: 1–11.

———. 1965. *Eupsychian Management: A Journal.* Homewood, Ill.: Dorsey Press.

EVANS, FREDERICK. Frederick William Evans (1808–1893) was born in Leominster, Worcestershire, in England. His father held a commission in the British army. When Frederick was four, his mother died, and the boy was cared for by her relatives, who sent him to school at Stourbridge. At the end of his formal schooling he lived with his aunts and uncles on a large and successful farm, Chadwick Hall, near Worcester. With his father and brother he sailed for the United States (1820) and settled in Binghamton, New York. He and his brother campaigned for reforms such as limited landholdings, abolition of monopolies and imprisonment for debt, female emancipation, and establishment of Sunday mail service. Such fragmented policies failed to gratify him, so he turned to Fourier's ideas and Owenism and walked 800 miles to join the community at Massilon, Ohio (1828). The community failed, and Evans went briefly to England, returned to the United States (1830), and joined a group of ex-Massilon freethinkers and reformers gathered around Robert Owen's (1771–1858) son, Robert Dale Owen (1801–1877). He surprised his fellows when, after a visit to New Lebanon, he suddenly converted to Shakerism (1830). He rose to chief elder of the New Lebanon novitiate by 1843 and eventually became the main publicist for the sect and one of its most prominent leaders and internal reformers. He restated the theology of the group and emphasized continuation of revelations and spiritual communications, arguing that with true revelation came self-denial and that revelations espousing licentiousness were fundamentally evil. He separated the sect, which looked backward, from the church, which was forward-looking. He wanted Shakers to be progressive, to reform the world, and to abandon the utopian ideals of transcending the world and living in isolation from it. To further his reformist views, Evans edited and wrote publications on radical reform in different fields, among them the *Bible of Reason*.

For sixty-three years he remained with North family at Mount Lebanon and for fifty-seven of those years presided over the family as an elder. He worked hard for the emancipation of slaves. He was a natural orator and a capable leader and, in time, became one the more prominent of Shaker leaders. He died at Mount Lebanon.

See Also Owen, Robert; Shakers, Shaking Quakers

Sources:

Johnson, Allen, and Dumas Malone, eds. 1930. *Dictionary of American Biography*. Vol. 3. New York: Charles Scribner's Sons.

Pitzer, Donald E. 1984. ''Collectivism, Community and Commitment: America's Religious Communal Utopias from the Shakers to Jonestown.'' In Peter Alexander and Roger Gill, eds., pp. 119–135. *Utopias*. London: Duckworth.

Whitworth, John McKelvie. 1975. *God's Blueprints: A Sociological Study of Three Utopian Sects*. London: Routledge and Kegan Paul.

EVANS, WILLIAM. William Evans (fl. 1843–1846) was born in Swansea and ran a newsdealer shop that sold socialist literature; he published the journal *The Potter's Examiner and Workman's Advocate* (1843). In the belief that England's industrial future was blighted, he recommended that potters should buy cheap land in the United States. He illustrated this with the example of the village of New Albion, Illinois. Also he warned that workers would be replaced at a remarkable pace by new technology and suggested that emigration to the United States would diminish the labor pool of potters and increase British demand for their employment. As a result the joint stock Emigration Company was formed by the County Trades Union of Operative Potters. Evans reprinted books to guide immigrants, encouraged subscribers and shareholders to support the company, and in 1846 sent an agent to buy the land. He went to Wisconsin and bought land, to be called Pottersville. Because the capital was short, and some conflict emerged between the settlers, Evans sailed back to England and began to include among the members of the community a wider range of craftsmen. He was partly successful, but the Pottersville venture failed. He tried to repeat the plan at Fox River in Wisconsin, but a lack of interest in Britain and poor soil at Fox River led this venture to fail also. Finally, misrepresentation, corruption, and incompetence were used to undermine the project and to illustrate that no longer was trade unionism a suitable basis for utopian ventures.

See Also Pottersville

Sources:

Armytage, Walter H. Green. 1961. *Heavens Below: Utopian Experiments in England 1560–1950*. London: Routledge and Kegan Paul.

Owen, Harold. 1901. *The Staffordshire Potter: With a Chapter on the Dangerous Process in the Potting Industry, by the Duchess of Sutherland*. Reprinted 1970. Bath: Kingsmead Reprints.

F

FABIANS. Fabians were a group of socialists who formed the Fabian Society (1884) and aimed for gradual social change. The Fabian Society was named after Fabius (d. 203 B.C.), a Roman dictator who fought Hannibal by avoiding direct engagement, and in time weakening the Carthaginians in skirmishes; similarly, the Fabians rejected revolutionary change or sudden reforms and for social change relied on propaganda, education, and discussion. Among its members were George Bernard Shaw (1856–1950), Sidney Webb (1859–1947), Beatrice Webb (1858–1943), George Douglas Howard Cole (1889–1956), Graham Wallas (1858–1932), and Herbert George Wells (1866–1946). Fabians thought their society reestablished socialism a generation after the death of Robert Owen (1771–1858). The gradualist and collectivist position of Fabians appeared in an essay by Mrs. A. Besant (1888) in response to an act that had created the county councils in Britain. The act divided England into districts controlled by a council. To Fabians this was a means by which socialism could be practiced through social reform and without the attendant anxiety of revolution. The reform that remained was to give every adult a vote in electing the councillors; reduce the term of office to one year; pay councillors so that they served the local community fully; and reduce legal restrictions on councillors so they could act freely to establish a small local government. Fabians thought this would form a community where no one would suffer the anxiety of struggling to survive. Twenty-five years later that anxiety was evident for many reasons, including the experience that the machinery of representative government, with frequent elections and party propaganda, exacerbated the social conflict and injustices that representative government was expected to overcome. Mass education was needed if representative government was to find a way to integrate property rights with cooperative working relationships. In the years to come Fabians would research these and other issues. Their numbers were not great in Britain— fewer than 3,000 by 1914—but today many intellectuals in the social sciences consider themselves Fabians, although they are not organized as such, because they support attempts to make the world a better place through gradual social reform supported by education for all and rational debate based on reliable social research.

See Also Cole, George Douglas Howard; Shaw, George Bernard; Wallas, Graham; Webb, Beatrice Martha; Webb, Sidney James; Wells, H. G.

Sources:

Beilharz, Peter. 1992. *Labour's Utopias: Bolshevism, Fabianism, Social Democracy.* London: Routledge.

Cole, Margaret I. P. 1964. *The Story of Fabian Socialism.* New York: Science Editions.

Hammond, Nicholas G. L., and Hayes H. Scullard, eds. 1970. *The Oxford Classical Dictionary.* Oxford: Clarendon Press.

MacKenzie, Norman, and Jeanne MacKenzie. 1977. *The Fabians.* New York: Simon and Schuster.

Miller, David, ed. 1987 *The Blackwell Encyclopedia of Political Thought.* Oxford: Blackwell.

Pèase, Edward R. 1963. *The History of the Fabian Society.* London: F. Cass.

Pimlott, Ben, ed. 1984. *Fabian Essays in Socialist Thought.* London: Heinemann.

Wallas, Graham. 1914. *The Great Society: A Psychological Analysis.* New York: Macmillan.

FAGE, DURAND. Durand Fage (fl.1680–1708) was born in Aubois in Languedoc and worked there as a weaver. In 1702 he was inspired by the sight of an eleven-year-old girl in great agitation, shivering all over, apparently possessed by some spirit. He became a soldier and prophet, but little is securely known of his career. He fought with, and led, the Camisards, a rebellious Protestant group from the Cevennes region in France (1702–1748). They were defeated, and he went to Switzerland, where shortly after his arrival he was expelled to Bernese territory. He fled to Basel and then to Holland. Within a month he was in London and there was found prophesying about the millennium. Declared an impostor, he returned to France.

See also Camisards

Sources:

Armytage, Walter Henry Green. 1961. *Heavens Below: Utopian Experiments in England 1560–1950.* London: Routledge and Kegan Paul.

Garrett, Clarke. 1987. *Spirit Possession and Popular Religion: From the Camisards to the Shakers.* Baltimore: Johns Hopkins University Press.

FAIRHOPE COLONY. Fairhope Colony was established on the shore of Mobile Bay, Alabama, in 1893 by four families from Des Moines, Iowa. They aimed to use Henry George's (1839–1897) single-tax principles under the existing laws. Land and ground rent were to be used in common and for the communal good; the colony was to own public utilities and operate them. It had a cooperative store, a steamer, and a wharf and exchange to trade in products and services. It was the Fairhope Industrial Association, later renamed the Fairhope Single Tax Corporation. The town of Fairhope was incorporated in 1908 on 11,000 acres, 40 percent of which belonged to the community; the remainder was owned privately. At first money for the purchase of land was raised with a membership fee of $200; afterward it was reduced to $100 and paid monthly in installments of $5. By 1915 about 130 leaseholders, each on a half acre, lived in dwellings on 120 plots. Many cooperative practices disappeared from the Fairhope Colony; however, it kept its cooperative spirit. It attracted the attention of Marie Howland (1835–1921), and Joseph Fels (1854–1914) donated thousands of dollars to this experiment.

See Also Fels, Joseph; George, Henry; Howland, Marie Stevens

Sources:

Alyea, Paul E., and R. Blanch. 1979. *Fairhope, 1894–1954: The Story of a Single Tax Colony*. Hoke: A.M.S. Press.

Fogarty, Robert S. 1990. *All Things New: American Communes and Utopian Movements 1860–1914*. Chicago: University of Chicago Press.

Gaston, Paul M. 1993. *Man and Mission: E. B. Gaston and the Origins of the Fairhope Single Tax Colony*. Montgomery, Ala.: Black Belt Press.

FARM ECO-VILLAGE, THE. The farm was founded in 1971 by Stephen Gaskin (fl. 1969–1995), who led a group of hippies from the Haight-Ashbury district of San Francisco in search of better living. Gaskin was teaching at San Francisco State University when he started a Monday night class to talk about why and how young people were changing their culture. Some class members decided to become a community. The group settled at Summertown in south-central Tennessee on 1,700 wooded acres. The number of followers increased from a few hundred to a peak of 1,400 in 1980. Early housing was the buses the members arrived in and military tents. Gradually, these were transformed into permanent structures. A great interest grew in building solar houses, and now the farm is involved in this activity commercially. The farm provides its own energy using wind generators and solar power; their food is vegetarian, with much reliance on soybean. Farming is organic, and composting is used for fertilizing. The community has its own paramedics, nurses, and midwives. In the early 1980s many members quit when they lost faith in Stephen Gaskin, debts rose, business ventures failed, and administration seemed incompetent. The farm reorganized its economy, allowing for private ownership of property. Now it has its own roads, water system, school, clinic, grocery store, repair shops, recreation facilities, government, and publishing house and makes electronic equipment and specialty food products. At present there are about 250 residents. The farm emphasizes social relations and actions rather than a particular ideology but entertains all versions of religion. Members use a special language to organize their work and social relations. They are attempting to become self-sufficient through intensive and technologically sophisticated farming; nevertheless, they need outside work. The community has a free communal store, dry goods store, laundromat, telephone system, and kitchen. It is the largest and best-known intentional community in the United States. Its spiritual commitment is to simple living, self-reliance, and the pioneering of social technologies and permaculture courses.

See Also Gaskin, Stephen; Permaculture

Sources:

Bates, Albert K. 1987. "Technological Innovation in the Farm Spiritual community, 1971–87." Paper presented at the National Historical Communital Studies Association, annual meeting, Bishop Hill, Ill., October.
Gaskin, Ina May. 1975. *Spiritual Midwifery*. Rev. ed., 1980. Summertown, Tenn.: Book.
Hall, John R. 1978. *The Ways Out: Utopian Communal Groups in an Age of Babylon*. London: Routledge and Kegan Paul.
Kern, Louis J. 1993. "Pronatalism, Midwifery and Synergistic Marriage: Spiritual Enlightenment and Sexual Ideology on the Farm (Tennessee)." In Wendy E. Chmielewski, Louis J. Kern, and Marlyn Klee-Hartzell, eds., pp. 201–220. *Women in Spiritual and Communitarian Societies in the U.S.* Syracuse, N.Y.: Syracuse University Press.
Popenoe, Cris, and Oliver Popenoe. 1984. *Seeds of Tomorrow*. San Francisco: Harper and Row.

FEDERATION OF EGALITARIAN COMMUNITIES. The Federation of Egalitarian Communities is a network of intentional communities in Virginia and Missouri that uphold democratic, nonviolent, secular, income-sharing societies. Members seek to share their ideas and experiences and to help others manage the problems of everyday life in a community. Visitors are welcome to take tours through the community, spend a week residing and working with members, or share community life on an internship basis. Members also go visiting and conduct workshops on the life spent in an intentional community. To publicize their community, they sell books and audiovisual materials and have newsletters and a Web site. The communities in Virginia are Twin Oaks in Louisa, Tekiah in Floyd, and Acorn in Mineral. In Missouri they are East Wind in Tecumseh and Sandhill and Dancing Rabbit/Skyhouse in Routledge.

See Also Twin Oaks

Sources:

Kinkade, Kathrine 1973. *A Walden Two Experiment: The First Five Years of Twin Oaks Community*. New York: Morrow.
———. 1994. *Is It Utopia Yet? An Insider's View of Twin Oaks Community in Its 26th Year*. Louisa, VA.: Twin Oaks Publications.

FELLOWSHIP FARM (PUENTE). Fellowship Farm was on seventy-five acres near Puente, California. In Santa Barbara, George Elmer Littlefield (fl.1862–1930) a utopian mystic, was asked to establish a new colony for the Los Angeles Fellowships Farms Company (1912). It had about fifty members in twelve families. The families took up about one acre each (1912–1913) and a share in the public utilities of the colony. Membership remained between fifty and sixty and practiced such eccentricities as nudism at home, and in Los Angeles some members went street-preaching. The landholdings proved to be uneconomic, and the colony dispersed as members left. Some bought larger holdings nearby. The sense of cooperation diminished as the equality of landholdings gave over to pressures for economy on large holdings. In 1927 the farm was taken over by a water utility, and the community disappeared.

    See Also Littlefield, George Elmer

Sources:

Fogarty, Robert S. 1990. *All Things New: American Communes and Utopian Movements 1860–1914.* Chicago: University of Chicago Press.
Hine, Robert V. 1953. *California's Utopian Colonies.* 1983 ed. Berkeley: University of California Press.

FELS, JOSEPH. Joseph Fels (1854–1914) was born of German Jewish parents in Halifax County, Virginia. Soon after, his parents settled in Yanceyville, North Carolina, and in 1865, they went to live in Richmond and in Baltimore. At age fifteen, Joseph quit school for business and worked for a year with his father producing hand soap and later went into partnership with another manufacturer. In 1889, he and his wife, Mary, joined the Society for Ethical Culture in Philadelphia, an organization that sought to advance enlightened philanthropy. With a strong belief in personal self-development, they quit the society and formed the Fellowship for Ethical Research and the Walt Whitman Fellowship. In 1893 Fels escaped the effects of the economic depression and bought an interest in a process of soap making from Naptha. After successful research and development the manufacture of hand soaps was established, and the Fels-Naptha plant eventually distributed its products internationally. While extending his exports in England, he was drawn to the ideas of Henry George (1839–1897). Land monopolies seemed the obvious cause of poverty, and a single tax—on landowners—was the obvious solution. He supported the Philadelphia Vacant Land Cultivation Association, which gave land to the unemployed to grow food. In 1894 he supported a similar scheme in Detroit. Although he lived in England, he gave $500 a year to the Philadelphia Association and remained a director (1900–1914). In 1895 he donated thousands of dollars to the Fairhope Colony on the shore of Mobile Bay, Alabama. He saw that settling and farming land lowered unemployment, but the small landholders were soon victims of avaricious landlords who raised the rents as the land became more productive. The better solution was vacant lot possession. At Hollesley Bay, Fels bought 1,300 acres for the unemployed to use; later at Maylands in Essex, he acquired 600 acres for the same purpose. He supported vacant lot farming in both London and Philadelphia. He became identified as a single-tax exponent (1905) and was given credit for obtaining the inclusion of land tax in the British budget of 1909.

He gave about $100,000 a year from his personal fortune for the promotion of the single-tax scheme in England and $25.000 in Canada, Europe, and Australia. One of his enterprises was to procure the translation of Henry George's *Progress and Poverty* into Chinese.

See Also George, Henry; Henry George League; Hollesley Bay Colony

Sources:

Dudden, Arthur Power. 1971. *Joseph Fels and the Single-Tax Movement*. Philadelphia: Temple University Press.
Johnson, Allen, and Dumas Malone, eds. 1930. *Dictionary of American Biography*. Vol. 3. New York: Charles Scribner's Sons.

FERM, ELIZABETH BYRNE. Elizabeth Byrne Ferm (1857–1944) was born in Illinois, married at twenty, and lived in New York. Objecting to her husband's dominating behavior, she left him and went to live with her mother in Brooklyn, where she began to care for her deceased sister's children. As a result her interest in child care and children's education developed. In the 1890s she attended a theosophy meeting where she met Alexis Ferm (1870–1971), a Swede who had come to New York in infancy and had studied and later lectured on education. They were married in 1898, and Elizabeth worked enthusiastically with her husband to establish free schools in New York (1901–1913). Neither accepted orthodox, organized education and its depressing impact on ideas and personal growth. They did not believe in having children indoctrinated and avoided intellectual pretensions. To them education was for a child's development, not for adults to teach. They lived on a farm in Connecticut until 1920, when they were persuaded by Harry Kelly (1871–1953) to run the Stelton school for children, which at the time was in chaos. The school was an important part of the Ferrer Colony, a utopian experiment in New York. Later, Joseph Cohen (1881–1953) asked them to take over the school entirely. They made drastic changes, raised the academic education level, and encouraged craft, manual training, and outdoor activities. They aimed to break down what they thought was an artificial barrier between schoolwork and everyday life. A conflict with the parents forced the Ferms to resign in 1925. The school and the Ferrer Colony remained separate; the school represented the inner road to individual liberation, while the colony took a political and social route to changing the world outside the individual.

See Also Cohen, Joseph; Ferrer Colony; Kelly, Harry

Sources:

Ferm, Mary Elizabeth (Byrne). 1949. *Freedom in Education*. New York: Lear.
Veysey, Laurence. 1973. *The Communal Experience: Anarchist and Mystical Counter-cultures in America*. New York: Harper and Row.

FERRER, GUARDIA FRANCISCO. Guardia Francisco Ferrer (1859–1909), born in Allela, near Barcelona, was self-educated and became a railway worker, freethinker, and fervent, strong supporter of the republican cause in Spain. While teaching Spanish in Paris (1886), he took up socialism, and with a legacy in 1901 he established a modern school in Barcelona (Escuela Moderna). It flourished, but because he had founded an anticlerical institution, he was thought to be seditious and was accused of planning to assassinate Spain's king and queen. The school was closed (1906), and he was imprisoned for one year. In 1909 he was visiting England when he was told of the Barcelona uprising. On his return he was arrested, charged with joining in the uprising, tried, convicted, and shot on the same day. International criticism followed, the Spanish ministry fell, and Ferrer was lauded as an anarchist and martyr of the Spanish republican cause. His name was given to the Ferrer Colony by a community of anarchists in New York (1915).

Sources:

Abbott, Leonard, ed. 1910. *Francisco Ferrer, His Life Work and Martyrdom*. 1987 Microfiche. Alexandria, Va.: Chadwyck-Healey.

Fogarty, Robert S. 1980. *Dictionary of American Communal and Utopian History*. Westport, Conn.: Greenwood Press.

Grossman, Rudolf. 1987. *Francisco Ferrer: sein Leben und sein Werk*. Trans. by Pierre Ramus. Microfilm. Alexandra, Va.: Chadwyck-Healey.

McCabe, Joseph. 1987. *The Martyrdom of Ferrer*. Alexandria, Va.: Chadwyck-Healey.

Oved, Yaacov. 1987. *Two Hundred Years of American Communes*. New Brunswick, N.J.: Transaction Books.

Veysey, Lawrence. 1973. *The Communal Experience*. New York: Harper and Row.

FERRER COLONY. The Ferrer Colony was part of a utopian movement originating from an experimental evening school at a cultural center in New York City (1915). It was founded by an anarchist community led by Harry Kelly (1871–1953), Joseph Cohen (1881–1953), and Leonard Abbott (1878–1953). They chose the name from the noted Spanish anarchist and socialist martyr Guardia Francisco Ferrer (1859–1909). The students came from the families of radical workers in the New York City garment industry. In spite of internal dissension the school survived for five years, and by 1918 the colony, which had moved to a new site in 1915, had dwellings for twenty families. The colony's Modern School was the stabilizing unit of the community and was organized by the radical educationist Elizabeth Byrne Ferm (1857–1944). The colony disbanded because of regular conflicts among members during World War II. By 1946 it had gone.

See Also Abbott, Leonard; Cohen, Joseph; Ferm, Elizabeth Byrne; Ferrer, Guardia Francisco; Kelly, Harry

Sources:

Dudley, Lavinia P. 1963. *The Encyclopedia Americana*. International ed. New York: Americana Corporation.

Fogarty, Robert S. 1980. *Dictionary of American Communal History*. Westport, Conn.: Greenwood Press.

FINDHORN COMMUNITY. Findhorn is an intentional community with a spiritual approach to solving the world's problems through a "network of light," that is, a spreading number of "spiritually attuned" people. A center of international education, Findhorn draws annually 3,000–6,000 visitors of many ethnic origins. In 1962 Eileen Caddy (b. 1917) and Peter Caddy (1917–1994) and his secretary, a Canadian, Dorothy Maclean (B.C. 1920) felt the call to establish a spiritual community near their hotel at Cluny Hill outside Findhorn, Scotland. Following Eileen Caddy's guidance, Peter Caddy's intuition, and Dorothy's spiritual interpretations the community operated for nine years. In her meditation in 1972 Eileen was told that she should stop giving guidance and that members would learn to become attuned to God's will themselves. In 1974, 150 members joined the community, and this doubled by 1978. Back in 1973 one and a half acres adjoining the trailer park where the Caddys lived was given to the community. The house was remodeled with a library, offices, meeting rooms, and a small sanctuary. In 1975 the community bought the run-down Cluny Hill Hotel for £60,000 to establish its security. On six acres the vast building was renamed Cluny Hill College and established as an educational center. The original trailer park property was acquired, as was a mansion known as Drumduan House. In 1980 a Garden School was started and attracted considerable interest. Findhorn members are expected to work thirty-three hours a week and to give two to three hours to departmental "attunement" each week and take part in kitchen cleaning, guest tours, and Sunday cooking. Slightly more than half of the foundation's net income comes from its educational programs, 10 percent from donations and members' fees; the rest comes from business operations, for example, trailer park, publications, and shop. During 1983 total income was over £1 million, and at the beginning of 1984 Findhorn had 167 members. Today Findhorn Foundation is a large part of six properties including Cluny College, the former hotel, and the caravan park. Each year 10,000 day visitors appear, and 4,000 people take part in residential programs of one week to six months.

See Also Caddy, Eileen and Peter

Sources:

Caddy, Eileen. 1978. *Foundations of Findhorn*. Forres, Scotland: Findhorn Foundation.
Findhorn Community. 1975. *The Findhorn Garden*. New York: Harper and Row.
Inglis, Mary. 1996. "Findhorn Foundation: Nature Spirits and New Age Business." In Bill Metcalf, ed., *Shared Visions, Shared Lives. Communal Living around the Globe*, Chapter 11. Forres, Scotland: Findhorn Press.
Maclean, Dorothy. 1990. *To Hear the Angels Sing*. Lindisfarne: Lindisfarne Press.
Popenoe, Cris, and Oliver Popenoe. 1984. *Seeds of Tomorrow*. San Francisco: Harper and Row.
Riddle, Carol. 1990. *The Findhorn Community: Creating a Human Dignity for the 21st Century*. Forres, Scotland: Findhorn Press.

Sheer, Arlene. 1984. "Findhorn, Scotland: The People Who Talk to Plants." In Ruby Rohrlich and Elaine Hoffman Baruch, eds., *Women in Search of Utopia: Mavericks and Myth Makers*, pp. 146–156. New York: Schocken Books.

Walker, Alex, ed. 1994. *The Kingdom Within; A Guide to the Spiritual Work of the Findhorn Community*. Forres, Scotland: Findhorn Foundation.

FINN VILLAGE. Finn Village was established at Mullumbimby in Brunswick Valley, northern New South Wales, Australia. It was built originally as a banana farming settlement in 1922. Failure of the banana crops ended the settlement, and other groups occupied the village. In 1972 Colin and Nancy Scattergood (fl. 1940–1976) arrived at Finn Village, and soon they were followed by others in search of an alternative lifestyle. The Scattergoods bought 160 hectares (400 acres) and leased it to people who they thought were interested in the alternative style of life that they themselves were seeking. The members of Finn Village lived separately rather than communally, but they formed a cooperative and committed themselves to mutual help. This they believed to be central to their style of living. By the end of the 1970s the community had begun to fade, members drifted away and took up different occupations, and Finn Village failed to attract new members.

Source:

Cock, Peter. 1979. *Alternative Australia: Communities of the Future?*, Chapter 3. Melbourne: Quartet Books.

FINNEY, CHARLES G. Charles G. Finney (1792–1875) was associated with the establishment of Oberlin College and its local community. He was raised in New York, studied law, and after a deep religious conversion turned to theology and in 1824 became a Presbyterian minister. After conducting amazing revivals in the eastern and middle states of the United States, he settled in New York City in 1832. In 1837 he aligned himself with Oberlin College and drew away from the Presbyterian community. He was the pastor of Oberlin's First Congregational Church (1835–1872) and was president of Oberlin College (1851–1866). He fought popularization of cheap amusements and railed against any gratifications and indulgences that might stand in the way of a revival of asceticism and churchgoing, for example, pleasures of tobacco, coffee, and tea. For this he was known as a New School Calvinist, an advocate of the Oberlin Theology, and often came under attack because of his belief in perfectionism. He published his lectures for Christians and edited the *Oberlin Quarterly Review*.

See Also Oberlin community

Sources:

Dupuis, Richard A. G., and Gaarth M. Rosell, eds. 1987. *The Memoirs of Charles G. Finney; The Complete Restored Text*. Annotated, critical ed. Grand Rapids, Mich.: Zondervan.

Hardman, Keith J. 1990. *Charles Grandison Finney, 1792–1875*. Durham, England: Evangelical Press.

Johnson, Allen, and Dumas Malone, eds. 1930. *Dictionary of American Biography*. Vol.
    3. New York: Charles Scribner's Sons.

FISHER, JAMES COWLEY MORGAN. James Cowley Morgan Fisher (1832–
1913) was born in Bristol, son of a magistrate, and at age fourteen ran away to
sea. In 1852 he went to the Goldfields of Ballarat, Australia, and later settled
in Nunawading outside Melbourne in Victoria. He married and had two sons.
After his first wife died, he remarried and had four more sons and four daughters. By 1863 he was leader in a Swedenborgian New Church of the First Born
and preached about a great spiritual influence coming to the Christian Israelites.
He practiced faith healing and exorcism among hundreds of followers. He was
known as the Nunawading Messiah and is said to have practiced polygamy. He
was scandalized in Melbourne for fraud and misrepresentation; nevertheless, he
could still hold positions on the boards of respectable local authorities. By 1900
his followers were drifting to the Western Australian goldfields, where they
selected over 20,000 acres. In 1904 Fisher arrived, built a church, and preached
regularly to his followers at New Jerusalem. The settlement had gained local
government support (1906). He married again in 1910. His settlement was seen
as a communal venture of Christianized Jews, a helpful brotherhood that adopted
the best features of communism. Following a serious head injury he became
demented and soon died. New Jerusalem blended into the local community after
Fisher's death.
    See Also New Jerusalem

Source:

Pike, Douglas, et al., eds. 1966–1990. *Australian Dictionary of Biography*. 12 vols., vol.
    4: 172. Carlton, Victoria: University of Melbourne Press.

FOLLETT, MARY PARKER. Mary Parker Follett (1868–1933) was born in
Quincy, Massachusetts, and educated at Thayer Academy and Radcliffe College
(1898). She attended Newnham College, Cambridge (1890–1891). Her first publication was a pamphlet, *The Speaker of the House of Representatives*, originally
an address given at Oxford. In Boston she began her public work at the Roxbury
Debating Club (1900) and helped get legislation passed for extended after-hours
use of the Boston public schools. This change became one foundation for a
widespread adult education movement. She established herself as political scientist and supporter of vocational guidance and became a close associate of
Lord Haldane (1856–1928), the English statesman and philosopher. Her aim
was for a better-ordered society in which individuals could live a full and sat-
isfying life, and she contributed to social experiments to find the most appropriate way to achieve this goal. Her main work was *The New State* (1918),
which guided the Peckham experiment in England. Also she published *Creative
Experience* (1924), her best-known work. It centered on teaching individuals to
appreciate and understand the views of others according to the principle of

"psychological interpenetration." From 1924 to 1933 she lived in England and studied industrial conditions by meeting often with industrialists and business-men. In 1926 and in 1928 she spoke at the Rowntree Lecture Conferences in Oxford and at the National Institute of Industrial Psychology, London. Although she was never in business herself, her *Creative Experience* showed she had a sound psychological understanding of the foundations of business administra-tion. She saw the League of Nations as a great opportunity to develop interna-tional relations on the basis of her fundamental management principle of "coordination" as the foundation of a well-organized human society. In England her final contribution to the subject of organization and management was a set of lectures in early 1933 for the Department of Business Administration at the London School of Economics. She died in Boston on her return to the United States that year.

See Also Peckham experiment; Rowntree, Benjamin Seebohm

Sources:

Graham, Pauline, ed. 1994. *Follett, Mary Parker: Prophet of Management—a Celebra-tion of Writings from the 1920s.* Boston: Harvard Business School Press.

Metcalf, Henry C., and L. Urwick. 1941. *Dynamic Administration: The Collective Papers of Mary Parker Follett.* London: Pitman.

Starr, Harris E., ed. 1944. *Dictionary of American Biography.* Supplement 1. New York: Charles Scribner's Sons.

FÖRSTER, BERNHARD. Bernhard Förster (c. 1844–1889) was the child of a Protestant pastor who died when Bernhard was young. The lad lived with his mother in Naumberg, became a schoolteacher, and moved on the fringes of Richard Wagner's (1818–1883) circle. In the Franco-Prussian War (1870–1871) he was awarded the Iron Cross and returned from military action to teach in Berlin. In 1876, after the Bayreuth Festival, Bernhard and his mother visited Elisabeth Nietzsche (1846–1935), enthused about the work of her brother, Fried-rich Nietzsche (1844–1900), especially its relevance to anti-Semitism and the needed purification and regeneration of the German culture. Förster founded the German People's Party of Anti-Semitism and attracted 6,000 to its first meeting (1881). He petitioned Otto Bismarck (1815–1898) to ban Jewish immigration to Germany and suspend all Jewish business activities on the assumption that they would destroy the nation. Förster was forced to resign from teaching. Im-mediately, he became a utopian activist and sought to purify humankind by supporting the emigration of Germans to colonize South America. He thought German colonies would check the expansion of the British empire, avoid the pernicious influence of Jews, and help Germany escape economic depression. With support from German bankers and industrialists he chose Paraguay for the first stage of creating a New Germany. Before he left, it was clear that Elisabeth Nietzsche had fallen in love with him and his ideas. He sailed in 1883, they wrote while he was at work in Paraguay, and he decided they should marry when he returned. They did and together produced his book *German Coloni-sation in the Upper La Plata District with Particular Reference to Paraguay: The Results of Detailed Practical Experience, Work and Travel 1883–1885*. In February 1886, with their Aryan pioneers, the couple set sail for New Germany in Paraguay. On a land grant fifty-five miles south of Conception they established themselves comfortably. However, the venture endured many hardships, and its economy failed. Many residents deserted the colony. Bernhard became ill, quit the colony, and suicided in 1889. Two years later his widow sold her interest in the venture.

See Also New Germany; Nietzsche, Theresa Elisabeth Alexandra

Source:

Macintyre, Ben. 1992. *Forgotten Fatherland: The Search for Elisabeth Nietzsche*. London: Macmillan.

FOUNTAIN GROVE. Fountain Grove was founded in 1876 by Thomas Lake Harris (1823–1906) two miles north of Santa Rosa, Sonoma County, California. Harris was a religious mystic and poet who had formed the Brotherhood of the New Life in the late 1850s, which melded ecclesiastical revolt, social reform, Christianity, spiritualism, and Swedenborgianism. Harris claimed he was chosen to announce the Second Coming of Christ. The community was on 700 acres bought by Harris, and later it increased by another 1,000 acres. It began as a dairy farm, but after five years it had taken to wine making on a large scale, for mystical reasons. Harris and a few of his closest followers lived in a large mansion. Other buildings housed about thirty people. Harris' comfortable lifestyle was supported by the wealth of some of his followers. Among them were Laurence Oliphant (1829–1888) and his mother, Lady Oliphant. Many members gave up their property and assets upon entering the colony. Community members would eat together and often dance and sing. Many controversial features of the colony were evident. The communal aspect of the group in not clear, because Harris owned all the property. In response he said the community was theosocialistic rather than communist. Harris interfered with family life, separating parents from their children or husbands from their wives if he felt that the relationships interfered with the harmony of the community. He believed that God was both male and female, because men and women were created in God's image. In 1891 scandals led to the community's being disbanded. The most important involved Alzine A. Chevaillier, a professional agitator who stridently accused Harris of making improper advances to her. The other scandal involved the publication of Margaret O. W. Oliphant's biography about her cousin Laurence, *Memoir of the Life of Laurence Oliphant* (1891), which suggests Harris was an immoral fake. The press and the local community seized on the scandals to name Harris a hypocrite and a fraudulent preacher of celibacy. In 1892 he married for the third time. His wife was Jane Lee Waring, who had been his secretary for thirty years. They left the colony for New York. Afterward

Fountain Grove became less a community and more a business and was dissolved in 1896. The winery continued for some time afterward.

See Also Brotherhood of the New Life; Harris, Thomas Lake

Sources:

Fogarty, Robert S. 1980. *Dictionary of American Communal History*. Westport, Conn.: Greenwood Press.

————. 1990. *All Things New: American Communes and Utopian Movements 1860–1914*. Chicago: University of Chicago Press.

Hine, Robert V. 1953. *California's Utopian Colonies*. 1983 ed. Berkeley: University of California Press.

FOURIER, CHARLES. François Marie Charles Fourier (1772–1837) was born into a family of French merchants of Besançon. The family forced him into commerce, and he went to Lyon to study banking (1789). He pursued commerce throughout Europe; he also found he was inventive and devised a musical notation and a railway with passenger carriages. While serving in the military (1794–1796), he planned a reform of adminstration that met with approval; later, he researched urban architecture to find reliable building improvements. In 1798 information about overpriced fruit led him to suspect a basic disorder lay in industrial organization, and he turned to the study of society to find it. When working as a clerk, he published his *The Theory of Four Movements* (1808), which stated that parallel to the natural order in the universe was a social order among humankind and that human identity developed through eight stages. At the highest stage humankind lived in harmony and expressed emotions freely. In 1812 he received an annuity from his mother's estate and thereafter had sufficient leisure to study and write. He published *A Treatise on Domestic Agricultural Association* (1822) and *The New Industrial and Social World* (1830). In condemning society for its competitiveness and waste, the work advocated utopian socialist communities. The basic unit of the utopian community was the phalanx, and in a nation many phalanxes would federate into a socialist nation. He advocated a world language and government. His converts appeared in France and the United States, where the noted examples were Brook Farm in Massachusetts (1841–1846) and the North American Phalanx, Red Bank, New Jersey. Forty such communities were established, but few lasted.

See Also Brook Farm Colony; Fourierist communities or phalanxes; North American Phalanx

Sources:

Beecher, Jonathan. 1986. *Charles Fourier: The Visionary and His World*. Berkeley: University of California Press.

Fogarty, Robert S. 1990. *All Things New: American Communes and Utopian Movements 1860–1914*. Chicago: University of Chicago Press.

Oved, Yaacov. 1987. *Two Hundred Years of American Communes*. New Brunswick, N.J.: Transaction Books.

Prevost, M., and Roman D'amat. 1986. *Dictionnaire de biographie Francaise*. Paris: Librairie Letouzey et Anè.

Riasanovsky, Nicholas. 1969. *The Teachings of Charles Fourier*. Berkeley: University of California Press.

Spencer, Michael C. 1981. *Charles Fourier*. Boston: Twayne.

Zeldin, David. 1969. *The Educational Ideas of Charles Fourier, 1772–1837*. London: Cass.

FOURIERIST COMMUNITIES OR PHALANXES. Fourierist communities or phalanxes constitute a socialist system proposed by François Marie Charles Fourier (1772–1837) for the reorganization of society. The small, cooperative communities or phalanxes would allow development of people's talents and expression of feelings. The basic unit of the utopian community was the phalanx, a group of 1,620 people living in common buildings or phalanstery, using about 5,000 acres and dividing and allocating work according to individual abilities. Phalanxes would eventually link and form one federation. Fourier also advocated a world language and government. His converts appeared in France and the United States, where the noted examples were Brook Farm Phalanx in Massachusetts (1845–1847) and the North American Phalanx, Red Bank, New Jersey (1843–1855), Sodus Bay Phalanx, New York (1844–1845), Ohio/American Phalanx near Bellaire in Ohio (1844–1845), and the Wisconsin Phalanx (1844–1850) in Ripon, Wisconsin. One of his U.S. utopias was established by Victor Prosper Considérant (1808–1893) at Considérant in Texas (1853–1869). Many communities were established, but few lasted.

See Also Brook Farm Colony; Considérant, Victor Prosper; Fourier, Charles; North American Phalanx

Sources:

Berry, Brian J. 1992. *America's Utopian Experiments: Communal Havens from Long-Wave Crises*. Hanover, N.H.: University Press of New England.

Guarneri, Carl J. 1991. *The Utopian Alternative: Fourierism in Nineteenth-Century America*. Ithaca, N.Y.: Cornell University Press.

———. 1994. "The Americanization of Utopia: Fourierism and the Dilemma of Utopian Dissent in the United States." *Utopian Studies* 5, no. 1: 72–88.

Kesten, Seymour 1993. *Utopian Episodes: Daily Life in Experimental Colonies Dedicated to Changing the World*. Syracuse, N.Y.: Syracuse University Press.

Oved, Yaacov. 1987. *Two Hundred Years of American Communes*. New Brunswick, N.J.: Transaction Books.

Pollard, Sidney, and John Salt, eds. 1971. *Robert Owen: Prophet of the Poor*. Lewisburg, Pa.: Bucknell University Press.

FOX, GEORGE. George Fox (1624–1691) was born in Fenny Drayton, Leicestershire, raised as a Puritan, and apprenticed to a shoemaker in Nottingham. In late adolescence he rebelled against the state control of the church and the formal organization of religion generally (1643). He would attend religious meetings and interrupt with declarations about "inner light," inveigh against the formalism of religious worship, and, Bible in hand, attack social conventions. He loathed priests, lawyers, and soldiers and, formally directed by God, would refused to doff his hat to any dignitary. It was revealed to him that he must preach brotherly love and announce the formation of a Society of Truth, later to be the Society of Friends. For this he was insulted, persecuted, and often imprisoned. By 1656, a year after he and his followers had rejected the oath of abjuration, over 1,000 of his followers were imprisoned. His *Journal* (1874) is a noted publication, and he is remembered largely for turgid, incoherent, and mystical preaching and teachings. He visited Scotland and Wales, married the widow of one of his followers, and went to Barbados, Jamaica, the United States, Holland, and Germany and was accompanied by William Penn (1644–1718), the English Quaker and reformer, and Robert Barclay (1648–1690), the first Quaker to marry in Scotland.

See Also Penn, William; Quakers

Sources:

Fox, George. 1852. *Journal.* 1952 ed. Cambridge: Cambridge University Press.

Gwyn, Douglas. 1986. *Apocalypse of the World: The Life and Message of George Fox, (1624–1691).* Richmond, Ind.: Friends United Press.

Ingle, Homer Larry. 1994. *First among Friends: George Fox and the Creation of Quakerism.* New York: Oxford University Press.

Pickvance, Joseph. 1989. *A Reader's Companion to George Fox's Journal.* London: Quaker House.

Ross, Hugh McG., ed. 1991. *George Fox Speaks for Himself: Texts That Reveal His Personality Hitherto Unpublished.* York: Sessions.

Wildes, Harry Emerson. 1965. *The Voice of the Lord: A Biography of George Fox.* Philadelphia: University of Pennsylvania Press.

Yolen, Jane H. 1972. *Friend: The Story of George Fox and the Quakers.* New York: Seabury Press.

FRANCIS OF ASSISI, SAINT. Saint Francis of Assisi (c. 1181–1226), the "Seraphic" Saint, was born in Umbria, Italy, the son of a cloth merchant of Assisi. His father hoped that Francis would follow him into the business, but Francis chose the military. In 1202 he fought in a war against Perugia, was imprisoned, fell ill on his escape, recovered, and went to serve papal forces under Count Gentile (1205). A series of visions and revelations formed his religious conversion. He returned to Assisi and was drawn to poverty, solitary prayer, and helping lepers. He renounced his father and material interests, broke with the family, worked to restore several chapels, and traveled and preached simple rules for living. In 1209 twelve mendicant friars sought approval of the Franciscan rules from Pope Innocent III (1160–1216). Tradition tells it was given, 16 April, the foundation day of the Franciscan Order. The basic rule was to follow Christ's beliefs and do as he had done; nevertheless, a view developed that Francis was one who primarily loved nature and poverty and practiced social work while he wandered and preached. In 1212 he began a second order, for women, the Poor Clares, named after Saint Clare (Clara) of Assisi, and later a third, the Order of Brothers and Sisters of Penance, which brought Franciscan ideas to the world generally. Shipwreck prevented his going to the Holy Land in 1212, and illness stopped him from visiting Spain. He visited Egypt (1219), impressed the sultan, and was allowed to visit holy places in Palestine. His order grew so rapidly in Italy that many disturbances relating to it required his attention and its reorganization. By 1224 he had withdrawn from external matters of the order to La Verna, where he is said to have had a vison of a seraph with six wings and endured the stigmata of crucifixion on his hands, feet, and side. For two years he lived in pain, blinded from an eye disease that he had contracted in the East. He died in Assisi and was canonized 16 July 1228. Francis' love of nature was later regarded as his major characteristic, and many artists painted him preaching in a utopian world to birds and small animals.

See Also Franciscans

Sources:

Bedoyere, Michael de la. 1962. *Francis: A Biography of the Saint of Assisi*. London: Collins.

Cunningham, Lawrence S. 1926. *Saint Francis of Assisi*. Boston: Twayne.

McCord, William. 1989. *Voyages to Utopia: From Monastery to Commune, the Search for the Perfect Society in Modern Times*. New York: W. W. Norton.

Sorrell, Roger D. 1988. *St. Francis of Assisi and Nature: Tradition and Innovation in Western Christian Attitudes towards the Environment*. New York: Oxford University Press.

FRANCISCANS. Franciscans constitute a practical, everyday, utopian community of lay brothers, friars, or novices of the mendicant order of the Roman Catholic Church (1209). They are bound to poverty, may carry no money with them, and are known as Minors or Minorites by virtue of their humility and Greyfriars from the original color of their habit. The "Conventual Franciscans," a branch of the order (1230), wear black and are permitted to have some income. Franciscans believe in the absolute primacy of Christ, so they imitate Jesus' deeds and teachings; they are ecclesiastical and emphasize a social mission and offer a personal example to others more than private contemplation. They uphold mysticism and suggest that God is present in all creatures and that humankind's destiny is in the hands of God. This has the effect of leading Franciscans to a state of joy, peace, and optimism. They are ascetic and assert that humankind must realize its state as creatures and imitate Christ, who became a member of humankind. Finally, they uphold reincarnationism and assert that it is not necessary to await the end of time for God's Coming. He is already here, present in all living things. This places great value on nature. From these principles flow the utopian aspects of life that emphasize simplicity, poverty, and the unrelenting desire to do good by consciously imitating Christ. They are unutopian in that they do not need to hope for a better world, because the world today enjoys the presence of God in all things. All people can be united with God simply by being absorbed by God's love, a state that can be achieved through revering nature.

See Also Francis of Assisi, Saint

Sources:

Editorial Staff, Catholic University of America, eds. 1967. *New Catholic Encyclopedia*, vol. 6. Washington, D.C.: Catholic University of America Press.

McCord, William. 1989. *Voyages to Utopia: From Monastery to Commune, the Search for the Perfect Society in Modern Times*. New York: W. W. Norton.

FREY, WILLIAM. William Frey, originally Vladimir Konstantinovich Geins (1839–1888), son of a soldier, was born at Odessa in Russia. William attended Military College but after receiving a commission, rejected an army career, rebelled against his authoritarian upbringing, and chose to be a scientist. Later, he was drawn to the ideas of Étienne Cabet (1788–1856), Robert Owen (1771–1858), Saint-Simon (1760–1825), and Charles Fourier (1772–1837), and is rumored to have been a member of the Land and Liberty Organization that planned to overthrow the government. At age twenty-seven he endured a severe mental crisis, probably because the revolution he supported had failed. He decided to emigrate. He was interested in the United States after reading about the Oneida Community. Before sailing he married (1868) and left Russia for Germany, intending to go to the United States. On landing in the United States, he took the name William Frey and wrote to Alcander Longley (1832–1918) and applied to be a member of the Icarian community of Reunion Colony. He arrived at the colony just as it was breaking up. After several attempts at community life, Frey was asked to lead a group of Jews in New Odessa (1882). Members of the organization did not accept Frey's leadership style (1884), and two years later he returned to Russia. By 1887 New Odessa had failed.

See Also Am Olam; Cedar Vale or Progressive Community; Longley, Alcander; New Odessa Community; Oneida Community; Reunion Colony

Sources:

Fogarty, Robert S. 1980. *Dictionary of American Communal History*. Westport, Conn.: Greenwood Press.

———. 1990. *All Things New: American Communes and Utopian Movements 1860–1914*. Chicago: University of Chicago Press.

Oved, Yaacov. 1987. *Two Hundred Years of American Communes*. New Brunswick, N.J.: Transaction Books.

Yarmolinsky, Avrahm. 1965. *A Russian's American Dream: A Memoir on William Frey*. Lawrence: University of Kansas Press.

FRIEND, DONALD. Donald Stuart Leslie Friend (1915–1989) was born and educated in Sydney, Australia, and studied art at the Royal Art Society of New South Wales (1933–1934), the Westminster Art School in London (1935–1936)

and Colarossi's in Paris. He joined the Australian Infantry Forces when he returned to Australia and served as a gunner in World War II. In 1945 he was official war artist. In 1955 he won the Blake Prize and lived in Sri Lanka (1957–1962) and on Bali (1966–1984). His work was satirical, often homoerotic, and based largely on the human figure. His illustrated diaries (1929–1932; 1942–1989) are in the National Library of Australia, Canberra. He helped found Hill End, an artist's colony in Australia that was based on a community that believed life and art coexist. It was established when Russell Drysdale and Friend stopped in 1947 at an old gold-mining town forty-five miles north of Bathurst, New South Wales.

See Also Drysdale, George Russell; Hill End

Sources:

McCulloch, Alan, and Susan McCulloch. 1994. *The Encyclopedia of Australian Art.* Sydney: Allen and Unwin.

Robb, Gwenda, and Elaine Smith. 1993. *Concise Dictionary of Australian Artists.* Edited by Robert Smith. Melbourne: Melbourne University Press.

Van Nunen, Linda. 1995. "Golden Summers: In a Harsh Environment, the Artists of Hill End Forged a New Vision of the Australian Landscape." *Time (Australia)* (2 August): 71–72.

FROEBEL, FRIEDRICH. Friedrich Froebel (1782–1852) was born at Oberweissbach, a village in the Thuringian forest, Germany. He was apprenticed to a forester and became a student of architecture before he went to Burgdorf, Switzerland, to study education with Johann Heinrich Pestalozzi (1742–1827). He studied at the universities of Jena, Göttingen, and Berlin. In 1813–1814 he served in campaigns against the French; afterward he established what he called the "Universal German Educational Institution" at Griesham, a Thuringian village (1816). In 1837 he founded the first kindergarten in Blankenburg in Thuringia. His system advocates the encouragement of learning rather than firm instruction, but his ideas and work met with much resistance at the time and were even forbidden by state law in Prussia. His theory and practice of education for preschool appeared in his *Die Menschenerziehung* (The Education of Man) in 1826. Because his work seemed unsystematic, dialectical, and contradictory, and his followers have interlarded some of his ideas with their own, his writings were not collected comprehensively, and his influence, though recognized, is not securely known.

See Also Froebelian kindergartens; Pestalozzi, Johann Heinrich

Sources:

Husen, Torsten, and T. Neville Postlethwaite. 1985. *The International Encyclopedia of Education Research and Studies.* Oxford: Pergamon.

Lilley, Irene, ed. 1967. *Friedrich Froebel: A Selection from His Writings.* Cambridge: Cambridge University Press.

McHenry, Robert, ed. 1992. *The New Encyclopedia Britannica*. Chicago: Encyclopedia Britannica.

Zusne, Leonard. 1984. *Biographical Dictionary of Psychology*. Westport, Conn.: Greenwood Press.

FROEBELIAN KINDERGARTENS. In Europe after 1850 kindergarten schools were established using free play, group work, singing, nature study, and outdoor activity. The themes are attributed to Friedrich Froebel (1782–1852). Such kindergartens assumed learning was to be enjoyed, not inculcated through dour, firm instruction; and because play is children's main activity, they learn best through games, some instruction in skills, family values, and nature study. However, those who carried forward Froebel's ideas replaced his principles with unbending rules of play, and strict discipline and also taught domestic work. These deviations probably occurred because, originally, the child's mother was present at the kindergarten. Consequently, toward the end of the nineteenth century American and British educators criticized the Froebelian approach for being too authoritarian (1898). In the twentieth century his original ideas were reintroduced and attached to art education and spiritual development in education. Froebel's ideas were romantic, related to a utopian world with God at its center, and emphasized individual development as a natural process. Children's education should be allowed to grow rather than be activated by prescriptions. Froebel advocated a law of education based on the power of nature and the authority of God. Through play children get to know the natural world. With such items as lines, points, cubes, cylinders, squares, splints, metal rings, peas, and straws, a child learns to grasp the objective features of the natural world. The structure of that world becomes internalized as the child perforates paper and folds it, weaves, draws, models clay, and pursues common playful activities in kindergarten. At the center of this internalization was the cube. The cube was Froebel's key to structuring the world. It provided diversity, unity, structure, identity, and insight. Also interaction between child and adult—rather than autocratic or progressive education principles administered in class—was the way to help children begin their education. Finally, he assumed children were innately good, and their development of a self through education was made secure by accepting God's authority.

See Also Froebel, Friedrich

Source:

Husén, Torsten, and T. Neville Postlethwaite. 1985. *The International Encyclopedia of Education Research and Studies*. Oxford: Pergamon.

FROGS' HOLLOW/MANDUKA. Frogs' Hollow/Manduka is an alternative community established in Queensland in 1978. It remains today as Manduka Community Settlement Cooperative Society Ltd. and has a dozen members. It is called "Frogs' Hollow" after the small settlement where the commune was first established. It is a land settlement cooperative with separate housing and joint land management; the community comprises nine adults aged from thirty-five to seventy-four, two children, and several tenants. The community was established by Jan Tilden and Jill Jordan with two women friends.

See Also Tilden, Jan

Source:

Tilden, Jan. 1995. "From Academic Exercises to Jumping Spiders." In Bill Metcalf, ed., *From Utopian Dreaming to Communal Reality: Cooperative Life Styles in Australia*, pp. 57–73. Sydney: University of New South Wales Press.

FRUITLANDS COLONY. Fruitlands was a short-lived colony of New England transcendentalists, among whom were Amos Bronson Alcott (1799–1888) and Charles Lane (1800–1870). When Alcott met Lane at Alcott House in Surrey, England, the two began plans for a similar colony in the United States where individuals could develop their higher spiritual nature. It was modeled on an earlier settlement, Wilkfarm. Lane supplied the capital to buy the land at Harvard, Massachusetts, and Fruitlands Colony began in June 1843. It lasted until the end of the year. The primary reason for its failure was financial. Fruitlands was put up for sale in 1844 but was sold two years later under mortgage for $1,700. Charles Lane was jailed for not paying taxes. When Fruitlands collapsed, he returned to England and married an erstwhile member of Robert Owen's Harmony Hall Colony.

See Also Alcott, Amos Bronson; Lane, Charles

Sources:

Armytage, Walter H. Green. 1961. *Heavens Below: Utopian Experiments in England 1560–1950*. London: Routledge and Kegan Paul.

Best, Arthur Eugene. 1970. *Backwoods Utopias: The Sectarian Origins and the Owenite Phase of Communitarian Socialism in America. 1663–1829*. 2d ed. Philadelphia: University of Pennsylvania Press.

Fogarty, Robert S. 1980. *Dictionary of American Communal History*. Westport, Conn.: Greenwood Press.

———. 1990. *All Things New: American Communes and Utopian Movements 1860–1914*. Chicago: University of Chicago Press.

Francis, Richard. 1997. *Transcendental Utopias: Individual and Community at Brook Farm, Fruitlands and Walden*. Ithaca, N.Y.: Cornell University Press.

Kesten, Seymour. 1993. *Utopian Episodes: Daily Life in Experimental Colonies Dedicated to Changing the World*. Syracuse, N.Y.: Syracuse University Press.

Kunitz, Stanley J., and Howard Haycraft, eds. 1938. *American Authors 1600–1900*. New York: Wilson.

Oved, Yaacov. 1987. *Two Hundred Years of American Communes*. New Brunswick, N.J.: Transaction Books.

Sears, Clara Endicott, comp. 1915. *Bronson Alcott's Fruitlands*. Boston: Houghton Mifflin. 2d ed., 1975, Philadelphia: Porcupine Press.

Who Was Who in America. Historical Volume 1607–1896. 1943. Chicago: Marquis.

G

GALLATIN, E. L. E. L. Gallatin (fl. 1828–1900) was born in St. Louis and became an apprentice saddler in Illinois. He set out for California in 1860 to find gold. Instead, he stopped in Colorado, became a saddler, and later worked in Montana (1864) and Wyoming (1881). The communal work schemes of the Colorado Cooperative Company, founded in 1894, attracted his attention, so he joined it (1895). Land was not owned communally, but work on the company's massive irrigation of desert acreage was planned as a community activity. In 1894 members for the scheme had been sought, news of the venture published in *The Altrurian*, and clubs established in Denver and elsewhere to attract people to the irrigation project. Internal disputes held up the work (1896–1897). Experiences in Topolobampo had taught one community member that common land-ownership would fail the people. Gallatin could see the value to the community of the irrigation scheme, so he advocated a cooperative work policy in the community rather than encouraging landholders to compete. Members also conflicted over their voting rights in the project. Members in the town were dissatisfied with the voting rights of those outside the town, especially residents of Denver. Gallatin argued that the project as a whole would fail if selfish individualism were allowed to undermine the working harmony in the community. A legal conflict arose in 1899, and in the next year Gallatin quit the colony. Notwithstanding, by 1910 the project had finished successfully and became a town company rather than a cooperative.

See Also Colorado Cooperative Company; Topolobampo Colony

Sources:

Fogarty, Robert S. 1980. *Dictionary of American Communal History*. Westport, Conn.: Greenwood Press.
Gallatin, E. L. 1900. *What Life Has Taught Me*. Denver: J. Frederic.

GANDHI, MOHANDAS K. Mohandas Karamchand Gandhi (1869–1948) was an Indian leader, born and raised in Porbandar, Kathiawar, where his father was dewan (prime minister). At age nineteen he studied law at University College London, was admitted to the bar (1889), and later established a legal practice in Bombay. Early, he was influenced by the Hindu sect Vaishnava and its special worship of its syncretic deity and by Jainism, a religion close to Buddhism, which aims to deliver one's spirit from the restrictions of the flesh by following knowledge, faith, and nonviolence. He left the practice to live on one pound a week in South Africa. In South Africa he spent twenty-one years opposing discriminatory legislation against Indians. He returned to India (1914), and while giving support to the British in World War I his interest grew in the Home Rule movement and independence from Britain. From 1922 to 1924 he was in jail for conspiracy, and in 1930 he led a 200-mile march to the sea to collect salt in defiance of the government monopoly. He was rearrested and, when released in 1931, attended the London Round Table Conferences on Indian constitutional reform. On his return to India he became known for his fasting as part of a nonviolent political campaign. He was jailed in 1942–1944, but in 1946 he negotiated with the British Cabinet Mission, which recommended the new constitutional structure and independence for India (1947). In Delhi Gandhi was assassinated by a Hindu fanatic. His beliefs melded Western ideas from Leo Tolstoy (1828–1910), John Ruskin (1819–1900), and Henry David Thoreau (1817–1862) with Jainism and Vaishnavism from India. These influences provided the elements of his religious and political utopianism. In Gandhi's utopia individuals would have overcome their delusions and desire for material possessions, be without pride, deceit, anger, and uncontrolled passion, hold women in deep respect, revere God, and regard the human body as sacred. People would honor one another, serve their fellows willingly, understand the depth of their misery, and think before speaking their mind. The goals of Gandhi's utopia were the pursuit of truth, equal rights, ready access to justice, and adequate food for all. This society could be achieved through nonviolent revolution. The proper way was to educate India's young in work-study camps that taught agricultural and craft skills for survival and a knowledge of the nation's cultural heritage. In India this utopia attracted many citizens, and they tried to bring it about in different ways. After he died, many followers formed a utopian movement of ''Gandhi's children.''

See Also ''Gandhi's children''

Sources:

Brown, Judith M. 1989. *Gandhi: Prisoner of Hope*. New Haven, Conn. Yale University Press.

Erickson, Erik H. 1970. *Gandhi's Truth*. London: Faber and Faber.

Fox, Richard G. 1989. *Gandhian Utopia: Experiment with Culture*. Boston: Beacon Press.

Kripalani, Krishna. 1968. *Gandhi: A Life*. New Delhi: Orient Longmans.

Ramashray, Roy. 1984. *Gandhi: Soundings in Political Philosophy*. Delhi: Chanakya.

Shirer, William L. 1979. *Gandhi: Memoir*. New York: Simon and Schuster.
Woodcock, George. 1972. *Gandhi*. London: Fontana Collins.

"GANDHI'S CHILDREN." "Gandhi's children" constituted a social movement for great change in Indian society, and among them were followers of Gandhi like Vinoba Bhave (1895–1982) and Jayaprakash Narayan (1902–1979), who, respectively, headed a nonviolent movement to have those with land pass their property over to those without and, contending for power with Indira Gandhi, led a social movement to improve Indian government and institute village democracy in special settlements. These utopian settlements and their followers were visited by McCord (1989), who found that Vinoba Bhave was thought to be a saint by millions of followers. On visiting one of Gandhi's original settlements where orthodox followers of his doctrines maintained their own community, he noted that automobiles were revered, while millions of Indians starved. In the Ashram he saw hundreds of adults concentrate attention on Gandhi's model of a community, devote themselves to nonviolence, vegetarianism, and meditation, sell small spinning wheels—Gandhi's symbol of self-sufficiency—to tourists, and spin and weave textiles. Those who opposed Gandhi's principles argued that modern technology could achieve their product in a fraction of the time. Gandhi argued that his principles and activities upheld local economic welfare and political democracy and that efficiency was of minor concern. These devoted followers of Gandhi's utopianism oppose mainstream India and its technology, warmongering, warfare, and industrialization of work and live modestly in their quest for a kingdom of heaven. Vinoba Bhave believed the nonviolent revolution should be motivated by a happy, positive, and extremely gentle search for the truth. He hoped the search would gradually create a new nation of self-sufficient village republics, free of government power. The best way was through the ballot box. Eventually, the state government would wither and go. Jayaprakash Narayan shared this view on village society and, after quitting party politics, in 1957 advocated a partyless democracy. Nevertheless, class distinctions and the caste system frustrated their policies, and education was not available to advance partyless democracy. So he organized a party to oppose Mrs. Gandhi. He advocated dismissing the legislature and police and substituting for them a people's assembly. Having tried communism and pursued socialist principles, he next turned to God and the power of love. Many reasons for the failure of Ghandi's children to effect a mental and social revolution have emerged in India, apart from the caste system and class differences. The goals set by Gandhi are not realistic; destructive nationalist policies are too strong; his followers are obsessed with their ideologies and have established political personalities to further them; villages, ashrams, and work camps are too poorly administered; interest in grassroots democracy fluctuates; revolutionary zeal is waning; protest methods to combat multinational firms are too vigorous; Gandhi's children do not appeal to the young; the land Vinoba Bhave gained for the peasants is too poor and small.

Sources:

Kalindi. 1994. *Moved by Love: The Memoirs of Vinoba Bhave*. Translated by Margery Sykes. Foxhole, Dartington, Totnes, and Devon: Green Books.

McCord, William. 1989. *Voyages to Utopia: From Monastery to Commune, the Search for the Perfect Society in Modern Times*. New York: W. W. Norton.

Ostergaard, Geoffrey. 1985. *Non-Violent Revolution in India*. New Delhi: Gandhi Peace Foundation.

Scarfe, A., and W. Scarfe. 1975. *J. P.: His Biography*. New Delhi: Orient Longman.

Shephard, Mark. 1987. *Gandhi Today: A Report on Mahatma Gandhi's Successors*. Arcata, Calif.: Simple Productions.

Weber, Thomas. 1996a. "Gandhi Is Dead: Long Live Gandhi: The Post-Gandhi Gandhian Movement in India." *Gandhi Marg* 18: 160–192.

———. 1996b. *Gandhi's Peace Army: The Shanti Sena and Unarmed Peacekeeping*. Syracuse, N.Y.: Syracuse University Press.

GARDEN CITY. The Garden City aimed to advance pleasure, function, and good health in urban life. It sprang from utopian motives underlying Robert Owen's (1771–1858) industrial villages, Edward Bellamy (1850–1898) and William Morris (1834–1896), Ebenezer Howard (1850–1928) and Raymond Unwin (1863–1940), and Patrick Geddes (1854–1932). The Garden City centered on issues of self-sufficiency, physical isolation, human regimentation, and population distribution. Robert Owen's industrial villages concept led to a scheme for Hygeia, city of health, outlined by Dr. Benjamin Ward Richardson (1828–1896), sanitary reformer (1875). Hygeia was to be built on a grid pattern of streets, washed daily, with no pubs or tobacconists. The idea was taken up and extended by Howard and published in his *Tomorrow; A Peaceful Path to Real Reform* (1898), later as *Garden Cities of Tomorrow*. Howard was influenced also by the model city of James Silk Buckingham (1786–1855). In Howard's plan 30,000 people were to live in a city on 6,000 acres divided into six wards, each enjoying town and country living. Cities were to be separated by 3,000-yard strips of open land. The plans for such cities in England were intended to reduce established towns to about 60,000 inhabitants each. The advantages were joy and freedom for the inhabitants, a just system of land tenure, promotion of brotherly goodwill, limited intrusion by government into private life, and the promotion of good relations between humankind and God. The planned Garden City originated also from early model villages like Copely (1853) and Saltaire (1863). Industrialists supported Garden Cities for different motives; some thought they would reduce industrial discontent, while others had a sincere interest in providing a better life for employees. Also the Garden City itself benefited the industrialists; wider streets not only brought more sunlight but also made police work easier; parks not only relieved the monotony of unending brick walls but also stimulated slothful employees; schools not only sharpened children's intellect but also taught voluntary obedience to directives from those in authority. Notable Garden Cities were Bedford Park (1880) with its tree-lined streets; Port

Sunlight (1888) and Bournville (1897) with their allotment gardens; New Earswick (1903) with use of the cul-de-sac; and the Hampstead Garden Suburb (1905) with delightful topography. Wythenshawe (1927–1941) was Ebenezer Howard's satellite city. In the United States the Garden City arose from pre–Great Fire Chicago and the ideas of the landscape architect who planned the layout of the Chicago World's Fair (1893), Frederick Law Olmstead (1822–1903). The Garden City movement flourished, lost a little support with the rise of the town-planning movement, and was taken up again in Britain by the Town and Country Planning Association after World War I and later spread to Australia.

See Also Bournville Experiment; Buckingham, James Silk; Buckingham's Plan for a Model Town; Hampstead Garden Suburb; Howard, Ebenezer; Letchworth; New Earswick; Port Sunlight; Saltaire

Sources:

Buder, Stanley. 1980. *Visionaries and Planners: The Garden City Movement and the Modern Community.* New York: Oxford University Press.

Creese, Walter L. 1992. *The Search for Environment: The Garden City Before and After.* Baltimore: Johns Hopkins University Press.

Freestone, Robert. 1989. *Model Communities: The Garden City Movement in Australia.* Melbourne: Nelson.

Galbraith, Margaret, and Gillian Pearson. 1982. *Elizabeth, Garden City.* Elizabeth, S. Australia: Corporation of the City of Elizabeth.

Marsh, Jan. 1982. *Back to the Land: The Pastoral Impulse in England, from 1880 to 1914.* London: Quartet.

Warburton, James W. 1983. *Payneham, Garden Village to City.* Payneham, S. Australia: Corporation of the City of Payneham.

GARNLWYD COMMUNITY. In July 1847 Garnlwyd estate near Swansea was made available for a community settlement. It was to be controlled by the Leeds Redemption Society. Initially, it would use ninety acres to support an agricultural community operating on scientific principles and, eventually, a printing industry and coal and lime mines. Plans were made to build houses and factories. The workers, known as "associates," would eat in communal dining rooms and work cooperatively to make superior shoes and garments far better than those made in a competitive market. These fine goods would be distributed and sold in Leeds. In the first year the community had fourteen members; to expand membership, in 1851 missionaries were deployed to seek new members, explaining that the community was a practical venture that could thrive like that of the sixty-year-old Shaker communities in the United States. A festival was held, a store was opened in Leeds to sell the community's produce, and membership rose. Nevertheless, by 1855 the original plan was found to be impossible, and the Leeds Redemption Society folded.

Source:

Armytage, Walter H. Green. 1961. *Heavens Below: Utopian Experiments in England 1560–1950.* London: Routledge and Kegan Paul.

GASKIN, STEPHEN. Stephen Gaskin (b. 1935), born in Denver, was educated at San Francisco State College (B.A., 1962; M.A., 1964). He was once a hard-drinking U.S. marine and used various drugs. In time he came to scorn most drugs. He was an instructor in creative writing and general semantics at San Francisco State College. He initiated a Monday night class that ran from 1967 to 1970. It was a weekly meeting of about 1,000–1,500 people who discussed politics, religion, drugs, sex, and love. A group of about 100 left San Francisco and went on a speaking tour of the United States. They settled at the Farm in Tennessee. Gaskin founded Plenty International, an overseas relief and development company. He is currently the general manager and production director of *The Birth Gazette*, a midwife quarterly.

See Also Farm Eco-Village, The

Sources:

Gaskin, Stephen. 1969. *Monday Night Class*. Summertown, Tenn.: Book.
———. 1972. *The Caravan*. New York: Random House.
———. 1974. *Hey Beatnik! This Is the Farm Book*. Summertown, Tenn.: Book.
———. 1985. *Rendered Infamous: Book of Political Reality*. Summertown, Tenn.: Book. Reprint, Westport, Conn.: Greenwood Press.
———. 1990. *Haight-Ashbury Flashbacks: Tales of the Sixties*. Berkely, Calif.: Ronin.

GAVIOTAS. Gaviotas was founded on the Colombian plains. In 1971 Paolo Lugari (b. 1944), the son of a tropical geographer, flew across the Andes behind Bogatá, over the Llanos, and noted that the savanna land made a perfect setting for a tropical civilization. He was concerned that the pressure of population would force citizens to live in poverty. A new model community was needed that used affordable modern technology to manage the problems of population growth. The model had to be suited to tropical conditions, not one drawn from the four-seasons climate of the Northern Hemisphere. Today visitors to Gaviotas notice windmills designed especially for the climate, steep roofs studded with solar panels, and buildings that are shaded with mango trees, and among them are observers studying the settlement to take home its utopian features for use in their own country. Gaviotas is a nonprofit foundation, a model of United Nations development. To support themselves the Gaviotans market their technology, not by patenting their inventions but by sharing them and producing innovative choices for sale. After studying fifty-six windmills, they chose one to suit their climate, and now it is used throughout South America. Also they use solar power widely, and a double-action pump instead of a piston pump to move water. Children's playground equipment serves as a water pump in many school yards to pump clean water to the community. In Gaviotas, schooling, housing, and health care are free; everyone can earn enough to avoid poverty, families are not too large to manage, and there is no crime. There are no police, no jails, and no theft; laws and written rules do not exist, only codes of common sense. When an individual breaks the code, he is ostracized. There is no adultery because free union of couples has replaced marriage. Gaviotas has no church, no religion, and no politicians. People respect each other's beliefs. Much farming is done hydroponically. Many people use cattle waste to produce methane for cooking, but most cook with solar power cookers. Hospitals are organized to admit the family of a patient as visitors, and while some members are with their ill relatives, others tend the medical herb garden. Also special timbers are grown to produce paint products and turpentine, and special value is given to a scheme to replace the rain forests. The Gaviotans do not claim that what they are doing is utopian: they call the place "topia," a real place, because to them "u-topia" implies the opposite. To Gaviotans God is in all natural things.

See Also Lugari, Paola

Sources:

Rosenblum, Art B. 1997. "All Things Considered (NPR): Utopia Rises out of the Colombian Plains." Transcript #1589, Segment #06. Philadelphia: Aquarian Research.

Weisman, Alan. 1997. *Gaviotas: A Village to Reinvent the World*. White River Junction, Vt.: Chelsea Green.

GEDDES, PATRICK. Patrick Geddes (1854–1932) was born at Ballater, Aberdeenshire, Scotland, and educated at Perth Academy. After working in a bank for a year, he studied under Thomas Henry Huxley (1825–1895) and later went to Paris to study zoology. He was appointed instructor at University College, London (1877–1878), and at age twenty-five went to Mexico, where suddenly he became blind. His slow recovery meant a career in biology was impossible. He compensated for this by undertaking the study of diagrammatic abstractions and an interest in self-government of university residences. After marriage he settled in Old Edinburgh and in 1892 purchased Outlook Tower for his sociological laboratory. From 1889 to 1914 he was a summer professor of biology at University College, Dundee. He also became interested in planning townships in Britain, Cyprus (1897), and India (1914–1923). He published *City Development* (1904), and his *Cities and Town Planning Exhibition* (1911) was mounted in Britain and, later, India and showed how rectilinear street design was ineffective and inefficient and ought to be replaced with street designs using gardens and sun courts. He advocated the use of social surveys to find what citizens wanted before building their towns. After his wife died, he settled in Montpelier and built Scots College. He was knighted in 1932. In his many plans for ideal industrial towns he sought two developments: one from the uplands bringing down open wedges of countryside into the cities and the second a move out of the cities to allow for recreational space with trees, gardens, and hedges. Such work illustrated his evolutionist dictum that one had to see many sides of life properly integrated from both a practical and a theoretical viewpoint.

See Also Garden City; Unwin, Raymond

Sources:

Armytage, Walter H. Green. 1961. *Heavens Below: Utopian Experiments in England 1560–1950*. London: Routledge and Kegan Paul.

Boardman, Philip. 1944. *Patrick Geddes, Maker of the Future*. Chapel Hill: University of North Carolina Press.

———. 1978. *The Worlds of Patrick Geddes: Biologist, Town Planner, Re-Educator, Peace-Warrior*. London: Routledge and Kegan Paul.

Geddes, Patrick. 1915. *Cities in Evolution*. London: Williams and Northgate.

Kitchen, P. 1975. *A Most Unsettling Person: An Introduction to the Ideas and Life of Patrick Geddes*. London: Victor Gollancz.

Legg, Leopold G. W., ed. 1949. *Dictionary of National Biography 1931–1940*. London: Oxford University Press.

Mairet, Philip. 1957. *Pioneer of Sociology: The Life and Letters of Patrick Geddes*. London: Lund Humphries.

Meller, Helen E. 1990. *Patrick Geddes: Social Evolutionist and City Planner*. London: Routledge.

GEORGE, HENRY. Henry George (1839–1897), the single-tax utopian, was born in Philadelphia, son of a customhouse clerk. He left school at thirteen and witnessed mutiny when shipped to India as a cabin boy. He became a journeyman printer of newspapers on the Californian and Canadian goldfields (1850s). He married and settled in California and became a journalist (1865), and an adviser to the state governor and briefly had his own newspaper to publish his ideas of economic reform. Poor and powerless in booming San Francisco, he dreamed of escaping to his own paradise. The experience of desperate poverty while supporting a family, combined with vivid examples of financial rapaciousness that came to his attention on the newspaper, led him to consider the need for great economic reforms. He saw that increasing poverty was accompanied by increasing national wealth. He believed poverty grew because rental of land and the increase in land values profited the few landholders, not the whole community whose efforts directly increased land values. In the belief that every person had the right to something on the earth's surface, he concluded a single tax on land would meet all the government's costs and leave a surplus. He first outlined his doctrine in a pamphlet, *Our Land and Land Policy* (1871). A full treatise followed in *Progress and Poverty* (1879), which sold millions of copies internationally and is still regarded as a fine study in economic theory and policy. As well as advocating a single tax on land, he opposed slavery and land speculation, supported free trade, opposed land monopoly, favored trade unions and high wages, but opposed socialism. He sailed to England and Europe, where his ideas were favorably studied by many, especially the Fabians. In 1886 he was an unsuccessful candidate for mayor of New York City, possibly because of electoral fraud; during a second attempt he died suddenly of a stroke.

See Also Fabians; Henry George League

Sources:

Baker, Charles A. 1955. *Henry George.* New York: Oxford University Press.
Cord, Steven B. 1965. *Henry George: Dreamer or Realist?* Philadelphia: University of Philadelphia Press.
Dudley, Lavinia P. 1963. *The Encyclopedia Americana.* International ed. New York: Americana Corporation.
Eatwell, John, Murray, Milgate, and Peter Newman. 1987. *The New Palgrave: A Dictionary of Economics.* London: Macmillan.
George, Henry. 1900. *The Life of Henry George.* 1960 ed. New York: R. Schalkenbach Foundation.
Johnson, Allen, and Dumas Malone, eds. 1931. *Dictionary of American Biography.* Vol. 4. New York: Charles Scribner's Sons.
Sills, David L., ed. 1968. *International Encyclopedia of the Social Sciences.* New York: Macmillan and Free Press.

GHOST DANCE. The Ghost Dance promises Native American dancers they will be united with deceased loved ones and freed of Euro-American oppression. In the late nineteenth century Native Americans faced a grim life of fatal diseases, lost hunting grounds, replacement of nomadic with agrarian culture, and loss of the sense of community, kinship, and spiritual world. The Ghost Dance answered the need to feel that these pressures and changes could be overcome by finding a meaning to their cultural changes and hope for a renewed world. Plains Indians formed dance camps well away from residential areas to help establish a sense of a new community; in the dance ritual knowledge was given to the young and instilled hope for a better future through visions and trances during the dance itself. In their social trances and singing the dancers felt invigorated, their daily actions were given fresh meaning, and old forms of behavior were reinterpreted. The Ghost Dancers would have utopian visions of white settlers failing, good hunting grounds flourishing once more, childhood games being replayed, and reuniting with familiar partners. The narrative of the Ghost Dance provided a complex history as well as a utopian promise to the practice of its well-established rituals.

Sources:

Hittman, Michael. 1992. "The 1890 Ghost Dance in Nevada." *American Indian Culture and Research Journal* 16: 123–166.
Lesser, Alexander. 1933. *The Pawnee Ghost Dance Hand Game.* 1969 ed. New York: Columbia University Press.
Mohrbacher, B. C. 1996. "The Whole World Is Coming: The 1890 Ghost Dance Movement as Utopia." *Utopian Studies* 7: 75–85.
Snodgrass, Mary Ellen. 1995. *Encyclopedia of Utopian Literature.* Santa Barbara, Calif.: ABC-CLIO.
Thornton, Russell. 1986. *We Shall Live Again: The 1870 and 1890 Ghost Dance Movements as Demographic Revitalization.* Cambridge: Cambridge University Press.

GILBERT, SAINT. Saint Gilbert (c. 1083–1189), born in England, was rejected as a youth at home, turned to learning, and after studies in Paris became a teacher. He worked as a clerk in the house of the bishop of Lincoln and was able to give his private income to the poor. He was ordained in 1123, became a parson at Sempringham, and established a home for girls (1148), following the monastic rules of Saint Benedict of Nursia (c. 480–570). Later, young men, lay sisters, clerics, and priests joined in the organization. Gilbert was highly esteemed by Henry II (1133–1189) and Queen Eleanor (1122–1204), who protected him against false and scandalous charges brought by once-trusted servants and officials. He retired from his abbacy long before his death, may have lived to be 100, and in 1202 was canonized by Pope Innocent III (1160–1216). Except for one house in Scotland the order throve only in England. Henry VIII (1491–1547) suppressed it, 1538–1540. Saint Gilbert's feast day is 4 February.

See Also Benedictines; Gilbertines

Source:

Stephen, Leslie, and Sydney Lee, eds. 1917. *The Dictionary of National Biography.* London: Oxford University Press.

GILBERTINES. Gilbertines are members of a Roman Catholic order founded at Sempringham, England (1148), where members would labor vigorously and perform four distinct functions. At first the home was to care for girls; later, young men were aligned with the convent to do the heavy labor; then, lay sisters were admitted to extend the religious work; and, finally, clerics and priests joined the organization. In this way it developed its four characteristic spheres of operation. Other, similarly organized establishments were founded, and in 1148 Pope Eugenius III approved the organization as an order.

Sources:

Graham, Rose. 1901. *Saint Gifford and Sempringham and the Gilbertines: A History of the Only English Monastic Order.* London: E. Stock.

McHenry, Robert, ed. 1992. *The New Encyclopedia Britannica.* Chicago: Encyclopedia Britannica.

GILMAN, CHARLOTTE PERKINS STETSON. Charlotte Perkins Gilman (1860–1935) was born in Hartford, Connecticut. Her father left the family, and she had an impoverished, unhappy childhood. She read avidly and worked as an art teacher and card painter. In 1884 she married the American artist Charles Walter Stetson (1858–1911) and had one child. They divorced in 1894, and six years later she married George, her cousin. She read anthropology, sociology, and economics with the aim of changing society for the better. Inspired by Edward Bellamy's *Looking Backward* (1888), she joined the Fabians and the Nationalist movement. In 1892 she published a fascinating short story about insanity, "The Yellow Wallpaper." In 1898 she published *Women and Economics*, which presented her belief that economic independence for women was essential for genuine social change. The book was translated into several languages, including Japanese. She thought women should enter the workforce, housing should be in collectives, and the kitchen should be centralized and in 1915 published her well-known fictional utopia, *Herland*, where three men discover a lost civilization on their exploration of Africa. The women bear children by parthenogenesis and are depicted as both intelligent and strong. Also she wrote for, edited, and published *Forerunner*, a magazine of social reform. In her writing between 1904 and 1928 she considered how we might improve city life and establish a rural utopia and advocated votes for women and the principles of women-only government, better education and remuneration for women, a place for women in business and high-level jobs for women in industry, specialized housekeeping and cooperation with men to reduce the drudgery of housekeeping, kitchen-free holiday cottages, health and welfare of babies, amenities for people of all ages, and a world whose nations were united. In her early work appear themes of racism and elitism. She died by her own hand while suffering from cancer. Recently, her life and work have attracted much attention.

See Also Herland

Sources:

Donaldson, Laura E. 1989. "The Eve of De-Construction: Charlotte Perkins Gilman and the Feminist Recreation of Paradise." *Women's Studies* 16: 373–387.

Hill, Mary A. 1980. *Charlotte Perkins Gilman: The Making of a Radical Feminist, 1860–1896*. Philadelphia: Temple University Press.

Kessler, Carol Farley. 1995. *Charlotte Perkins Gilman: Her Progress toward Utopia with Selected Writings*. Syracuse, N.Y.: Syracuse University Press.

Lane, Ann J. 1990. *To "Herland" and Beyond: The Life and Works of Charlotte Perkins Gilman*. New York: Pantheon.

———. ed. 1968. *Charlotte Perkins Gilman Reader*. New York: Pantheon. Reprinted, Westport, Conn.: Greenwood Press.

Levitas, Ruth. 1995. "Who Holds the Hose: Domestic Labour in the Work of Bellamy, Gilman, and Morris." *Utopian Studies* 6: 65–84.

Meyering, Sheryl L. 1988. *Charlotte Perkins Gilman: The Woman and Her Work*. Ann Arbor, Mich.: UMI Research Press.

Scharnhorst, Gary. 1985. *Charlotte Perkins Gilman*. Boston: Twayne.

Starr, Harris E., ed. 1944. *Dictionary of American Biography*. Supplement 1. New York: Charles Scribner's Sons.

GODWIN, WILLIAM. William Godwin (1756–1836), born in Wisbech, North Cambridgeshire, into a large, prosperous, middle-class family, was raised in Norfolk. His family had been Dissenters for several generations. He attended Hoxton, a Dissenting Academy in London (1773–1778), became a Dissenting minister and a republican. In 1785 he associated with extreme Whigs and turned to atheism. In 1789 the French Revolution deeply affected him, and in 1793 he published *An Enquiry concerning Political Justice*, his contribution to the cause of freedom and equality. It subverted the law, especially the marriage law, and deprecated violence and so vividly challenged fundamental assumptions of contemporary moral and political thought that he became known as the philosophical representative of English radicals. Godwin's politics led Samuel Coleridge (1772–1832), Robert Southey (1774–1843), and others to plan their utopian pantisocracy in the United States. In March 1797 he married Mary Wollstonecraft (1759–1797), novelist, historian, essayist, and reviewer whom he had met six year earlier. In September 1797, ten days after the birth of their daughter, she died. He started a publishing business in 1805; it did not prosper and eventually folded (1822). In 1833 he was appointed yeoman-usher of the Exchequer. As a leading eighteenth-century English radical who advocated overthrowing the established government systems, the family, religion, and accumulated private property, he was influenced by Jean-Jacques Rousseau (1712–1778) and the French Encyclopedists; in turn, he influenced the poets William Wordsworth (1770–1850), Coleridge, Percy Shelley (1792–1822), and Lord Byron (1788–1824). His ideas are well summarized in the Preface to Shelley's *Revolt of Islam* (1818), a poem that espouses the cause of liberty and love. Among Godwin's works are two novels, *The Adventures of Caleb Williams* (1794) and *St. Leon* (1799), and *A History of the Commonwealth* (1824–1828).

   See Also Coleridge, Samuel Taylor; Pantisocracy; Rousseau, Jean-Jacques; Southey, Robert

Sources:

Magnussen, Magnus, and Rosemary Goring, eds. 1990. *Chambers Biographical Dictionary.* 5th ed. Edinburgh: Chambers.
Marshall, Peter H. 1984. *William Godwin.* New Haven, Conn.: Yale University Press.

GOLDING, WILLIAM GERALD. William Gerald Golding (1911–1993) was born in Cornwall, England, and educated at Marlborough Grammar School and Oxford University. He studied science, turned to English literature, and published *Poems* (1935). He became an actor, playwright, and theater director and in World War II served in the Royal Navy. For fifteen years afterward he taught English and philosophy at a private school in Salisbury. His *Lord of the Flies* (1954), a dystopian novel that sharply criticizes war, political opportunism, and oppression, made him famous internationally. The book was filmed (1963, 1989). He said the work drew on his experience in the Royal Navy and as a teacher of young boys in a private English school. His *The Inheritors* (1955) also dwells on mob violence and humankind's malice and spite. *Pincher Martin* (1956) is a study of greed and self-delusion of a drowning man tormented by his past. He published *Free Fall* (1959) and *The Spire* (1964), a symbolic account of the building of the spire of Salisbury Cathedral. Over the next ten years Golding wrote four novels, and in 1979 his *Darkness Visible* appeared. He wrote film scripts, short stories, and *The Ends of the Earth*, a sea trilogy about a callow aristocrat on a voyage to Australia, comprising *Rites of Passage* (1980), *Close*

Quarters (1987), and *Fire Down Below* (1989). The first of these won the Booker Prize (1983). In 1984 he published *The Paper Men*. In 1983 he won the Nobel Prize in literature and was knighted in 1988. He aimed to put the characters in his novels into extreme situations, observe the evil they do and the sins they suffer, and do this in a mythmaker's style, well beyond the constraints of Christian morality.

See Also Dystopia; *Lord of the Flies*

Sources:

Carey, John, ed. 1986. *William Golding: The Man and His Books. A Tribute to His 75th Birthday*. London: Faber.

Crompton, Don A., and Julia Briggs. *A View from the Spire: William Golding's Later Novels*. New York: Blackwell.

Gekoski, R. A. and Peter A. Grogan. 1994. *William Golding: A Bibliography, 1934–1993*. London: Deutsch.

Kinkead-Weekes, Mark, and Ian Gregor. 1984. *William Golding: A Critical Study*. London: Faber.

Magnussen, Magnus, and Rosemary Goring eds. 1990. *Chambers Biographical Dictionary*. 5th ed. Edinburgh: Chambers.

Ousby, Ian, ed. 1988. *The Cambridge Guide to Literature in English*. Rev. ed., 1995. Cambridge: Cambridge University Press.

Snodgrass, Mary Ellen. 1995. *Encyclopedia of Utopian Literature*. Santa Barbara, Calif.: ABC-CLIO.

Subbaroa, V. V. 1987. *William Golding: A Study*. London: Oriental University Press.

Tiger, Virginia. 1974. *William Golding: The Dark Fields of Discovery*. London: Calder and Boyars.

GOODMAN, BARRY. Barry Goodman (fl. 1930–1996) was born in Sydney, Australia, into a middle-class family, was educated at Sydney Grammar School, and studied engineering at Sydney University (c. 1946–1950). Unemployment in the 1930s gave him a strong feeling for self-sufficiency, frugality, and helpfulness. In his early twenties he studied at a theological college and became a lay preacher but later found religion largely irrelevant to everyday life. He worked as an engineer in various industries and was impressed by the effect of informal organization on work. In 1970 he quit industry when he noted that stress was contributing regularly to the death of his peers in management. Yearning to be a farmer, he learned some aspects of the work and at age forty-two bought a farm 100 km (sixty miles) south of Sydney. It was not financially viable. In 1977 he did a biography workshop that helped him assess his life. Afterward he joined an intentional community for social healing, separated from his wife, found a new partner, and with her in 1984 left the community to be the site manager of another residential development in northern New South Wales. It was clearly destined to fail. Barry resigned and shortly after was drawn to permaculture and settled at Crystal Waters with others who shared similar interests (1986). Goodman felt that two moves—the first from city to country and the second from nuclear family to community—were two decisive events in his life. Today he sees his role as a grandfather of Crystal Waters, enjoys advising members, feels it is his important place, and believes he has learned to accept the world rather than expect better from it. He upholds permaculture ideas and values the feelings he found in the work of Buddha, Tao, and the Syrian American symbolist poet and painter Kahlil Gibran (1883–1931), especially his well-known *The Prophet* (1923).

See Also Crystal Waters; Permaculture

Source:

Goodman, Barry. 1995. "From Grey-Suited Engineer to Birthday-Suited Hippie." In Bill Metcalf, ed., *From Utopian Dreaming to Communal Reality: Cooperative Life Styles in Australia*, pp. 127–139. Sydney: University of New South Wales Press.

GRAMEEN BANK. Grameen Bank means "village bank" in Bangladesh. On his return to Bangladesh from Ph.D. studies in the United States in 1972, Dr. Muhammad Yunus met Sophia Kahtoon, twenty-two. She lived in poverty, making bamboo stools for two cents each. Her poverty was due to her debt to the trader who sold her the materials for the stools at a price so high that she had to borrow the amount from him. She was his bonded laborer. Yunus found she needed U.S.$27 to break the conditions set by the bond. He did not want to simply give her the money, so he sought a loan from a bank. The bank refused, saying people in poverty were not worthy of credit. In time Yunus arranged to borrow U.S.$300 from a bank, offering himself as guarantor. He lent the money to Sophia and several other women. All was repaid, and the young women escaped their round of poverty. When he approached the banks again, Yunus found their policy toward the poor in Bangladesh had not changed. In 1983 he got a license to operate a bank, the Grameen Bank. Today the bank has over 2 million borrowers and over 1,000 branches and last year lent U.S.$400 million (in Bangladesh currency). For twelve years the Grameen Bank maintained a repayment record of 98 percent. Over the last twelve years the repayment record of the Industrial Bank of Bangladesh has been less than 10 percent. Today no bank will lend to the poor because they are not creditworthy. They will lend only to the rich. The Grameen Bank operates on the following principles: lend to the poorest of the poor (94 percent of the bank's clients are women); loans are without collateral; the bank does not advise borrowers on how to use loans; the bank helps and supports its borrowers to succeed; the bank serves the poor, not other banking activities; the bank meets all costs from interest income. The bank has branches worldwide, 200 in the United States, with its center in Chicago, and claims to have the personal support of the Belgian and Spanish royal families and U.S. president. Today ten different corporate bodies serving the poor are connected to the Grameen Bank, including the Grameen Education Foundation and the Grameen Securities Ltd.

See Also Yunus, Muhammad

Sources:

Bornstein, David. 1996. *The Price of a Dream*. Dhaka, Bangladesh: University Press;
     New York: Simon and Schuster.
Todd, Helen. 1996. *Women at the Center: Grameen Bank Borrowers after One Decade*.
     Boulder, Colo. Westview Press.
Yunus, Muhammad. 1997a. "Barefoot Banking: The Importance of Women." *Perma-
     culture International Journal* 65: 39–41.
———. 1997b. "Barefoot Banking. The Story of the Grameen Bank Which Is Helping
     the World's Poor Build a Future." *Permaculture International Journal* 64:23–
     27.

GREAVES, JAMES PIERREPONT. James Pierrepont Greaves (1777–1842)
was a merchant who was bankrupted by the Berlin and Milan Decrees (1806),
rebuilt his business, and left for Yverdun, where he studied Pestalozzian ideas
of education (1817). With Johann Pestalozzi (1746–1827) he met Robert Owen
(1771–1858). Both men had a common concern for infant education. Greaves
spent four years teaching English at the universities of Basel and Tübingen, and
in 1825 he returned to England. He founded the London Infant School Society,
became its secretary, and promoted Pestalozzi's educational principles. In 1827
he published *Three Hundred Maxims for the Consideration of Parents, Physical
and Metaphysical Hints for Everybody*, and *The Contrasting Magazine*, a teaching device in comparative education. Amos Bronson Alcott (1799–1888) was
much taken with Greaves' views on infant education. Greaves also worked to
alleviate social problems of unemployment in Randwick, Gloucestershire, by
using a system of payments by tokens that were exchanged for food, clothing,
and tools (1832). He was a mystic, and his mysticism in education centered on
the soul and deity. He asserted the deity introduced virtues like love into the
soul, which in time would heighten people's interests in humankind generally.
He became known as the "Sacred Socialist." To him humankind lived by three
maxims: the external or physical; the inward or intellectual; and the spiritual or
moral. Life's aim was for one to live on a high moral plane. This could be
achieved through vegetarianism, drinking water, celibacy, and cold water therapy. All social ills could be attributed to humankind's failure to obey these
principles. Also he was much drawn to Jakob Boehme's (1575–1624) ideas.
Financial support for his work came from a clique of wealthy women, and
intellectual rapport came from disciples, among whom were many disaffected
Owenites. Toward the end of his life he was at Alcott House, Ham Common
in Surrey, a community and a boarding school run by his followers, including
Charles Lane (1800–1870). When Lane went with Alcott to establish Fruitlands
in Harvard, Massachusetts, Alcott House was reorganized according to the ascetic, vegetarian, and transcendental principles of Greaves and named the First
Concordium.

     See Also Alcott, Amos Bronson; Alcott House or School and the First Con-
cordium; Boehme, Jakob; Pestalozzi, Johann Heinrich

Sources:

Armytage, Walter H. Green. 1961. *Heavens Below: Utopian Experiments in England 1560–1950*. London: Routledge and Kegan Paul.
Harrison, John F. C. 1969. *Robert Owen and the Owenites in Britain and America: Quest for the New Moral World*. New York: Charles Scribner's Sons.
Stephen, Leslie, and Sydney Lee, eds. 1917. *The Dictionary of National Biography*. London: Oxford University Press.

GREELEY, HORACE. Horace Greeley (1811–1872) learned the trade of a printer when he was apprenticed in the office of the *Northern Spectator*, East Poultney, Vermont. In 1831 he came to New York City as a journeyman and five years later married, wrote for Whig newspapers, and edited the *Jeffersonian* (1838). Following the 1837 panic he sought to help people by encouraging them to join utopian communes, like those of Charles Fourier (1772–1837). The *Jeffersonian* was an influential Whig campaign weekly that ran for a year. Greeley launched his *New York Tribune* in 1841, and in five years it was the best all-round newspaper in New York City. Its news was gathered energetically, and published in good taste at a high moral and intellectual level. Greeley's views were fiercely expressed; he was an egalitarian who opposed monopoly of any kind, especially the domination of one class over another. He espoused Fourierism and the agrarian movement, and supported cooperative shops and labor unions, and fought capital punishment and the unrestricted sale of liquor. At the beginning of the Civil War (1861–1865) he supported the Union, demanded no concessions be made to slavery, and opposed Lincoln's policy of conciliating the border states. In 1864 his reputation fell when he hesitated to support Lincoln because his activities to promote peace were ill advised. The liberal Republicans at Cincinnati, Ohio, nominated him in May 1870 for president, but his campaign carried only six states, and he was deeply hurt by the abuse against him during the campaign. His wife died shortly afterward, and, a broken man, he died insane. He helped draw up the constitution of the North American Phalanx with Albert Brisbane (1809–1890), a notable American utopian and Owenite.

See Also Brisbane, Albert; Fourier, Charles

Sources:

Hale, William Harlan. 1950. *Horace Greeley: Voice of the People*. New York: Harper.
Lunde, Erik S. 1981. *Horace Greeley*. Boston: Twayne.
Oved, Yaacov. 1987. *Two Hundred Years of American Communes*. New Brunswick, N.J.: Transaction Books.
Schulze, Susanne. 1992. *Horace Greeley. A Bio-Bibliography*. Westport, Conn.: Greenwood Press.
Sothern, Charles. 1915. *Horace Greeley and Other Pioneers of socialism*. New York: M. Kennerley.
Van Deusen, Glyndon Garlock. 1953. *Horace Greeley: Nineteenth-Century Crusader*. Philadelphia: University of Pennsylvania Press.

GREENPEACE. Greenpeace, an international organization, has since 15 September 1971 considered earth its utopia and defends it by nonviolent means.

The organization became public with the action of a few Vancouver conservationists who left home on the *Phyllis Cormack*, a rickety, old twenty-four-meter fishing boat, decked with a Greenpeace sign, making for Amchitka, a small island off Alaska. Even though it was highly prone to earthquakes, it had become the site for U.S. nuclear bomb tests. Frightened by the icy waters, stormy seas, and the chances of being contaminated by the radiation from the bomb, the Greenpeace members sailed toward the area in protest and broadcast to a local radio station: "Our goal is a very simple, clear and direct one—to bring about a confrontation between the people of death and the people of life. We insist on conserving the environment for our children and future generations." They were arrested. But only one more bomb was detonated there because the Greenpeace protest had raised public opinion strongly against further nuclear testing in such a dangerous place. For twenty-five years Greenpeace's influence spread as its growing membership organized many environmental protests. Greenpeace upholds principles of biodiversity and protests against the impact of using hazardous chemicals generally and the conditions that exacerbate the greenhouse effect on climate change. It encourages scientific research and production of environmentally sound goods, services, and practices. Greenpeace practices a Quaker principle of bearing witness in protest against conflict. For example, members of Greenpeace have witnessed whaling activities, marine pollution, supported reuse, recycle, and reduce principles for consumption, aimed to use less fossil fuel for public transport, witnessed the arrival and departure of nuclear-powered vessels in harbors around the world, blocked outflow pipes to prevent discharging dangerous chemicals into the sea, decried the use of drift nets in fishing, protested against fossil fuel for energy production, protested against nuclear testing in the South Pacific, prevented shipping of waste lead batteries to underdeveloped countries as bogus recycling, and disgraced chemical firms that persist in producing and distributing ozone-depleting gases for refrigerators.

See Also Quakers

Sources:

Brown, Michael and John May. 1991. *The Greenpeace Story.* 2d, rev. ed. New York: Dorling Kindersley.

Eayrs, James G. 1973. *Greenpeace and Her Enemies.* Toronto: Anasi.

Knight, Stephen. 1988. *Icebound: The Greenpeace Expedition to Antarctica.* Auckland, New Zealand: Century Hutchinson.

Leggett, Jeremy, ed. 1990. *Global Warming: The Greenpeace Report.* Oxford: Oxford University Press.

May, John. 1989. *The Greenpeace Book of the Nuclear Age: The Hidden History, the Human Cost.* London: Gollencz.

GRONLUND, LAURENCE. Laurence Gronlund (1846–1899) was born and educated in Denmark and graduated from the University of Copenhagen (1865). Instead of studying law, he emigrated to the United States (1867) and taught German in Milwaukee. He finished his law studies and was admitted to the bar

(Chicago, 1869). He practiced briefly, then turned vigorously to socialist studies, and was drawn to Blaise Pascal's (1623–1662) *Pensées* (1699), notes for a posthumously published casebook on Christian truths. He wrote *The Coming Revolution: Its Principles* (1878) and his most valuable work, *The Cooperative Commonwealth* (1884). He disliked extravagance, loathed vindictiveness, and was motivated by the principles of German social democracy. He believed the wage system exploited labor and predicted its downfall in the evolution of socialism. His work was the first in English to present the origins of social democracy in Germany and the ideas of Karl Marx (1818–1883), with Gronlund's modifications and refinements. Recognized in the United States as a prominent exponent of collectivism and likened to Edward Bellamy (1850–1898), he became a popular writer and lecturer and much influenced Julius A. Wayland (1854–1912), founder of Ruskin Colony. He published frequently on socialism, wrote on the inadequacies of Henry George's (1839–1897) single-tax scheme, and was elected to the executive committee of the Socialist Labor Party (1888). To Gronlund socialism was a religion that should replace the capitalist wage system and unify the divisive industrial society of his day. His utopian prescription appeared in 1898 with his *New Economy: A Peaceable Solution to the Social Problem* and his *Socializing a State*. He died after serving briefly on the labor staff of the *New York Journal*.

    See Also Bellamy, Edward; Ruskin Colony; Social democracy; Wayland, Julius A.

Sources:

Fogarty, Robert S. 1990. *All Things New: American Communes and Utopian Movements 1860–1914*. Chicago: University of Chicago Press.
Johnson, Allen, and Dumas Malone, eds. 1931. *Dictionary of American Biography*. Vol. 4. New York: Charles Scribner's Sons.
Oved, Yaacov. 1987. *Two Hundred Years of American Communes*. New Brunswick, N.J.: Transaction Books.

GUILD OF ST. GEORGE AND ST. GEORGE'S FARM, ABBEYDALE, OR TOTLEY FARM. The guild was formed in 1871 by John Ruskin (1819–1900) with two trustees. It was registered as a company seven years later. It was Ruskin's attempt to battle injustices of his day. His policy was to take an acre of ground, make it attractive, and produce and distribute food for those who needed it without charging rent. He wanted land bought for well-instructed laborers to work, while companions of the guild would own and manage the land. The farm would be administered by a master, through provincial marshals, and by laborers. Companions of the guild would give the farm one-tenth of their income, and the wealth of the farm would be carried in the ornaments made by guildsmen; every estate would have a school, and members would use the guild's special currency for exchange. In April 1876 on a visit to Sheffield John Ruskin enthused a group of workers with his ideas on communism. One suggested that there be established a commune largely dependent on boot making. Later, seeing they accepted the ideas behind his Guild of St. George, Ruskin made available the funds to get thirteen acres near Sheffield, where St. George's Farm was established as a self-governing Christian organization. It would be run by the Life Guards of the New Life ("Fors Clavigera," as Ruskin called them). The task for community members was to produce fine shoes, make their financial accounts public, and find a custodian to manage their affairs. After the two trustees resigned, Ruskin was solely responsible for what he called Abbeydale, St. George's Farm, or Totley Farm outside Sheffield. On the farm most laborers made shoes and, as Life Guards of the New Life, under Ruskin's direction, developed a form of self-government. Work was oriented toward customer satisfaction, but the items to be produced were determined by the shoemakers themselves. They were to choose a master for themselves, and William Harrison Riley (fl. 1870s) was their choice. But Riley failed as a controller of Abbeydale, so Ruskin took over and sent his gardener from London to manage the estate as a vegetable and botanical garden. For five years the farm lost seventy pounds a year, and in 1884 the farm management was again replaced. The nonsectarian community comprised ten men and three women who rented 180 acres, opened three quarries, and put the fruits of their work into the common stock. They leased the land for twenty-one years. It languished, was later revived, and in 1929 was purchased for a nursery and a market garden rather than a utopian farm. In 1979 it was operating not as a commune but as St. George's Nurseries. Today the guild supports many environmental projects and advances research into alternative agricultural economics. It is a registered charity (1994) that welcomes visitors and upholds Ruskin's ideas of being aware of the environment and having a visual appreciation of it.

See Also Riley, William Harrison; Ruskin, John

Sources:

Armytage, Walter H. Green. 1961. *Heavens Below: Utopian Experiments in England 1560–1950*. London: Routledge and Kegan Paul.

Harris, Anthony. 1985. *Why Have Our Little Girls Large Shoes? Ruskin and the Guild of St George*. London: Brentham Press.

Marsh, Jan. 1982. *Back to the Land: The Pastoral Impulse in England, from 1880 to 1914*. London: Quartet.

H

HAMPSTEAD GARDEN SUBURB. Hampstead Garden Suburb, England, is a utopian Garden City founded by Henrietta Barnett (1851–1936). The aim of the suburb was to preserve the beauty of Hampstead Heath, make a community for people with a secure life and an interest in nature, and be a bridge between social classes. It took shape in 1907. Hampstead Heath was the common of the manor of Hampstead (1680) with 336 acres. During the eighteenth century the heath area decreased as Hampstead Town grew in response to the popularity of its salubrious spa. After 1823 digging for sand reduced the ground level of the heath. Between 1829 and 1871 many claims were made to develop the Heath but with little success. Between 1871 and 1971 a constant battle was waged to save the heath from extensive urban development. In 1889 the London County Council became responsible for the care of Hampstead Heath; but in 1896 it raised a public outcry when attempts were made to tidy the heath. In the next year the Hampstead Heath Protection Society was formed to preserve the natural beauty of the heath. More land was bought, and the area of the heath was increased (1899–1902). In 1905 the urban railway tube was to reach Hampstead, and two stations were to be built. Eton College, owner of nearby Wyldes Farm, planned to develop the farm with residences when the tube stations were opened at Heath End. At Heath End Mrs. Barnett had a holiday cottage with a fine view. The railway plans and the housing development meant that her view would be lost and that the character of Hampstead Heath would change. So, with the secretary of the Hampstead Protection Society, Mrs. Barnett formed the Hampstead Heath Extension Council. The council took an option over eighty acres of Eton College farm for £48,000. At her request Eton College changed the area that she wanted to conserve and reduced the price to £36,000. An agreement was made in 1904, and money was collected for this purpose. More problems arose when the London County Council demanded fees incurred in building the roads. Finally, the extension cost almost £44,000. During World War I a few building allotments were allowed on the heath. The boundaries of the heath from Gospel Oak, Dartmouth Park, Highgate, and Turner's Wood around to Child's Hill now comprise gardenlike residential areas with playing fields, golf courses, gardens, tennis courts, schools, and hospitals in leafy settings. By 1971 Hampstead Heath covered 802 acres and today is a highly sought-after residential area of London.

See Also Barnett, Henrietta; Garden City

Sources:

Farmer, Alan. 1984. *Hampstead Heath.* New Barnet: Historical.

Gill, Roger. 1984. "In England's Green and Pleasant Land." In Peter Alexander and Roger Gill, eds., pp. 109–117. *Utopias.* London: Duckworth.

Ilkin, C. W. 1971. *Hampstead Heath Centenary 1871–1971: How the Heath Was Saved for the People.* London: Greater London Council.

Marsh, Jan. 1982. *Back to the Land: The Pastoral Impulse in England, from 1880 to 1914.* London: Quartet.

HANDMAID'S TALE, THE. In her *The Handmaid's Tale* (1985) Margaret Atwood (b.1939) depicts the United States replaced with the Republic of Gilead and dominated by the U.S. religious Right. It is a place where sexual liberation has given over to cold puritanism and the denigration of most women. A totalitarian state, Gilead is described in a document about the life of a "handmaid," and sexuality is the central theme. In Gilead successful men are issued with women of differing statuses: "wives" manage men's domestic affairs; "marthas" are their servants; "handmaids" are their sex objects. "Econowives" play all roles for men who are less successful. "Aunts" train and control the handmaids, while "Jezebels" service foreign dignitaries. The remainder, "unwomen," work in low and hazardous occupations, for example, as cleaners of toxic waste areas in Gilead's colonies. In Gilead women are kept illiterate; not even Scrabble is allowed, and the signs for shoppers are all in symbols. The central character, a handmaid, "Offred"—she serves a commander called "Fred"—tells the reader she is nothing but a two-legged womb used for breeding. In Gilead love is not allowed, and pleasure is denied any part in sexual contact. Nevertheless, Offred and her commander develop a close relationship, but always under his icy control. Religion in Gilead is also a matter for political domination, the Bible is a seditious document, and television is devoted to religious propaganda and distorted news reports. Having wiped out its past, Gilead is testimony to the failure of Western civilization to learn from its history. In the epilogue it is 2195, and Offred's manuscript is being discussed. The reader can find a little hope in this dystopia. Gilead has had at least one escapee, the author of the manuscript. Perhaps the future is not so dark; perhaps we are not condemned by ignorance of the past to endless night?

See Also Atwood, Margaret; Dystopia

Sources:

Atwood, Margaret. 1985. *The Handmaid's Tale*. London: Jonathan Cape.
Booker, M. Keith. 1994. *Dystopian Literature: A Theory and Research Guide*. Westport, Conn.: Greenwood Press.
Dodson, Danita J. 1997. " 'We Lived in the Blank White Space': Rewriting the Paradigm of Denial in Atwood's *The Handmaid's Tale*." *Utopian Studies* 8, no. 2: 67–86.
Fitting, Peter. 1990. "The Turn from Utopia to Recent Feminist Fiction." In Libby Falk Jones and Sarah Wimpster Goodwin, eds., *Feminism, Utopia and Narrative*, pp. 141–158. Knoxville: University of Tennessee Press.
Hansot, Elisabeth. 1996. "Selves, Survival, and Resistance in 'The Handmaid's Tale.' " *Utopian Studies* 5, no. 2: 56–69.
Kellerer, David. 1989. "Margaret Atwood's 'The Handmaid's Tale': A Contextual Utopia." *Science-Fiction Studies* 16: 209–217.
Malak, Amin. 1987. "Margaret Atwood's 'The Handmaid's Tale' and the Dystopian Tradition." *Canadian Literature* 112: 9–16.
Snodgrass, Mary Ellen. 1995. *Encyclopedia of Utopian literature*. Santa Barbara, Calif.: ABC-CLIO.
Stillman, Peter S., and S. Ann Jonson. 1996. "Identity, Complicity and Resistance in 'The Handmaid's Tale.' " *Utopian Studies* 5, no. 2: 70–86.

HARMONIA. Harmonia was a spiritualist colony (1853–1863) established at Kiantone, New York. In 1850 a local blacksmith learned, while in a trance, that near a local spring had once been a perfect, free-love society. On receipt of some spring water, John Murray Spear (1804–1877), a former Universalist minister who had been active in reforming Boston prisons, was drawn to the site, intending it to be place of great harmony. In 1853, ten octagonal houses were erected, and Harmonia was established as a summer commune for twenty to forty members. The community, sometimes known as Kiantone Community, the Domaine, or the Association of Beneficents, lived on 123 acres with two springs; community members believed the springs had special healing qualities and magnetic forces. The women members were devoted feminists. In 1858 at a convention on the site, speakers denounced marriage and family relations, and advocated raising women's status and freedom and striving for a perfect social order. Once a member of Brook Farm, John Orvis (1816–1897) was one of the leaders of Harmonia. On a voyage down the Mississippi to achieve world peace, colonists founded Patriot, Indiana, and settled July 1860. By 1863 Harmonia at Kiantone was gone.

See Also Orvis, John; Spear, John Murray

Source:

Fogarty, Robert S. 1980. *Dictionary of American Communal History*. Westport, Conn.: Greenwood Press.

HARMONY INDUSTRIAL ASSOCIATION, OR HARMONA. Harmona was near Tantallon on the Qu'Appelle River, Qu'Appelle valley, Saskatchewan (c.

1895–1900). The association was inspired by John Ruskin (1819–1900), William Morris (1834–1896), Edward Bellamy (1850–1898), and some Calvinist farmers who set about constituting a cooperative community that idealized brotherhood (1895). In opposition to the nineteenth-century exploitative and fraudulent capitalist system they designed a self-sufficient community of private homes, factories, mills, and retailing outlets as well as schools, recreational services, and welfare services. Members could own up to 5 of the community's 500 shares, each one valued at $200, and were rewarded with profits commensurate with their participation. A complete system of checks and balances, rewards and obligations provided for a communistic style of equality within the community. Entry and membership were rigorously managed by the group using autocratic methods of social control. Not more than fifty people managed to participate. Because there were no goods or services for the community to sell, the cost of operations exceeded income, and this financial problem brought the colony to an end within two years.

Sources:

Johnson, Gilbert. 1951. "The Harmony Industrial Association: A Pioneer Cooperative." *Saskatchewan History* 4: 11–21.
Rasporich, Anthony W. 1992. "Utopian Ideals and Community Settlements in Western Canada 1880–1914." In R. Douglas Francis and Howard Palmer, eds., *The Prairie West: Historical Readings*, 2d ed., pp. 338–361. Edmonton, Alberta: Pica Pica Press.

HARMONY SOCIETY. Harmony Society was a communistic, religious body organized by George Rapp (1770–1847) in Würtemberg. The members aimed to reform modern society by applying to it a literal interpretation of the New Testament. The New Testament indicated to them that it was best to revive the practices of the primitive church. In Würtemberg the local religious authorities were not sympathetic, so Rapp and a band of believers emigrated to Pennsylvania (1803) and on Connoquenessing Creek in Butler County established a settlement they called "Harmony." Known as "Harmonists," the members cultivated the land, wove cloth, and through other industries acquired much wealth. In 1815 the community moved to 27,000 acres along the Wabash River in Indiana, where they became prosperous and called the settlement "New Harmony." The property at New Harmony was sold to Robert Owen (1771–1858) in 1824, and the Harmonists moved to Beaver County, Pennsylvania, and built the village "Economy" on the Ohio, near Pittsburgh, and later a new village, Harmony. They held all property in common and strongly discouraged marriage and sexual intercourse and believed the Second Coming of Christ was imminent and that, ultimately, the human race would be saved. In seeking the Second Coming of Jesus Christ, they quickly amassed much wealth for the Lord's use; members practiced self-denial, celibacy, and tight economy. They were noted for marching to work in the field, a band leading their way. With assets worth millions—farms, vineyards, dairies, railroad, and bank shares—they waited, well prepared for the Second Coming. After 1825, in an effort to halt any possible corrupting influence that might ensue from vast wealth, its business agent sought to hide information that the community was greatly prospering. Even so they became collective millionaires. Rapp was a strong leader and dictator to the community, and on his death in 1847 a merchant took over the leadership. But their numbers fell, and by 1906 the community had gone.

See Also Economy; Rapp, George

Sources:

Arndt, Karl J. R. 1972. *George Rapp's Harmony Society 1758–1847.* Cranbury, N.J.: Associated University Presses.

———. 1980. *Harmony on the Connoquenessing, 1803–1815.* Worcester, Mass.: Harmony Society Press.

Fogarty, Robert S. 1980. *Dictionary of American Communal History.* Westport, Conn.: Greenwood Press.

———. 1990. *All Things New: American Communes and Utopian Movements 1860–1914.* Chicago: University of Chicago Press.

Oved, Yaacov. 1987. *Two Hundred Years of American Communes.* New Brunswick, N.J.: Transaction Books.

Pitzer, Donald E., and Josephine M. Elliott. 1979. "New Harmony's First Utopians." *Indiana Magazine of History* 75 (September): 224–300.

HARRIMAN, JOB. Job Harriman (1861–1925) was born in Indiana and lived on a farm until he was eighteen. He went to school at North Western Christian University, later Butler College, Indianapolis, and studied for the ministry. After leaving college, he found many of his ideas uncongenial to religion. He decided to study law at Colorado College, Colorado Springs. He was admitted to practice in 1885 in Indiana; next year he moved to California. In 1890 his growing interest in socialism led him to join a Nationalist Club in San Francisco. In the Socialist Labor Party in San Francisco he worked his way up and joined the Altruians and their colonization schemes, which pursued the principles of a consumer's cooperative. He was the socialist nominee for governor of California in 1898 but was not elected. In 1899 he accepted nomination for the presidency of the United States from the Socialist-Laborites. When the Socialist Labor Party and the social democrats united, he was dropped to the vice presidential position. During the campaign he learned that the socialist movement needed an economic, rather than a political, base and began to support enrollment in labor unions as a requirement for membership with the Socialist Party. During the political campaign (1910) the *Times* attacked Harriman and his labor supporters. When a bomb exploded at the back of the *Times'* building, and twenty men were killed, labor supporters were prime suspects. Two were arrested, and Harriman accepted the position of chief councillor for the defense. The men confessed, so the case did not come to court. Harriman was so upset he quit politics. Nevertheless, still holding a strong belief in socialism, Harriman began to search southern California to establish a community based on socialist ideas and formed the Llano del Rio Company (1914).

See Also Altruria; Llano del Rio Company

Sources:

Fogarty, Robert S. 1980. *Dictionary of American Communal History*. Westport, Conn.: Greenwood Press.

Hine, Robert V., ed. 1983. *California's Utopian Colonies*. Los Angeles: University of California Press.

Oved, Yaacov. 1987. *Two Hundred Years of American Communes*. New Brunswick, N.J.: Transaction Books.

Who Was Who in America. 1966. Vol. 1, 1897–1942. Chicago: Marquis.

HARRIS, THOMAS LAKE. Thomas Lake Harris (1823–1906) was born at Fenny Stratford, Buckinghamshire, England, and as a young child was taken by his parents to settle in Utica, New York, where his father was a grocer and auctioneer. His mother died four years later. His stepmother treated him harshly, and Thomas dwelled much upon the memory of his true mother. He was befriended by the Universalist minister in the town, frequently visited him, and eventually lived there, writing poetry and articles for Universalist journals, and when studying for the Baptist ministry he was converted to Universalism (1843). In 1845 he married and became a pastor of the Fourth Universalist Society in New York City. After the death of his wife in 1850 he began lecturing on spiritualism and entering trances while communicating with the celestial world. At these times he would compose long, mystical poems on the theme of celestial love. In 1851 he established the first of his settlements, Mountain Cove, which was assumed to be the original site of the Garden of Eden. It closed due to internal conflicts in 1853. In 1855 he married his second wife, Kenley Waters. In about 1858 he founded the Church of the Good Shepherd, using doctrines of Charles Fourier (1772–1837) and Swedenborg (1688–1772). He and his wife went to England, and, on their return, Harris established a second spiritualist colony at Wassaic, New York (1861), and called the community Amenia, or the Brotherhood of the New Life. In 1867 the group moved to 1,600-acre tract near Brocton in New York. In 1876 he founded Fountain Grove in California. After the death of his second wife (1883) Harris married his secretary, Jane Lee Waring, known as "Dovie," a wealthy and prominent member of Fountain Grove Community (1892). Controversy embroiled this venture, and Harris was denounced as a fraud and hypocrite. People who liked Harris and knew him seemed to have been impressed by the prophetic force of his personality as well as by his remarkable eloquence and poetic gifts. He and his new wife left for New York. At one time he had about 2,000 adherents.

See Also Brotherhood of the New Life; Fountain Grove

Sources:

Fogarty, Robert. 1990. *All Things New: American Communes and Utopian Movements 1860–1914*. Chicago: University of Chicago Press.

Hinds, William Alfred. 1908. *American Communities and Co-Operative Colonies*. 3d ed. Chicago: C. H. Kerr. [Original ed. 1878]. 1975 ed., Philadelphia: Porcupine Press.

Hine, Robert V. 1953. *California's Utopian Colonies*. 1983 ed. Berkeley: University of California Press.

Johnson, Allen, and Dumas Malone, eds. 1931. *Dictionary of American Biography*. Vol. 4. New York: Charles Scribner's Sons.

Kirk, John Foster, ed. 1865. *Allibone's Critical Dictionary of English Literature and British and American Authors*. Supplement, vol. 2. Reprint of 1891 ed. Detroit: Gale Research.

Schneider, Herbert W., and George Lawton. 1942. *A Prophet and a Pilgrim: Being the Incredible History of Thomas Lake Harris and Laurence Oliphant*. Reprinted, 1970. New York: Columbia University Press.

HASIDIC COMMUNITY. Hasid, a sect of Orthodox Jews, was founded in eighteenth-century Poland. It bases its beliefs on deep feeling and its ideas on ancient Jewish mystical traditions of pantheism as in the Cabala (Hebrew for "traditions"). By upholding piety and ecstatic prayer and denouncing intellectual attitudes to life, charismatic leaders of the sect in Eastern Europe spread their influence in the face of strong resistance. Hasidic men are known by their conservative suits and broad-brimmed hats characteristic of eighteenth-century dress. Today Hasidic beliefs are not widely accepted among Jews. In the United States among the Hasidic communities are Boyaner, Lubavitcher, and Satmar. Hasidism assumes messianic hope, and their leaders, Rebbes, claim special access to the Messiah and special means to bring him forth and sometimes claim to be either the Messiah or in his lineage. They aim to change or return the corrupt world to its pre-messianic state. In the United States Satmar and Lubavitcher are well known. Satmar established themselves in a settlement called Kiryas Joel (City of Yoel) at Monroe, Orange County. To them isolation is a shield from untoward external forces. Since 1983 they have given much attention to children who are disabled, and their attempt to use public funds for this purpose has attracted unsuccessful litigation. It was alleged the community was using U.S. democracy to advance its goals because they believed disabilities in children are evidence of divine visitations. Hasidic communities thrive on charismatic leadership of a spiritual leader who fulfills the messianic wishes of members. Recently, the Lubavitcher leaders stressed the value of religious activism in bringing back the Messiah. The community assumes it has the answer to causing messianic redemption: involve all Jews in Jewish law. In this the Lubavitcher differ from the Satmar, who prefer to control visions in the past, while the Lubavitcher appear to look to the future. Some critics suggest that confusion in Hasidic orientation is caused by tensions and ambiguities in the U.S. family, working, and political life, all of which dog the Hassim and exacerbate their divisiveness, rivalries, and excessively passionate loyalties.

Source:

Mintz, Jerome R. 1992. *Hasidic People: A Place in the New World*. Cambridge: Harvard University Press.

HASKELL, BURNETTE. Burnette G. Haskell (1857–1907) was born in Sierra County, northern California, into a family of wealthy landowners, descendants from early Puritan settlers in New England. His parents sent him to Oberlin College, Ohio. He attended the University of Illinois and the University of California, read law in his uncle's law firm, and was admitted to the California bar (1879). He turned to journalism, became interested in socialism, and supported the labor movement. He led independent social movements on the Pacific Coast of the United States in the 1880s and the 1890s. He founded the Sailors' Union of the Pacific (1885) and, with James J. Martin (fl. 1884–1914), established the Kaweah Cooperative Community (1885–1892) and also led the Californian Bellamyite movement. He helped form the International Working Men's Association. Jealousies and much ideological and religious argument split the community, apparently because of Haskell's argumentative temperament. Most members supported Martin. In 1890 the community, Kaweah, was incorporated into the new Sequoia National Park, and the community declined. As a Democrat in 1880, Haskell had tried to enter politics, and between 1892 and 1896 he became a Populist and, later, a Republican. In 1900 President William McKinley (1843–1901) named him a notary public in Alaska. In 1903 he returned to California, where, unable to find work, he lived in poverty and occasionally found employment as a proofreader on the *Oakland Tribune*.

See Also Kaweah Co-operative Commonwealth; Martin, James J.

Sources:

Fogarty, Robert S. 1980. *Dictionary of American Communal History*. Westport, Conn.: Greenwood Press.

Hine, Robert V. 1953. *California's Utopian Colonies*. 1983 ed. Berkeley: University of California Press.

Johnpol, Bernard K., and Harvey Klehr, eds. 1986. *Biographical Dictionary of the American Left*. Westport, Conn.: Greenwood Press.

Oved, Yaacov. 1987. *Two Hundred Years of American Communes*. New Brunswick, N.J.: Transaction Books.

HEIDELBERG SCHOOL. The Heidelberg School was a colony of artists who together deliberately sought to make a place in Australian art for Australian artists rather than allowing the prevailing idealization of European art to dominate the culture and taste in Australian painting. The group was established in the countryside east of Melbourne, Victoria, in Box Hill (c.1885) by Tom Roberts (1856–1931), Frederick McCubbin (1855–1917), and Louis Abrahams (1852–1903). Later, they were joined by Charles Conder (1868–1909), Arthur Streeton (1867–1943), Walter Withers (1854–1914), Clara Southern (1861–1940), and Jane Sutherland (1855–1928). They also painted near Mentone by the sea and in the country north of Melbourne, around Eaglemont and Heidelberg from which the group was given its name. Their work represented an Australian interpretation of plein-air painting. Many of the impressions of the Eaglemont group were painted on cedar, cigar box lids and were shown in the

1889 Impressionist Exhibition, which was controversial at the time. In 1890 the original group dissolved, but Walter Withers and others continued to paint in the Heidelberg area afterward.

See Also Conder, Charles Edward; McCubbin, Frederick; Roberts, Thomas William; Streeton, Arthur Ernest

Sources:

McCulloch, Susan, and Alan McCulloch. 1994. *The Encyclopedia of Australian Art.* Sydney: Allen and Unwin.
Robb, Gwenda, and Elaine Smith. 1993. *Concise Dictionary of Australian Art.* Edited by Robert Smith. Melbourne: Melbourne University Press.
Splatt, William, and Dugald McLellan. 1986. *The Heidelberg School: The Golden Summer of Australian Painting.* Melbourne: Lloyd O'Neil.

HELICON HALL COLONY. Helicon Hall Colony was planned by Upton B. Sinclair (1878–1968) as a cooperative for a group of young literary couples near Englewood, New Jersey. A few months after the plan was announced, June 1906, the Colony was established in a former boys' school on the western edge of the Palisades. It comprised forty six adults and fifteen children, including Harry Sinclair Lewis (1885–1951), later to be noted for his *Main Street* (1920) and *Babbit* (1922), and other promising writers. A fire ended the dreamlike socialist colony in 1907 after only six months.

See Also Sinclair, Upton

Source:

Fogarty, Robert S. 1980. *Dictionary of American Communal History.* Westport, Conn.: Greenwood Press.

HELLER, MARIA. Maria Magdelene Engelliebe Heller (1841–1906) was born in Wilhelmsdorf, Silesia. Her father was a gardener. In 1855, when confirmed in the Lutheran Church, she was considered quite mad. She had visions, made prophecies, spoke poorly, and was ugly, but she had the respect of simple peasants, some of whom vowed that God spoke through her. She, too, believed this, especially when in a trance. In one trance God told her to gather her followers and emigrate to Australia. In 1875 she landed at Melbourne, Victoria, and with fifty to seventy-five followers established Hill Plains, a community near Benalla, central Victoria. Later that year her whole community was ill with malnutrition and scurvy. Johann Krumnow (1811–1880), leader of Herrnhut German community, offered to accommodate her and her followers. By August 1876 Heller and Krumnow were at swords' points over leadership of the augmented community, and she was charged with being a dangerous lunatic for having tried to assault Krumnow with a rock. In court much evidence indicated she was erratic, emotional, more religiously possessed than insane, and probably epileptic. Found not guilty, she was bound to keep the peace on a bond of ten pounds. Curiously, Krumnow offered himself as surety for another twenty pounds. She left Herrnhut for Tabor in November 1876, married, and no longer claimed God's gifts. Her remaining followers drifted into groups of German farmers in the Hamilton district of Victoria.

See Also Herrnhut Commune; Hill Plains; Krumnow, Johann Frederick

Source:

Meyer, C. 1978. "Two Communes in Nineteenth-Century Victoria." *The Victorian Historical Journal* 49: 204–205.

HENRY GEORGE LEAGUE. The Henry George League attracted followers of economic principles for radical, nonrevolutionary redistribution of wealth through taxation—especially the "single tax"—on land. The modern mix economy owes much to Henry George's (1839–1897) best-selling reform tract *Poverty and Progress* (1879), which gave birth to an antimonopoly movement in the 1880s. George attributed worsening economic inequalities in the United States to unearned profits from rent on land. The remedy he proposed was the single tax, a levy on rent that would eliminate the unintended consequences of the industrializing United States. *The Standard* (1886–1892) won national prominence for its author and gave strength to his two unsuccessful New York mayoralty campaigns. George lectured extensively in the United States and abroad and in England influenced the circle of intellectuals who later founded the Fabian Society. Few economists of reputation supported George's plans, and his ideas had no significant practical result. Even so, his forceful emphasis on privilege, his demand for equal opportunity, and his systematic economic analysis stimulated orderly reform. In the United States Tahanto was the first of a series of single-tax colonies that flourished (1909–1934). Fiske Warren (1862–1937), a paper manufacturer, established the colony thirty-two miles west of Boston. Joseph Fels (1854–1914) was also a notable supporter of the single-tax principle.

See Also Fairhope Colony; Fels, Joseph; George, Henry; Warren, Fiske

Sources:

Cayton, Mary, Elliot Gorn, and Peter Williams, eds. 1993. *Encyclopaedia of American Social History*. New York: Charles Scribner's Sons.

Eatwell, John, Murray Milgate, and Peter Newman. 1987. *The New Palgrave: A Dictionary of Economics*. London: Macmillan.

Jones, Peter d' A. 1991. *Henry George and British Socialism*. New York: Garland Press.

Miller, Timothy. 1990. *American Communes: 1860–1960*. New York: Garland.

Sills, David L., ed. 1968. *International Encyclopedia of the Social Sciences*. New York: Macmillan and Free Press.

Wenzer, Kenneth C. 1997. *I: Henry George Centennial Trilogy; II: An Anthology of Tolstoy's Spiritual Economics; III An Anthology of Single Land Tax*. Rochester, N.Y.: University of Rochester Press.

HERLAND. *Herland* (1915), a utopian novel by the American feminist Charlotte Perkins Gilman (1860–1935), is an important early contribution to women's utopian literature, and includes many ideas that are commonplace today (Kessler, 1995). Three men, Vandyck, Terry, and Jeff, explore Africa and fly into a hidden civilization, Herland. It has existed well without men for 2,000 years. The women are capable, intelligent, and strong and bear children by parthenogenesis. Vandyck is the typically reasonable man, and Terry is sexy, knows, and shows it, while Jeff overestimates women in an effort to manage his feelings toward them. They are the three male types that characterize Western, patriarchal society before World War I. On flying into Herland, the three men are captured and examined as potentially useful objects for Herland's civilization. The society is open-minded, looks forward to change, often rewrites its laws in response to advancing knowledge, alters children's pastimes to ensure they accept change, and advances educational programs to refresh the women's lively intellects and busy activities. Love, devotion, and friendship dominate relations between the people of Herland. At the center of the Herland utopia are a high value on motherhood and insouciance toward sex. The society coheres in outlook, operations, and goals. Little government is required. The primary norm for this cohesive society is that all women mother all children. Consequently, separate areas of interest and activity are integrated, for example, drama with religion, education with drama, music with dancing, education with music, and so on. Because of their Western backgrounds, the three men find Herland society difficult to understand. Compared with Herland, their own society seems amusing and comical. The sexy Terry becomes the center of a dark comedy when the women of Herland consider he might be employed to explore bisexual reproduction. The protective and husbandly Jeff is shown that his apparently normal urges are unnecessary for women, who can look after themselves, while a little understanding of Herland begins to dawn on Vandyck. The author has each man undergo an intellectual courtship and marry. She illustrates how Herland differs from other societies. The three husbands believe marriage implies the man possesses the woman he has sex with; the three wives believe marriage is merely a means to promote social unity, while sex is an uncalled-for alternative to parthenogenesis. In frustration Terry attacks his wife, and their conflict leads him to decide to leave Herland and fly to the civilization he knows. Vandyck, the pilot, must accompany him; his wife decides to come with the two men. There is a sequel to the novel, *With Her in Ourland*.

See Also Gilman, Charlotte Perkins Stetson

Sources:

Gilman, Charlotte Perkins. 1997. *With Her in Ourland: Sequel to Herland*. Edited by Mary Jo Deegan and Michael R. Hill. Westport, Conn.: Greenwood Press.

Karpinsky, Joanne B., ed. 1992. *Critical essays on Charlotte Perkins Gilman*. Boston: G. K. Hall.

Kessler, Carol Farley. 1995. "Review Essay: Recent Work on Charlotte Perkins Gilman." *Utopian Studies* 6: 102–107.

HERRNHUT COMMUNE. Herrnhut was the first commune in Australia's white history and was established in September 1853 close to Hamilton in the colony of Victoria. It was founded by Johann Frederick Krumnow (1811–1880), who named it after a Saxony town where, since 1722, Moravian Brethren had established themselves. Krumnow had twelve followers who accepted the apostolic doctrine, vowed to defend it, and accepted Krumnow as their leader and teacher. Herrnhut aimed to care for the physical and spiritual welfare of its members and of destitutes. Members came from Lobethal, South Australia, and built homes, a church, and a communal kitchen. The Herrnhut members shared all money and property, but authority was kept by Krumnow himself. The community was in great conflict when its membership was augmented by people from Hill Plains community and their leader, Maria Heller (1841–1906), in 1876. When Krumnow died, there were few members at Herrnhut, and the land was heavily in debt. Frau Elmore took over but was unable to inspire the members to the same degree as Krumnow, and the community finally collapsed. The community was not able to get enough new members or retain the current members' children to survive the death of the first generation of members. After forty-four years it was sold in 1889. By 1931 only three houses remained on the site. Probably the physical isolation and the leadership of Krumnow helped Herrnhut survive longer than any other early Australian commune.

See Also Heller, Maria; Hill Plains; Krumnow, Johann Frederick

Sources:

Blake, L. J. 1966. "Village Settlements." *The Victorian Historical Journal* 37: 189–201.
Metcalf, Bill, ed. 1995. *From Utopian Dreaming to Communal Reality: Cooperative Life Styles in Australia.* Sydney: University of New South Wales Press.
Meyer, C. 1978. "Two Communes in Nineteenth-Century Victoria." *The Victorian Historical Journal* 49: 204–205.

HERTZKA, THEODOR. Theodor Hertzka (1845–1924) was born in Budapest and became an economist and journalist. He was editor in chief of the Budapest daily *Magyar Hirlap* (1901). He published two novels, *Freeland; A Social Anticipation* (1889) and *A Visit to Freeland or the New Paradise Regained* (1894). The novels describe a utopian colony in Kenya that upholds peace, equality, public participation in policy making, freedom, culture, and beauty. Europeans are impressed, and both sides of politics, left and right, are converted to the ideal of Freeland. The colony specified the need for a constitution, free entry to all applicants, and the establishment of a board of directors to run the venture, meetings of members, and the payment of a maintenance income for those who cannot work. The central aim of the work was to avoid the pitfalls of both communism and capitalism. At the Equality Colony on Puget Sound, Washington, Alexander Horr (1871–1947) employed principles from *Freeland*. Hertzka founded an international movement and an attempt to establish a utopian community in Africa, but it failed (1893). At first Hertzka's work also interested Theodor Herzl (1860–1904), but later he thought the plan unworkable.

See Also Equality Colony; Herzl, Theodor; Horr, Alexander

Sources:

Hertzka, Theodor. 1889. *Freeland; A Social Anticipation*. English translation by the British Freeland Association, 1891. New York: Appleton. Translated by Arthur Ransom, 1972, New York: Gordon Press.

————. *A Visit to Freeland or the New Paradise Regained*. English translation of *Freiland: ein sociales Zukunftsbild* by Arthur Ransom published by the British Freeland Association, 1894. London: Reeves.

Oved, Yaacov. 1987. *Two Hundred Years of American Communes*. New Brunswick, N.J.: Transaction Books.

Roth, Cecil E., ed. 1971. *Encyclopedia Judaica*. New York: Macmillan.

Snodgrass, Mary Ellen. 1995. *Encyclopedia of Utopian Literature*. Santa Barbara, Calif.: ABC-CLIO.

HERZL, THEODOR. Theodor Herzl (1860–1904) was born in Budapest into a middle-class, Jewish family. As a youth he was interested in writing and technology, and in 1878, following the death of his sister, his family moved to Vienna. He studied law at the University of Vienna and for a year worked as a lawyer in Vienna and Salzburg. He decided to be a writer. He married Julie Naschauer (1868–1907), daughter of a wealthy businessman (1889), had three children, and separated from his wife in the 1890s. He lived in Paris (1891–1895), where he was much affected by the rise of anti-Semitism, and concluded the problem could be solved best by a mass exodus and resettlement of Jews on their own territory. In 1894 he published *The New Ghetto*, an idealized account of the new Jew, aristocratic, virtuous, and one who dies an honorable death in defense of Jewish ideals. In 1895 in *Der Judenstaat* he outlined his plan for a Jewish state. Although influential Jews in Western Europe did not support him, he remained confident the project was feasible. With some changes the plan was published in 1896. His main support came from students in Austria and neighbors from the Movevei Zion. At the first Zionist Congress, Basel, 1897, Herzl was elected president of the World Zionist Organization and remained so until his death from heart failure. In 1903 he published *Altneuland*. The book attracted many followers from Eastern Europe and was influential in the founding of the real Jewish state. Herzl's diaries are published in English and German.

See Also Altneuland; Zionism

Sources:

Beller, Steven. 1991. *Herzl*. London: Halban.

Elon, Amos. 1975. *Herzl*. London: Weidenfeld and Nicolson.

Falk, Israel. 1993. *The King of the Jews: A Psychoanalytic Biography of Theodor Herzl*. Lanham, M.: University Press of America.

Herzl, Theodor. 1903. *Altneuland*. Leipzig: H. Seeman. *Old-Newland*. Translated by Lotte Levensohn. 1941. New York: Bloch.

————. 1941. *The Diaries of Theodor Herzl*. 1962 ed. New York: Scopus.

Loewenberg, Peter. 1971. ''Theodor Herzl: A Psychoanalytic Study in Charismatic Political Leadership.'' In Benjamin B. Wolman, *The Psychoanalytic Interpretation of History*. New York: Basic Books.

―――. 1983. ''Theodor Herzl: Nationalism and Politics.'' In Peter Loewenberg, *Decoding the Past: The Psychohistorical Approach*. 1996 reprint. New Brunswick, N.J.: Transaction.

Pawel, Ernst. 1989. *The Labyrinth of Exile: A Life of Theodor Herzl*. New York: Farrar, Straus, and Giroux.

Stephen, Leslie, and Sydney Lee, eds. 1917. *The Dictionary of National Biography*. London: Oxford University Press.

HILL END. Hill End is an artist's colony in Australia that was based on a community that believed life and art coexist. It was established when George Russell Drysdale (1912–1981) and Donald Friend (1915–1989) went to explore New South Wales (1947). They stopped at an old gold-mining town, Hill End, forty-five miles north of Bathurst, New South Wales. On arriving, they found a handful of townsfolk living on the memory of 50,000 inhabitants and fabulous tales of gold strikes, fossicking, and rabbiting. Eventually, the Hill End artists' colony included Margaret Olley (b.1923), David Strachan (1919–1970), Jeffrey Smart (b. 1921), Jean Bellette (1909–1991), and her husband, the art critic and painter Paul Haefliger (1914–1982). The colony grew and included Brett Whiteley (1939–1992), John Olsen (b. 1928), and John Firth-Smith (b. 1943). In 1995 Rothschild (Australia) sponsored an exhibition of their work, *The Artists of Hill End: Art and Landscape*, at the Art Gallery, Sydney, New South Wales. They depicted the harsh realities of the country and its eerie isolation, and some saw it as a surreal wasteland of the mind. Special paintings of this group were Drysdale's *The Cricketers* (1948), noted for the bowler's frozen delivery, and the haunting *Nuns' Picnic* (1957) by Smart. For years Donald Friend lived at Hill End in a wattle-and-daub hut and produced his noted *Hill End Bacchanal* (1948). Margaret Olley's *Back Buildings* (1948) and Whiteley's *Hill End* (1985–1990) celebrate the town. The group's work represented a cycle of boom, bust, abandonment, and renewal; now a new generation of artists has established itself there through an artist-in-residency program at the Haefliger cottage. Today some artists believe that Hill End is being reinvented, where life and art coexist more spontaneously than ever before.

See Also Drysdale, George Russell; Friend, Donald

Sources:

McCulloch, Alan, and Susan McCulloch. 1994. *The Encyclopedia of Australian Art*. Sydney: Allen and Unwin.

Robb, Gwenda, and Elaine Smith. 1993. *Concise Dictionary of Australian Artists*. Edited by Robert Smith. Melbourne: Melbourne University Press.

Van Nunen, Linda. 1995. ''Golden Summers: In a Harsh Environment, the Artists of Hill End Forged a New Vision of the Australian Landscape.'' *Time (Australia)* (2 August): 71–72.

Wilson, Gavin. 1995. *The Artists of Hill End: Art, Life and Landscape.* Sydney: Art
    Gallery of New South Wales.

HILL PLAINS. Hill Plains, a German community, was established by Maria
Heller (1841–1906), near Benalla, central Victoria, Australia (1875). She had
no money. Presumably, her followers pooled their funds to purchase the land.
It seemed most members were old women and children. They agreed to give
their labor so they could live and worship on the land with her. By the end of
the year about sixty acres were under wheat, but the farm implements and horses
had to be sold to buy food. The community comprised two campsites, one of
ten and the other of over forty. Although both camps were clean, visitors noticed
the members seemed ill. By December 1875 one baby had died, and many other
members suffered from scurvy. They had no money to pay a doctor and relied
on Maria and her grasp of God's will. Food and medicine were sent from Benalla, thirty miles away. Early in 1876 all residents accepted the offer of Johann
Krumnow (1811–1880), leader of Herrnhut, another German community many
miles distant, to join his followers. Conflict between Heller and Krumnow
quickly arose and led to a court case. Heller quit the joint community. Her
followers went to Tabor or other nearby German communities.

See Also Heller, Maria; Herrnhut Commune; Krumnow, Johann Frederick

Source:

Meyer, C. 1978. "Two Communes in Nineteenth-Century Victoria." *The Victorian
    Historical Journal* 49: 204–205.

HINDENBURG, PAUL VON. Paul Ludwig Hans Anton von Beneckendorff
und Hindenburg (1847–1934) was born into a Prussian Junker family, Posen;
educated as a cadet at Wahlstatt and Berlin, he had a successful military career,
became a general (1903), and entered retirement in 1911. In World War I he
came out of retirement and defeated the Russian armies at Tannenburg (1914)
and Masurian Lakes (1915). Unsuccessful on the Western front, he supervised
the German army's retreats in the summer of 1918. In February 1925, when
Friedrich Ebert (1871–1925) died, Germany was without an accepted leader,
and Hindenburg, a national hero, was pressed to become Germany's president.
In April 1925 he announced his candidature, was elected, and sworn in 12 May
1925. As a father figure to many Germans, he was a conservative supporter of
the Weimar Republic and valuable opposition to Adolf Hitler, whom he defeated
for election as president in 1932. In 1933 support for the Weimar Republic was
low, and democratic government was losing favor because the chancellor could
not find support for a reliable governing coalition. Also, Hitler, head of the
popular National Socialists, was demanding that he be made Germany's chancellor, and there were rumors of an army putsch, a Nazi putsch, and a general
strike. Under great pressure, Hindenburg, eighty-six, appointed Hitler Germany's
chancellor, 30 January 1933, in the belief that his influence would be limited.

In fact, the appointment brought German democracy to an end. On Hindenburg's death Hitler combined the roles of chancellor of the Reichstag—Germany's parliament—and the role of the president and made himself Germany's dictator.

See Also Ebert, Friedrich; Hitler, Adolf; Weimar Republic

Sources:

Asprey, Robert B. 1993. *The German High Command at War: Hindenburg and Ludendorff and the First World War*. London: Little, Brown.

Dorpalen, Andreas. 1964. *Hindenburg and the Weimar Republic*. Princeton: Princeton University Press.

Magnussen, Magnus, and Rosemary Goring, eds. 1990. *Chambers Biographical Dictionary*. 5th ed. Edinburgh: Chambers.

Shirer, William L. 1960. *The Rise and Fall of the Third Reich: A History of Nazi Germany*. London: Secker and Warburg.

HITLER, ADOLF. Adolf Hitler (1889–1945) was born in Braunau-am-Inn, Austria, son of Alois Hitler (formerly, Schickelgruber) and his third wife, Klara Poelz. He first worked in Munich as an architect's draftsman, joined the German army in 1914, became a corporal, and was wounded during World War I. While still in the army he joined a socialist group, German Workers' Party, and quickly rose to leadership. Eventually, he changed the name to the Nazi Party. As a result of political crises in Germany during the early 1930s he became chancellor with a coalition government (30 January, 1933). In March 1933 he had passed the "Law for Removing the Distress of the People and Reich," known as the "Enabling Law"; it gave the Reich cabinet, which Hitler controlled, the power of legislation, control of the budget, approval of foreign treaties, and the power to amend the constitution. The law was to be in effect for only four years. On the death of President Hindenburg (1934) Hitler became both president and chancellor; finally, he became a totalitarian dictator with personal control of the German military as well as the German parliament. Political parties other than the Nazis were forbidden, trade unions were suppressed, free speech was curbed, and the secret police were expanded. Jews, Russians, and communists were declared Germany's enemies. In 1936 Hitler began his campaign to conquer Europe by marching into the Rhineland. Britain was obliged to declare war on Germany in 1939 after the Nazi invasion of Poland. By 1941 Hitler's army occupied most of Western Europe. After the entry of the United States into the war and the Allied invasion of Europe, the German advances were limited, and eventually in 1945 Germany was defeated, and Hitler died.

See Also Hindenburg, Paul Von; Hitler's Germany; Weimar Republic

Sources:

Bullock, Alan L. G. 1952. *A Study in Tyranny*. Rev., 1990. Harmondsworth: Penguin.

———. 1992. *Hitler and Stalin: Parallel Lives*. New York: Knopf.

Fest, Joachim C. 1974. *Hitler*. London: Weidenfeld and Nicolson.

Waite, Robert G. L. 1978. *Psychopathic God: Adolf Hitler*. New York: American Library.

HITLER'S GERMANY. Hitler's Germany (1933–1945), the Third Reich, a utopian state that was thought to have a future of a thousand years, is often regarded, as is Stalin's Russia, as a model for modern dystopia. It is characterized by a personal dictatorship, militant anti-Semitic nationalism, subordination of all institutions to a one-party state (especially the press, politics, art, family, industry, religion, leisure, education), a foreign policy of unlimited territorial expansion through military invasion, and racial policy of purification through genocide and murder. Today Hitler's Germany is noted for the Holocaust, the most evil of all political acts in the twentieth century. Countless books have appeared on the Third Reich of Germany; the most popular and comprehensive was by William Shirer (1960), who lived in and wrote about Germany as its utopian Third Reich rose and fell.

See Also Hitler, Adolf

Sources:

Grunberger, Richard. 1974. *A Social History of the Third Reich.* Middlesex, England: Penguin.

James, Donald, and Warren Shaw. 1987. *A Dictionary of the Third Reich.* London: Grafton.

Shirer, William L. 1960. *The Rise and Fall of the Third Reich: A History of Nazi Germany.* London: Secker and Warburg.

Snyder, Louis L., ed. 1981. *Third Reich; A Documentary History.* Chicago: Nelson-Hall.

HODSON, WILLIAM. William Hodson (fl. 1830–1841) was a farmer of Brimstone Hill, a Methodist preacher who married his deceased wife's sister, a practice frowned upon in his local community. He aimed for elimination of envy and conflict, which he thought were the cause of social distinctions, by forming an ideal community where "each for all" was the guiding principle. He was supported at first by Owenites, but later they preferred their own, more orthodox scheme of community development. He became the president and agricultural director of Manea Fen, which prospered so well that it appeared on the way to repaying him his loan within three years of operation. Late in 1839 he toured England, recruiting new members for the community. He believed that his Manea Fen Community was so successful that English socialists and utopians had no longer any need to look to Australia, New Zealand, or the United States. Communitarian settlement in Britain was a far better alternative. He gave up the presidency of Manea Fen to proselytize for the community and uphold its sober, hardworking, businesslike and democratic administration. But by Christmas 1840 his ability to finance the community was threatened, and community members sought to replace him because he was unfit to be a trustee. Hodson argued with the communitarians, and the latter decided to take over the formal management of the community. Before they could, he took away the books. The community split, considerable conflict emerged, and at the end of February in 1841 he was shot.

See Also Manea Fen; Owenite communities

Source:

Armytage, Walter Henry Green. 1961. *Heavens Below: Utopian Experiments in England 1560–1950*. London: Routledge and Kegan Paul.

HOEDADS. Hoedads is a worker-owned forest labor cooperative advocating and practicing radical reafforestation in Eugene, Oregon. With over 300 members, in the early 1980s it was part of the timber industry of the Pacific Northwest. It reafforested under contract to the U.S. Departments of Agriculture and the Interior. The group was founded in 1970 and grew until 1977, when limits were put on membership. Its political influence was established when a supporter, Jerry Rust (fl. 1970–1983) was unexpectedly elected Lane County commissioner in 1976. He was the first president of the Hoedads, and with members' support he beat the fourteen-year incumbent. From this success the Hoedads learned they could affect local community attitudes with their lobbying and conservationist principles relating to herbicide and pesticide research. The cooperative is divided into crews; each crew has a representative in the council, and each of the members has a vote. The council is like a board of directors, elects its president and treasurer annually, meets regularly, and distributes its minutes to all crews. Work crews are small and organized in a collectivist, democratic structure; members live together and rely on working as a team. Crews meet before each new tree-planting contract to discuss and vote on aspects of the contract. The crews believe in collective action rather than in debate on competitive and individualistic employment conditions. The whole cooperative meets regularly, and the full membership votes on controversial policy issues. The activities of the Hoedads have influenced development of other worker cooperatives nearby.

Sources:

Hartzell, Hal, Jr. 1987. *Birth of a Cooperative: Hoedads Inc., a Worker Owned Cooperative Forest Labor Camp*. Eugene, Ore.: Hugolosi.
Jackall, Robert, and Henry M. Levin. 1984. *Worker Cooperatives in America*. Berkeley: University of California Press.

HOLLESLEY BAY COLONY. Hollesley Bay Colony was a labor colony established with the support of the "single tax" advocate Joseph Fels (1854–1914). The colony had a large set of spacious buildings that housed 335 men, homes for farmers on 1,300 acres, thirty cottages, a swimming pool, farm buildings, a wharf, a warehouse on the riverfront, workshops, and a light tramway. Its depressed and dependent inmates led Beatrice Webb (1858–1943) to write unfavorably about the scheme, and the local government was not impressed by its work. Nevertheless, it benefited 11,000 workers until 1914, when Fels died. It continued until 1938, when it was sold for £85,000 and reconverted into a deterrent workhouse.

See Also Fels, Joseph; Webb, Beatrice Martha

Sources:

Armytage, Walter Henry Green. 1961. *Heavens Below: Utopian Experiments in England 1560–1950*. London: Routledge and Kegan Paul.
Dudden, Arthur Power. 1971. *Joseph Fels and the Single Tax Movement*. Philadelphia: Temple University Press.
Fels, Mary. 1916. *Joseph Fels, His Life and Work*. Rev. ed., 1940. New York: Doubleday, Doran.

HOLLOW MEADOWS (SHEFFIELD EXPERIMENT). Hollow Meadows, a workhouse farm experiment on forty-eight acres of reclaimable moorland, was established at Hollow Meadows in 1848. The land was to be worked, reclaimed, and later sublet for profit. Free labor was to be used from the pauper population in Sheffield. A Board of Guardians governed the experiment for which groups of ten men were expected to work diligently, 8:00 A.M. to 5:30 P.M. daily, with no time for resting, under a paid supervisor. Half a day per week was allowed for family visits. By 1854 twenty-two acres had been reclaimed and planted with root crops; in 1853 the experiment had achieved a surplus of sixty pounds. The experiment showed paupers' labor to be productive. The venture was supported vigorously by Isaac Ironside (fl. 1800–1869), a champion of such agrarian communities, for its astounding moral accomplishments, so elevating and humanizing and in tune with the principle ''he that will work not neither shall he eat.'' But when economic conditions improved in Britain, interest in agrarian experiments like Hollow Meadows waned. In May 1851 the Poor Law Commission announced that it had found the management at Hollow Meadows to be irregular and lax. Earlier conflict had arisen between some of the members on the board and the farm manager, who openly shared Ironside's democratic views. The manager was dismissed, and all reclaimable land was sublet to private farmers. Although Ironside supported the view that part of the Hollow Meadows experiment could be self-supporting, in 1854 the Board of Guardians was inclined to lease land to private farmers only. By 1861, fifty acres had been reclaimed and let, and Ironside's influence was no longer clear. The experiment was not repeated on a larger scale, nor did others seek to follow its principles. A year later it became an industrial school for problem pupils in the Sheffield School Board System of Education.

See Also Ironside, Isaac

Sources:

Armytage, Walter Henry Green. 1961. *Heavens Below: Utopian Experiments in England 1560–1950*. London: Routledge and Kegan Paul.
Salt, John. 1960. ''Isaac Ironside and the Hollow Meadows Farm Experiment.'' *Yorkshire Bulletin of Economic and Social Research* 12: 45–51.

HOLY CATHOLIC APOSTOLIC CHURCH (IRVINGITES). The Holy Catholic Apostolic Church, also known as the Catholic Apostolic Church, was a community established by the adherents of Edward Irving (1792–1834) in 1832 after he had been removed from his religious post. He had outraged his church for giving credence to the mystical tongues uttered by a woman in his flock. Twelve of the founders—apostles—of the Apostolic Catholic Church met formally in 1835. Shortly afterward they went on missions to the United States and Continental Europe and helped spread Tractarianism and a growing interest in Catholic doctrines. Their practices were drawn from Roman Catholic, Greek, and Anglican rites. They prepared themselves for the Second Coming, due in 1864, healed the sick with ''sealing'' the wounds (Revelation 7:3), and reintroduced the use of holy water. Often in Holland and Germany their work had to be kept secret; they even gained adherents from among some Roman Catholic priests, and the Prussian nobility provided even more followers. In 1901, after the last of the twelve apostles died, the impact of the church diminished in Great Britain, but in the United States and Germany adherents can still be found. After the founder's death the members of the community became known as Irvingites, a title they thought unacceptable. In London the community had its chief home in a fine Gothic building in Gordon Square.

See Also Irving, Edward

Sources:

Cross, L. A., and E. A. Livingstone. 1997. *The Oxford Dictionary of the Christian Church*. 3d ed. New York: Oxford University Press.

Douglas, James D., ed. 1974. *The New International Dictionary of the Christian Church*. Exeter: Paternoster Press.

Shaw, Plato Ernest. 1946. *The Catholic Apostolic Church, Sometimes Called Irvingite: An Historical Study*. New York: King's Crown Press.

HOLY CITY. Holy City was a colony of thirty followers of the Perfect Christian Divine Way. William E. Riker (1873–1952) was the founder. The colony practiced celibacy at its settlement in central California in the Santa Cruz Mountains, midway between San Jose and Santa Cruz. The community began in 1919, provided housing, clothing, meals, and the means of production to its members, and attracted 200 converts. Riker controlled the government of the Holy City, and its economy was based on agriculture, trade, and mechanics. Members were not paid for work other than getting what they needed at the community's expense. Men and women were segregated, members did not marry, no children were born, and the community's natural future was left to destiny. The community declined, and only twelve remained in 1952, after Riker was charged with sedition.

See Also Riker, William E.

Sources:

Fogarty, Robert S. 1980. *Dictionary of American Communal History*. Westport, Conn.: Greenwood Press.

Hine, Robert V. 1953. *California's Utopian Colonies*. 1983 ed. Berkeley: University of California Press.

HOLYOAK, GEORGE. George Jacob Holyoak (1817–1906) was born into a large Birmingham family in England. He was the eldest son and the second of thirteen children of a notable engineer. Apprenticed to a tinsmith, George later worked at his father's Eagle Foundry as a whitesmith. His father had bought some new machinery for making bone buttons and put his son in charge. He was interested in social reform, joined the Birmingham Reform League (1830), and in the following year joined the Chartist movement. At age seventeen, George became a student at the Old Mechanics' Institute, studied mathematics, and began making mechanical instruments. In 1837 he attended meetings addressed by Robert Owen (1771–1858) and in 1838 enrolled in the Owenite Association of All Classes of All Nations. He was present at the great Chartist riots known as "the Bull Ring Riots" in Birmingham (1839). In 1840 he accepted an invitation from the Owenites of Worcester to work for them at their Hall of Science, one of many centers of educational and propagandist work. Under such influences Holyoak became a rationalist. In 1841 he was one of the editors of *The Oracle of Reason*, published in Bristol. After making a flippant reference to the deity, he was arrested and jailed. A report of the trial was published in 1842, and in 1851 Holyoak wrote *The History of the Last Trial by Jury for Atheism in England*. After his release from prison he drifted away from Owenism.

See Also Owen, Robert; Owenism

Sources:

Fogarty, Robert S. 1990. *All Things New: American Communes and Utopian Movements 1860–1914.* Chicago: University of Chicago Press.
Lee, Sidney, ed. 1920. *Dictionary of National Biography.* Supplement 1901–1911. Oxford, U.K.: Oxford University Press.

HOME COLONY. Home Colony emerged from the failure of Glennis Cooperative Industrial Company (1894–96), a colony on Puget Sound, Washington, that had been inspired by the Bellamy Nationalist movement. It was established by three erstwhile members of the Glennis Cooperative in 1898. They objected to the authoritarianism of the administration. The original group of 40 rose to 54 in a year, reached 155 by 1906, and swelled to 230 by 1910. The colony emphasized individualism and personal freedom—unusual characteristics of communal life—and encouraged free love, free speech, and freedom of ideas. They acquired land and formed the Mutual Home Association, which allowed members to buy between one and two acres to be held in trust by the association; the proceeds were used to purchase more land. In 1909 the Mutual Home Association altered its articles of association to allow members to own property rather than have it held for them in trust. The colony published a weekly anarchist paper, *Discontent: Mother of Progress, New Era*, and *The Agitator*. In 1901, the editors were arrested for publishing obscene material, and the paper closed down, only to be replaced with the *Demonstrator*. From the Ruskin Colony, which had failed in Tennessee, the Cooperative Brotherhood, the Puget Sound Cooperative Colony, and the Equality Colony, reconverted socialists arrived to join the Home Colony. Visitors came from the Koreshans in Chicago, and Elbert Hubbard (1856–1915) of the Roycrofters appeared. Following the assassination of President McKinley (1901) the Home Colony was the butt of much press criticism and was followed by a decline in the spirit of cooperation in the Colony. After World War I, Home Colony became more like a conventional rural community.

See Also Bellamy, Edward; Equality Colony; Hubbard, Elbert Green; Roycrofters; Ruskin Colony

Sources:

Fogarty, Robert S. 1980. *Dictionary of American Communal History*. Westport, Conn.: Greenwood Press.

———. 1990 *All Things New: American Communes and Utopian Movements 1860–1914*. Chicago: University of Chicago Press.

LeWarne, Charles Pierce. 1975. *Utopias on Puget Sound, 1885–1915*. Seattle: University of Washington Press.

Oved, Yaacov. 1987. *Two Hundred Years of American Communes*. New Brunswick, N.J.: Transaction Books.

HOPEDALE COMMUNITY. Hopedale Community was named after the expectations of its founder, Adin Ballou (1803–1890). In January 1851 Ballou and thirty-one associates formed a joint-stock organization to establish ''an order of human society based on the sublime ideas of the Fatherhood of God and the Brotherhood of Man as taught and illustrated in the Gospel of Jesus Christ'' (Ballou, 1897). With a capital of $4,000, 250 acres were purchased in the town of Milford and afterward increased to 600 acres. They advocated nonresistance and promised to abstain from hatred, murder, liquor, military and civil activities, and voting. Road making, building, and various industrial enterprises, including farmwork, provided the economic basis for the community, and religious services were held regularly in the community chapel. A good library and a school were established. In 1856 the membership of Hopedale reached 110, and the joint-stock property was set at $40,000. Ballou edited *The Practical Christian*, and in 1852 he retired. The new community president, with his brother, a recent member of the community, owned three-fourths of the community stock. They decided to withdraw their share of the enterprise. No one could find the funds to make up their share, so the community ended as an economic venture. They invested in the Hopedale Manufacturing Company, became wealthy, and, in time, changed the town from a community of idealists into a modern manufacturing center, the location of the Draper Company. As a moral association the community lasted until 1868, when it merged with the Hopedale Parish, a Unitarian organization of which Adin Ballou remained pastor until 1880. He believed the basic cause of the Hopedale Community's failure was moral, not financial. In its material ambitions lay the germ of its failure. After being encouraged, its members withdrew from community supervision. Eventually, the Draper Company developed an improved loom, which was used to great advantage in the U.S. South, where labor costs were less than those in New England.

See Also Ballou, Adin

Sources:

Ballou, Adin. 1897. *History of the Hopedale Community*. Lowell, Mass.: Thompson and Hill. Reprinted 1972, Philadelphia: Porcupine Press.
Johnson, Allen, ed. 1927. *Dictionary of American Biography*. Vol. 1. New York: Charles Scribner's Sons.
Kersten, Seymour R. 1993. *Utopian Episodes: Daily Life in Experimental Colonies Dedicated to Changing the World*. Syracuse, N.Y.: Syracuse University Press.
Oved, Yaacov. 1987. *Two Hundred Years of American Communes*. New Brunswick, N.J.: Transaction Books.
Perry, Lewis. 1973. *Radical Abolitionism*. Ithaca, N.Y.: Cornell University Press.

HORR, ALEXANDER. Alexander Horr (1871–1947) was born in Hungary and raised an Orthodox Jew. In the 1880s he came to the United States and joined the Freeland Central Association, a group that promoted ideas outlined in Theodor Herzka's *Freeland* (1891). In 1904 Horr published the introduction to the U.S. edition of Hertzka's work. That year Horr joined the Equality Colony on Puget Sound, Washington and, following Hertzka's ideas, reorganized the ailing community. Nevertheless, the community divided, and during one conflict Horr was assaulted (1905). By 1907 the community had fallen into so much internal strife that it was dissolved by court order. Horr went to San Francisco, where he was a member of the Socialist Party, and ran for governor, having put aside his anarchist principles.

See Also Equality Colony; Hertzka, Theodor

Sources:

Fogarty, Robert S. 1980. *Dictionary of American Communal History*. Westport, Conn.: Greenwood Press.
Le Warne, Charles Pierce. 1975. *Utopias on Puget Sound, 1885–1915*. Seattle: University of Washington Press.
Oved, Yaacov. 1987. *Two Hundred Years of American Communes*. New Brunswick, N.J.: Transaction Books.

HOUSE OF DAVID. The Israelite House of David (1903–1928) was founded at Benton Harbor in Berrien County, Michigan, by "Queen Mary and King Benjamin Purnell." The House of David took its origin from the Hebrew Scriptures. Almost 500 followers were there in 1907, and membership peaked at close to 1,000. Some members sailed from Australia and England. The community owned 1,000 acres with many large buildings, including an auditorium, cannery, steam laundry, carpenter shop, tailor shop, coach factory, automobile garage, and power plant. In 1916, when Benjamin's older brother, Jesus, did not arrive as predicted, the community split and by 1920 was involved in a lawsuit. Purnell died in 1929, and the commune was divided between Queen Mary's group, which established the City of David, and another, which continued as the House of David.

See Also Purnell, Benjamin

Source:

Fogarty, Robert. 1990. *All Things New: American Communes and Utopian Movements 1860–1914*. Chicago: University of Chicago Press.

HOWARD, EBENEZER. Ebenezer Howard (1850–1928) originated the Garden City movement and founded Letchworth and Welwyn. He was born in London, son of a confectioner, and was educated at a private boarding school. He worked as a clerk in the city of London. In 1872 he sailed for New York and, after a few months working on a farm, went to Chicago and joined the staff of the official stenographers to the law courts. He returned to England in 1887 and established his own business as a shorthand writer in the law courts. In his late thirties Howard imagined his England as a beautiful land with a canopy of sky, the sun, the wind and the rain, and the dew all embodying a divine love. He drew on the ideas of Edward Bellamy (1850–1898), Henry George (1839–1897), the Fellowship of the New Life, James Silk Buckingham (1786–1855), George Bernard Shaw (1856–1950), Sidney Webb (1859–1947), and Beatrice Webb (1858–1943). Also he was much influenced by the sanitary reformer Dr. Benjamin Ward Richardson (1828–1896) and his *Hygeia* (1875). In 1898, after reading Bellamy's *Looking Backward* (1888), he worked for a new civilization based on service to the community rather than self-interest by building new towns not for profit of individuals but for the interests of inhabitants. He wrote *Tomorrow, a Peaceful Path to Real Reform* (1898), which was republished as *Garden Cities of Tomorrow* (1902). He aimed to remedy overcrowding and unhealthy living conditions due to excessive expansion of large cities. The towns were to be industrial and residential, well planned, limited in size, surrounded by a rural belt with residences within easy reach, and enjoying the advantages of a civilized town life as well as access to the countryside. It was essential in his scheme of ''Garden Cities'' that the town should own the land on which it was situated. He planned a town in about 1888 and called it ''Rurisville,'' but he did not like its French and Latin connotations, so he chose ''Garden City.'' In June 1899 was founded the Garden City Association, and the Garden City Ltd. was incorporated (1903), and Letchworth, Howard's first utopia, began. The association grew rapidly, and in 1919 Howard repeated his work and developed Welwyn in Hertfordshire. Although he was awarded an officer of the Order of the British Empire (OBE) in 1924 and knighted in 1927, he remained poor all his life and until he was seventy had to work as a shorthand writer to support his family. He died at home in Welwyn in 1928.

See Also Bellamy, Edward; Buckingham, James Silk; Garden City; George, Henry; Letchworth; Shaw, George Bernard; Webb, Beatrice Martha; Webb, Sidney James

Sources:

Beevers, Robert. 1987. *The Garden City Utopia: A Critical Biography of Ebenezer Howard*. London: Macmillan.

Buder, Stanley. 1990. *Visionaries and Planners: The Garden City Movement and the Modern Community*. New York: Oxford University Press.

Fishman, Robert. 1977. *Urban Utopias in the Twentieth Century: Ebenezer Howard, Frank Lloyd Wright, and Le Corbusier*. 1982 ed. Cambridge: MIT Press.

Howard, Ebenezer. 1898. *Tomorrow, a Peaceful Path to Real Reform*. London. With a Preface by F. J. Osborne, 1965. Reprinted as *Garden Cities of Tomorrow*, 1902, Cambridge: MIT Press.

Macfadyen, Dugald. 1933. *Sir Ebenezer Howard and the Town Planning Movement*. Manchester: Manchester University Press.

Marsh, Jan. 1982. *Back to the Land: The Pastoral Impulse in England, from 1880 to 1914*. London: Quartet.

McGill, David. 1994. *Lower Hut: The First Garden City*. Lower Hut, New Zealand: Lower Hut City Council.

Weaver, John R. H. ed. 1937. *Dictionary of National Biography 1922–1930*. London: Oxford University Press.

HOWELLS, WILLIAM DEAN. William Dean Howells (1837–1920) was born in Martin's Ferry, Ohio, and at nine began work in his father's printery. Later he was a compositor for the *Ohio State Journal* (1856–1861), wrote poetry, and published a biography of Abraham Lincoln. Writing for *Harper's Magazine* (1886–1891), he became a noted critic and social commentator. Howells was distressed by the absence of a sense of community between workers and employers and hoped that a form of Christian socialism would arise that would create a genuine democracy and communitarian society. He felt community building should become a national policy to ameliorate the industrial class war. In 1894 he published *A Traveler from Altruria*, and its sequel in 1907 was *Through the Eye of a Needle*. The first of these works sketched a utopia, Altruria. One summer, the commentator in the novel, Mr. Homos from Altruria, is a hotel guest of U.S. novelist. Homos says that in Altruria people grew tired of the industrial war; they voted out capitalism and voted in Christian socialism and led an essentially communitarian existence. Altruria is a nation that comprises many villages in which brotherhood is the dominant relationship. Each community is self-sufficient, based on farming, and its workers are protected from competition by the abolition of cities and factories and are secured against financial exploitation and greed by the elimination of money. A central store has everything an Altrurian could want. No person works for another, except voluntarily. No one owns anything; everyone has the right to use anything he or she can. Altrurians live the life of professional socialists, free of dogma and bitter party politics, and everyone is opposed to war. Villages themselves have little intellectual life; so Altrurians travel to their administrative and cultural centers on fast, electrified public transport. Howells' ideas were taken up by Christian socialists in 1894, and, like Edward Bellamy's *Looking Backward* (1888), Howell's work stimulated other communitarian novels. At the time his work was second in influence only to Bellamy's. He belonged to the Brotherhood of the Cooperative Commonwealth, which supported Equality on Puget Sound (1897). Howells wrote short stories, thirty-one plays, and autobiographical works and was well known for his realistic character studies and his insistence on realism in fiction.

See Also Altruria

Sources:

Firkins, Oscar W. 1924. *William Dean Howells: A Study.* Cambridge: Harvard University Press.

Howells, Mildred, ed. 1928. *Life in Letters of William Dean Howells.* 2 vols. Garden City, N.Y: Doubleday, Doran.

Howells, William Dean. 1893. *My Year in a Log Cabin.* New York: Harper and Brothers.

Oved, Yaacov. 1987. *Two Hundred Years of American Communes.* New Brunswick, N.J.: Transaction Books.

Snodgrass, Mary Ellen. 1995. *Encyclopedia of Utopian Literature.* Santa Barbara, Calif.: ABC-CLIO.

Spann, Edward K. 1989. *Brotherly Tomorrows: Movements for a Cooperative Society in America 1820–1920.* New York: Columbia University Press.

HOWLAND, EDWARD. Edward Howland (1832–1890), born in Charleston, South Carolina, into a cotton merchant family, was privately educated and graduated from Harvard College (1853). He cofounded a literary journal, the *New York Saturday Press*, and by 1869, when the journal folded, he had become a devoted Fourierist. In 1865 he married Marie Stevens Case (1835–1921), and they settled in Hammonton, New Jersey, where he wrote on social reform. As a freelance writer he produced a life of Ulysses Grant (1868) and commentaries on travel in North America and the railroads. He was elected state master in southern New Jersey (1873), and when he and his wife became acquainted with Albert K. Owen (1847–1916), they became greatly interested in his Topolobampo Bay Colony. Howland wrote on the experiment in industrial relations at Guise in France (1876), indicating how conflict could be managed, and industrial harmony could be achieved. Owen wanted Howland's views on industrial reorganization, and in the 1880s Marie and Edward publicized Owen's scheme and jointly edited *Integral Cooperation.* Edward suffered locomotor ataxia and with his wife went to live in Topolobampo, believing the climate would benefit his health. He was a strong supporter of social cooperation and thought it would save civilization from excessive strife. He died at the colony.

See Also Howland, Marie Stevens; Owen, Albert Kimsey; Topolobampo Colony

Sources:

Fogarty, Robert. 1990. *All Things New: American Communes and Utopian Movements 1860–1914*. Chicago: University of Chicago Press.
Howland, Edward. 1874. *The Palace of Industry: Or the Workingmen's Home*. New York: Leavitt.
———. 1893. Topolobampo Collection, 1872–1910. Special Collections, Geisel Library, University of California, San Diego.

HOWLAND, MARIE STEVENS. Marie Stevens Howland (1835–1921) had to begin work at age twelve in a textile mill, Lowell, Massachusetts, after her father died (1847). In the 1850s she went to New York City, where she worked as a teacher and married a lawyer. During the late 1850s she lived at Unity House, where she met Edward Howland (1832–1890). She had a varied life and became interested in photography and free love. She divorced and in 1864 married Howland, and they went for a year to J. B. Godwin's Familisterie during the Civil War (1861–1865). In 1868 the Howlands settled at Hammonton, New Jersey, where their home became a part of the radical Hammonton Vineland. Among their visitors were Albert Brisbane (1809–1890) and Albert Kimsey Owen (1847–1916) and other social radicals from New York and Philadelphia. She published a utopian romance, *Papa's Own Girl* (1874), which went through three editions and was mooted to be a prototype for Edward Bellamy's *Looking Backward* (1888). The Howlands were strong supporters of the scheme for Pacific City at Topolobampo and joined the Topolobampo Colony. Marie left the colony in 1894 after the scheme failed and went to Fairhope Colony in Alabama, the single-tax settlement, which followed the ideas of Henry George (1839–1897). She became the colony's librarian and wrote for the Fairhope *Courier*.

See Also Bellamy, Edward; Brisbane, Albert; Fairhope Colony; George, Henry; Howland, Edward; Owen, Albert Kimsey; Topolobampo Colony; Unity House

Sources:

Fogarty, Robert S. 1990. *All Things New: American Communes and Utopian Movements 1860–1914*. Chicago: University of Chicago Press.
Spann, Edward K. 1989. *Brotherly Tomorrows: Movements for a Cooperative Society in America 1820–1920*. New York: Columbia University Press.

HUBBARD, ELBERT GREEN. Elbert Green Hubbard (1856–1915) was born in Bloomington, Indiana. In Chicago he worked as a journalist (1872–1876) and wrote advertising copy. After travels in Europe (1895) he settled in East Aurora, Erie County, New York, where he established the Roycroft shops for handicrafts and the Roycroft Printing Shop and Press. It was named after the noted seventeenth-century printer Thomas Roycroft (fl. 1654–1677), who was appointed by Charles II as king's printer of Oriental languages and who produced the polyglot Bible (1654–1657) and edited many classics. The shop supported and developed many artisans and artists who formed a community and were known as "Roycrofters." Hubbard founded *The Philistine*, a pocket-sized magazine of social reform and criticism that he printed, edited, and maintained until his death. In 1908 he founded the *FRA*, a larger magazine. He printed *Little Journeys to the Homes of Good Men and Great* (1894), a miscellany of biographical sketches. He also wrote novels and essays. He was the author of *A Message to Garcia*, a plea for efficiency and duty based on an incident during the Spanish-American War (1898). Sometimes he wrote under the name of FRA, Elbertus. His social reform and utopian interest in craft, printing, and art were inspired by William Morris (1834–1896) and his Kelmscott Press in England. He and his wife died when the Germans torpedoed the *Luisitania*, April 1915. His works were reprinted by John T. Hoyle (fl. 1873–1928).

See Also Morris, William; Roycrofters

Sources:

Chernow, Barbara A., and George A. Vallasi. 1993. *The Columbia Encyclopedia*. 5th ed. New York: Columbia University Press.
Fogarty, Robert S. 1980. *Dictionary of American Communal History*. Westport, Conn.: Greenwood Press.
Hoyle, John Thomas. 1915. *In Memoriam. Elbert and Alice Hubbard*. East Aurora, N.Y.: Roycrofters.

HUGHES, THOMAS. Thomas Hughes (1822–1896), born in Uffington, Berkshire, was educated at Rugby and Oriel College at Oxford. In 1848 he married and was called to the bar. Between 1865 and 1874 he was a Liberal member of Parliament and aligned himself with the Christian socialists and supported trade unionism and the establishment of the Workingmen's College, London. He was principal of the college (1872–1883) and helped found a model settlement in Tennessee, which flourished for seven years. On a visit to the United States (1879), he and some friends bought a large estate in Tennessee for the establishment of a model community, to be called "Rugby." The purchasers were not accurately informed about the productive value of the estate and became deeply distressed by the inadequacy of their purchase. Hughes quit the enterprise. He wrote *Tom Brown's Schooldays* (1856), which was based on his experiences at Rugby under Dr. Thomas Arnold, who was headmaster. He wrote a sequel, *Tom Brown at Oxford* (1861), and several biographies in social studies.

See Also Rugby Colony

Sources:

Drabble, Margaret, ed. 1985. *The Oxford Companion to English Literature*. 5th ed. New York: Oxford University Press.
Fogarty, Robert. 1990. *All Things New: American Communes and Utopian Movements 1860–1914*. Chicago: University of Chicago Press.
Lee, Sidney, ed. 1920. *Dictionary of National Biography: Supplement 1901–1911*. London: Oxford University Press.

Magnussen, Magnus, Rosemary Goring, and John O. Thorn, eds. 1990. *Chambers Biographical Dictionary*. Edinburgh: Chambers.

HUNTSMAN, MASON T. Mason T. Huntsman (fl. 1880s) was born in Stroudsburg, Pennsylvania. His parents died when he was eight, and he lived for ten years with a farming family. At thirty-one he underwent a religious conversion and changed his name to Paul Blandin Mason. He let his hair and beard grow and had the appearance of a prophet. In 1887 he began to attack the village of Park Ridge, New Jersey, as immoral and corrupt. In response the residents attacked his home and trimmed his beard and long hair. ''Brother Paul,'' as he was known, was arrested for Sabbath-breaking, conspiracy to defraud, kidnapping, rape, and running a disorderly house. In 1889 he was in prison for blasphemy and impersonating the Savior. Also he abducted two young women after persuading them to follow his quietist religious beliefs. After his release from prison he established Lord's Farm at Woodcliff, New Jersey. Locals called community members the ''Angel Dancers'' because they allegedly danced nude. Lord's Farm was known also as Woodcliff Community. Eventually, he was evicted by his brother, and shortly afterward Lord's Farm was disbanded.

See Also Woodcliff Community

Sources:

Fogarty, Robert S. 1980. *Dictionary of American Communal History*. Westport, Conn.: Greenwood Press.
Schroeder, Theodore. 1919. *Anarchism and the Lord's Farm*. (Microform) Reprinted, 1987. Alexandria: Chadwyck-Healey.

HUTTER, JACOB. Jacob Hutter (d. 1536) was born at Moos in the South Tyrol. Some say he had little basic education; others, that he was well educated. He became a wandering Swiss hatmaker—his name means ''hatter'' Early in life he joined the Anabaptists and in 1529 became their leader. He advocated the practice of adult baptism, rejection of oaths, passivism, and nonassimilation. From 1531 he led the Hutterian Brethren in Moravia, a haven for the sect. He helped organize a refuge for his followers and formed communities of them near Auspitz. The pattern of organization was retained, but Hutter was persecuted and for safety fled for the Tyrol, where he was captured, tortured, and put to death at the stake. Communities that had found asylum in Moravia under his leadership established settlements based on the communal ownership of property. They were persecuted and wandered extensively, and some of their descendants emigrated to the United States.

See Also Hutterites

Sources:

Eliade, Mircea, ed. 1987. *Encyclopedia of Religion*. New York: Macmillan.
Melton, Gordon, ed. 1989. *The Encyclopedia of American Religions*. Detroit, Mich.: Gale Research.

Oved, Yaacov. 1987. *Two Hundred Years of American Communes*. New Brunswick, N.J.: Transaction Books.

HUTTERITES. Hutterites were Anabaptists who escaped religious persecution in Central Europe in the fourteenth century and fled to the Tyrol and Moravia. They rejected the practice and belief in baptism, emphasized community ownership of goods, and modeled their religion on the primitive church of Jerusalem. Their name comes from Jacob Hutter (d. 1536). They lived modestly on collective farms of 60–150 members, educating their children and keeping away from local politics. Persecuted in Middle Europe and unable to get religious tolerance in Russia, approximately 800 Hutterites migrated to the United States between 1874 and 1876. Half settled on family farms, eventually affiliated with the Mennonite Church, and ceased to be part of the Hutterite community; the others established three colonies or ''leut'' (German for ''people'') in South Dakota. Each leut or community was named for its founder: Schmiedeleut, after Michael Waldner, a ''schmeide'' (German for ''blacksmith''), is the oldest of the leuts (1850s); Dariusleut, after Walter Darius, a preacher; and Lehrerleut. Schmiedleut was established in Bon Homme (1874), Dariusleut was founded in Silver Lake (1874–1875), and Lehrerleut was established in Old Elm Spring (1877). Each community organized, disciplined, and administered its religious and communal life in its own way. The growing numbers in each community led to the communities' being divided. When a colony reached 100–150, it would split and establish a new colony. Families would stay intact and form units as the base of the new settlement; the old commune would buy more land and clear it, and when membership reached 150, the planned split occurred, and a new settlement emerged. Lots were cast to determine membership for the new colony. By 1918 the Schmiedeleut had founded nine colonies. During World War I local communities rejected Hutterites because they were Germans and pacifists. Gradually, they abandoned their colonies and relocated in Manitoba, for example, Buffalo Colony, later the James Valley Colony. In 1983 there were 138 Schmiedeleut colonies in the United States; often neighbors still disapprove of their pacifism, misinterpret their culture, suspect their German lifestyle, and disapprove of their high birthrate. They live from agriculture and chicken farming and occupy over 100 colonies in Canada and the High Plains states, and their number is over 25,000. Notable colonies are Pincher Creek Colony, Canada; Spokane Colony; in Washington state, Warden, Stahlville, and Marlin; and others are being established. Communities are self-sufficient economically and careful when they buy from outside the community and have sufficient funds to meet the expectations of a growing population. They use a traditional division of labor—men labor on farms, women in the home—and the community members are closely related through religion, the German language, and educational practices (Fogarty, 1980). Hutterites have suffered for their pacifism but have not lost their community through it. In 1898 during the Spanish-American War the Dariusleut established a colony in their dominion city, Manitoba, with the intention of moving to Canada should military conscription be introduced. Jamesville Colony, the second Hutterite Colony of the Dariusleut, was raided by locals in 1918 for refusing to buy war bonds in support of U.S. efforts in World War I. When the community could not achieve the status of conscientious objectors, they moved to Alberta, Canada. Some Hutterites were put in Alcatraz Prison for refusing to wear military uniforms. In response many others emigrated to Canada. In 1935 some returned to the United States, while others remained in Canada. After World War II there were nineteen communities. They flourish today. In the United States and Canada the well-known settlements are Bon Homme, Silver Lake, Old Elmspring, Kutter Colony, Redlands (Alberta), Walls Creek, Maxwell Colony (Alberta), Milford Colony, Milltown Colony, New Elmspring (Alberta), Spink Colony (Alberta), Wolf Creek (Alberta), Spring Creek (Alberta), Tidioute, Tripp, and Warren Range (Alberta). Hutterites have attracted many scholarly studies.

See Also Hutter, Jacob

Sources:

Berry, Brian J. 1992. *America's Utopian Experiments: Communal Havens from Long-Wave Crises.* Hanover, N.H.: University Press of New England.

Clasen, Claus P. 1972. *Anabaptism: A Social History 1525–1618: Switzerland, Moravia, South and Central Germany.* Ithaca, N.Y.: Cornell University Press.

Erasmus, Childs. 1977. *In Search of the Common Good: Utopian Experiment Past and Present.* New York: Free Press.

Flint, David. 1975. *The Hutterites: A Study in Prejudice.* Toronto: Oxford University Press.

Fogarty, Robert S. 1980. *Dictionary of American Communal and Utopian History.* Westport, Conn.: Greenwood Press.

Hosteller, John A. 1974. *Hutterite Society.* Baltimore: Johns Hopkins University Press.

Hosteller, John A., and Gertrude Huntington. 1967. *The Hutterites in North America.* New York: Holt, Rinehart, and Winston.

Janzen, William. 1990. *Limits on Liberty.* London: University of Toronto Press.

———. 1992. "Limits on Liberty: The Experience of Mennonite, Hutterite and Doukhobor Communities in Canada." *University of Toronto Law Journal* 42: 239–246.

Lanbach, Ruth Baer. 1993. "Colony Girl: A Hutterite Childhood." In Wendy E. Chmielewski, Louis J. Kern, and Marlyn Klee-Hartzell, eds., *Women in Spiritual and Communitarian Societies in the U.S.*, pp. 241–255. Syracuse, N.Y.: Syracuse University Press.

Lippy, Charles H., and Peter W. Williams, eds. 1988. *Encyclopedia of American Religious Experience.* New York: Charles Scribner's Sons.

Oved, Yaacov. 1987. *Two Hundred Years of American Communes.* New Brunswick, N.J.: Transaction Books.

Packull, Werner O. 1995. *Hutterite Beginnings: Communitarian Experiments during the Reformation.* Baltimore: Johns Hopkins University Press.

Peters, Victor. 1965. *All Things Common: The Hutterite Way of Life.* Minneapolis: University of Minnesota Press.

————. 1987. *The Dynamics of Hutterite Society.* Edmonton: University of Alberta Press.

Pickering, William S. F. 1982. *The Hutterites: Christians Who Practice a Communal Way of Life.* London: Ward Lock Educational.

Rexroth, Kenneth. 1974. *Communalism: From Its Origins to the Twentieth Century.* New York: Seabury Press.

Youmans, Vance Joseph. 1995. *The Plough and the Pen: Paul S. Gross and the Establishment of the Spokane Hutterian Bretheren.* Boone, N.C.: Parkway.

HUXLEY, ALDOUS. Aldous Leonard Huxley (1894–1963) was the grandson of Thomas Henry Huxley (1825–1895), the noted British scientist and mentor to Herbert George Wells (1866–1946). Aldous was educated at Eton, studied at Oxford, and found his aspirations to science limited by eye disease. He befriended Lady Ottoline Morrell (1873–1938) and other literary, political, and intellectual luminaries and wrote for John M. Murry's (1889–1957) *The Antheneum* in 1919 and a series of celebrated and amusing satires and novels about his wayward acquaintances and associates, for example, *Chrome Yellow* (1921), *Antic Hay* (1923), and *Point and Counter Point* (1928). He lived in Italy in the 1920s. In 1926 his visit to the United States confirmed a hostile view he held toward mass production as established by Henry Ford (1863–1947) and the luxuriant hedonism evident among residents of Los Angeles and southern California. In 1926–1927 his elitist view of politics changed when he renewed his acquaintance with D. H. Lawrence (1885–1930) and witnessed firsthand the degeneration of Italy's politics into brutal fascism. In 1932 he published *Brave New World*, his most noted work, and later *Eyeless in Gaza* (1936). To save his eyesight and feeling much defeated by his unsuccessful efforts to promote pacifism, Huxley went to live in California. He published *Doors of Perception* (1954) and his later experiments with mind-altering drugs, *Heaven and Hell* (1956). In *Brave New World Revisited* (1958) he reviewed his pessimistic approach to utopia in *Brave New World* and considered it may be with us sooner than expected. Later, he published a positive utopian novel, *Island* (1962), in which a spiritual belief system is successfully applied to everyday life.

See Also Brave New World; Dystopia; Murry, John Middleton

Sources:

Beauchamp, Gorman. 1990. "*Island*: Aldous Huxley's Psychedelic Utopia." *Utopian Studies* 1: 57–72.

Bedford, Sybille. 1973–1974. *Aldous Huxley: A Biography.* 2 vols. London: Chatto and Windus/Collins.

Deery, June. 1996. *Aldous Huxley and the Mysticism of Science.* London: Macmillan.

Huxley, Aldous L. 1932. *Brave New World.* 1950 ed. with new foreword by author. London: Chatto and Windus.

————. 1958. *Brave New World Revisited.* London: Chatto and Windus.

Kumar, Krishan. 1987. *Utopia and Anti-Utopia in Modern Times*. Oxford: Basil Black-
    well.
Snodgrass, Mary Ellen. 1995. *Encyclopedia of Utopian Literature*. Santa Barbara, Calif.:
    ABC-CLIO.

I

ICARIAN MOVEMENT. The Icarian movement comprises several U.S. communities originally organized in 1848 by the French utopian socialist Étienne Cabet (1788–1856) and based on his ideas in *Voyage en Icarie* (1840). The Icarian movement of Étienne Cabet is a story of utopian dreams and splitting communities. In general, the communities dreamed of a society that placed all economic activity under the guidance and control of elected officials and made the family the only other politically influential unit. Icarian communities comprise several major splinter groups: the first was established for three months in Texas in 1848; the Texas community went to an abandoned Mormon settlement, Nauvoo, Illinois, for eleven years, 1849–1860; at Nauvoo emerged the Cheltenham group, which went to suburban St. Louis for six years, 1858–1864, while others from Nauvoo went to Corning, Iowa, for eighteen years, 1860–1878; a conservative splinter group at Corning formed New Icaria for twenty years, 1878–1898, while a progressive splinter group at Corning formed Jeune Icarie (Young Icaria) for eight years, 1878–1886; from the Jeune Icarie community emerged a final splinter group that went to Cloverdale, California, and formed Icaria Speranza for five years, 1881–1886.

See Also Cabet, Étienne; Cheltenham; Corning; Speranza; Texas-Nauvoo

Sources:

Fogarty, Robert S. 1980. *Dictionary of American Communal History.* Westport, Conn.: Greenwood Press.

Hine, Robert V. 1953. *California's Utopian Colonies.* 1983 ed. Berkeley: University of California Press.

Kesten, Seymour. 1993. *Utopian Episodes: Daily Life in Experimental Colonies Dedicated to Changing the World.* Syracuse, N.Y.: Syracuse University Press.

Mumford, Lewis. 1922. *The Story of Utopias.* 1962. New York: Viking.

Oved, Yaacov. 1987. *Two Hundred Years of American Communes.* New Brunswick, N.J.: Transaction Books.

Snodgrass, Mary Ellen. 1995. *Encyclopedia of Utopian Literature*. Santa Barbara, Calif.: ABC-CLIO.

Sutton, Robert P. 1994. *Les Icariens: The Utopian Dream in Europe and America*. Urbana: University of Illinois Press.

INDUSTRIAL VILLAGES. Industrial villages were utopian experiments that offered inhabitants a planned alternative to the residential sprawl in manufacturing centers that had appeared in the wake of the fast-growing industrialization of work, that is, the rapid transformation of work from farm to factory (c. 1750–1920). The industrial villages provided a practical example for a better urban life. The ideas of dissenting individuals during the seventeenth century combined with millennial dreams to produce a flurry of small villages. Many of them were developed by Quaker families that had been successful in business and felt they gained from the labor of those who were treated badly. In these villages the housing was sound, the holdings were small, and each boasted a garden; inhabitants were sometimes ensured against illness, the vagaries of old age, and unemployment; shops and mills were operated as cooperatives; and education and medical care were free. To residents the price was paternalistic control based on what had been practiced under manorial life. These began around 1700 and continued through the era of Robert Owen (1771–1858) to the advent of the New Towns. The industrial village was utopian instrument of social reform in Victorian England. Port Sunlight, Bournville, and New Earswick were models for industrial city expansion—in them the concerns for work, welfare, and environment were blended—and given to an overarching body. The second function of these villages was to provide a working model that could be refined and extended to meet the aims of the industrialist.

See Also Bournville Experiment; New Earswick; Port Sunlight

Sources:

Fishman, Robert. 1977. *Urban Utopias in the Twentieth Century: Ebenezer Howard, Frank Lloyd Wright, and Le Corbusier*. 1982 ed. Cambridge: MIT Press.

Gill, Roger. 1984. "In England's Green and Pleasant Land." In Peter Alexander and Roger Gill, eds., *Utopias*, pp. 109–117. London: Duckworth.

Grubb, Isobel. 1930. *Quakerism and Industry before 1800*. London: Williams and Norgate.

Meller, Helen E., ed. 1979. *The Ideal City*. Leicester: Leicester University Press.

Raistrick, Arthur. 1938. *Two Centuries of Industrial Welfare: The London (Quaker) Lead Company 1692–1905; The Social Policy and Work of the Governor and Company for Smelting Down Lead etc.* Rev. ed. 1977. Buxton, England: Moorland.

Stein, Clarence S. 1957. *Towards New Towns for America*. Cambridge, Mass: MIT Press.

IRONSIDE, ISAAC. Isaac Ironside (fl. 1800–1869) was born in Masborough of working-class parents, was educated at a Lancastrian School, and age twelve was apprenticed to a stove-grate fitter. He worked hard and with enterprise became a successful estate agent and railway shareholder and made a fortune.

In 1830, ambitious to rise socially, he aligned himself with radical Whigs and wanted the vote for everyone but in time became disillusioned with his associates' middle-class attitudes to social reform and turned vigorously to Chartism and the Owenites. To Ironside Robert Owen's (1771–1858) ideas would lead to universal happiness. In 1839 he visited Manea Fen. By 1842 he considered seriously the founding of Hollow Meadows Community, a utopian farm that would remove from the workhouse the poor of Sheffield and have them do dignified agricultural work. After seeing the failure of Owen's Queenwood venture, Ironside modified his plans for Hollow Meadows and pursued them with vigor. He was never officially associated with Hollow Meadows, but in public he insisted that it was the most effective means to employ and benefit both physically and morally, hundreds of impoverished unemployed in Sheffield. In May 1848 the poor were on the edge of rebellion in Sheffield. Ironside demanded an inquiry into the efficacy of the workhouse as a means to solve the problem of poverty because the system was failing, and inmates were in despair, wretched and hungry. He pressured the Sheffield Board of Guardians, which was responsible for administering the Poor Laws in the district for many years, to support the Hollow Meadows venture. To a degree they followed his advice, but with great misgiving. By 1853, after some success, the Guardians defeated Ironside's efforts to have all paupers transferred from the workhouse to Hollow Meadows. By 1854 over fifty acres of the farm were reclaimed and sublet. The venture was a failure for Ironside, and for years his vigorous efforts to relieve the poor were denigrated. In 1869, for all his eccentricities, demagoguery, and socialist theories, he was accused of trying to establish Hollow Meadows as an abode of love!

See Also Hollow Meadows (Sheffield Experiment); Manea Fen; Owen, Robert; Owenite communities

Source:

Salt, John. 1960. ''Isaac Ironside and the Hollow Meadows Farm Experiment.'' *Yorkshire Bulletin of Economic and Social Research* 12: 45–51.

IRVING, EDWARD. Edward Irving (1792–1834), born at Annan, Dumfries, in Scotland, was tutored privately and graduated from the University of Edinburgh (1809). He taught mathematics for two years and became a licensed preacher in the Church of Scotland (1815). In 1822 Irving was minister of the Caledonian Asylum chapel in Hatton Garden, London, where he became a popular preacher. Many of his eloquent sermons were published in *For the Oracles of God* (1823). His popularity fell when, in 1825, he predicted the Second Coming for 1864. Later, he was charged with heresy for his radical views in his *Doctrine of the Incarnation Opened* (1828) and especially on the human nature of Christ in his tract *The Orthodox and Catholic Doctrine of Our Lord's Human Nature* (1830). Later that year came evidence of unknown tongues speaking religious truths. Consequently, he was prosecuted for heresy; he was found not guilty, but in

1832 he was removed from the pulpit. His followers—including at one time Robert Owen (1771–1858)—gathered and later called themselves the Holy Catholic Apostolic Church, and Irving was their head. Nevertheless, his status as a clergyman was removed in Scotland (1833). He still preached widely and on his return to London from Scotland found himself deposed from his own congregation. Shortly after, he died, and twelve members of the Holy Catholic Apostolic Church carried his work forward and became known as "Irvingites."

See Also Holy Catholic Apostolic Church (Irvingites)

Sources:

Dallimore, Arnold. 1983. *The Life of Edward Irving: The Forerunner of the Charismatic Movement.* Edinburgh: Banner of Truth Trust.

Oliphant, Margaret O. W. 1860. *The Life of Edward Irving: Minister of the National Scotch Church, London: Illustrated by His Journals and Correspondence.* London: Hurst and Blackett.

Stephen, Leslie, and Sydney Lee, eds. 1917. *The Dictionary of National Biography.* London: Oxford University Press.

Whitely, Henry C. 1955. *Blinded Eagle: An Introduction to the Life and Teaching of Edward Irving.* London: S.C.M. Press.

ISRAELITES (NEW HOUSE OF ISRAEL). The Israelites (New House of Israel) was a Canadian sect known as the Flying Roll, which settled on 144 acres donated to them by a family in East Texas. The group comprised vegetarians, followed Mosaic Law, and recruited seventy-five local families (1900). In the community they built a church called New House of Israel. The men had long hair and beards. When the high priest died, no one took the leadership, the families moved away, and in the early 1920s Israel was a ghost town in Texas.

See Also Purnell, Benjamin

Source:

Fogarty, Robert S. 1980. *Dictionary of American Communal History.* Westport, Conn.: Greenwood Press.

ITTOEN—FRIENDS OF THE LIGHT. Ittoen, meaning "garden of one light," can be found in the suburbs of the old imperial city of Kyoto, Japan. Established in 1905 by one of Japan's leading spiritual teachers of the twentieth century, it has a membership of over 200 people who are devoted to a spiritual way of life. The founder, Tenko Nishida (1872–1968), came from a well-to-do merchant family. At age twenty, with only a primary school education, he chose, in place of military service, to help cultivate land in the underdeveloped northern island of Hokkaido. Under the encouragement of the governor of his district, he induced 100 families to join him and rent 2,000 acres. At thirty-two he left his family and home behind, spent several days meditating in a small Buddhist temple, and decided to undertake the life of Roto, that is, a homeless beggar. In time he advocated homelessness, unpaid service to others, and no possessions.

Roto is now defined by Ittoen as the spiritual state of an individual who is not attached to knowledge, pride, or worldly love and does not feel resentful of physical or mental suffering. Nonattachment affords a true spiritual freedom, in the same way as homelessness offers a true physical freedom. In 1928 on the hillside above Yamashina, Kyoto, twenty-five acres were given to the movement, and the community flourished with the admission of new members and the birth of their children. On Tenko's death the administration of Ittoen passed to his grandson, Takeshi Nishida. Today Ittoen receives occasional bequests or gifts of money, and at present virtually all of its support comes from its various highly successful business enterprises. The oldest of these is the printing department, which began in 1927. It prints a monthly magazine with a circulation of 1,600 among the Friends of Light, and much of its work is for business outside the community. The agricultural department sells, primarily by mail, more than sixty varieties of rice seed. There are large greenhouses growing a variety of vegetables, and they also raise and sell bamboo shoots and mushrooms.

Source:

Popenoe, Cris, and Oliver Popenoe. 1984. *Seeds of Tomorrow*. San Francisco: Harper and Row.

J

JANCO, MARCEL. Marcel Janco (1895–1984), a noted Dadaist painter, was commissioned by the Israeli government to search the mountains of Israel to find a place for a national park. In the hills around Mount Carmel he came across a stone village that had been deserted by the Arabs when fleeing the Israeli militia during the Israeli war of independence. Feeling deeply that the village ought to be preserved, Janco proposed that it would be a fine site for an artists' colony. On 1 May 1953, with artists from Haifa and Tel Aviv, Janco entered the ruined stone village. People chose their homesites and began work. The group members spent the week in the city, working at their normal jobs, and spent each weekend to rebuild the village. From the ruins emerged Ein-Hod, an artists' utopia, and Janco became its first mayor.

See Also Ein-Hod

Source:

Popenoe, Cris, and Oliver Popenoe. 1984. *Seeds of Tomorrow*. San Francisco: Harper and Row.

JANSSON, ERIK. Erik Jansson (1808–1850) was a controversial, strict, and autocratic religious leader from Sweden. In 1845 he had to flee New York because he was about to be jailed for the second time. In 1846, 700 of his followers joined him at Bishop Hill Colony in Illinois. In 1850 he was shot to death by the lover of a colonist whom he had forbidden to marry.

See Also Bishop Hill Colony

Source:

Fogarty, Robert. 1990. *All Things New: American Communes and Utopian Movements 1860–1914*. Chicago: University of Chicago Press.

JARLANBAH. Jarlanbah is an Australian eco-village, Jarlanbah Eco-Regional Association (JERA), in the subtropical mountains of northern New South Wales near the Queensland border. It is on the fringe of the existing Nimbin Community formed in the 1970s. Half is held in common, and the remainder is divided into forty-three twenty-two hectare (fifty-five acres) blocks for private ownership. Less than half the area will be used for residences. The community plans to have a hall, library, laundry, playground, and recreational facilities. Members are part owners of common ground and facilities. The houses are sited and designed to maximize the use of new technologies of waste disposal and power supply and to fit into the landscape. On the common ground dams have been built to regenerate the rain forest, woodlots have been set aside for cabinetmaking, and timber has been planted for sustainable commercial ventures. Corridors of orchards line the roads, and solar houses are clustered to blend into the environs. The community has been designed according to the principles of permaculture. It has built a community cooperative where goods and labor are bartered. The community was alienated at first from the Nimbin Community due to the former's free enterprise values and opposition to traditional development methods and their contribution to urban sprawl. Jarlanbah aims to provide a cooperative life that enriches, rather than depletes, both humankind and the environment. For this reason at least one member from each dwelling is expected to learn permaculture.

See Also Permaculture

Sources:

Lloyd, Graham. 1994. "Nimbin, the Happening." *Herald Sun Weekend*, 3 September: 8–9.
Trainer, Ted. 1995. *The Conserver Society: Alternatives for Sustainability*. London: Zed Books.

JEHOVAH'S WITNESSES. Jehovah's Witnesses are a utopian religious movement founded in 1872 that follows the *Bible* in its literal sense. Through its identification with God—sometimes in a grandiose delusion of greatness—the movement promotes the idea of a religious utopia in heaven after the world has come to an end. The movement was established by Charles Taze Russell (1852–1916) and Joseph Franklin ("Judge") Rutherford (1869–1942). Members reject the Holy Trinity, the deity of Jesus Christ, the Holy Spirit, all military service, and blood transfusions. As the world comes to an end, believers assert, there will be 144,000 Jehovah's Witnesses forming the elect in heaven. Active believers are noted for the zeal of their door-to-door proselytizing. With worldwide printeries the movement follows an effective propaganda campaign under the name of "Watch Tower Bible and Tract Society." The movement is named after Jehovah, God's personal name, which was revealed to be the case by Moses on Mount Horeb (Exodus 3:13–15). The term comes from Hebrew Yahweh, *Y H V H*. Among the Jews the word became too sacred to be uttered, so from

c. 300 B.C. it was replaced with "Adonai," meaning "Lord" in Hebrew. Later, the vowels *A O A* were inserted between the four letters of *Y H V H*, and Yaweh became the term for God; later, this appeared as "Jehovah," God's personal name.

Sources:

Cross, L. A., and E. A. Livingstone. 1997. *The Oxford Dictionary of the Christian Church.* 3d ed. New York: Oxford University Press.

Douglas, James D., ed. 1974. The New International Dictionary of the Christian Church. Exeter: Paternoster Press.

Penton, M. James. 1985. *The Story of Jehovah's Witnesses.* Toronto: University of Toronto Press.

Stroup, Herbert H. 1945. *The Jehovah's Witnesses.* New York: Columbia University Press.

Zusne, Leonard. 1987. *Eponyms in Psychology: A Dictionary and Sourcebook.* Westport, Conn.: Greenwood Press.

JERUSALEM. Jerusalem was a community established by the Society of Universal Friends (1788) and founded by Jemima Wilkinson (1753–1819), the "Public Universal Friend." The members accepted the statements by Jemima that she was divinely inspired because in 1774 she had been raised from the dead. In 1789 she and her followers from Connecticut, Massachusetts, and Rhode Island decided to leave home to establish a community in Yates County, New York. In this community there would be no marriages, and all things were to be held in common, as had been so with the early followers of Christ. She led over 100 followers 500 miles to their Jerusalem. Only briefly did her Jerusalem survive its founder.

See Also Wilkinson, Jemima

Sources:

Fogarty, Robert S. 1980. *Dictionary of American Communal History.* Westport, Conn.: Greenwood Press.

Hudson, David. 1821. *History of Jemima Wilkinson: A Preacheress of the Eighteenth Century; Containing an Authentic Narrative of Her Life and Character, and of the Rise, Progress and Conclusion of Her Ministry.* Geneva, Ontario, and New York: S. P. Hull. Later published as *Memoir of Jemima Wilkinson.* 1844. Bath, N.Y.: R. L. Underhill.

Wisbey, Herbert Andrew, Jr. 1964. *Pioneer Prophetess: Jemima Wilkinson, the Publick Universal Friend.* Ithaca, N. Y.: Cornell University Press.

JOHN LEWIS PARTNERSHIP. The John Lewis Partnership, protected by a trust, was organized in 1918–1920 and administers a large British department store and its branches in the interests of its employees; it now belongs to all who work in the firm, and they share in its prosperity.

See Also Lewis, John Spedan

Sources:

Flanders, Allen, Ruth Pomeranz, and Joan Woodward. 1968. *Experiment in Industrial Democracy: A Study of the John Lewis Partnership.* London: Faber and Faber.
Marsh, Arthur. 1979. *Concise Encyclopedia of Industrial Relations.* Westmead, Farnborough, and Hants: Gower.

JOHNSON, SAMUEL. Samuel Johnson (1709–1784), son of a bookseller, was born in Lichfield, Staffordshire. He read voraciously. He was educated at the local grammar school and attended Pembroke College, Oxford (1728–1731), left without a degree, taught before marrying a widow, twenty years his senior, and opened a school with her in Lichfield. It failed and he was forced to live in London and do hack writing for a living (1738–1746). An incessant reader from childhood, he indulged this passion further as he cataloged the great library of the earl of Oxford. In 1747 he wrote a prospectus for a dictionary of the English language, and worked on it for eight years, and when it appeared, he was awarded an M.A. at Oxford (1755). Meanwhile, he wrote biographical pieces, poems, commentaries, and moral essays. In 1752 his wife died, his mental depression deepened, and he became noted for being ever more peevish and slovenly in dress, eccentric, indolent, and arrogant. Living in Grub Street (now Milton Street), London, he was England's celebrated man of letters, literary dictator of England. In the Latin tradition he wrote essays, satires, poems, and, in a neo-classical style, with its Latinate, awkward, and generally complicated style, produced fiction, classical tragedies, and criticism. He received a doctorate at Oxford (1775) and, when offered patronage by the English statesman and man of letters Lord Chesterfield (1694–1773), indignantly refused and continued to write to earn a living. On the death of his mother in 1759 he wrote his didactic, utopian, moral fable *Rasselas, Prince of Abyssinia* (1759) in one week to offset the costs of her funeral. Material for the work had become available to Johnson when he translated from the French *A Voyage to Abyssinia* (1735) written by a Portuguese missionary. The work describes a young and isolated group's unsuccessful search for happiness, an experience also denied Johnson for a lifetime. In the following year, when George III (1738–1820) became king, Johnson received a pension sufficient for his financial security. In 1763 he met James Boswell (1740–1795), a Scot, who became a friend and would write Johnson's biography, the most revered in English literature. Dr. Johnson established a literary circle in London (1764) and published a critical edition of Shakespeare's plays and a ten-volume study of noted English poets (1779–1781). In his final years the unexpected marriage of a much-loved woman friend, recently widowed (1781), depressed him further. He died unwell and miserable and was buried at Westminster Abbey. His outstanding literary reputation was enhanced by the publication of Boswell's *Life of Doctor Johnson LL.D* (1791).

See Also Rasselas, Prince of Abyssinia

Sources:

Cunningham, J. S. 1982. *Samuel Johnson: The Vanity of Human Wishes and Rasselas.* London: Arnold.
Irwin, George. 1971. *Samuel Johnson: A Personality in Conflict.* Auckland: Auckland University Press.
Ousby, Ian, ed. 1988. *The Cambridge Guide to Literature in English.* 1995 ed. Cambridge: Cambridge University Press.
Snodgrass, Mary Ellen. 1995. *Encyclopedia of Utopian Literature.* Santa Barbara, Calif.: ABC-CLIO.
Wain, John. 1974. *Samuel Johnson.* London: Macmillan.

JONES, JAMES WARREN. James Warren Jones (1931–1977) was born in Lynn, Indiana. His mother was the center of family life, and she behaved toward the child as if he were destined to be a savior. As a boy he practiced the skills of an authoritarian preacher with his age peers. In the late 1950s he founded the Peoples Temple in Indiana. He preached racial brotherhood and helping the poor. In 1965 the growing congregation moved to California. In 1977 the Peoples Temple sought refuge from criticism to a compound, Jonestown, in Guyana, where in November, following the visit and murder of a U.S. congressman, Senator Leo J. Ryan, Jim Jones mustered his followers, announced the killing of Ryan and others, and began a "revolutionary suicide," a ritual that had earlier been rehearsed.

See Also Jonestown (Peoples Temple)

Sources:

King, Martin. 1993. *Preacher of Death.* Melbourne: Penguin.
Klineman, George, Sherman Butler, and David Conn. 1980. *The Cult That Died: The Tragedy of Jim Jones and the Peoples Temple.* New York: Putnam.
Lindsey, Robert. 1978a. "How Jim Jones Gained His Power over Followers." *New York Times Biographical Service* 9 (November): 1052–1055.
———. 1978b. "Jim Jones—from Poverty to Power over Many Lives." *New York Times,* 26 November.
McCormick, Maaga, and Catherine Wessinger. 1988. *Hearing the Voices of Jonestown.* Syracuse, N.Y.: Syracuse University Press.
Reston, James, Jr. 1981. *Our Father Who Art in Hell: The Life and Death of Jim Jones.* New York: Times Books.

JONESTOWN (PEOPLES TEMPLE). Jonestown is a symbol of a dystopian horror that involved a mass suicide-murder among members of a religious cult in Guyana at Jonestown. In 1977 in response to newspaper and magazine criticism of James Warren Jones' (1931–1977) politics—antiracism, anti-capitalism, antinuclear arms—the Peoples Temple congregation left the United States and established a compound in the jungle of Guyana. In November 1977 Senator Leo J. Ryan went to Guyana to investigate charges that Jones was holding people against their will. When attempting to leave after the investigation, Ryan and others were shot to death. Shortly afterward Jones led a suicide-murder ritual in which he poisoned most of his followers. Over 900 members of the Peoples Temple settlement died when, under the direction of their religious leader, they drank poison. Official investigators, survivors, and defectors provided information and social psychological studies of the once-loved utopian community. Jonestown attracted many interpretations and analyses in an effort to understand why such a horrible disaster took place. It is often compared with a similar event at Waco, Texas.

See Also Dystopia; Jones, James Warren

Sources:

Ahlberg, Sture. 1986. *Messianic Movements: A Comparative Analysis of the Sabbations, the Peoples Temple, and the Unification Church.* Stockholm: Almqvist and Wiksell International.

Barker, Eileen. 1986. "Religious Movements: Cult and Anti-Cult since Jonestown." *American Review of Sociology* 12: 329–346.

Chidester, David. 1988. *Salvation and Suicide: An Interpretation of Jim Jones, the Peoples Temple, and Jonestown.* Bloomington.: Indiana University Press.

Endleman, Robert. 1993. *Jonestown and the Manson Family: Race, Sexuality and Collective Madness.* New York: Psyche Press.

Feinsod, Ethan, and Odell Rhodes. 1981. *Awake in a Nightmare: Jonestown, the Only Eyewitness Account.* New York: Norton.

Hall, John R. 1987. *Gone from the Promised Land: Jonestown in American Cultural History.* New Brunswick, N.J.: Transaction Books.

Kilduff, Marshal, and R. Jevers. 1978. *Suicide Cult: The Inside Story of the People's Temple Sect and the Massacre in Guyana.* New York: Bantam Books.

Kroth, Jerry. 1992. *Omens and Oracles: Collective Psychology in the Nuclear Age.* New York: Praeger.

Moore, Rebecca. 1986. *The Jonestown Letters: Correspondence of the Moore Family, 1970–1985.* Lewiston, N.Y.: Edwin Mellen Press.

———. 1988. *In Defense of Peoples Temple.* Lewiston, N.Y.: Edwin Mellen Press.

Moore, Rebecca, and Fielding McGehee III, eds. 1989. *New Religious Movements, Mass Suicide and the Peoples Temple.* Lewiston, N.Y.: Edwin Mellen Press.

Osherow, Neal. 1984. "Making sense of the Non-Sensical: An Analysis of Jonestown." In Elliot Aronson, ed., *Readings about the Social Animal*, pp. 68–86. New York: W. H. Freeman.

Ulman, Richard B., and D. Wilfred Abse. 1983. "The Group Psychology of Mass Madness: Jonestown." *Political Psychology* 4: 637–662.

U.S. Congress House Committee on Foreign Affairs. 1979. *The Assassination of Representative Leo J. Ryan and the Jonestown Guyana Tragedy.* Washington, D.C.: U.S. Government Printing Office.

Wooden, Kenneth. 1981. *The Children of Jonestown.* New York: McGraw-Hill.

K

KAFKA, FRANZ. Franz Kafka (1883–1924) was born in Prague and graduated in law but never practiced. He worked in a government insurance office, wrote prolifically, and published little. Before he died of tuberculosis—his last years were in a sanatorium—he asked a friend born in Prague, the Austrian novelist, poet and dramatist Max Brod (1884–1968), to destroy all his scripts. Instead, between 1935 and 1937 Brod published Kafka's work. The work reflects Kafka's view of stark tragedy tinged with dark, strange humor and a classic beauty. He is noted for his imagery of individuals' isolation, bewilderment at their loss of identity in an evil world of oppressive red tape, meaningless bureaucracy, and inner rebellion against such pressures. He used strange and absurd settings, emphasized alienation, guilt, and shame as prime motives, and drew characters that were in constant fear of being watched and followed by distant authorities. His influence on the Western literature that examines the impact of institutional life has been deep and broad. *Der Prozess* (*The Trial*, 1925, trans. 1937) and *Das Schloss* (*The Castle*, 1926, trans. 1937) are his two best-known works. In both novels the hero is placed under official duress and, despite the most apparently sensible efforts, can never learn why. Today the two novels are outstanding works of dystopian fiction.

See Also Castle, The; Dystopia; *Trial, The*

Sources:

Brod, Max, ed. 1948. *The Diaries of Franz Kafka*. New York: Schocken.

———. 1960. *Franz Kafka: A Biography*. Translated. G. Humphreys Roberts and Richard Winston. New York: Schocken.

Glatzer, Nahum N., ed. 1974. *I Am a Memory Come Alive: Autobiographical Writings of Franz Kafka*. New York: Schocken.

Hawkins, Joyce M., ed. 1986. *The Oxford Reference Dictionary*. Oxford: Clarendon.

Hayman, Ronald. 1982. *Kafka: A Biography*. New York: Oxford University Press.

Pawel, Ernst. 1984. *The Nightmare of Reason: A Life of Franz Kafka*. New York: Harper. 1992 ed. New York: Noonday, Farrar, Straus, and Giroux.

KALEVAN KANSA. Kalevan Kansa was a short-lived utopian commune founded by a Finn, Matti Kurikka (1863–1915), on the coast of Queensland, Australia. Early in 1900 Kurikka began a long march with his devoted followers from the Queensland coast near Cooktown to establish a utopia on the Gulf of Carpentaria. Many members starved and had to eat wild honey and roots to survive. As distress and misery deepened among his followers, he was blamed for their feelings, and many deserted him. He felt he had to arm himself against possible attack. By July 1900 the experiment was over. The Queensland government had supported the venture and agreed that Kurikka had been honest and well meaning but quite impractical; some of his fellow countrymen thought that his efforts were based on a dream rather than reality and that Kurrika's attitude to women brought the experiment down, as well as his unconventional views on communal child raising.

See Also Kurikka, Matti; Sojntula

Source:

Metcalf, Bill, ed. 1995. *From Utopian Dreaming to Communal Reality: Cooperative Life Styles in Australia*. Sydney: University of New South Wales Press.

KANSAS COOPERATIVE FARM. Kansas Cooperative Farm was the original name of a community known as Silkville and as Prairie Home Colony. In 1869 the articles of association of the Kansas Cooperative Farm were drawn up. It throve in Silkville, Kansas (1870–1884).

See Also Boissiere, Ernest Valeton de; Prairie Home Colony

Source:

Fogarty, Robert S. 1980. *Dictionary of American Communal History*. Westport, Conn.: Greenwood Press.

KAWEAH CO-OPERATIVE COMMONWEALTH. Kaweah Co-operative Commonwealth flourished in California (1885–1892). James J. Martin (fl. 1884–1914) and Burnette G. Haskell (1857–1907), two militant labor leaders of the International Working Men's Association in San Francisco, organized Kaweah socialist colony after reading *Co-operative Commonwealth* (1884) by Laurence Gronlund (1846–1899). The book translated Karl Marx (1818–1883) into practical terms for Americans. Over forty men, mainly skilled laborers from trade unions, claimed 600 acres of the timber mills of Sierra Nevada in Tulare County. They took advantage of the Timber Act (1878) and the Homestead Act (1862). The community was named Kaweah Colony after the river flowing through the acreage. Members were a curious group of dress-reform cranks, artists, vegetarians, word purists, musicians, anticapitalists, Bellamyites, spiritualists, orthodox Christians, and intelligent book readers. Members were advised to read works by Gronlund, Albert Kimsey Owen (1847–1916), and Marie Stevens Howland (1835–1921). The colony flourished between 1885 and 1892 and comprised 400 members, most of whom were affiliated with the Bellamy movement. Edward Bellamy (1850–1898) thought the commonwealth could not succeed unless it was placed on a national footing. The economy was based on time spent at work: no work, no food. All workers got thirty cents an hour. Membership cost $500: $100 in cash, the rest in labor or goods. Until cabins were built, residents lived in tents. They built a dining-meeting hall, cabins, school, kindergarten, print shop, blacksmith, barn, and sheds. They had literary and scientific discussions, held dances and picnics, and went swimming. Through the great forest they built a magnificent road. In 1890 Gronlund himself joined as a nonresident member and was made the commonwealth's secretary. Because funds were not available to bring him and his family from Boston to California, he did not serve locally as secretary in the colony. Conflicts over the legal identity of the colony led to its being turned from a voluntary association into the Kaweah Co-operative Commonwealth Company of California Limited, a joint-stock company. Members divided over trivial matters and were poorly led, and finally the whole community was threatened by external interests that wanted access to the magnificent timberland they occupied. The community was charged with illegal tree felling and mail fraud. By November 1891 the time-work system had all but collapsed. In April 1892 the socialist dream dissolved, and after the U.S. government evicted the community, the area eventually became the Sequoia National Park.

See Also Bellamy, Edward; Haskell, Burnette; Howland, Marie Stevens; Martin, James J.; Marx, Karl; Owen, Albert Kimsey

Sources:

Fogarty, Robert S. 1980. *Dictionary of American Communal History*. Westport, Conn.: Greenwood Press.

Hine, Robert V. 1953. *California's Utopian Colonies*. 1983 ed. Berkeley: University of California Press.

Johnpol, Bernard K., and Harvey Klehr, eds. 1986. *Biographical Dictionary of the American Left*. Westport, Conn.: Greenwood Press.

Oved, Yaacov. 1987. *Two Hundred Years of American Communes*. New Brunswick, N.J.: Transaction Books.

KEIL, WILHELM. Wilhelm Keil (1812–1877) was born and raised in Europe and in the mid-1830s emigrated to the United States. He earned his living in New York as a tailor. Next he turned to medicine, even though he had no medical education and was not officially registered as a doctor. He practiced medicine effectively because he was a persuasive character and could convince his listeners to concentrate on their health. He broadened his knowledge of chemistry and, following the craft of witch doctors, learned how to prepare several exotic medicines. By combining these skills with his intuitive understanding of human beings, he began to cure patients and was called ''Doc'' by many people. Some evidence suggests he became a preacher in the Methodist Church, which later he quit to form a sect of his own based on his belief that he was one of the witnesses mentioned in the Book of Revelation. In 1844 Keil and his followers went to establish their Christian community, Beth El, in northeastern Missouri. Keil appeared to be a benevolent autocrat and a dictator. He and his followers had no definite tenets since he refused to form any theories, regarded the Bible as their theoretical foundation, and maintained that their communal practices should grow spontaneously. About 250 members left during 1847 because of Keil. Under his rule the colony grew to 1,000 members on 4,000 acres by the early 1850s. In 1853 a small group left Beth El to explore Oregon County and to select a location for a new home. They chose a tract of land on the Willapa River at Aurora, Oregon. In 1855 Keil moved to Oregon himself and remained a strong force there until 1871, when colony pressure forced him to relinquish the colony lands to individual owners.

See Also Beth El Community

Sources:

Fogarty, Robert S. 1980. *Dictionary of American Communal History*. Westport, Conn.: Greenwood Press.

Nordhoff, Charles. 1875. *The Communist Societies of the United States*. 1961 ed. New York: Hillare House.

Oved, Iaacov. 1987. *Two Hundred Years of American Communes*. New Brunswick, N.J.: Transaction Books.

KELLY, HARRY. Harry Kelly (c. 1871–1953) was raised in Missouri, his father having died when Harry was only five years old. To support the family, Harry had to leave school. He learned the printing trade. At age twenty he had become a wanderer, drifting from city to city. In 1894 he settled briefly in Boston and was drawn to anarchism. He went to New York and was the first organizer of the Ferrer organization, promoted its anarchist cause, and maintained its daily operations. In 1915 with Joseph Cohen (1881–1953) and Leonard Abbott (1878–1953) he helped the Ferrer organization move to Stelton, New Jersey, to establish itself as a school-centered colony. In 1923 he left the colony and in 1925 started the Mohegan Colony at Lake Mohegan, New York, and later the Mount Airy Colony at Harmon, New York. The first was like Stelton and had its own school, but Mount Airy did not. Kelly died in New Rochelle.

See Also Abbott, Leonard; Cohen, Joseph; Ferrer Colony

Sources:

Fogarty, Robert S. 1980. *Dictionary of American Communal History*. Westport, Conn.: Greenwood Press.

Veysey, Laurence. 1973. *The Communal Experience: Anarchist and Mystical Counter-Cultures in America*. New York: Harper and Row.

KELPIUS, JOHANN. Johann Kelpius (1673–1708) was born in Halwegen, Germany, and died at Coxsackie, Pennsylvania. He was educated in Tübingen and graduated from the University of Altdorf near Nuremberg (1689) with a Ph.D. in liberal arts and mathematics. Shortly afterward he published philosophical papers and was drawn to the Pietists' movement. At age twenty he founded the "Society of the Women of the Wilderness" and led forty members to the United States, where he helped found the "Women in the Wilderness Community." The move to the United States was taken in the belief that in 1694 the kingdom of heaven would establish itself on earth. When it did not, Kelpius simply postponed the millennium and kept his following. After he died, the community disintegrated.

See Also Women in the Wilderness Community

Sources:

Fogarty, Robert S. 1980. *Dictionary of American Communal History.* Westport, Conn.: Greenwood Press.

Oved, Yaacov. 1987. *Two Hundred Years of American Communes.* New Brunswick, N.J.: Transaction Books.

KENDAL. Kendal, an Owenite community, was established in 1826 with worshipers who had lived together well before they had become familiar with the ideas of Robert Owen (1771–1858). Unlike many Owenites, they made no agreement among themselves to uphold egalitarianism, so questions about the equality of duties, opportunities, and rights never vexed them, as it had others. Also, their leader, Samuel Underhill (1776–1859), who followed Owenite principles, denied the superiority of one religious persuasion over another. In its first year Kendal was more like a traditional utopian community than an Owenite gathering. In 1827 the colonists at Forestville, Coxsackie, New York, emigrated to Kendal Community. Kendal lasted longer than other Owenite communities. This could be explained by their common religious bond and because the question of equality did not arise to divide them. However, according to one Kendal resident, only a freakish summer fever in 1828 killed the heads of seven families and ended the experiment at Kendal. But, according to records of the community meetings, what destroyed the community was the members' inability to get along with each other. In the fall of 1828 members asked to be released from the community, and one by one they moved away. So the equality they had sought could not be realized.

See Also Owen, Robert

Sources:

Harrison, John F. C. 1969. *Robert Owen and the Owenites in Britain and America: Quest for the New Moral World.* New York: Charles Scribner's Sons.

Kesten, Seymour. 1993. *Utopian Episodes: Daily Life in Experimental Colonies Dedicated to Changing the World.* Syracuse, N.Y.: Syracuse University Press.

Kolmerten, Carol A. 1990. *Women in Utopia.* Bloomington: Indiana University Press.

Oved, Yaacov. 1987. *Two Hundred Years of American Communes*. New Brunswick, N.J.: Transaction Books.

Pitzer, Donald E., ed. 1972. *Robert Owen's American Legacy*. Indianapolis: Indiana Historical Society.

KENWORTHY, JOHN COLEMAN. John Coleman Kenworthy (1861–c. 1934), Ph.D., an English leader of radical Christians, was born in Liverpool and was much influenced by, or collaborated with, anarchists and communitarians like Thomas Carlyle (1795–1881), John Ruskin (1819–1900), Henry George (1839–1897), and Peter Kropotkin (1842–1921), the Russian exile. In 1890 on his way to the United States to help establish utopian rural communities, Kenworthy read Leo Tolstoy's (1828–1910) work and was deeply impressed. In eighteen months he returned to settle in Canning Town for two years, hoping to establish a cooperative society with Mansfield House University Settlement. These ideas and experiences led to his writing *The Anatomy of Misery, Plain Lectures on Economics* (1893). Also in 1893 he published essays and addresses, *The Christian Revolt*. In 1894 appeared his *From Bondage to Brotherhood*. In June 1884 he opened a Brotherhood Church at Croydon for intellectuals seeking spiritual regeneration. Also he published a magazine, *New Order*, which collected and disseminated information on intentional communities worldwide. He wanted to plan for what he called the ''right social order'' for appropriate members who should actively confront capitalist organization with fraternal organization and see that divisions in society—its ''wounds,'' he called them—must be healed from within. This would require psychological honesty, economic socialism, political communism, and militant pacifism. Kenworthy wrote to the Doukhobors' leader Peter V. Verigin—Peter the Lordly—(1859–1924), who was drawn to Kenworthy's ideas of a Christian brotherhood and called his Russian followers ''the Christian Community of Universal Brothers.'' In the winter of 1895–1896 he went to Moscow, where Leo Tolstoy gave him the rights to publish and benefit from some of Tolstoy's writings in English. Kenworthy gave moral and material aid to the migration of Doukhobors, a much persecuted group of religious pacifists, to Cyprus and later to Canada (1899). In February 1897 he helped establish Purleigh Colony on lines that Tolstoy had given. Kenworthy endorsed many of its anarchist principles and built a house at the colony (1898). Kenworthy's account of meeting Tolstoy appeared as *A Pilgrimage to Tolstoy* (1896) and a biography, *Tolstoy: His Life and Works* (1902). At the end of his life Kenworthy was confined to a lunatic asylum. Kenworthy promoted the English Land Colonisation Society (1893) to help city dwellers escape urban blight.

    See Also Bracher, Samuel V.; Doukhobors; Purleigh Colony; Tolstoy, Leo; Tolstoyan communities

Sources:

Armytage, Walter Henry Green. 1961. *Heavens Below: Utopian Experiments in England 1560–1950*. London: Routledge and Kegan Paul.

Who Was Who in Literature 1906–1934. Reprinted, 1979. Detroit: Gale Research.
Woodcock, George, and Ivan Avakumovic. 1968. *The Doukhobors.* London: Faber and
　　Faber.

KHRUSHCHEV, NIKITA SERGEYEVICH. Nikita Sergeyevich Khrushchev
(1894–1971) was born in Kalinkova, in Kursk Province, son of a miner and
peasant. He was a farm laborer, plumber, and locksmith and joined the Communist Party in 1918; by 1929 he had been trained as a party organizer. He
became a member of the Central Committee of the party (1934) and secretary
of the Moscow District Party Committee (1934–1938), was elected to the Polit-
buro (1939), and made general secretary of the Ukraine (1938–1946, 1947–
1953). When the Ukraine was occupied by Nazi Germany he was a lieutenant
general. He became the premier of the Ukraine (1944–1947) and secretary of
the Communist Party (1953–1964). Meantime, he eliminated the top levels of
its leadership and replaced his own nominee, Nikolai A. Bulganin (1895–1975)
as premier (1958–1964). He was forced out of office in October 1965.

Sources:

Frankland, Mark. 1966. *Khrushchev.* Harmondsworth: Penguin.
Martin, Kingsley, ed. 1958. *The Vital Letters of Russell, Khrushchev, Dulles, with an
　　Introduction by Kingsley Martin.* London: MacGibbon and Kee.
Medveder, Roy A. 1982. *Khrushchev.* Translated by Brian Pearce. Oxford: Blackwell.
Pistrak, Lazar. 1961. *The Grand Tactician: Khrushchev's Rise to Power.* New York:
　　Praeger.
Taubman, William, ed. and trans. 1990. *Khrushchev on Khrushchev: An Inside Account
　　of the Man and His Era by His Son Sergei Khrushchev.* Boston: Little, Brown.

KHRUSHCHEV'S RUSSIA. In 1956 Nikita Krushchev (1894–1971) presented
a utopian vision for a pure society in communist Russia to be established in the
early 1960s. The outline was given to eighty-one representatives of the Communist Party governments meeting in Moscow. It assumed the Communist Party
would always direct the future of society; it denounced Stalin's totalitarianism
and rejected his "cult of the individual," preferring a pure collective leadership;
and a peaceful coexistence with capitalism until it was defeated; and it announced that a timetable would be laid down for the attainment of communism
everywhere. It was announced that Russia was completing its goal of building
world socialism and would continue to lead other communist nations to this
goal. For many years this vision held the attention of communist-inspired intellectuals and social moralists. It ended when Krushchev was sent into political
obscurity in 1965.

See Also Khrushchev, Nikita Sergeyevich

Sources:

Chotinery, Barbara A. 1984. *Khrushchev's Party Reform: Coalition Building and Insti-
　　tutional Innovation.* Westport, Conn.: Greenwood.

Dallan, David J. 1964. *From Purge to Coexistence: Essays on Stalin's and Khrushchev's Russia.* Chicago: H. Regnery.

Frankland, Mark, trans. 1979. *Khrushchev, Nikita: Anatomy of Terror.* London: Greenwood.

Medveder, Roy A., and Zhores A. Medveder. 1976. *Krushchev: The Years in Power.* New York: Columbia University Press.

KIBBUTZ. A kibbutz (meaning "in-gathering") is a modern form of Jewish settlement that began early in the twentieth century. The kibbutz emerged under the guidance of the World Zionist organization when Jews began to emigrate to Palestine (1880s) and reconstruct Jewish society based on a close connection with the land, brotherhood, equality, and mutual help. Earlier Jewish settlements all over the world had similar utopian ideals. The Marranos settled in Colombia in the sixteenth century; the Sephardim settled in Costa Rica in the eighteenth century; there was a Jewish society in China that traced back to the ninth and tenth centuries; German Jews arrived in Guatemala in 1848, and the first communal group was established in 1870. In Peru in 1870 a group of European Jewry formed the Sociedad de Beneficencia Israelita. In East Africa the first Jewish settlers came to Nairobi in 1903, and the first community was founded in 1904. In the 1880s in Palestine, Jews settled on farms bought with funds given by wealthy Jewish families; professional agronomists provided technical supervision. From this grew the kibbutz movement. The first was a community, Deganiah ("God's wheat"), comprising two women and ten men who settled on 750 acres on the east bank of the Jordan at the Sea of Galilee (1907). They were an extended family who took meals communally. The Israeli statesman and soldier Moshe Dayan (1915–1981) was the first child born there. Similar settlements emerged, and the kibbutz movement began and led to a significant element in the establishment of the state of Israel today. The original group did not want to follow the form of early Jewish settlements. Instead, the group rebelled against the arbitrary methods of the manager and received reluctant permission to establish their own farm without administrator, supervisor, or overseer. The group wanted a utopian communal way of life based on equality, no private ownership of the means of production, no exploitation of labor, and use of the production, property, and functions of the kibbutz for each according to his or her ability and to each according to his or her needs. Finally, the group wanted mutual aid and mutual responsibility so they were free from worries over their family life. Also all people should have a say and the right to vote on issues that might affect everyone. Since 1907 much has changed, and different kinds of kibbutzim have developed, and some early utopian principles have been undermined or thwarted. For example, people do not share all their possessions; some have bank accounts and electric appliances while others do not. Originally, their life was based on agriculture, but whenever it failed, manufacturing began. Many are now in debt to banks. Outsiders were admitted to help make uneconomic activities viable, and large salaries were paid to consultants and managers. People did not have to seek the advice or views of kibbutz members for the decisions that would affect the kibbutz. Today there are debates about raising the morale of kibbutz members, encouraging them to work harder and cut down on waste, privatization principles, whether to seek mutual aid and cooperation, offering large rewards for greater efforts, and finding ways to adapt to changes in the outside world. Many scholars have written on kibbutzim.

See Also Altneuland; Herzl, Theodor; Yodfat

Sources:

Bedford, John. 1990. *Kibbutz Volunteer*. Oxford: Vacation Work.

Bowes, A. M. 1989. *Kibbutz Goshen*. Prospect Heights, Ill.: Waveland Press.

Dror, Yuval. 1994. "Social Education—Bridging between Education and Social Systems; Owen's Utopian Education and Kibbutz Education Today—a Comparison." *Utopian Studies* 5, no. 2: 87–102.

Le Selle, Sallie. 1972. *The Family Communes and Utopian Societies*. New York: Harper and Row.

Lerman, Antony, ed. 1989. *The Jewish Communities of the World*. London: Macmillan.

McCord, William. 1989. *Voyages to Utopia: From Monastery to Commune, the Search for the Perfect Society in Modern Times*. New York: W. W. Norton.

Near, Henry. 1992. *The Kibbutz Movement: A History*. 2 vols. New York: Oxford University Press.

Oved, Yaacov. 1987. *Two Hundred Years of American Communes*. New Brunswick, N.J.: Transaction Books.

Spiro, Melford E. 1956. *Kibbutz: Venture into Utopia*. Boston: Harvard University Press. 1963 ed., New York: Schocken.

Rabin, A. I. 1973. "Kibbutz Child-Rearing and Personality Development." In Rosabeth Moss Kanter, *Communes: Creating and Managing the Collective Life*, pp. 381–392. New York: Harper and Row.

Warhurst, Christopher. 1994. "The End of Another Utopia? The Israeli Kibbutz and Its Industry in a Period of Transition." *Utopian Studies* 5, no. 2: 103–121.

Yassour, Avraham. 1995. *Change: Values and Institutions in a Modern, Changing Kibbutz*. Haifa, Israel: University of Haifa Press.

KINGDOM OF HEAVEN COLONY. The Kingdom of Heaven Colony was established on 480 acres near Walla Walla, Washington, by William W. Davies (1833–1906) in 1867. With forty followers Davies had come from a Mormon community in Utah after the death in 1862 of its leader, Joseph Morris (fl. 1848–1862), when the settlement had been overrun. The colony was a communal settlement, all property was held in common, the fruits of labor were shared equitably, and provisions and goods were regarded as common stock. The colony lasted until 1880, when Davies' two young sons died of diphtheria. He had declared the boys to be the reincarnation of Jesus Christ and God the Father, respectively. The death of the boys, dissension about the colony, and various legal proceedings led to the colony's demise later that year.

See Also Davies, William W.

Sources:

Fogarty, Robert. 1990. *All Things New: American Communes and Utopian Movements 1860–1914*. Chicago: University of Chicago Press.
Miller, Timothy. 1990. *American Communes: 1860–1960*. New York: Garland.

KINGDOM OF MATTHIAS. The Kingdom of Matthias, also known as Mount Zion, was a notorious community of perfectionists established in 1833 at Sing Sing. The community members would cavort naked, marry spiritually, and freely exchange sexual partners. Also they used prayer to raise the dead under the influence of Robert Matthias (fl. 1830s). Their policy of free love scandalized the neighbors. The community's leader, Matthias, fled to New York, an earlier leader took over the community, died shortly afterward, and the community went to Manhattan to follow its free love practices under Matthias. Matthias was bribed to leave the community and disappeared after a notorious trial.

See Also Matthias, Robert; Truth, Sojourner

Sources:

Fogarty, Robert. 1990. *All Things New: American Communes and Utopian Movements 1860–1914*. Chicago: University of Chicago Press.
Johnson, Paul E., and Sean Wilentz. 1994. *The Kingdom of Matthias*. New York: Oxford University Press.

KIRTLAND COMMUNITY. Kirtland Community, an early Mormon community, was founded in February 1830 in Lake County, Ohio, by Sidney Rigdon (1793–1876). Although Rigdon was the main force behind the community, he resided at Independence, Missouri, during the early months of the community. Rigdon claimed that Mormonism was the true Apostolic Church after he read *The Book of Mormon*. From that time the congregation and the community established at Kirtland followed Rigdon and Mormonism. In 1831 Joseph Smith (1805–1844) went to Kirtland, and it became the church's headquarters. Between 1832 and 1837 Kirtland faced considerable debt. Also, Rigdon and Smith had been instructed by revelations to establish a center of Mormons at Independence, Missouri. Soon followers at Kirtland were not happy with the decision to use Missouri as the headquarters. Bitterness arose between Mormons in Missouri and Ohio, as well as among members of the Kirtland Community. All followers were admonished to purify themselves of their jealousies about where the headquarters might be. Then conflict within the Mormon communities was matched by that between Mormons and non-Mormons in the local community. By the end of 1833 Rigdon and Smith were themselves at odds. Nevertheless, the temple was completed at Kirtland by 1836. But the debts incurred by the Mormon Church were so great they could not be maintained through agricultural production. The community attempted to form a bank, but that failed; they tried other methods of raising and saving money but again had no success. In January

1838 Rigdon and Smith fled to escape the mob violence that seemed imminent. The conflict over the pattern of community life they should adopt split the community and made its future stability precarious. The communal phase ended when Joseph Smith stated: "Thou shalt not take thy brother's garment. Thou shalt pay for that which thou shalt receive of thy brother."

See Also Mormons; Rigdon, Sidney; Smith, Joseph

Sources:

McKiernan, Mark. 1979. *The Voice of One Crying in the Wilderness: Sidney Rigdon, Religious Reformer: 1793–1876.* Lawrence, Kan.: Herald House.

Wagoner, Richard S. 1994. *Sidney Rigdon: A Portrait of Religious Excess.* Salt Lake City, Utah: Signature Books.

KORESH, DAVID. David Koresh (1960–1993), a musician, led a religious sect, the Branch Davidians, who believed him to be Jesus Christ. On 2 March 1993, nine miles outside Waco, Texas, his sect was attacked by the U.S. Federal Bureau of Alcohol, Tobacco, and Firearms, which intended to arrest Koresh because he was so heavily armed. They stormed his compound, Mount Carmel, and four agents died, while many were wounded in the compound, including Koresh, who demanded his religious music be played over radio before he would release small children held captive in his compound. To understand Koresh and his perception of his identity and mission, it is necessary to know that the Book of Revelation, 5:2, states: "Who is worthy to pen the scroll and to loose its seals?" The text identifies a figure, the "Lamb," or the "Root of David"; he alone is able to open the book that is sealed with the Seven Seals (Revelation 5:5). Koresh claimed that he was that "Lamb" of Revelation who takes and opens the sealed book. Christians have traditionally understood this as a clear and exclusive reference to Jesus Christ. Koresh argued otherwise. He stated that the entire Book of Revelation, though revealed by Jesus and written by John the Divine in the first century, was to be understood and accomplished only shortly before the end of history. When the Seven Seals are opened, four horses are revealed—red, white, black, and the pale horse of death. An apocalypse ensues, and in time heaven is revealed. Koresh died during the attack on his headquarters outside Waco.

See Also Branch Davidians; Jonestown (Peoples Temple)

Sources:

Gibbs, Nancy. 1993. " 'Oh, My God' Fire Storm in Waco." *Time* (Australia), 3 May: 22–44.

King, Martin. 1993. *Preacher of Death: The Shocking Inside Story of David Koresh and the Waco Siege.* New York: Signet Books.

Tabar, James D., and Eugene V. Gallagher. 1995. *Why Waco: Cults and the Battle for Religious Freedom in America.* Berkeley: University of California Press.

Valdemar, Richard. 1994. *Siege at Waco.* London: Constable.

Wright, Stuart A., ed. 1995. *Armageddon in Waco: Critical Perspectives in the Branch Davidian Conflict.* Chicago: University of Chicago Press.

KORESHANS AND KORESHAN UNITY. Koreshans constituted a group that took its name from "koresh," Hebrew for "Cyrus," the first name of the group's founder, Cyrus R. Teed (1839–1908). He was a visionary doctor and mystic who advocated cellular cosmology. In 1886, shortly after he was elected president of the National Association of Mental Science, Teed began to plan a utopian community based on his teachings. Teed and his followers established a cooperative home and formed Koreshan Unity, a celibate organization, in Chicago. At the cooperative home they published the *Guiding Star*, later known as *Flaming Sword*. Also he established a cooperative business organization, the Bureau of Equitable Commerce, which was intended to encourage laborers to join the organization. In 1894 Teed rechristened himself "Koresh," and outlined further his community philosophy, Koreshanty. It claimed to explain the true astronomical, religious system by which the universe functioned and by which men should live. According to the theory, the earth is a hollow sphere, and humans live inside it, with their feet pointing outward from the center, and the horizon curves upward on all sides. This system was known as cellular cosmology. By the turn of the century Koreshanty had many adherents. To advance his work Teed decided to establish his great city, the center of Koreshanty, a new Jerusalem, at Estero, a few miles south of Fort Myers, Florida, on the Bay of Mexico, where the climate was mild, and communal living was tolerated. In 1903 the whole community left Chicago for Florida. At its peak the Koreshan Unity organization had over 4,000 members, and 300 residents lived on 6,000 acres. The community established its own press and published periodicals, books, and pamphlets. Teed claimed to have 10,000 members throughout the United States, but his community in Florida never had more than 200 members. In 1906 Teed entered a political dispute with several of the politicians in Fort Myers, and the community fell into disrepute. Although Koreshanty survived Teed's death, it did not develop further. In 1949 publications were reduced because the press was burned down. In 1961 the surviving leadership transferred the property to the state of Florida. The community is remembered by a historical site at Estero today. The community had no connection with David Koresh (1960–1993).

Sources:

Fogarty, Robert S. 1980. *Dictionary of American Communal History*. Westport, Conn.: Greenwood Press.
Hill, Samuel S., ed. 1984. *Encyclopedia of Religion in the South*. Macon, Ga.: Mercer University Press.
Kanter, R. M. 1972. *Commitment and Community*. Cambridge: Harvard University Press.
Kitch, Sally L. 1989. *Chaste Liberation: Celibacy and Female Cultural Status*. Champaign: University of Illinois Press.
Melton, J. Gordon. 1989. *Encyclopedia of American Religions*. Chicago: Gale Research.

KRISTENSTAET. Kristenstaet was established in January 1928 in Hood County, fifty miles southwest of Fort Worth, Texas. Its members upheld self-help and mutual assistance and were never socialists or communists, nor did they consider their isolated community to be a utopia. The colony produced a monthly magazine, *The Interpreter*. Outsiders thought Kristenstaet looked like a utopia caught in the capitalism of the 1930s depression. On 1 January 1928, a Dane, John B. Christensen, founded the town of Kristenstaet, naming it after himself. He was a farmer, lawyer, and colonizer. When he proposed the settlement, Christensen was told that he would fail because the land was often flooded. Originally, he thought the settlement should be restricted to American Scandinavians, and although others joined, the label "Danish Settlement" adhered to their community. Twelve thousand acres were cleared for cultivation; 6,000 were for pasture, and the remainder for hay, corn, cotton, and peanuts. The main industries were farming and ranching. Keen to avoid anything going to waste, the community established as one of the first industrial enterprises a sawmill according to their policy of biproduct industries. Also they grew large acreages of pecan, cottonwood, cedar, elm, oak, and hackberry. Some of the timber was used with native stone to construct houses and industrial plants, the surplus being turned to charcoal for sale. Cream, poultry, eggs, butter, hogs, and cattle also brought in revenue to the colony. Kristenstaet had its own currency, and it was used mostly in exchange among the residents themselves. A labor pool was used in which the men, having done their own work on the farm or in the factory, could go find additional employment. They received $2–2.50 a day in Kristenstaet coin. The community declined as the 1930s depression came to an end, and in late 1970 some of the stone buildings were all that remained as relics. Today some of the community's 6,000 acres are covered by water near the dam on the Brazos River built by the Brazos River Authority.

See Also Christensen, John B.

Source:

Fischer, Ernest G. 1980. *Marxists and Utopias in Texas*. Burnet, Tex.: Eakin Press.

KRUMNOW, JOHANN FREDERICK. Johann Frederick Krumnow (1811–1880) was born in Posen, Prussia. He was short and severely handicapped and spoke so indistinctly that he could never realize his dream to become a Lutheran pastor, so he became a tailor. In 1839 he emigrated to South Australia to escape religious domination by the Prussian State Church. He had a hypnotic power of persuasion and continued to seek influence among Lutherans and held meetings in private homes. Among older Lutherans were some who felt he could exorcise the devil. When he preached that Moravian Brotherhood should include communal ownership, Germans in South Australia rejected his ideas, and after much conflict he was excommunicated from the Lutheran Church. He went to Victoria (1851), worked as a tailor in Newtown (now Collingwood) near Melbourne, and preached successfully to the superstitious and hysterical. In 1853 he bought 1,584 acres near Hamilton and established Herrnhut Community. Although the members ate communally, Krumnow would eat alone in his cabin; also, he alone administered the community finances; but community stock and labor were shared. He became an excellent sheep shearer, taught locals the craft, and organized work teams to a strict schedule. Another Moravian commune, Hill Plains, which had been established near Benalla in central Victoria, became unable to feed itself or cope with scurvy, and Krumnow offered to accommodate them (c. 1875–1876). Shortly after the Hill Plains community arrived, its leader, Maria Heller (1841–1906), conflicted with Krumnow over joint leadership of the expanded community. Some members left when Maria Heller quit not long after arriving at Herrnhut. By 1885 only a few remained. In time, after many legal conflicts over the ownership and mortgage of Herrnhut's land, the property was sold (1889). Some members believed Krumnow had used his golden tongue to swindle them of their share of the land, taken advantage of simple folk, overestimated his abilities, and even claimed that he could fly. Unknown to the community, he had put the title in his name, not the community's. Krumnow was a strong, charismatic leader, and this was largely responsible for the longevity of Herrnhut.

See Also Heller, Maria; Herrnhut Commune; Hill Plains

Sources:

Blake, L. J. 1966. "Village Settlements." *The Victorian Historical Journal* 37: 189–201.

Metcalf, Bill, ed. 1995. *From Utopian Dreaming to Communal Reality: Cooperative Life Styles in Australia.* Sydney: University of New South Wales Press.

Meyer, C. 1978. "Two Communes in Nineteenth-Century Victoria." *The Victorian Historical Journal* 49: 204–205.

KURIKKA, MATTI. Matti Kurikka (1863–1915) was born in Ingria into a well-to-do Finnish family. He studied at the University of Helsinki, where he was drawn to socialism. He edited a Finnish newspaper in Viipuri, published books, and visited Denmark and Germany. In 1896 he worked for a Finnish labor newspaper, *Tyomies* (The Worker). Within a year he gave the paper a strong nationalist orientation, offended the Finnish establishment, and had become a recognized labor leader. As the paper prospered, he was under pressure from the Marxists, who pushed his socialist work aside in favor of a revolutionary approach to social change. To avoid conflict, he went to Australia to seek a better world by founding a utopian socialist community (1899) where harmony would replace social evil, especially the oppression of tyrants. The Queensland government was supporting utopian endeavors and gave him and his seventy-eight followers free rail travel to the site of their choice. A small camp was established near Chillagoe, and they named it El Dorado. They cut wood for railway sleepers and planned to save and buy land by the sea. Unable to speak fluent English, they were exploited by employers and other workers. More problems arose: the climate was too hot, they cut the wrong timber, food was inadequate, and workers were not competent to do what was required. In time the government realized Kurikka was not following their policies, worried about his utopian, socialistic, and communal interests, and, in view of recent failures of twelve similar communities, decided his attempts should not be supported. A poor administrator, Kurikka squandered their funds, and some followers had to endure much hardship. Because his followers had so little money, Kurikka began playing music for money in Cooktown pubs and talking fervently of his utopian schemes. With twenty-seven followers Kurikka headed for the northern coast of Queensland along the Gulf of Carpentaria. They left their families behind. The journey was too long, the grasslands were impenetrable, the climate was too hot, and the adventurers felt they would starve to death. By June 1899 Kurikka decided his plans for a utopian community would fail. In anger he blamed Australians, whom he thought were prejudiced, unfriendly, vulgar drunks. In August 1900 he quit Australia for Nanaimo, Vancouver, in Canada. There also his plans for a utopian community were not a success. He was thought to be an honest, well-meaning theorist but hopelessly impractical. Others considered him a gifted, intelligent leader but obstinate, headstrong, impatient, and restless. He was a poor organizer who made enemies easily, womanized, and held eccentric views on private property, women's roles, and the education of children. Some Finnish followers thought his sexual philosophy confusing because it advocated that those who lived together should not have intercourse, that the father of a child should not be the man who lived with the child's mother, and that all children should be raised by the commune members and live apart from their biological parents in a children's home.

See Also Kalevan Kansa; Sojntula

Sources:

Koivukangas, Olavi. 1974. *Scandinavian Immigration and Settlement in Australia before World War II*. Turku: Institute for Migration (Migration Studies C 2).

———. 1986. *Sea, Gold and Sugarcane; Attraction versus Distance, Finns in Australia, 1851–1947*. Turku: Institute for Migration (Migration Studies, 0356–780X, C 8).

Metcalf, Bill, ed. 1995. *From Utopian Dreaming to Communal Reality: Cooperative Life Styles in Australia*, pp. 31–33. Sydney: University of New South Wales Press.

L

LA JOLLA—CAPITALIST UTOPIA. In 1887 La Jolla was a small beach paradise for artists and writers on a barren peninsula near San Diego, California. By 1905 it had 1,300 residents; between 1920 and the early 1950s it became a village of 11,000. Thereafter, its population grew rapidly to 30,000, and in the 1980s there was little space for newcomers. In the late 1980s only 400 plots of land remained in the 1877 section of La Jolla, and each sold for about $1 million an acre. In 1987 the lowest price for a house was $275,000, and prices rose to $11.5 million for the finest home. La Jolla had become a capitalist's utopia and symbolized the California dream, where retired intellectuals and otherwise wealthy folk watched rolling surf from mansions hugging the cliffs. The village of La Jolla had a perfect climate, expansive beaches, and closely shaved suburban lawns. This was the ideal culture to which Americans aspired to achieve. Its founders were enterprising capitalists who helped La Jolla become one of the wealthiest places in their world, on a green, lush, no-longer-barren peninsula, beside one of the largest cities in California. It achieved independence from San Diego by imposing strict zoning laws. It became a stronghold of white Protestants, supported by wealth acquired elsewhere, living in opulent residences; and, following probably illegal discriminatory practices with the aid of a more or less private police force, they have kept Asians, blacks, and Hispanics away from La Jolla beach and its elegant recreational facilities.

Sources:

De Murguia, Valdemar. 1986. *Capital Flight and Economic Crisis: Mexican Post-Devaluation Exiles in a California Community*. San Diego.: Center for U.S. Mexican Studies.
McCord, William. 1989. *Voyages to Utopia: From Monastery to Commune, the Search for the Perfect Society in Modern Times*. New York: W. W. Norton.
Schaelchlin, Patricia A. 1988. *La Jolla: The Story of a Community, 1887–1987*. La Jolla: Friends of the La Jolla Library.

LABADIE, JEAN. Jean de Labadie (1610–1674), the seventh child in his family, was so delicate in infancy that he had to be dressed in red in order to be seen among the grass and flowers of the garden. When young, he showed a considerable interest in learning and memorizing prayers and the catechism, and at seven he joined his brothers at the Jesuit College, Bordeaux. At the time the College de La Madeleine was in disarray, and armed students fought among themselves. Labadie completed his early education with the Jesuits, entered the order as a novice (1625), and in 1628 entered the subdiaconate. At Bordeaux for three years he studied the Scriptures, philosophy, and rhetoric and became a leader of his peers. They felt he had the aura of a saint when he addressed them. In 1639 he fell ill, left the Jesuits, and became a preacher at parishes all over France. In 1650 he joined the Reformed Church and preached on the European continent, notably in Holland, and with fifty-five followers he settled in Herford, Westphalia. The Catholic Church was much angered by his controversial beliefs and outspoken preaching and accused him of heresy. He escaped their pursuit, converted to Calvinism, and became an ambivalent figure as he preached in Europe, loved by some, reviled by others. He died in Germany in 1674.

See Also Labadists

Sources:

Cross, L. A., and E. A. Livingstone. 1997. *The Oxford Dictionary of the Christian Church.* 3d ed. New York: Oxford University Press.

Oved, Yaacov. 1987. *Two Hundred Years of American Communes.* New Brunswick, N.J.: Transaction Books.

Saxby, T. J. 1987. *The Quest for the New Jerusalem: Jean de Labadie and the Labadists, 1610–1744.* Dortrecht, Netherlands: Martinus Nijhoff.

LABADISTS. Labadists were followers of the preacher Jean de Labadie (1610–1674). In 1675, after the death of their leader, the Labadists reinstated their community on Dutch soil, having had to leave Germany due to hostility toward their church. A community, Wieuwerd, was formed at Walta-slat and approached by road from Leeuwarden, Bolsward, or Sneek. The community was modeled on the Jerusalem Church after Pentecost, which was thought to be the purest manifestation of the Kingdom of God. To serve this community all members had to sacrifice their time, possessions, abilities, affections, and will to the work of the Lord. So those who sought membership had to arrange the sale of any property they held outside the province. This was taken as proof of their detachment from worldly goods and entitled them to full membership. Members wore modest, simple clothing, no jewelry or braided hair. Women wore a habit made of coarse frieze and had their hair tied back and covered like that of a nun. Men wore rough peasant smocks for work and worshiped in a dark costume. All members worked on the community estate and built new residences as their numbers rose. Their cottage industry became self-sufficient, and they exported the surplus. Cloth manufacture, the carding of wool, and cotton milling flourished. They had a tannery, a bakery, a brewery, and a printing press. They manufactured soap as well as pills for the treatment of fever—Labadie Pills— which provided much income to the community. A contingent came to the United States in 1683. Wieuwerd had three classes of members: visitors were welcomed with special accommodations; probationers had accommodations in cramped cells of four or five; the "elete" (elite), numbering 250 at the peak of the Labadists' growth, lived in great comfort. Labadists believed in the extreme Pietist view that only by being inspired by the Holy Spirit could one understand the Bible. They rarely celebrated the Eucharist; and marriage with an unregenerate individual was not binding. Beginning in 1690, unrelenting hostility with the Dutch Reformed Church affected the community's finances and spiritual life. Also the growing acceptance of Pietism—a religious creed close to that of Labadists—took members from the community. In the epidemic of 1691 one Labadist died every two weeks, July through September, and the community itself seemed near death. Because they organized in communes, they survived fifty years after their leader's death.

Sources:

Cross, L. A., and E. A. Livingstone. 1997. *The Oxford Dictionary of the Christian Church*. 3d ed. New York: Oxford University Press.

Fogarty, Robert S. 1990. *All Things New: American Communes and Utopian Movements 1860–1914*. Chicago: University of Chicago Press.

Saxby, T. J. 1987. *The Quest for the New Jerusalem: Jean de Labadie and the Labadists, 1610–1744*. Dordrecht, Netherlands: Martinus Nijhoff.

LANCASTER, JOSEPH. Joseph Lancaster (1778–1838), an English educator, was born at Southwark, London. He opened his own school (1798) and later moved to larger premises (1801). He believed that education should be available to all children regardless of their ability to pay; since he could not afford to hire teachers, he developed the monitorial system, which is based on a method used by Andrew Bell (1753–1832), a superintendent of Madras Male Orphan Asylum, India (1789). Lancaster traveled throughout Britain lecturing and raising funds for the establishment of new Lancasterian schools and published a pamphlet describing his method, *Improvements in Education* (1803). In 1818 he was bankrupt and emigrated to the United States, where he carried on his work, especially in New York state. Lancaster himself was forced out of the school organization for financial mismanagement and other personal reasons. He died in New York. The schools were taken over by the New York school authorities (1853).

See Also: Bell, Andrew; Lancasterian school

Sources:

Aldrich, Richard and Peter Gordon. 1987. *Dictionary of British Educationists*. London: Woburn Press.

Magnussen, Magnus, and Rosemary Goring, eds. 1990. *Chambers Biographical Dictionary.* 5th ed. Edinburgh: Chambers.
Preece, Warren E., ed. 1965. *Encyclopedia Britannica.* Chicago: Encyclopedia Britannica.
Smith, Benjamin. 1903. *The Century Cyclopaedia of Names.* London: Times.
Stephen, Leslie, and Sydney Lee, eds. 1917. *The Dictionary of National Biography.* London: Oxford University Press.

LANCASTERIAN SCHOOL. A Lancasterian school uses a teaching system that employs monitors in place of teachers in order to extend public education to those who are in poverty and unable to pay for their children's education. The system was established in India in 1789 by Andrew Bell, superintendent of Madras Male Orphan Asylum, and taken up in Britain by Joseph Lancaster (1778–1838). It centers on a monitorial system that was intended to help children learn from others without using adult teachers. Their wages were too high. The method is described in Lancaster's *Improvements in Education* (1803). In 1811 in England 30,000 pupils attended ninety-five Lancasterian schools; but by 1818 Lancaster was bankrupt. He sailed to New York, where over sixty of his monitor schools were founded. They flourished until the early 1850s, when, due to financial mismanagement, they were taken over by the New York state authorities and continued to be one of the most favored methods of mass education among impoverished areas of industrialized society.

See Also Bell, Andrew; Lancaster, Joseph

Sources:

Aldrich, Richard, and Peter Gordon. 1987. *Dictionary of British Educationists.* London: Woburn Press.
McHenry, Robert, ed. 1992. *The New Encyclopedia Britannica.* Chicago: Encyclopedia Britannica.
Stephen, Leslie, and Sydney Lee, eds. 1917. *The Dictionary of National Biography.* London: Oxford University Press.

LANE, CHARLES. Charles Lane (1800–1870) was born in Hackney, Middlesex, England, became editor of *The London Merchant Current,* and developed his interests in social reform during the 1840s. In 1842, at Alcott House, he met the U.S. educational reformer and transcendentalist Amos Bronson Alcott (1799–1888), who shared many of his views. At that time Lane was editing the *Healthian,* a dietary magazine, for the group that attended Alcott House. Bronson, Lane, and others decided to establish a colony of Alcott House in the United States that would uphold the values and practices of good health, both physical and spiritual. Lane provided the funds to purchase a property at Harvard, Massachusetts, to be known as "Fruitlands." The social structure of the colony was to revolve around Lane's "consociate family," a group with similar views that provided members with intellectual support needed to maintain a positive approach to examining their inner life. A vegetarian, Lane would not use any animal products, even wool, nor would he use cotton; he banned tobacco and liquor and pursued the water cure for therapy. Alcott was much taken with Lane's views, and Fruitlands began in June 1843. Unlike Alcott, others felt Lane to be too austere and lacking a sense of humor, while Abigail Alcott could not tolerate the consociate family. Lane gave the impression of being both skillful and witty, much devoted to eating uncooked vegetables, and insistent that others follow his high moral standards. When financial problems arose, Fruitlands failed, and Lane was jailed for not paying taxes. In 1844 Lane briefly joined the Shakers at Harvard and looked around for other communities to interest him, and in 1846, the year Fruitlands was sold, he returned to England and married a woman who had once been an Owenite.

See Also Alcott, Amos Bronson; Alcott House or School and the First Concordium; Fruitlands Colony

Source:

Fogarty, Robert S. 1980. *Dictionary of American Communal History*. Westport, Conn.: Greenwood Press.

LANE, WILLIAM. William Lane (1861–1917) was born in Bristol, England, eldest of five sons and one daughter. His mother was English, and his father an Irish Protestant. Until he drank the profits of his successful business, Lane's father was a landscape gardener. When Lane's mother died, his teacher gave William funds to work his passage to Canada, where he had an operation that improved his misshapen foot but left him always lame and in need of a walking stick. After working for a printer, Will became a news reporter in 1881. He married in 1884, visited England briefly, and sailed to Brisbane in June 1885. Familiar with the writings of Karl Marx (1818–1883) and Adam Smith (1723–1790), he wrote "Labour Notes" for the *Observer* and soon established himself among trade union members and officials. He founded the Bellamy Society, a group of utopian idealists who were much impressed with some ideas in Edward Bellamy's (1850–1898) *Looking Backward: 2000–1887* (1888) and Theodor Hertzka's (1845–1924) *Freeland—a Social Anticipation* (1891). Through the local Trade and Labour Council Lane began promoting the founding of state-supported village settlements. To advance the cause he launched *Boomerang*, a blatantly anti-Chinese newspaper that throve on exposing prostitutes, the inadequacies of doctors, and foibles of the upper classes. He sold his interest in the paper and became editor of the *Worker* and, under the pseudonym of John Miller, promoted idealistic socialism and cooperative communcs of a thousand inhabitants based on "simplicity and art, as opposed to Bellamy's luxury." In May 1891 one of Lane's associates visited South America to discuss establishing a community in Argentina. In October that year Lane published the policy of the New Australian Cooperative Settlement Association. After gaining support in many rural areas, the venture became a reality, and settlements were organized and established not in Argentina but Paraguay. After ending his participation in the settlements in 1899, Lane went to New Zealand, and wrote for a conservative newspaper until his death in 1917.

See Also Cosme; New Australia

Sources:

Armytage, Walter Henry Green. 1961. *Heavens Below: Utopian Experiments in England 1560–1950.* London: Routledge and Kegan Paul.

Graham, Stewart. 1912. *Where Socialism Failed.* London: John Murray.

Lake, Marilyn. 1986. "Socialism and Manhood: The Case of William Lane." *Labour History* 50: 54–62.

Lane, W. (Pseud. "John Miller"). *The Workingman's Paradise.* Sydney: Edwards Dunlop.

Pike, Douglas, et al., eds. 1966–1990. *Australian Dictionary of Biography.* 12 vols. Carlton, Victoria: University of Melbourne Press.

Singer, I, and L. J. Berens. 1894. *New Australia: A Criticism.* Sydney: T. H. Houghton.

Souter, Gavin. 1968. *A Peculiar People: The Australians in Paraguay.* Sydney: Angus and Robertson.

LAWRENCE, D. H. David Herbert Lawrence (1885–1930) was born in Nottinghamshire, England, the child of a brutal alcoholic, coal miner, and puritanical schoolteacher. His childhood was extremely unhappy. He was educated at Nottingham University College, held a teaching certificate (1908), and taught school in Derbyshire (1902–1906) and at Davidson Road School in Croydon (1908–1911). His first novel was *The White Peacock* (1911). During World War I in 1915 he hoped to emigrate to the United States, where he planned to found a colony of like-minded individuals, called "Rananim." For his novel *The Lost Girl* (1920) he received the Tait Black Memorial Prize from Edinburgh University (1921). He also wrote short stories, plays, nonfiction, and travel sketches. Many of his works were filmed after World War II; several novels were the subject of court cases for obscenity. Among the most notable novels are *Sons and Lovers* (1913) and *Lady Chatterley's Lover* (1928). He suffered long from tuberculosis, witnessed the banning of many of his books, and after 1909 traveled to Italy, Australia, Ceylon, France, the Pacific, Mexico, and the United States to find a congenial life and companionship. Some critics objected to his overbearing and hortative style, incessant attacks on institutions, and the tendency to sacrifice character for moralizing in his literary work. In his politics he developed a sociopolitical style that was given his name—Lawrentian. This centered on a love for nature rather than technology, a deep preference for tenderness in the place of sophistication, and a strong rejection of pornography in the face of frank sexuality. The term also referred to the cryptofascist political views that the novelist is reputed to have adopted at his life's end. Lawrence's novels search for new forms of sensibility and human relations that are made accessible by the increased awareness of, and value placed on, bodily sensation. His unrealized utopia was more a psychological haven than a place of escape.

See Also Rananim

Sources:

Burgess, Anthony. 1985. *Flame into Being: The Life and Work of D. H. Lawrence*. London: Heinemann.

Delavenay, Emile. 1972. *D. H. Lawrence: The Man and His Work, the Formative Years 1885–1919*. London: Heinemann.

Kermode, Frank. 1973. *Lawrence*. London: Fontana Collins.

May, Hal, ed. 1987. *Contemporary Authors*. Vol. 121. Detroit: Gale Research.

Seeber, Hans Ulrich. 1995. "Utopian Mentality in George Eliot's *Middlemarch* (1871–72) and D. H. Lawrence's *The Rainbow*." *Utopian Studies* 6: 30–39.

LEADE, JANE. Jane Leade (1623–1704) was born in Norfolk, England, and when young claimed to have heard a miraculous voice and consequently devoted herself to religion. In 1644, aged twenty-one, she married William Leade, who died shortly after their daughter was born. In London Jane lived in seclusion, where she was deeply impressed by the mystic revelations of Jakob Boehme (1575–1624) and recorded her prophetic visions in a diary, which she published in 1670 as *A Fountain of Gardens*. In that year she met Dr. John Pordage (1608–1698). She published *The Heavenly Cloud* (1681) and *The Revelation of Revelations* (1683). In 1693 one of her books reached Holland, and after its translation her reputation was established in the Netherlands. A young Oxford scholar, Francis Lee (1661–1719), met her in England and was impressed by her spirituality; in turn, she adopted him as her son and adviser. Mrs. Leade became blind, and Lee took over all her correspondence and married her daughter, and, it was alleged, this marriage was in obedience to divine order. Mrs. Leade dictated works to Francis Lee, who edited them with prefaces of his own and sometimes with verses by Richard Roach (1662–1730). Around Mrs. Leade and Lee gathered a group of London theosophists who called themselves Philadelphians. Many others congregated in Holland and Germany. In 1696 Mrs. Leade printed a *Message to the Philadelphian Society Whither Soever Dispersed over the Whole Earth*, and in 1697 her followers drafted a constitution. At West Moreland House her followers resolved to publish quarterly *Transactions*, but only one appeared. At the end of her life Mrs. Leade lived in poverty but was offered some relief by Baron Kniphousen, a German sympathizer, who gave her 400 gulden a year. She lived in a poor house in Stepney, and in 1702 she published her own *Funeral Testimony*. A month after her death Francis Lee, who had attended her faithfully, wrote *The Last Hours of Jane Leade, by an Eye and Ear Witness*. This account was translated into German.

See Also Boehme, Jakob; Lee, Francis; Philadelphians

Sources:

Magnussen, Magnus, and Rosemary Goring, eds. 1990. *Chambers Biographical Dictionary*. 5th ed. Edinburgh: Chambers.

Stephen, Leslie, and Sydney Lee, eds. 1917. *The Dictionary of National Biography*. Vol. II. London: Oxford University Press.

LEE, ANN. Ann Lee (?1742–1784) was born in Manchester, second of eight children in a blacksmith's large family. An uneducated teenager, she worked in a textile mill and at age twenty was a cook in an infirmary. At twenty-two she joined the religious dissenters Jane and James Wardley (fl. 1747–1774), Quaker tailors. They had been much influenced by radical Calvinists, the Camisards, who had fled France after the revocation of the Edict of Nantes (1685), which had guaranteed the freedom of conscience to Protestants. Four years later Ann married one of her father's employee blacksmiths. She had four stillborn children. The experience affected her physical and mental health, and she turned to the Wardleys to support her passionate condemnation of sex. She proclaimed her views to the Wardleys' followers, and her outbursts against lust, organized religion, and worldliness attracted many. At meetings they would become agitated, and their shaking became a frequently used means to curb wickedness before God. Her preaching was attacked as witchcraft, and mobs came to brutalize her listeners for condoning her heresy and blasphemy. Ann was imprisoned. In jail she had marvelous revelations, was filled with Christ's spirit, became aware of the Second Coming, and felt Christ speak through her. After her release, Shakers were no longer molested, and Ann was a martyr to Wardleys' followers. She came to her new faith not through theology and organization of followers but through support due to her spellbinding addresses. She stated that only confession would regenerate one's life, and the price was celibacy; that wars, poverty, slavery, and depravity were due to concupiscence, the greatest evil; that it must be exposed as an ugly serpent, so as to save humankind. She felt called by God to set up his church in the United States. With a few followers she went to the United States (1774) and claimed on arrival to have been commissioned to spread God's word. Near Albany in New York, at Niskeyuna (later Watervliet) on the Hudson River, her followers established a settlement while she labored in New York. By 1780 people began coming to hear her speak. Later, droves of people came to hear her preach about the filthy gratification and deceit of men and women who seduced and tempted one another and forever after suffered from envy, jealousy, murder, rape, war, poverty, shame, disgrace, and wretchedness. Privately, she accepted marriage provided it was chaste and aimed to serve the community rather than personal passion. She advocated economy, kindness, and hospitality and converted some people to believe in her ability to perceive unconfessed guilt. As the consequence of confession she witnessed frenzied shaking, convulsing, and trembling. Also she was subject to much harassment during her preaching tours. The work exhausted her, and soon after the death of her brother, she herself became ill and died. She helped lay the foundation of twenty-four settlements in nine states with tens of thousands of inhabitants. Fourteen lasted over 100 years, and several remain in Maine and New Hampshire.

See Also Camisards; Shakers, Shaking Quakers; Wardley, Jane and James

Sources:

Andrews, Edward Deeming. 1963. *The People Called Shakers: A Search for the Perfect Society*. New York: Dover.
Oved, Yaacov. 1987. *Two Hundred Years of American Communes*. New Brunswick, N.J.: Transaction Books.
Whitworth, John McKelvie. 1975. *God's Blueprints: A Sociological Study of Three Utopian Sects*. London: Routledge and Kegan Paul.

LEE, FRANCIS. Francis Lee (1661–1719) was born in Cobham, Surrey. Both his parents died when Lee was an infant. In 1675 he was educated at Merchant Tailors' School and entered Oxford in 1679 (B.A., 1683, M.A., 1687). He was appointed chaplain to Lord Stawell, Sommerton, Somerset (1691), and a tutor to his son. In 1691 he studied medicine at the University of Leyden and practiced in Venice. He became acquainted with the writings of Mrs. Jane Leade (1623–1704), became a devoted disciple, arranged and published her manuscripts, and married her daughter. In 1697 he founded the Philadelphian Society. With Richard Roach (1662–1730) in 1697 he wrote and published *Theosophical Transactions*. The society's meetings were so large that they were moved from Baldwin's Gardens to West Moreland House. Between Lee and Henry Dodwell (1641–1711) argument arose because of Lee's approach to the society. This conflict continued until 1701. Dodwell's arguments and those of others in 1702 probably led to the demise of the Philadelphian Society in 1703. In 1708 Francis Lee became a member of the London College of Physicians. He died in 1719 after contracting a fever in Flanders, where he had been attending to business.

See Also Leade, Jane; Philadephians

Sources:

Stephen, Leslie, and Sydney Lee, eds. 1917. *The Dictionary of National Biography*. London: Oxford University Press.

LEE KUAN YEW. Lee Kuan Yew (b. 1923), born in Singapore, came from a wealthy Chinese family. He studied law in England and returned to Singapore to practice in 1951. An avowed anticommunist, he went into politics and was elected to the Singapore legislative assembly in 1955 as founder of the moderate, anticommunist People's Action Party (1954). In 1959 he became the nation's first prime minister and ruled as such for forty years. In 1965 he oversaw Singapore's becoming an independent nation within the British Commonwealth. With industry and probity Lee chose capitalism for the nation's economy, encouraged investment by multinational corporations, slashed trade union influence, reduced government revenue through taxes, and advocated vigorous entrepreneurial activities. He believed that through the free market and industrious enterprise, Singapore could become the most productive nation with the highest standard of living in Asia. The People's Action Party dominated Singapore's politics 1968–1980, and Lee was seen by more liberal nations as a powerful autocrat. The party's power diminished slightly when the Worker's Party managed to get members elected to Parliament. In 1990 Lee Kuan Yew was replaced by Goh Chock Tong and in 1992 gave up the chairmanship of the party he had founded.

See Also Singapore as a Confucian-Capitalist Utopia

Sources:

Josey, Alex. 1968. *Lee Kuan Yew*. Singapore: D. Moore Press.
McCord, William. 1989. *Voyages to Utopia: From Monastery to Commune, the Search for the Perfect Society in Modern Times*. New York: W. W. Norton.

LENIN, NIKOLAI VLADIMIR. Nikolai Vladimir Ilich Lenin was originally Vladimir Ilich Ulyanov (1870–1924). He was born at Simbirsk (now Ulyanovsk) on the Volga River. His father was a provincial inspector of schools, his mother came from a medical family, and Lenin was educated at the local secondary school. After being raised in a happy home, in 1887 he graduated from secondary school with distinction, but that year his older brother Aleksandr was executed for involvement in a plot to assassinate the oppressive czar Alexander III (1845–1894). A few months later Lenin was expelled from the University of Kazan after participating in student demonstrations. He studied law at the University of St. Petersburg and in 1893 joined the growing revolutionary movement. In 1897 he was arrested and exiled to Siberia, where he studied and wrote. In 1889 he formed a small discussion circle to consider the ideas of Karl Marx (1818–1883). In 1900 Lenin left Russia to live in London and write pamphlets outlining Marxism and to edit the Russian social democrat newspaper while in exile. He founded the revolutionary newspaper *Iskra*, which was smuggled into Russia by agents. In the March revolution of 1917 he returned and attempted to get its leadership, failed, and was forced to take refuge in Finland. During the food riots of 1917 he returned to Russia and urged that the current "capitalist revolution" be turned into a "socialist revolution." With Bolshevik support he was able to gain power and establish a dictatorship by gradually eliminating the opposition. He established a government, the Council of People's Commissars, nationalized the banks, means of production, distribution, and exchange, and redistributed land to peasants, and made Russia withdraw from World War I. In 1921 he introduced his New Economic Policy, and it restored a degree of capitalism to Russia. In 1923, after suffering two debilitating strokes the year before, he was wounded by anti-Bolsheviks in their attempt to assassinate him. He died the following year. His name is legendary in the communist world, where he is known as humankind's greatest genius.

See Also Bolshevism; Leninist Russia; Marx, Karl

Sources:

Conquest, Robert. 1972. *Lenin*. London: Fontana.
Harding, Neil. 1977, 1981. *Lenin's Political Thought*. 2 vols. London: Macmillan.

Hill, Christopher. 1978. *Lenin and the Russian Revolution*. London: English University Press.

Rice, Christopher. 1990. *Lenin: Portrait of a Professional Revolutionary*. London: Cassell.

Schapiro, Leonard, and Peter Reddaway, eds. 1967. *Lenin*. London: Pall Mall Press.

Ulam, Adam B. 1965. *Lenin and the Bolsheviks: The Intellectual and Political History of the Triumph of Communism in Russia*. London: Secker and Warburg.

LENINIST RUSSIA. Leninist Russia was the major national expression of Marxism that followed the 1917 revolution until Lenin's death, 1924. Among other propositions it held that capitalism was an international and imperialist force that led to international wars and consequently promoted conditions for a national revolution and, second, that to overthrow capitalism in any state, a revolutionary political party must rise to power before the proletariat can take over.

See Also Bolshevism; Lenin, Nikolai Vladimir; Stalin, Joseph; Stalinist Russia

Sources:

Beilharz, Peter. 1992. *Labour's Utopias: Bolshevism, Fabianism, Social Democracy*. London: Routledge.

Meyer, Alfred. 1957. *Leninism*. New York: Praeger.

Miller, David, ed. 1987. *The Blackwell Encyclopedia of Political Thought*. Oxford: Blackwell.

LEONGATHA LABOR COLONY. Leongatha Labor Colony was the most successful of many utopian experiments during the 1890s depression in Victoria, Australia. It belonged to an antiutopian tradition of employing workhouse labor. A heavily timbered site, eighty miles southeast of Melbourne was chosen to establish the colony. It was to be supported by public subscription and sale of produce, but instead it had to be subsidized by the government (1893–1898). The colony mainly existed to give unemployed men temporary work at subsistence wages. Middle-class Melbournians saw the colony was a utopian lifestyle for the undeserving poor, while the poor saw it more as an English workhouse. The colony was not self-supporting as planned, and skilled agricultural labor had to be brought in. In its first year the average stay was about three months. Altogether nearly 3,500 unemployed people and families settled communally in Leongatha. In April 1903 the colony was closed by government proclamation. When poverty did not disappear the venture was reproclaimed in 1904. It offered a cheap way to ensure that men did not starve. Men were dismissed from the colony as soon as they had earned £2. The colony cost the government almost £21,000 and helped 9,300 people over twenty-six years. It ceased in May 1919, the government took it over for veterans of World War I, and the land was given to soldiers who had served the British empire.

See Also Tucker, Horace Finn; Tucker Village Settlements

Sources:

Kennedy, R. E. W. 1968. "The Leongatha Labor Colony: Founding an Anti-utopia."
    Labour History 14: 54–58.
Metcalf, Bill, ed. 1995. *From Utopian Dreaming to Communal Reality: Cooperative Life
    Styles in Australia*. Sydney: University of New South Wales Press.

LETCHWORTH. Letchworth was the first Garden City. The Garden City Company was formed with £20,000 share capital under Ebenezer Howard (1850–1928) and six directors. The Garden City (1904) at Letchworth in Hertfordshire was established on 3,818 acres, and cost £155,587. It was designed with effective sanitation and given a rail link forty-two minutes from London. Inaugurated in October 1903 and begun in the summer of 1904, Letchworth was managed by the company shareholders. It became a model for residential development. It had cottages for those who wanted expensive housing and cheap cottages at £150 each. Residents were known as open-plan lovers, rose gardeners, lovers of herbaceous borders, and prone to strange crazes and lifestyles. Natural features of the region were preserved, and some residents aimed for self-sufficiency. At first the residents voted against having a bar; they settled for the Skittles Inn, with its cocoa and other nonintoxicating drinks. Many residents were vegetarians. Craftwork spread quickly. Skills included bookbinding and printing, corset making, handloom weaving, pottery, and upholstery. There were an engineering firm that made cars and a progressive school for children, and J. M. Dent established its Arden Press. Plans included electrification only for heat and light, all services underground, and inward sloping roads with central drains. Two Derbyshire architects, Raymond Unwin (1863–1940) and Barry Parker (1867–1947), designed the suburb in keeping with Howard's ideas. John Ruskin's (1819–1900) supporters were drawn to Howard's application of his policies. Letchworth attracted many enthusiasts for Tolstoy's (1828–1910) villages and members from the Fellowship of the New Life. Aiming for rural-urban settlement with light industry and spacious residential areas, Letchworth was to be like a utopia of clean, pure air, flowers, and perpetual sunshine. It was followed by other Garden Cities, Welwyn, Stevenage, Harlow, and Hatfield.

See Also Garden City; Howard, Ebenezer; Parker, Richard Barry; Unwin, Raymond

Sources:

Armytage, Walter H. Green. 1961. *Heavens Below: Utopian Experiments in England
    1560–1950*. London: Routledge and Kegan Paul.
Gill, Roger. 1984. "In England's Green and Pleasant Land." In Peter Alexander and
    Roger Gill, eds., *Utopias*, pp. 109–117. London: Duckworth.
Marsh, Jan. 1982. *Back to the Land: The Pastoral Impulse in England, from 1880 to
    1914*. London: Quartet.

LETS. LETS stands for Local Employment Trading System, Local Energy Transfer System, Local Exchange Trading System, and Labour Exchange Trading System. In the 1970s, a Scot, Michael Linton (fl. 1967–1997), emigrated from Britain to the west coast of Canada. Early in the 1980s he founded the original LETS group in the Comox Valley on Vancouver Island. He then established Landsmen Community Services Ltd. The system involves the exchange of goods and services without using legal tender. Exchange is denominated in terms of the official currency, for example, dollars or pounds, or, as is more usually the case, as a locally nominated unit of exchange, called, say, a "pool" or "nugget." LETS groups are voluntary, self-help schemes with independent democratic organizations run on a nonprofit basis. Each group produces a directory of members, and describes the range of services and goods they regularly offer, for example, "Sally . . . [phone number]—carpentry, baby-sitting, organically grown herbs." This directory facilitates multilateral exchanges within the group; every time an exchange takes place, the relevant credit and debit are logged onto a computerized accounting system. Therefore, money is not physically necessary for an exchange to take place. The system is not barter—which is unilateral exchange—nor is it conventional trade where money arises in all its familiar functions. Today there are hundreds of LETS groups around the world, all based on Linton's practical model. Often these groups develop ancillary functions, taxing their members to create a charitable poor fund, providing skills training, and even establishing credit union-style lending institutions. Sometimes the local unit of account functions as quasi-legal tender, goods and services being exchanged at market rates. Other groups make a more radical departure from conventional market/money systems and assess all work, from the provision of medical services, to gardening and baby-sitting as equally remunerative. In 1991 LETS Blue Mountains was established in the state of New South Wales, Australia, and has been reported to be the most expansive and intensive LETS group in the world.

Sources:

Furnell, Peter. 1994. "No Time to Waste." *TOES (The Other Economic Summit, Australia) Newsletter* 2 (Spring): 10–15.
Trainer, Ted. 1995. *The Conserver Society: Alternatives for Sustainability*. London: Zed Books.

LEVER, WILLIAM H. William Hesketh Lever (1851–1925) was born in Baltin, Lancashire, the eldest son of a wholesale and retail grocer. William was educated at a private school in Baltin, studied at the Church Institute, and underwent commercial training. He decided to train on his own account and chose the name "Sunlight" to register a new soap made mainly from vegetable oils instead of tallow. The demand for this soap grew rapidly, and in 1887 he founded a center for his soap works near where his employees would live. He bought 52 acres, later extended to 500, in Cheshire, and in March 1888 the new town of Port Sunlight was established. Manufacturing began in 1889. His model township, Port Sunlight, was run as a benevolent autocracy. He introduced profit sharing, planned houses, and gardens and established various social and sporting amenities for his employees' benefit. In 1890 a public company was formed, and after many amalgamations, either by purchase or by interchange of shares, Lever gained great control over the soap-making industry. He became wealthy and was a noted philanthropist. To find and supply raw materials for his companies, Lever sought a supply of palm oil and palm kernel oil in West Africa and in 1910 in Nigeria established mills that were later extended into the Belgian Congo. In 1911 he was made a baronet, and in 1917 he was made a peer, Baron Leverhulme, a combination of his own and his wife's name. In 1922 he was a viscount.

See Also Lewis Island, North and South, and Harris Islands; Port Sunlight

Sources:

Gill, Roger. 1984. ''In England's Green and Pleasant Land.'' In Peter Alexander and Roger Gill, eds., *Utopias*, pp. 109–117. London: Duckworth.
Jolly, W. P. 1976. *Lord Leverhulme: A Biography*. London: Constable.
Lever, William H. 1927. *Viscount Leverhulme by His Son*. London: Allen and Unwin.
Weaver, John R. H., ed. 1937. *Dictionary of National Biography 1922–1930*. London: Oxford University Press.

LEWIS, JOHN SPEDAN. John Spedan Lewis (1885–1963), son of John Lewis, founder of the London department store Peter Jones, was educated at Westminster and at home. After being disillusioned about his father's commercial success, hearing that he, his father, and his brother received annually far more from the business than the total salary and wages bill, and noting the repressive and inefficient management practices in the firm, young John considered the value of a business partnership with the employees. While recovering from a riding accident, he had the idea that shares instead of cash should be distributed to those who worked for the firm. When young John succeeded his father and overcame his intense opposition, the John Lewis Partnership was organized (1918–1920). After his father's death, John worked for twenty-seven years to secure the partnership, which belongs to all who work in the firm and share in its prosperity.

Sources:

Jeremy, D. J., and C. Shaw, eds., *Dictionary of Business Biography: A Biographical Dictionary of Business Leaders Active in Britain in the Period of 1860–1980*. London: Butterworths.
Lewis, John S. 1948. *Partnership for All*. London: Kerr-Cros.
———. 1954. *Fairer Shares*. London: Staples.

LEWIS ISLAND, NORTH AND SOUTH, AND HARRIS ISLANDS. These islands were owned by William Hesketh Lever (1851–1925). In 1917 he purchased the island of Lewis and followed this with a purchase in 1919 of the islands of North and South Harris. He aimed to improve the economy of the

Western Isles of Scotland generally and to raise the living conditions of the local crofter population with plans for a fishing industry on the islands. Lewis was to be the Port Sunlight of fishing. To market the fish, Lever bought 350 fish shops in British towns. He had difficulties about tenure and occupation of the land and met opposition from the crofters of Lewis. The scheme was abandoned in 1923. When he left, he offered, as a gift to the town of Stornoway, much of the land that he had acquired. Consequently, Lewis failed, but the fish distribution became MacFisheries in the Unilever Group.

See Also Lever, William H.; Port Sunlight

Source:

Marsh, Jan. 1982. *Back to the Land: The Pastoral Impulse in England, from 1880 to 1914.* London: Quartet.

LIEBKNECHT, KARL. Karl Liebknecht (1871–1919) was the son of the German socialist Wilhelm Liebknecht (1826–1900), who founded the Social Democratic Party (1875). Karl studied law, practiced as a barrister, and served in the Prussia Guard but turned from his conservative views to socialism in 1904 when defending a group of agitators in Königsberg. In 1907 he was imprisoned for sedition. In 1912 he was elected to the Reichstag but in 1916 was expelled and then imprisoned again. He was one of a few socialists who refused to support World War I and was an associate of Rosa Luxemburg (1871–1919). In 1918 he helped her turn the Spartakusbund (Spartacus League) into the German Communist Party. He is reported to have said of his work, ''We are fighting for the gates of heaven!'' Luxemburg and he were murdered by army officers during the abortive Berlin workers' uprising in 1919.

See Also Luxemburg, Rosa; Social democracy; Spartacists

Sources:

Magnussen, Magnus, and Rosemary Goring, eds. 1990. *Chambers Biographical Dictionary.* 5th ed. Edinburgh: Chambers.
Muzenberg, Will, ed. 1927. *Speeches of Karl Liebknecht with a Biographical Sketch.* New York: International.

LINDISFARNE ASSOCIATION. Lindisfarne Association is an international community established in 1972 by William Irwin Thompson (b. 1938) for individuals and groups to foster a new planetary culture. Lindisfarne's name comes from an ancient Celtic Monastery established on Holy Island, Northumbria, 635. The association assumes the world is locked in conflict between religions, nations, classes, peoples, and institutions; and that self and society do not adequately describe cultural reality or the proper relation between nation and culture. Lindisfarne aims to transform and conserve human culture. Transformation will be through uniting people—religious leaders, scientists, ecologists, architects, artists, and businesspeople—to help them accept challenges of new technologies in the creation of new world cultures. Conservation will be through integrating the humanities at a time of commercial debasement of scholarship, art, and religion. This will be done with an association of intellectuals and scholars like those of the fifteenth century who fostered the Renaissance and those of the seventh century who fostered the rise of Christendom. In their time all worked for long-term change using compassion rather than political and economic imperatives. The association transforms individuals through contemplative education and the realization of an inner harmony of all religions and tribes, fostering a new, healthier balance between nature and culture and illuminating the spiritual foundation of governments. In practice it supports replacing competition in art, science, and knowledge with collaboration and the development of technologies in an economy that upholds conservation instead of consumption; and supports establishing metaindustrial villages and convivial cities. The association headquarters is in the Cathedral Church of St. John the Divine, New York City. The association has fellows who have made outstanding contributions to the expression of the new planetary culture. Activities began in Southampton, Long Island, August 1973, where a resident staff lived communally on a thirteen-acre facility and offered educational services to the Greater New York area through seminars, residential courses, and conferences. From 1976 to 1979 Lindisfarne was centered on the Episcopal Landmark Church in Manhattan, where scholarly lectures and seminars were held that resulted in publication of important works such as Bateson's *Mind and Nature* (1979), Mitchell's *Megalithomania* (1982), Thompson's *Darkness and Scattered Light* (1978), and the script for Andre Gregory's film *My Dinner with Andre* (1983). The association became a self-organizing and self-sustaining network whose members shared not so much a community as an ecology. After the publication of several books the Lindisfarne Association established its own Lindisfarne Press, Great Barrington, Massachusetts, and its *Lindisfarne Letter*. Fellows of the association may use the Lindisfarne Mountain Retreat in New Mexico.

See Also Thompson, William Irwin

Sources:

Lindisfarne Association. 1973. *An Outline of the Lindisfarne Association.* New York: Lindisfarne Center.
Thompson, William Irwin. 1973. *Passages about Earth: An Exploration of the New Planetary Culture.* 1981 ed. New York: Harper Colophon.

LITTLE LANDERS COLONIES. The first Little Landers Colony was established in 1909 in Tiajuana Valley, about fourteen miles south of San Diego, facing the Mexican hills. Named San Ysidro, it claimed to show that "a little land and a living, surely, is better than desperate struggle and wealth, possibly." This was the belief of William E. Smythe (1861–1922), who in the ten years before World War I, argued that people could support themselves and their families on an acre of irrigated ground. Many believed him, and he led a group of Californians, "Little Landers." Also he had the support of the California

Promotion Committee. About twelve families answered Smythe's call in 1909, and the colony was established on 120 acres. Early in 1910, 38 families had joined the colony, and by the fourth year the colony had 116 families and 300 people. Most people were middle-aged or elderly. Each family held only as much land as it could work without needing added help. Usually, the area was only one acre, which was worked intensively and with diversified crops heavily fertilized. The community was not formally organized, and members cooperated with each other as far as each member wanted. The colonists were helped in getting full value for their produce when one of them collected the day's output in a horse and buggy and sold the fruit and vegetables in the streets of San Diego. Later, they bought a truck and in the center of San Diego sold produce at a cooperative store. By 1916 four more Little Landers Colonies had been established and imitated the parent group in San Diego. Colonists felt convinced that their settlements would become permanent and that their social ideals were secure. Other settlements were Runnymede near Pao Lato; Hayward Heath in Alameda County; and colonies in San Fernando Valley and at Cupertino, San Jose. In 1916 a flood swept the valley, and many houses were lost. Slowly, the colonists found their holdings were too small to be economical, and the Little Landers movement slowly disintegrated, especially during the boom years of World War I, when more, better paid jobs became available. The Little Landers were utopian colonies in the sense that they withdrew from society and incorporated a social message; nevertheless, they did not practice communal ownership of land or means of production or even communal housing and dining, as is often the case with utopian life.

See Also: Smythe, William Ellsworth

Sources:

Fogarty, Robert S. 1980. *Dictionary of American Communal History*. Westport, Conn.: Greenwood Press.

Hine, Robert V., ed. 1983 *California's Utopian Colonies*. Los Angeles: University of California Press.

LITTLEFIELD, GEORGE ELMER. Rev. George Elmer Littlefield (fl. c. 1862–1930) was a mystical utopian associated with utopian communities in the United States. In 1882 he was working as a printer in Boston. At age twenty-six he met Edward Bellamy (1850–1898), joined the Nationalist Club, and entered Harvard University. By 1892 he was a unitarian minister. In 1910 he bought the Fellowship Farm at Westwood, Massachusetts, where he organized a short-lived utopian colony and established the Ariel Press. In 1912 at the request of Los Angeles dentist Kate D. Buck, who believed a small holding within the boundaries of a cooperative colony was an excellent antidote to the poisonous city life in California, Littlefield agreed to find her locations and followers for her scheme, the Los Angeles Fellowship Farms Company (1912). At a seventy-five-acre site at Puente near Santa Barbara, California, he established what Kate

Buck wanted. Twelve families lasted there until they found the holdings were too small to survive. In 1927 the farm was taken over by a water utility and disappeared. In 1930 Littlefield established a magazine, *Joy*.

See Also Fellowship Farm (Puente)

Sources:

Bedford, Henry. 1966. *Socialism and the Workers of Massachusetts*. Amherst: University of Massachusetts Press.

Fogarty, Robert S. 1990. *All Things New: American Communes and Utopian Movements 1860–1914*. Chicago: University of Chicago Press.

Hine, Robert, V. 1983. *California's Utopian Colonies*. Los Angeles: University of California Press.

Littlefield, George Elmer. 1911. *The Fellowship Farm Plan: How One Fellow Makes an Honest Living on the Land and Is a Free Man*. Westwood, Mass.: Ariel Press on Fellowship Farm.

———. 1928. *Illumination and Love*. Santa Barbara, Calif.: Red Rose Press.

LLANO DEL RIO COMPANY. The Llano del Rio Company was a cooperative colony (1914–1918) for socialists and labor union members. They were led by Job Harriman (1861–1925), an active socialist in California's politics since the early 1890s who had helped to establish Altruria. With five other families Harriman settled on 2,000 acres of desert land forty-five miles northeast of Los Angeles in Antelope Valley. The name of the company was taken from the Spanish name of a nearby creek. Within a year a hundred families came, and by 1917 the membership of the community was 900, of whom 175 were enrolled in the Llano school. Members were recruited to the colony through the magazine *The Western Comrade*. The colony's industries grew as much as its social life; many members worked as day laborers for neighboring farmers because the colony's operations were small and unprofitable. Conflict between nonresident directors and resident members, financial difficulties, and lawsuits against the colony combined to bring an end to Llano del Rio. In 1917 forty remaining members moved to a new community in Louisiana.

See also Altruria; Harriman, Job

Sources:

Fogarty, Robert S. 1990. *All Things New: American Communes and Utopian Movements 1860–1914*. Chicago: University of Chicago Press.

Hine, Robert V., ed. 1983. *California's Utopian Colonies*. Los Angeles: University of California Press.

Oved, Yaacov. 1987. *Two Hundred Years of American Communes*. New Brunswick, N.J.: Transaction Books.

LLOYD, HENRY DEMAREST. Henry Demarest Lloyd (1847–1903) was born in New York, studied at Columbia University and lectured on political economy, and was a student of law and admitted to the bar (1869). In 1872 he worked on the *Chicago Tribune* until 1885: toward the end of his work on the paper he joined its editorial staff. Thereafter, he devoted his time to writing, primarily as an economist. Among his publications are *A Strike of Millionaires against Miners, the Story of Spring Valley* (1894), *Wealth against Commonwealth* (1894), and *Labor Copartnership* (1899). In these works he mentions visits to cooperative shops and farms in Great Britain. He published *A Country without Strikes*, (1900), which describes the workings of arbitration in New Zealand, and *A Sovereign People* (1907), which was a study of democracy in Switzerland. He published *Men, the Workers* (1909), *Lords of Industry* (1910), and *Mazzini and Other Essays* (1910). His specialty was the study of labor. He advocated cooperation rather than competition between employers and employees and supported a socialistic control of industry. His writing was interesting and influential, even though it was largely the product of research into court records and other documents. He wrote vividly and forcefully. A prominent suppporter of utopian communes, he described himself as a socialist-anarchist individual, collectivist-individualist, communist, cooperativist, and aristocratic democrat.

See Also Anarchist Utopias

Sources:

Dudley, Lavinia P. 1963. *The Encyclopedia Americana*. International ed. New York: Americana Corporation.

Fogarty, Robert S. 1980. *Dictionary of American Communal History*. Westport, Conn.: Greenwood Press.

Lloyd, Henry Demarest. 1909. *Men, the Workers*. New York: Doubleday, Page.

Munslow, Alun, and Owen R. Ashton, eds. 1995. *Henry Demarest Lloyd's Critiques of American Capitalism, 1881–1903*. Lewiston: E. Mellen Press.

Oved, Yaacov. 1987. *Two Hundred Years of American Communes*. New Brunswick, N.J.: Transaction Books.

LONGLEY, ALCANDER. Alcander Longley (1832–1918) was born in Oxford, Ohio. In 1867 he and his family became probationary members of Icaria, the colony founded by Étienne Cabet (1788–1856) in Iowa, but withdrew after a few months. Longley had early adopted Fourieristic ideas, but after trying to organize several utopian colonies along the lines of cooperatives, he turned to communism. He established a communistic Icarian community in Missouri, Reunion Colony, which failed in 1867. In January 1868 he began to publish *The Communist*, which presented his own program of social reform and communist activities throughout the United States. In 1885, he changed the publication's name to *The Altruist* and continued publication until May 1917. For nearly fifty years he persisted in issuing his paper, despite the problems that he met, and working for the organization of ideal communities. Between 1868 and 1885 he tried five times to establish a communist society in Missouri. He worked at his trade during the intervals between these social experiments in the composing room of another St. Louis newspaper. He was always interested in political methods for the improvement of a society and was active in the Socialist Labor

Party of St. Louis. He married three times and had three children by his first wife.

See Also Reunion Colony

Sources:

Fogarty, Robert S. 1990. *All Things New: American Communes and Utopian Movements 1860–1914*. Chicago: University of Chicago Press.

Hine, Robert V. 1953. *California's Utopian Colonies*. 1983 ed. Berkeley: University of California Press.

Malone, Dumas, ed. 1933. *Dictionary of American Biography*. Vol. 6. New York: Charles Scribner's Sons.

Oved, Yaacov. 1987. *Two Hundred Years of American Communes*. New Brunswick, N.J.: Transaction Books.

LOOKING BACKWARD: 2000–1887. *Looking Backward: 2000–1887*, published in 1888 by Edward Bellamy (1850–1898), tells of a wealthy Bostonian, Julian West, who goes into a hypnotic sleep in 1887 and wakes in 2000. He falls in love with Edith—the name of his fiancée when he lived in 1887—who, with her father and friends, takes him on a tour of Boston, which now thrives in a utopian commonwealth. But for small personal items, private ownership in this commonwealth has disappeared; the people share the wealth of the nation and contribute to it as best they can in a comfortable, well-trained industrial army. Compulsion has given over to cooperation; because there is enough to live on, there is no fighting for, or hoarding of, scarce resources; it is not necessary for anyone to dominate; crime has been reduced by economic security and a healthy moral development; and the level of culture has risen remarkably. In his dreams Julian now sees the old society as unjust and its people as ruthless and driven by greed. Over 113 years these changes occurred without suffering or the distress of revolution because, in essence, humankind is good and deservedly attains and enjoys its noblest achievement—a social order that is both humane and rational. On publication in 1888 this utopia appeared eminently reasonable when compared with the irrational economic liberalism and terrifying industrial warfare that enhanced the wealth of the rich and the poverty of the dispossessed. The work's political impact was enormous. In two years it sold over 300,000 copies. Its principles were used to establish the Nationalist Party and 150 Bellamy Clubs, the first in Boston itself. The author founded the *New Nation* and spent his life furthering social reform and emphasizing small town virtues and a sense of community. With newspapers and campaigns, a movement emerged, and plans were made for the nation's citizens to own society's means of exchange, production, and distribution of goods and services. The movement attracted both conservative and radical interests. The impact of the book spread to Continental Europe, Russia, and Britain. *Looking Backward* was highly rated among the most influential books on social order published between 1885 and 1935. Its most noted contemporary critic was William Morris (1834–1896).

See Also Bellamy, Edward

Sources:

Bellamy, Edward. 1888. *Looking Backward: 2000–1887*. Boston: Tichnor. Edited with an introduction and notes by Robert C. Elliott, 1966, Boston: Houghton Mifflin (Riverside Editions). Edited with an introduction by Cecelia Tichi, 1982, New York: Penguin American Library. Edited with an introduction by Daniel H. Borus, 1995, New York: Bedford Series in Culture and History, St. Martin's Press.
———. 1897. *Equality*. Reprint 1970. New York: A.M.S. Press.
Geoghegan, Vincent. 1992. "The Utopian Past: Memory and History in Edward Bellamy's *Looking Backward* and William Morris's *News from Nowhere*." *Utopian Studies* 3, no. 2: 75–90.
Kumar, Krishan. 1987. *Utopia and Anti-utopia in Modern Times*. Oxford: Basil Blackwell.
Morris, William. 1899. "Looking Backward." *Commonweal* 5, 180: 194–195.
Murdoch, Norman H. 1992. "Rose Culture and Social Reform: Edward Bellamy's *Looking Backward* and William Booth's *Darkest England and the Way Out*." *Utopian Studies*, 3, no. 2: 91–101.
Patai, Daphne. 1989. *Looking Backward, 1988–1888: Essays on Edward Bellamy*. Amherst: University of Massachusetts Press.
Sadler, Elizabeth. 1944. "One Book's Influence: Edward Bellamy's 'Looking Backward.' " *New England Quarterly* 17: 530–555.

LORD OF THE FLIES. *Lord of the Flies* was the first published novel of William Gerald Golding (1911–1993). It is a fable of schoolboy adventures. A plane crashes on a desert island during a nuclear war. The survivors are schoolboys. At first the story suggests a new start for human civilization. But two factions emerge among the schoolboys: one is led by Jack, the totalitarian, and the other by Ralph, the democrat. In time they become savages, vindictive and barbaric to each other. The fat boy, Piggy, is tortured physically and psychologically and murdered with Simon, the symbol of Christ. A destroyer rescues the boys. Not until then does Ralph, Piggy's friend, see the breadth of the depravity that the boys experienced on the island. Golding took the idea for his realistic and dystopian fable from his years of teaching small boys at a private school in England and his service in the Royal Navy. He wanted to show that society's flaws take their origins from individuals, especially the natural tendency to aggression. The book made Golding an international writer immediately. The novel is an outstanding example of dystopian fiction. It was filmed in 1962–1963 by the notable British stage director Peter S. P. Brook (b. 1925) and met great acclaim.

See Also Dystopia; Golding, William Gerald

Sources:

Booker, M. Keith. 1994. *Dystopian Literature: A Theory and Research Guide*. Westport, Conn.: Greenwood.
Ousby, Ian, ed. 1988. *The Cambridge Guide to Literature in English*. 1995 ed. Cambridge: Cambridge University Press.

Magnussen, Magnus, and Rosemary Goring, eds. 1990. *Chambers Biographical Dictionary*. 5th ed. Edinburgh: Chambers.
Snodgrass, Mary Ellen. 1995. *Encyclopedia of Utopian Literature*. Santa Barbara, Calif.: ABC-CLIO.

LOVELL, ROBERT. Robert Lovell (c. 1770–1796) was born at Bristol, son of a wealthy Quaker. He was a poet and participator in the pantisocracy project of Robert Southey (1774–1843) and Samuel Taylor Coleridge (1772–1834). He married a beautiful actress, Mary Fricker, in 1794. Robert Southey became engaged to Mary Fricker's sister Edith, and Samuel Coleridge to another sister, Sara, whom he married in 1795. Next to their love of poetry Lovell and his two friends were deeply involved with their project for a utopia on the banks of the Susquehanna. Lovell was to bring his wife and his brother and sisters and his in-laws the Frickers. The plan had all but collapsed before Lovell's death in April 1796. His father refused to assist his daughter-in-law, Mary, after Robert's death because she had been an actress. It was left to Robert Southey to assist her and her infant son. She lived with Southey and, after his death, with his daughter Kate until her own death at the age of ninety. The son, Robert Lovell the younger, became a printer in London in 1824. He later went to Italy and disappeared without a trace.

See Also Coleridge, Samuel Taylor; Pantisocracy; Southey, Robert

Source:

Lee, Sidney, ed. 1920. *Dictionary of National Biography: Supplement 1901–1911*. London: Oxford University Press.

LUGARI, PAOLA. Paolo Lugari (b. 1944) was born in Popayán, Colombia, and educated at home. His father, a geographer, engineer, and attorney from Italy, had visited Colombia, decided to stay, and married into one of the country's finest families. Young Paolo was raised in the company of Colombia's notables and as a youth often sat at the table with diplomats and important politicians and joined them in discussing the country's future with government ministers. The future of Colombia and its plans for development and the happiness and welfare of its citizens were significant topics of discussion to Paolo. At the university in Bogotá he passed exams easily, became a noted orator, and received a United Nations scholarship to study development in the Far East. After studying how Filipinos had devised rare uses of animal and vegetable waste to make fuel, he returned to Colombia (1965) and was given the task of planning the development of Chocó, a tropical wilderness along Colombia's Pacific coast, where it was envisaged that deep rivers could be turned into a canal to rival the Panama Canal. Lugari did not agree that linking the Atlantic and Pacific was as important to Colombians as maintaining the unique heritage and environs of Chocó. Later, his uncle, the minister responsible for public works, invited Lugari to fly over barren land of the Orinocan llanos (prairie) in eastern Colombia. The land was to be given to wandering coffee farmers from the rich western slopes of the Andes who had been displaced from their lands and were fleeing Colombia's violent civil war. To the casual observer nothing of value would grow on the hot plains, there were no adequate roads, and in the rainy season malaria abounded. On this inhospitable savanna Paolo Lugari founded Gaviotas in 1972.

See Also Gaviotas

Source:

Weisman, Alan. 1997. *Gaviotas: A Village to Reinvent the World.* White River Junction, Vt.: Chelsea Green.

LUNACHARSKY, ANATOLY VASIL'YEVICH. Anatoly Vasil'yevich Luna-charsky (1875–1933) was born in Ukraine (Poltava), the son of an official, and educated at Kiev High School and Zurich University. While studying at Kiev High School, he joined the Social Democratic Circle (1892) and a year later moved to Switzerland, all the while maintaining close contact with a "liberation of labor" group. He studied natural science and philosophy, returned to Russia in 1897, and became a member of the RSDRP (Russian Social-Democratic Workers' Party). After the second RSDRP congress he sided with the Bolshe-viks. He was deported in 1898 for his revolutionary activities. He went into exile in Vologola and Pot'na (1901–1903). In 1904 he went to Geneva and joined the editorial staff of the Bolshevik newspapers *Vpered* (Forward) and, later, *Proletary.* In 1905 he returned to Petersburg and became an agitator who helped to edit the legal Bolshevik news, *Novayazhizn.* With Maxim Gorky (1868–1936) and Aleksandr Bogdanov (1873–1928) he established an advanced school for the elite Russian factory employees at Capri (1909). Lenin (1870–1924) opposed the project, and it was closed. After drifting for a short time Lunacharsky returned to Russia and after 1913 worked for the Bolshevik news-paper *Pravda.* In 1917 he was admitted to the Bolshevik group of the RSDRP. During the civil war he was a member of the Revolutionary Military Council. From 1927 he went abroad on diplomatic missions, was a cofounder and a member of the Sverlov Communist Academy, and helped reorganize higher and secondary education in the USSR. He had always thought religion and Marxism were compatible and published *Religion and Socialism* (1911). In his utopian view religion gave socialism an ethical foundation, made God and humankind equivalent, and, through revolution, gave humankind a means to attain God-like status. Such a belief promoted a culture with a proletarian base, provided its members were educated enough to see that socialism could light the way to a new world. He was a member of the USSR Academy of Science from 1930. He was buried by the Kremlin Wall on Moscow's Red Square.

See Also Bolshevism

Sources:

Beilharz, Peter, ed. 1992. *Social Theory: A Guide to Central Thinkers.* Sydney: Allen and Unwin.

McHenry, Robert, ed. 1992. *The New Encyclopedia Britannica*. Chicago: Encyclopedia Britannica.
Schulz, Heinrich E., Paul K. Urban, and Andrew I. Lebed, eds. 1972. *Who Was Who in the U.S.S.R.* Metuchen, N.J.: Scarecrow Press.

LUXEMBURG, ROSA. Rosa Luxemburg (1871–1919), born in Zamość, Poland, converted to communism in 1890 and, while serving an underground cause, helped establish the Polish Social Democratic Party, later to be the Polish Communist Party. She was an effective orator and writer and published *Social Reform or Revolution* (1889). After moving to Berlin in 1898 she became a leader of the left-wing social democrats. Her associate was Karl Liebknecht (1871–1919), with whom she formed the Spartakusbund (Spartacus League) at the outbreak of World War I. Her revolutionary activities forced her to spend most of the war in prison. After an abortive attempt to influence the Republican government of Friedrich Ebert (1871–1925), the social democrat who ruled Germany and led the nation into the Weimar Republic, Luxemburg was murdered by army officers during a workers' demonstration in Berlin.

See Also Ebert, Friedrich; Liebknecht, Karl; Social democracy; Spartacists

Sources:

Abrahams, Richard. 1989. *Rosa Luxemburg: A Life for the International*. Oxford: Berg.
Basso, Lelio. 1975. *Rosa Luxemburg: A Reappraisal*. Translated by Douglas Parmee. New York: Praeger.
Bronner, Stephen E. 1981. *A Revolutionary for Our Times: Rosa Luxemburg*. London: Pluto.
Ettinger, Ernst. 1986. *Rosa Luxemburg*. Boston: Beacon Press.
Frölich, Paul. 1940. *Rosa Luxemburg*. 1970 ed. Translated by Edward Fitzgerald. London: Gollancz.
Geras, Norman. 1976. *The Legacy of Rosa Luxemburg*. London: New Left Books.
Magnussen, Magnus, and Rosemary Goring, eds. 1990. *Chambers Biographical Dictionary*. 5th ed. Edinburgh: Chambers.
Nettl, J. Peter. 1966. *Rosa Luxemburg*. 2 vols. London: Oxford University Press.
Nye, Andrea. 1994. *Philosophia: The Thought of Rosa Luxemburg, Simone Weil and Hannah Arendt*. New York: Routledge.

M

MANDALA. Mandala was established by an eccentric ex-nun, Carla, in 1975 on 112 hectares (275 acres) near Warwick in Queensland. Bill Smale (b. 1944) and his wife were also founders of Mandala, which now is a thirty-five-member alternative community with anarchist qualities. To begin with, Carla, thirty-six, was the leading light until a strong team of members interested in participatory democracy ousted her. Although the community has experienced a large turnover of participants, eight founding members remain. For a long time it held together with little collective effort, and relative individualism prevailed, but in the late 1980s the community deliberated over becoming intentional and more communal. Today active members predominate, one result being the establishment of an Environmental Education Centre and the reorganization of the group as Mandala Community P/L (Proprietary Limited), in November 1993.

See Also Smale, Bill

Source:

Smale, Bill. 1995. "From Outrage to Insight." In Bill Metcalf, ed., *From Utopian Dreaming to Communal Reality: Cooperative Life Styles in Australia*, pp. 99–114. Sydney: University of New South Wales Press.

MANEA FEN. Manea Fen, an Owenite agricultural community, was established in Cambridgeshire on a small estate plus acreage nearby belonging to William Hodson (fl. 1838–1840). The Manea Fen trustees called themselves "communists," with a motto "all amongst us is ours." They sought recruits of sober, honest, and industrious character. The estate was under their management by July 1839. They built houses, a communal kitchen, dormitories, and married quarters, laid a railway, constructed a brick kiln, a clay pit, and an observatory, and announced plans for seventy-two cottages. Edward Thomas Craig (1804–1894), a pioneer in cooperation, taught school. A cricket ground was laid, a gymnasium was put to use, and a laboratory was planned. At first the local community was hostile to these developments, but Manea Fen flourished and recruited more skilled workers. With power tools they built a windmill and then later bought 1,000 fruit trees. The community flourished so well that many members expected the capital that they had borrowed would be repaid in three years. Also their self-government was successful, and members hoped that not long after their first year the community would have 700 members. At Manea Fen money was replaced with labor notes that could be cashed at the community store. The members designed and produced uniforms for men and women. Plans were made for three more pottery kilns and a school. Four directors were appointed to deal with visitors who came to inspect the venture. With its strong agricultural base, Manea Fen developed a close relationship with Tytherly, a more orthodox Owenite community with educational interests. Moves were made to unite the fifty members of Manea Fen and the small group at Tytherly. But conflict grew among the leaders over this scheme, and at Christmas 1840 evidence of financial problems emerged, and questions were raised about William Hodson's leadership. The community split into two groups: one supported Hodson, and the other did not. In February 1841 Hodson was shot. Terrorist conflict and brutal destruction of property followed. Most members resigned, and Manea Fen ended.

See Also Craig, Edward Thomas; Hodson, William; Tytherly

Sources:

Armytage, Walter Henry Green. 1961. *Heavens Below: Utopian Experiments in England 1560–1950*. London: Routledge and Kegan Paul.
Harrison, John F. C. 1969. *Robert Owen and the Owenites in Britain and America: Quest for the New Moral World*. New York: Charles Scribner's Sons.

MARION, ELIE. Elie Marion (fl. 1708) was a French prophet who wandered through Europe at the command of the Holy Spirit and for a time helped lead the Camisards, a Protestant peasant group in the Cevannes region of France. After predicting that London would burn and the world would end, Marion was convicted of both profanity and terrorism.

See Also Camisards; Fage, Durand

Source:

Garrett, Clarke. 1987. *Spirit Possession and Popular Religion: From the Camisards to the Shakers*. Baltimore: Johns Hopkins University Press.

MARTIN, JAMES J. James J. Martin (fl. 1884–1914) helped establish with Brunette Haskell (1857–1907) the Industrial Co-operative Union of Kaweah (1885–1892) in California. Martin and Haskell were two labor leaders of the International Working Men's Association in San Francisco. The credit for this cooperative is given largely to Haskell, not to Martin. The Kaweah venture failed, partly due to conflict between the two men. Afterward Martin organized a utopian colony, United Self Helpers, in Vancouver, British Columbia (1912), and later another colony in Tasmania, Australia (1914).

See Also Haskell, Burnette; Kaweah Co-operative Commonwealth

Sources:

Fogarty, Robert S. 1980. *Dictionary of American Communal History.* Westport, Conn.: Greenwood Press.

Hine, Robert V. 1953. *California's Utopian Colonies.* 1983 ed. Berkeley: University of California Press.

Johnpol, Bernard K., and Harvey Klehr, eds. 1986. *Biographical Dictionary of the American Left.* Westport, Conn.: Greenwood Press.

Oved, Yaacov. 1987. *Two Hundred Years of American Communes.* New Brunswick, N.J.: Transaction Books.

MARX, KARL. Karl Marx (1818–1883) was a German economist and revolutionary socialist, born at Trier. His family were middle-class and gave him many advantages, including a sound education. He studied history and philosophy at the universities of Bonn (1835–1836) and Berlin (1836–1841), received his doctorate from the University of Jena (1842), and worked as a journalist. After a year he went to Paris and joined political radicals with whom he agreed that, under capitalism, alienation of humankind abounded, and the proletariat must become the major agent of revolutionary social change. His own radicalism attracted attention of the Prussian government, and he was forced to go to Brussels (1845). He organized the German Communist League with help from Friedrich Engels (1820–1895), who would become a lifelong associate, colleague, and support. They collaborated on *German Ideology*, published posthumously, which stated fully the materialist view of history. In 1847–1848 he wrote the *Communist Manifesto*, a powerful revolutionary call to workers to unite and attack capitalists, concluding: "The proletarians have nothing to lose but their chains. They have a world to win. Working men of all countries unite!" In 1848 he was expelled from Europe and lived in England until his death. He was supported financially by Engels and worked in the British Museum preparing for publication of one of the most influential works ever written, *Das Kapital* (3 vols.; 1867, 1884, 1894). In this work he developed his ideas of surplus value, conflict between economic classes, and the exploitation of labor and predicted that capitalism would be superseded by socialism and that in time the state would wither away as a classless, communist society emerged. Communists had the role of easing the pain of this development. He returned to politics and appeared as a leader at the First International (Workingmen's Association) in 1862 and remained an influence until the association split in 1872, when anarchists gained an upper hand. Some critics argue that Marxism has given rise to widely unacceptable and even inhuman political systems. Current supporters partly agree but also assert that human brutishness rather than Marxist ideals was responsible for the failure, especially in Russia. Notwithstanding, Marx's ideas have greatly influenced social sciences, and the secular followers of his thought outnumber those of any other political persuasion.

See Also Marxist community

Sources:

Carver, Terrell. 1988. *A Marx Dictionary*. Cambridge: Polity.
————, ed. 1991. *The Cambridge Companion to Marx*. Cambridge: Cambridge University Press.
Little, Daniel. 1986. *The Scientific Marx*. Minneapolis: University of Minnesota Press.
McLellan, David. 1975. *Marx*. London: Fontana.
Sills, David L., ed. 1968. *International Encyclopedia of the Social Sciences*. New York: Macmillan and Free Press.
Singer, Peter 1980. *Marx*. Oxford: Oxford University Press.

MARXIST COMMUNITY. A Marxist community assumes that economic factors (forces and relations of production) are the major contributors to cultural change. Change occurs in stages: social revolution, a class struggle between those who have variable access to economic production, and the formation of economic institutions and an ideology to maintain them. Also it is believed the society will survive where, through common ownership of economic production, bitter, envy-driven conflict is prevented, for example, as in a socialist or communist society. Finally, it assumes a capitalist society is transitory and may become a socialist or communist society through either violent revolution or liberal and humane means. The *Communist Manifesto* rejected utopian social experiments because they deadened the class struggle and were the basis of reactionary sects. Although utopia generally was not accepted, Marx's writings do contain utopias. The utopian society of the craftsman appears in his *Paris Manuscripts* (1844), where alienated workers live in an ideal political economy. In *The German Ideology* (1845) Marx's ideas are cognate with those of Charles Fourier (1772–1837) in that they again oppose the alienation that emerges from an oppressive division of labor. In the *Grundrisse* (1857–1858) Marx advocates a workingmen's utopia of creative labor in a criticism of Adam Smith (1723–1790) and advances the view that work fulfills a human need. In the third volume of *Das Kapital* utopian freedom for labor is extended beyond work to an ideology justifying freedom at work and advocating a variety of socialism where workers participate in work-related decisions. Variations on these themes appear as Marxist-Leninism, Neo-Marxism, Stalinism, and Maoism.

See Also Marx, Karl

Sources:

Beilharz, Peter. 1992. *Labour's Utopias: Bolshevism, Fabianism, Social Democracy*. London: Routledge. Pp. 7–14 for a summary of Marx's views on utopias.
Brzezinski, Zbigniew. 1990. *The Grand Failure: The Birth and Death of Communism in the Twentieth Century*. London: Macdonald.

Kolakowski, Leszek. 1978. *Main Currents of Marxism: Its Rise, Growth and Dissolution*. Translated by P. S. Falb. 3 vols. Oxford: Clarendon Press.

Lichtheim, George. 1961. *Marxism: An Historical and Critical Study*. Rev. ed., 1967. London: Routledge and Kegan Paul.

McLellan, David. 1980. *Marxism after Marx: An Introduction*. London: Macmillan.

Schapiro, Leonard B. 1960. *The Communist Party of the Soviet Union*. 2d rev. ed., 1970. London: Eyre and Spottiswood.

MARYKNOLL. Maryknoll was begun in 1949 by the Australian National Catholic Rural movement. Founded in 1939, the movement envisaged small communities with members living in a natural habitat, enjoying a diversified farm economy, self-sufficient in food. The model for the community came from the European village. The town was built as a cooperative village on 250 hectares (620 acres) forty-two miles southeast of Melbourne, Victoria. At Maryknoll houses were built in a circle around the church, school, and community hall. With sound business advice from the Catholic Church, screen-printing and joinery firms and a soft-drink factory were established. Community members had three kinds of work: paid jobs, part-time work on their holdings, and part-time work for the community. The pioneers lived in a community on a poor farm with no water or power and with many children. The community grew from seven families in 1950 to seventy, all Catholics at first. In the early 1950s the community split when the Australian Labor Party divided over its relations to communism, and a Catholic working-class party developed, the Democratic Labor Party (DLP). In the late 1960s Maryknoll opened its membership to non-Catholics but always remained a DLP stronghold. In the early 1980s it became clear that the younger generation did not want to continue the cooperative community life their elders had established. The community's money was divided around the original shareholders, and Maryknoll became like any other town community. By 1995 it had only forty-five families and had lost some of its sense of communality. Nevertheless, its spirit is flourishing today. The remaining original community members showed much compassion when they welcomed a new community, the Windana Society's thirty-bed therapeutic community for drug addicts.

Sources:

Heinrichs, Paul. 1998. "Remembering Maryknoll: Santamaria's Rural Religious Commune Is Almost Forgotten." *The Sunday Age* (Melbourne), 8 March, The News: 8.

Metcalf, Bill, ed. 1995. *From Utopian Dreaming to Communal Reality: Cooperative Life Styles in Australia*, p. 36. Sydney: University of New South Wales Press.

Santamaria, B. A. 1981. *Against the Tide*, pp. 49–50. Melbourne: Oxford University Press.

MASLOW, ABRAHAM H. Abraham Harold Maslow (1908–1970) was born in Brooklyn, New York, and educated at the City College of New York, Cornell

University, and the University of Wisconsin. In 1948 he began teaching humanistic psychology at Brandeis University in Massachusetts. He assumed that humans are wanting animals and that once a need, desire, or want is gratified, another takes over; that is, when satisfied, lower-order needs (food, shelter) are replaced by higher-order needs (social contact). In unusual cases the highest order of need satisfaction centered on the powerful drive for self-actualization—the need to become all that one is capable of. Maslow became deeply interested in the lives of self-actualizing people and how they differed from others. They seemed to enjoy an unusual state of psychological health and to free themselves from the labels and prejudices thrust upon them by others; they tended to be realistic and act with little anxiety or defensiveness and enjoyed an intense awareness of themselves, joy, insight, and what became known as "peak experiences." Maslow described these experiences in his *Toward a Psychology of Being* (1962). Because they had become free of the powerful competitive need that dominates most humankind, these people were politically stable. Such people could well be suited to the formation of a special utopia. Maslow approached this possibility with his outline of Eupsychia. In 1967 Maslow was named humanist of the year by the American Humanist Association. Also in 1967, he was elected president of the American Psychological Association. He wrote about a utopia, Eupsychia, where people were permissive, wish-respecting and wish-gratifying. He died in Menlo Park, California.

See Also Eupsychia

Sources:

Garraty, John A., and Mark C. Carnes, eds. 1988. *Dictionary of American Biography.* Supplement 8. New York: Charles Scribner's Sons and Collier Macmillan.

Hoffman, Edward. 1988. *The Right to Be Human: A Biography of Abraham Maslow.* Los Angeles: J. P. Tarcher.

Lowry, Richard J., and Jonathan Freedman, eds. 1982. *The Journals of Abraham Maslow.* Lexington, Mass.: Lewis.

MATTHIAS, ROBERT. Robert Matthias (fl. 1830s) led a notorious community of perfectionists in New York in the 1830s. An earlier leader of the community, the merchant Elija Pierson, who had become a religious fanatic and tried to reincarnate his wife through prayer, attracted some perfectionists by leading them to believe that prayers, combined with controlled fantasies, would make it possible for them to become apostles who could cure the sick and use prayer to bring back the dead. In May 1832 he was approached by Robert Matthias, self-appointed Prophet of God and Jews, who joined Pierson's community and soon took over as its leader. In August 1833, at Sing Sing, two of Matthias' followers provided acreage for the community. In the community the members bathed together, enjoyed shameless nakedness, replaced marriage with a spiritual matching, and swapped sleeping partners. They called the community Mount Zion, and the neighbors were scandalized by its free love policy. Matthias fled to New York City, and Pierson took over the community. But he died—perhaps poisoned by Matthias—and with its free love practices the community came to Manhattan. Benjamin Folger, who had given the land at Sing Sing to the community, offered to pay Matthias $630 if he left the community. When he did, Folger told the police that Matthias had stolen the money. The police caught Matthias and charged him with fraud and embezzlement. Strangely, Matthias was tried instead for the murder of Pierson. He was acquitted and later found guilty of assault, was jailed for three months, and then disappeared.

See Also Kingdom of Matthias; Truth, Sojourner

Sources:

Fogarty, Robert S. 1990. *All Things New: American Communes and Utopian Movements 1860–1914*. Chicago: University of Chicago Press.
Johnson, Paul E., and Sean Wilentz. 1994. *The Kingdom of Matthias*. New York: Oxford University Press.

MAXWELL COMMUNITY. The Maxwell Community, named after Robert Owen's (1771–1858) house in New Lanark, was founded in Canada in the late 1820s. The founder, Henry Jones (fl. 1820–1827), a retired naval officer from Devonshire, had heard Owen speak in the early 1820s, visited New Lanark, and decided he wanted to use his fortune to establish a similar community in Canada. He found a suitable site of 10,000 acres on the shores of Lake Huron, Lamberton County, Ontario. In 1827, with many families dedicated to establishing Owen's "social system," he returned to Canada. Members of the community held possessions in common. During the years that the community flourished, Jones used his funds to build a communal house, separate apartments for each family, a common kitchen, school, and a general store. At Maxwell the women worked together preparing the food, while the men worked in groups to clear the community's land. In the early 1830s the community disbanded because plentiful, cheap land attracted many members of the community who wanted to work their own holdings, and, some say, a fire destroyed the main community house.

See Also Owen, Robert; Owenism; Owenite communities

Sources:

Fogarty, Robert S. 1980. *Dictionary of American Communal History*. Westport, Conn.: Greenwood Press.
Harrison, John F. C. 1969. *Robert Owen and the Owenites in Britain and America: Quest for the New Moral World*. New York: Charles Scribner's Sons.
Kolmerten, Carol A. 1990. *Women in Utopia*. Bloomington: Indiana University Press.

McCUBBIN, FREDERICK. Frederick McCubbin (1855–1917), an Australian artist, was born in Melbourne, Victoria, and attended the Artisans' School of Design in Carlton (1867–1870) and afterward the artist's school of the National Gallery of Victoria (1872–1886). He studied there at night until 1877 and then became a full-time painter. In 1886 he was appointed a teacher of drawing at the school. He married Ann Moriarty (1889) and had seven children. In 1885 he established with Tom Roberts (1856–1931) and Louis Abrahams (1852–1903) the first artist's camp at Box Hill, outside Melbourne, later to be known as the Heidelberg School. At this time he painted large subjects, and not until 1907, when he visited Europe, under the influence of Roberts, did his work become more impressionistic. Outstanding works such as *The Pioneers* and *The Lost Child* date from his Box Hill period. He remained as drawing master at the National Gallery of Victoria from 1886 until he died.

See Also Conder, Charles Edward; Heidelberg School; Roberts, Thomas William; Streeton, Arthur Ernest

Sources:

McCulloch, Susan, and Alan McCulloch. 1994. *The Encyclopedia of Australian Art.* Sydney: Allen and Unwin.
Magnussen, Magnus, Rosemary Goring, and John O. Thorn, eds. 1990. *Chambers Biographical Dictionary.* Edinburgh: Chambers.
Splatt, William, and Dugald McLellan. 1986. *The Heidelberg School: The Golden Summer of Australian Painting.* Melbourne: Lloyd O'Neil.

McWHIRTER, MARTHA WHITE. Martha White McWhirter (1827–1904) was born in Jackson County, Tennessee, and joined the Methodist Church when she was sixteen. For twenty-five years she was an active supporter of the Church, married in 1845, and went with her family to Belton, Texas. After the death of her brother and two of her children in 1866 she became convinced that God was punishing her. In 1867 she heard God's voice, and she began to attend Methodist prayer meetings. Shortly afterward a Pentecostal baptism led her to believe that she was sanctified in the tradition of the perfectionists. She began to hold weekly prayer meetings for the women of the town and preached sanctification. The women followers (sisters) practiced celibacy, and this led to marriage breakdowns. Many separated from their husbands, escaping violent, unhappy marriages, while others felt they were forced to leave the household of unsanctified husbands. The community cared for the children as a group. Martha founded the Women's Commonwealth (1874), which achieved economic independence by 1879. They established a hotel in Belton with an inheritance from one of the sisters and founded Belton's public library. In 1898 the community moved to Washington, D.C., where they managed and occupied their boardinghouse. Martha McWhirter was their leader, and when she died, the community faded, moved to their Maryland farm, and lasted only ten more years.

See Also Women's Commonwealth (Sanctificationists)

Sources:

Fischer, Ernest G. 1980. *Marxists and Utopias in Texas.* Burnett, Tex.: Eakin Press.
Fogarty, Robert. 1990. *All Things New: American Communes and Utopian Movements 1860–1914.* Chicago: University of Chicago Press.

James, Eleanor. 1975. "Martha White McWhirter (1827–1904)." In Evelyn M. Carring-
    ton, ed., *Women in Early Texas*, pp. 180–190. Austin, Tex.: Jenkins.
Moment, Gairdner B., and Otto F. Kraushoar, eds. 1980. *Utopias, the American Expe-
    rience*. London: Scarecrow Press.

MEEKER, NATHANIEL COOK. Nathaniel Cook Meeker (1817–1879), was
born in Euclid, near Cleveland, Ohio. He was educated in Oberlin and Hudson.
From the early 1830s until 1870 he was a wanderer, changing his residence and
work often. He worked for a newspaper in New Orleans, a teacher in Euclid, a
writer in New York, and a teacher in Allentown, Pennsylvania (1842), and at
Orange, New Jersey (1843), and in 1844 he ran a business store at Euclid. He
was interested in the teachings of Charles Fourier (1772–1837) and lectured on
his ideas and joined the Fourierist Trumball Phalanx in Ohio. He worked on the
farm, lectured, taught school, prospered, and learned how much cooperative
people would tolerate. He found that three years were enough on a cooperative
farm and in 1849 went back to business in Euclid. He opened a store also in
Hiram. In 1865 he was on the staff of The *New York Tribune* as the agricultural
editor, and with the support of the newspaper's editor, Horace Greeley (1811–
1872) he launched Union Colony, December 1869. Union Colony banned sa-
loons and billiard halls and opened a school and library. Neighbors thought that
the colonists were cranks and that Meeker, tall, awkward, and slow-speaking,
was a tactless eccentric. He found it difficult to settle but remained for eight
years. In 1878 he took an appointment as an Indian agent at the White River
Reservation. Because he lacked any tact or understanding, he had difficulties
with the Native Americans; those who were hostile to his plans, Utes, rode in
and killed him and all the other white men in the agency.

  See Also: Greeley, Horace; Union Colony

Sources:

Hayden, Dolores. 1976. *Seven American Utopias*. Cambridge: MIT Press.
Malone, Dumas, ed. 1933. *Dictionary of American Biography*. Vol. 6. New York: Charles
    Scribner's Sons.

MEMNONIA INSTITUTE. Memnonia Institute was established in 1856, Yellow Springs, Ohio, and lasted about one year. It was established as a "school
of life" by Thomas Low Nichols (1815–1901) and his wife, Mary Sargeant
Neal Gove Nichols (1810–1884), after they left Modern Times on Long Island.
The president of Antioch College thought the institute was a colony of free love;
in fact, it followed Charles Fourier's (1772–1837) ideas at first, then turned to
asceticism, fasting, and spiritual penance. The institute was apparently named
after Voltaire's play about the folly of having too much wisdom. Its twenty
members grew less and less Fourierist and ever more religious, and after six
months most of them joined the Roman Catholic Church.

  See Also Modern Times; Nichols, Mary Sargeant Neal Gove; Nichols,
Thomas Low

Source:

Fogarty, Robert S. 1980. *Dictionary of American Communal History*. Westport, Conn.:
    Greenwood Press.

MÉNILMONTANT. Ménilmontant was a utopian community that espoused the
ideas of Claude Henri Saint-Simon (1760–1825) in France. Barthèlemey Prosper
Enfantin (1796–1864) led followers of Saint-Simon, called himself the ''Supreme Father'' of the church of the Saint-Simonians, and in the 1830s helped
them establish a utopian community outside Paris at Ménilmontant. After much
gossip, a court case, and extensive scandal, the community was disbanded amid
charges that they were a band of free-love advocates.

    See Also Enfantin, Barthèlemey Prosper; Saint-Simon, Claude Henri de Rou-
vroy, Comte de

Source:

Kanter, Rosabeth Moss. 1973. *Communes: Creating and Managing the Collective Life*.
    New York: Harper and Row.

MENNONITES. Mennonites, members of a sixteenth-century Protestant sect,
combine some of the characteristics of the Baptists and the Friends. Through
the use of evangelism, dividing and splitting into groups, and natural population
growth, they spread through Europe. When subject to excessive political, religious, and economic oppression in Europe, they curbed extremism and fanaticism
within their ranks and thereby maintained their identity, immigrated to the
United States, and emerged as Anabaptist-Mennonites or Hutterites, Amish, and
simply Mennonites. They believe that mature and reflective religious experience
lies at the base of community life and that community life shapes a special
identity or sense of individuality. Their original, unique religious ideas centered
on the belief that baptism should be administered only by confession of faith.
This makes baptism inappropriate for infants. Also they refuse to take oaths to
bear arms; they condemn divorce and refuse to act out of revenge. Their basic
religious belief is in Christianity and that they, through congregating to reflect
upon their religious experiences, can restore the church to its pure and original
state. This can best be done by founding a commonwealth, whose members vow
to put God first. To begin with, every generation is taught fundamental traditions, symbols to uphold, and importance of cohesive interpersonal relations
and binding obligations in the community. The communities reject the need for
an overarching state, nation, or a state church or the need to participate in any
state activities; they advocate a separate existence for their members in a peaceful, well-disciplined community. Also they support the right of all humankind
to do as they do and a continuous program of aid to all those in need outside
the community. Many scholars have studied the social life and history of Mennonites, and the literature on their communities is vast.

    See Also Simons, Menno

Sources:

Fretz, J. Winfield. 1989. *The Waterloo Mennonites: A Community in Paradox*. Waterloo: Wilfrid Laurier University Press.

Janzen, William. 1992. ''Limits on Liberty: The Experience of Mennonite, Hutterite and Doukhobor Communities in Canada.'' *University of Toronto Law Journal* 42: 239–246.

Oved, Yaacov. 1987. *Two Hundred Years of American Communes*. New Brunswick, N.J.: Transaction Books.

Redekop, Calvin. 1989. *Mennonite Society*. Baltimore: Johns Hopkins University Press.

Redekop, Calvin, and Sam Steiner. 1986. *Mennonite Identity: Historical and Contemporary Perspective*. Lanham, Md.: University Press of America.

METLAKATLA PASS. Metlakatla Pass, Canada, is at an ancestral Tsimshian village where William Duncan (1832–1918) created a utopian Christian Indian settlement in 1862. He led several hundred Indians to the sites to escape a smallpox epidemic. The settlement was prosperous, and Duncan's ideas were widely recognized, respected, and imitated. However, the community split when the Anglican Church at Victoria sent a new bishop to Metlakatla who undermined Duncan's authority and disagreed with the idea of secular progress in the Christian community and its failure to offer communion to converts. In 1887 the divided villagers took sides, and many Tsimshian established another independent Christian utopia at New Metlakatla, Annette Island, Alaska.

See Also Duncan, William

Source:

Halpenny, Frances G., ed. 1990. *Dictionary of Canadian Biography*. Toronto: University of Toronto Press and Les Presses de L'Université Laval.

METZ, CHRISTIAN. Christian Metz (1794–1867) was born in Neuwied, Prussia, and his family moved to Ronneburg, Hesse (1801), where they were members of the Community of True Inspiration, a group much influenced by German mystics and Pietists. At the time membership in the Community of True Inspiration was declining. In 1817 Metz had the truth revealed to him during a religious revival, and later he was recognized as the community leader, inspired by God to secure the community's future. Early in the 1840s he led a group of Inspirationists who had been under regular attack for their beliefs by local religious authorities. After preaching in Saxony and Switzerland in 1842, fleeing both the pressures of government and the rising rents, he and his followers emigrated to the United States. On Metz's death his Amana Community was thriving with its own factories, stores, churches, and schools on about 25,000 acres in Iowa.

See Also Amana Colonies

Sources:

Fogarty, Robert S. 1990. *All Things New: American Communes and Utopian Movements 1860–1914*. Chicago: University of Chicago Press.

Johnson, Allen, ed. 1927. *Dictionary of American Biography.* Vol. 1. New York: Charles
    Scribner's Sons.
Oved, Yaacov. 1987. *Two Hundred Years of American Communes.* New Brunswick, N.J.:
    Transaction Books.

MODERN TIMES. Modern Times, a community established on Long Island by
Josiah Warren (1798–1874), was one of the first anarchist communities in the
United States. Its members practiced free love during the 1850s, and the community lasted for about twenty years. After 1880, as the flow of German and
Russian emigrants to the United States increased, many of them Jews, the anarchist movement changed and developed conventional social revolutionary interests.

    See Also Anarchist Utopias; Equity Colony; Time Store; Utopia; Warren,
Josiah

Sources:

Fogarty, Robert S. 1980. *Dictionary of American Communal History.* Westport, Conn.:
    Greenwood Press.
Kesten, Seymour. 1993. *Utopian Episodes: Daily Life in Experimental Colonies Dedi-
    cated to Changing the World.* Syracuse, N.Y.: Syracuse University Press.
Oved, Yaacov. 1987. *Two Hundred Years of American Communes.* New Brunswick, N.J.:
    Transaction Books.
Veysey, Laurence. 1973. *The Communal Experience: Anarchist and Mystical Counter-
    cultures in America.* New York: Harper and Row.

MODJESKA, HELENA. Helena Modjeska (1840–1909), née Helena Opid, born
in Kraków, Poland, became a notable actress in her homeland (1865–1878).
Around her formed a group of Polish dissidents who wished to escape the censorship of Polish theater. At the time Helena was unwell. The group emigrated
to California and formed a colony to escape oppression and to advance a healthier lifestyle. The colony lasted six months, and most colonists returned home.
With her family Helena stayed in the United States, improved her English, and
acted in *Camille, Mary Stuart,* and several Shakespearean plays. She also appeared on the British stage. In 1893 she spoke out publicly at the Columbian
Exposition in Chicago against oppression in Poland. She died in California and
was buried in Kraków.

    See Also Modjeska's Colony

Sources:

Fogarty, Robert S. 1980. *Dictionary of American Communal History.* Westport, Conn.:
    Greenwood Press.
Hine, Robert V. 1953. *California's Utopian Colonies.* 1983 ed. Berkeley: University of
    California Press.
Magnussen, Magnus, and Rosemary Goring, eds. 1990. *Chambers Biographical
    Dictionary.* 5th ed. Edinburgh: Chambers.

MODJESKA'S COLONY. Modjeska's Colony had about thirty Polish émigrés, mainly artists and intellectuals who aimed to escape censorship of the theater in Poland and settle near Anaheim in Santa Ana Valley, California (1877–1878). The colony was named after Helena Modjeska (1840–1909), a notable actress around whom the group's activities revolved. Basing their scheme on Brook Farm in Massachusetts, the community also sought a healthier style of life. The émigrés expected a civilized setting for their new life. Pamphlets from the Department of Agriculture in Washington led them to anticipate a reasonably comfortable setting. They were misled. Not only were the amenities poor and the housing inadequate, but also the setting was far too plain and ordinary for them. The community members had insufficient finances, lacked the farming skills needed to milk cows and kill animals for food, and often had their goods taken by neighbors. The colony lasted only six months. Most colonists returned home. The community appears in Modjeska's *Memories and Impressions* (1910).

Sources:

Fogarty, Robert S. 1980. *Dictionary of American Communal History*. Westport, Conn.: Greenwood Press.
Hine, Robert V. 1953. *California's Utopian Colonies*. 1983 ed. Berkeley: University of California Press.
Starr, Kevin. 1973. *America and the Californian Dream: 1850–1915*. New York: Oxford University Press.

MOLLISON, BILL. William C. Mollison (fl.1940–1998) was born in the small Tasmanian fishing village of Stanley, and at age fifteen he left school to help manage the family bakery. Later he worked as a seaman, millworker, tractor-driver, and glassblower; he worked nine years at the Wildlife Survey Section of the Commonwealth Scientific and Industrial Research Organisation (CSIRO), the Tasmanian Museum, and the Inland Fisheries Commission. In 1968 he became a tutor at the University of Tasmania and later a senior lecturer in environmental psychology. He published papers on the genealogy of Tasmanian Aborigines and on lower vertebrates of Tasmania. He returned to Tasmania to write a treatise on Tasmanian Aborigines and in 1978, with David Holmgen, developed the concept of permaculture and spread the idea around the world. Permaculture was conceived as the conscious design and maintenance of agriculturally productive ecosystems that were diverse, stable, and resilient and involved the harmonious integration of landscape and people for food, energy, shelter, material and nonmaterial needs in a sustainable way. In 1986 Mollison wrote that "without Permaculture agriculture there is no possibility of a stable social order." With permaculture individuals work with nature, follow thoughtful observations, and promote functional relations between elements of ecosystems. Permaculture has advocates in over 100 countries and publishes *Permaculture International Journal*.

See Also Permaculture

Sources:

Mollison, Bill C. 1988. *Permaculture: Designer's Manual*. Twalgum, New South Wales: Tagari.

———. 1996. *Travels in Dreams "One Fatfoot after the Other": The Autobiography of Bill Mollison*. Twalgum, New South Wales: Tagari.

MONDRAGÓN COOPERATIVES. The Mondragón cooperatives began in northern Spain, southeast of Bilboa in the valleys of Guipuzcoa Province. Mondragón is the center of more than 100 employee-owned cooperatives, Spain's major producer of microchips, and the country's largest appliance maker. The network covers three provinces of the Basque territory. It began in 1943, when Father José Maria Arizmendiarrieta (1915–1976) founded a technical school; in 1956 the first cooperative was established. They make kitchen products under the name FAGOR. FAGOR emerged from the group Ulgor, an eponym made from the first letter of the names of five engineers who founded the group in 1956. All five were students of Father Arizmendiarrieta. Every member who is hired to work in the cooperative lends a prescribed sum to it and gets a fixed interest rate. They are paid with wages, 6 percent fixed interest on capital, and profits on the cooperative's shares, until the member's retirement. The labor market sets the wage level, limited by a 6:1 ratio between highest and lowest wage levels. The original levels were 3:1. Managers are appointed for four years by an elected Supervisory Board, accountable to the cooperative's General Assembly. Another elected body, the Social Council, attends to members' needs as workers rather than owners. Management is accountable to the latter and works with the former. The cooperative's bank unites the members, provides capital, expert advice, and planning assistance, and, through agreement with members, effectively controls most of the cooperative's policies, especially compensation. In the cooperative network are a research institute that studies new technologies, a pension scheme, an educational system, and a division that encourages new product development. Each is governed by boards accountable to the member cooperatives in the network, as well as to their own working shareholders. The cooperative is linked with the Basque nationalist movement, and the school system teaches the Basque language and nationalist values. The growth rate of the cooperative was four times that of Spain's industrial output 1976–1983. In the 1976–1986 recession, when 150,000 Basque jobs were lost, the cooperative created 4,200 jobs, and no member lacked employment or assistance. The cooperative guards against abuse and exploitation, advances the security of rewards, extends its elaborate secondary cooperative networks, and furthers a sense of moral achievement. It is a middle-class familial utopia, with benefits for both personal and communal life in housing, schools, social welfare, and health programs. Participative action research on the cooperative has grown from Mondragón's collaboration with Cornell University and the efforts of William Foote Whyte (1989, 1991).

See Also Arizmendiarrieta, José Maria

Sources:

Hoover, Kenneth R. 1992. "Mondragón's Answers to Utopia's Problems." *Utopian Studies* 3, no. 2: 1–20.

McCord, William. 1989. *Voyages to Utopia: From Monastery to Commune, the Search for the Perfect Society in Modern Times.* New York: W. W. Norton.

Meek, Christopher, and Warner Woodworth. 1991. "Technical Training and Enterprise: Mondragón's Educational System and Its Implications for Other Cooperatives." *Economic and Industrial Democracy* 11, no. 4: 505–528.

Whyte, William F., and Kathleen K. Whyte. 1988. *Making Mondragón: The Growth and Dynamics of the Worker Cooperative Complex.* 2d ed., 1991. Ithaca, N.Y.: Cornell University ILR Press.

MONTE-CRISTO. Monte-Cristo, a lavish chateau, was built by the French novelist Alexandre Dumas, "Dumas pére" (1802–1870), on thirteen acres of forest above the Seine Valley. It was to be a small retreat where he could write far enough from Paris to avoid crowds of curious onlookers. Under guidance from the architect Hippolyte Durand (1809–1881), Dumas was so carried away with the construction that by 1847 the private utopia had become a "paradise on earth in miniature." Its budget rose from 48,000 francs to over 200,000. In the summer of 1847, fifty guests were invited to the housewarming, but over 550 gate-crashed. At the time one observer wrote that the building was ostentatious, lacked taste, and was obviously built by one whose morals were ruled by extravagance. In a year Monte-Cristo bankrupted Dumas, having engorged over half a million francs. Under pressure from his creditors Dumas sold his personal utopia for one-seventh of what it had cost him. In 1970, after years of neglect, it was to be demolished, but following an appeal led by a noted French historian, Monte-Cristo was bought by the nearby townships, restored, and opened to the public.

Source:

Foote-Greenwell, Victoria. 1996. "Alexandre Dumas: One for All." *Smithsonian* 27, no. 4: 110–122.

MONTESSORI, MARIA. Maria Montessori (1870–1952) studied at the University of Rome and was the first woman in Italy to graduate in medicine (1894). In 1898 she opened the Orthophrenic School, a special school for mentally retarded children, and in 1907 established her first "Casa dei Bambini" (Children's House), a school for normal children aged from three to seven. In Italy and other countries many schools used what came to be called the "Montessori method." In 1933 she left Italy for Spain and later founded training schools in the Netherlands and India before returning to the University of Rome (1947). She wrote *The Montessori Method* (1912) and *The Advanced Montessori Method* (1917).

See Also Montessori school

Sources:

Kramer, Rita. 1976. *Maria Montessori: A Biography*. New York: Putnam.
Montessori, Maria. 1912. *The Montessori Method*. 1964 ed. New York: Schocken.
Zusne, Leonard. 1984. *Biographical Dictionary of Psychology*. Westport, Conn.: Green-
    wood Press.

MONTESSORI SCHOOL. The Montessori method of teaching and learning
was developed by Maria Montessori (1870–1952). The first Italian woman graduate in medicine, she worked in psychiatric clinics, where she became interested
in teaching retarded and disadvantaged children. In 1900, after being appointed
director of a demonstration school for retarded children, she began to use special
teaching methods. The teacher became more of an observer, guide, and gentle
leader than a strong, controlling instructor. Her classroom was prepared with
learning aids that she designed. Also she encouraged spontaneity among the
children and freedom from authoritarian restraint in class. Her method was so
successful that apparently retarded children passed their exams as well as normal
children. Next Montessori went to teach children in the slums of Rome. Again
her methods were hugely successful. Word of her methods spread, and in 1909
she began to hold training seminars. In 1911 the first of these in the United
States was established at Tarrytown, New York. Thereafter, Montessori schools
were established worldwide, and her ideas gradually crept into progressive education. Today her methods are commonplace in modern schools.

Sources:

Deighton, Lee C., ed. 1971. *The Encyclopedia of Education*. New York: Macmillan and
    Free Press.
Devine, Elizabeth, Michael Held, James Vinson, and George Walsh, eds. 1983. *Thinkers
    of the Twentieth Century: A Biographical, Bibliographical and Critical
    Dictionary*. London: Macmillan.
Husen, Torsten, and T. Neville Postlethwaite. 1985. *The International Encyclopedia of
    Education Research and Studies*. Oxford: Pergamon.

MOON, SUN MYUNG. Sun Myung Moon (b.1920) was born in northwest
Korea. His family joined the Presbyterian Church and rejected the Shinto faith
of the Japanese invaders (1930). A sensitive boy, Sun Myung Moon was educated in Seoul and trained at the Pentecostal Church, and in 1936, Jesus came
to him. He studied Western and Eastern religious figures and principles of all
religions. Later in Tokyo he studied electrical engineering (1938) and also
worked to undermine the Japanese rule in Korea. After World War II he returned
to Korea, but his spiritual work was crushed by the new communist regime, and
he was imprisoned until 1950, when the United Nations forces liberated him.
He fled south, attracted followers, and began writing his *Divine Principle* (1957,
1973) about God's unchanging truths and integrating Christian and Oriental
religious principles. He entered business, which later provided for the church;
also he started an international mission, which by 1959 had established itself in

the United States as the Freedom Leadership Foundation (1969). In 1971 Moon brought his "Day of Hope" message to the United States, moved his head-quarters to Tarrytown, New York, and claimed that of 3 million followers, 40,000 were in the United States. On his 1973 visit he attracted large audiences and supported President Richard Nixon (1913–1994), arguing he should be for-given for Watergate. Moon's proselytizing led to an investigation, with parents suing him for alienating their children. His Unification Church and its business practices were scandalized and investigated, and Moon's name was linked with the autocratic rule of South Korea, the "Koreagate" (1977–1978). By 1976 he had ended his personal ministry in the United States. In 1982 Moon was found guilty of tax evasion, fined $25,000, and sentenced to eighteen months in prison; in September 1983 his conviction was upheld by a federal court of appeals in New York City. In 1988 he was still officiating at the mass weddings of his followers in South Korea and claiming to be fighting communism and restoring moral virtues to the world. For almost ten years Moon gave no interviews and late in 1989 broke his silence with an interview in Seoul, South Korea. In 1990 he visited Moscow and gave a speech titled "True Unification and One World," which stated he and the companies of the Unification Church in thirty-five coun-tries were planning to make vast commercial investments in Russia as they had already done fifty miles from Hong Kong inside southern China. The companies dealt in weapons, soft drinks, car parts, computers, and fish.

Sources:

Chernow, Barbara A., and George A. Vallasi. 1993. *The Columbia Encyclopedia*. 5th ed. New York: Columbia University Press.
Moritz, Charles, ed. 1983. *Current Biography Yearbook*. New York: Wilson.
Owen, Roger J. 1982. *The Moonies: A Critical Look at a Controversial Group*. London: Ward Lock Educational.
Sandars, S. W. 1991. "Moon over Moscow." *National Review* 43 (15 April): 39–41.

MOONIES (UNIFICATION CHURCH). Moonies, officially the Holy Spirit Association for Unification Church and widely known as the Unification Church, is a religious sect formed in 1954 in Korea by Sun Myung Moon (b.1920). He moved to the United States in 1971 and established its headquarters at Tarry-town, New York. His followers believe Moon is a messiah, and he claims to have communication with Buddha, Jesus, Moses, and Abraham. The Unification Church has utopian ideals and practices and claims variously to undermine com-munism by working devotedly to establish God's truths and to integrate Oriental and Occidental religious traditions and beliefs. In spite of its noble mission to free the world of conflict, the Unification Church, through its leader, has been involved in diverse businesses, given support to Richard Nixon at the time of the Watergate crisis, alienated children from their parents, been found guilty of tax evasion, produced mass weddings through matchmaking, made commercial investments with Russia since the fall of the Berlin Wall, associated with the

South Korean intelligence agency, and established relations with arms dealing inside southern China. The headquarters of the church is now in New York City. In United States there are about 5,000 members. Today the term "Moonies" is often used in a derogatory way, because their leader and his business ventures, which are synonymous with the church, have become suspect. The Moonies have attracted much research and publicity.

See Also Moon, Sun Myung

Sources:

Bethell, T. 1990. "Moon over Moscow." *The American Spectator* 23 (June): 9–11.

Chryssides, Geroge D. 1991. *The Advent of Sun Myung Moon: The Origins, Beliefs and Practices of the Unification Church.* London: Macmillan.

Clift, E., and M. Miller. 1988. "Rev. Moon's Political Moves." *Newsweek* (15 February): 31.

Cooper, N. 1989. "Rev. Moon's Rising Son." *Newsweek* 111 (11 April): 39.

Green, M. L. 1993. "Moonstruck in Connecticut." *Christianity Today* 37 (21 June): 54.

Holt, T. Harvey 1989. "A View of the Moonrise." *Conservative Digest* 15 (January–February): 36–37.

Judis, John B. 1989. "Rev. Moon's Rising Political Influence." *U.S. News and World Report* 106 (27 March): 27–29.

Mass, Peter. 1990. "Moon over Moscow." *The New Republic* 203 (19 November): 7–8.

MOORA COOPERATIVE. The Moora Cooperative is in Healesville, Victoria, Australia. In 1972 a small planning group created a manifesto for itself, and Moora was registered as a community settlement society. Two years later they bought 245 hectares (600 acres) of bush-farming land in a mountainous area outside Melbourne, Victoria. The land had buildings that provided communal living areas; housing was planned in clusters, and management was by elected directors. Today fifty people live there. They wanted no connection to the state electricity grid and use solar energy. Their founder claims that while seven members wrote the manifesto, he and his woman partner were the founding father and mother of the community, with all the power and responsibility that this entailed. They decided on a cooperative, rather than a communal, structure to allow for diversity and privacy. The cooperative is particularly concerned to preserve the bush environment. Members own shares with an option to build or buy homes. The community has a primary school and a bus to other schools.

Sources:

Cock, Peter. 1979. *Alternative Australia: Communities of the Future?*, Chapter 5. Melbourne: Quartet Books.

———. 1995. "From Communal Theory to Echo-Spiritual Practice." In Bill Metcalf, ed., *From Utopian Dreaming to Communal Reality: Cooperative Life Styles in Australia*, pp. 153–169. Sydney: University of New South Wales Press.

Cock, Peter, and Robert Rich. 1993. *A Community's Experience of Living with Appro-*

priate Energy Technology: A Case Study of Moora Cooperative, Victoria. Clayton, Victoria: Graduate School of Environmental Science, Monash University.

MOORABBEE COMMUNE. Moorabbee was an Australian urban commune comprising five couples. It was established in 1972 in suburban Melbourne, Victoria, and lasted for two and a half years. The couples came from Protestant, middle-class backgrounds, were university-educated, and employed as professionals, ages twenty-one to thirty. The group moved into a rented house. It was an old brick, Edwardian mansion of two stories with spacious rooms and high ceilings and had once been used as a rooming house. The residents agreed to pool their material resources and money, divide the house into communal and private areas, and hold regular meetings to discuss plans and make joint decisions. It was important that cooking and cleaning were rostered and members share tasks equally between men and women. The first year was regarded as a trial year. During that time two couples had babies. In time meetings became less frequent, and, when held, the atmosphere was ever more tense. After the first trial year three couples quit, and the remaining two couples advertised for replacements. With occasional changes the group lasted another eighteen months before coming to an end. There seemed to be no specific conflict or falling out between the couples. The founding couple simply moved on, and this essentially bourgeois, urban community evaporated.

Source:

Cock, Peter. 1979. *Alternative Australia: Communities of the Future?*, Chapter 4. Melbourne: Quartet Books.

MORAVIAN BETHLEHEM. In Pennsylvania, the Moravians established several communities, one of which was Bethlehem. They came from Germany, where the Moravian Brethren had been organized and led by Count Nikolaus Ludwig von Zinzendorf (1700–1769). In Bethlehem the Moravians employed both communal organization and a narrow family economy in their guiding principles. Founded in 1742, for twenty years the community banned private ownership of property, upheld minimal family ties, and lived primarily in "choirs," that is, same-sex peer groups. The communal economy was dissolved when the whole Moravian Church faced great financial problems; thereafter, the system based itself on the nuclear family until about 1818. The community was economically stable until 1844, when it faced another economic crisis and decided to open membership to non-Moravians. Gradually, in the Bethlehem community women had leadership and managerial positions; communal living gave over to family life; membership increased by proselytizing and missionary work. Other Moravian communities were established at Wachovia Tract in North Carolina and Lititz and Nazareth in Pennsylvania.

See Also Zinzendorf, Count Nikolaus Ludwig Graf von

Sources:

Gollin, Gilliam. 1967. *Moravians in Two Worlds: A Study of Changing Communities.* New York: Columbia University Press.
Smaby, Beverly P. 1988. *The Transformation of Moravian Bethlehem: From Communal Mission to Family Economy.* Philadelphia: University of Pennsylvania Press.

MORE, THOMAS. Thomas More (1478–1535), the son of a judge, was born in London, was educated at Oxford in law and afterward spent four years in prayer and devotion at Charterhouse. In Parliament from 1504, More was undersheriff in London (1510–1518), and Henry VIII (1491–1547) placed him in three important posts; master of requests (1514), treasurer of the Exchequer, (1521), and duchy of Lancaster (1525). Also from 1518 he was a member of the Privy Council. He was knighted in 1521, appointed speaker of the House of Commons (1523), and in 1529 reluctantly accepted the position of lord chancellor. His approach to work was simple and elementary, and he sought reforms among the clergy but had no wish to cross them. In 1532, when Henry VIII made himself head of the church, More would not recognize the self-appointment, because to him the pope was the head of the church. In 1534 More was imprisoned for a year after refusing to swear to the Act of Succession, an oath on the supremacy of Henry VIII. For this More was beheaded for treason. His Latin *Utopia* (1516; trans. English, 1551) placed him among the great Renaissance humanists. He was much influenced by the ideas of John Colet (c. 1467–1519) and Erasmus (c. 1446–1536), who later became his friend.

See Also Utopia

Sources:

Fortier, Mardelle L., and Robert F. Fortier. 1992. *The Utopian Thought of St. Thomas More and Its Development in Literature.* Lewiston, Maine: Edwin Mellin Press.
Kenny, Anthony. 1983. *Thomas More.* Oxford: Oxford University Press.
Marius, Richard. 1984. *Thomas More: A Biography.* New York: Knopf.
Reynolds, Ernest. 1968. *The Fields Is Won: The Life and Death of Saint Thomas More.* London: Burns.
Ridley, Jasper. 1982. *The Statesman and the Fanatic: Thomas Wolsey and Thomas More.* London: Constable.

MOREVILLE COMMUNITORIUM. Moreville Communitorium was established in a house at Hanwell by Goodwyn Barmby (1820–1881). It was a utopian experiment based on his views of the four stages of history. The experiment was given a strong religious foundation with a profound sense of duty to the communist state.

See Also Barmby, John Goodwyn

Source:

Armytage, Walter Henry Green. 1961. *Heavens Below: Utopian Experiments in England 1560–1950.* London: Routledge and Kegan Paul.

MORMONS. Mormons are members of the Church of Jesus Christ of the Latter-Day Saints. Members are taught that after his Resurrection Jesus came to the United States to teach the indigenes, a tribe of Israel, because the Christian church elsewhere had renounced the faith. In 1820 God restored his "latter-day" religion by sending Moroni, an angel, to show new Scriptures to Joseph Smith (1805–1844), farmworker near Palmyra, New York. The Scriptures, in reformed Egyptian, were returned to heaven, and Joseph, whom God had visited—as did Jesus and four saints as well as John the Baptist—translated and published them as *The Book of Mormon* (1830). The book is named after Mormon, an ancient prophet in North America, and accepted by Mormons as part of Christian Scriptures. In the face of violence, scorn, and ridicule—Mark Twain (1835–1910) would call *The Book of Mormon* "chloroform in print"—converts to Mormonism flocked to the new church. At Kirtland, Ohio, its center flourished, and Zion was built in Missouri—now a Mormon shrine, "Adam-ondi-Ahman," two hours north of Kansas City. Missourians rose against the new church in 1838; the community moved to Nauvoo, near the Mississippi River in Illinois, and by 1843 had attracted 20,000 members. Smith began to take to himself "spiritual wives." With his brother he was jailed in nearby Carthage, where 150 masked men went to murder them in 1844. Brigham Young (1801–1877), a follower since 1832 who had been to Britain, where he and other apostles had converted 2,000 Mormon proselytes (1839–1842), took over the church from other factions. In 1847, after much local conflict, Young led his followers to the valley of the Great Salt Lake in Utah. There the church flourished. Based on agriculture and manufacturing, with the help of spreading railways, roads, and bridges, Mormon wealth expanded. The U.S. president made Young the state's governor until 1857. That year concern about polygamy in the United States centered attention on the Mormons, and a military force was sent to put down the practice and replace Young. In 1890, the polygamy issue, which bedeviled the church, was formally repudiated. Recent research shows it continued into the early 1900s and that Smith, a polygamist, had even dabbled in occultism. Many Mormons remained in the U.S. Midwest, where Independence, Missouri, became the church headquarters, and Joseph Smith (1832–1914), son of the founder, became its head. The church was restructured and renamed the Reorganized Church of Jesus Christ of Latter-Day Saints. In the course of the changes Young's faction was denounced; the current church claimed to be the proper successor to the original; and missionary work led to a loose, but clear, membership around the world of over 1 million by 1950 and over 9 million by 1996. Now almost 5 million are in the United States, over 2 million in South America, 600,000 in Asia, over 750,000 in Mexico, and almost 400,000 in both Europe and Central America, and the church enjoys an annual income of nearly U.S.$6 billion. The Mormons turned 150 in August 1997 and are now the most commercially successful creed in the United States. Many Mormon practices offend other Christians: non-Mormons may not worship in Mormon temples; Mormons wear special undergarments when worshiping; marriages are sealed beyond death to eternity; the dead may be baptized to ensure non-Mormon ancestors the chance of salvation; the Lord's Supper uses water, not wine; the president of the Mormon Church may have revelations that overrule previous revelations from God. Today Mormons believe in only one God, although they accept that other gods may be in other worlds; Mormons reject original sin, so its expiation through Christ's death is irrelevant; humankind—but mainly men—may ideally become as God. To other Christian sects Mormonism is heresy. Modern growth of Mormon wealth is attributed not so much to the absence of guilt arising from original sin but to the intense purposiveness and sociability of members. Every Mormon is visited monthly by two others. Their practice upholds the honesty, chastity, fidelity, and hard work that are basic to commercial expansion. Mormon life is subject to white, abstemious, male domination, even though black people have been allowed into the church since 1978. As practicing utopians, Mormons are revered for caring for their own, insisting on self-reliance until support is obviously needed, providing stores to serve welfare needs, and furnishing those stores with the money saved by fasting for two meals each month. Mormons and Quakers have been compared, as they are the two most materially successful religious utopias on record (McCord, 1989).

See Also Kirtland Community; Morris, Joseph; Rigdon, Sidney; Smith, Joseph; Young, Brigham

Sources:

Allen, James V., and Glen M. Leonard. 1976. *The Story of the Latter-Day Saints*. Salt Lake City, Utah: Desert Books.

Arrington, Leonard J., and Davis Bitton. 1979. *The Mormon Experience: A History of the Latter-Day Saints*. New York: Knopf. 1992 ed., Chicago: University of Illinois Press.

Berry, Brian J. 1992. *America's Utopian Experiments: Communal Havens from Long-Wave Crises*. Hanover, N.H.: University Press of New England.

Ludlow, Daniel H., ed. 1992. *Encyclopedia of Mormonism*. New York: Macmillan.

Marquis, Kathy. 1993. "Diamond-Cut Diamond: The Mormon Wife vs. the True Woman, 1840–1890." In Wendy E. Chmielewski, Louis J. Kern, and Marilyn Klee-Hartzell, eds., *Women in Spiritual and Communitarian Societies in the U.S.*, pp. 169–181. Syracuse, N.Y.: Syracuse University Press.

Mauss, Armand L. 1984. "Sociological Perspectives on the Mormon Subculture." *Annual Review of Sociology* 10: 437–460.

McCord, William. 1989. *Voyages to Utopia: From Monastery to Commune, the Search for the Perfect Society in Modern Times*, pp. 189–193. New York: W. W. Norton.

Snodgrass, Mary Ellen. 1995. *Encyclopedia of Utopian Literature*. Santa Barbara, Calif.: ABC-CLIO.

Van Biema, David. 1997. "Kingdom Come: The Empire of the Mormons." *Time*, 150 (August 4):50–57.

MORRIS, JOSEPH. Joseph Morris (fl. 1848–1862) was born in England and converted by missionaries to Mormonism in 1848. He sailed to the United States and in 1854 reached Salt Lake City, claiming he had had revelations that persisted while he was in Utah. Along the bank of the Weber River he established a settlement in 1861 about thirty miles from Salt Lake City. They became known as "Morrisites." By 1862 the settlement consisted of a few hundred. Members believed in reincarnation and the Second Coming. Within a year its membership topped several hundred, but in the summer that year it was overrun by a territorial posse of Mormons following an armed battle. Morris was killed, and many of his followers scattered. Several communities of Morrisites established themselves, and some of their leaders claimed to have Morris' prophetic authority. Some factions and leaders could still be found in the 1950s, but none ever had the success that the originator enjoyed.

See Also Mormons

Sources:

Anderson C. Le Roy. 1981. *For Christ Will Come Tomorrow: The Saga of the Morrisites.* Logan: Utah State University Press.
Miller, Timothy. 1990. *American Communes: 1860–1960.* New York: Garland.

MORRIS, WILLIAM. William Morris (1834–1896), born into a middle-class family in Walthamstow, outside London, was educated at Marlborough School and studied at Exeter College, Oxford. After desultory studies for a career in the church he turned to architecture, married an artist's model (1859), and, much influenced by Pre-Raphaelite colleagues, established in 1861 an architectural firm, Morris, Marshall, Faulkner and Company. The firm changed entirely the art of house decoration and furnishings in Great Britain. He published poetry and studied and published works on the literature of heroes in Iceland, where he visited in 1871 and 1873. He translated Virgil's *Aeneid* (1875) and Homer's *Odyssey* (1887). His approach to the craft of house design and building led him to place high value on Gothic architecture and various medieval crafts and turned him against the mass production techniques of the Victorian period of industrialization. In 1883 he joined the Social Democratic Federation and became a zealous socialist, publishing *The Dream of John Bull* (1888) and his most noted utopian romance, *News from Nowhere* (1891). He wrote a scathing critique of Bellamy's *Looking Backward*; he thought Bellamy's work reflected his personality more than a mature view of socialism because it lacked a sense of history and art and distorted socialism by assuming that present-day life could be made gratifying once misery, waste, and injustice were eased out of the world to allow a professional middle class to thrive. Morris did not agree with Bellamy's view that society could evolve into a well-trained industrial army free of the irrationalities of capitalism, greed, and anxiety. In 1890 Morris established Kelmscott Press and for it designed clear typefaces and wide, elaborate borders. The press published many of his works and classical English literature. Toward the end of his life he published much poetry and romantic novels.

See Also Bellamy, Edward; *News from Nowhere*

Sources:

Aho, Gary L. 1985. *William Morris: A Reference Guide*. Boston: G. K. Hall.

Coleman, Stephen, and Paddy O'Sullivan. 1990. *William Morris and News from Nowhere: A Vision for Our Time*. Bideford: Green Books.

Coote, Stephen. 1990. *William Morris: His Life and Work*. London: Garamond.

Geoghegan, Vincent. 1992. ''The Utopian Past: Memory and History in Edward Bellamy's *Looking Backward* and William Morris's *News from Nowhere*.'' *Utopian Studies* 3, no. 1: 76–90.

Glasier, John Bruce. 1921. *William Morris and the Early Days of the Socialist Movement*. London: Longmans, Green.

Harvey, Charles, and Jon Press. 1996. *Art, Enterprise and Ethics; The Life and Works of William Morris*. London: Frank Cass.

Kirchhoff, Frederick. 1990. *William Morris: The Construction of the Male Self, 1856–1872*. Athens: Ohio University Press.

Kumar, Krishan. 1994. ''A Pilgrimage of Hope: William Morris's Journey to Utopia.'' *Utopian Studies* 5, no. 1: 89–107.

Latham, David, and Sheila Latham, eds. 1991. *An Annotated Critical Bibliography of William Morris*. New York: St. Martin's Press.

Lindsay, Jack. 1991. *William Morris: Dreamer of Dreams*. London: Nine Elms Press.

McCarthy, Fiona. 1995. *William Morris: A Life for Our Time*. London: Faber and Faber.

Meir, Paul. 1978. *William Morris: The Marxist Dreamer*. 2 vols. Translated from the French by Frank Grubb. Brighton: Harvester.

MORRONE, PIETRO DEL. Pietro del Morrone, Pope Celestine V (1215–1296), an ascetic and formerly a Benedictine, became a hermit and about 1235 lived in the Abruzzi mountains. He attracted followers, who later became known as Celestines and whom he brought eventually into the Benedictine Order. He lived austerely in imitation of Saint John the Baptist. Ending a two-year dispute among the cardinals over who ought to follow Nicholas IV as pope, he was elected 5 July 1294. Not a strong character, Celestine V was dominated by Charles II, king of Naples, who insisted the pope be in Naples. Celestine V granted privileges to all who asked and gave the cardinals all the duties of his papal office while he lived in his cell. Because his reign was so chaotic, and he was victim to so many opportunists, he abdicated after five months and in December ordered a new election for pope. Dante thought him a coward for his indecision and in the first part of *Divina Commedia* (1300–1311) placed him at the entrance to hell. Celestine V was canonized in 1313.

See Also Benedictines; Celestines

Sources:

Delaney, John, and James Tobin, eds. 1961. *Dictionary of Catholic Biography*. Garden City, N.Y.: Doubleday.

McDonald, William, ed. 1967. *New Catholic Encyclopedia*. New York: McGraw-Hill.

McHenry, Robert, ed. 1992. *The New Encyclopedia Britannica*. Chicago: Encyclopedia Britannica.

MUGGLETON, LODOWICKE. Lodowicke Muggleton (1609–1698) was a journeyman tailor who, with his cousin John Reeve (1608–1658), founded the Muggletons (c.1651). Before the English civil war (1642–1652) Muggleton was much influenced by the Puritans and beliefs of the Ranters. Early Puritans wanted to omit making the sign of the cross in baptism; the ring in marriage omitted from church services; only educated men admitted to the ministry; bishops prevented from enjoying the benefices that they never administered; and men not excommunicated by minor officials over trifling matters. Later Puritans would boycott dramas as immoral, allow only limited access at home to poetry, and view the court of Charles II a place of lust and intemperance. Muggleton's sect believed in the personal inspiration of the founders, who claimed to be the two witnesses in Revelation, xi, 3–6. Muggleton was Aaron, while Reeve was Moses. Their *Transcendent Spirituall Treatise* was published in 1652. They were condemned as blasphemous, and Muggleton was pilloried, put in prison, and fined but carried forward their work after Reeves' death. The sect flourished for 200 years.

Sources:

Cross, L. A., and E. A. Livingstone. 1997. *The Oxford Dictionary of the Christian Church*. 3d ed. New York: Oxford University Press.

Douglas, James D., ed. 1974. *The New International Dictionary of the Christian Church*. Exeter: Paternoster Press.

Magnussen, Magnus, and Rosemary Goring, eds. 1990. *Chambers Biographical Dictionary*. 5th ed. Edinburgh: Chambers.

Powell, Nathaniel. 1983. *A True Account of the Trial and Sufferings of Lodowick Muggleton: One of the Two Last Prophets and Witnesses of the Spirit: Left by Our Friend Powell, Who Witnessed the Trial and All His Sufferings*. Facsimile of 1808 publication. York: Michael Cole.

MUGGLETONIANS. The Muggletonians inherited the speculative work of John Robbins (fl.1651), who planned with his wife to lead a community of 114,000 to the Holy Land. He believed he had been on earth as Melchizedek some time before Adam. Ten of his community in Ling Alley, Moorfields, were imprisoned in Clerkwell Prison, May 1651. Also the Muggletonians were preceded by Thomas Tany (fl. 1649–1650), a goldsmith who announced he would lead the Jews—of whom he made himself a member—to the Holy Land and then as high priest build a temple there. To this effect he claimed to be the heir to the throne and established a tent city at Eltham. The expedition was diverted when he claimed the crown of France (1654), burned the tents and all chattels at Lambeth, and sailed for Holland.

See Also Muggleton, Lodowicke

Source:

Armytage, Walter Henry Green. 1961. *Heavens Below: Utopian Experiments in England 1560–1950*. London: Routledge and Kegan Paul.

MURPHY, MICHAEL. Michael Murphy (b. 1930) was born in Salinas, California, completed his B.A. at Stanford University (1952), and did military service (1953–1954). He graduated in philosophy (1955–1956) at Stanford. In India he studied at Sri Aurobindo Ashram (1956–1957). He began Esalen in 1962 on 175 acres of his family's property. He married in 1975. Among his writings are *Golf in the Kingdom* (1972), *Jacob Atabet: A Speculative Fiction* (1977), and *The Appalachian Dulcimer Book* (1976). He helped initiate the Soviet American Exchange program at Esalen. He is the chairman of the Esalen Board of Trustees.

See Also Esalen

Source:

Locher, F. C. ed. 1978. *Contemporary Authors*. Vols. 73–76. Detroit: Gale Research.

MURRY, JOHN MIDDLETON. John Middleton Murry (1889–1957) was born at Peckham, London, the elder son of John Murry, clerk in the Inland Revenue Department. Through scholarships young John was educated at Oxford University in literature (1910–1912). In 1911 he met Katherine Mansfield (1888–1923); they married in 1918, **and he introduced** her work through *The Adelphi*, which he founded and edited (1923). After writing for the *Westminster Gazette* and *Nation* (1912–1913), Murry worked in political intelligence in the War Office and was awarded an officer of the Order of the British Empire (OBE) (1920). He was an associate of D. H. Lawrence (1885–1930), who was much interested in establishing a utopia, but Murry could not see how it could be achieved. In 1923 Murry's wife died, and he became deeply depressed. Later, he felt a spiritual rebirth. He established *The Adelphi*, meaning "brothers," and named it for the small group who helped found the journal. He controlled its publication until 1948. Through it he presented a pacifist's view of global issues. In his personal search for a messiah he published *To the Unknown God: Essays Towards a Religion* (1924). Following Lawrence's death in 1930 Murry read Karl Marx (1818–1883) and concluded that among socialists the idea of community was religious, because it assumed the human ego must be sacrificed for a finer order of life. He founded the Adelphi Centre at the Oaks at Langham, near Colchester (1935–1936). He published his late wife's letters, diaries, and a biography (1932) and his autobiography, *Between Two Worlds* (1935). The Adelphi Centre ended when Murry joined the Peace Pledge Union in 1937. The Center became a home for Basque children. Murry bought twenty-two acres to house and care for aged wartime evacuees and to unite the pacifist movement with pacifist land communities, which had begun to develop around the British countryside. The Air Ministry acquired Murry's land, so he decided to establish his own community, Thelnetham. He wanted to establish many village communities as attractive as those inhabited by the upper classes in Britain in the nineteenth century. Thelnetham also failed. In 1954 he published a critical biography of Jonathan Swift and died three years later. Shortly before dying he wrote, "I have at the Adelphi Centre proved the failure of socialism and the prodigious difficulty of creating a new co-operative ethos . . . we have learned, by hard experience, how little it is possible to achieve.''

See Also Lawrence, D. H.; Oaks, The; Thelnetham

Sources:

Armytage, Walter Henry Green. 1961. *Heavens Below: Utopian Experiments in England 1560–1950*. London: Routledge and Kegan Paul.
Lea, F. A. 1959. *The Life of John Middleton Murry*. London: Methuen.
May, Hal, ed. 1986. *Contemporary Authors*. Vol. 118. Detroit: Gale Research.

MURTHO. Murtho was one of thirteen Australian village settlements that were established under the South Australian Government Land Act of 1893. Others were Gillen, Holder, Kingston, Lyrup, Moorook, New Era, New Residence, Pyap, Ramco, and Waikerie. All were founded along the Murray River between Renmark and Morgan. Two others were Mount Remarkable, situated fifty miles north of Adelaide, and Nangkita, thirty miles to the south. Modeled on New Australia, the community in Paraguay, Murtho was the most utopian of the settlements in that the land and other means of production were held in common, individuals owned personal effects, and the joining fees were the same. Married members contributed sixty pounds, unmarried forty pounds. Harry Taylor (1873–1932), noted socialist who accompanied the utopians to Paraguay and lived at Cosmé, briefly lived at Murtho and noted how it seemed like New Australia, Paraguay. Murtho started with ten families, ten single men, and three single women. It was one of few settlements where women were allowed to vote. All settlements declined and eventually failed; communal ownership was replaced by private property, social responsibilities gave over to individual interests, membership fell, and in 1902 the act that established the settlements was repealed. Taylor thought the communities also failed because members were untutored in communal living. Further, the land was often not arable, droughts were frequent, irrigation failed, work was wasted, the wrong trees were planted, the cooperative was poorly administered, and government support was inadequate.

See Also New Australia; Taylor, Harry Samuel; Village Settlements of South Australia

Sources:

Metcalf, Bill, ed. 1995. *From Utopian Dreaming to Communal Reality: Cooperative Life Styles in Australia*. Sydney: University of New South Wales Press.
Pike, Douglas, et al., eds. 1966–1990. *Australian Dictionary of Biography*. 12 vols. Carlton, Victoria: University of Melbourne Press.
Souter, Gavin. 1981. *A Peculiar People*. Sydney: Sydney University Press.

N

NASHOBA. Nashoba was a short-lived Owenite communal experiment in Tennessee (1825–1827) established by a wealthy Scot, Frances Wright (1795–1852). On seeing Robert Owen (1771–1858) and his sons founding New Harmony, Wright assumed the same principles could be applied to found a model community that would show free labor was more economical than slavery. Tennessee was the most likely state for the scheme to gain support. In the fall of 1825, Wright met Andrew Jackson (1767–1845)—later to be president of the United States—in Nashville, and he suggested buying land along the Wolf River, fifteen miles from the village of Memphis, which he and his partners had founded. Frances Wright purchased 2,000 acres and a house in Memphis and had built two log cabins on the property, which she named Nashoba, the Native American Chickasaw for "wolf." They cleared fifteen acres for potatoes, corn, and cotton; visitors were welcome, and Frances Wright hoped black and white people, especially skilled workers, would join the small community. It opened officially 3 March 1826, with Frances and a few close followers and a handful of slaves. But it was a dream in need of people and money and a strong spiritual commitment that was characteristic of the religious utopian communities that were being founded at that time in the United States. Freedom for slaves, cooperation between people, and her generosity were not enough to sustain Nashoba, and it closed in 1827.

See Also Wright, Frances

Sources:

Bestor, Arthur Eugene, Jr. 1970. *Backwoods Utopias: The Sectarian Origins and Owenite Phases of Communitarian Socialism in America, 1663–1829.* 2d enlarged ed. Philadelphia: University of Pennsylvania Press.
Eckhardt, Celia Morris. 1984. *Fanny Wright: Rebel in America.* Cambridge: Harvard University Press.

Egerton, John. 1977. *Visions of Utopia: Nashoba, Rugby, Ruskin, and the "New Communities" in Tennessee's Past.* Knoxville: University of Tennessee Press.

Oved, Yaacov. 1987. *Two Hundred Years of American Communes.* New Brunswick, N.J.: Transaction Books.

NEALE, JEPH. When Jeph Neale (fl. 1969–1997) and his Australian wife failed in 1969 to find a nonsuburban homesite outside Melbourne, Victoria, they were advised to consider a scheme mooted for Bend of Islands, north of the city. The scheme aimed to save about eighty acres from degrading urban development. At a meeting of fifteen similarly minded people, they set aside $300 to support the venture (1969) and, like others, were excited by the chance to share the land and activities of an alternative to suburban life. Twenty-six years Jeph said he learned much about bush ecology, conservation practices, and relations between species of plants and animals, weather, fire management in the bush, local government, and land management, none of which he felt were understood by those who build conventional houses in the suburbs. Today, living on a modest income, he and his artist partner feel their lifestyle is the envy of many visitors to the cooperative, Round the Bend.

See Also Berryman, Margaret; Ealey, E. H. M.; Round the Bend Conservation Co-operative

NEILL, A. S. Alexander Sutherland Neill (1883–1973), son of a schoolmaster, was born in Kingsmuir, Scotland. His upbringing was repressive. He was a pupil teacher at Kingsmuir (1899–1903). In Fife he was an assistant master at Kingskettle School (1903–1906) and Newport Public School (1906–1908). He studied English at Edinburgh University and briefly turned to publishing before being appointed headmaster at Gretna Public School (1914–1917). After World War I, in Hampstead he taught at King Alfred School (1918–1920) and edited *New Era* (1920–1921). At Hellerau near Salzburg he started a community school. Eventually, it settled in Leiston, Suffolk, as Summerhill School (1927) for both boys and girls. Neill put great emphasis on emotions in learning, especially love. Summerhill's organization was antiauthoritarian and followed a progressive and liberal teaching ideology. The school was popular among middle-class American parents and had remarkably successful results with problem children, who were given private lessons as an educational form of psychotherapy. Neill, a somewhat cantankerous character, was the most radical of Britain's progressive schoolmasters and publicized his ideas in many books, for example, *A Dominie's Log* (1916) and *Neill! Neill! Orange Peel!* (1973).

See Also Summerhill

Sources:

Croall, Jonathan. 1983. *Neill of Summerhill: The Permanent Rebel.* London: Routledge and Kegan Paul.

———, ed. 1983. *All the Best Neill: Letters from Summerhill.* London: Deutsch.

Neill, Alexander S. 1962. *Summerhill: A Radical Approach to Education.* London: Gol-
    lancz.
Placzek, Beverley R., ed. 1982. *Record of a Friendship: The Correspondence between
    Wilhelm Reich and A. S. Neill: 1936–1957.* London: Gollancz.
Walmsley, John. 1969. *Neill and Summerhill: A Man and His Work; A Pictorial Study.*
    Baltimore: Penguin.

NEW ATLANTIS. *New Atlantis* is an allegorical romance by Francis Bacon
(1561–1626), written between 1614 and 1618, about an imaginary island on
which is a philosophical commonwealth that seeks to cultivate a civilization
securely established on knowledge gained through natural science. Inspired by
More's *Utopia* (1516), this fable describes a journey to the island and its paternalistic government. The work owes much also to Plato's (c. 427–348 B.C.)
Critias and *Timaeus*, which describe the mythical isle of Atlantis, which was
overwhelmed by an earthquake in the Atlantic Ocean and sank more than 9,000
years ago. In *New Atlantis* the island is Bensalem, off the U.S. coast, where an
unknown, secretive, and advanced culture has great knowledge of present civilization. Blown off their course to the Orient, visitors arrive and are put into
the House of Strangers, where they learn that the island's inhabitants had been
brought to a pure form of Christianity. The Society of Solomon's House is at
the core of the island culture. In the house scientific knowledge holds the greatest
claim to authority. Its members are scientists who, in their search for wisdom,
travel and study books on all sources of knowledge. Also they have made advanced machinery of various kinds, for example, refrigeration, oxygen tanks,
telephones, artificial flowers, airplanes, submarines. They practice vivisection,
cross-breed plants, and produce optical illusions. Ambassadors are sent abroad,
called ''Merchants of Light,'' to inform others of the developments on the
happy, isolated commonwealth. Bacon's work is noted mainly for its interest in
expanding achievements in human society. In the history of utopian fiction it is
widely regarded as the great inspiration to work for a practical realization of an
ideal society through scientific knowledge and technological endeavor.
    See Also Bacon, Francis

Sources:

Bacon, Francis. 1627. *The Advancement of Learning and New Atlantis.* Edited by Arthur
    Johnston, 1974. Oxford: Clarendon Press.
Kumar, Krishan. 1987. *Utopia and Anti-Utopia in Modern Times.* Oxford: Basil Black-
    well.
Morely, Henry, ed. 1886. *Ideal Commonwealths: Plutarch's Lycurgus, More's Utopia,
    Bacon's New Atlantis, Campanella's City of the Sun, and a Fragment of Hall's
    Mundus Alter et Idem, with an Introduction by Henry Morely.* London: G. Rout-
    ledge. Reprinted, 1968. Port Washington, N.Y.: Kennikat Press.
Snodgrass, Mary Ellen. 1995. *Encyclopedia of Utopian Literature.* Santa Barbara, Calif.:
    ABC-CLIO.

Weinberger, Jerry. 1976. "Science and Rule in Bacon's Utopia: An Introduction to the
    Reading of *New Atlantis.*" *American Political Science Review* 70: 865–885.

NEW AUSTRALIA. In July 1893, 220 Australians sailed on the *Royal Tar* to South America to establish the utopian settlement New Australia. The venture was a response to economic depression, bank closures, industrial strikes, ruthless oppression of workers' leaders, and dreams of a harmonious society. The movement was led by William Lane (1861–1917), a utopian socialist who wrote for workers' papers and established the New Australian Cooperative Settlement Association. It advocated communal ownership of property and the saving of capital and communal maintenance of children under parental guardianship. Surplus wealth would be divided equally among adults, and women were to rank equally with men. There would be no non-English-speaking members, no de facto marriages, and no members of dubious reputation, and no member was allowed to oppose socialism. Members were to enjoy freedom of speech, religious worship, and leisure activities; but there would be no alcohol and no Chinese. Distant Paraguay was chosen to discourage the weak from seeking membership in the association. Before the *Royal Tar* reached South America, Lane's autocratic, tactless, and intolerant manner had alienated many passengers. Not long after arriving, the settlers were frustrated by the unexpectedly harsh environs, inadequate supply of capital for the venture, and the distance from markets. These frustrations combined with Lane's uncompromising views on the use of alcohol and on the settlers' sexual relationships with the locals to divide the settlement. In 1894 a group broke away and settled at Cosme forty-five miles away. In 1899 Lane, tired and depressed, severed his connection with the venture and left the settlement to a core of the original residents. Over the years 700 people came to live; at New Australia the most there at any one time was about 200; at Cosme the maximum reached about 130. Altogether, about 600 made the journey, and 100 years later their descendants live there.

See Also Lane, William

Sources:

Armytage, Walter Henry Green. 1961. *Heavens Below: Utopian Experiments in England
    1560–1950.* London: Routledge and Kegan Paul.
Graham, Stewart. 1912. *Where Socialism Failed.* London: John Murray.
Lake, Marilyn 1986. "Socialism and Manhood: The Case of William Lane." *Labour
    History* 50: 54–62.
Lane, W. (Pseud. "John Miller"). 1892. *The Workingman's Paradise.* Sydney: Edwards
    Dunlop.
Pike, Douglas, et al., eds. 1966–1990. *Australian Dictionary of Biography.* 12 vols.
    Carlton, Victoria: University of Melbourne Press.
Ross, L. R. M. 1937. *William Lane and the Australian Labor Movement.* Sydney: N.P.
Singer, I, and L. J. Berens. 1894. *New Australia: A Criticism.* Sydney: T. H. Houghton.
Souter, Gavin. 1968. *A Peculiar People: The Australians in Paraguay.* Sydney: Angus
    and Robertson.

Warren, Harris Gaylord. 1985. *Rebirth of the Paraguayan Republic*. Pittsburgh: University of Pittsburgh Press.
Whitehead, Anne. 1997. *Paradise Mislaid: In Search of the Australian Tribe of Paraguay*. St. Lucia, Queensland: University of Queensland Press and Penguin.
Wilding, Michael. 1984. *The Paraguayan Experiment*. Ringwood, Victoria, Australia: Penguin.

NEW EARSWICK. New Earswick is a British urban community at York established in 1902 in the Garden City tradition of Ebenezer Howard (1850–1928) by Joseph Rowntree (1836–1925), the industrialist and social reformer, born himself in York. Raymond Unwin (1863–1940) and Richard Barry Parker (1867–1947) designed the suburb as a Garden City.

See Also Garden City; Howard, Ebenezer; Parker, Richard Barry; Unwin, Raymond

Sources:

Gill, Roger. 1984 "In England's Green and Pleasant land." In Peter Alexander and Roger Gill, eds., *Utopias*, pp. 109–117. London: Duckworth.
Marsh, Jan. 1982. *Back to the Land: The Pastoral Impulse in England, from 1880 to 1914*. London: Quartet.

NEW GERMANY. New Germany was a German colony established in Paraguay in 1891. In the 1880s Germany was much interested in founding colonies in South America. Prominent Germans went to study Paraguay as a possible country for colonization. They tended to be anti-Semitic, Aryan schemes that explicitly excluded Jews. Most schemes met with little success, but New Germany lasted for several years. In 1886 Bernhard Förster (c.1844–1889) and his wife, Elisabeth (1846–1935)—sister of Friedrich Nietzsche—sailed to Paraguay to establish New Germany, known also by the Spanish name "Nueva Germania." Six hundred square kilometers were chosen, and after a month of negotiations agreement was reached with the Paraguayan government. In 1888 the Försters took possession of their mansion, Försterhof, while at the same time discontent spread among the impoverished colonists over their poor housing. In the first two years forty families sailed for New Germany, and 25 percent quit by July 1888. Of the 100 town plots, only 30 were sold. The scheme required finding 110 families in a year, so Elisabeth and Bernhard Förster spent much of their time begging the president of Paraguay and private supporters in Germany to fund the venture. One colonist, Julius Klingbeil, who arrived in 1888, returned to Germany to denounce the venture as a fraud in his *Revelations concerning Bernard Förster's Colony New Germany* (1889). The book demonstrated to Germans what had been known only to the few lost, bewildered German peasants in the heart of the Paraguayan jungle: the new Aryan republic was a sham, and the Försters were arrogant swindlers. Förster denounced Klingbeil, went to live in a hotel in San Dan Deno, drank heavily, and suicided. In 1890 the venture was bought by a corporation of businessmen from England, Spain, Denmark,

Italy, Germany, and Paraguay. Elisabeth returned to Germany and worked to secure the future of the colony of New Germany in Paraguay (1891). In August 1892 she returned only to see colonists trickling away. She was blamed personally for the venture's failure, sold her house, and left Paraguay forever August 1893, still appealing for its financial support. The ruins of Försterhof were being used as a pigsty in 1991.

See Also Förster, Bernhard; Nietzsche, Theresa Elisabeth Alexandra

Sources:

Warren, Harris Gaylord. 1985. *Rebirth of the Paraguayan Republic.* Pittsburgh: University of Pittsburgh Press.

Macintyre, Ben. 1992. *Forgotten Fatherland: The Search for Elisabeth Nietzsche.* London: Macmillan.

NEW HARMONY COMMUNITY. This community was founded by Robert Owen (1771–1858) on the Wabash River in Posey County, Indiana, in 1825. In his opening address he said: "I have come to this country to introduce an entire New State of society: to change it from the ignorant selfish system to an enlightened social system, to gradually unite all interests into one and remove all cause of contest between individuals." The members of the new society were to share equally in the labor of production and in the rewards of their common industry. Owen himself had purchased the town of Harmony from the Rappites for approximately $150,000; the constitution was prepared by him, and he retained the right to appoint a committee that was to "direct and manage the affairs of this society." Within three weeks 800 people had gathered at the little village of Wabash, and at the year's end the population was 1,000. The drawing up of a "permanent constitution" was begun in January 1826, and most members subscribed to the new constitution. But within the first month branch societies began breaking away from the main community. Owen was asked to assume directorship, but that did very little to stop the disintegration of his community, and in May 1827 he delivered his farewell address and was forced to admit that his dream had failed to materialize and that the great experiment had fallen through.

See Also Owen, Robert; Owen, Robert Dale and brothers

Sources:

Bestor, Arthur Eugene, Jr. 1970. *Backwoods Utopias: The Sectarian Origins and Owenite Phases of Communitarian Socialism in America, 1663–1829.* 2d, enlarged ed. Philadelphia: University of Pennsylvania Press.

Fogarty, Robert S. 1980. *Dictionary of American Communal History.* Westport, Conn.: Greenwood Press.

Harrison, John F. C. 1969. *Robert Owen and the Owenites in Britain and America: Quest for the New Moral World.* New York: Charles Scribner's Sons.

Kesten, Seymour R. 1993. *Utopian Episodes: Daily Life in Experimental Colonies Dedicated to Changing the World.* Syracuse N.Y.: Syracuse University Press.

Oved, Yaacov. 1987. *Two Hundred Years of American Communes*. New Brunswick, N.J.: Transaction Books.

Pars, Thomas Clinton, Jr., and Sarah Pars. 1933. *New Harmony: An Adventure in Happiness, the Papers of Thomas and Sarah Pars*. 1973 ed. Clifton, N.J.: A. M. Kelley.

Pitzer, Donald E., ed. 1971. *Robert Owen's American Legacy*. Indianapolis: Indiana Historical Society.

Pollard, Sidney, and John Salt, eds. 1971. *Robert Owen: Prophet of the Poor*. Lewisburg, Pa.: Bucknell University Press.

NEW ITALY. New Italy was established by Italian immigrants in New South Wales, Australia, near Woodburn in 1882. In 1888, with 250 residents, the experiment had its own school, church, business, and winery, an almost self-sufficient economy. Vineyards had been planted, and it was hoped the wine industry would rival that of South Australia. With the help of government funds a silk industry was established, and the silk won first prize at the Sydney exhibition in 1889 and at Milan in 1906. However, the industry was not profitable, and it collapsed. As the original settlers died, so did their socialist ideals, and the members born in Australia chose individual, rather than communal, property for their future. In 1933 the school closed, in 1945 the church was burned down, and in 1955 the last of the residents died.

Sources:

Clifford, F. 1889. *New Italy: A Brief Sketch of a New and Thriving Community*. Sydney: Government Printer.

Metcalf, Bill, ed. 1995. *From Utopian Dreaming to Communal Reality: Cooperative Life Styles in Australia*. Sydney: University of New South Wales Press.

NEW JERUSALEM. New Jerusalem was a Jewish Christian community established by James Fisher (1832–1913) in Western Australia twenty-four miles east of Narrogin. Founded on 4,000 acres, the community comprised seventy members, who later selected a further 20,000 acres. At first 10 percent was cropped, and later 30 percent was cleared for farming. Their industry and the success of their spiritual unity under Fisher's leadership provided New Jerusalem with a good name even to skeptical government officials. Fisher, known as a ''fascinating messianic'' leader, enjoyed revelations by Christ until an accident curtailed his power as a leader. The community ended when he died in 1913.

See Also Fisher, James Cowley Morgan

Sources:

Metcalf, Bill, ed. 1995. *From Utopian Dreaming to Communal Reality: Cooperative Life Styles in Australia*. Sydney: University of New South Wales Press.

Pike, Douglas, et al., eds. 1966–1990. *Australian Dictionary of Biography*. 12 vols. Carlton, Victoria: University of Melbourne Press.

NEW LANARK. At New Lanark, Scotland, in his model company town Robert Owen (1771–1858) created a successful community publicized in his *A New View of Society* (1813). His aim was to make a model industrial community, a "happy valley" set against the disorder and despair of the early industrial age. As a pioneer of welfare capitalism, he soon won public attention with the provision of pensions, cheap housing, and medical care for workers and cut their hours of labor to below the prevailing practice. Instead of higher wages he provided an environment that kept his people dependent on him, in a tidy, orderly, and enclosed organization; all inhabitants, as Owen later said, were "united and working together as one machine proceeding day by day with the regularity of clockwork." In his autobiography he wrote about New Lanark, saying that "the superior condition of the schools, mills, establishments generally, was effected without religious interference and by the dictates of common sense, applied to the study of humanity, of its natural wants and of the easy natural means of supplying these wants." At New Lanark education became the center of his socialist ideas and their application. Infants were admitted to his school as soon as they could walk and graduated into the mill at age twelve. About 1,300 people, in families, constituted the community. Approximately 500 children had come from poorhouses and charities in Edinburgh and Glasgow and were mostly between the age of five and ten years. These people had been surrounded by deplorable living conditions that Owen assumed had powerfully distorted their characters and behavior. Between 1814 and 1829 the New Lanark experiment gained international recognition for illustrating the value of welfare capitalism. Around the world many attempts were made to replicate the venture. Although he remained a partner in the New Lanark concern until 1828, Robert Owen broke his ties with his model company town in 1825.

See Also Owen, Robert; Owen, Robert Dale and brothers; Owenism; Owenite communities

Sources:

Harrison, John F. C. 1969. *Robert Owen and the Owenites in Britain and America: Quest for the New Moral World.* New York: Charles Scribner's Sons.
Podmore, Frank. 1906. *Robert Owen: A Biography.* London: Allen and Unwin.
Pollard, Sidney, and John Salt, eds. 1971. *Robert Owen: Prophet of the Poor.* Lewisburg, Pa.: Bucknell University Press.
Spann, Edward K. 1989. *Brotherly Tomorrows: Movements for a Cooperative Society in America 1820–1920.* New York: Columbia University Press.

NEW ODESSA COMMUNITY. New Odessa Community established itself on 780 acres in the woods of southwestern Oregon after a short stay in New York to raise funds. It was part of Am Olam community, a Jewish colony, and comprised sixty young people, aged twenty-one to thirty, from Odessa. They began the venture after William Frey (fl. 1839–1884), a non-Jewish Russian, who had established communes in the Midwest, for example, Cedar Vale Community, became their leader. Religion was not important in the community. About one year after the community began, an ideological split occurred between a group that supported Frey and emphasized positivism and another group opposing it. Frey and a few followers departed. Some returned to New York to launch a common household with a cooperative laundry that lasted another five years. New Odessa Community flourished between 1883 and 1887.

See Also Am Olam; Cedar Vale or Progressive Community; Frey, William

Sources:

Fogarty, Robert S. 1980. *Dictionary of American Communal History.* Westport, Conn.: Greenwood Press.
————. 1990. *All Things New: American Communes and Utopian Movements 1860–1914.* Chicago: University of Chicago Press.
Oved, Yaacov. 1987. *Two Hundred Years of American Communes.* New Brunswick, N.J.: Transaction Books.

NEWBROUGH, JOHN BALLOU. John Ballou Newbrough (1827–1891) was born near Wooster, on the Ohio frontier, and left home at sixteen to work for a dentist in Cleveland. He graduated from Cincinnati Dental College (1849), shortly afterward joined the gold rush for California, and in 1851 went seeking gold in Australia, where he made a great fortune. For six years he traveled. He returned to Cincinnati to practice medicine and dentistry and took up spiritualism. In Scotland in 1860 he married Rachel Turnbull and brought his bride to Philadelphia, where he practiced dentistry until 1862, then moved to New York. He is thought to have invented the rubber plate and wrote *A Catechism on Human Teeth* (1869) recommending tooth decay could be managed with cleanliness and temperance in eating. Meanwhile, his interest in spiritualism grew. He led a convention of spiritualists in New York City in 1883. He believed spiritualism was a force that could be integrated with principles of social reform. He wrote *The Oahspe* (1882), a mystical book; it was allegedly written by spirits using Newbrough's hands. He and his disciples founded the Shalam Colony (1884) to care for and raise foundlings and orphan children to better the world as adults. He wanted to go to New Mexico, his wife refused, and they were divorced. He married Frances Van de Water, who helped him with the Shalam Colony. When he died in 1891, the colony seemed to be prospering, but shortly afterward it became a financial burden to his wife and her new husband. By 1901 it had closed.

See Also Shalam Colony

Sources:

Fogarty, Robert S. 1980. *Dictionary of American Communal History.* Westport, Conn.: Greenwood Press.
————. 1990. *All Things New: American Communes and Utopian Movements 1860–1914.* Chicago: University of Chicago Press.

Hastings, James, ed. 1930. *Encyclopedia of Ethics and Religion.* Vol. 9. New York: Charles Scribner's Sons.

Malone, Dumas, ed. 1934. *Dictionary of American Biography.* Vol. 7. New York: Charles Scribner's Sons.

NEWS FROM NOWHERE. In 1891 William Morris (1834–1896) published a noted utopian romance, *News from Nowhere* (1891), outlining his socialist ideas. By socialism he meant a condition of society in which there were neither rich nor poor, neither masters nor their underlings, neither unemployed nor over-worked citizens, none worked wastefully, all humankind lived under equal circumstances, and each individual understood that harm done to one citizen injured all others. To Morris such a society would be best called a "common-wealth." The work was serialized January to October 1890 in *Commonweal,* a socialist weekly published by William Morris himself. The plot emerges in three parts. Morris dreams and awakes at his Hammersmith house during the twenty-first century in a communist society. In his travels through London he finds many changes, the most notable being that the Houses of Parliament are a dung market. At the center of the work is a discussion with an elderly historian on the details of how the world became the way it is. It seems that a violent revolution took place (1952), newspapers disappeared, railways were abandoned, an interest in history faded, politics became a thing of the past, and organized religion evaporated while a pagan form of religious pastimes reappeared. The final part centers on a river journey up the Thames beyond Oxford to celebrate the hay-making season. It is taken as riposte or direct repudiation of Edward Bellamy's *Looking Backward* (1888), which Morris reviewed critically in his *Commonweal* in 1889. Unlike Bellamy's workers, Morris' citizens revert to work with few machines and no managers or factories. Morris' book did not affect his country's politics as Bellamy's book did; nevertheless, the work was seminal and was reprinted eight times before Morris died. Also it was translated into Italian. Dismissed at the time by socialist academics for its sentimental and medieval settings, today it is becoming regarded as an important criticism of capitalist values and is gaining followers among the members of the environ-mentalist and feminist movements, as well as modern educationists who see the school of today as one that ignores children's learning.

See Also Bellamy, Edward; Morris, William

Sources:

Levitas, Ruth. 1990. *The Concept of Utopia,* Chapter 5. London: Philip Allan.

McMaster, Rowland. 1991. "Tensions in Paradise: Anarchism, Civilisation, and Pleasure in Morris's *News from Nowhere.*" *English Studies in Canada* 17: 73–87.

Morris, William. 1891. *News from Nowhere: Or an Epoch of Rest: Being Some Chapters from a Utopian Romance.* London: Reeves and Turner.

Parrinder, Patrick. 1991. "News from the Land of No News." *Foundation* 51: 29–37.

Snodgrass, Mary Ellen. 1995. *Encyclopedia of Utopian Literature.* Santa Barbara, Calif.: ABC-CLIO.

Thompson, Edward P. 1977. *William Morris: Romantic to Revolutionary.* London: Merlin.

Thompson, Paul. 1967. *The Work of William Morris.* London: Oxford University Press.

NICHOLS, MARY SARGEANT NEAL GOVE. Mary Sargeant Neal Gove Nichols (1810–1884) was born in Goffstown, New Hampshire. She was raised in Craftsbury, Vermont, where her parents moved when she was a small child. Reading widely, she educated herself and developed a special interest in anatomy and physiology, in the face of ridicule from her peers. She persisted in her studies and taught at a local school, published stories and poetry in local papers, and announced she believed that she was on some special mission in this world. In 1831 she married Hiram Gove, of Weare, New Hampshire, and separated from him in 1840 because she opposed his beliefs and way of life. After divorcing him in 1848, she married Thomas L. Nichols (1815–1901) and became a water-cure physician, reformer, and supporter of mesmerism, spiritualism, temperance, dress reform, and Fourierism. They had one child and taught in a school in New York for water-cure practitioners (1851–1853) and then together edited a monthly magazine in Cincinnati, Ohio, that stated a theory underlying the freedom of love. In 1854 they published a volume, *Marriage: Its History, Character and Results.* Later, she published *Mary Lyndon: Or Revelations of a Life* (1855), a personal account of her own life. She and her husband settled in England when the Civil War (1861–1865) began.

See Also Memnonia Institute; Nichols, Thomas Low

Sources:

Hopkins, Joseph G. E., ed. 1964. *Concise Dictionary of American Biography.* New York: Charles Scribner's Sons.

Malone, Dumas, ed. 1934. *Dictionary of American Biography.* Vol. 7. New York: Charles Scribner's Sons.

NICHOLS, THOMAS LOW. Thomas Low Nichols (1815–1901), born at Oxford, New Hampshire, was descended from early English settlers in Massachusetts. He began studying medicine at Dartmouth College but abandoned it for journalism and served his apprenticeship on newspapers in New York and Lowell. In 1837 he became the editor and part proprietor of a political newspaper called the *Buffalonian* and wrote so vehemently that he was given four months in prison for libel. He published *Journal in Jail* (1840), a lively account of his experiences in prison. He completed his medical studies in New York and in 1848 married a divorcée, Mary Gove (1810–1884). He and his wife founded a school for the training of water-cure practitioners. With Mary, he wrote and published several books on health and other reforms and propagandized for a number of spiritualist doctrines in *Nichols' Journal* and *Nichols' Monthly* (1853–1857). They established the Memnonia Institute, a "school of life" (1856), in Yellow Springs, Ohio, after they left Modern Times, Josiah Warren's

(1798–1874) free-love, anarchist community on Long Island. The institute lasted about one year. The Nichols then converted to Roman Catholicism and for two years afterward gave lectures on hygiene in Catholic institutions in the Mississippi Valley. He and his wife disapproved of the Civil War (1861–1865) and settled in England, where he published books on food reform and *Forty Years of American Life* (1864).

See Also Memnonia Institute; Modern Times; Nichols, Mary Sergeant Neal Gove

Sources:

Allibone, S. Austin. 1872. *A Political Dictionary of English Literature*. Reprinted, 1965. Detroit: Gale Research.

Fogarty, Robert S. 1980. *Dictionary of American Communal History*. Westport, Conn.: Greenwood Press.

Kunitz, Stanley J., and Howard Haycraft, eds. 1938. *American Authors 1600–1900*. New York: H. W. Wilson.

Malone, Dumas, ed. 1934. *Dictionary of American Biography*. Vol. 7. New York: Charles Scribner's Sons.

NIETZSCHE, THERESA ELISABETH ALEXANDRA. Theresa Elisabeth Alexandra Nietzsche (1846–1935), born in Saxony, was only two when her father died. She and her brother Friedrich were raised by a young mother in Naumberg in a household of old women. The three came to despise women and revere men. As she matured, Elisabeth acquired an ambivalent view of men, deferring to their heroic service to humanity and beguiling and manipulating them into meeting her demands. She excelled in her private school education. In 1869 her inheritance from her grandmother made Elisabeth financially independent, and she went to Leipzig to study and improve her English. Through her brilliant brother, Friedrich Nietzsche (1844–1900), with whom she considered establishing a utopian community of scholars, she met Richard Wagner (1813–1883) and Bernhard Förster (1844?–1889), a passionate anti-Semite. In 1885 she married Förster after his visit to Paraguay, where he planned to establish New Germany, a vegetarian's utopia untainted with Jewish blood. Together they published *German Colonisation in the Upper La Plata District with Particular Reference to Paraguay: The Results of Detailed Practical Experience, Work and Travel 1883–1885* (1886). In February 1886 with their Aryan pioneers they sailed for Paraguay. The journey of one month was extremely difficult (1886). The utopian venture failed, although in August 1893 she was still appealing for financial support for the colony. After her husband's death in 1889 Elisabeth—who, as a child, was known as Lisbeth, Lichen, and Llana, as an adult in Paraguay, known as Eli, and finally, as Elisabeth Förster-Nietzsche—spent her life spreading her late brother's ideas and developing close relations with Benito Mussolini (1883–1945) and Adolf Hitler (1889–1945) and their plans for Europe.

See also Förster, Bernhard; New Germany

Sources:

Macintyre, Ben. 1992. *Forgotten Fatherland: The Search for Elisabeth Nietzsche*. London: Macmillan.
Warren, Harris Gaylord. 1985. *Rebirth of the Paraguayan Republic*. Pittsburgh: University of Pittsburgh Press.

NIMBIN. Nimbin, a small Australian village in northern New South Wales, seemed like a ghost town until 1973. Around the village were regions of deep spiritual interest to indigenous Australians, who know the place as "Gnymbunge." Suddenly, Nimbin became the center of alternative lifestyle activists after the ten-day Aquarius Festival, 1973. By 1974 the village of Nimbin had attracted national and international attention and became known as Australia's counterculture capital. The community began with members who, feeling a sense of union and love for each other, believed they constituted a modern tribe with ideals for a better life. They were university graduates and professionals, disillusioned by mainstream values, the threat of nuclear war, signs of a hopeless future, and a lack of meaning among life's opportunities. Initially, they were willing to share caravan accommodations, and live in tents with no electricity or running water. Many artistic and otherwise talented people joined them, all seeking a new kind of life for their offspring. People came and went, some experimenting with drugs and sexual freedom, others meditating and promoting vegetarianism. By 1995 the population was 10,000–12,000. Heroin traders openly touted their wares, but most were not community members. The community divided; a major group lived well away from the old township, and the others in the town. At first, housing was essentially communal; today many of the original members live in their own homes but maintain they have never dropped their primary reasons—artistic and creative—for gathering at Nimbin. Many of the children, raised in an idyllic setting of waterfalls, rain forests, and extended families, left the community to find a conventional alternative to Nimbin's utopianism. Glad to have been raised at Nimbin, many return for vacations. When they see how warm, caring, confident, and open their children are, the original parents of the Nimbin movement feel the social experiment has been a success. Today among the cottage industries at Nimbin are metalworking, toy making, ceramics, stonemasonry, sculpture, and candle making. Members of the community include solicitors, dentists, architects, filmmakers, university teachers, and organic and conventional farmers.

See Also Tuntable Falls Co-ordination Co-operative

Sources:

Alexander, Brian W. 1990. *Nimbin: A Photographic Essay*. Lismore, New South Wales: W. B. Alexander.
Cock, Peter. 1979. *Alternative Australia: Communities of the Future?* Melbourne: Quartet Books.

Constine, Gloria. 1995. "From a London Slum to Nimbin's Magic." In Bill Metcalf, ed., *From Utopian Dreaming to Communal Reality: Cooperative Life Styles in Australia*, pp. 74–83. Sydney: University of New South Wales Press.

Johnston, Donald S. 1982. *Nimbin Centenary: 1882–1982*. Nimbin, New South Wales: Bush Design.

Powys, Jennifer J. 1981. *Aspects of Land Use and Part Time Farming in Northern New South Wales*. Armidale, New South Wales: University of New England.

NINETEEN EIGHTY-FOUR. *Nineteen Eighty-Four*, a 1949 novel by George Orwell (1903–1950), depicts a world of three superpowers dominated by a totalitarian state. War is perpetuated to maintain the balance of power between the superpowers and centers on the Oceania. Through the life of Winston, the reader glimpses a fantasy of totalitarian Britain in the mid-1940s. Oceania, ruled by one political party, uses torture, public execution, spies in families, thought police, and doublethink slogans like "war is peace" and "freedom is slavery." Big Brother rules the party, omniscient, omnipotent, omnipresent, infallible, and unseen; his name and image are on stamps, coins, cigarette wrappings, and posters, but he and his origins are obscure. Sex is constrained, puritanically, love is almost banished, fresh information is ideological "newspeak," history is constantly revised to suit the present, and individual judgment is unstable, unverifiable, and distorted. Life is dominated by a shortage of goods, all of which are of poor quality. The urban landscape is pitted with bomb craters and scattered with half-demolished buildings. Winston is an official at the Ministry of Truth. After his brief love affair Winston Smith is arrested by the Thought Police, tortured, and brainwashed, and on his release his hopeless struggle for truth and decency fails when he finally submits to the totalitarian controls of the state. He is sentenced to die for having unacceptable ideas in a state that offers no hope, privacy, or permission to individuals to hold deviant or unorthodox thoughts. The book depicts a dystopia in which the police state has been perfected, and power is the only important concern. The work has produced a catalog of interpretations: prophecy, allegory, satire, parody, religion; final testament, autobiography, personal product of depression and pessimism; a warning of worse to come; a Western weapon in the Cold War, stick to beat Stalin with; antisocialist; a treatise in support of socialism, fascism, democracy; a disquisition on the corruption of power; a perversion of centralized economy; an attack on totalitarianism for the sake of democracy. As a warning and a prophecy, the work owes much to Wells' *When the Sleeper Awakes* (1899), Jack London's *The Iron Heel* (1907), Zamyatin's *We*, and Huxley's *Brave New World*. Terms like "newspeak," "doublethink," and "Big Brother" have secure places in the English language. The novel was filmed in 1955 and again in 1984; the latter is the better film and stars John Hurt as Winston Smith and the late Richard Burton as the interrogator.

See Also Brave New World; Dystopia; Huxley, Aldous; Orwell, George; *We*; Wells, H. G.; Zamyatin, Evgeny Ivanovich

Sources:

Booker, M. Keith. 1994. *Dystopian Literature: A Theory and Research Guide*. Westport, Conn.: Greenwood Press.

Kumar, Krishan. 1987. *Utopia and Anti-Utopia in Modern Times*. Oxford: Basil Blackwell.

Snodgrass, Mary Ellen. 1995. *Encyclopedia of Utopian Literature*. Santa Barbara, Calif.: ABC-CLIO.

NORTH AMERICAN PHALANX. The North American Phalanx was established in 1843 near Red Bank, New Jersey, and initially espoused the principles of Fourierism. In principle the basic unit of the utopian community was the phalanx, a group of 1,620 people living in common buildings or phalanstery, using about 5,000 acres, and dividing work according to individual abilities. In theory phalanxes would eventually link and form one federation. In Red Bank the leaders were not well schooled in Fourier's ideas, failed to educate their own members, and instead presented them with simple messages. Without an understanding of Fourier's fundamentals, the community fell into doctrinal conflict, became confused, and began to split. Conflicts centered on the division of profits. However, a few years before the community disintegrated, members decided on an equal income to all, to be adjusted for differences in the type of work performed. At the outset the community also suffered from a lack of funds. Members wanted to avoid debt but could see they would never advance without some initial borrowing. Also the North American Phalanx's Industrial Council was unable to grasp the complexity of Fourier's operation schedules. Each night it had to meet to consider work plans for the following day, because next day at breakfast the day's work had to be drawn up and assigned to members. This was not what Fourier had envisaged. He wanted members to do what suited and attracted them as individuals. The community ended in 1855.

See Also Fourier, Charles; Fourierist communities or phalanxes

Sources:

Kesten, Seymour. 1993. *Utopian Episodes: Daily Life in Experimental Colonies Dedicated to Changing the World*. Syracuse, N.Y.: Syracuse University Press.

Oved, Yaacov. 1987. *Two Hundred Years of American Communes*. New Brunswick, N.J.: Transaction Books.

Swann, Norma Lippincott. 1973. "Work and Community in the North American Phalanx." In Rosabeth Moss Kanter, *Communes: Creating and Managing the Collective Life*, pp. 257–263. New York: Harper and Row.

NORTON COLONY. Norton Colony was a short-lived anarchist colony formed in 1893 by Hugh Mapleton (fl. 1893–1900) and Herbert Stansfield (fl. 1876–1900), an art student, on the grounds of Norton Hall, owned by a retired lace maker from Nottingham. They were much influenced by Edward Carpenter (1844–1929). By 1898 there were seven colonists, nonsmoking, teetotal vegetarians. They lived in the gardener's cottage, grew lettuce, made sandals, and sold their products from door to door. The colony followed no prescribed rules except that at the communal breakfast they planned the day's work. Occasionally, they made enough to have a little pocket money. On one hand, they were called cranks because they made sandals and sang at their work, but, on the other, they were feted by many visitors from Sheffield. Their policy was to remain small and hope that several similar small groups would arise nearby and that, later, the groups might form a larger community of like-minded anarchists. The colony closed after seven years when the lease ended in 1900. Nevertheless, several members continued to follow the practices they had established in the colony. Some joined other similar groups, while Hugh and his brother Henry Mapleton began manufacturing vegetarian food and eventually became one of the most successful firms in Great Britain. Stansfield became a professor of industrial design in Toronto, while another member became a food and drug inspector in Sheffield.

See Also Carpenter, Edward

Sources:

Armytage, Walter H. Green. 1961. *Heavens Below: Utopian Experiments in England 1560–1950.* London: Routledge and Kegan Paul.
Marsh, Jan. 1982. *Back to the Land: The Pastoral Impulse in England, from 1880 to 1914.* London: Quartet.

NOYES, JOHN HUMPHREY. John Humphrey Noyes (1811–1886) was born in Brattleboro, Vermont, and attended Dartmouth College (1826); skeptical of revivalism, he took up legal studies until 1831, when he suddenly converted from law to theological studies after intense criticism from his peers. Licensed to preach (1833), he believed he was a member of an elite of true Christians with direct contact with God. Plagued by depression and hallucinations that he might be a heretic, he often fell ill from fanatasizing about his strengths and weaknesses. He finally concluded that he was sinless. In 1834 he helped found *The Perfectionist*, which published his theology. In 1835 he was involved in an affair at the perfectionist community in Brimfield, Massachusetts. From personal doubts as to whether sex had taken place, Noyes concluded that true Christianity required a life of order and discipline. His preaching met with a poor response. He began evangelizing and established the Putney Bible School, but it failed to get support. He married an ardent follower (1838). His regular suffering showed him he was God's only true carrier of the Christian message. However, the Brimfield scandal had damaged his theological reputation and led to his break with the perfectionists and developed in him an infantile view of sexual relations and the belief that the nation and the world were corrupt. After his marriage, Noyes founded the Putney Association, which by 1847 had forty-five members who subordinated their will to his charisma and powers of healing. He publicized the difference between his theology and the other sects—perfectionists, Millerites, Shakers—and in 1847 asserted the world of the perfectionists was ready for his Kingdom of Heaven. In 1846 Noyes had established the secret principle of "complex marriage"—sharing of spouses by designated pairs of married couples—as a solution to his wife's suffering from both fruitless pregnancies and his ideas on contraception. In the summer of 1847 the complex marriage became public, and Noyes was arrested and charged with adultery and fornication. On bail he fled to New York, the Putney Association folded, and in February 1848 he called followers to the Oneida Community. He stayed with the community until May 1849, established it firmly, and then went to Brooklyn until 1854, during which time he published his social theories. From 1855 to 1865 he returned to Oneida to purify the membership and to establish it financially. After 1860 he became less a radical reformer and more a gradualist and planned to regenerate society with special breeding of an elite; however, his sexual, economic, and communistic policies gave way under his followers' doubts about their purpose. Splits developed in the community, and he found that his charisma and other social controls were not effective. At age sixty-seven, in June 1879, he deserted the Oneida Community without a word. He feared prosecution by a group of Presbyterians and attacks on his leadership from inside the community and a weakening of his influence among his followers.

See Also Oneida community

Sources:

Klaw, Spencer. 1993. *Without Sin: The Life and Death of the Oneida Community.* New York: Penguin Books.

Noyes, George Wallingford. 1923. *Religious Experience of John Humphrey Noyes.* New York: Macmillan.

Oved, Yaacov. 1987. *Two Hundred years of American Communes.* New Brunswick, N.J.: Transaction Books.

Whitworth, John McKelvie. 1975. *God's Blueprints: A Sociological Study of Three Utopian Sects.* London: Routledge and Kegan Paul.

O

OAKS, THE. The Oaks was an English utopian community at the Adelphi Center of John Middleton Murry (1889–1957). This was to be a house on spacious grounds staffed by a dozen men and women. Half were recruited from among the unemployed, and their task was to establish a self-sufficient community with its own workshops and center for conferences largely attended by socialists. His journal, *The Adelphi*, would be associated with the scheme. Murry established the Oaks at Langham, near Colchester (1935–1936), as a monastic retreat for genuine socialists, not those who used socialism as a political support for their careers. In the community, Murry felt people could learn cooperation in ordinary work, take on duties according to their abilities, and contribute to community well-being and make it largely self-supporting. In such a community Murry believed social and Christian principles could be integrated. Murry invested £1,000; others put in £800. He lived at the Oaks in 1936 with his fourth de facto wife. A limited liability company was established, ''the Adelphi School Company,'' for the education of adults and children, all according to Murry's own principles. In 1937 he returned to his third de facto wife, and the Adelphi Center closed. The property was given to the Peace Pledge Union as a home for Basque refugee children. During World War II Murry was back in control and turned the institution into a haven for elderly wartime evacuees from London, who worked the property as a market garden.

See Also Murry, John Middleton; Thelnetham

Source:

Armytage, Walter H. Green. 1961. *Heavens Below: Utopian Experiments in England 1560–1950*. London: Routledge and Kegan Paul.

OBERLIN COMMUNITY. Oberlin was a residential community of perfectionists in Oberlin, Lorain County, Ohio. They believed that it is always possible for individuals to become free of sin in their own lifetime through religious conversion and willpower. Charles G. Finney (1792–1875), a professor of theology, was their chief spokesman in Oberlin Community. It is a college town founded in 1833 by Rev. John J. Shipherd (1802–1844) and Philo Penfield Stewart (1798–1868) as a community that was committed to the highest level of thinking and a plain life. It was named after Jean Frederick Oberlin (1740–1826), a pastor from Alsace who had taught widely in France. Oberlin College, intimately linked with the Oberlin Community, was strongly reformist, advocated coeducation and the integration of different races, and was so deeply opposed to slavery that it became a stopover in the Underground Railway, an escape route for slaves seeking freedom in Canada.

See Also Finney, Charles G.

Sources:

Dudley, Lavinia P. 1963. *The Encyclopedia Americana*. International ed. New York: Americana Corporation.
Hurka, Thomas. 1993. *Perfectionism*. New York: Oxford University Press.
McHenry, Robert, ed. 1992. *The New Encyclopedia Britannica*. Chicago: Encyclopedia Britannica.

O'CONNOR, FEARGUS. Feargus O'Connor (1794–1855), was born in Cork, Ireland, and educated at Trinity College, Dublin, and called to the Irish bar. His life's work was spent attempting to introduce land reform in Great Britain. O'Connor aimed for a stable, peasant, proprietary class in England. In 1833 he was a member of Parliament (MP) for Cork, and for two years in Parliament he failed to introduce the land reform bill, left Parliament, and went to Manchester. He established the radical paper *Northern Star* (1837) and was secretary of the Great Northern Union of Working Men and a supporter of the ideas followed by Robert Owen (1771–1858). He published propaganda on the practical management of small farms. In 1838 many radical movements consolidated, and members adopted the "People's Charter of the Working Men's Association" and became known as Chartists. O'Connor's paper was the organ of Chartism. At the Chartist Conventions of 1843 and 1844 he argued for a land reform scheme that assumed all land once belonged to the people and had been usurped by kings, princes, and lords. In 1845 In Brussels he focused much attention on his message and received a signed approval from Karl Marx (1818–1883), Friedrich Engels (1820–1895), and others, and in March 1846 he gave his name to O'Connorville near Watford. Later that year he bought an estate, Lowbands, and established a bank—Land and Labour Bank—and in 1846 he formally changed the name of the Chartist Co-operative Land Company to the National Land Company. Because he preferred cooperation in working relationships to socialism, some leading Chartists opposed him, for they saw in him a threat to the Chartist principle of the nationalizing of land and property. But from the success of several Chartist Land Colonies that he established and supported, he gained many adherents. In 1847, as member of Parliament (MP) for Nottingham, he vigorously supported the six-point Chartist program and signed a contract for the sixth Chartist Land Colony at Dodford. He sought not only land reform and the charter but also a peasant republic for Great Britain. To achieve this he had a petition with an alleged 5 million signatures taken to the House of Commons. It was a farce; there were only a million or so, and many were false signatures. This was early evidence of his impaired mental health. In 1848 a Parliamentary Committee of Inquiry found that evidence recently collected by the Poor Law Commission showed that all the Chartist Land Colonies had been managed badly, and irregularities in financial administration seemed much like fraud. The Chartist movement collapsed. In response O'Connor worked vigorously to restore confidence in his schemes. He failed and was taken to court. He behaved erratically, seemed inconsistent in his policies, and confused many. Even his persuasive, overwhelming oratory failed him, and in 1851 his work was wound up, the Land Company was liquidated, and a year later O'Connor's mental health required he be committed to an asylum. A few years later 50,000 people attended his funeral.

See Also Chartist Land Colonies

Sources:

Armytage, W. H. G. 1961. *Heavens Below: Utopian Experiments in England 1560–1950.* London: Routledge and Kegan Paul.

Jones, Barry. 1989. *The Macmillan Dictionary of Biography.* Melbourne: Macmillan.

Morris, William, ed. 1965–1966. *Grolier Universal Encyclopedia.* New York: American Book-Stratford Press.

Smith, Benjamin. 1903. *The Century Cyclopedia of Names.* London: Times.

Stephen, Leslie, and Sydney Lee, eds. 1917. *The Dictionary of National Biography.* London: Oxford University Press.

OLEANA. Oleana was a planned community in western Pennsylvania supported by the singer and violinist Ole Bull (1810–1880) and named for him and his wife, Ana. It failed, and in response local wags composed a song about a failed utopia, "Oleana." In the 1950s the Kingston Trio also wrote a song about it. Ole Bull was a Norwegian violinist who made the first of his five tours in the U.S. in 1843. He encouraged nationalism among United States composers and created such works as "Grand March to the Memory of Washington," "Niagara," and "Solitude of the Prairie." He figures as the musician in Henry Wadsworth Longfellow's (1807–1882) "Tales of a Wayside Inn" (1874). In 1852 he established the short-lived Norwegian colony Oleana in Pennsylvania. *Oleanna* is the title of a recent drama about trust and betrayal between a woman student and man teacher at a university. It was inspired by the utopia, an item read in the *New York Times* about an argument between a man and his wife, and the public debate centering on the sexual harassment charges central to the Clarence Thomas–Anita Hill hearings (1991). The play was written by David Mamet and performed at Cambridge in Boston, London, and San Francisco

(1994). A film was made of the play in 1996. Mamet added an extra *n* to the play's title because he thought it looked better.

Sources:

Broderson, Elizabeth. 1994. " 'Tis but a Word and a Blow." *Performing Arts*, 7 June: 7.
Hart, James D., ed. 1983. *The Oxford Companion to American Literature*. 5th ed. New York: Oxford University Press.

OLOWO. Olowo Village was one of five established on Africa's Atlantic coast, 1947–1956. The founders were protesting against the killing of twins, a movement that began in western Nigeria in 1942. At first 2,000 members were attracted to the community, but the numbers halved in about twelve months. It was part of the Aladura prophetic movement, which gave the community a religious base. With strong authoritarian leadership and the belief that economic development ensured immortality and salvation, the villagers thrived. They were led by Apostles who first settled there in 1945. First the villagers built huts on stilts, then connected them with boardwalks, also on stilts. In 1949 the Apostles finished a seven-mile canal using communal labor. In 1953 they bought an electric generator. In the mid-1950s a telephone system was installed, several factories were established, and about twenty-five seacraft, many large passenger boats, and several motorized fishing boats were built with little external finance. By 1957 the community was reputed to have the highest living standard in Nigeria. During this development other villages were established: Mimo (1948) by a prophet, Mimo, who did not want to be a member of Olowo; the fourth was Talika, established in 1950; and the fifth was a small theocracy founded in 1951 by a prophet who quit Mimo. Then came a period of great and sudden decline, the sense of community evaporated, the economy stagnated, and the outside world seduced the inhabitants. In 1968 private enterprise was introduced, and for the first time people were paid wages. In time many refused to work unless paid, and soon they began to compete with one another in the labor market. The family reemerged as the prime unit of the village, and the villages became stratified into rich and poor. Soon people began to leave and look for work elsewhere. By 1972 the community was finished.

Source:

Barrett, Stanley R. 1977. *The Rise and Fall of an African Utopia*. Waterloo, Ontario, Canada: Wilfrid Laurier University Press.

ONEIDA COMMUNITY. Oneida, a religious community, was formally established in 1848 by John Humphrey Noyes (1811–1886) with support from his associates, who believed in working to make their lives an example of what good humankind could achieve, that is, perfectionists. Oneida was based on the belief that God had started to develop his kingdom in the United States, that the spirit of heaven would inoculate the kingdom's subjects from sin, and that the work would be done under an enlightened theocracy. By the end of 1848 the community had 87 members, a third under fifteen years. In June 1879 the community of 300 lost its leader when he fled to Canada in fear that he might be charged with criminal activities. In 1880 the community's property was transferred to a corporation, and former members received stock. Meanwhile, Noyes lived in Canada in a house overlooking Niagara Falls. During its thirty years the Oneida Community followed the social and sexual theories of its leader, driven largely by his missionary zeal. He upheld male sexual continence in a pattern of complex marriage with special sexual practices for different social levels in the community. Selective breeding or "stirpiculture" was advocated, as were healing by faith and the use of group pressure known as "mutual criticism." At first Noyes was radical in his insistence on these and other practices; later, he became more of a gradualist. Authority in the community centered on Noyes' God-given charisma; the economy of Oneida, although shaky at first, was based on minor craft industries—brooms, seats, sewing silk—and became secure through the manufacture of traps, especially after the depression of 1857–1858, and following the Civil War (1861–1865). After 1870, Noyes' health declined, members became more educated and began to question Noyes' restraints on their social and sexual interests, and his authority weakened. Noyes himself became threatened with charges of statutory rape. Clergy outside the community saw Oneida as a utopia of obscenity. When Noyes fled, the community collapsed. The Oneida Community has attracted much scholarly research.

See also Noyes, John Humphrey; Towner, James William

Sources:

Berry, Brian J. 1992. *America's Utopian Experiments: Communal Havens from Long-Wave Crises.* Hanover, N.H.: University Press of New England.

Carden, Maren Lockwood. 1969. *Oneida: Utopian Community to Modern Corporation.* Baltimore: Johns Hopkins University Press.

Fogarty, Robert S., ed. 1994. *Special Love/Special Sex: An Oneida Community Diary.* Syracuse, N.Y.: Syracuse University Press.

Hayden, Dolores. 1976. *Seven American Utopias: The Architecture of Communitarian Socialism, 1790–1975.* Cambridge: MIT Press.

Klaw, Spencer. 1993. *Without Sin: The Life and Death of the Oneida Community.* New York: Penguin Books.

Klee-Hartzell, Marlyn. 1993. "Family Love, True Womanliness, Motherhood, and the Socialization of Girls in the Oneida Community." In Wendy E. Chmielewski, Louis J. Kern, and Marlyn Klee-Hartzell, eds., *Women in Spiritual and Communitarian Societies in the U.S.*, pp. 182–200. Syracuse, N.Y.: Syracuse University Press.

Lockwood, Maren. 1971. *Oneida: Utopian Community to Modern Corporation.* Baltimore: Johns Hopkins University Press.

Noyes, Constance. 1970. *Oneida Community: An Autobiography 1851–1876.* Syracuse, N.Y.: Syracuse University Press.

Noyes, Corinna Ackley. 1960. *The Days of My Youth*. Kenwood, N.Y.: Mansion House.
Noyes, Pierrepont B. 1937. *My Father's House: An Oneida Boyhood*. New York: Farrar and Rinehart.
Oved, Yaacov. 1987. *Two Hundred Years of American Communes*. New Brunswick, N.J.: Transaction Books.
Parker, Robert Allerton. 1935. *A Yankee Saint: John Humphrey Noyes and the Oneida Community*. Reprinted, 1972. New York: Putnam.
Stegner, Wallace. 1964. *The Gathering of Zion: The Story of the Mormon Trail*. New York: McGraw-Hill.
Whitworth, John McKelvie. 1975. *God's Blueprints: A Sociological Study of Three Utopian Sects*. London: Routledge and Kegan Paul.

ORBISTON. Orbiston was the third and most successful Owenite experiment of Abram Combe (1785–1827). On 291 acres nine miles east of Glasgow on the Calder River, Scotland, the experiment was based on a passion for communal living and a plan for a four-story building with a common kitchen, dining room, leisure rooms, and schools. Only adults' bed-sitting rooms were private. By October 1825, 125 shares of £250 had been bought. Newspapers advertised for members, and a weekly magazine appeared. Skeptics dubbed the venture "Babylon." After one year the community's tenants discussed self-government and agreed to abide by principles of the Sermon on the Mount. Early a problem arose when people were not paid for their work, skilled or otherwise; so a value had to be put on all persons' working hours, and their activities were classified. A foundry was established as an independent venture with special benefits for its proprietors and the workers involved. Also members worked in a flourishing market garden, a dairy, and a cobbler's shop. The community prospered, and membership reached 250. In 1826 the community divided in conflict between the idea of full community of property and limited ownership of the successful foundry. A compromise was reached, and the community stabilized; but another split emerged between Abram Combe, who tended to tolerate all people and their activities, and those who resented members of the community who did not seem to work hard. This difference was settled when a school was established. The community grew to 290 members. A reservoir was built to supply water, and sewage was used to fertilize the garden. Printers, growers of produce, and foundry workers flourished; but those who were inclined to communism—weavers, tailors, and shoemakers—did not. Jealousy arose over the distribution of food. Morale declined sharply, so a new system of work was introduced. But in 1827, when Combe died, and his brother assumed management of the experiment, the mortgagees pressed for their funds. He advised the members to leave. The community dispersed, and the land was sold.

See Also Combe, Abram; Owenite communities

Sources:

Armytage, Walter Henry Green. 1961. *Heavens Below: Utopian Experiments in England 1560–1950*. London: Routledge and Kegan Paul.

Cullen, Alex. 1910. *Adventures in Socialism, New Lanark Establishment Orbiston Community*. Glasgow: Smith.

Jones, Benjamin. 1894. *Co-operative Production*. Oxford: Clarendon Press.

Harrison, John F. C. 1969. *Robert Owen and the Owenites in Britain and America: Quest for the New Moral World*. New York: Charles Scribner's Sons.

Pollard, Sidney, and John Salt, eds. 1971. *Robert Owen: Prophet of the Poor*. Lewisburg, Pa.: Bucknell University Press.

ORVIS, JOHN. John Orvis (1816–1897) was born in Boston into a Hicksite Quaker family, attended Oberlin College, and in the 1830s went to Boston, where he became involved with antislavery groups. In 1844 he joined Brook Farm and worked with the farming group and wrote for *The Harbinger*. As a lecturer he toured New England for Brook Farm and Fourierism. After leaving the colony, he sold insurance and sewing machines, and in 1862 he went to England to study. Following his return Orvis promoted association with Sovereigns of Industry. He was elected Sovereigns' president in 1873, became one of its national lecturers, and edited *The Sovereigns of Industry Bulletin*. He was a labor agitator who defended the trade unions even while he was an active member of the Knights of Labor. In the 1890s he joined the Nationalist movement and continued his interest in cooperation.

See Also Brook Farm Colony

Sources:

Fogarty, Robert S. 1980. *Dictionary of American Communal History*. Westport, Conn.: Greenwood Press.

Moment, Gairdner B., and Otto F. Kraushaa, eds. 1980. *Utopias: The American Experience*. Metuchen, N.J.: Scarecrow Press.

Montgomery, David. 1967. *Beyond Equality*. New York: Knopf.

Oved, Yaacov. 1987. *Two Hundred Years of American Communes*. New Brunswick, N.J.: Transaction Books.

Swift, Lindsay. 1961. *Brook Farm*. Reprint. New York: Corinth Books.

ORWELL, GEORGE. George Orwell (1903–1950) is the pseudonym of Eric Arthur Blair, British novelist and essayist. He was born in Bengal, brought to England, and educated at Eton. He served in the Indian Imperial Police in Burma (1922–1927), but loathing of imperialism and a passion for writing led him to resign. These experiences appear in his first novel, *Burmese Days* (1934). *Down and Out in Paris and London* (1933) tells of his years of poverty that followed. Four novels published in the next five years were all evidence of his deep socialist beliefs. He was a democratic socialist who hated totalitarianism; he was disillusioned with the aims and methods of communists, and in the Spanish civil war (1935–1937) he fought for the loyalists. He recorded the hardships of war in *Homage to Catalonia* (1938). In 1945 he published *Animal Farm*, a satire on Stalinism, and in 1949 published *Nineteen Eighty-Four*, a dreadful view of a totalitarian future ruled by Big Brother. He insisted that *Nineteen Eighty-Four* showed that if the world powers prepare for total war, develop new weapons like atom bombs, and accept totalitarian attitudes, then civilization would be unbearable. Orwell acknowledged a debt to Evgeny Ivanovich Zamyatin (1884–1937), the Russian novelist who published *We* (1924).

See Also Animal Farm; Brave New World; Dystopia; Huxley, Aldous; *Nineteen Eighty-Four; We*; Wells, H. G.; Zamyatin, Evgeny Ivanovich

Sources:

Buitenhuis, Peter, and Ira B. Nadel, eds. 1988. *George Orwell: A Reassessment*. New York: St. Martin's Press.
Crick, Bernard. 1981. *George Orwell: A Life*. London: Secker and Warburg.
Crick, Bernard, and Audrey Coppard. 1984. *Orwell Remembered*. London: British Broadcasting Corporation.
Fleischmann, Wolfgang B. 1971. *Encyclopedia of World Literature in the 20th Century*. New York: Frederick Ungar.
Gottlieb, Erika. 1992. "Review Essay: Orwell in the 1980s." *Utopian Studies* 3, no. 1: 109–120.
Rose, Jonathan, ed. 1992. *The Revised Orwell*. East Lansing: Michigan State University Press.
Sheldon, Michael. 1991. *Orwell: The Authorized Biography*. London: Heinemann.
Snodgrass, Mary Ellen. 1995. *Encyclopedia of Utopian Literature*. Santa Barbara, Calif.: ABC-CLIO.

OSCHWALD, AMBROSE. Ambrose Oschwald (1801–1873) was born in Mundelfingen, Baden, Germany, and died at the St. Nazianz Community in Wisconsin, which he helped to found. He was educated at the University of Freiburg (1833–1834) and was ordained a priest (1833). In 1848 he published *Mystischen Schriften*, which was condemned by the local archbishop of Baden for outrageous predictions and errors. That year he also published *Revelations of St. Methodius*, which predicted a new Jerusalem before 1900. His writings led him to be relieved of his parish (1849). He organized his followers into the Spiritual Magnetic Association, with St. Gregory Nazianzen as patron. He studied medicine (1852–1854) and botany at Munich and in 1854 advised his followers to imitate St. Gregory and flee the wickedness of this world and think about themselves. So, in May 1854, he and over 100 followers sailed for the United States and founded the St. Nazianz Colony at Manitowoc County, Wisconsin. His outstanding spiritual and temporal leadership, his pastoral skills, and his medical training held together the unusual Roman Catholic experiment in utopian communal life. When he died, his followers drifted apart, and the colony dispersed well before 1900, the appointed year for the new Jerusalem.

See Also St. Nazianz Community

Sources:

Beck, Frank. 1959. "Christian Communists in America: A History of the Colony of Saint Nazianz, Wisconsin." M.A. thesis, St. Paul Seminary.

Fogarty, Robert S. 1980. *Dictionary of American Communal History.* Westport, Conn.:
    Greenwood Press.

OWEN, ALBERT KIMSEY. Albert Kimsey Owen (1847–1916) was born in
Chester, Pennsylvania, into a Quaker family. His father was a physician and
sent Albert to study engineering at Jefferson College, where he graduated in
1867. Before beginning as a railroad engineer he worked as city manager in his
hometown. In 1871 he helped develop the Clear Creek Canyon Railroad and
the expanding township of Colorado Springs. In the following year he surveyed
land for a railroad in Mexico on the west coast and explored Topolobampo Bay.
For the next twenty years he promoted a railway scheme that was intended to
join the emerging western economy of the United States with that of the Orient
through a harbor at Topolobampo. He sought special financial aid from the U.S.
and Mexican governments and got special help from members in the Greenback
Club, Pennsylvania. In 1885 he organized the Credit Foncier Company to establish small settlements on the routes from east to west and a large city, Pacific
City, at the terminal on Topolobampo Bay. Many people were interested in his
venture, including Marie Howland (1835–1921). Owen used his newspaper, *Integral Cooperation*, to attract 200 colonists to Topolobampo Bay Colony in late
1886. By 1892 nearly 500 residents had settled. The colony did not succeed
because members could not cope with the tropical conditions, conflict within
the community, and the absence of Owen, its leader. Owen continued plans for
social reform, and he considered developing a rapid transit system. In his *Dream
of an Ideal City* (1897) appears Owen's vision of Topolobampo as an ideal
community with such features as fulfilling work, an absence of vice and crime,
quiet and attractive environment, rewarding educational opportunities, good, cooperative relations, fine architecture, and freedom from poverty.

See Also Howland, Marie Stevens; Topolobampo Colony

Sources:

Fogarty, Robert S. 1980. *Dictionary of American Communal History.* Westport, Conn.:
    Greenwood Press.
————. 1990. *All Things New: American Communes and Utopian Movements 1860–
    1914.* Chicago: University of Chicago Press.

OWEN, ROBERT. Robert Owen (1771–1858), born at Newton, Montgomery
Shire in north Wales, was the son of a saddler who was also an ironmonger and
served as the town postmaster. The boy was largely self-educated, not religious,
and seemed precocious and independent. At ten he began an apprenticeship, was
much impressed by modern technologies, and took advantage of all opportunities
he was given. In 1784 he visited New Lanark to inspect a cotton mill and by
1800 had acquired it. At New Lanark he experimented with management principles based on justice and kindness. After ten years he had a prosperous business with 2,000 workers (including 500 young paupers) and had all but

eradicated theft and alcoholism among his employees by offering them reasonable standards of living and some education. He cut working hours to twelve a day, and with paternal discipline he enforced cleanliness, winter curfews and fines for drunkenness and provided medical care, a sick fund, and public eating facilities. He sought to reform character and create a moral, humane, kind, active, and educated workforce. He was successful, but his views and practices met resistance from his peers when he sought to extend his reforms to all society and create a new social system (i.e., socialism). He formed a plan, toured to promote it, and published a refinement of it in his *Report to the County of Lanark* (1820). In 1825 he bought for £40,000 (80 percent of his fortune from New Lanark) the established community of Harmony from the Rappites, a Pietist German sect, in the United States. New Harmony, as he called it, failed as a utopian venture. In England, Orbiston, the first Owenite community, also failed. Nevertheless, in his name, the Owenite movement spread in Britain, well outside his personal control, and was dominated by communitarianism. He tried to curb attempts to change industrial society that he disagreed with and in time began to support labor exchanges and trade unions. To him labor was the source of wealth. He campaigned for an eight-hour day, but he failed as leader of the working class, largely because of his paternalistic leadership style. Later, he established the democratically organized Rational Society—the short title of the organization—and toured for it through England, France, and the United States as a socialist, speaking on an array of popular topics. The society established Queenwood, a utopian community for 700 members (1839), but its building was so extravagant, and its funds so poorly deployed that by 1844 the venture bankrupted the Rational Society, and Owenism ended. Owen tried to revive his following in the United States and France without success. In his final years Owen gave many speeches on social reform, until finally he was carried from the stage, half conscious, midway through an address he was giving to the National Association for the Advancement of Social Science meeting in Liverpool. A month later he died. His ideas and work attracted many scholars in the social sciences.

See Also Kendal; Nashoba; New Harmony Community; New Lanark; Orbiston; Owen, Robert Dale and brothers; Owenism; Owenite communities; Valley Forge; Yellow Springs Community

Sources:

Claeys, Gregory. 1989. *Citizens and Saints: Politics and Anti-Politics in Early British Socialism*. Cambridge: Polity Press.
———, ed. 1987. *Machinery, Money and the Millennium: From Moral Economy to Socialism, 1815–1860*. Cambridge: Polity Press.
———. 1993. *Selective Works of Robert Owen*. London: William Pickering. Vol. 1, *Early writings*; Vol. 2, *The Development of Socialism*; Vol. 3, *The Book of the New Moral World*; Vol. 4, *The Life of Robert Owen*.
Cole, George Douglas Howard. 1966. *The Life of Robert Owen*. 3d. ed. Hamden, Conn: Archon Books.
Fischer, Ernest. 1980. *Marxists and Utopias in Texas*. Burnet, Tex.: Eakin Press.

Harrison, John F. C. 1969. *Robert Owen and the Owenites in Britain and America: Quest for the New Moral World*. New York: Charles Scribner's Sons.

McCabe, Joseph. 1920. *Robert Owen*. London: Watts.

Podmore, Frank. 1906. *Robert Owen: A Biography*. London: Allen and Unwin.

Oved, Yaacov. 1987. *Two Hundred Years of American Communes*. New Brunswick, N.J.: Transaction Books.

Owen, Robert. 1813–1816. *A New View of Society or Essays on the Principle of the Formation of the Human Character and the Application of the Principle to Practice. And a Report to the County of Lanark*. 1970 ed., introduced by V.A.C. Gatrell. Harmondsworth: Penguin Books.

Spann, Edward K. 1989. *Brotherly Tomorrows: Movements for a Cooperative Society in America 1820–1920*. New York: Columbia University Press.

Taylor, Anne. 1987. *Visions of Harmony*. Oxford: Clarendon Press.

OWEN, ROBERT DALE AND BROTHERS. Robert Dale Owen (1801–1877) was born in Glasgow, the eldest son of Robert Owen (1771–1858), and in 1825 he accompanied his father and his brother William Dale Owen (1802–c.1842) to the United States to help establish New Harmony in Indiana. He edited the *New Harmony Gazette* and taught at the school in New Harmony. He went to New York, edited the *Free Enquirer* (1829), and on his return to Indiana in 1832 entered politics, introduced the bill for the founding of the Smithsonian Institution, and eventually was U.S. minister to Naples (1853–1858). In his work to abolish slavery he wrote *The Policy of Emancipation* (1863) and *The Wrong Slavery* (1864). In 1874 he published his autobiography, revealing he was a wanderer, a fine educationist, and deeply spiritual. He died after a period of mental ill health. William Dale Owen was mechanically minded and, like his elder brother, was educated at Hofwyl, Switzerland, and went to live at New Harmony. He was left in charge in the autumn of 1826 but could not manage the community, largely because of his father's earlier attempts to bring equality into the settlement too quickly. There were difficult administrative problems about admission to membership of unsuitable applicants to the community, and unclear rules about private property at the settlement. He was angry with his father's impractical model for New Harmony. But he settled there, married (1837), and died about 1841 or 1842. William kept a record of his efforts in *Diary of 1824–25* (1906). David Dale Owen (1807–1860), third son of Robert Owen, was born in Scotland and also educated in Switzerland. He went with his father to New Harmony, Indiana. In 1831 he returned to London University to study geology and medicine. In 1837 he became state geologist in Indiana. In 1847 he was a U.S. geologist and studied the geology of the Cape Land District (1847–1852). Two years later he was made state geologist of Kentucky, then Arkansas (1857), and died in 1860 from overwork and malaria. Richard Owen (1810–1890) arrived in New Harmony when he was eighteen and taught there and ran a steam flour mill. He assisted his brother David with geological surveys and on his death succeeded him as the state's geologist (1860). He fought in the Civil War (1861–1865) and afterward became a professor of natural science at Western Military Institute of Kentucky and published reports and addresses on education and ethics and died at age eighty.

See Also New Harmony; Owen, Robert

Sources:

Armytage, Walter H. Green. 1961. *Heavens Below: Utopian Experiments in England 1560–1950.* London: Routledge and Kegan Paul.
Cole, George D. H. 1925. *The Life of Robert Owen.* 3d ed. London: Cass.
Fogarty, Robert S. 1980. *Dictionary of American Communal History.* Westport, Conn.: Greenwood Press.
Harrison, John F. C. 1969. *Robert Owen and the Owenites in Britain and America: Quest for the New Moral World.* New York: Charles Scribner's Sons.
Malone, Dumas, ed. 1934. *Dictionary of American Biography.* Vol. 7. New York: Charles Scribner's Sons.
Oved, Yaacov. 1987. *Two Hundred Years of American Communes.* New Brunswick, N.J.: Transaction Books.
Owen, Robert Dale. 1874. *Threading My Way: An Autobiography.* London: Trübner.
Podmore, Frank. 1906. *Robert Owen: A Biography.* Reprinted, 1923. London: Allen and Unwin.

OWENISM. Owenism is the political thought of Robert Owen (1771–1858) that guided utopian ventures. It assumes, first, that human ideas and actions are determined largely by the environment. Consequently, character is formed *for* an individual, not *by* one. Influenced by William Godwin (1756–1836), Owen believed the issue of free will was at the center of moral life. To him prevailing religious thought assumed that since humans were entirely responsible for their own acts, they should be sanctioned accordingly. Owen believed such a view of humankind led to misery through poverty. He thought if the environment were improved, then the individual would flourish, and any other sort of reward system was pointless. Human nature could be improved, and New Lanark was Owen's proof. Second, he believed that all society had to be reformed with a uniform set of rural/urban communities. Competition had to be replaced with cooperation and the holding of property in common. Economic justice could be achieved in practice by using not money but labor notes. The abolition of the false division of labor between worker and capitalist was also necessary. Mechanization of work did not need the division of labor to be productive; it needed modern machinery without the division of labor. In consequence, justice, morality, and equality would be enjoyed by all, the daily hours of work could be reduced, and education would be enjoyed by everyone. Machinery would produce far more than consumers would use, so competition would not be necessary and would vanish. The new moral world involved people's having the same responsibility and privileges and the same opportunity for education. Responsibilities would differ for each person at different stages of his or her life. For this reason society should be structured according to age, and responsibility and privileges allocated accordingly. As a result, since all would be well educated to the level appropriate to their age and hold and relinquish positions of authority on that basis, problems of dependency would evaporate, and all people through their lifetime would be guaranteed equal rights and experience both justice and happiness. Government by age would rid civilization of the inequities of monarchy and aristocracy. Owen wanted to see socialism introduced not through revolution, mass protest, or extending the franchise but by providing exemplary communities as models for society. To give power to the poor and the working class over the rich simply replaced one group of oppressors with another. Democratic politics would form a society that was hostile, competitive, unharmonious, noisy, and irrational and would create divisive electioneering. Party politics to Owen was a social evil: it should be replaced with socialism where childish interests and the hostile use of power were replaced by sociability and the absence of anger. He wanted to eliminate war and other less dangerous forms of political conflict, eradicate evils of industrial civilization—alcoholism and theft—and promote harmony among religions and in marriage. Universal education was the way. His ideas appear in the cooperative movement, model towns, and Garden Cities, and all systems of thought that challenge capitalism, and they underlie liberal socialism, justice in exchange, Fabianism, and social engineering and appear in the ideas of Marx and Engels. His ideas seek to avoid the excesses of laissez-faire beliefs, identify the failings of centralized planning, uphold the value of general education, assume the appropriateness of rule by the elders, outline the dangers of social idealism, environmentalism, feminism, and profit sharing, and condemn the inefficiencies of the divisions of labor.

See Also Owen, Robert; Owenite communities

Sources:

Claeys, Gregory, ed. 1993. *Selective Works of Robert Owen*. London: William Pickering. Vol. 1, *Early Writings*; Vol. 2, *The Development of Socialism*; Vol. 3, *The Book of the New Moral World*; Vol. 4, *The Life of Robert Owen*.

Owen, Robert. 1813–1816. *A New View of Society or Essays on the Principle of the Formation of the Human Character and the Application of the Principle to Practice. And a Report to the County of Lanark*. 1970 ed., introduced by V.A.C. Gatrell. Harmondsworth: Penguin Books.

OWENITE COMMUNITIES. During the 1820s some Americans, excited by Robert Owen's (1771–1858) ideas, helped create an Owenite community. At least seven attempts were made to establish Owenite communities, and at least seven more Owenite societies formed that never became fully fledged communities. In the United States the best known are Yellow Springs, the Friendly Association for Mutual Interests (Valley Forge), Franklin Community or Haverstraw Community, Forestville or Coxsackie, Nashoba, Blue Springs Kendal. The first of these Owenite communities created in the United States by American reformers was the Yellow Springs Community located in Greene County, Ohio. Robert Owen lectured to a large Cincinnati audience where Daniel Rowe was a minister of a local Swedenborg church. Rowe heard Owen talk about advantages of his system, and when Owen returned to Cincinnati in June that year, he found that Rowe and his followers were intelligent, liberal, generous, cultivated, wealthy, and well educated and had already made arrangements to begin the Yellow Springs Community. In July, Rowe and seventy-five families, including professional men, teachers, merchants, mechanics, farmers, and laborers, went to Greene County, Ohio, where they purchased more than 800 acres. They formed an overnight community based on shared interests and agreed that all additional property they might later acquire would be added to the common trust for the benefit of all. The community soon disbanded because, according to the community leaders, social equality became an impossible goal, and the women especially were dissatisfied when they found the equality proposed by the Owenites was dysfunctional, and they alone had to perform the ceaseless domestic tasks so necessary for communal survival. Put another way, if women were to insist upon genuine equality in utopian communal life, then no community could run smoothly.

Sources:

Berry, Brian J. 1992. *America's Utopian Experiments: Communal Havens from Long-Wave Crises.* Hanover, N.H.: University Press of New England.

Harrison, John F. C. 1969. *Robert Owen and the Owenites in Britain and America: Quest for the New Moral World.* New York: Charles Scribner's Sons.

Harsin, Jill. 1984. "Housework and Utopia: Women in the Owenite Socialist Communities." In Ruby Rohrlich and Elaine Hoffman Baruch, eds., *Women in Search of Utopia: Mavericks and Mythmakers*, pp. 73–84. New York: Schocken Books.

Kolmerton, Carol A. 1990. *Women in Utopia, the Ideology of Gender in the American Owenite Communities in Utopia*, Chapter 4. Bloomington: Indiana University Press.

———. 1993. "Women's Experiences in American Owenite Communities." In Wendy E. Chmielewski, Louis J. Kern, and Marilyn Klee Hartzell, eds., *Women in Spiritual and Communitarian Societies in the U.S.*, pp. 38–51. Syracuse, N.Y.: Syracuse University Press.

Oved, Yaacov. 1987. *Two Hundred Years of American Communes.* New Brunswick, N.J.: Transaction Books.

P

PANTISOCRACY. The pantisocracy was a utopian community planned by Samuel Taylor Coleridge (1772–1834), Robert Lovell (c.1770–1796), and Robert Southey (1774–1843) in 1794. It was based on the theories of Jean-Jacques Rousseau (1712–1778) and William Godwin's (1756–1836) *An Enquiry concerning Political Justice* (1793). It was to be in the United States. In a pantisocracy a noble man would lead a noble life and be respected for his abilities. The scheme was to form a community to which each member would contribute two to three hours' labor daily; leisure would be spent in discussion, study, and educating children. Each member would contribute £125. The group learned that for £600 they could buy 1,000 cleared acres in Pennsylvania on the Susquehanna River, free of hostile Native Americans. In March 1795 they would sail to the United States, establish themselves, and preach pantisocracy, equal government by all, and "Aspheterism," Southey's term for the denial of private property. Also they believed that in the United States they could live from writing. The party would include various friends and relations and an apothecary, about twenty-seven all told. Problems arose about a month before they were due to sail. Southey wanted to take an aunt as his servant, but Coleridge would have nothing to do with servitude in a pantisocracy. In the party there were five daughters of a sugar manufacturer from Bath, Fricker. Two were betrothed, one to Southey and one to Lovell, while a third was picked by Southey for Coleridge to marry. At the time Coleridge was wooing the daughter of a theater manager in Cambridge and did not love Southey's choice for him. Also money for the scheme was short; Southey began to lecture in Bristol. In February 1795 Southey's enthusiasm for the venture waned, while Coleridge felt the Fricker family were unsuited to life in a pantisocracy. Furthermore, Lovell's death led Southey to quit the scheme. Coleridge took up an interest in the mystical ideas of Jakob Boehme (1575–1624). Finally, Coleridge, Southey, and another of the latter's friends married a Fricker girl each. The scheme folded, and in time the term "pantisocracy" became a derogatory term for wild utopian schemes and ventures.

See Also Boehme, Jakob; Coleridge, Samuel Taylor; Godwin, William; Lovell, Robert; Rousseau, Jean-Jacques; Southey, Robert

Sources:

Armytage, Walter H. Green. 1961. *Heavens Below: Utopian Experiments in England 1560–1950*. London: Routledge and Kegan Paul.

PARAMAHANSA YOGANANDA. Paramahansa Yogananda (1893–1952) was born in India. He became a guru and published his *Autobiography of a Yogi* (1946), one of the few written by a yogi about himself. He was an important disciple of Sri Yuktesnari Giri, whom he revered after his own mother died when he was only eleven years old. Giri sent him as special missionary to the West in 1920. The book, which is largely about modern Hindu saints, thought, and spiritual life, attracted many followers to him and helped to continue his work after his death. He acquired several new properties: a retreat in the desert at Twentynine Palms, California, where he would go for periods of seclusion to work on his writings; a church in Long Beach, California; and another in Phoenix, Arizona. He had many thousands of disciples worldwide when he died. He was largely responsible for opening the West to much of the spiritual teachings of Hindus.

See Also Ananda Co-operative Village; Swami Kriyananda

Sources:

Yogananda, Paramahansa. 1946. *Autobiography of a Yogi*. 1971 ed. Los Angeles: Self-Realization Fellowship.
Walters, Donald. 1977. *The Path: Autobiography of a Western Yogi (Swami Kriyananda)*. Nevada City, Calif.: Ananda.

PARKER, CRITCHLEY. Critchley Parker (1911–1942), born in Melbourne, Australia, the only child of an influential publisher of business journals, lived comfortably on an allowance from the family. His father was an expert on mining and fisheries and a close associate of some influential Jews. Critchley had no occupation. Although he was a capable bush walker and hiker in Australia and abroad, Parker was declared unfit for war service in 1940. Parker was not a Jew, but he had a deep interest in the welfare of refugees from Europe and deep concern for Tasmania's economy, where he wanted to establish a utopian venture modeled on Soviet communal life. He believed that since Tasmania was rich in minerals, the venture could rely heavily on mining, and after it was well established, manufacturing industries and sporting and scholarly ventures should be pursued. Tasmanian mountains and rivers were well suited to building hydroelectric power stations. He also valued athletics, play reading, music contests, and scientific expeditions. He was a good-natured idealist with a vision for a new Jerusalem. He befriended and was much influenced by a charming and pretty Jewish journalist, Caroline Isaacson (d. 1962), several years his senior. Jewish leaders considered the utopian scheme unusual, coming as it did from a Gentile in Australia, but in time agreed to support it. Parker went to Tasmania to examine the southwest wilderness more closely near Port Davey. Government officials would not go with him to study further the environs of Port Davey at that time because the weather was too harsh for a trek through dense bush and across difficult terrain. They were right. Critchley died from starvation and exposure in a most inhospitable environment. His body was not found for four months. In 1944, the Australian government rejected a similar venture for 50,000 Jews to settle in Australia's East Kimberley region, and this decision made the Tasmanian venture a closed issue.

See Also Poynduk

Source:

Rubinstein, Hilary L. 1990. "Critchley Parker (1911–42): Australian Martyr for Jewish Refugees." *Journal of the Australian Jewish Historical Society* 9: 56–68.

PARKER, RICHARD BARRY. Richard Barry Parker (1867–1947) went to school at Ashover in Derbyshire and then to T. C. Simmonds' "Àteliér of Art" and later to the South Kensington School of Art. From 1889 to 1892 he worked for the architect A. Faulkner Armitage (1849–1937). He designed the Parker family home, "Moorlands" (1894). He became friends with Raymond Unwin (1863–1940). They were half cousins. Together they designed St. Andrews Church, Barrow Hill, and shortly afterward formed their notable partnership and became founding architects of many Garden Cities in England. The first was Letchworth (1904).

See Also Howard, Ebenezer; Letchworth; Unwin, Raymond

Sources:

Gray, A. Stuart. 1986. *Edwardian Architecture: A Biographical Dictionary.* Des Moines: University of Iowa Press.

Jackson, Frank. 1985. *Sir Raymond Unwin: Architect, Planner and Visionary.* London: Zwemmer.

Miller, Mervyn. 1992. *Raymond Unwin: Garden Cities and Town Planning.* Leicester, U.K.: Leicester University Press.

PAYNE, EDWARD BIRON. Edward Biron Payne (1845–1923) was born in Vermont and educated at schools in Connecticut and Illinois. His father was a Congregationalist minister. He attended Iowa College and later graduated from Oberlin College (1874). In 1875 he went to Berkeley, California, and until 1880 served there as a congregationalist minister. Suddenly, he became so dissatisfied with Congregationalists that he resigned, became a Unitarian, and returned to New England. In Massachusetts and New Hampshire he had parishes, and he worked with labor groups as well. He contracted tuberculosis and was forced back to the milder Berkeley climate, where, in 1890, he was head of the first

Unitarian congregation. He became a popular speaker and was much attracted by the ethics of the Social Gospel, and soon he became a leading Christian socialist. Although he never became the full-time resident of the Altruria Colony, he served in the role of president and chief publicist. He edited the *Altrurian* (1894–1896), a newspaper of social reform. Despite help from a network of Altrurian clubs in California, the colony dispersed in January 1895 because it could not maintain itself economically. Later, Payne edited *Coming Light* (1898–1899).

See Also Altruria

Sources:

Fogarty, Robert S. 1980. *Dictionary of American Communal History*. Westport, Conn.: Greenwood Press.
Hine, Robert V. 1953. *California's Utopian Colonies*. 1983 ed. Berkeley: University of California Press.

PECCEI, AURELIO. Aurelio Peccei (1900–1983) was born in Turin and educated at its university. In 1930 he joined the Fiat Company and later established the firm in Argentina (1953), where he served as head until 1973. Also he was managing director and vice chairman of Olivetti from 1964 to 1973. He met with the head of the Organization for Economic Cooperation and Development in Paris, Alexander King, in 1967, and they agreed that the world lacked political leadership adequate to the task of controlling population growth and its consequences for depleting natural resources, poverty, and pollution. At the Accademia dei Lincei in Rome, April 1968, he formed the Club of Rome. It would have only 100 members: scientists, industrialists, educationists, statesmen, and economists. Its structure would be informal, because Peccei believed too many organizations in the world were ineffectively managed. It was called the Club of Rome because Peccei lived in Rome and founded it in Rome. The club's first report, *The Limits of Growth* (1972), employed an advanced computer program to show a great disaster was coming within a century unless a balance was struck in the world between population growth and industrial output. Critics thought it false and argued that with the appropriate technology, management, and a little intelligence, economic growth could continue without disaster. After twelve years Peccei thought that every indicator showed the world was in a worse than expected state in 1984 and that sacrifices had to be made. He is noted for having raised the social conscience of Italian businessmen and linked academic and community life. Always an optimist, toward the end of his life he was drawn to the idea of a Japanese professor for a ''human revolution'' to change the world. Such a change, he felt, required broad experience and a capacity to listen to people from different cultures, and, because everyone lived in the same world, it was important to get many different perspectives.

See Also Club of Rome

Sources:

Pauli, Gunther, A. 1988. *Crusader for the Future*. New York: Pergamon Press.
Peccei, Aurelio. 1969. *The Chasm Ahead*. New York: Macmillan.
———. 1977. The Human Quality. New York: Pergamon Press.
———. 1981. *One Hundred Pages for the Future*. New York: Pergamon Press.
Waggoner, Walter H. 1984. ''Aurelio Peccei, Italian Executive and Founder of a Forum,
    Is Dead.'' *New York Times Biographical Service* 15 (March): 380.

PECKHAM EXPERIMENT. The Peckham experiment was a neighborhood organization based on ideas in *The New State* (1918) by Mary Parker Follett
(1868–1933) and established to support primarily the health needs of the local
urban community. In 1926 at a small house in Queen's Road, Peckham, England, 100 families agreed to pay one shilling each for periodic health examinations. By 1935 the community had a health center, gymnasium, nursery,
theater, consulting rooms on the top floor, dressing rooms and laboratories, and
a cafeteria on the lower floor. It was the first health center of its kind, cost
£7,000 to run, and in 1939 had 3,000 members in 875 families. During World
War II it was converted to a factory. After World War II the National Health
Scheme made the Peckham experiment unnecessary.

See Also Follett, Mary Parker

Sources:

Armytage, Walter H. Green. 1961. *Heavens Below: Utopian Experiments in England
    1560–1950*. London: Routledge and Kegan Paul.
Comerford, John. 1947. *Health the Unknown: The Story of the Peckham Experiment*.
    London: Hamilton.
Follett, Mary Parker. 1918. *The New State: Group Organization, the Solution of Popular
    Government*. 1923 ed. New York: Longmans.
Stallibrass, Alison. 1989. *Being Me and Also Us*. Edinburgh: Scottish Academic Press.

PENN, WILLIAM. William Penn (1644–1718) was the son of an admiral, Sir
William Penn (1621–1670). Young William was raised in a puritanical family,
matriculated from Oxford, and was expelled in 1661 for refusing to conform to
the restored Anglican Church; in despair his father sent him to Paris. The lad
saw action in the Dutch War. On his return William studied law and in 1666
was sent to administer his father's estates in Cork, where he was converted to
Quakerism. He was imprisoned for his *Sandy Foundation Shaken* (1668), which
outlined a new gospel. After his father won his release, and William endured
further terms of imprisonment, the young man toured Holland and Germany
preaching Quakerism. His father was owed a debt by King Charles II (1630–
1685). In 1681, in lieu of it, William was given the territory ''Pensilvania''
(Pennsylvania). As a Quaker trustee, he wanted to establish a model commonwealth based on Quaker principles. In 1682, he called together an assembly of
the ''Free Society of Traders of Pennsylvania'' and allowed them to enact a
constitution, a ''Great Charter.'' It vested many of the powers of government

in representatives of the people. Penn accepted this scheme and sailed to the United States in 1682, spoke with the indigenous Americans at the site of Philadelphia, and for two years governed tolerantly. He returned to England (1684–1699) to battle religious persecution of Quakers. On returning to Pennsylvania, he found its constitution had not functioned well and noted the evils of slavery, although he himself had slaves. He returned to England in 1701, witnessed much bitter political conflict, and feared his province and territories in the United States would become Crown Colonies. He fell into debt, was imprisoned (1708), and was forced to mortgage his property rights to the Crown.

See Also Pennsylvania; Quakers

Sources:

Dunn, Mary Maples. 1967. *William Penn: Politics and Conscience*. Princeton: Princeton University Press.

Dunn, Richard, and Mary M. Dunn, eds. 1986. *The World of William Penn*. Philadelphia: University of Pennsylvania Press.

Endy, Melvin B. 1973. *William Penn and Early Quakerism*. Princeton: Princeton University Press.

Illack, Joseph E. 1965. *William Penn, the Politician. His Relations with the English Government*. Ithaca, N.Y.: Cornell University Press.

Magnussen, Magnus, and Rosemary Goring, eds. 1990. *Chambers Biographical Dictionary*. 5th ed. Edinburgh: Chambers.

Stephen, Leslie, and Sydney Lee, eds. 1917. *The Dictionary of National Biography*. London: Oxford University Press.

PENNSYLVANIA. Sir William Penn (1621–1670) was owed a debt by King Charles II (1630–1685), and in 1681, in lieu of it, his son William Penn (1644–1718) was given the territory ''Pensilvania'' (Pennsylvania) to honor the old admiral and to establish a colony for young William's coreligionists, largely persecuted Quakers. A Great Charter was drawn up that gave many government powers to the settlers of the territory. The colony was peopled early by Germans who had suffered during the cruel invasion of the Rhineland by the armies of Louis XIV (1638–1715), the persecution of Lutherans and other sects, and the tyranny of local German princes. At the turn of the century, when religious freedom was offered to settlers under the regime of Queen Anne (1665–1714) and her successors, immigration from Germany grew rapidly. William Penn advertised guarantees of religious freedom and in doing so attracted attention of the Dunkers, Amish, Pietists, and Mennonites in the United States. One of the earliest groups settled in 1683 and made Germantown a center of handicrafts, and the Rittenhouse family established paper mills. A great influx began after 1700 up the Mohawk Valley in New York, into New Brunswick. In time thousands would come each year from Germany and Switzerland. In 1739 a German newspaper was published in Germantown. Also the Scotch Irish came to Pennsylvania, fleeing oppression and the Anglican establishment and the English laws prohibiting manufacture in the weaving industry of Ireland. In his plan for Philadelphia, Penn upheld what would be the Garden City concept as an ideal, used the grid pattern, and insisted each house be surrounded by a half acre of ground. This was a fundamental change from land use in Europe.

See Also Garden City; Penn, William; Quakers

Sources:

Bronner, Edwin B. 1962. *William Penn's Holy Experiment: The Founding of Pennsylvania.* New York: Temple University Press.

Buranelli, Vincent. 1962. *The King and the Quaker: A Study of William Penn and James II.* Philadelphia: University of Pennsylvania Press.

Gill, Roger. 1984. "In England's Green and Pleasant Land." In Peter Alexander and Roger Gill, eds., *Utopias*, pp. 109–117. London: Duckworth.

Janney, S. M. 1852. *Life of William Penn.* Philadelphia: Hogan, Perkins.

Soderlund, Jean R., ed. 1983. *William Penn and the Founding of Pennsylvania, 1680–1684; A Documentary History.* Philadelphia: University of Pennsylvania Press.

PERMACULTURE. Permaculture is a form of agriculture that uses a beneficial assembly of plants and animals in relation to human settlements, mostly aimed toward household and community self-reliance. Its aim is to unite systems for long-term sustenance; it requires careful thinking about the environment and use of resources and need gratification and seeks to establish productive environments for food, energy, shelter, material, and nonmaterial needs and social and economic infrastructures to support them. It was first developed in two books, *Permaculture I* and *Permaculture II*, by Bill Mollison and David Holmgren in Tasmania in 1974. Its social philosophy is based on a belief in cooperation with nature and each other and care for the earth and people, and this is done by designing diverse, stable, resilient natural ecosystems, regeneration of damaged land, and the preservation of existing ecosystems. The individual philosophy is based on resourceful self-reliance regarding local and global issues. Since 1974 permaculture has been used worldwide and has become a social movement. In the United States the Farm pursues permaculture principles, the *Permaculture International Journal* has been established, and countless books are available for following permaculture principles in private gardens.

See Also Crystal Waters; Farm Eco-Village, The; Mollison, Bill

Sources:

Mollison, Bill C. 1979. *Permaculture II: Practical Design and Further Theory in Permanent Agriculture.* Stanley, Tasmania: Tagari Books.

———. 1988. *Permaculture: Designer's Manual.* Twalgum, New South Wales: Tagari.

———. 1990. *Permaculture: A Practical Guide for a Sustainable Future.* Washington, D.C.: Island Press.

Mollison, Bill C., and David Holmgren. 1978. *Permaculture I: A Perennial for Human Settlements.* Environmental Psychology, Hobart, Tasmania: University of Tasmania.

Mollison, Bill C., with Reny Mia Slay. c. 1991. *Introduction to Permaculture.* Twalgum, New South Wales: Tagari.

Whitefield, Patrick. 1993. *Permaculture in a Nut Shell*. Twalgum, New South Wales: Tagari.

PESTALOZZI, JOHANN HEINRICH. Johann Heinrich Pestalozzi (1746–1827), born into a wealthy family of Zurich, studied theology and law and later turned his attention to agriculture. He was devoted to the education of the people and in 1775 established a school on his estate. At his school, pupils were encouraged to observe and reason and develop an interest in their studies. Jean-Jacques Rousseau's (1712–1778) ideas contributed much to the system. It failed to draw financial support by popular subscription, so Pestalozzi was obliged to give up the plan in 1780. The first account of his method of instruction was published about this time, but his principal literary work was *Lienhardt and Gertrude; A Book for the People*, which he wrote between 1781 and 1785. In 1798 with support from the government he founded an educational institution for poor people at Stanz. It was abandoned in 1799. He then took charge of a school at Burgdorf, 1804–1825. His collected works were published in sixteen volumes between 1869 and 1872.

See Also Pestalozzian School

Sources:

Green, John A. 1912. *The Life and Work of Pestalozzi*. Baltimore: Warwick and York.
———. ed. 1914. *Pestalozzi's Educational Writings*. Reprinted, 1969. New York: Longman, Green.
Krusi, Hermann. 1875. *Pestalozzi: His Life, Work and Influence*. Cincinnati: Wilson, Hinkle.
Silber, Kate. 1973. *Pestalozzi*. 2d ed. London: Routledge and Kegan Paul.
Zusne, Leonard. 1984. *Biographical Dictionary of Psychology*. Westport, Conn.: Greenwood Press.

PESTALOZZIAN SCHOOL. A Pestalozzian school follows the principles suggested by the Swiss educator Johann Heinrich Pestalozzi (1746–1827). His principles of education emphasize the role of mother, sensory experience, and the immediate environment in the development of ideas and the coherence of thinking among children. They contradict authoritarian and other oppressive techniques of extracting obedience from children and provide the foundation of modern elementary education. His school assumes a natural order in human development based on concrete experience and the cultivation of individual differences in aptitude and ability. It opposes memorization and discipline and replaces them with love and understanding of the child's own world. Tactile experiences are fundamental to teaching natural science to the young. At the same time as learning factual and technical knowledge, moral education is valued, as is the idea that the social world can and should be reformed to make a better world. To Pestalozzi education was an instrument of social reform. Teacher training methods were changed due to the experiences of teachers in Pestalozzi schools, and teaching became a unified science of learning. The ideas were used in Russia, also by the German philosopher Johann Gottlieb Fichte (1762–1814), and later in England by Rev. Charles Mayo (1792–1846), who opened a boarding school using Pestalozzian methods at Epsom (1822–1826) and Cheam (1826–1846) with help from his sister Elizabeth Mayo (1793–1865).

See Also Pestalozzi, Johann Heinrich

Sources:

Dudley, Lavinia P. 1963. *The Encyclopedia Americana.* International ed. New York: Americana Corporation.

Heafford, Michael R. 1967. *Pestalozzi: His Thought and Its Relevance Today.* London: Methuen.

Magnussen, Magnus, Rosemary Goring, and John O. Thorn, eds. 1990. *Chambers Biographical Dictionary.* Edinburgh: Chambers.

McHenry, Robert, ed. 1992. *The New Encyclopedia Britannica.* Chicago: Encyclopedia Britannica.

Monroe, Will S. 1907. *History of the Pestalozzian Movement in the United States.* Reprinted, 1969. Syracuse, N.Y.: C. W. Bardeen.

PHILADELPHIANS. Philadelphians were members of a chiliastic community, the Philadelphian Society, a short-lived Böhmenist sect. It comprised followers of Mrs. Jane Leade (1623–1704), who witnessed her husband die after having been swindled and reduced to poverty. Afterward she had visions that she recorded in *A Fountain of Gardens* (1670). To her the Resurrection of Christ was imminent, as she wrote in *The Heavenly Cloud Now Breaking* (1684). She published several chiliastic tracts in the 1690s and had many more visions. She was influenced by John Pordage (1607–1681), a millenarian, and following his death used his unpublished tracts to augment her own. The Philadelphian Society's constitution was set down in 1697 and was supported with funds from Germany, where Jane Leade's writing was taken seriously. The society's meetings were so crowded that they were moved from Baldwin's Gardens to West Moreland House. In 1703 the Philadelphians broke up, due in part to conflicts between Henry Dodwell (1641–1711), Francis Lee (1661–1719), and others.

See Also Dodwell, Henry; Leade, Jane; Lee, Francis; Roach, Richard

Sources:

Armytage, Walter Henry Green. 1961. *Heavens Below: Utopian Experiments in England 1560–1950.* London: Routledge and Kegan Paul.

Magnussen, Magnus, and Rosemary Goring, eds. 1990. *Chambers Biographical Dictionary.* 5th ed. Edinburgh: Chambers.

Stephen, Leslie, and Sydney Lee, eds. 1917. *The Dictionary of National Biography.* London: Oxford University Press.

PITT TOWN. Pitt Town was one of three Australian communal settlements established by a government-appointed board of control in 1893–1894. In New South Wales, Pitt Town is noted for being the largest project in utopian experimentation in Australia's history. It comprised 100 households with 500 members on 800 hectares (2,000 acres). Most members were unemployed workers from Sydney who, with little experience, built 120 homes, planted 1,800 fruit trees and, over 18,000 grape vines, and cleared a quarter of their land for farming. They fenced the land, dug dams, built a sawmill and a church and a dairy. By the end of 1895 numbers had dwindled, and the community survived only on selling firewood to residents of Sydney. The community divided: the majority was against communalism, and this ended the experiment in the middle of 1896. Other utopian experiments in New South Wales were at Bega and Wilberforce.

See Also Village Settlements of South Australia

Source:

Metcalf, Bill, ed. 1995. *From Utopian Dreaming to Communal Reality: Cooperative Life Styles in Australia.* Sydney: University of New South Wales Press.

PLATO. Plato (c. 427–347 B.C.) became a pupil (407 B.C.) and later a friend of Socrates (469–399 B.C.). From 388 B.C. he lived at the court of Dionysius the Elder (431–367 B.C.), the tyrant of Syracuse and a patron of poets and philosophers. When he returned to Athens, Plato founded the Academy and taught philosophy and mathematics until he died. He visited Syracuse twice more and in vain sought to realize his political ideals. His work appears in dialogues and epistles. The early dialogues concern the defense of Socrates (*Apology*), whether or not virtue can be taught (*Meno*), and the absolute character of right and wrong (*Gorgias*). The conversations are dialogues with Socrates and treat a problem by raising related issues and examining basic philosophical questions about knowing and living. Assuming a harmony in the universe, Plato taught a philosophy to understand and show rational patterns in relations between the cosmos, the state, and the soul. Among his great dialogues was *The Republic*, which shows that by considering justice in the state, one can understand justice in the individual, its relation to the idea of the Good, the principle that guides both truth and order. *The Republic* argues that philosophers are the best rulers because through the study of dialectics—the scientific method of constant inquiry—only they can grasp the harmonious relations between the elements of the universe. In his *The Republic*, the classes of society—philosophers, warriors, laborers—willingly and cooperatively enjoy the results of their efforts. In his *Phaedo*, Plato shows the philosopher traveling through death to eternity; in the *Symposium* true lovers ascend poetically to beauty, forever; in *The Laws*, a long utopian work like *The Republic*, Plato presents a practical outline of the nature of the state. Plato considered most problems that humankind faced and has become one of the most influential thinkers in Western civilization.

See Also Republic, The

Sources:

Dawson, Doyne. 1992. *Cities of the Gods: Communist Utopias in Greek Thought.* New York: Oxford University Press.

Snodgrass, Mary Ellen. 1995. *Encyclopedia of Utopian Literature*. Santa Barbara, Calif.: ABC-CLIO.

Taylor, Alfred Edward. 1927. *Plato: The Man and His Work*. London: Methuen.

Vlastos, Gregory. 1973. *Platonic Studies*. Princeton: Princeton University Press.

POINT LOMA. Point Loma is an another name for the Universal Brotherhood of the Theosophical Society. It was established at Point Loma on 330 acres of a peninsula protecting San Diego Bay, California, and was the first of three splinter theosophical groups originating with Helena Petrovna Blavatsky's (1831–1891) theosophy. The society was led by Katherine Tingley (1847–1929) after the death of Blavatsky. It blended Eastern mysticism and New England transcendentalism. During the 1890s the society supported the reform movements based on Edward Bellamy's (1850–1898) *Nationalism* (1895) in New York. Membership reached 500 by 1910; 300 were children at the Raja-Yoja School, an important educational experiment begun at Point Loma in 1901. During 1901–1902, seventy-five children were recruited from Cuba. The colony at Point Loma prospered initially and began to decline in the mid-1920s. In 1942 all its holdings were sold, and many left Point Loma; the remaining theosophists moved to Covina near Los Angeles.

See Also Bellamy, Edward; Blavatsky, Helena Petrovna Hahn; Tingley, Katherine Augusta Westcott

Sources:

Fogarty, Robert S. 1980. *Dictionary of American Communal History*. Westport, Conn.: Greenwood Press.

Hine, Robert V. 1953. *California's Utopian Colonies*. 1983 ed. Berkeley: University of California Press.

PORT SUNLIGHT. Port Sunlight is one of Britain's Garden Cities. In 1888, the successful soap manufacturer from Warrington, William Hesketh Lever (1851–1925) began to erect employees' houses at Port Sunlight, Wirrel, near Birkenhead and Liverpool. It was different from earlier similar ventures in that it was planned as a village, spacious and green, open and self-contained, quiet, and set apart from the industrial world of the day. On one side were the factory and works—chimneys, railway sidings, wharves—where Lever soaps were made (1890–1910) with the efficiency and profitability of modern capitalist methods. On the other side, behind a neo-classical facade, houses were well protected from the sight of the industrial activities and buildings. Sited tastefully on the 130 acres were half-timbered cottages with side and front lawns and tree-lined paths. The architecture owed much to the Cheshire Manor house, Renaissance style, and the elegant English village with its red sandstone church, Tudor-style coach inn, men's clubs, half-timbered library, and various halls for the pursuit of arts and crafts and a school. Port Sunlight has the Lady Lever Art Gallery with many fine nineteenth-century British paintings, sculptures, tapestries, Napoleonic mementos, and fine chinoiserie. To the regret of the Lever family few of the working classes showed much interest in the art they displayed in the gallery. Today Port Sunlight is Unilever's European soap factory, and the village amazes its visitors for its leafy, film-studio setting.

See Also Lever, William H.

Source:

Marsh, Jan. 1982. *Back to the Land: The Pastoral Impulse in England, from 1880 to 1914*. London: Quartet.

POTTERSVILLE. Pottersville was a community of potters in Wisconsin who settled in 1846–1848 with 134 British immigrants on 1,600 acres. The original plan was devised by William Evans (fl. 1843–1846) with the Trades Union of Operative Potters, Staffordshire. New technology was being forced on unwitting employees in the pottery trade. It was hoped that 500 of the 7,000 members of the union would pay £1 each for a share in a joint-stock emigration company and a shilling per week thereafter. However, the money did not appear, and another £3,000 was required. Division grew between potters when one group found they could adapt to the new technology applied to pottery in Staffordshire. They decided to stay at their work, so they quit the original union and formed one of their own. While Evans lectured groups on the persecution of Staffordshire potters and the reduction of their minimal wages, in the United States divisions appeared among the emigrants. Legal problems arose over land-ownership as well as personal problems that centered on the climate, inadequate water, sandy soil, and threatening Indians. It seemed many emigrants were not willing to work hard, and further attempts to establish potters' communities also failed at this time.

See Also Evans, William

Source:

Armytage, Walter Henry Green. 1961. *Heavens Below: Utopian Experiments in England 1560–1950*. London: Routledge and Kegan Paul.

POUNDBERRY. Poundberry is an urban village on a lush green hillside in rural Dorset. It is the consequence of efforts by Charles, Prince of Wales (b. 1948), to show that rural architectural traditions can be cognate with modern life. The urban village is on the outskirts of Dorchester on a 160-hectare (400-acre) site sold off by the prince's duchy of Cornwall estate. The homes are designed to be flint-stone cottages and Georgian stone houses and mix luxurious accommodations with low-rent cottages. The ideas are based on *A Vision of Britain* (1989) by Prince Charles himself, who asserts that countryside development should enhance and never detract from the immediate landscape and should aim to promote a sense of community within both economic and residential activities. The prince is well known for his dislike of modern architecture, and to benefit the profession, he set up his own Institute of Architecture. Closely involved with the establishment of Poundberry, he even helped to choose the bricks and streetlights. In Poundberry a high-technology farm occupies a converted Victorian farmhouse, while sheep graze in nearby fields. Wrought-iron wall lamps glow in the streets all night long. When completed, Poundberry will have 2,500 houses—over 100 are now built—small craft shops, and a village pub. Prince Charles often visits Poundberry to reinforce the creation of the village atmosphere and sense of identity and an urban setting. To some it appears like a model village from a novel by Thomas Hardy (1840–1928), the nineteenth-century British century novelist, but without the thatched roofs and horses in the streets. Critics regard it a kind of Disneyland, built according to retrograde principles of architecture, an imitation of the past, and a variety of architecture that has no place being built today. Others who are equally critical are pleased to see the prince do something about his architectural beliefs after his strong criticism of the proposed extension of the eighteenth-century National Gallery as being a "monstrous carbuncle."

See also Charles, Prince of Wales

Sources:

Charles, Prince of Wales. 1989. *A Vison of Britain: A Personal Vision of Architecture.* London: Doubleday.
Serjeant, Jill. 1997. "Charles's Designer Village Taking Shape in the Hills." *The Age* (16 June): A9.

POYNDUK. Poynduk was a utopian settlement planned for Tasmania in the early 1940s by Critchley Parker (1911–1942). Attracted to the Soviet economic system, Parker proposed a settlement, Poynduk, in southwest Tasmania, near Port Davey, which could thrive on local mineral deposits. It was to be named after an Aboriginal leader. Members of the settlement were to be Jewish refugees from Europe. Tasmania was chosen because many of its inhabitants had left to serve the military in Europe and on the Australian mainland. Jews were chosen because of their economic success in establishing settlements in Palestine. The Tasmanian government supported the scheme. Parker advocated the settlement have a thirty-five-hour working week, a month's vacation on full pay, and attractive recreational facilities. At first the settlers would import their food until they became self-sufficient. From Czechoslovakia would come Jews skilled in iron and steel manufacture, and they would establish a canning industry and ultimately produce wool and cotton goods and even Scotch whiskey. Port Davey would become the "Paris of Australia" because it would adopt the culture of French Jews. Their efforts would also help fur, leather, and flax industries to prosper. Members of the settlement would agree to work at Poynduk for ten years or be legally proceeded against. The settlement would be modeled on the collective ownership system of the USSR, and experts would be called to meet on the plans for its first five years. It would become a center of cultural pursuits, sporting achievements, trade fairs, and a focus of learning because of its great university, staffed with highly paid professors, and attractive scholarships to draw young scholars from China, Japan, Java, India, Arabia, South America, and Africa. Social justice and social welfare would be dominant values at Poynduk. The scheme died with the death of Parker, due partly to the Australian government's policies toward Jewish refugees' settling in Australia at that time.

See Also Parker, Critchley

Sources:

Gettler, Leon. 1993. *An Unpromised Land.* Fremantle, Western Australia: Fremantle Arts Center Press.
Metcalf, Bill, ed. 1995. *From Utopian Dreaming to Communal Reality: Cooperative Life Styles in Australia.* Sydney: University of New South Wales Press.
Rubinstein, Hilary L. 1990. "Critchley Parker (1911–42): Australian Martyr for Jewish Refugees." *Journal of the Australian Jewish Historical Society* 9: 56–68.

PRAIRIE HOME COLONY. Prairie Home Colony was originally the Kansas Cooperative Farm and was also called Silkville because it was established in Silkville, Williamsburg township, Franklin County, Kansas (1870–1884). The community began making silk in 1869, but the colony began officially in 1870. It was one of the last attempts at Fourierist experiments in the United States and was established by Ernest Valeton de Boissiere (1810–1894) with Albert Brisbane (1809–1890), Elijah P. Grant (1808–1894), and others. Articles of association of the Kansas Co-operative Farm were drawn up in 1869; 3,500 acres were bought in Franklin County, Kansas, and $29,000 was promised for the scheme. However, in June 1869 the scheme seemed a failure, and Brisbane and Grant quit. In 1870, with the help of Horace Greeley (1811–1872), an account was published of the project under the leadership of de Boissiere. French immigrants were already well established in the northeast of Kansas, and the colony attracted forty experts in silk production. Notable U.S. families were in the community, including the erstwhile president of the North American Phalanx. In 1873 Grant issued a prospectus, *The Prairie Home Association and Corporation based on an Attractive Industry*, which indicated that socialists would be welcome in their communal venture. Buildings were erected, and silk was produced, exhibited, and praised at the Centenary Exposition in Philadelphia (1876). Until 1882 the community flourished. Later, they found their silk production no longer profitable. The cooperative features of the community were never fully developed, in 1884 De Boisseire went home to France, and in 1886 the community ended.

See Also Boissiere, Ernest Valeton de; Brisbane, Albert; Fourierist communities or phalanxes; Greeley, Horace

Sources:

Fogarty, Robert S. 1980. *Dictionary of American Communal History.* Westport, Conn.: Greenwood Press.
Miller, Timothy. 1990. *American Communes: 1860–1960.* New York: Garland.

PRAIRIE HOME COMMUNITY. The Prairie Home Community was an anarchist group that formed under no formal authority and allowed members to do much as they wanted. It was based on Fourierist principles that had been discussed at a socialist convention in New York (1843). Delegates organized a group of 130 after they made their way back to the West, and they settled in Logan County, Ohio, on 500 acres of forest in undulating country. Members came from the Quakers and English and German socialist groups. Most were farmers. They had no constitution and advocated the greatest of individual choices and a libertarian way of life. The community lasted about a year.

Sources:

Oved, Yaacov. 1987. *Two Hundred Years of American Communes*. New Brunswick, N.J.: Transaction Books.
Veysey, Laurence. 1973. *The Communal Experience: Anarchist and Mystical Counter-cultures in America*. New York: Harper and Row.

PRAYING VILLAGES. Praying villages were established by John Eliot (1604–1690) as pastoral communities. After learning the language of Native Americans he made his first pastoral visit to them October 1646 at Nonantum in Massachusetts. He gave a sermon in the Native American dialect but prayed in English. This was an early attempt at what was thought then to be the ''civilizing'' of Native American converts. Later, Eliot established settlements that provided Native Americans with industrial occupations, homes and clothing, and a form of self-government that would allow them to enjoy the comfort and security white settlers had. Eliot sought the approval of fellow ministers in his attempts to draw Native Americans into Christian religion. In New England a law was passed July 1649 to establish a corporation to promote and propagate the gospel among Indians, and in 1651 the first township was established at Natick, a township of ''praying Indians.'' Under Eliot's supervision fourteen similar settlements were founded. At nearby Roxbury and Natick he provided the villages with clothing and other necessities that his pupils had donated. The first Native American church was founded at Natick (1660) and maintained until its last pastor died, 1716.
See Also Eliot, John

Sources:

Fogarty, Robert. 1990. *All Things New: American Communes and Utopian Movements 1860–1914*. Chicago: University of Chicago Press.

PREOBRAZHENSKY, EVGENII A. Evgenii Aleksevich Preobrazhensky (1886–1937) was born in Bolhkov, Orel Gouvt, Russia. Although his father was a priest, the lad became an atheist when he turned fourteen. From 1912 he was a Bolshevik Party agitator and collaborated with Vladimir Lenin (1870–1924). Until 1927 he was an editor of *Pravda* and the chairman of the finance committee attached to the Central Committee. In 1927 he was expelled from the Communist Party altogether. In 1929 he was readmitted to the party, only to be expelled in 1933, admitted again, and expelled permanently in 1936. With Nikolay Bukharin (1888–1928) he wrote the *ABC of Communism* (1922) and was largely responsible for Russia's industrialization plans, followed at the expense of peasants. In 1937 he was arrested and shot to death.

See Also Bogdanov, Aleksandr; Bolshevism; Bukharin, Nikolay Ivanovich

Source:

Vronskaya, Jeanne, and Vladimir Chuguev. 1992. *The Biographical Dictionary of the Former Russian Soviet Union*. London: Bowker-Saur.

PRESHIL SCHOOL. Preshil is Australia's longest surviving progressive school and defines clearly an alternative to the prevailing system of Australian education, public and private. The school respects the children, and its members are not locked into roles of teacher and pupil. Preshil takes into account social and emotional requirements of its children as well as their intellectual needs. The school was founded in 1931 by Greta Lyttle (1875–1944) with a small group of children in her living room in a house in Barkers Road, Melbourne, Victoria. She was interested in theosophy and had taught at St. Andrews in Kew, a nearby suburb; and when she left, she took a group of children with her. She was influenced by Friedrich Froebel (1782–1852), Maria Montessori (1870–1952), and the Indian philosopher Rabindranath Tagore (1861–1941). In 1932 the school had eighty pupils. In 1933, after being inspected for a day by officials from the Victorian Education Department, the school was registered. In 1944 Margaret Lyttle (b. 1913) took over the school when her aunt died. In 1994, after fifty years at the school, Margaret Lyttle retired at age eighty-one. She was known affectionately as "Mug." Those who prefer formalized education systems have asserted that at Preshil anything goes, and children do as they like. This is far from the truth. In a bushlike setting, the school buildings have been designed and built to meet the needs of growing children rather than to control methods of instruction; classes are planned for small groups of individuals rather than large age cohorts; children learn from being given special programs to which they contribute; class timetables are determined more by the children's level of interest and commitment to learning than by a schedule of periods; organized sport and religious instruction are not imposed on the children; sometimes groups gather to play sport and find other schools for competitors; parents contribute to the maintenance of school buildings and the financial management of school operations; annually, children flock together to write plays and musicals, which they produce and direct to large audiences. Preshil has been the model for many similar schools during the last sixty years.

See Also Froebel, Friedrich; Montessori, Maria

Sources:

Rosh-White, Naomi. 1994. *School Matters: The Preshil Alternative to Education*. Melbourne: Reed.

PRINCE, HENRY JAMES. Henry James Prince (1811–1899) was born in Bath and studied medicine. He discontinued medical studies due to illness and took up Anglican orders under the influence of a middle-aged spinster whom he later married. Shortly after he became a minister, his wife died. Prince stirred his congregation so enthusiastically that his religious services were held on weekdays as well as Sunday. In 1842 the local religious authorities had him replaced by one of his friends, George Thomas, an enthusiast for Prince's ideas. Thomas' friend, a rich civil engineer, William Cobbe, endowed a chapel at Spaxton in Somerset near Bridgewater. In 1849, with help from three of his congregation who had married to financial advantage and with William Cobbe, Henry Prince established at Spaxton the Community of the Son of Man. Its members were free of sin because membership itself entailed salvation of both soul and body. Members were religious visionaries who shared their possessions and, as some thought, their women. The community was known as Agapemone, ''abode of love.''

See Also Community of the Son of Man

Sources:

Armytage, Walter Henry Green. 1961. *Heavens Below: Utopian Experiments in England 1560–1950*. London: Routledge and Kegan Paul.

Magnussen, Magnus, Rosemary Goring, and John O. Thorn, eds. 1990. *Chambers Biographical Dictionary*. Edinburgh: Chambers.

PROUDHON, PIERRE JOSEPH. Pierre Joseph Proudhon (1809–1865) was born in Besançon, France. He became a compositor and helped devise a new technique of typography. He edited Bible notes in Hebrew and typeset *The New Industrial and Social World* (1830) by Charles Fourier (1772–1937), whose ideas captivated him. He published a work on the principles of grammar (1838) and contributed to *Encyclopédia catholique*. He published a paper, *What Is property?* (1840), on the idea that when owners of property charged rent to their tenants, those owners were, in fact, thieves of labor. Support for such an attack on the ownership of property led to his trial for holding revolutionary opinions that endangered the stability of the state. He was found not guilty (1842) and four years later published his *Système des contradictions économiques*. His socialist opinions secured his election to the Seine Department during the 1848 revolution in France. Afterward he published more radical proposals, seeking to advance the cause of great social changes by establishing a bank that did not charge its creditors interest. It was a financial failure. For his wildly inflammatory and anarchistic statements he was imprisoned for three years but escaped to Geneva. In the belief that his jail term would serve his revolutionary cause he came back to France and accepted imprisonment, during which he published much revolutionary literature, including guidelines for socialist/anarchistic insurrections. When released in 1852, he was charged again for his anarchism and jailed for another three years. He fled to Belgium and was given amnesty in

1860. In short, he advanced ideals of justice, freedom, and equality; he assumed humankind would somehow grow in moral stature when such ideals were met, and that in time all government and rule by law would be redundant. His grandest ideal was the fulfillment of the individual's personal development. Such utopian views preceded and conflicted with the ideas of Karl Marx (1818–1883), did not support revolution or dictatorship of the proletariat as the means of social change, abhorred coercive, autocratically run bureaucracies, and in their place advocated the Fourierist idea of a federation of communes. He had won a mass following at the time of his death, and his ideas lived through an ardent follower, Mikhail Bakunin (1814–1876), to shape the anarchist ideology of Saint Émilion.

See Also Bakunin, Mikhail; Fourier, Charles; Saint Émilion

Sources:

Magnussen, Magnus, Rosemary Goring, and John O. Thorn, eds. 1990. *Chambers Biographical Dictionary.* Edinburgh: Chambers.

McCord, William. 1989. *Voyages to Utopia: From Monastery to Commune, the Search for the Perfect Society in Modern Times.* New York: W. W. Norton.

Woodcock, George. 1962. *Anarchism.* Cleveland: World.

PULLMAN, GEORGE MORTIMER. George Mortimer Pullman (1831–1897), one of ten children, was born at Brocton, New York. At fourteen he left school and learned the cabinetmaker's trade and worked with his brother. In 1855 he went to Chicago, where he filled various construction contracts with great success and became interested in making long railway journeys less tedious. In 1859 he remodeled two ordinary railway carriages into sleeping cars for a journey from Chicago to Bloomington, Indiana. But the railway companies were slow to adopt the idea. Pullman went to Colorado to become a storekeeper. In 1863 he returned and, with help from a friend, constructed the first of the famous sleeping cars that bear his name. He married in 1867 and had four children. He also developed a dining car (1868), a chair car (1875), and a vestibule car (1887). His firm was based in Detroit and had plants throughout the United States. He founded the industrial town of Pullman in Illinois. It was built by Pullman for his employees, finished in 1881, ran for sixteen years, and was believed to be one of the healthiest environments in the world. He invested in other car plants, became a philanthropist, and left $1.2 million for a free manual training school at Pullman.

See Also Pullman Village

Sources:

Buder, Stanley. 1967. *Pullman: An Experiment in Industrial Order and Community Planning: 1890–1930.* New York: Oxford University Press.

Fogarty, Robert S. 1990. *All Things New: American Communes and Utopian Movements 1860–1914.* Chicago: University of Chicago Press.

Malone, Dumas, ed. 1935. *Dictionary of American Biography*. Vol. 8. New York: Charles
Scribner's Sons.
Morel, Julian. 1983. *Pullman: The Pullman Car Company, Its Services, Cars and
Traditions*. Newton Abbot: David and Charles.

PULLMAN VILLAGE. Pullman Village was an industrial town created,
planned, and built by George Mortimer Pullman (1831–1897) with good taste
and forethought. The plan called for 320 dwellings, and, unlike Chicago's industrial sprawl and uneven growth, it was to be an aesthetic town that would
impress its community and refine life around the factory. All commercial, industrial, and residential buildings were designed to be both practical and orna-
mental. Construction began on the town and factory in May 1880, and by June
1881, 654 residents were settled. By September 1884 the cost of the town was
$8 million, and it comprised 1,400 dwellings. To Pullman it was the most perfect
city in the world. The town became well known and was compared favorably
with model company towns in Europe, for example, Saltaire in England, Guise
in France, and Esse near the Krupp's work in Germany. Pullman's company
did not wish to subsidize the town beyond the initial investment, so its costs
were to be borne by the inhabitants. Rents in Pullman, with a surcharge for
beauty, were an economic constant. Residents had no choice. But the population
of 12,500 was not stable because the breadwinners were unable to own their
own homes. Pullman was convinced that his town could not survive if the houses
were sold to the inhabitants, and he were to lose control of their appearance.
The influence of the company and the absence of any self-government were
probably the main weakness of the town. Residents had all things done for them
and nothing by them; they had no deep commitment to the town's future; and
the town took on many of the characteristics of a feudal institution. In 1894 the
Pullman plant employees went on strike because wages had been cut, and rents
had not been lowered. By mid-June hundreds of families were moving in search
of new work. The Pullman Company remained indifferent to public opinion. A
boycott of all Pullman cars by the American Railway Union spread the strike,
prolonged it, and cost the workers $360,000 in wages and a great loss to the
company. The fame of the Pullman Village showed how a company could lead
a community with technology, business organization, and social responsibility;
however, this image faded as Pullman Village became synonymous with serious
labor conflict.

See Also Pullman, George Mortimer

Sources:

Buyer, Stanley. 1967. *Pullman: An Experiment in Industrial Order and Community Plan-
ning 1880–1930*. New York: Oxford University Press.
Hayden, Delores. 1976. *Seven American Utopias: The Architecture of Communitarian
Socialism, 1790–1975*. Cambridge: MIT Press.
Morel, Julian. 1983. *Pullman: The Pullman Car Company, Its Services, Cars and
Traditions*. New Abbot: David and Charles.

PURLEIGH COLONY. Purleigh Colony was established in February 1897 on a twenty-three-acre estate near Purleigh, south of Malden in England. The members kept a goat, grew grapes and tomatoes, made bricks, and built their own cottages. The colony functioned according to the free anarchist principles endorsed by John C. Kenworthy (1861–c.1934), who himself built a house there in 1898. It was organized along lines that Leo Tolstoy (1828–1910) had stated for communities. As the membership grew—fifteen were at the colony, and sixty-five scattered nearby—they met weekly to discuss plans. Decisions were made unanimously. There were no rules; everyone was held in check by the opinions of others and his or her own good sense. They supported worthy causes. A contingent of Russian exiles visited the colony, and Purleigh members collected £1,000 to help the Doukhobors in Canada. By 1898 many people wanted to join the colony, which had by now four acres of market gardens, a 100-foot greenhouse, many new buildings, 200 apple trees, and 250 gooseberry bushes. Members aimed for a better and truer life for humanity; some decided not to hold legal title to property, others would no use money, some protested against railways, other shunned the use of postage stamps. In 1898 arguments arose about the admission of tramps to the colony. Other divisions grew, and by 1899 Purleigh was deeply conflicted. Glasshouse crops flourished, but outdoor crops failed; members seemed to be shirking their duties. In the end several of the more enthusiastic founders quit the colony and rode their bicycles from London to the Cotswolds to found another community. Tolstoy thought the structure of the colony did not match the beliefs of the inmates; others pointed to the insanity of members, bad temperedness, and a lack of character.

See Also Doukhobors; Kenworthy, John Coleman; Tolstoyan communities

Sources:

Armytage, Walter Henry Green. 1961. *Heavens Below: Utopian Experiments in England 1560–1950.* London: Routledge and Kegan Paul.
Marsh, Jan. 1982. *Back to the Land: The Pastoral Impulse in England, from 1880 to 1914.* London: Quartet.

PURNELL, BENJAMIN. Benjamin Purnell (1861–1927) was born in Greenup City in Kentucky. He had little education, married a girl from Kentucky in 1877, and became a traveling preacher. In 1880 he was living in Ohio and Indiana and married for a second time without divorcing his first wife. In 1892 he joined an Anglo-Israelite sect, the New House of Israel. When the colony broke up in 1895, Purnell became its leader. He was rejected by the sect; nevertheless, he maintained his messianic mission by publishing a pamphlet, *Star of Bethlehem*, from a small village in Ohio. He moved to Benton Harbor, Michigan (1903), and founded the House of David. This celibate colony aimed to be a ''gathering-in'' place where Purnell prophesied the millennium for the year 1905. Many believers came from Australia, where there was already an Israelite congregation. By 1910 there were 300 members in the House of David. Around Benton

Harbor they ran farms and several businesses and operated an amusement park. After World War I they established a famous baseball team, toured the Midwest, and were noted for wearing long beards. Purnell and his wife were king and queen of the colony and ruled it autocratically. Around them spread rumors of sexual irregularities in their celibate community, but neither state nor federal investigations could gather substantial evidence to convict them. In 1921 dissident members sued Purnell. He went into hiding and was hunted throughout the nation. Faithful members sheltered him, and he never left the colony's headquarters. In 1923 the state of Michigan held a legal inquiry into Purnell's activities, and he was charged with seducing young women, defrauding members of the House of David, and perpetrating a great religious hoax. In the colony it was known that Purnell enjoyed sexual relations with many young women, but, since it was thought he was divine, such activity was condoned. He died during the long trial in 1927.

See Also House of David

Sources:

Fogarty, Robert. 1990. *All Things New: American Communes and Utopian Movements 1860–1914*. Chicago: University of Chicago Press.

Q

QARAMITAH (KARMATHIANS). Qaramitah or Karmathians were a Muslim sect in the Middle East, pantheistic and socialistic, that throve in the ninth century. Their name comes from Hamdan ben-Ashath Karmat (fl. c. 850–900), a poor laborer who professed to be a prophet. He was converted to the Ismaili movement and began missionary activities about 873. The rural populace gave him the name Qarmat, meaning "short-legged" or "red-eyed." He became a missionary in Kufa, the leading apostle of the Karmathians or Qaramitah. The group left the Ismaili movement, and because it threatened the Abbasid caliphate and terrorized southern Iraq, it was regarded as a socialist threat and later was falsely accused of practicing communal ownership of women and property. Principally, the people aimed for a better future by establishing an equitable form of government. Some groups experimented with communism while others were similar to an oligarchic state, for example, Bahrain in the tenth century. The followers were mainly peasants, but in their military actions they had the support of some Bedouin tribesmen. They regarded the Koran as an allegorical book and rejected all revelation, fasting, and prayer. Between 951 and 1078 the sect fought wars with the Fatimid in Cairo and with Baghdad; the Qaramitah disappeared in 1077–1078 and their communities were absorbed by others. Some sources suggest the Druze grew from this sect.

Sources:

Brewer, Ebenezer Cobham. 1970. *Brewer's Dictionary of Phrase and Fable*. Centenary ed. Revised by Ivor H. Evans. New York: Harper and Row.
Eliade, Mircea, ed. 1987. *Encyclopedia of Religion*. New York: Macmillan.
Gibb, Hamilton A. R., et al., eds. 1960. *The Encyclopedia of Islam*. Leiden: Brill.
McHenry, Robert, ed. 1992. *The New Encyclopedia Britannica*. Chicago: Encyclopedia Britannica.
Smith, Benjamin. 1903. *The Century Cyclopedia of Names*. London: Times.

QUAKERS. ''Quakers'' was the name given derisively to members of the Society of Friends, established by George Fox (1624–1691). Quakers believe that
by means of the Inner Light—the light of God in every person—Christ works
directly on the soul, and for this reason all trappings of institutionalized religion—ministers, priests, dogma—are unnecessary. Meetings begin in silence;
members wait for the Inner Light to stir one of them and allow others to witness
proof of the speaker's enlightenment, commitment to God, and desire to serve
humankind. Beginning about 1648–1650 Quakers were much feared in England
for their dispensing with creeds, professional clergy, and traditional ways of
worship. They were persecuted for blasphemy. They could be identified by their
plain dress, distinct speech, and open meetings. The origin of their name is not
clear; George Fox claimed that at his arraignment for blasphemy at Derby he
had enjoined the judge to quake and tremble at the word of the Lord. Other
evidence shows the word was in use earlier. For this reason some people believe
the term arose in reference to the religious trembling under the stress of religious
fervor at meetings. Quakers are noted for using ''thou'' instead of ''you,'' because in seventeenth-century England it indicated the speaker was affirming
humankind's equality when addressing a familiar or socially inferior person.
Persecution ended in 1689 with the Toleration Act. Today their worship is characterized by calm and silence. Quakers believe in the equality of sexes, free
will, temperance, charity, antislavery, democratic unity, open-mindedness, honesty. They oppose the tyranny of oppressive authority from both autocrats and
the masses. They abjure dishonest business practices, war, capital punishment,
totalitarian and dictatorial use of power, and proselytizing. Their utopian ideas
aimed to eradicate poverty, abolish slavery, build a new society—notably, Pennsylvania, their ''holy experiment''—educate poor children, treat mental patients
humanely, support votes for women, uphold sex education and planned parenthood, extend tertiary education, and serve as medical aides on the battlefield.
Today they offer sanctuary, help establish nuclear-free zones, and support total
disarmament and the abolition of military spending. They helped pursue peace
in Ireland, Costa Rica, and Vietnam.

   See Also Fox, George; Penn, William

Sources:

Comfort, William Wistar. 1952. *The Quaker Way of Life*. Philadelphia: American Friends
      Service Committee.
Loukes, Harold. 1960. *The Discovery of Quakerism*. London: G. G. Harrap.
McCord, William. 1989. *Voyages to Utopia: From Monastery to Commune, the Search
      for the Perfect Society in Modern Times*. New York: W. W. Norton.

R

RALAHINE. Ralahine Agricultural and Manufacturing Cooperative Association was a pioneering cooperative society founded in November 1831 on the estate of John Scott Vandeleur (fl. 1828–1831), at Ralahine, County Clare, Ireland. After the murder of a ruthless steward by angry peasants on his 618-acre estate near Limerick, John Scott Vandeleur decided to experiment on his property following the principles of Robert Owen (1771–1858) at New Lanark. Vandeleur hired Edward Thomas Craig (1804–1894) to help and built a large dining hall and six cottages. In November 1831 Craig and Vandeleur proposed a draft of association for the community that included members' jointly owning capital, education for all children, a higher standard of living for all members, and welfare for the sick, aged, and impoverished. The peasants were encouraged to renounce the conflict surrounding them and cooperate for the good of everyone. Vandeleur hoped the scheme would help him get higher rents and assuage the peasants' anger. Another goal was to induce peasants to give up their local agrarian secret societies for a better life offered by Vandeleur. In the beginning the commune comprised twenty-one single adult men, seven married men and their wives, five single women, four orphan boys, three orphan girls, and five children under the age of nine. A committee of nine elected twice a year governed the commune, and under an agreement between Vandeleur and the commune, the estate and property were to remain his for a rent of £700 a year until the cooperative could acquire the capital to purchase the land. For stock and equipment the commune was paid £200 per year. The peasants' duties were assigned by an elected committee rather than a brutal autocratic steward; a suggestion book was adopted; weekly meetings of workers discussed the constitution; and cardboard vouchers were used as money. Ralahine made a pioneering effort in the kindergarten tradition by having children go to an infant school every day of the week. Conflict all but ceased, and as the new sobriety and industriousness spread, it showed peasants can organize for a peaceful working life. Ralahine lasted two years. Vandeleur, a secret, compulsive gambler, wagered his fortune and estate in Dublin clubs, in the autumn of 1833 had a losing streak, and fled the country, leaving great debt. His creditors refused to recognize the commune and seized the estate, and the experiment, which had attracted international attention, collapsed.

See Also Craig, Edward Thomas

Sources:

Armytage, Walter Henry Green. 1961. *Heavens Below: Utopian Experiments in England 1560–1950*. London: Routledge and Kegan Paul.

Craig, Edward Thomas. 1882. *The Irish Land and Labour Question Illustrated in History of Ralahine and Cooperative Farming*. London: Trübner.

———. 1920. *An Irish Commune: The History of Ralahine*. Dublin: M. Lester.

Hickey, D. J., and J. E. Doherty, eds. 1980. *A Dictionary of Irish History since 1800*. Dublin: Gill and Macmillan.

Holyoake, G. J. 1906. *A History of Cooperation*. London: T. Fisher Unwin.

Pare, William. 1870. *Cooperative Agriculture: A Solution of the Land Question as Exemplified in the History of Ralahine Cooperative Agricultural Association, County Clare Ireland*. London: Longmans, Green, Reader, and Dyer.

Pollard, Sidney and John, Salt. eds. 1971. *Robert Owen: Prophet of the Poor*. Lewisburg, Pa.: Bucknell University Press.

Wallace, Alfred R. 1900. *Studies Scientific and Social*. London: Macmillan.

RANANIM. Rananim was a utopian scheme devised by D. H. Lawrence (1885–1930) with the help of Lady Cynthia, daughter-in-law of England's prime minister, Antony Asquith. Lawrence planned to emigrate to the United States, where he would found a colony of people who thought like as he did. On 18 January, 1915 he wrote, ''I want to gather together about twenty souls and sail away from this world of war and squalor and found a little colony where there shall be no money but a sort of communism as far as the necessaries of life go and some real decency.'' To prepare for emigration, he read American authors and wrote critical essays on them. Also he began to consider some psychological ideas that would later appear in his novels and poetry and provide the foundation for his utopia. To Bertrand Russell (1872–1970) he wrote in December 1915 that he thought in men and women there was a kind of consciousness that was unrelated to the brain and the central nervous system. He emphasized the importance of the sexual connection between men and women and its role in arousing what he called the blood consciousness of people. During the war years he and his German-born wife were assumed to be German agents, and feeling life in England could no longer be tolerated, they went to Italy in 1919. They sailed to Ceylon, Australia, and the United States. In 1923 they returned home to England, where he was so miserable early in 1924 that they went back to New Mexico, to the Kiowa Ranch, where he had hoped to establish ''Rananim.'' The ranch is near Taos and had been given to his wife by Lawrence's patroness.

At the ranch Lawrence fell ill with tuberculosis. They went to Europe in search of a cure, and he died in Vence, near Nice, France, in 1930.

See Also Lawrence, D. H.

Sources:

Kunitz, Stanley, and Howard Haycraft, eds. 1942. *Twentieth Century Authors.* New York: H. W. Wilson.

May, Hal, ed. 1987. *Contemporary Authors.* Vol. 121. Detroit: Gale Research.

Ousby, Ian. ed. 1995. *The Cambridge Guide to Literature in English.* 1995 ed. Cambridge: Cambridge University Press.

RANCHO RAJNEESH. Rancho Rajneesh was a utopian experiment established in 1981 by Bhagwan Shree Rajneesh (b. 1931), known as the "rich man's guru," who earlier had founded a spiritual movement from humble origins in India. The experiment covered 64,229 acres near Antelope, Oregon. Within one year of its being established the experiment had a road system, modern, prefabricated houses, storage buildings, a sewage disposal system, electricity, water supplies, and a dairy. In April 1982 work began on a spacious administrative block, and in May the largest solar greenhouse in the United States went into construction, covering more than 2 acres. That July the inaugural celebration was held. Two thousand tents were erected for an expected attendance of 7,000 visitors. It became a multinational, multimillion-dollar business. Bhagwan was arrested in North Carolina, in October 1985, charged with violations of U.S. immigration laws, was found guilty, received a ten-year suspended sentence, and was fined $400,000. The Oregon property of 100 square miles, capable of housing 5,000 people, was offered for sale in November 1985—price $40 million. The sale included an airplane, mobile homes, satellite television equipment, a beauty salon, gambling tables, and place settings for 20,000. Rancho Rajneesh was closed. Four thousand followers, who had worked a sixteen-hour day for four years to create an ecologically sound paradise, scattered to their home countries. There are many Rajneesh establishments around the world.

See Also Bhagwan Shree Rajneesh

Sources:

Aveling, Harry. 1994. *The Laughing Swamis.* Delhi: Motilal Bararsidass.

Carter, Lewis F. 1990. *Charisma and Control in Rajneeshpuram: The Role of Shared Values in the Creation of a Community.* Cambridge: Cambridge University Press.

Mullan, Bob. 1983. *Life as Laughter: Following Bhagwan Shree Rajneesh.* London: Routledge and Kegan Paul.

Palmer, Susan J., and Arvind Sharma. 1993. *The Rajneesh Papers.* Delhi: Motilal Bararsidass.

Strelley, Kate. 1987. *The Ultimate Game.* San Francisco: Harper and Row.

RAPP, GEORGE. George Rapp (1757–1847) founded and led the Harmony Society. He was born at Iptingen in Würtemberg, bordering the Rhine in the old province of Swabia. His father was a farmer and vinedresser. George had a local school education in south Germany, learned geography, reading, writing, and arithmetic, and then left school to help his father on the farm in summer and to work as a weaver in the winter. He married a farmer's daughter and had two children, later to become members of the Harmony Society. As a youth George Rapp read the Bible and compared conditions of people among whom he lived with the social order appearing in the New Testament. Unhappy with the lifelessness of the church, he began to preach to small groups of friends in his home. He thought of reforming modern society according to a literal interpretation of the New Testament. Local clergy resented his interference with their work, persecuted his adherents, and fined them, and some were imprisoned and denounced as "Separatists," a name they were willing to accept. Rapp gathered 300 families and in 1803 emigrated to the United States, where they hoped to secure freedom of worship and revive practices of the primitive church. That year Rapp sailed for Baltimore with his son John and bought 5,000 acres twenty-five miles north of Pittsburgh in the valley of Connoquenessing. Three hundred of Rapp's people landed in Baltimore on 4 July 1804 and were followed six weeks later by another 300. They formed the Harmony Society, agreed to pool their possessions and work for the whole community and uphold celibacy, and were happy to name their settlement "Harmony." They cultivated the land, wove cloth, and through other industries acquired much wealth. In 1815 the community moved to land along the Wabash River in Indiana, where they became prosperous and called the settlement "New Harmony." The property at New Harmony was sold to Robert Owen (1771–1858) in 1824, and the Harmonists moved to Beaver County, Pennsylvania, and built the village of Economy (1824–1905). When George Rapp, spirited head and strong leader of the community, died, a merchant became the chief trustee of the Harmony Society, Romelius L. Bäker (1794–1868).

See Also Economy; Harmony Society

Sources:

Arndt, Karl J. R. 1972. *George Rapp's Successors and Material Heirs, 1847–1916.* Rutherford, N.J.: Fairleigh Dickinson University Press.

Berry, Brian J. 1992. *America's Utopian Experiments: Communal Havens from Long-Wave Crises.* Hanover, N.H.: University Press of New England.

Bowden, Henry W. 1977. *Dictionary of American Religious Biography.* Westport, Conn.: Greenwood Press.

Cross, Frank L. 1974. *The Oxford Dictionary of the Christian Church.* 2d ed. New York: Oxford University Press.

Dudley, Lavinia P. 1963. *The Encyclopedia Americana.* International ed. New York: Americana Corporation.

Fogarty, Robert S. 1980. *Dictionary of American Communal and Utopian History.* Westport, Conn.: Greenwood Press.

Nordhoff, Charles. 1961. *The Communistic Societies of the United States.* New York: Hillary House.

RARITAN BAY UNION. Raritan Bay Union was encouraged by Marcus Spring (1810–1874) and established at Perth Amboy, New Jersey, in 1852. When religious missionaries appeared at the North American Phalanx (1843–1855) and proselytized, many freethinkers became angry, and in 1852 between thirty and forty families went to Eagleswood (now part of Perth Amboy) to organize another community that did not emphasize Fourierism so much. Raritan Bay Union began well by employing most of its funds for social experimentation. They raised $40,000, and much of it was used to build a grand edifice, 250 feet high. The community aimed for the best in industry, education, and social life, which they believed had not been present at the North American Phalanx. People of culture and education were drawn to the community. However promising and well endowed, the community had no clear ideological commitment, and it began to fragment. In 1855 Spring bought shares in the venture as dissatisfaction among members rose. The union disbanded at about this time.

  See Also Spring, Marcus

Sources:

Fogarty, Robert S. 1980. *Dictionary of American Communal History*. Westport, Conn.: Greenwood Press.

Oved, Yaacov. 1987. *Two Hundred Years of American Communes*. New Brunswick, N.J.: Transaction Books.

Spann, Edward K. 1989. *Brotherly Tomorrows: Movements for a Cooperative Society in America 1820–1920*. New York: Columbia University Press.

RASSELAS, PRINCE OF ABYSSINIA. *Rasselas, Prince of Abyssinia* is a romantic, philosophical novel by Samuel Johnson (1709–1784). In three parts, the novel describes the search for happiness by Rasselas, son of the emperor and prince of Abyssinia. The emperor of Abyssinia has confined his children to the Happy Valley. The prince, his sister, Nekayah, and her friend Pekuah escape with the sage Imlac and travel from Suez to Cairo searching for what humankind calls happiness. They are filled with theoretical anticipations and pointless meditation. After meeting all manner of people, the searchers fail to find anyone happy. Their observations on happiness are deeply contradictory. Arabs capture Pekuah at the pyramids. When she is returned, the three young travelers decide what would actually make them completely happy. The prince chooses to be the administrator of a little kingdom that sensibly dispenses justice; Nekayah decides on knowledge; and Pekuah chooses convent life. Eventually, they return to Happy Valley knowing that they can never have their original wish. The story lacks substance but has common sense and humor and gently treats idealism and youthful innocence. It is aphoristic but does not come down on one side or the other; instead, it offers paradoxes that prevent the characters from making tidy decisions. For example, monks whom we would assume would be secure in life are certain only that life is hard; the Sultan, whom we would imagine is powerful, is racked by suspicion and finds the great wisdom of a philosopher will not help him overcome melancholia. The work tells the readers that they are responsible for their choices in life and that overthinking is not to be preferred to decisive action. The mood of the work reflects the author's chronic depression, much exacerbated by the death of his mother in 1759.

See Also Johnson, Samuel

Sources:

Johnson, Samuel. 1759. *The History of Rasselas, Prince of Abissinia*. Edited with an in introduction by Geoffrey Tillotson and Brian Jenkins. 1971. London: Oxford University Press.
Ousby, Ian, ed. 1988. *The Cambridge Guide to Literature in English*. 1995 ed. Cambridge: Cambridge University Press.
Snodgrass, Mary Ellen. 1995. *Encyclopedia of Utopian Literature*. Santa Barbara, Calif.: ABC-CLIO.

REED, JAMES FRAZIER. James Frazier Reed (c.1800–1847), thought to have been descended from Polish aristocracy, the Reedowskys, was a fierce and haughty character. He was born in Northern Ireland but since boyhood had lived in the United States, and served in the Black Hawk campaign in the same company as Abraham Lincoln (1809–1865). In Illinois he manufactured furniture and was a railroads merchant. A mature, wealthy man, he led the Donner–Reed Party (1846–1847), but a day after the caravan began its journey, George Donner (c. 1785–1847), not Reed, was elected as the party's leader. Nevertheless, the caravan was known at the time as "Messrs. Reed and Donner's company."

See Also Donner, George; Donner Party

Sources:

Madsen, David, and Bruce Hawkins. 1990. *Excavation of the Donner Reed Wagons*. Salt Lake City: University of Utah Press.
Stewart, George R. 1960. *Ordeal by Hunger*. Lincoln: University of Nebraska Press.

REEVE, JOHN. John Reeve (1608–1658) and his cousin Lodowicke Muggleton (1609–1698), damning all predecessors and advocating a new divine dispensation, stated the three commissions of the Lord regarding Moses and the prophets, Jesus and the apostles, and two witnesses in Revelation 11. Reeve was the first "messenger," and Muggleton was the "mouth," and in 1652 they identified themselves as the two witnesses in Revelation 11:3. Muggleton carried their utopian work forward after Reeve's death in 1658, insisting that the devil became incarnate in Eve and denying the Holy Trinity. For his efforts he was imprisoned at Chesterfield (1663) and London (1677). The Muggletonians established and maintained a reading room at Bishop Gate, London, in his memory for many years after he died.

See Also Muggleton, Lodowicke; Muggletonians

Source:

Armytage, Walter Henry Green. 1961. *Heavens Below: Utopian Experiments in England 1560–1950*. London: Routledge and Kegan Paul.

REPUBLIC, THE. *The Republic* by Plato starts the literary history of utopias. It is a dialogue that applies Plato's ethics to the ideal state. Socrates reports of a discussion that he had with a sophist, Thrasymachus, Glaucon and Adeimantus, two of Plato's brothers, and Polemarchus and his elderly father, Cephalus. The friendly, casual gathering takes place at Cephalus' house. The topic drifts to justice, which many try to define but never meet the scrutiny of Socrates. He suggests that justice may be found in a discussion of the state and through books 2, 3, and 4 traces the evolution of the ideal state. The ideal state is an aristocracy with guardians who have been carefully selected from among trained philosophers. Next, Socrates turns to the original question about the definition of justice; however, the others are more interested in the problem of the ideal state. In book 5 he discusses ideas on the community of women and children among the guardians. He says that the sketch of the ideal state was undertaken for only experimental reasons and that it may never be possible to realize the ideal state. All that can be hoped for is an approximation to the ideal. In books 6 and 7 he talks about the education of the philosophers and how it is related to the development of their character. In book 8 he argues that differences of character correspond to types of political system: aristocracy, timocracy, oligarchy, democracy, despotism. He suggests how these states succeed and replace each other in practice. In book 9 he concludes that the just man will guide himself by reference to the ideal state. He suggests that perhaps a pattern of the ideal state may be found in heaven; its relevance to earthly existence is unimportant. In book 10 Plato returns to a discussion of poetry, a topic he had considered when discussing education, and concludes that the influence of poetry is wholly bad and, with the exceptions of hymns and praises for the great men, should not be part of the ideal state. He then argues that nothing, not even vices, can destroy the soul; it is immortal. Rewards that the just rulers may expect after death appear in the apocalyptic myth of Er, who glimpsed life beyond death and returned to tell humankind of the punishments and the rewards of life after death and of the governance of the universe. The work does consider some benefits for citizens: state-supported education and education for women. But the education is for the children of the Guardians, not workers, and although women can have education, they are still a form of property. In many ways Plato's commonwealth seems like a modern dystopia (Booker, 1994) with its absolute power of philosopher kings, state ownership of art and rejection of poetry, training in state ideology, use of women selectively for breeding, inferiority of children as such, use of slavery, and the sacrifice of individual happiness to the general good. But such criticisms seem inappropriate because the work is more a philosophical discussion than a blueprint for an ideal world or a better world, and its relevance is limited by the period in which it was written.

See Also Plato

Sources:

Booker, M. Keith. 1994. *Dystopian Literature: A Theory and Research Guide*. Westport, Conn.: Greenwood.

Mumford, Lewis. 1922. *The Story of Utopias*. 1962 ed. New York: Viking.

Plato. 1902. *The Republic*. Cambridge: Cambridge University Press.

Ross, William D. 1951. *Plato's Theory of Ideas*. Oxford: Clarendon Press.

Russell, Bertrand. 1946. *The Problem of Philosophy*. London: Oxford University Press.

Snodgrass, Mary Ellen. 1995. *Encyclopedia of Utopian Literature*. Santa Barbara, Calif.: ABC-CLIO.

Starnes, Colin. 1990. *The New Republic: A Commentary on Book I of More's "Utopia" Showing Its Relations to Plato's "Republic."* Ontario, Canada: Wilfrid Laurier University Press.

REUNION COLONY. Reunion Colony, or "True Family," was a community established in Jasper County, Missouri. Under the influence of Icarian communism, Alcander Longley (1832–1918) established this commune after staying for eight months at the Icarian Community in Iowa (1867). The community comprised only twenty-seven adults, most of whom had heard Longley's call for a community convention in his *The Communist*, published in St. Louis. Troubled by mortgage payments for the forty acres and the development of an opposing faction, the colony ended in 1870.

See Also Icarian movement; Longley, Alcander

Sources:

Fogarty, Robert S. 1980. *Dictionary of American Communal History*. Westport, Conn.: Greenwood Press.

Hine, Robert V. 1953. *California's Utopian Colonies*. 1983 ed. Berkeley: University of California Press.

REUNION, LA. La Reunion (1853–1869) was one of two Fourierist colonies with a French, rather than U.S., leadership. It was established about four miles west of Dallas, Texas (1855–1859), by people who loathed political and religious oppression and compulsory military service. Various historians have described it as socialistic, communistic, and capitalistic. Victor Prosper Considérant (1808–1893) was a leading theorist of Fourierism. He met Albert Brisbane (1809–1890), the American associationist. In May 1853, with others, they went to Texas, and Considérant sent back glowing, exaggerated descriptions of the land. He organized the European Society for the Colonisation of Texas (1854) when he returned to France from the United States. Its aim was to establish a colony in Texas, named La Reunion. They bought over 6,000 acres. In February 1855 the first large contingent of French, Belgians, Swiss, and Germans sailed aboard a U.S. ship. It seems that the colony was doomed from the start. The 1854 drought continued through 1856; livestock starved or died of thirst; the late freeze of 1856 and the drought ruined the growing season, and remaining crops were devoured by grasshoppers. The investors wanted their expected 6 percent interest and blamed Considérant, who, in turn, blamed the Paris office for sending unsuitable immigrants. Approximately 300 emigrated (1855–1856). Among them bad feeling developed, and hostility grew toward their neighbors. Few farmers worked the soil, while the many intellectuals, artists, musicians, and lawyers engaged in their favorite activity, hunting. In January 1859 one of the Paris managers of La Reunion came to study the colony and concluded that the society should be dissolved. Today huge cement plants occupy the ground in west Dallas County where the French colonists hoped to grow grapes.

See Also Brisbane, Albert; Considérant, Victor Prosper

Sources:

Fischer, Ernest G. 1980. *Marxists and Utopias in Texas.* Burnet, Tex.: Eakin Press.
Fogarty, Robert S. 1980. *Dictionary of American Communal History.* Westport, Conn.: Greenwood Press.
Kesten, Seymour. 1993. *Utopian Episodes: Daily Life in Experimental Colonies Dedicated to Changing the World.* Syracuse, N.Y.: Syracuse University Press.

RIGDON, SIDNEY. Sidney Rigdon (1793–1876) was born at St. Clair, Allegheny County, New York, into a Baptist family. He educated himself, worked first as a printer, and later studied for the ministry: he was licensed to preach by the Baptist Church, 1819. In January 1822 he was pastor of the First Church in Pittsburgh. However, because of his association with Alexander Campbell (1788–1866), who founded the Disciples of Christ Church, Rigdon lost his pastorate in Pittsburgh (1824) and had to work as a tanner. But in 1826 he was able to accept another pastorate at Mentor, Ohio. In Ohio he led revival meetings (1828–1829) and until 1830, when he broke with the Campbellites over questions of doctrine, considered organizing a community. After reading Joseph Smith's *Book of Mormon*, he made his decision, and with Joseph Smith (1805–1844) formed a colony at Kirtland in Ohio in 1831, where all property was held in common, as was the case in the early Christian Church. In the community were established a store, a mill, and a bank. Smith appointed himself president of the bank, and Rigdon was cashier. In 1835, after much conflict within the church when the bank failed, Smith and Rigdon fled at night to avoid arrest and their pursuing creditors. They joined other Mormons in Caldwell County in the Far West. Rigdon became renowned for his vigorous denunciations against persecutors of ''God's Chosen People.'' Smith and Rigdon were found guilty of treason, murder, and felony and imprisoned. In 1844, when Joseph Smith was shot at Carthage, Illinois, Rigdon sought the leadership of the Mormon sect, but the community leaders turned instead to Brigham Young (1801–1877). In response Rigdon established a new church, and the Mormons excommunicated him. His followers deserted him within two years. In 1863 he founded the Church of Jesus Christ and the Children of Zion. It lasted until the 1880s. His final years were spent in misery and emotional imbalance. He died in Friendship, New York.

See Also Kirtland Community; Mormons; Smith, Joseph

Sources:

McKiernan, Mark. 1979. *The Voice of One Crying in the Wilderness: Sydney Rigdon Religious Reform: 1793–1876*. Lawrence: University of Kansas, Herald House.
Van Orden, Bruce A. 1992. "Sidney Rigdon." In Daniel H. Ludlow, *Encyclopedia of Mormonism*, pp. 1233–1235. Vol. 3. New York: Macmillan.
Wagoner, Richard S. 1994. *Sidney Rigdon: Portrait of Religious Excess*. Salt Lake City, Utah: Signature Books.
Wilson, James, and John Fiske, eds. 1889. *Appletons Cyclopaedia of American Biography*. New York: Appleton.

RIKER, WILLIAM E. William E. Riker (1873–1952), born in Oakdale, California, became a mechanic in San Francisco. He preached in the street, claiming authority for his Perfect Christian Divine Way from a curious understanding of cataclysms and divine experiences and God's revelations (1909). His attitude to African Americans was like that of the Ku Klux Klan. He believed white people should rule the world. In Santa Cruz he bought land for his Holy City (1918) and, published a monthly paper, the *Enlightener*, and a tract on *The Philosophy of the Nerves Revealed* as well as *World Peace and How to Have It*. Riker sought a political career and ran unsuccessfully for state governor four times. He was also charged at various times with murder, breach of promise, tax evasion, dangerous driving, and fraud. Membership of his community declined, and only twelve remained in 1952, after Riker was charged with sedition.

See Also Holy City

Sources:

Fogarty, Robert S. 1980. *Dictionary of American Communal History*. Westport, Conn.: Greenwood Press.
Hine, Robert V.1953. *California's Utopian Colonies*. 1983 ed. Berkeley: University of California Press.

RILEY, WILLIAM HARRISON. William Harrison Riley (fl. 1870s) was the son of a preacher in Manchester, England. He learned engraving and went to the United States for three years and returned to Britain as a commercial traveler for his father in the cloth printing business. After another visit to the United States he became an active socialist and returned to England in 1870 with experience as a journalist. By 1875 he was in Bristol and had published his *Yankee Letters to British Workmen*, had joined the International Working Men's Association, and had begun publishing the *International Herald*, later, the *Republican Herald* (1874) and later still, the *Herald* and *Helpmate* (1875) He and his wife helped manage a mutual-help club in Britain until they objected so much to the sale of alcohol on the premises that they left and established the Social Improvement Institute. After it failed, he went to Sheffield, announced he was a Christian socialist, and published briefly the *Socialist* (1877). The journal presented a draft of the British Constitution with five important proposals for a utopian world: the aim for utopias is human happiness; this can be achieved by the duty to labor; all property and products of Britain are owned by Britain; the basic needs for living should be distributed to all citizens according to need; citizens are free to do as they choose, provided no one's rights are threatened. Riley was seen as a superior visionary. He took the role of custodian or master at the Totley Commune, a farm that followed the principles of the St. George's Guild. He so alienated its committee of management and John Ruskin (1819–1900), its major supporter, that he left and emigrated to the United States with his family and lived on a farm in Townend Center, Massachusetts.

See Also Guild of St. George and St. George's Farm, Abbeydale, or Totley Farm; Ruskin, John

Source:

Armytage, Walter Henry Green. 1961. *Heavens Below: Utopian Experiments in England 1560–1950*. London: Routledge and Kegan Paul.

RIPLEY, GEORGE. George Ripley (1802–1880) was born in Greenfield, Massachusetts, and educated at Harvard (1823) and the Harvard Divinity School (1826). He was minister of Purchase Street Church in Boston (1826–1841). Strongly influenced by German theology and French philosophy, Ripley edited *Specimens of Foreign Standard Literature* with F. H. Hedge (1838), which was translations of Victor Cousin (1792–1867), Théodore Jouffroy (1796–1842), and others who had considerable influence on the intellectual life of New England. He defended his views, which arose from a controversy on the philosophy of religion, in his *Letters on the Latest Form of Infidelity* (1840). He founded and edited *The Dial* (1840) with Sarah Margaret Fuller (1810–1850). In 1841 he resigned from the ministry and with twenty other members of the Transcendental Club moved to West Roxbury, where he became president of the experiment in communal living, Brook Farm. He did not support the regimentation that often accompanied the practice of socialism and with others at Brook Farm accepted a new constitution that made the community a Fourierist phalanx (1844) and haven for U.S. transcendentalists such as Amos Bronson Alcott (1700–1888). U.S. transcendentalism was a movement of philosophical idealism that reached its peak in New England during the 1840s. Transcendentalists objected to the coolness and detachment of eighteenth-century empiricism and its reliance on the sense of immediate experience to establish the truth. Transcendentalists believed in the supremacy of mind and preferred and defended intuition as the way to truth. In New England, transcendentalism was never well organized, produced no coherent philosophy, and stood mainly for self-expression. Brook Farm, the Transcendental Club, and *The Dial* were three of their specific projects. George Ripley taught mathematics and philosophy at Brook Farm and worked on the farm itself. Brook Farm was destroyed by fire and fell into debt. Heavily involved in debt due to the financial collapse of Brook Farm, Ripley went to New York City and became a literary critic on the *New York Tribune* (1849). He soon became an outstanding influence in the world of letters. He was one of the founders of *Harpers New Monthly Magazine* (1850) and, with Charles A. Dana (1819–1897), brought out the first volume, in 1858, of *The New American Cyclopedia* (sixteen volumes, 1858–1863). It was later revised as the *American Cyclopedia* (1873–1876). Extensive and frequent travel in Europe enriched his inner resources (1866, 1869, and 1870), and he met many authors whose work he had praised.

See Also Alcott, Amos Bronson; Brook Farm Colony; Dana, Charles Anderson

Sources:

Magnussen, Magnus, and Rosemary Goring, eds. 1990. *Chambers Biographical Dictionary*. 5th ed. Edinburgh: Chambers.

Malone, Dumas, ed. 1935. *Dictionary of American Biography*. Vol. 8. New York: Charles Scribner's Sons.

RIVERSIDE COMMUNITY. Riverside Community began in New Zealand in 1941. Hubert and Marion Holdaway (fl. 1900–1960) gave a 38-acre farm for the venture, 4 acres in hardwood timber, and the rest pasture. Hubert had two other orchards to support the scheme. He led the local Methodist community, and most of his workers were women or were men awaiting detention or appeal for being pacifists during wartime. In 1946–1947 several ex-commanding officers and their wives joined Riverside, and by 1949 it had seven young couples and a few single men, mainly Methodists, Quakers, and some Anglicans. Riverside Community bought acreage from Hubert's brother and now had 500 acres. In May 1953 the Riverside Community Trust Board was incorporated, and all assets were transferred to it in December 1955. Hubert Holdaway had been a veteran of World War I and became dedicated to the repudiation of war, the abolition of private property and private profit, and the placement of a limitation on income in an attempt to achieve equality of income. The first years of the community's existence were very difficult because New Zealand was involved in World War II, and many of the men were imprisoned for resisting the military draft. Under Holdaway's leadership land was cleared, and creating the farm community was work mainly for the women. In 1984 the community had seventy members and a net worth of about $1 million. All teetotaling Methodists, the founders emphasized Christian commitment and practice and expected one another to attend church regularly. As public attitudes changed, and the community attracted new members, it relaxed its requirements for admission. The community settled for a simple affirmation of Christian belief. Even so, this rule was too restrictive, and in recent years atheists and Jews have become members. The community setting is idyllic; it is thirty miles from the town of Nelson at the north end of the South Island of New Zealand. Twenty houses and a church constitute the village; there are a hostel, which accommodates thirty guests, a hall, and office buildings. The main source of income is apples. The community also produces boysenberries, pears, beef, mutton, timber, wool, and milk. The emphasis at Riverside is on economic success, but not self-sufficiency. Organic vegetables are grown for the members' consumption, but commercial crops are not grown organically. The community sells its products through different co-operatives. Originally, the community had planned to combine farming with small manufacturing industries, for example, printing and weaving. The orchards became so labor-intensive that the manufacturing industries were not established. Originally, Riverside was a limited company on land owned by one of the members in partnership with his brother, who owned nearby land. When the brother decided to move, the community bought his land, and the operation became a charitable religious trust. To join the community, an individual or a family makes an application as probationary members for one year. Once ac-cepted, their assets are made over to the community. In return they receive free housing, telephone, and electricity and free fruit and vegetables in season, and each person gets five eggs per week, subsidized meat and honey, and a small amount of cash. They are expected to work the same hours as other farmers in New Zealand, and by and large they enjoy a normal family life. The Christian feature of Riverside has lapsed, but it is still committed to peace, justice, and nonviolence. It is New Zealand's oldest intentional community.

Sources:

Palmer, Chris. 1996. "Riverside: Escapism or Realism." In Bill Metcalf, *Shared Visions, Shared Lives: Communal Living around the Globe*, pp. 53–61. Forres, Scotland: Findhorn Press.

Popenoe, Cris, and Oliver Popenoe. 1984. *Seeds of Tomorrow*. San Francisco: Harper and Row.

Rain, Lynn. 1991. *Community, the Story of Riverside, 1941–1991*. Lower Moutere, New Zealand: Riverside Community.

ROACH, RICHARD. Richard Roach (1662–1730), born in London, went to Merchant Taylors' School (1677), where he met Francis Lee (1661–1719). In 1681 he went to Oxford and graduated from St. John's College (B.A., 1686; M.A., 1688). He became a priest (1689) and graduated bachelor of divinity (1695). He was rector at St. Augustine's, Hackney, until he died. Roach was much interested in mysticism and came under the influence of Jane Leade (1623–1704). In 1697, with his friend Francis Lee, he helped found the Phila-delphian Society, and that year they wrote and published *Theosophical Trans-*

actions. He wrote many articles on mysticism and published extracts from Jane Leade's writings, for example, *The Imperial Standard of the Messiah Triumphant. Coming Now in the Power and the Kingdom of His Father, to Reign with His Saints on Earth* (1728).

See Also Leade, Jane; Lee, Francis; Philadelphians

Sources

Stephen, Leslie, and Sydney Lee, eds. 1917. *The Dictionary of National Biography.* London: Oxford University Press.

ROBERTS, THOMAS WILLIAM. Thomas William "Tom" Roberts (1856–1931) was born in Dorchester, England, and landed in Melbourne, Victoria, Australia, 1869. While working as a photographer's studio assistant he attended night classes at East Collingwood School of Design (1873–1874) and studied at the National Gallery of Victoria School (1875–1880) and the Royal Academy Schools of London (1881–1882). He met Frederick McCubbin (1855–1917) and Louis Abrahams (1852–1903) at the National Gallery School. After studies in London, Roberts traveled through Europe, where he was introduced to French impressionism. In 1885 he returned to Australia and with McCubbin and Abrahams established an artist's camp in Box Hill, outside Melbourne. It became known as the Heidelberg School. He helped establish the Australian Artist's Association and organized the controversial *Impressions Exhibition* (1890). Travels to New South Wales in the late 1880s led to his most famous works, *Shearing the Rams* and *The Breakaway.* He went to live in Sydney and between 1891 and 1896 established a camp with Arthur Streeton (1867–1943). Roberts married Elizabeth Williamson (1896), and they had one son. In the early twentieth century he traveled to Holland and Italy and during World War I served as a hospital orderly.

See Also Conder, Charles Edward; Heidelberg School; McCubbin, Frederick

Source:

Splatt, William, and Dugald McLellan. 1986. *The Heidelberg School: The Golden Summer of Australian Painting.* Melbourne: Lloyd O'Neil.

ROBINSON, FRED. Fred Robinson (c. 1891–1983), a sugar farmer in Australia who failed during the 1930s depression, began training in New Age awareness with a teacher who said he had had incarnated from another planet and had come to earth to help lay the grounds for the establishment of the New Age. Fred trained until 1950 and then toured the east coast of Australia, lecturing on unidentified flying objects (UFOs) and the New Age. He seemed an inspirational character, charismatic and affectionate, and encouraged listeners to establish their utopian communities. He himself tried four times to establish a community but failed. In 1962 he met his wife, Mary Robinson (b. 1911), and they established an information center about New Age matters twenty miles (thirty-two kilometers) south of Perth, Western Australia. In 1971 they started a series of national lecture tours and then settled on the farm at Balingup.

See Also Universal Brotherhood

Source:

Popenoe, Cris, and Oliver Popenoe. 1984. *Seeds of Tomorrow*. San Francisco: Harper and Row.

ROSENTHAL, HERMAN. Herman Rosenthal (1843–1917) was born in Friedrichsstadt, a province of Courland, Russia. He was educated in Courland and became a competent linguist in Hebrew, German, and Russian. He mastered the literature of each language. At age sixteen he began writing poetry of his own and translating into German poems by notable Russian poets. During the Russo-Turkish War (1877–1878) he served in the Russian Red Cross and received the society's medal for his services. In 1881, soon after coming to the United States, he began to bring forward a plan to found agricultural colonies for Russian Jews who had been compelled to emigrate to the United States because of the czarist repressive regime. He founded the first agricultural colony of Russian Jews, Sicily Island, in Catahoula parish, Louisiana, December 1881. In South Dakota he organized another, Cremieux (1882–1889), and in 1891 became a prominent administrator of a settlement in Woodbine, New Jersey. As a German poet, English essayist, and scholar of Hebrew and Russian, he used all four languages to ease the burdens of the oppressed and shed light on the history of the Jews in Russia and Poland. From 1898 Rosenthal headed the Slavonic Department of the New York Public Library.

See Also Am Olam; Sicily Island Colony

Sources:

Malone, Dumas, ed. 1935. *Dictionary of American Biography*. 1963 ed. New York: Charles Scribner's Sons.
Roth, Cecil E., ed. 1971. *Encyclopedia Judaica*. New York: Macmillan.

ROUND THE BEND CONSERVATION CO-OPERATIVE. The Round the Bend Conservation Co-operative was founded in the early 1970s. A group of conservationists were concerned about the conventional development of land northeast of Melbourne, Australia. They pooled their money and bought 326 acres (132 hectares). A cooperative was registered as a community settlement society under the Co-operation Act of 1958 with a permit to build thirty-two houses. In 1996 there were eighteen houses, and two more were planned. The community aimed to live in the Australian bushland with as little impact on the environment as possible. Most members maintain kitchen gardens using wastewater on transpiration beds. Under this system all household waste passed through a septic system from the house into a garden transpiration bed and evaporated or was absorbed into the plants. The cooperative has its own rules for land management and conservation. Cats and dogs are not permitted within the cooperative because of the threat to native birds and wildlife. Only native plants are allowed for revegetation, and house designs are approved in consultation with neighbors to ensure they blend with the environment. The prospective buyers of land must be approved by the directors, learn about the cooperative's culture, and are not allowed to use the land as security for a mortgage. Among the members are musicians, artists, engineers, bureaucrats, and tradespeople. Most built their homes with their own hands. Over the years the cooperative has spoken out on various issues affecting the cooperative and surrounding area. In the mid-1970s it won a fight with the state electricity commission to install underground electricity to minimize visual impact and reduce the risk of wild fires in the bushland. In addition to speaking out on local issues such as proposed subdivisions and rezoning of special areas, the cooperative supported like-minded organizations such as the Australian Conservation Foundation.

See Also Berryman, Margaret; Ealey, E.H.M.; Neale, Jeph

Source:

Cock, Peter. 1979. *Alternative Australia: Communities of the Future?*, Chapter 5. Melbourne: Quartet Books.

ROUSSEAU, JEAN-JACQUES. Jean-Jacques Rousseau (1712–1778), a political philosopher, educationist, and essayist, was born in Geneva. His mother died at his birth, and in 1722 his father left him in the care of relatives. Except for his reading of Plutarch's *Lives* and some Calvinist sermons, he had no education and was raised largely on bitter experiences. His attempts at work were unsuccessful. He converted to Catholicism and was sent to Turin, Italy. He gained considerable knowledge of Italian music by joining the local choir school. In 1741 he went to Paris and earned a living doing secretarial work and copying music and began a lifelong association with a maid at his hotel. They had five children, all of whom were sent to the foundling hospital. He composed an opera and became acquainted with François Voltaire (1694–1778) and Denis Diderot (1713–1784). In 1750 he won an essay competition by the Academy of Dijon on whether arts and science had purified humankind. He maintained they had not, that humankind had been seduced from its natural state and had its freedoms curtailed. Parisians treated him as a celebrity for this. He returned to Geneva and Calvinism and began his novel *La Nouvelle Héloise* (1761). On returning to Paris, he lived with his old love and her mother in Montmorency, but later moved to Luxembourg (1757). In 1762 he produced his masterpiece *Du Contrat Social*, which proposed a social contract whereby citizens surrender their rights and possessions to the ''general will'' to achieve the ''impartial good.'' The same year he published *Émile*, his novel on education, and later accepted an invitation from David Hume (1711–1776) to settle in England (1766–1767) where he wrote most of his frank *Confessions* (1771). Suffering persecution mania and hypersensitivity, he lost his English friends, and on returning to Paris (1770), he lived in poverty as a copyist and wrote wearisome ramblings to justify his past. Insane, he died at Ermenoville, 2 July, 1778, from thrombosis. In 1794 his remains were placed with Voltaire's in the Panthéon. Rousseau's writings presaged Romanticism, and his ideas underpinned much of German and English idealism early in the nineteenth century.

Sources:

Dent, N. J. H. 1988. *Rousseau: An Introduction to His Psychological, Social and Political Theory*. New York: Blackwell.
Launay, Michel. 1968. *Rousseau*. Paris: Presses universitaires de France.
Miller, James. 1984. *Rousseau: Dreams of Democracy*. New York: Yale University Press.
Morely, John. 1873. *Rousseau*. 2 vols. London: Chapman Hall.
Rousseau, Jean-Jacques. 1966. "The People of the Ideal Commonwealth and the Expression of their Good Will." Reprinted in Frank E. Manuel, and Futzie P. Manuel, eds., *French Utopias: An Anthology of Ideal Societies*, pp .117–130. New York: Free Press.
Wokler, Robert. 1992. *A Rousseau Dictionary*. Oxford: Blackwell References.
———. 1995. *Rousseau*. Oxford: Oxford University Press.

ROWNTREE, BENJAMIN SEEBOHM. Benjamin Seebohm Rowntree (1871–1954), son of Joseph Rowntree (1836–1925), studied at Owens College (later, University of Manchester) and entered his father's firm, H. I. Rowntree and Company, in 1889. Greatly influenced by his father's philanthropic views, he carried them forward for life. He was mainly interested in labor–management relations and introduced the eight-hour working day in his firms in 1896, a pension scheme in 1906, and other amenities like the five-day working week (1919). He wanted to promote humane conditions of high industrial efficiency. In 1895 he was greatly affected by what he saw of the slums of Newcastle upon Tyne. In 1901 he published *Poverty, a Study of Town Life*. It was a pioneering study in empirical industrial sociology that showed that 28 percent of the population fell below an arbitrary level of minimum income and that fundamental poverty was widespread in York. He worked to establish that a social welfare policy was vital to good government and national prosperity. Also he studied unemployment, business organization, and gambling. David Lloyd George (1863–1945), Welsh social reformer, chancellor of the Exchequer (1908–1915), and prime minister of Britain (1916–1922), appointed Rowntree to the Land Enquiry Committee (1912–1914). During World War I he directed the welfare department of the Ministry of Munitions. After the war he was the chairman of H. I. Rowntree and Company.

See Also New Earswick; Rowntree, Joseph; Unwin, Raymond

Sources:

Briggs, Asa. 1961. *Social Thoughts and Social Action: A Study of the Work of Seebohm Rowntree*. London: Longmans.

Williams, E. T., and Helen M. Palmer, eds. 1971. *Dictionary of National Biography 1951–1960*. London: Oxford University Press.

ROWNTREE, JOSEPH. Joseph Rowntree (1836–1925) was born in York, son of Joseph Rowntree (1801–1859), a Quaker educationist. He worked in his father's grocery business and in 1869 entered into partnership with his brother to manufacture cocoa. On his brother's death Joseph became sole owner of the firm. He aimed to ameliorate the brutal employment and living conditions of many workers during the Industrial Revolution in Britain. He wanted his employees to work reasonable hours for reasonable wages and to be consulted about their employment conditions. Also he provided for periods of unemployment, old age, and widows' pensions and introduced social workers to his factory in 1891. Appalled by his son Seebohm's views on poverty in York, he bought 123 acres outside the city in 1901 to establish New Earswick. He employed Raymond Unwin (1863–1940) as its architect and developed the idea of the neighborhood unit. It was to have social and intellectual resources, and adult education services and uphold temperance. In general, he supported the idea of finding out the causes of social problems rather than simply treating their manifestations.

See Also New Earswick; Rowntree, Benjamin Seebohm; Unwin Raymond

Sources:

Gill, Roger. 1984. "In England's Green and Pleasant Land." In Peter Alexander and Roger Gill, eds., *Utopias*, pp. 109–117. London: Duckworth.

Vernon, Anne. 1958. *A Quaker Businessman: The Life of Joseph Rowntree, 1836–1925*. London: Allen and Unwin.

Weaver, John R. H., ed. 1937. *Dictionary of National Biography 1922–1930*. London: Oxford University Press.

ROYCROFTERS. The Roycrofters Community was established by Elbert Green Hubbard (1856–1915) in East Aurora, in New York in 1895 as a semi-communistic corporation whose members shared the profits. Community members worked on a farm and in a bank, a printing plant, a book bindery, a furniture factory, and a blacksmith's shop. Membership fluctuated between 300 and 500 hundred people, and sometimes up to 1,000 locals were employed in activities of the Roycrofters. Some members lived at the Roycroft Inn, a phalanstery. The community received substantial income from the sales of Hubbard's *A Message to Garcia* (1898), a pamphlet on duty and efficiency relating to an incident during the Spanish-American War. Hubbard died aboard the *Lusitania* (1915), and thereafter the community became a commercial enterprise noted for outstanding handicrafts. The community magazine, *The Roycrofter* (1926–1932), was devoted to Roycroft ideals. The company closed in 1939.

See Also Home Colony; Hubbard, Elbert Green

Source:

Fogarty, Robert S. 1980. *Dictionary of American Communal History*. Westport, Conn.: Greenwood Press.

RUDOLF STEINER SCHOOL. A Rudolf Steiner school for children has a strong spiritual and humanistic outlook on education and special educational methods. It was once known in the United States as the Waldorf method. The first Rudolf Steiner school was established as the Waldorf School in 1919 for the children of employees of the Waldorf-Astoria cigarette factory in Stuttgart. From Rudolf Steiner's (1861–1925) ideas developed the Waldorf School movement, homes for disabled and maladjusted children, a form of therapy, biodynamic agriculture, centers of scientific and mathematical research, eurythmy, and schools of most cultural arts. Steiner emphasized the educational value of playacting, art, and mythmaking for children. The Waldorf schools taught children to find their own outlook for adulthood, to realize their full potential, and to make fruitful relationships. Each class has a teacher who moves forward with the group, thereby helping the children with problems of authority as well as schoolroom subjects. Closed by the Nazis, the school reopened in 1945, and the movement spread to most European countries, the United States, Canada, Australia, New Zealand, South Africa, and South America.

See Also Steiner, Rudolf

Sources:

Blisher, Edward, ed. 1969. *Blond's Encyclopedia of Education*. London: Blond Educational.

Richards, Mary C. 1980. *Towards Wholeness: Rudolf Steiner Education in America*. Middletown, Conn: Wesleyan University Press.

RUGBY COLONY. Rugby Colony flourished in Rugby, Tennessee (1880–1887). An English reformer, Thomas Hughes (1822–1896), founded the cooperative venture in 1879 on a visit with friends to the United States. It was established on the Cumberland Plateau in eastern Tennessee. By 1884 it had 400 members, forty-two buildings, a church, school, library, and hotel. However, the land was not as productive as the community was led to anticipate. Disappointed with their scheme, the early settlers and investors quit, and Hughes abandoned it altogether. The cooperative features gradually declined; its governing board, the original source of funds, reorganized in 1892 and turned the venture into a landholding company. With her youngest son, Hughes' mother went to live at Rugby and died there ten years later.

See Also Hughes, Thomas

Source:

Fogarty, Robert S. 1980. *Dictionary of American Communal History*. Westport, Conn.: Greenwood Press.

RUSKIN, JOHN. John Ruskin (1819–1900), son of a London wine merchant, was tutored at home, had a religious upbringing, which he later rejected, and studied at Oxford (1836). He turned to the publicizing of art in his *Modern Painters* (1843), toured Europe often, and wrote on social mores and good taste. He became a noted art critic, an advocate of the Pre-Raphaelites. After 1860 he took a critical look at the social impact of rapacious capitalism and the too rapid adoption of new technology at work. He developed his own variety of Christian communism, which he published in *Unto This Last* (1862), a criticism of the simple view of relations between supply and demand. To him society was basically rotten, had to be disposed of, and should be rebuilt. He objected to modern utopianism because it would turn men into unproductive animals by raising technology to heroic status. He was the first Slade Professor of Fine Arts at Oxford, lectured on art, and outlined his social philosophy in his papers for British workers and laborers, *Fors Clavigera* (1871–1874). He used his fortune to establish the St. George's Guild, a nonprofit shop in Paddington Street whose members used their money to support Ruskin schools. He gave up the professorship, wrote his life story, *Praeterita*, and launched his final attack on the uncivilized use of modern technology by criticizing the railways for their desecration of England's rural beauty. In 1864, after his father left him a fortune, Ruskin bought three houses near Marylebone and gave them to Octavia Hill (1838–1912) to be run on community lines. The success of the venture extended the work to Lambeth, Southwark, and Deptford. From Europe women came to be trained by her. Her work led to the establishment of the National Trust. Another follower of Ruskin was Patrick Geddes (1854–1932), the urban sociologist. At Oxford was founded Ruskin College, largely worked in communal style by students—no servants, save a cook—and some critics thought Ruskin's ideas helped form Guild socialism. The author D. H. Lawrence (1885–1930) was much affected by Ruskin's work, and Ruskin's influence spread to the United States. In 1900 the Ruskin movement comprised twenty-three affiliated societies and 200 members. William Morris (1834–1896), the socialist, followed Ruskin's ideas—ignoring the religious element—by working to integrate socialism and Christianity.

See Also Geddes, Patrick; Guild of St. George and St. George's Farm, Abbeydale, or Totley Farm; Lawrence, D. H.; Ruskin Colony

Sources:

Beetz, Kirk H. H. 1976. *John Ruskin: A Bibliography*. Metuchen, N.J.: Scarecrow Press.
Fellows, Jay. 1981. *Ruskin's Maze: Mastery and Madness in His Art*. Princeton: Princeton University Press.
Hilton, Tim. 1985. *John Ruskin: The Early Years: 1819–1859*. New Haven, Conn.: Yale University Press.
Hinds, William A. 1878. *American Communities*. 1962 ed. New York: Corinth Books.
Hunt, John Dixon. 1982. *The Wider Sea: A Life of John Ruskin*. London: J. M. Dent and Sons.

Kemp, Wolfgang. 1991. *The Desire of My Eyes: A Life of John Ruskin.* Translated by
    Jan van Heurck. London: HarperCollins.
Landow, George P. 1985. *Ruskin.* Oxford: Oxford University Press.
Wise, Thomas J., and James P. Smart. 1893. *A Complete Bibliography of the Writings
    in Prose of John Ruskin with a List of the More Important Ruskiniana.* 1964 ed.
    London: Dawsons of Pall Mall.

RUSKIN COLONY. The first Ruskin Colony was founded by Julius A. Wayland (1854–1912), publisher of a socialist weekly, *The Coming Nation.* Funds
from the weekly, which sold 50,000 copies (1894), helped found the colony on
two 500-acre tracts, fifty miles west of Nashville, Tennessee. The colony bought
more property of 800 acres in Yellow Creek Valley late in 1895. The population
of the colony increased to 200, with most adults being age thirty and forty. They
came from over thirty-two states, primarily Ohio and Pennsylvania. Membership
turnover was constant between 1894 and 1899. In the fall of 1897 and early
1898 some families abandoned the colony and reformed at Dixie on the Tennessee River. This branch lasted until the end of the year. The members were
middle-class city dwellers and intellectual socialists who fell into conflict with
the more recent members who had come from the depressed rural areas. Most
members voted to abolish the Ruskin Cooperative Association and create a new
colony to be known as the Ruskin Commonwealth. Having lost their land in
Tennessee, the major group of the Ruskin Cooperative Association joined the
Duke colonists who had already settled a year earlier in Georgia. When they
dissolved their organization, the Duke colonists became members of the Ruskin
Commonwealth. Also, a dozen families quit and joined the single-tax colony at
Fairhope; others moved to another socialist colony at Burley in Washington;
and some deserted communal life altogether. With a membership of 300, the
new Ruskin Colony republished *The Coming Nation.* Despite their efforts to
establish themselves, before they could completely organize their community,
fire, malaria, and suspicious neighbors prevented their success (1899–1901).
    See Also Fairhope Colony; Wayland, Julius A.

Sources:

Fogarty, Robert S. 1980. *Dictionary of American Communal History.* Westport, Conn.:
    Greenwood Press.
Oved, Yaacov. 1987. *Two Hundred Years of American Communes.* New Brunswick, N.J.:
    Transaction Books.

RUSSIA AS UTOPIA. To some critics the USSR, like the United States, was
an enormous, but failed, utopia. In the 1980s corruption and repression in Russia
were rife, and with the end of communist government as such came a seemingly
chaotic form of government whose empire crumbled at the edges as each of the
Russian satellites and nearby regions sought its autonomy and unique way of
life. The subject is discussed by Kumar in his *Utopianism* (1991, pp. 81–85)
and his *Utopia and Anti-Utopia* (1987, Chapter 3). A further argument is that

attempts to achieve total freedom from all oppression will itself lead to totalitarianism. This is so because to develop human abilities such that they achieve common goals, it is necessary that all humankind have a rational grasp of interpersonal relations and the relation between individuals and all natural phenomena; this requires all human actions to focus on only one goal: the maintenance of the species. Such a focus omits the observation that humans differ in both their original endowment and their daily management of civilized life. Consequently, total freedom can be upheld only by keeping some humans unfree (Walicki, 1995). The outcome is totalitarian control, which too often permits dictatorship like that in Russia (1917–1989). A more positive view assumes that utopia proper starts in eighteenth-century Russia, as shown by the extensive utopian and antiutopian literature from that time until the present (Heller and Niqueux, 1995).

See Also United States as Utopia

Sources:

Heller, Leonid, and Michel Niqueux. 1995. *Histoire de l'utopie Russia.* Paris: Presses Universitaires de France.

Holloway, M. 1951. *Heavens on Earth: Utopian Communities in America: 1680–1880.* New York: Dover.

Holstun, James. 1987. *A Rational Millennium: Puritan Utopias of Seventeenth-Century England and America.* New York: Oxford University Press.

Kumar, Krishan. 1987. *Utopia and Anti-utopia in Modern Times.* Oxford: Basil Blackwell.

———. 1991. *Utopianism.* Milton Keynes: Open University Press.

Walicki, Andrzej. 1995. *Marxism and the Leap to the Kingdom of Freedom: The Rise and Fall of the Communist Utopia.* Stanford, Calif.: Stanford University Press.

S

SAINT ÉMILION. Saint Émilion was an anarchist alternative to the modern commune, established near Tours in France (1946). It was supported by a factory that made motorcycles. The workers bought the factory from its past owner, a Vichy collaborator who was escaping France after World War II. The leader of the community was ''Jacques,'' an ex-Jesuit and onetime steelworker who earlier had been a poet and a prisoner in a Nazi concentration camp. The factory employed approximately 300 workers. They rotated their jobs annually. The firm prospered. The group paid no taxes to the government; it had its own justice system agreed on by the whole community. An elected governing council was responsible for day-to-day decisions; major decisions required unanimity. All workers got the same pay, and profits were distributed to social benefits, for reinvestment, and to retire debts. The group agreed on educational classes organized for the workers in history, sewing, politics, and literature. The members did not live communally, nor did they have a collective school. Their political beliefs were a mixture of anarchism and related socialist beliefs; major intellectual influences can be traced to Pierre Joseph Proudhon (1809–1865), Peter Kropotkin (1842–1921), and Mikhail Bakunin (1814–1876). In general, the community opposed authoritarian controls; was anti-institutional, for example, opposed church and corporate organization; and assumed that fundamental changes can be made in human nature; and that industrial civilization had destroyed human dignity and limited people's scope for self-regulation. The workers lost control of their factory when the commune was destroyed by the involvement of the automobile maker Citröen. Citröen offered to rent the factory and provide new machinery and hire the workers. This split the community. The offer was accepted against advice from Jacques. Some members left the group, and in time the community dispersed.

See Also Bakunin, Mikhail; Proudhon, Pierre Joseph

Source:

Mc Cord, William. 1989. *Voyages to Utopia: From Monastery to Commune, the Search for the Perfect Society in Modern Times.* New York: W. W. Norton.

ST. NAZIANZ COMMUNITY. St. Nazianz Community was the only Roman Catholic intentional community founded in the United States. It was established at St. Nazianz, Manitowac County, Wisconsin, by a group of 113 German immigrants from Baden (1854–1874). Father Ambrose Oschwald (1801–1873) was the leader. The community had 3,840 acres, all property was held in common, and all labor was given without any return other than clothing and food. At its peak the community comprised 450 members, 180 of whom were married. The married members were given their share of the property after 1873, when Oschwald died. Later, the remaining property was taken over by a Catholic order, the Capitalist Society of Our Divine Saviour.

See Also Oschwald, Ambrose

Sources:

Fogarty, Robert S. 1980. *Dictionary of American Communal History.* Westport, Conn.: Greenwood Press.

Pitzer, Donald E. 1984. "Collectivism, Community and Commitment: America's Religious Communal Utopias from the Shakers to Jonestown." In P. Alexander and R. Gill, eds., *Utopias,* pp. 119–135. London: Duckworth.

SAINT-SIMON, CLAUDE HENRI DE ROUVROY, COMTE DE. Claude Henri de Rouvroy, Comte de Saint-Simon was born at Paris into an ancient, noble, but impoverished family. He served as a volunteer in the American Revolution (1776), but his aristocratic birth prevented him from playing a prominent part in the French Revolution. After making a fortune by speculating in confiscated lands, he devoted his time to the study of philosophy. The latter years of his life were spent in poverty because he wasted his fortune in costly experiments. The major exposition of his ideas appears in his *Nouveau Christianisme* (1825).

See Also Saint-Simonism

Sources:

Ansart, Pierre. 1969. *Saint-Simon.* Paris: Presses universitaires de France.

Saint-Simon, Claude-Henri de. 1966. "A Golden Rule for Posterity." Reprinted in Frank E. Manuel, and Futzie P. Manuel, eds., *French Utopias: An Anthology of Ideal Societies,* pp. 259–298. New York: Free Press.

SAINT-SIMONISM. Saint-Simonism was a utopian ideology for a state system of socialist government and became the founding policy of French socialism. The overarching belief was that humankind should strive for an organic society in a form advantageous to the greatest number. The ideology was developed by the followers of Claude Henri de Rouvroy, Comte de Saint-Simon (1760–1825) on the following assumptions: the state should possess all property; inheritance of property should be abolished; the distribution of the products of labor should not be equal, but instead all persons should be rewarded according to the service they rendered the state; consequently, active, able individuals would receive a larger share than the slow and less competent. Society should be reordered on the basis of a new spiritual power or new religion that could meet requirements of an imminent industrial age. The process of industrialization should be seen as benefiting humankind, and, since differences between labor and capital were not as important as some commentators claimed, the old feudal and military systems should be superseded by an industrial order led by industrial chiefs. At the same time society should be given spiritual direction with a new religion, that is, one based not on the traditional authority of the church but on the true and reliable knowledge emanating from science. Through this new religion society could be revitalized by all its members' accepting the belief to love one another. These utopian ideas are often assumed to connect the social philosophies of the eighteenth century with those of the nineteenth century.

See Also Saint-Simon, Claude Henri de Rouvroy, Comte de

Sources:

Beilharz, Peter. 1992. *Labour's Utopias: Bolshevism, Fabianism, Social Democracy.* London: Routledge.
Coser, Lewis A. 1977. *Masters of Sociological Thought.* New York: Harcourt Brace Jovanovich.
Cross, Frank L. 1974. *The Oxford Dictionary of the Christian Church.* 2d ed. New York: Oxford University Press.
Durkheim, Emile. 1959. *Socialism and Saint-Simon.* London: Routledge and Kegan Paul.
Holloway, Mark. 1951. *Heavens on Earth.* London: Turnstile Press.
Pollard, Sidney, and John Salt, eds. 1971. *Robert Owen: Prophet of the Poor.* Lewisburg, Pa., Bucknell University Press.

SALT, TITUS. Titus Salt (1803–1876), son of a cloth merchant of Morely, West Riding of Yorkshire, was educated at Heath Grammar School in Wakefield and worked as a wool dealer in Bradford for his father. The business expanded rapidly, and in 1836 Salt had several mills manufacturing worster wool, pioneered the use of alpaca in cloth making, and subsequently acquired great wealth. In 1850 he decided to move his workers from the polluted Bradford, of which he was mayor, to Saltaire, a model town that he had build for them by in 1853. It was an industrial utopia where all amenities—save alcohol—were available to employees. He was the mayor of Bradford (1848), a Liberal member of Parliament (1859–1861), and in 1869 was made a baronet. On his death his wife and son, according to Salt's will, created the Salt Trust and left the control of the institute and schools at Saltaire to the governors; in 1887 the control of the hospital and poorhouse and £30,000 were also transferred to the governors. He was sketched as Mr. Trafford in Disraeli's *Sybil: Or the Two Nations* (1845).

See Also Saltaire

Sources:

Armytage, Walter H. Green. 1961. *Heavens Below: Utopian Experiments in England 1560–1950*. London: Routledge and Kegan Paul.
Crystal, David, ed. 1994. *The Cambridge Biographical Encyclopedia*. Cambridge University Press.
Magnussen, Magnus, Rosemary Goring, and John O. Thorn, eds. 1990. *Chambers Biographical Dictionary*. Edinburgh: Chambers.
Reynolds, Jack. 1983. *The Great Paternalist: Titus Salt and the Growth of 19th Century Bradford*. London: Temple Smith and Oxford University Press.
Stephen, Leslie, and Sydney Lee, eds. 1917. *The Dictionary of National Biography*. London: Oxford University Press.

SALTAIRE. Saltaire was a community built for the workers of Titus Salt (1803–1876) in the valley of the Aire where the London–Glasgow Railway and Leeds–Liverpool Canal joined. It was a model town begun late in 1851 near Bradford, and in two years the first stage was finished. Saltaire, the model manufacturing town of the world, opened 20 September 1853. The buildings were arranged like the letter *T*, built in Italian style, with a very long, large room on the sixth floor and with great plate glass windows. Fresh air and good light were available to workers, and the noise of machines was comparatively quiet beneath the floor. The stem of the *T* comprised warehouses. Around the big *T* and covering twenty-six acres were built 800 houses, each with its kitchen, scullery, living room, and pantry. Streets were lined with shops, schools, literary institutes, and other amenities. It was an industrial utopia that integrated work, home, and leisure. No alcohol was allowed because Titus Salt believed lust and beer together produced social problems.

See Also Salt, Titus

Sources:

Armytage, Walter Henry Green. 1961. *Heavens Below: Utopian Experiments in England 1560–1950*. London: Routledge and Kegan Paul.
Boase, Frederic. 1965. *Modern English Biography*. Vol. 3. London: Frank Cass.
Gill, Roger. 1984. ''In England's Green and Pleasant Land.'' In Peter Alexander and Roger Gill, eds., *Utopias*, pp. 109–117. London: Duckworth.
Reynolds, Jack. 1983. *The Great Paternalist: Titus Salt and the Growth of Nineteenth Century Bradford*. Great Britain: Maurice Temple Smith and University of Bradford.

SALVATION ARMY COLONIES. Salvation Army Colonies were intended to help the urban unemployed by providing the chance to work on the land (1898–1910). They valued the family and a cooperative, rather than competitive, view of the economy. For that reason the colonies were often thought to be utopian. It was also assumed that disadvantaged people could become productive simply by being given a fresh start. The ideas for rural colonies emerged from William Booth's (1829–1912) *In Darkest England and the Way Out* (1890). In 1896

Frederick Booth Tucker, commander of the Salvation Army in the United States, put his ideas for rural colonies into action. Three were founded: Fort Amity, Colorado; Romie, California; and Fort Herrick, Ohio. Fort Amity was the most successful. Settlers were selected for their potential as farmers. They received ten acres, a horse, and basic implements and had to cultivate land. They enjoyed high moral support, but little economic cooperation arose between families. By 1903 the colony had 450 residents. Because of excessive alkaline deposits, the crops failed in 1909, and the scheme folded in 1910. With other colonies the selection of land raised problems.

Sources:

Fogarty, Robert S. 1980. *Dictionary of American Communal History*. Westport, Conn.: Greenwood Press.
————. 1990. *All Things New: American Communes and Utopian Movements 1860–1914*. Chicago: University of Chicago Press.

SANCTIFICATIONISTS. *See* McWhirter, Martha; Women's Commonwealth (Sanctificationists)

SANDEMAN, ROBERT. Robert Sandeman (1718–1771) was born at Perth, Scotland, and studied at the University of Edinburgh, where he was much influenced by John Glas (or Glass) (1695–1773) and became an elder in the Glassite Church (1744). He was a linen manufacturer (1734–1744) in a partnership with his two brothers. He was a son-in-law and zealous disciple of John Glas, the founder of the Glasites, a group that had formed in protest against the Church of Scotland in 1728. Their major belief was that ''the bare work of Jesus Christ without a Deed or Thought on the Part of Man is sufficient to present the chief of Sinners spotless before God.'' This was Sandeman's epitaph. He became known for his controversial publications, one of which was *Letters on Theron and Aspasio*, addressed to the author and published in Edinburgh in 1757. Sandeman also promoted the U.S. colonies, sailed to the United States (1764), and began preaching in many New England towns. He settled in Danbury, Connecticut, where the largest group of his supporters emerged. The sect of Glasites came to bear his name from 1764 to 1771. He and his followers were strongly opposed by the prominent New England ministers for rejecting the Covenant of Grace and the doctrine of justification by faith as an act of regeneration. These religious figures tried to force him out of town as an ''undesirable transient.'' He stayed and died in Danbury.

See Also Sandemanians

Sources:

Magnussen, Magnus, and Rosemary Goring, eds. 1990. *Chambers Biographical Dictionary*. 5th ed. Edinburgh: Chambers.
Malone, Dumas, ed. 1935. *Dictionary of American Biography*. Vol. 8. New York: Charles Scribner's Sons.

Sandeman, Robert. 1758. *Some Thoughts on Christianity*. London: D. Nottage.
———. 1857. *Discourses on Passages in Scriptures*. Dundee: George Sandeman.
Smith, Benjamin. 1903. *The Century Cyclopedia of Names*. London: Times.

SANDEMANIANS. Sandemanians were Glasites (or Glassites), followers of the U.S. religious sect who practiced the community of goods, abstinence from blood and from things strangled, love feasts, and weekly celebrations of communion. They were named Sandemanians after their leader in the United States, Robert Sandeman (1718–1771). The sect flourished until 1900 on the basis of agreement between members rather than majority voting and was organized by coequal presbyters who followed members' decisions. They practiced foot washing, infant baptism, and excommunication. Membership was low because conditions of membership were strict, and the church controlled its members' private funds.

See Also Sandeman, Robert

Sources:

Cross, Frank L. 1974. *The Oxford Dictionary of the Christian Church*. 2d ed. New York: Oxford University Press.
Douglas, James D., ed. 1974. *The New International Dictionary of the Christian Church*. Exeter: Paternoster Press.
Hastings, James. 1913. *Encyclopedia of Religion and Ethics*. New York: Charles Scribner's Sons.

SANTA ROSA. Santa Rosa was an alternative name for, and the site of, the New Eden of the West better known as the Fountain Grove Community of the Brotherhood of the New Life. The brotherhood was led by Thomas Lake Harris (1823–1906).

See Also Brotherhood of the New Life; Fountain Grove; Harris, Thomas Lake

Sources:

Fogarty, Robert. 1990. *All Things New: American Communes and Utopian Movements 1860–1914*. Chicago: University of Chicago Press.
Hine, Robert V. 1953. *California's Utopian Colonies*. 1983 ed. Berkeley: University of California Press.
Spann, Edward K. 1989. *Brotherly Tomorrows: Movements for a Cooperative Society in America*. New York: Columbia University Press.

SCANLON, JOSEPH NORBETT. Joseph Norbett Scanlon (c.1899–1956) was a cost accountant, professional boxer, steelworker, and union official. In 1936 he unionized steelworkers and became president of the local union. In 1938 he presented his plan to the La Pointe Machine Tool Company to help its productivity and to benefit the union members in the plant. Because work in the steel industry had damaged his health, Scanlon accepted a professorship at Massachusetts Institute of Technology (1946) to develop further his scheme in the hope that it would improve industrial relations in the United States.

See Also Scanlon Plan

Sources:

"Obituary: Joseph Scanlon." 1956. *New York Times*, 11 February: 11.
Wren, Daniel A. 1994. *The Evolution of Management Thought*. 4th ed. New York: Wiley.

SCANLON PLAN. The Scanlon Plan was a suggestion plan in U.S. industry that sought to cut operating costs and benefit workers as a group for their suggestions. In 1938 after consulting with steelworkers at the nearly bankrupt La Pointe Machine Tool Company, Joseph Norbett Scanlon (c. 1899–1956) outlined a productivity plan that gave workers, as a group rather than individuals, rewards for suggestions they might make to improve the efficiency of operations. Stressing cooperation rather than competition, the plan helped save the firm and encouraged further union–management cooperation in costs reduction. Participation in decisions to help the firm gave the workers a sense of belonging to the organization. The Scanlon Plan differed from other similar schemes in that it rewarded groups, not individuals, used management–union committees to suggest changes, and had workers share not in greater profits but in reduced operating costs.

See Also Scanlon, Joseph Norbett

Source:

Lesieur, Frederick G., ed. 1958. *The Scanlon Plan: A Frontier in Labor–Management Cooperation*. New York: Wiley, Cambridge: MIT Press.

SCHETTERLY, HENRY. Henry Schetterly (fl. 1844–1848) was born and educated in Germany and became the founding secretary of the Alphadelphia Industrial Association. On arriving at the association he brought with him the appurtenances of a medical doctor, including laboratory equipment, chemical supplies, a globe, and astronomical instruments. It is not known whether he had any qualifications as a doctor, although he was referred to by that title. He became the editor of the *Tocsin*, the association's newspaper, as well as secretary of the association. He seemed more interested in raising the literary tone of the newspaper than attending to the vital needs of the association members. With the other leaders of the association he worked hard to increase the number of subscribers to the *Tocsin* and was upbraided for giving too much effort to the task and allowing agents outside the community to advance the subscription rate. The *Tocsin* took up much of Schetterly's time, appears to have had literary pretensions well beyond the understanding of its illiterate members, and carried much critical writing on Fourierism, which put much emphasis on the immediate utility of their association's activities for members. Schetterly charged Fourier,

Alphadelphia's mentor, with infidelity by ascribing powers to the planets and stars, which were normally considered God's bailiwick.

See Also Alphadelphia

Source:

Kesten, Seymour. 1993. *Utopian Episodes: Daily Life in Experimental Colonies Dedicated to Changing the World.* Syracuse, N.Y.: Syracuse University Press.

SCHUMAN, ROBERT. Robert Schuman (1886–1963) was born in Luxembourg into a well-to-do family and was educated at German-language schools. He studied at the universities of Bonn, Berlin, and Munich and graduated in law from the University of Strasbourg. He practiced law in Metz. He spent World War I in prison, refusing to enter combat. Afterward he was elected to the French Chamber of Deputies and for seventeen years was head of the Assembly Finance Division. In 1940 he was arrested by the Gestapo, escaped, and worked for the French underground resistance. In 1946 he was France's finance minister and introduced an austerity campaign. He became prime minister, 1947; and in 1950 he advanced a plan to pool the coal and steel resources that had been in dispute in Europe. He successfully weathered the electoral reforms of Charles de Gaulle (1890–1970) and in November 1958 was reelected to the French National Assembly. He was elected president of the Strasbourg European Assembly (1958–1960) and awarded the Charlemagne Prize.

Sources:

Magnussen, Magnus, and Rosemary Goring, eds. 1990. *Chambers Biographical Dictionary.* 5th ed. Edinburgh: Chambers.

Moritz, Charles ed. 1963. *Current Biography Yearbook.* New York: Wilson.

Rothe, Anna, ed. 1948. *Current Biography Yearbook.* New York: Wilson.

SCHUMAN PLAN. The Schuman Plan was devised by Jean Monnet (1888–1979), head of the French Planning Agency, and was implemented by Robert Schuman (1886–1963), the French foreign minister for the European Coal and Steel Community (ECSC) (1950). The idea behind the plan was to reduce the strict economic controls imposed on Germany after World War II, so as to allow West Germany's economic contribution to benefit Western Europe. The plan involved the proposed establishment of a common market for coal and steel, with an independent governing authority. This led to the establishment of the European Coal and Steel Community in 1952. It aimed for economic and military unity in Europe and for a rapprochement between France and Germany so the two would not go to war again. ECSC comprised six nations of Europe: France, West Germany, Italy, Belgium, the Netherlands, and Luxembourg. They established an economic union for Europe. In the 1950s the removal of trade barriers led to a great increase in the trade of coal and steel. In 1973 Denmark, Ireland, and the United Kingdom joined the community; Greece joined in 1981, followed in 1986 by Portugal and Spain. At this time the European Economic

Community merged with the ECSC and the European Atomic Energy Community and formed the European Community.

Sources:

Bullen, Roger, M. E. Pelley, et al. eds. 1986. *The Schuman Plan, the Council of Europe and Western European Integration: May 1950–December 1952*. London: HMSO.

Dell, Edmund. 1995. *The Schuman Plan and the British Abdication of Leadership in Europe*. Oxford: Oxford University Press.

Diebold, William. 1959. *The Schuman Plan: A Study in Economic Cooperation, 1950–59*. New York: Praeger.

SCOTT, ANNIE ELIZA DORA. Annie Eliza Dora Scott (1884–1979), born in England, was twelve when her father died in 1897. She planned to be a teacher, but on advice that her eyes were inadequate to the task, she worked caring for babies while her mother took in student boarders. In 1912 Ernest Bader (1890–1982) took a room in the Scott house. They were married in 1915. She became a nurse. They pursued business interests in the Scott Bader Company, and she became a director and attended board meetings, and, in addition to the traditional work of a wife, she helped Ernest with his English. She was not so much a power behind the throne as a support to it in their work. All her life she traveled with him and took part in the many humanistic causes he pursued.

See Also Bader, Ernest; Scott Bader Commonwealth

Sources:

Hoe, Susanna. 1978. *The Man Who Gave His Company Away: A Biography of Ernest Scott Bader, Founder of Scott Bader Commonwealth*. London: Heinemann.

Jeremy, David J. 1984. "Ernest Bader." In D. J. Jeremy and C. Shaw, eds., *Dictionary of Business Biography: A Biographical Dictionary of Business Leaders in Britain in the Period of 1860–1980*. London: Butterworths.

SCOTT BADER COMMONWEALTH. The Scott Bader Commonwealth was a British collaborative management–worker organization established after World War II that aimed to limit conflict at work and enhance employment conditions for all members of an industrial community. The commonwealth was established by Ernest Bader (1890–1982) and his wife, Annie Scott Bader (1884–1979), in the belief that business should serve society, and social conflict could be resolved through common ownership of industrial assets. Influenced by similar ideas from Europe, he and his wife established the Scott Bader Commonwealth Ltd., a charity that held 90 percent of the capital of Scott Bader Ltd. and decided how the firm's profits were to be distributed. Bader's patriarchal control of the commonwealth lasted until 1963, when a Quaker sociologist, Fred H. Blum (1968), completed an action research study of the organization, and power in the commonwealth was moved from Bader himself to a self-governing work community.

See Also Bader, Ernest; Scott, Annie Eliza Dora

Sources:

Blum, Fred H. 1968. *Work and Community: The Scott Bader Commonwealth and the Quest for a New Order*. London: Routledge and Kegan Paul.
Wilken, Folkert. 1965. *The Liberation of Work: The Elimination of Strikes and Strife in Industry through Associative Organization of Enterprise*. London: Routledge and Kegan Paul.

SEARCH CONFERENCE. The Search Conference is a participative method for changing human organizations so they can achieve desirable and possible futures. The method is an alternative to the conventional planning in traditional organizations that uses elite groups—often supported by expert staff advice and external consultants—as the locus of control in a chain of command. By contrast the Search Conference draws together people who normally work together to establish plans for the system they share. They use a responsive and effective social interaction rather than impose or have imposed directives from above. In three days the Search Conference devises a long-term strategy plan, achievable aims, and schemes for concrete procedures to achieve those aims. The Search Conference assumes its participants are purposive, are able to seek ideals together, are powerfully moved by a sense of common purpose, and can shift from points of conflict to common ground. The first Search Conference was held 10–16 July 1960 at Barford House, Warwick, England, by London's Tavistock Institute of Human Relations. It was planned by two of its senior staff, Fred E. Emery (1925–1997) and Eric L. Trist (1909–1993). The problem was to change two large organizations. The senior executives of the Bristol and Siddley aeroengine companies were directed by the British government to create a single operating firm. Over the next ten years eleven more Search Conferences were held involving, for example, the National Farmers Association in England and diplomats in an international conflict in Southeast Asia. Thereafter the Search Conference technique was developed further in Canberra, Australia (1970–1982), and was used in Holland, Norway, France, and Canada. By 1993 it was well established in North America. It is now recognized as an ideal method for working toward a better future for communities, regions, industrial organizations, private companies, and government agencies. The conference has three phases, involves between twenty and thirty participants, and lasts three days. First, participants appreciate their group, community, or organizational environment by considering desirable and possible futures; second, the participants analyze the history of the system, its present and desired future; third, they integrate the system with its environment and deal specifically with constraints and devise strategies and plans for the future action. For many years the Search Conference has been used and taught by Dr. Merrelyn Emery in conjunction with her husband, Dr. Fred Emery, at the Australian National University, Canberra, Australia.

See Also Emery, Frederick E.; Trist, Eric Lansdown

Sources:

Emery, Merrelyn. 1996. "The Search Conference: Design and Management of Learning." In Fred E. Emery, Hugh Murray, and Beulah Trist, eds., *The Social Engagement of Social Science: A Tavistock Anthology: A Socio-Ecological Perspective*. Vol. 3. Philadelphia: University of Pennsylvania Press.

Emery, Merrelyn, and Ronald E. Purser. 1996. *The Search Conference: A Powerful Method for Planning Organizational Change and Community Action*. San Francisco: Jossey-Bass.

Weisbord, Marvin R., et al. 1992. *Discovering Common Ground: How Future Search Conferences Bring People Together to Achieve Breakthrough Innovation, Empowerment, Shared Vison and Collaborative Action*. San Francisco: Berrett-Koehler.

SEMCO. Semco is an egalitarian workplace with utopian features established in São Paulo, Brazil. It manufactures many goods, including maritime pumps, dishwashers, air conditioners, mixers, and blenders. In 1982 this traditionally organized business was taken over by Ricardo Semler (b. 1959), the son of its founder, Antonio Curt Semler (b. 1912). In 1985 Ricardo began to reorganize the firm along lines familiar in modern social and psychological literature on organizational behavior and development. Beginning with a cure for "time sickness"—the failure to use work time effectively—Ricardo Semler brought changes to the firm, including increases in worker control over jobs; reduction in supervisory and corporate staff; elimination of data processing, training, and quality control departments; excising twelve layers of bureaucracy and the replacement of the pyramid organization with concentric circles; making all employees counselors, partners, coordinators, or associates; eliminating corruption involving government agencies. Today the company is run by representative, democratically appointed committees; flexitime is a principle used by all employees; memos have only one page; sabbaticals and job rotation are universal; job security is never used; profit sharing is widespread; risk taking is encouraged with salary packages; there are fewer petty rules, like dress codes or travel regulations; employees set salary levels and pay increases, establish their own companies within the firm, and may compete with it; the business comprises units of no more than fifty people; there are no secretaries, personnel assistants, or other servile, dead-end work; all employees are taught all aspects of the business, including financial matters; working at home is encouraged; there is no organization chart; employees determine hiring practices; workers change their own immediate work environments; unions are accepted fully; strikes occur rarely, and striking employees are never subject to discrimination; no prizes are given for suggestions; there are no management perks, like car parking, special dining facilities, toilets; the aim of the firm is not to promote socialism or capitalism but to make people look forward to coming to work in the morning.

See Also Semler, Antonio Curt; Semler, Ricardo

Sources:

Semler, Ricardo. 1993. *Maverick! The Success Story behind the World's Most Unusual Workplace*. 1994 ed. London: Arrow.

SEMLER, ANTONIO CURT. Antonio Curt Semler (b.1912) was born in Vienna, son of a dentist; Antonio graduated in engineering at Vienna Polytechnic University, and in 1937 he joined Du Pont in Argentina, survived the political reign of Juan Peron Sosa (1895–1974), and became plant manager. In 1952 he visited São Paulo and married another Austrian exile, Renee Weinmann. In 1954 he planned Semler and Company to make an oil separating machine. In the late 1950s and 1960s Brazil's economy grew at 7 percent annually, and Semler and Company prospered immensely. Later, Semco began making marine pumps. Antonio established a traditionally organized firm that expanded as Brazil did. In 1980 Antonio handed over the firm to his son, Ricardo Semler (b. 1960).

See Also Semco; Semler, Ricardo

Sources:

Semler, Ricardo. 1993. *Maverick! The Success Story behind the World's Most Unusual Workplace*. 1994 ed. London: Arrow.

SEMLER, RICARDO. Ricardo Semler (b. 1959) was born and raised in São Paulo. He was a popular boy at school and developed musical talents. At age sixteen he worked during a summer vacation at his father's firm, Semco, but found he preferred to play guitar. Later he went to law school in São Paulo and in 1980 worked at Semco to begin the transition from his father's control to his own. While his father went on vacation, Ricardo instituted a ''Great Purge,'' fired fifteen senior executives, and next day hired an energetic Italian financial administrator. For the remaining year they scurried to banks to get enough cash to keep the firm going. In time Semco diversified, quickly attracted many lucrative contracts, and brashly extended the company's operations. After some success and several more managerial changes he hired an executive in human resources with a background in progressive education and eighteen years' training at Ford. In 1985 Semler began to reorganize Semco by replacing its autocratic controls with a participative ideology that questioned traditional values, in particular, problems of the unplanned use of time and the fear of delegation and replaceability. In ten years this led to the establishment of an entirely new organization for the company. Now it aims to make people look forward to coming to work each day. The company has been a remarkable financial success.

See Also Semco; Semler, Antonio Curt

Sources:

Semler, Ricardo. 1993. *Maverick! The Success Story behind the World's Most Unusual Workplace*. 1994 ed. London: Arrow.

SETTLEMENT HOUSE OF HENRY STREET, HULL HOUSE. The Settlement House of Henry Street was established in New York in 1895 by Lillian Wald (1869–1940) and Jane Addams (1860–1935) with financial support from Jacob Schiff (1847–1920). The original Settlement House, Chicago's Hull House, had been founded in 1889 by Jane Addams. At the Henry Street settlement the first activists were several permanent residents and nurses who were interested in public health and welfare programs. The welfare programs involved city playgrounds and health centers. The activists lobbied for local government officials to take over health and welfare responsibilities and later pressed for these services to be taken up under President Theodore Roosevelt's (1858–1919) adminstration. The programs involved hundreds of nurses who held radical views about the value of alternative and preventive medicine. Among these policies was the visiting home nurse service. The women who were seeking these social changes were imprisoned for suffrage activities and were labeled "reds" and "traitors." They also contributed to the establishment of the National Women's Trade Union League, the Children's Bureau, the National Association for the Advancement of Colored People, and the Women's Peace Party and other antiwar organizations.

See Also Addams, Jane; Wald, Lillian

Source:

Cook, Blanch Wiesen. 1984. "A Utopian Female Support Network: The Case of the Henry Street Settlement." In Ruby Rohrlich and Elaine Hoffman Baruch, eds., *Women in Search of Utopia: Mavericks and Myth Makers.* New York: Schocken Books.

SHAKERS, SHAKING QUAKERS. Shakers were a religious community that separated from the Quakers and were first led by Jane and James Wardley (fl. 1747–1774). They used the Quaker meeting technique of silent meditation and broke in with passionate anticlerical revelations, loud declamations, and much trembling by "Mother Jane," as she became known. In 1758 at Balton they were joined by Ann Lee (c.1742–1784). They became known as the "Shaking Quakers" because they danced and uttered loudly in strange voices. Eventually, Ann Lee, an intense evangelist, became their leader. She had married a blacksmith, had four miscarriages, and had been imprisoned for shaking at the tabernacle. In visions she saw the sons of Adam and Eve, was driven to believe in celibacy, and earned the sobriquet of "Mother Ann" and "Bride of the Land." A vision told her to go to the United States. She sailed with her family in 1774, and she established a network of Shaker communities at Watervliet and New Lebanon in New York state in 1787; Hancock, West Tittsfield, Massachusetts in 1793; and New Gloucester, Maine in 1784. New Lebanon became the largest and, until it dissolved in 1947, had over 3,000 members. In the nineteenth century eight communities were founded and eleven paracommunities also. The literature on American Shakers is vast, and the Shaker settlements in the United

States have became tourist attractions, where early Shaker life is depicted in fascinating detail.

See Also Lee, Ann; Wardley, Jane and James

Sources:

Andrews, Edward Deeming. 1953. *The People Called Shakers: A Search for the Perfect Society.* 1963 ed. New York: Dover.

Armytage, Walter H. Green. 1961. *Heavens Below: Utopian Experiments in England 1560–1950.* London: Routledge and Kegan Paul.

Berry, Brian J. 1992. *America's Utopian Experiments: Communal Havens from Long-Wave Crises.* Hanover, N.H.: University Press of New England.

Brewer, Priscilla J. 1990. "Review Essay. Shaker Voices: The New Scholarship." *Utopian Studies* 1: 144–150.

———. 1993. "Tho' of the Weaker Sex: A Re-Assessment of Gender Equality among the Shakers." In Wendy E. Chmielewski, Louis J. Kern, and Marlyn Klee-Hartzell, eds., *Women in Spiritual and Communitarian Societies in the U.S.*, pp. 133–149. Syracuse, N.Y.: Syracuse University Press.

Fogarty, Robert S. 1990. *All Things New: American Communes and Utopian Movements 1860–1914.* Chicago: University of Chicago Press.

Gordon, Beverly. 1993. "Shaker Fancy Goods: Women's Work and Presentation of Self in the Community Context in the Victorian Era." In Wendy E. Chmielewski, Louis J. Kern and Marlyn Klee-Hartzell, eds., *Women in Spiritual and Communitarian Societies in the U.S.*, pp. 89–103. Syracuse, N.Y.: Syracuse University Press.

Humez, Jean McMahon, ed. 1981. *Gifts of Power: The Writings of Rebecca Jackson, Black Visionary, Shaker Eldress.* Amherst: University of Massachusetts Press.

Nickless, Karen K., and Pamela J. Nickless. 1993. "Sexual Equality and Economic Authority: The Shaker Experience, 1784–1900." In Wendy E. Chmielewski, Louis J. Kern, and Marlyn Klee-Hartzell, eds., *Women in Spiritual and Communitarian Societies in the U.S.*, pp. 119–132. Syracuse, N.Y.: Syracuse University Press.

Oved, Yaacov. 1987. *Two Hundred Years of American Communes.* New Brunswick, N.J.: Transaction Books.

Rohrlich, Ruby 1984. "The Shakers: Gender Equality in Hierarchy." In Ruby Rohrlich, and Elaine Hoffman Baruch, eds., *Women in Search of Utopia: Mavericks and Mythmakers*, pp. 54–61. New York: Schocken Books.

Spencer, Sylvia Minott. 1973. "My Memories of the Shakers." In Rosabeth Moss Kanter, *Communes: Creating and Managing the Collective Life*, pp. 375–380. New York: Harper and Row.

Stein, Stephen J. 1992. *The Shaker Experience in America: A History of the United Society of Believers.* New Haven Conn.: Yale University Press.

Whitworth, John McKelvie. 1975. *God's Blueprints: A Sociological Study of Three Utopian Sects.* London: Routledge and Kegan Paul.

SHALAM COLONY. Shalam was a community of leading spiritualists in New York City in 1883 that gave rise to Shalam Colony (1884) at Dona Ana, on 1,500 acres in the Mesilla Valley on the east bank of the Rio Grande, New Mexico. It was led by John Ballou Newbrough (1827–1891). Using abandoned children as members, it integrated social reform and spiritualism with family values. It was partly funded by several philanthropists, including Elizabeth Rowell Thompson (1821–1899), who would see in the scheme a practical application of her ideas on the role of children for the future. Twenty of Newbrough's disciples sought to care for and raise fifty small, lost children (1887–1901) at the Children's Land of Shalam. The founders assumed that much conflict in society would give over to benevolence if the very young were educated in virtue and industry. Newbrough wanted a new race, free of helplessness and poverty, the causes of crime; he would gather orphans, abandoned children from all races and nationalities to be raised from infancy in communities where they lived on a pure diet—no fish, no flesh. Children were drawn from foundling homes, some were donated, and others were picked up at police precincts. Andrew M. Howland, whaling magnate, who married Mrs. Newbrough after her husband's death, provided most of the funds. The mission began to falter after Newbrough's death in 1891, when a second colony, Levitica, was founded nearby to cater to single and married adults and their children who sought isolation so they could work and live in their own way. Trainloads came to settle, and within two years Andrew Howland faced bankruptcy. The venture lasted until 1901, when its drain on the wealth of the Howlands made it no longer viable. By 1901 Shalam was over. The Howlands placed the children in private homes and orphanages in Denver and Dallas and departed Shalam in 1907.

See Also Newbrough, John Ballou; Thompson, Elizabeth Rowell

Sources:

Fogarty, Robert S. 1980. *Dictionary of American Communal History*. Westport, Conn.: Greenwood Press.
———. 1990. *All Things New: American Communes and Utopian Movements 1860–1914*. Chicago: University of Chicago Press.

SHAW, GEORGE BERNARD. George Bernard Shaw (1856–1950) was born in Dublin, Ireland, had a desultory education, learned music from his mother, and by reading and visiting the National Gallery of Dublin taught himself much about literature and art. He worked as an office boy and later a cashier for an estate agent and went to London. He published five novels (1879–1883) with little success. In 1884 he joined the newly founded Fabian Society, and his friend Sidney Webb (1859–1947) joined in 1885, and before long they were its most influential members. They helped ensure that the British Labor Party did not become dominated by Marxist beliefs in social change. He edited *Fabian Essays in Socialism* (1889). His main work was done in the theater. His plays were performed with great success (1904–1907) at London's Court Theater, his reputation grew, and in 1925 he was awarded the Nobel Prize in literature. His social satires on the English character and British institutions amused his countrymen immensely. He was regarded as a crank for his vegetarianism and abstinence from alcohol; conservatives were shocked by his free thought, socialism, views on the war production industry and medical profession, and liberal attitudes to sexual relations (e.g., *Mrs. Warren's Profession*). Few social institutions escaped his witty analysis and criticism. His approach to socialism was driven by a utopian need for order in the community, and he loathed poverty and ill health for their untidiness and thought both should be abolished. His politics were far from democratic; he admired forceful, dictatorial folk, saw himself as an aristocrat of good taste and intellectual wisdom, and enjoyed expressing his individualistic temperament. Today his fiction reads like polemical rationalizations or propagandistic advocacy for old causes—rights of women, vegetarianism, stupidity of war—largely because they are accepted alternatives, make good sense, or have been revised into a more correct form.

See Also Fabians; Wallas, Graham; Webb, Sidney James

Sources:

Ganz, Arthur. 1983. *George Bernard Shaw*. New York: Grove.

Hammond, Nicholas G. L., and Howard H. Scullard, eds. 1985. *The Oxford Companion to English Literature*. Oxford: Clarendon Press.

Holroyd, Michael. 1979. *The Genius of Shaw: A Symposium*. London: Hodder and Stoughton.

———. 1988–1992. *Bernard Shaw*. 4 vols.; one-vol. ed., 1997. London: Chatto and Windus.

Legg, Leopold G. W., and E. T. Williams, eds. 1959. *Dictionary of National Biography 1941–1950*. London: Oxford University Press.

Mathews, John F. 1969. *George Bernard Shaw*. New York: Columbia University Press.

Ousby, Ian. ed. 1988. *The Cambridge Guide to Literature in English*. Cambridge: Cambridge University Press.

Snodgrass, Mary Ellen. 1995. *Encyclopedia of Utopian Literature*. Santa Barbara, Calif.: ABC-CLIO.

SICILY ISLAND COLONY. Sicily Island Colony was established at Sicily Island in Louisiana. It was the first agricultural colony of Russian Jews in the United States, comprised twenty-five families under the leadership of Herman Rosenthal (1843–1917), and included some single men, mostly from Kiev. They settled on a 2,800-acre colony that had been chosen by the New York branch of the Alliance Israelite Universelle, which also provided some of the funding. The colonists did not like the seclusion of the site. The Mississippi flooded in the spring of 1882, and everything was lost. The members scattered, but a small group under Rosenthal left for South Dakota to try again.

See Also Am Olam; Rosenthal, Herman

Sources:

Fogarty, Robert S. 1980. *Dictionary of American Communal History*. Westport, Conn.: Greenwood Press.

SILKVILLE. Silkville is another name for Prairie Home Colony. Originally, this colony was the Kansas Cooperative Farm, established in Silkville, Kansas, on Fourierist principles (1870–1884) by Ernest Valeton de Boissiere (1810–1894).
  See Also Boissiere, Ernest Valeton de, Prairie Home Colony

Source:

Fogarty, Robert S. 1980. *Dictionary of American Communal History.* Westport, Conn.:
  Greenwood Press.

SIMONS, MENNO. Menno Simons or Symons (1496–1561) was born at Witmarsum, Friesland, Holland. He became a parish priest. In 1536 he renounced the Roman Catholic Church, joined the Anabaptists, and helped protect and reorganize persecuted religious communities in the Netherlands and its neighbors. Often he would enter local disputes and would have to move on. He valued a community where members were committed to a new life that had been sealed by adult baptism. He was chief founder of the Mennonites, who took his name. They believed in the administration of baptism only upon confession of faith and therefore did not baptize infants; they refused to take oaths to bear arms and condemned every kind of revenge, as well as divorce. He wanted followers to marry within the community and withdraw from the trivia of secular activities. He distrusted intellectualizing religion, took the Scriptures literally, and rejected abstractions like the Trinity. The first congregation formed in Zurich (1525). The sect spread through Switzerland and the south of Germany and Austria and had a large following at Augsburg and Strasburg. The sect had many divisions, and the more fanatical were repressed. Many Mennonites migrated to the United States and built their first churches in Pennsylvania in the late 1680s.
  See Also Mennonites

Sources:

Cross, L. A., and E. A. Livingstone. 1997. *The Oxford Dictionary of the Christian
  Church.* 3d ed. New York: Oxford University Press.
Douglas, James D., ed. 1974. *The New International Dictionary of the Christian Church.*
  Exeter: Paternoster Press.
Horst, Irvis B. 1962. *A Bibliography of Menno Simons.* Nieuwkoop: B. de Graaf.
MacMaster, Richard K. 1983. *Land, Piety, Peoplehood: The Establishment of Mennonite
  Communities in America 1683–1790.* Scottdale, Pa.: Herald Press.
McHenry, Robert, ed. 1992. *The New Encyclopedia Britannica.* Chicago: Encyclopedia
  Britannica.
Redekop, Calvin. 1989. *Mennonite Society.* Baltimore: Johns Hopkins University Press.

SINCLAIR, UPTON. Upton Beall Sinclair (1878–1968) was born in Baltimore, and when he was ten years old, his family moved to New York. He graduated from New York City College (1897) and, shortly after beginning to study law at Columbia University, turned to politics and literature. He supported himself by writing adventure stories while a student. In 1902 he joined the

Socialist Party and moved to Princeton. In 1904 his novel *The Jungle* exposed the unhealthy conditions of the meat packing industry in Chicago. With the royalties from the novel he started a cooperative colony, Helicon Hall at Helicon, Englewood, New Jersey (1906–1907). From New York some notables came to visit. It was seen more as a pretentious gathering of aristocratic itinerants than a community to change society because it used servants and followed a rather luxurious lifestyle with little of the customary asceticism of a utopia. His socialist attitudes were evident in his *Metropolis* (1908), *King Coal* (1917), *Oil!* (1927), and *Boston* (1928). In 1917, opposing its antiwar policy, he quit the Socialist Party but later rejoined in opposition to President Woodrow Wilson's (1856–1924) postwar policies. In California he ran for the House of Representatives as a socialist (1920), for the U.S. Senate (1922), and for governor (1926 and 1930). He was never successful. In 1934 he left the Socialist Party once more and ran as the Democratic candidate for governor with the EPIC slogan— "End Poverty in California." Frank Merriam (1865–1955) was the successful Republican incumbent. Among his other reform interests were temperance, the American Civil Liberties Union, and cooperative societies. His novel *Co-op* (1935) outlines the difficulties and the gains to be made from cooperation rather than competition in organizations. He is noted for writing an eleven-volume series on "Lanny Budd": it began in 1940 with *World's End* and included the Pulitzer Prize-winner *Dragons' Teeth* (1942) and *A World to Win* (1946); also he published *The Return of Lanny Budd* (1952).

See also EPIC Plan; Helicon Hall Colony

Sources:

Bloodsworth, William A. 1977. *Upton Sinclair*. Boston: Twayne.

Garraty, John A., ed. 1977. *Dictionary of American Biography*. Supplement 8. New York: Charles Scribner's Sons.

Harris, Leon. 1975. *Upton Sinclair: American Rebel*. New York: Thomas Y. Crowell.

Herms, Dieter, ed. 1990. *Upton Sinclair: Literature and Social Reform*. New York: Peter Lang.

Sinclair, Upton Beall. 1962. *The Autobiography of Upton Sinclair*. New York: Harcourt, Brace, and World.

Yoder, Jon A. 1975. *Upton Sinclair*. New York: Ungar.

SINGAPORE AS A CONFUCIAN-CAPITALIST UTOPIA. Singapore is a one-island nation at the tip of the Malay Peninsula, joined to the Malaysian mainland by a causeway, and has associated with it fifty-seven small islands. In 1819 it was leased from the sultan of Johore to the British East India Company, was placed under British Crown rule in 1858, and became part of the Straits Settlements (1867–1942). As a poverty-stricken port under British rule it was occupied by the Japanese during World War II (1942–1945). In 1945 the Singaporese and the Malays chose not to return to colonial domination. They sought self-determination, and it was granted in 1957. Singapore remained part of the Federation of Malaysia (1963) until antagonism between Malays and Chinese arose over alleged preferential treatment of Malays by Malaysia's federal government. The 1.7 million Chinese wanted their prime minister, Lee Kuan Yew (b. 1923), to have Singapore secede from Malaysia and to discuss the policy with Malaysia's Tengku Abdul Rahman (1903–1990) and arrive at some amicable agreement. In 1961 together they had formed "Greater Malaysia" to prevent left-wing groups' gaining control of Singapore. The Chinese of Singapore achieved their aim in August 1965, and Singapore became an independent nation within the British Commonwealth. The British maintained its base of 50,000 servicemen on Singapore until October 1971, when the Royal Navy warships departed, ending Britain's Far East command. Lee's People's Action Party dominated Singapore's one-chamber Parliament between 1968 and 1980. Lee chose capitalism for the nation's economy, welcomed multinational companies, curbed the power of trade unions, cut taxes, and supported free enterprise. He believed that through the free market Singapore would become the most productive nation with the highest standard of living in Asia—a truly utopian achievement— outside Brunei and Japan. It exports electronics, petroleum products, rubber, machinery, and vehicles. In 1984 an opposition, the Worker's Party, was able to get deputies elected to Parliament, and gradually Lee's personal control was eroded until he took firm action and conveniently found the leader of the Worker's Party guilty of perjury in November 1986. In 1990 Lee Kuan Yew was replaced by Goh Chock Tong, and the political system remains a liberal democracy with strict limits on dissent. Today it comprises 240 square miles of jungle, factories, skyscrapers, and beaches, and its people speak Chinese, Malay, Tamil, Hindi, and English and worship as Confucians, Buddhists, Taoists, Hindus, Christians, and Islamists. Citizens enjoy free medical care and education; tropical diseases are well under control; population growth is close to 1 percent; and by 1989 life expectancy had been raised to seventy-four years. Over 80 percent of the population read two of the nation's four official languages.

See Also Lee Kuan Yew

Sources:

Chew, Ernest C. T., and Edwin Lee, eds. 1991. *A History of Singapore*. New York: Oxford University Press.

International Council on Archives. 1989. *Guide to the Sources of History in Singapore*. Singapore: National Archives.

McCord, William. 1989. *Voyages to Utopia: From Monastery to Commune, the Search for the Perfect Society in Modern Times*. New York: W. W. Norton.

McHenry, Robert, ed. 1992. *The New Encyclopedia Britannica*. Chicago: Encyclopedia Britannica.

Turnbull, C. Mary. 1989. *A History of Singapore*. Rev. ed. New York: Oxford University Press.

SKANEATELES COMMUNITY. Skaneateles Community was a communal society originating in Mottville, Onandaga County, New York (1843–1846), under John Anderson Collins (c. 1810–1890). He forbade organized religion. It was a

Fourierist phalanx and joint-stock association whose members held reform meetings in and around Syracuse. The proposed constitution appeared in April, and by November a 300-acre site had been bought for $15,000, and thirty-six people were involved. Collins issued a statement of principles emphasizing anarchist politics and community of ownership, prohibiting consumption of meat, narcotics, and alcohol, and suggesting a philosophy of free love. The community wanted no coercion, militarism, taxation, or a legal system. Members preferred settling disputes peacefully. By early 1844 the colony had started farming and had adopted Fourierism to guide its philosophy. By 1846 after much hard work the community members had doubled the value of their property. A dispute arose between Collins and one of the original settlers, a Syracuse lawyer, who quit, disapproving of Collins' radical social views. Their dispute weakened the colony, and Collins, tired of the venture, withdrew. Although the community was unable to resolve disputes among its major leaders, it was noted among the phalanxes for its financial success. Those who left the community after a religious quarrel joined the Oneida community.

See Also Collins, John Anderson; Oneida community

Sources:

Fogarty, Robert S. 1980. *Dictionary of American Communal History.* Westport, Conn.: Greenwood Press.

Oved, Yaacov. 1987. *Two Hundred Years of American Communes.* New Brunswick, N.J.: Transaction Books.

Veysey, Laurence. 1973. *The Communal Experience: Anarchist and Mystical Countercultures in America.* New York: Harper and Row.

SKINNER, B. F. Burrhus Frederic Skinner (1904–1990) was born in Susquehanna, Pennsylvania, and educated at Hamilton College and Harvard University. He taught at Harvard (1931–1936) and Minnesota University (1936–1945) and returned to Harvard for the rest of his academic career. He took the ideas of John Broadus Watson (1878–1958) on the study of behavior and refined, clarified, and extended them in research into radical behaviorism. To Skinner psychology was best advanced through the scientific study of behavior and the removal from scientific psychology of mentalistic concepts. He devised a simple Skinner Box for the study of animal psychology, and the principles he discovered have been applied to the study of human learning. He wrote prolifically, and his influence on U.S. psychology has been immense. He influenced ideas on education by showing that by accommodating to the learner's needs and using regular and immediate feedback, learning becomes more efficient and effective. He applied the principles of learning that he established in the laboratory to the establishment of a new approach to child raising in *Walden Two* (1948), a utopian U.S. community that has attracted much attention for over forty years. He wrote the book, with the provisional title "The Sun Is but a Morning Star," in response to a deep personal crisis about his identity after disappointing reviews of his *The Behavior of Organisms* (1939), and when war-time projects and the understanding of his scientific research into operant (naturally occurring) behavior met with little acceptance. Although he did not believe that the writing of *Walden Two* or any literature was in itself of therapeutic value, in his case evidence is clear that working on the book helped him to resolve his midlife identity crisis (Elms, 1981). He wrote his long autobiography and was honored by the American Psychological Association (1958) and awarded its Gold Medal (1971) as well as the National Medal of Science (1968). In 1976 he reconsidered his views of *Walden Two*.

See Also Walden Two

Sources:

Elms, Alan C. 1981. "Skinner's Dark Year and *Walden Two.*" *American Psychologist* 36: 470–479. Reprinted in Alan C. Elms, 1994, *Uncovering Lives; The Uneasy Alliance of Biography and Psychology*. New York: Oxford University Press.
Skinner, B. Fred. 1967. "Autobiography." In E. G. Boring and G. Lindzey, eds., *A History of Psychology in Autobiography*. Vol. 5. New York: Appleton-Century-Crofts.
———. 1976. *Particulars of My Life*. New York: Knopf.
———. 1979. *The Shaping of a Behaviorist*. New York: Knopf.

SMALE, BILL. Bill Smale (b. 1944) was born in Liverpool, England, and raised in Devon and Liverpool by an affectionate Welsh mother and a distant, sometimes drunken English father. He attended grammar school and became an imitation of the British middle class, without its values. He drifted from one clerk's job to another until 1964, when he married and escaped to Australia, where he anticipated he could forge a secure identity in a classless society. Instead, he became another British misfit in Brisbane, like the one he had been in Devon. Bill turned to anarchist and utopian literature. In 1977 he entered communal life, a hippie house opposite his own in the inner suburbs of Brisbane. Within three months his own house was as open to the world as the hippies' place across the road. It filled with beautiful young proletarians, some silly, New Age, ignorant, and superstitious but all enjoying an enviable self-confidence. After two years and one police raid, Bill and his wife felt they wanted to settle in a rural holding. This was established in 1975, when Mandala was founded. A thirty-six-year-old ex-nun, a much conflicted individual, beautiful yet sinister, childlike but intelligent, had gotten 112 hectares (275 acres) southwest of Brisbane. She and her man wanted Bill and his wife to join them and help make a community. They planned to live by establishing a garment industry on the acreage. Bill and his wife sold their house, took their two children to England for three months, and, on returning at Christmas 1975, joined the eccentric ex-nun at Mandala. They built a house, grappled with the ex-nun's outlandish claims to authority, and salvaged the tottering community from under her. Using his bookkeeping skills and methods of participatory democracy, Bill kept the community reasonably stable. The struggle drained much from him, as he battled with problems of other people's pride and self-denial, spasms of despair and torment, and a tempest as the ex-nun and her man quit. Out of the dottiness and eccentricities of the founders emerged for Bill a secure disdain for the middle class and their social climbing, a deep acceptance of feminist principles, and a well-regulated, practical, anarchist community.

See Also Mandala

Source:

Smale, Bill. 1995. "From Outrage to Insight." In Bill Metcalf, ed., *From Utopian Dreaming to Communal Reality: Cooperative Life Styles in Australia*, pp. 99–114. Sydney: University of New South Wales Press.

SMITH, JOSEPH. Joseph Smith (1805–1844) was born in Sharon, Vermont. In 1820 he received a call as a prophet at Manchester, New York, and three years later he said that an angel told him about a hidden gospel on golden plates with two stones that could help to translate it from the "reformed" Egyptian. On 22 September 1827, at night, the sacred records were delivered to him. *The Book of Mormon* (1830) describes the history of the United States from colonization—a time of the confusion of tongues— to the fifth century of the Christian era. The book is said to have been written by a prophet named Mormon. The Church of the Latter-Day Saints was founded in Fayette, in New York (1830), and won converts despite much general hostility. In 1831 he announced the unique "United Order," a plan for the Latter-Day Saints (Mormons) at Kirtland, Ohio. The United Order was one of the earliest communal economic plans suggest by an American that melded cooperation with capitalism. Each head of a Mormon family was to give all possessions to the bishop and in return receive an inheritance to keep his family through efforts of private enterprise. The strict order was abandoned by most Mormons for a practical tithe of 10 percent. Its headquarters was established at Kirtland, Ohio, and it built Zion in Missouri. In 1838, during a riot against the Mormons in Missouri, Smith was arrested, a common practice for him by now. In 1840 the Mormon community moved to Illinois, founded Nauvoo, and within three years had 20,000 followers. Smith started having "spiritual wives." He was imprisoned with his brother Hyrum. In June 1844, 150 masked men broke into the jail in Carthage and shot them to death. The Mormons then chose Brigham Young (1801–1877) as their leader, and the Mormons moved west to Utah.

See Also Kirtland Community; Mormons; Young, Brigham

Sources:

Beardsley, Harry. 1931. *Joseph Smith and His Mormon Empire*. Boston: Houghton Mifflin.

Hill, Donna, ed. 1977. *Joseph Smith, the First Mormon*. Garden City, N.Y.: Doubleday.

Magnussen, Magnus, and Rosemary Goring, eds. 1990. *Chambers Biographical Dictionary*. 5th ed. Edinburgh: Chambers.

SMYTHE, WILLIAM ELLSWORTH. William Ellsworth Smythe (1861–1922) was born in Worcester, Massachusetts, and became a notable writer and editor and organized a colony in California, the "Little Landers." In 1891, as editor of the *Irrigation Age*, he organized conferences in Nebraska on irrigation, and in 1893 he planned a national conference in Los Angeles to consider water problems. He lectured widely on irrigation in western institutions and under the auspices of the Water and Forest Association and the Californian Constructive League on behalf of a radical form of water laws and the adoption of the Australian system of land settlement, 1901–1902. He believed that irrigation was the proper way to use water and that conservation policies would promote the rational use of land in the U.S. West. In southern California he believed it possible to establish a colony, Little Landers, where a family could live on one acre of irrigated land, if large sections of land were irrigated cooperatively. He was a Democratic candidate for Congress in 1902. In 1909 he launched the Little Landers Colony at San Ysido; Little Landers of Los Angeles, 1913; Runnymede, 1916. He founded the magazine *Little Lands* in 1916. No venture survived or could maintain a cooperative principle of land use. In 1915 the first settlement was lost to floods, and in 1917 Smythe turned to the American Homesteaders Organization, which supported workers who wanted to buy land and build their own home. Smythe published several books on irrigation and conservation: *The Conquest of Arid America* (1900), *Constructive Democracy* (1905), the *History of San Diego* (1907), *City Homes on Country Lanes* (1921), and *Homelanders of America* (1921).

See Also Little Landers Colonies

Sources:

Fogarty, Robert S. 1980. *Dictionary of American Communal History.* Westport, Conn.: Greenwood Press.
Hine, Robert V. 1953. *California's Utopian Colonies.* 1983 ed. Berkeley: University of California Press.

SNOW HILL NUNNERY. Snow Hill Nunnery was a group of fifty members organized and incorporated as the German Seventh Day Baptist Church in 1814. They settled at Schneeberg, now Snow Hill, Maryland, in one of the richest agricultural counties in the United States. The church itself had been established in 1709 by Swiss and French parishioners and later by the Germans in Franklin County, southeast Pennsylvania on the Susquehanna River. The community was established in 1798 and organized into three congregations of separate brother- and sisterhoods and modeled on the failed Ephrata Colony. Their spiritual leader and guide was Peter Lehman (1757–1823), who was from an Amish family in Glades, Somerset County, Pennsylvania, and who had joined the Ephrata Colony in the early 1770s before entering the Snow Hill Community in 1798. The congregations sought a communal life dominated by simplicity and informed by the mysticism practiced at Ephrata. Several celibate dwellings, a community house, and chapels were erected (1814–1843). Between 1820 and 1840, when the community flourished vigorously, the number of members was no more than forty. Printing and working the land were their major activities. Shortly after the Civil War (1861–1864) the community declined and disappeared. The monastic order was dissolved in 1900 and became a church society.

See Also Ephratans

Sources:

Fogarty, Robert S. 1980. *Dictionary of American Communal History*. Westport, Conn.: Greenwood Press.
Oved, Yaacov. 1987. *Two Hundred Years of American Communes*. New Brunswick, N.J.: Transaction Books.

SOCIAL DEMOCRACY. Social democracy is a political ideology with many intellectual and practical forms and today is accepted as the most prominent heir to humanist utopian thought and the many attempts to make the world a better place. It is often linked to events late in the nineteenth century, when August Bebel (1840–1914) founded the German Social Democratic Workers' Party (1869). In 1875 from it emerged the German Social Democrat Party. Early in the twentieth century social democracy spread through Austria, Belgium, the Netherlands, Hungary, Poland, and Russia, and in Britain the Labor Party owed much to the social democrat tradition. Social democracy became a distinct ideology when espoused by followers of Karl Marx (1818–1883). In Britain H. M. Hyndman (1842–1921), a conservative stockbroker and political figure, led the Socialist Democratic Federation, which in 1911 became the British Socialist Party. Under Vladimir Lenin (1870–1924), Bolsheviks constituted the Russian Democrat Party. After the Russian revolution (1917), when Lenin took control, a split grew between those who sought socialist goals through revolution and others who preferred the gradual reforming of society and its economy through Parliament. Reforming socialists were those who joined the Fabians in Britain, and preferred *réformisme* in France and revisionism in Germany. In Russia social democrats demanded their country follow the parliamentary method to socialism and avoid costly violence and oppressive dictatorship. They upheld civil rights and the freedom and independence of trade unions. In recent years social democrats have supported the welfare state and asserted that the state should maintain national prosperity and justice. This assumes market forces should be checked wherever injustices arise due to their fluctuations. Northern Ireland formed its Social Democratic Labor Party (1970), aimed for Irish unification, and distanced itself from the violence of the Irish Republican Army (IRA), preferring a constitutional, conciliatory method for Irish reform. Recently, in Britain the Social Democratic Party formed with disaffected members of the British Labor Party (1981–1990). In June 1990 David Owen (b.1938), its leader from 1983, and a majority of members voted to dissolve it. Today the fundamental beliefs on social democracy constitute a utopian image of a future society where work is at the center of personal development and a protection for personal identity. Between individuals cooperation—taking part in joint activities harmoniously—is upheld, as are voluntary membership in all associations—unions, clubs, societies—and basic support for those members in need. The modern social democracy supports a humane or civilized form of capitalism, combined with social and liberal reform. Religion would give over to a systematic organization of social labor; education would be for life rather than qualifications for a post in capitalist and government bureaucracies; and experience would be given the same status as educational achievement. The preferred knowledge would be scientific. Work would be done in large-scale units, but under decentralized control; technology would be used to cut the burden of labor; all people would be obliged to work but would have the choice of an occupation; work would be done as much for enjoyment as productivity; mental and physical labor would be integrated; women would have exactly the same political and economic status as men; no person would be tied for his or her working life to one occupation; freedom at work would come by increasing production rather than restricting consumption; as citizens, people would integrate their rights with their duties; cities would become the centers of utopian social democracies, but this change would evolve, not come suddenly. In such a social democratic society the miseries of capitalism—poverty, maldistribution of wealth, ungratifying work—would evaporate. Nowadays, intellectuals are divided on the future of social democracy. Optimists hope for it and agree it is an unfulfilled project; pessimists believe it will fail as did the Weimar Republic, which was followed by Hitler's Germany and afterward by the problematic social administration of modern Germany. The intellectual origins of social democracy belong with the history of the great utopian thinkers, especially those of the eighteenth and nineteenth centuries, and can be traced through More's *Utopia*, to the social philosophers at the time of the French Revolution (1789–1815), the ideas and work of, for example, Robert Owen (1771–1858) and his followers, Saint-Simon (1760–1825), Karl Marx and Friedrich Engels (1820–1895), Charles Fourier (1772–1837), Étienne Cabet (1778–1856), Edward Bellamy (1850–1898), Max Weber (1864–1920), Sidney (1859–1947) and Beatrice (1858–1943) Webb, Richard H. Tawney (1880–1962), Leon Trotsky 1879–1940), and William H. Beveridge (1879–1963).

Sources:

Beilharz, Peter. 1992. *Labour's Utopias: Bolshevism, Fabianism, Social Democracy.*
        London: Routledge.
Owen, David. 1981. *Face the Future.* Rev. ed. Oxford: Oxford University Press.
Vaizey, John E. 1971. *Social Democracy.* London: Weidenfeld and Nicolson.

SOCIETY OF BROTHERS (BRUDERHOF). Society of Brothers (Bruderhof) is a utopian sect established in Sannerz, Germany (1920) with later communities in Liechtenstein, England, Paraguay, Uruguay, and the United States. Only three communities existed in the early 1970s, all in the United States. Through Ebhard

Arnold (1883–1935) the German sect reestablished itself in the Rhone Mountains in 1927. The Bruderhof lived in poverty because their land use had a low yield of crops, some land was taken for debts, and funds were used to meet the requirements of the needy. They published books on Christian studies of the forthcoming new order and developed a shaky alliance with Hutterites in late 1930. The Nazis took total control of education and religious institutions in Germany after 1933, so the Bruderhof moved to establish a community at Liechtenstein. The Gestapo closed down the Bruderhof in the Rhone Mountains in 1937. After the founder's death in 1935 the Liechtenstein group went to England to found a community at Ashton Keynes, Wiltshire. After World War II began, the English Bruderhof were permitted to leave Britain and emigrate to the only country that would have them, Paraguay (1941), where they established several small communities based on the Primavera Estate. In ten years their numbers rose to 600, and in 1952 a group established a small community near Montevideo, Uruguay. Those who remained in Britain established the Wheathill Bruderhof (1942) and the Bulstrode Community outside London (1958). After World War II the South American members developed a working relationship with Quakers in the United States and in 1954, north of New York City, established the Woodcrest Community at Rifton. In Pennsylvania, Oak Lake was founded (1957), and Evergreen was founded in Connecticut. Wheathill Community closed in 1960, and Bulstrode closed in 1966. The Bruderhof purged dissenters and purified itself by expulsion (1958–1962). Its formal organization, techniques of control, religious practices and economic principles, family and educational policies, and relations with the outside world are described by Whitworth (1975, pp. 181–209).

See Also Arnold, Eberhard; Bruderhof

Sources:

Armytage, Walter H. Green. 1959. "The Wheathill Bruderhof 1942–58." *American Journal of Economics and Sociology* 18: 285–294.

———. 1961. *Heavens Below: Utopian Experiments in England 1560–1950*. London: Routledge and Kegan Paul.

Arnold, Emmy. 1963. *Torches Together*. Woodcrest, Rifton, N.Y.: Plough Publishing House.

Fretz, Josph Winfield. 1962. *Immigrant Group Settlements in Paraguay: A Study of the Sociology of Colonization*. North Newton, Kans.: Bethel College.

Merchant, W. 1952a. "The Bruderhof Communities—I." *Co-operative Living* 3, no. 2: 13–15.

———. 1952b. "The Bruderhof Communities—II." *Co-operative Living* 3, no. 3: 4–6.

———. 1952c. "The Bruderhof Communities—III." *Co-operative Living* 4, no. 1: 8–11.

Oved, Yaacov. 1987. *Two Hundred Years of American Communes*. New Brunswick, N.J.: Transaction Books.

Whitworth, John McK. 1971. "The Bruderhof in England: A Chapter in the History of a Utopian Sect." *Year Book of Sociology of Religion in Britain*, no. 4: 84–101.

———. 1975. *God's Blueprints: A Sociological Study of Three Utopian Sects*. London: Routledge and Kegan Paul.

SOJNTULA. Sojntula, British Columbia, was a Finnish utopia on Malcolm Island whose members sought escape from the mines of Vancouver Island. They aimed to advance their children's education under the leadership of Matti Kurikka (1863–1915). In Australia Kurikka found alcohol had thwarted his attempt to establish utopian settlements near Chillagoe, Queensland (1899); he also thought churches should not be permitted in a utopian venture and held unusual views on sexual practices. Temperance and anticlericalism were the main principles governing Sojntula. Workers received a standard wage and their board. Even though its cultural interests were well supported, the venture failed because the Kalevan Kansan Colonisation Association, its founder, was not competent in financial management. Also the settlement failed to establish its fishing and lumbering business soundly, and in 1903 a fire damaged property severely. That year Kurikka departed, the community declined, and debts rose, and finally the settlement collapsed in 1904, when a bridge-building venture, which was planned to relieve the community of debt, failed to meet its costs. Much blame was heaped on Kurikka, who was criticized for his attitude to free love and financial mismanagement. When it failed, the community of 250 split ideologically, and one faction tried unsuccessfully to establish another utopia in Fraser Valley.

See Also Kurikka, Matti

Sources:

Kolehmainem, John. 1941. "Harmony Island: A Finnish Utopian Venture in British Columbia." *British Columbia Historical Quarterly* 5, no. 2: 114.

Rasporich, Anthony W. 1992. "Utopian Ideals and Community Settlements in Western Canada 1880–1914." In R. Douglas, ed., *The Prairie West: Historical Readings*, pp. 338–361. Edmonton: Pica Pica Press.

Wilson, Donald J. 1973. "Matti Kurikka: Finnish-Canadian Intellectual." *British Columbia Studies* 20: 65.

SOUTHCOTT, JOANNA. Joanna Southcott (1750–1814) was born in Gittisham, East Devon, the fourth daughter of a poor farmer. Until she was forty, she worked as a dairy maid, and domestic servant and, later, as an upholsterer. Close study of the Bible underpinned her detailed knowledge of even its most obscure books. At Christmas 1791 she joined the Wesleyans. On Easter Monday 1792 she predicted the locusts of Abaddon would envelop the world. An established religious visionary, she retired to her sister's home in Devon, where she began to write her prophecies, in a "mixture of doggerel verse and rambling prose." As early as 1794 she had identified herself with the woman in Revelation XII. In 1801 she invested £100, her life savings, in printing *The Strange Effects of Faith*, the first of her many books and pamphlets. The printer included two shillings and sixpence in his invoice "for correcting the spelling and grammar of the prophesies.'' She eventually moved to London, where at High House, Paddington, she began to attract the faithful, eventually gaining an estimated 20,000 adherents. In October 1802 she foretold that she would give birth to Shiloh, the Prince of Peace, the second Christ. Her fame grew rapidly in 1803–1804; she organized her followers to observe the Sabbath and the Jewish practice of using only "clean" meat. Beginning in 1802, for a fee, she issued seals and signed papers for those who accepted her writings. The seal ensured the recipient would inherit the Tree of Life and be redeemed from sin and become an heir of both God and Jesus Christ. A chapel was opened for her in Southwark in the spring of 1805. Before her death she had published sixty-five books and circulated enough manuscripts to fill many more. Her box of writings weighed 156 pounds and was kept by her disciples, the Southcottians. In October 1813 she went into seclusion, intending to give birth to the Prince of Peace, and in March 1814, aged sixty-four, fell sick, died of dropsy in December, and was buried at St. John's Wood. At that time she had thousands of followers and had published *A Warning* (1803) and the *Book of Wonders* (1813–1814).

See Also Southcottians

Sources:

Balleine, George R. 1956. *Past Finding Out: The Tragic Story of Joanna Southcott and Her Successors*. London: S.P.C.K.

Hopkins, James K. 1982. *A Woman to Deliver Her People: Joanna Southcott and English Millenarianism in an Era of Revolution*. Austin: University of Texas Press.

Magnussen, Magnus, and Rosemary Goring, eds. 1990. *Chambers Biographical Dictionary*. 5th ed. Edinburgh: Chambers.

Seymour, Alice, ed. 1909. *The Express, Containing the Life and Divine Writings of the Late Joanna Southcott*. 1916 ed. London: Simpkin, Marshall.

Stephen, Leslie and Sydney Lee, eds. 1917. *The Dictionary of National Biography*. London: Oxford University Press.

Todd, Janet, ed. 1985. *A Dictionary of British and American Women Writers 1660–1800*. Totowa, N.J.: Rowman and Allanheld.

SOUTHCOTTIANS. Southcottians, an early nineteenth-century religious community, followed Joanna Southcott (1750–1814), who claimed she would give birth to a Prince of Peace as indicated in Revelation XII: "and there appeared a great wonder in heaven, a woman with the sun and the moon at her feet and upon her head a crown of twelve stars. And she being with child cried, travailing in birth and pained to be delivered . . . and she brought forth a man child who was to rule all nations with a rod of iron; and her child was caught up unto God and to his throne." Among her followers, mainly artisans and a few genteel folk, were an estimated 20,000 who bought from her a seal that gave them high hopes of being among the 144,000 elect. They had a chapel in London after 1805. After her death the movement survived under different leaders and had followers in the United States, Canada, and Australia. Southcott's adherents believed she had been chosen to be God's perfectly obedient servant and that she would announce that Jesus would end the world's evil, which had been forced upon humankind by a temptress in the Garden of Eden. In time all women would make all men good by giving birth to the spiritual children of God. Southcott herself would be the model for this happy event. She died, making this prediction, at age sixty-four. Her sealed box of prophecies was not to be opened unless twenty-four bishops were present. The box was opened before only one bishop in 1927. It contained trivia. Some believers think the wrong box was opened. Pandora Society members are still waiting. The Southcottians are probably extinct today.

See Also Southcott, Joanna

Sources:

Cross, L. A., and E. A. Livingstone. 1997. *The Oxford Dictionary of the Christian Church.* 3d ed. New York: Oxford University Press.
Douglas, James D., ed. 1974. *The New International Dictionary of the Christian Church.* Exeter: Paternoster Press.
Harrison, John F. C. 1979. *The Second Coming: Popular Millenarianism, 1780–1850.* New Brunswick, N.J.: Rutgers University Press.
Hastings, James. 1920. *Encyclopedia of Religion and Ethics.* Edinburgh: T. and J. Clark.

SOUTHEY, ROBERT. Robert Southey (1774–1843) was born in Bristol. His father was a linen draper. Much of his upbringing was under the strict care of maiden aunt Miss Tyler, who influenced his bleak view of life. At age fifteen, when the French Revolution began, he became a passionate sympathizer of the revolutionary cause. He was expelled from Westminster School for writing an attack against flogging. In 1792 at Balliol College, Oxford, he met Samuel Taylor Coleridge (1772–1834), then an undergraduate at Cambridge, who converted him to Unitarianism and pantisocracy. He, Coleridge, and Southey's friend Robert Lovell (c.1770–1796) evolved a plan for a settlement in the United States to be run on egalitarian, pantisocratic principles. Southey married Edith Fricker in November 1795. The pantisocracy plan fell through after Lovell's death in April 1796. Deeply affected by the loss, the Southeys went to Lisbon for two years and later in 1800 visited Spain. In 1803 Southey went to live in Greta Hall in Keswick, North England, where Coleridge was already living with his wife, Sarah, Edith's sister. In 1809 he began thirty years' work as a regular contributor to the *Quarterly*, expounding his views on the measures necessary to save the country. In 1813 he accepted the office of poet laureate. Some of his published works were *Life of Wesley* (1820), *Visions of Judgment* (1821), and two commonplace books, *Omniana* (1812) and *The Doctor* (1837). He took no active part in politics, preferring to stay at his Keswick retreat as the kindly head of his own pantisocratic republic. His eldest son, Herbert, died at age nine in 1816, and the loss greatly affected Southey. His wife was even more severely affected by the death of their daughter in 1826, and she died in a lunatic asylum in 1837. In 1839 Southey was married a second time to poet Caroline Bowles, but shortly after, he became demented and died in March 1843. Four of his seven children survived.

See Also Coleridge, Samuel Taylor; Lovell, Robert; Pantisocracy

Sources:

Carnall, Geoffrey. 1964. *Robert Southey.* London: Longmans, Green.
Stephen, Leslie, and Sydney Lee, eds. 1917. *The Dictionary of National Biography.* London: Oxford University Press.

SPARTACISTS. Spartacists (Spartakusbund) were left-wing revolutionaries among Germany's social democrats during the summer of 1915. They supported the communist revolution of 1918, when the German Communist Party was established. They took their name from Spartacus (d. 71 B.C.), a Roman gladiator who led a revolt of 90,000 slaves, army deserters, and renegades and withstood the Roman army for two years. The leaders of the modern Spartacists, or Spartacus League, were Rosa Luxemburg (1871–1919) and Karl Liebknecht (1871–1919), who had parted from the social democrats in Germany, 1917, called for the end of World War I, and supported Bolsheviks in the Russian revolution and the toppling of Germany's government in favor of workers' and soldiers' Soviets. In 1919 the Spartacists reorganized as the Communist Party of Germany and attacked violently the Republican government of Friedrich Ebert (1871–1925) after the kaiser had abdicated (November 1918). Luxemburg and Liebknecht were both murdered by army officers in the German Freikorps, January 1919, during the Berlin workers' revolt.

See Also Ebert, Friedrich; Liebknecht, Karl; Luxemburg, Rosa; Social democracy

Sources:

Geras, Norman. 1976. *The Legacy of Rosa Luxemburg.* London: N.L.B.
Howard, Dick, ed. 1971. *Selected Political Writings of Rosa Luxemburg.* New York: Monthly Review Press.
Wieczynski, Joseph, ed. 1984. *The Modern Encyclopedia of Russian and Soviet History.* Gulf Breeze, Fla.: Academic International Press.

SPEAR, JOHN MURRAY. John Murray Spear (1804–1877) founded Harmonia, a model community. Little is known about his early life. He was a Universalist minister, and during the 1840s, he and his brother Charles were active in prison reform. They published a weekly, *The Prisoner's Friend.* In 1852 Spear began to receive spirit messages instructing him to make radical changes to society and establish a model community. A year later he received further spirit messages indicating where and how to begin a colony that upheld universal harmony. Directives on house design and various social reforms came from heaven for a colony called Harmonia, the Association of Beneficents, or the Domaine. It was located near the village of Kiantone, Chautauqa County, New York. It comprised ten oval and octagonal houses. The National Spiritualists Convention was held at the site in 1855, and rumors scandalized the local community by suggesting spiritualism and free love were synonymous, a common view among Americans in the 1850s. In 1859 Spear received another spirit message urging him to organize a group to be called "the Sacred Order of Unionists" to promote world government. A small group set out on the steamer *Cleopatra* for New Orleans, and on the way they established a colony at Sacred Patriot, Indiana. By 1861 they had spent all their money, and the Sacred Order entered the sewing machine business with help from John Orvis (1816–1897). The scheme failed, and by 1863 Orvis had dissolved the order. Spear and his wife divorced, and he married a member of the community in 1863. Spear then moved to London, where he met with notable spiritualists. In 1877 he returned to the United States, where he died soon after.

See Also Harmonia; Orvis, John

Sources:

Fogarty, Robert S. 1980. *Dictionary of American Communal History*. Westport, Conn.: Greenwood Press.

Myerson, Joel. 1978. *Brook Farm: An Annotated Bibliography and Resources Guide*. New York: Garland.

SPENCE, THOMAS. Thomas Spence (1750–1814) was born in Newcastle upon Tyne, one of nineteen children, and was taught to read by his father. He became a clerk, teacher, and bookseller. A lawsuit between the corporation and freemen of his hometown concerning some common land is said to have first turned Spence's attention to the question of land reform, his life's mission. In 1775 he submitted his views on land tenure to the Philosophical Society in a paper, "The Real Rights of Man." In 1801 the attorney general filed information against Spence for writing and publishing a seditious libel, *The Restorer of Society to Its Natural State*. Spence was imprisoned for twelve months. His disciples were known as Spenceans. In 1816 Spence's plan was revived, and the Society of Spencean Philanthropists was established. The Spenceans considered other social issues of the day besides land reform, and one of their notable projects was to petition Parliament to do away with machines.

See Also Spensonia

Source:

Stephen, Leslie, and Sydney Lee, eds. 1917. *The Dictionary of National Biography*. London: Oxford University Press.

SPENSONIA. Spensonia was a British utopia proposed by Thomas Spence (1750–1814). He recommended that the inhabitants of every parish should form a corporation in which the land should be forever vested. Parish officers would collect rents, deduct state and local expenses, and divide the rest among the parishioners. There would be no tolls or taxes levied beyond rent; all goods, manufactures, and employment would be duty-free, and public libraries in schools would be supported from the local fund. Every man would have to serve in a militia, and each year the parish would choose a representative for a national assembly. Every five days there would be a day of rest. These proposals were often printed and sold in a London pamphlet in 1796 as *The Meridian Sun of Liberty*.

See Also Spence, Thomas

Sources:

Spence, Thomas. 1795. *Description of Spensonia. Constitution of Spensonis.* Leamington Spa: Courier Press.

————. c. 1796. *The Restorer of Society to Its Natural State. In a Series of Letters to a Fellow Citizen. Including the Constitution of Spensonia: A Country in Fairy-Land Situated between Utopia and Oceania Brought from Thence by Captain Swallow.* 4th ed. Ascribed in the text to Mr. Spence. [Microform, 1987] Alexandria, Va.: Chadwyck-Healey.

SPERANZA. Speranza was an Icarian community. From the Jeune Icarie Community emerged an Icarian splinter group that went to Cloverdale, California, and formed Icaria Speranza for five years, 1881–1886. Fifty-five families joined the group in 1884 on 900 acres of land seventy-five miles north of San Francisco. It was the last of the Icarian splinter groups. They accepted and followed Icarian practices except that their constitution permitted some private ownership. The commune was dissolved, and the property was divided among the members once they realized that neither funds nor members were likely to be transferred from Jeune Icarie.

See Also Cabet, Étienne; Cheltenham; Corning; Icarian movement, Texas-Nauvoo

Sources:

Fogarty, Robert S. 1980. *Dictionary of American Communal History.* Westport, Conn.: Greenwood Press.

Hine, Robert V. 1953. *California's Utopian Colonies.* 1983 ed. Berkeley: University of California Press.

Oved, Yaacov. 1987. *Two Hundred Years of American Communes.* New Brunswick, N.J.: Transaction Books.

SPINELLI, ALTIERO. Altiero Spinelli (1907–1986) was born in Rome and became a strong opponent of the Italian dictator Benito Mussolini (1883–1945). An intellectual and political activist, Spinelli spent much time in prison and was confined to an island off the coast of Rome and Naples (1927–1943). On his release he was active in the Italian underground resistance. He advocated following the precise thinking of British federalists and helped in secret to draft a plan for resolving conflict in Europe with resistance workers from eight countries of Europe, including Germany. He founded the European Federalist movement (1943), was elected to the Italian Parliament (1946), and from 1961 to

1964 was at the Center for Advanced International Studies. He also founded the Institute of International Affairs (Rome). He was director in 1966. He was a member of the European Commission (1970–1976) and a member of the European Parliament from 1976. In Brussels he was appointed commissioner for European Communities (1976–1979), was elected a deputy on the communist list, and became a member of the Foreign Affairs Commission. He worked for a utopian scheme to unify Europe—Spinelli Initiative. It was partly realized in the Single European Act (1986). Because the act was not as comprehensive as his original plan, Spinelli criticized it vigorously. Among the books that he published were *The Eurocrats* (1966) and *The European Adventure* (1973). In 1984 he published his autobiography.

Sources:

Coppa, Frank J. 1985. *Dictionary of Modern Italian History*. Westport, Conn.: Greenwood Press.
Groeg, Otto J. 1980. *Who's Who in Italy*. 3d ed. Milan: Who's Who in Italy.
Keesing's Contemporary Archives: Record of World Events. 1986. Entry 34629. London: Keesings.
McHenry, Robert, ed. 1992. *The New Encyclopedia Britannica*. Chicago: Encyclopedia Britannica.
Who's Who 1986. London: A. and C. Black.

SPINELLI INITIATIVE. A utopian scheme, plan, or movement—Movimento Federalista Europeo—for a Federal European Community. The plan proposed more power for European, rather than nation-based, institutions in Europe, for example, European Parliament and the European Economic Commission. The plan was basic to the Draft Treaty on European Union that the European Parliament endorsed in February 1984; the plan led in January 1986 to the Single European Act. In time this policy was taken up in the Maastricht Treaty.
   See Also Spinelli, Altiero

Sources:

Barav, Arni, ed. 1993. *Commentary on the EC Community and the Single European Act*. Oxford: Clarendon Press.
Burgess, Michael, ed. 1986. *Federalism and Federation in Western Europe*. London: Croom Helm.
Glaesner, H. J. 1988. *The Single European Act*. Luxembourg: Office for Official Publications of the European Communities.

SPIRIT FRUIT SOCIETY. The Spirit Fruit Society began as a gathering of thirteen people in a colony of spiritualists and theosophists. Toward the end of the century Jacob Beilhart (1867–1908) organized the gathering and preached that there is one universal spirit; that humankind is undeveloped; that it has yet to manifest its fruit; and that the full fruit of humankind is to attain a Christlike state. People would achieve this state and receive the Spirit Fruit, the Spirit of Christ, if they acted unselfishly and did good works. In 1901 Beilhart incorporated the Spirit Fruit Society at home with his family in Lisbon, Ohio. This small group believed in freedom, including sexual freedom. ''The Home,'' as the gathering was called by neighbors, was criticized in newspapers because it renounced conventional marriage. Neighborhood pressure forced Beilhart and his followers to leave the farm and Lisbon in 1905, and they relocated on ninety acres at Ingleside, northwest of Chicago. The members built a spacious mansion for themselves and a barn. After Beilhart died, the colony continued without a clear leader. In 1913 they moved to a rural landholding, Hilltop Ranch, near Santa Cruz, California. The society survived, but membership declined, and by the late 1920s it had all but vanished due to personality conflicts and the death of its members. The society was dissolved in 1930.

See Also Beilhart, Jacob

Sources:

Fogarty, Robert S. 1980. *Dictionary of American Communal History.* Westport, Conn.: Greenwood Press.

Grant, Roger H. 1988. *Spirit Fruit: A Gentle Utopia.* DeKalb: Northern Illinois University Press.

Murphy, James L. 1989. *The Reluctant Radicals: Jacob Beilhart and the Spirit Fruit Society.* Lanham, Md.: University Press of America.

SPRING, MARCUS. Marcus Spring (1810–1874) was born in Northbridge, Massachusetts, and came from a Congregationalist and Unitarian background. He attended Uxbridge Academy and in adulthood became a Quaker. In 1831 he went to New York, where he was a successful cotton merchant and took great interest in reform movements. He and his wife were frequent travelers and gave support to many cooperative projects. He was one of the oldest and largest of the nonresident stockholders in the North American Phalanx, and he raised his share in it to $6,000 in the early 1850s. He was never a resident, but he built a summer house on the property. Although the community's economic success pleased him, Spring felt the social and cultural progress of the community and its spiritual development had failed. He persuaded some of the members to establish a new community, the Raritan Bay Union, Perth Amboy, New Jersey (1852). This move cost the North American Phalanx a quarter of its membership and capital; consequently, in 1855 its creditors agreed to liquidate the phalanx. The property was sold, and the stockholders got back about 57 percent of their investment. Also the Raritan Bay Union was not a success because the idea of a collective economy was abandoned for the principle of individual independence. Spring spent $40,000 on the erection of a large stone phalansetry, later to be used as a school, and it was built across a substantial lawn from a spacious family dwelling. He lived on the site of the Raritan Bay Union until he died in the spring of 1874.

See Also Raritan Bay Union

Source:

Hayden, Delores. 1976. *Seven American Utopias*. Cambridge: MIT Press.
Spann, Edward K. 1989. *Brotherly Tomorrows: Movements for a Cooperative Society in America 1820–1920*. New York: Columbia University Press.

STAKHANOV, ALEXEI GRIGORIEVICH. Alexei Grigorievich Stakhanov (c.1905–1977) was born in Lugovaia, Orel Province. As a brakeman, he worked at the Tsentral'naia-Irmino Mine, Kadievka (Donbas), in 1927, and later he became a pneumatic drill operator, or cutter, in a coal mine (1933). In 1935, after completing a course for cutters at the mine, he set a record on 30–31 August by extracting 102 tons of coal in a six-hour night shift. This was over fourteen times the quota of seven tons. He and his timberman achieved this by efficient division of their labor. Stalin (1879–1953) is alleged to have praised his efforts, and this ensured that the achievement attracted enough support throughout the Soviet Union to provide a basis for the Stakhanovite movement. After becoming a member of the Communist Party, he studied at Moscow's Industrial Academy (1936–1941), was a mine chief for two years, and worked at the Ministry of Coal Industry (1943–1957). From 1957 to 1959 he was deputy director of the Chistiakovan-tratsil Trust; and in 1959 he was assistant chief engineer of Mine Administration. In 1970 he was made a Hero of Soviet Labor and retired in 1974.

See Also Stakhanovite movement

Sources:

Magnussen, Magnus, and Rosemary Goring, eds. 1990. *Chambers Biographical Dictionary*. 5th ed. Edinburgh: Chambers.
Wieczynski, Joseph, ed. 1984. *The Modern Encyclopedia of Russian and Soviet History*. Gulf Breeze, Fl. Academic International Press.

STAKHANOVITE MOVEMENT. The Stakhanovite movement was a utopian scheme to improve the work of the Russian worker by setting a good example. It was named for Alexei Grigorievich Stakhanov (c.1905–1977). The movement had utopian aims and comprised workers, engineers and technicians who aimed to raise the productivity of labor. After World War II engineers in Western mining ventures were drawn to the Stakhanovite principles and tried to introduce them in their mines. Often they were met with strong resistance by unions. Work was organized into brigades, sections, and units—not unlike shock troops—and achieved remarkably high levels of productivity during the Second Five Year Plan (1933–1937) and World War II. It followed principles of one man to two machines, combinations of functions allocated to one position, and accelerated production and construction rates.

See Also Stakhanov, Alexei Grigorievich

Source:

Prokhorov, A. M., ed. 1980. *Great Soviet Encyclopedia*. New York: Macmillan.

STALIN, JOSEPH. Joseph Stalin, pseudonym of Iosif Vissarionovich Dzhugashvili (1879–1953), was born near Tiflis, Georgia, the son of a shoemaker. He attended a theological seminary near Tiflis but was expelled for spreading Marxist propaganda. In 1896 he joined the Social Democratic Party and sided with the Bolsheviks after the party split in 1903; he was often exiled to Siberia for political activity (1904–1913) but always managed to escape. He took the name Stalin, "Man of Steel," from activities before the Russian revolution. A close associate of Lenin, Stalin took part in the 1917 revolution and became a member of its military council (1920–1923). Following Lenin's death (1924) Stalin established himself as Russia's dictator and is now held fully responsible for murderous purges in most aspects of Russian life during his rule. Following the Nazi invasion of Russia in 1941 he became commissar for defense and chairman of the Council People's Commissars, thus taking over supreme direction of military operations. In 1943 he was created marshal of the Soviet Union. Until his death he held personal power over all Russia.

Sources:

Bullock, Alan. 1991. *Hitler and Stalin: Parallel Lives*. London: HarperCollins.
Franklin, Bruce, ed. 1973. *The Essential Stalin*. London: Croom Helm.
Jonge, Alex de. 1986. *Stalin*. London: Collins.
Lacqueur, Walter. 1990. *Stalin: The Glasnost Revelations*. London: Unwin Hyman.
McNeal, Robert Hatch. 1988. *Stalin: Man and Ruler*. Basingstoke: Macmillan and St. Antony's College, Oxford.
Tucker, Robert C. 1990. *Stalin in Power: The Revolution from Above, 1928–1941*. New York: Norton.

STALINIST RUSSIA. Stalinist Russia (1924–1953) involved the collectivization of agriculture and the industrialization of Russia's secondary industry by the use of murderous purges and forced labor camps; secret policy making and brutal forms of bureaucratic terrorism; the development of a personality cult favoring Stalin as hero; a foreign policy of hostility to all capitalism; and the revision of all history and literature to this end. The reversal of Stalinism began with de-Stalinization (February 1956) in Nikita Khrushchev's (1894–1971) "secret" speech against Stalin's personal reign of terror and the separation of Stalinism from earlier conceptions of Marxist ideology.

See Also Khrushchev, Nikita Sergeyevich; Stalin, Joseph

Sources:

Cohen, Stephen F. 1985. *Rethinking the Soviet Experience*. New York: Oxford University Press.
Kumar, Krishan. 1987. *Utopia and Anti-Utopia in Modern Times*, pp. 381–383. Oxford: Basil Blackwell.
———. 1991. *Utopianism*, pp. 84–85, 79. Milton Keynes: Open University Press.
Tucker, Robert C. 1990. *Stalin in Power*. New York: Norton.

STEINER, RUDOLF. Rudolf Steiner (1861–1925), an Austrian social philosopher, scientist, and artist, was the son of a railway stationmaster. He was educated in Vienna, much of it through his own efforts; he edited Goethe's scientific writings and published his Ph.D. thesis, *Truth and Science*, and, in 1894, *The Philosophy of Freedom*. After studying Goethe's ideas closely, he turned to theosophy and eventually developed his anthroposophy. Anthroposophy has mystical and spiritual features, rejects materialism, and aims to develop the whole person, intellectually and socially, as well as spiritually. He believed people are reincarnated often before they are fully self-aware. He edited a journal in Berlin, lectured at a workingman's college, and studied the knowledge produced by man's higher self. In 1912–1913 he founded the Anthroposophical Society and in 1913 began to build his first school of spiritual science. He lectured on the arts and on medicine; he reintroduced to medicine the concept of the "humors." Steiner's main contribution was to give a detailed account of child development—later confirmed by prominent child psychologists—and a curriculum designed to support the development of the child, with strong emphasis on the physical as well as psychological aspects of maturation. He also lectured on agriculture, introducing the effects of the lunar cycle on plant growth. He built the Goethanum, Dornach, Switzerland, the world center for anthroposophy.

See Also Rudolf Steiner school

Sources:

Babel, Ulrich, and Craig Giddens, comps. 1977–1979. *Bibliographical Reference List of the Published Works of Rudolf Steiner*. English trans. London: Rudolf Steiner Press.

Davy, John, ed. 1975. *Work Arising from the Life of Rudolf Steiner*. London: Rudolf Steiner Press.

McDermott, Robert A., ed. 1984. *The Essential Steiner: Basic Writings of Rudolf Steiner*. San Francisco: Harper and Row.

Wilson, Colin. 1985. *Steiner: The Man and His Vision*. Wellingborough: Aquarian Press.

STELLE. Stelle ("place" in German) was founded in Illinois, about seventy-five miles south of Chicago in 1973 by Richard Kieninger (b.1927). It was built in preparation for doomsday predicted for the year 2000. Kieninger was directed by the Brotherhoods and aimed to survive the prediction and bring about a postapocryphal Kingdom of God. Stelle had forty-four houses and around 125 people (1984). The group itself was begun by Kieninger and his wife, Gail, in 1963. Its membership and capital gradually increased until 1970, when the group purchased 240 acres south of Chicago. They built a factory to support their woodworking industry and began building houses, streets, and footpaths. They also have a large water purification plant. Stelle Industries became the profit wing of the organization, and the Stelle Group is a nonprofit organization. In the early 1970s splits in the group opened further with the breakdown of the Kieninger marriage and subsequent divorce in 1976. Richard left temporarily and established a small community, Adelphi, in Texas. Gail left permanently. The group believes in the importance of the interaction between the physical environment and people's actions and thoughts. The community members live in earthquake-proof houses, and they aim to develop a self-sufficient economy and store food and all the necessities in preparation for doomsday. At the age of three and four, children are taught to read and write, and they go to school in the community school, where learning is generally at an accelerated level. In the early 1980s economic problems forced the community to allow nonresident members to join the community. Kieninger's life story, *The Ultimate Frontier* (1963), is the central text for the community and was written under the pen name Eklal Kueshana.

Source:

Popenoe, Cris, and Oliver Popenoe. 1984. *Seeds of Tomorrow*. San Francisco: Harper and Row.

STRAIGHT, DOROTHY WHITNEY. Dorothy Whitney Straight (1887–1968) was born in Washington, D.C., the daughter of William Collins Whitney (1841–1904), secretary of the navy in the Democratic administration of President Grover Cleveland (1837–1908). Both her parents were immensely wealthy. When Dorothy was six, her mother died, and eleven years later her father died. At seventeen Dorothy was an orphan and an heiress. During her late teens and early twenties she traveled to Europe and developed a personal interest in the Junior League, the suffragette movement, and the Women's Trade Union League. In 1911 she married Willard Dickerman Straight (1880–1918). Together they established *The New Republic*, a radical journal read widely by liberal-minded intellectuals. She was left a widow with three children when her husband died from the worldwide scourge of influenza (1918). A few years later she met and married Leonard Elmhirst (1893–1974) and funded his work in India, where he was working to reestablish impoverished rural villages. They shared an interest in progressive education and decided to establish a school with modern education policies in an experimental and utopian manner. In 1925 they married and purchased Dartington Hall in Devon. The following year they began a boarding school, where Dorothy worked and lived until her death.

See Also Dartington Hall; Elmhirst; Leonard Knight

Sources:

Kidel, Mark. 1990. *Beyond the Classroom: Dartington's Experiments in Education*. Devon, U.K.: Green Books.
Popenoe, Cris, and Oliver Popenoe. 1984. *Seeds of Tomorrow*. San Francisco: Harper and Row.
Straight, Michael Whitney. 1983. *After Long Silence*. New York: Norton.
Young, Michael D. 1982. *The Elmhirsts of Dartington: The Creation of a Utopian Community*. London: Routledge and Kegan Paul.

STRAIGHT EDGE INDUSTRIAL SETTLEMENT. The Straight Edge Industrial Settlement was an experiment in cooperative enterprise that flourished between 1899 and 1918 in New York City. A small group of about a dozen made up the commune in the beginning. The founder was Wilbur F. Copeland (fl. 1869–1899). Copeland had been associated with the Christian Commonwealth and established a School of Methods for the Application of the Teachings of Jesus to Business and Society. The settlement was a trade school that taught cooperation and the social skills needed to work effectively with others; also it ran cooperative farms on Staten Island and in Alpine, New Jersey. Communal life was abandoned in 1906, although the industrial organization existed until 1918.

See Also Copeland, Wilbur F.

Sources:

Fogarty, Robert S. 1980. *Dictionary of American Communal History*. Westport, Conn.: Greenwood Press.
———. 1990. *All Things New: American Communes and Utopian Movements 1860–1914*. Chicago: University of Chicago Press.

STRANG, JAMES JESSE. James Jesse Strang (1813–1856), born in Scipio, New York, was noted as a leader of a Mormon sect of Strangites. In 1836 he married. He became a postmaster and edited *Randolf Herald* in western New York. In 1843 he went to Wisconsin and took up Mormonism in 1844. When the founder and prophet of Mormonism died in June 1844, a struggle arose over the succession, and Strang was one of the aspiring prophets. He attracted a considerable following, and with the aid of angelic visitations and the unearthing of golden plates and other unusual phenomena characteristic of the Mormon sect, he developed the holy city of Voree, near the town of Burlington, Wisconsin (1844–1849), and many of his followers scattered throughout the country. His attention was diverted to the Beaver Islands in Lake Michigan, where in 1849 the city of St. James was founded as his new holy city. In 1850, the Kingdom of God on Earth was proclaimed formally, and Strang considered himself God's vice-regent who was called upon to establish God's rule in the world. Strang was a competent public speaker, a man of considerable shrewdness, and for six years he dominated several thousand subjects in his kingdom. He was murdered by disgruntled conspirators, and his followers were robbed and driven into exile in 1856 by a frontier mob.

See Also Beaver Island

Sources:

Beaver Island Historical Society. 1981. *The Journal of Beaver Island History*. 2 vols. St. James: Beaver Island Historical Society.
Fogarty, Robert S. 1980. *Dictionary of American Communal History*. Westport, Conn.: Greenwood Press.

Gilbert, Bill. 1995. "America's Only King Made Beaver Island His Promised Land." *Smithsonian* 26, no. 4: 85–92.

Malone, Dumas, ed. 1935. *Dictionary of American Biography*. Vol. 9. New York: Charles Scribner's Sons.

Quaife, Milo M. 1930. *The Kingdom of Saint James: A Narrative of the Mormons*. New Haven, Conn. Yale University Press.

Van Noord, Roger. 1988. *King of Beaver Island: The Life and Assassination of James Jesse Strang*. Bloomington: University of Illinois Press.

STREETON, ARTHUR ERNEST. Arthur Ernest Streeton (1867–1943) studied art at the National Gallery of Victoria School (1882–1888) while he worked as an apprentice lithographer. At Mentone, a seaside suburb south of Melbourne, Australia, he met Tom Roberts (1856–1931) and Frederick McCubbin (1855–1917). They invited Ernest to join their painting camps, and he worked at Eaglemont for a time and painted his *Golden Summer*. They constitute the Heidelberg School in Australian art. In 1890 he moved to Sydney and lived at a camp with Roberts. At the turn of the century he sailed to Europe and returned briefly in 1906–1907 to exhibit his paintings. He was most successful. In 1918 he was appointed the official war artist and returned to Australia permanently in 1923. In 1928 he won the Wynne Prize, and from 1929 he became the art critic in Melbourne for *The Argus*. For his services to Australian art he was knighted in 1937.

See Also Conder, Charles Edward; Heidelberg School; McCubbin, Frederick; Roberts, Thomas William

Sources:

McCulloch, Susan, and Alan McCulloch. 1994. *The Encyclopedia of Australian Art*. Sydney: Allen and Unwin.

Splatt, William, and Dugald McLellan. 1986. *The Heidelberg School: The Golden Summer of Australian Painting*. Melbourne: Lloyd O'Neil.

SUMMERHILL. Summerhill School was a progressive British education community based on freedom, democracy, and self-determination. It advocated replacing autocratic authority in class with self-determination, and learning/teaching was rewarded by the gratification of human needs, interests, and curiosity rather than by pain of physical punishment. The community assumed that maturity is impeded by punishment, because it engenders fear, anger, and outrage, which naturally cripple human curiosity and achievement. On one hand, the child's task is to learn respect for the adult, never to intrude upon or abuse the adult's goodwill, or to use childish pressure to manipulate the adult; on the other hand, the adult teacher must be sincere, worthy of trust, and reliable and never lie. As a result, in its own time, the child learns to forgo its primary tie with parents, finds their substitutes in society, acquires true independence, and understands the world intellectually and emotionally. The school was founded by A. S. Neill (1883–1973) in 1927 after working on a community school in

Salzburg. Originally, it was an experiment at Leiston, Suffolk, 100 miles from London. Children entered school at age five to twelve years and left at sixteen. Half boys, half girls, the school population of fifty pupils forms three age groups: five to seven, eight to ten, and eleven to fifteen, years. Members of each group have a housemother, are accommodated two to four to a room, and are entirely responsible for their housekeeping and dress. Because the experimental aim was to make the school fit the child, Neill and his wife put aside the conventional views on classroom discipline, and moral and religious instruction and assumed the child was innately good, wise, and realistic. Lessons were optional, children were free to enter and leave class, and timetables were for teachers only. Classes varied according to age and interest; consequently, children learned what they wanted to learn, some set about learning quickly, some loafed, and others played and worked intermittently. The children acquired self-confidence and developed the playful as well as productive sides to their schoolwork. Because some Summerhill children wanted to go to a university, they were offered instruction in examinations and whatever was necessary to achieve required standards, usually after age fourteen.

See Also Neill, A. S.

Sources:

Hemmings, Ray. 1972. *Fifty Years of Freedom: A Study of the Development of the Ideas of A. S. Neill.* London: Allen and Unwin.
Lamb, Albert, ed. 1992. *The New Summerhill.* London: Penguin.
Neill, Alexander S. 1960. *Summerhill: A Radical Approach to Education.* New York: Hart.
————. 1967. *Talking of Summerhill.* London: Gollancz.
Segefjord, Bjarne. 1970. *Summerhill Diary.* Translated from Danish by Maurice Michael. London: Gollancz.

SWAMI KRIYANANDA. James Donald Walters (b. 1926) was born in Telaejen, a small Anglo-American colony on the oil fields of Romania where his father worked for Esso as an oil geologist. He was educated at home by a governess, and at age eleven began two years at a Quaker School for boys in England. When he reached thirteen, his family returned to the United States. He attended Kent School in Connecticut, a church school run by Episcopalian monks, and afterward he went to the local high school at Scarsdale, where he graduated in 1943. He went to Haverford, a Quaker college, for two years and then Brown University. He became a disciple of Paramahansa Yogananda after reading his *The Autobiography of a Yogi* (1946). In 1955 he was universally reborn as Swami Kriyananda when he was initiated into the ancient Swami order of India.

See Also Ananda Co-operative Village

Source:

Walters, Donald J. 1977. *The Path: Autobiography of a Western Yogi (Swami Kriyananda.* Nevada City, Calif.: Ananda.

SWEDENBORG, EMMANUEL. Emmanuel Swedenborg (1688–1772) was born in Stockholm, the son of Jesper Svedborg. The name was changed to Swedenborg when the family was ennobled in 1719. After studies at Uppsala in technology and engineering and travels in Europe, Swedenborg was appointed by Charles XII of Sweden (1682–1718) to a post on the Swedish Board of Mines (1716). With his mathematical ability he anticipated many subsequent hypotheses and discoveries, for example, nebular theory, magnetic theory, the machine gun, and airplane; he wrote on sluices, docks, and astronomy, and some claim he founded crystallography. He published three outstanding works, one a mixture of metaphysics and metallurgy and two others on anatomy and physiology. After feeling he was in direct contact with the angels and the spirit world through dreams and visions and in his conscious life (1743–1745), he decided God was calling him to spread his ideas among humankind through the New Church. In 1747 he resigned from the Board of Mines to make a comprehensive study of the Scriptures. He wrote thirty works on spiritual revelations. Among them three stand out: *Arcana Coelestia* (1749–1756), *De Coelo et eius Mirabilibus et de Inferno* (1758), and *Vera Christiana Religio* (1771). His best work is reputed to be *Divine Love and Wisdom* (1763). He did not personally found the Swedenborgians. In London in 1787 the Swedenborg New Jerusalem Church first met, was organized, and from that time spread through the world on the basis of his teachings, Swedenborgianism.

See Also Swedenborg New Jerusalem Church

Sources:

Cross, Frank L. 1974. *The Oxford Dictionary of the Christian Church*. 2d ed. New York: Oxford University Press.

Jonsson, Inge. 1971. *Emanuel Swedenborg*. New York: Twayne.

Magnussen, Magnus, and Rosemary Goring, eds. 1990. *Chambers Biographical Dictionary*. 5th ed. Edinburgh: Chambers.

McHenry, Robert, ed. 1992. *The New Encyclopedia Britannica*. Chicago: Encyclopedia Britannica.

Trobridge, George. 1974. *Swedenborg: Life and Teaching*. London: Swedenborg Society.

Zusne, Leonard. 1984. *Biographical Dictionary of Psychology*. Westport, Conn.: Greenwood.

SWEDENBORG NEW JERUSALEM CHURCH. In the Swedenborg New Jerusalem Church members are known as Swedenborgians after Emmanuel Swedenborg (1688–1772), who considered that his writings would be the basis of a New Church relating to the New Jerusalem from the Revelation of Saint John the Divine in the last book of the New Testament, 21: 2. In the course of stating what was revealed to him, Saint John says that he saw a new heaven and a new earth, and this was because the first heaven and the first earth had passed away, and the sea also had gone. Then he swears, "I, John saw the Holy City, New Jerusalem, coming down from God out of heaven, prepared as a bride adorned for her husband." The first New Church was opened in 1788 in Great East

Cheap, London. Since 1789 a general conference of the New Church has met annually except for the periods 1794–1806 and 1809–1814. In Baltimore a society was established (1792), and the General Convention of the New Jerusalem in America was founded in Philadelphia in 1817. In 1897 a separate group established the General Church of the New Jerusalem. Members learn that the Scriptures should be taught and interpreted spiritually, and from these teachings emerge basic principles to the preaching in the church. The British General Conference and the U.S. General Convention are controlled by an annually appointed general council and a ministerial council, while the general church is governed by bishops. The New Church has missions abroad, particularly in Africa and in Australia, where a conference is closely connected with that in Britain. In the United States the influence of the New Church is widespread.

See Also Swedenborg, Emmanuel

Sources:

Fogarty, Robert S. 1990. *All Things New: American Communes and Utopian Movements 1860–1914*. Chicago: University of Chicago Press.
McHenry, Robert, ed. 1992. *The New Encyclopedia Britannica*. Chicago: Encyclopedia Britannica.

SYMBIONESE LIBERATION ARMY. In November 1973, The Symbionese Liberation Army (SLA), a band of urban guerrillas, assassinated the superintendent of schools for Oakland, California. On 4 February 1974 the group kidnapped Patricia Hearst, nineteen, daughter of William Randolph Hearst (1863–1951), the wealthy publisher. The SLA published a revolutionary program to overthrow the forces of fascism and reaction. In a series of ransom notes sent to Hearst the group demanded food be distributed to the poor of San Francisco in return for Patricia Hearst's return. Patricia Hearst announced in a taped message that accompanied the notes that she was a prisoner of war, and the Federal Bureau of Investigation (FBI) feared she had been brainwashed. She appeared to participate in a bank robbery with other SLA members. Another woman seemed to be training a gun on Patricia, which suggested she was acting under duress. Earlier, she issued a statement that she had joined the group and had taken the name Tania, 3 April 1974. The SLA hideout was found in May that year and led to the shooting of six inhabitants in a house. The FBI finally captured Tania and Bill and Emily Harris. Patricia denied that she had been a willing convert to the SLA, although the Harrises disputed this. In September 1975 she was refused bail following bank robbery charges, for which a year later she was jailed for seven years. She was freed on five years' probation in May 1977, and in November 1977 her conviction for robbery was upheld. She appealed for a review of her sentence, but the Supreme Court turned down her appeal in April 1978. President Carter commuted her jail sentence, and on 1 February 1979 she was released from prison.

Source:

Hall, John R. 1978. *The Ways Out: Utopian Communal Groups in an Age of Babylon*. London: Routledge and Kegan Paul.

T

TAHITI. Tahiti enjoys the image of being a natural utopia similar to that commonly found in early literary utopian novels. It is the largest of the Society Islands of French Polynesia in the Pacific Ocean. In this image food is bountiful, the climate is superb, politics are just, sexual relations between men and women are open and free, and no person toils or labors. In brief, life on Tahiti is simple, peaceful, and harmonious. This image emerged from reports and imaginings of seamen (1767–1787) and was cultivated by Robert Louis Stevenson (1850–1894), the Scottish author, 100 years later and by other writers as they depicted the life of the French painter Paul Gauguin (1848–1903), who lived on Tahiti briefly (1895–1901). The image of Tahiti as a Pacific paradise has attracted tourists for almost 100 years. Nevertheless, this romantic tourist image contrasts with anthropological evidence on Tahiti. Life on Tahiti has not been as cooperative, kindly, generous, and considerate as the image would have one believe. Theft, petty wars, limited free love, subordination of women to men, slavery, duplicity, infanticide, human sacrifice, boredom, lack of dignity, corruption, savagery, brutality, desire for glory, and grave diseases were as commonplace among Tahitians as among those who came to Tahiti and brought their own shameful hypocrisy, sickness, and violence in the name of Western civilization. Tahiti was made a French protectorate (1843) and colony (1880), and after World War II, Tahitians had French citizenship. In the 1980s, when the population of Tahiti had reached 116,000, the French used their Polynesian islands to test hydrogen bombs until 1996.

Sources:

Diderot, Denis. 1796. ''Love in Tahiti.'' Reprinted in Frank E. Manuel and Futzie P. Manuel, eds. 1966. *French Utopias: An Anthology of Ideal Societies*, pp. 149–166. New York: Free Press.
Dodd, Edward. 1983. *The Rape of Tahiti*. New York: Dodd, Mead.
Haldane, Charlotte Franklin. 1963. *Tempest over Tahiti*. London: Constable.

Henry, Teuira. 1928. *Ancient Tahiti*. Reprinted, 1971. New York: Kraus.
Langdon, Robert. 1968. *Tahiti: Island of Love*. 3d ed. Sydney: Pacific.
McCord, William. 1989. *Voyages to Utopia: From Monastery to Commune, the Search for the Perfect Society in Modern Times*. New York: W. W. Norton.
Newbury, Colin. 1980. *Tahiti Nui: Change and Survival in French Polynesia, 1767–1945*. Honolulu: University of Hawaii Press.
Snodgrass, Mary Ellen. 1995. *Encyclopedia of Utopian Literature*. Santa Barbara, Calif.: ABC-CLIO.

TAYLOR, HARRY SAMUEL. Harry Samuel Taylor (1873–1932) was born in North Adelaide, South Australia, and won a scholarship to Prince Alfred College, Adelaide, where he later taught (1887–1891). He quit teaching to tour the colony to advocate the single-tax theory of Henry George (1839–1897). He became the secretary of the South Australian Single Tax League, editing its journal, *Pioneer*. In 1893, much persuaded by William Lane (1861–1917) and the plan for New Australia, he sailed with the first Christian socialists to Paraguay and returned soon after to organize the next wave of emigrants. On returning to Paraguay, he saw the split among the settlers and followed Lane to Cosme (1894–1896). He wrote the *Porpoise*, the ship's journal for the second voyage, by hand and in Cosme would read aloud the *Cosme Evening Notes*, a cheerful account of the community and its leader. Forced to return to Adelaide after his father's death in 1895, he sailed via England and visited with H. G. Wells (1866–1946), the British socialist utopian and writer of science fiction. On arriving home, Taylor worked at Murtho, a utopian commune, one of the village settlements on the upper Murray River established in 1893 in South Australia. Illness shortened his stay. He married, became a fruit grower and later a dairy farmer, edited the *Mildura Cultivator*, and then bought the *Renmark Pioneer* (1905). Thereafter, he was an influential publisher who used his newspapers to advance many causes, rural, urban, national, and international. He was a friend of both conservatives and labor supporters, supported postwar soldier settlement schemes for World War I veterans, and stood for freedom, brotherhood, and the White Australia policy. He became a lay preacher, sat on many local committees and boards, and espoused advanced education in rural districts and the extension of the railways to the country. Immaculate, generous, forgiving, widely read, this genial and intelligent character impressed many with his idealism.

See Also Lane, William; Murtho; New Australia

Sources:

Pike, Douglas, et al. 1966–1990. *Australian Dictionary of Biography*. 12 vols. Carlton, Victoria: University of Melbourne Press.
Souter, Gavin. 1968. *A Peculiar People*. 1981 ed. Sydney: Sydney University Press.

TAZAWA, SEISHIRO. Seishiro Tazawa (1884–1966) and his son founded Yamatoyama, now a large intentional community in Japan. Seishiro Tazawa was a wealthy trader who had followed his father into business. By middle age he had become absorbed in spirituality (1924) and was a recognized healer. Seishiro's father left him an estate that enabled him and his family to live an ascetic life. One of his three children was a daughter who wrote down revelations identifying "the deity of Yamatoyama" and the importance of institutionalizing a spiritual lifestyle. In attempting this, he was persecuted by government, and his missionary efforts were reviled until his son, Yasuaburo, joined him in 1946 and helped his father realize plans for the intentional community of Yamatoyama. Yasuaburo became leader of the community when his father died.

See Also Yamatoyama

Source:

Popenoe, Cris, and Oliver Popenoe. 1984. *Seeds of Tomorrow*. San Francisco: Harper and Row.

TEED, CYRUS READ. Cyrus Read Teed (1839–1906) was a physician and metaphysician who devised the religious ideology "cellular cosmology." He tried without success to establish a small colony in Moravia, New York, where he practiced as a physician. He visited Economy in 1878 to study its organization and success. In 1869 Teed had a spiritual awakening, and he felt he was directed from his medical career in New York to lead a movement to cure the mind. The name "Koreshan" was his transliteration of "Cyrus" from the Hebrew. He believed his spirit had inhabited the body of Cyrus of Persia (fl. 553–529 B.C.) as well as other notables. His teachings constituted the basis of Koreshanty and used the terms of orthodox Christianity. He and his disciples moved to Chicago and established a church (1886), Assembly of the Covenant and the World's College of Life Educational Institution. Teed's cosmology assumed that the earth's surface was concave; that man lives on the inside of a sphere, not on a ball in space; that earth is not 4.5 billion years old but eternal; that God is an eternal being living in the central brain cells of the aggregate of humanity; that in one eternal form God is both male and female; that Jesus Christ was God perpetuating himself in a human form and was created by a process of virgin birth—parthenogenesis. Teed rechristened himself Koresh in 1894, and his followers established Koresh Unity, a community in Florida.

See also: Economy; Koreshans and Koreshan Unity

Sources:

Fogarty, Robert S. 1990. *All Things New: American Communes and Utopian Movements 1860–1914*. Chicago: University of Chicago Press.

Kitch, Sally L. 1989. *Chaste Liberation: Celibacy and Female Cultural Status*. Champaign: University of Illinois Press.

TEXAS-NAUVOO. Texas-Nauvoo was the original Icarian community organized by the French socialist Étienne Cabet (1788–1856). In May 1847 he decided to realize his dream of a socialist utopia by founding a colony, Icaria.

Without having seen the land, he purchased a million acres in the Red River Valley in Texas, and 1,500 men embarked for the new land after agreeing to accept Cabet as undisputed leader for ten years. When it tried to get to the site the advance party of sixty-nine discovered the route almost impassable, the site an uninhabited desert, totally unsuited to agriculture. The Texas settlement would last only four months, largely because of illness. In 1849 Cabet denounced his followers for their carelessness and came to the United States. He led the second party of Icarians to Nauvoo, Illinois, where they purchased a settlement that the Mormons had developed and later evacuated, and there, joined by the first group of Icarians from Red River Valley, Cabet established the Icarian community securely (1849–1859). They prospered until 1856, when the membership began to fluctuate, factions emerged, and, because of Cabet's arbitrary rule, he was voted out of the position of president. Accompanied by his loyal followers, Cabet left the Nauvoo community to establish a new colony, Cheltenham. He died shortly afterward.

See Also Cabet, Étienne; Cheltenham; Corning; Icarian movement; Speranza

Sources:

Egbert, D. D., and Persons Stow, eds. 1952. *Socialism and American Life*. Princeton: Princeton University Press.

Fogarty, Robert S. 1980. *Dictionary of American Communal History*. Westport, Conn.: Greenwood Press.

Oved, Yaacov. 1987. *Two Hundred Years of American Communes*. New Brunswick, N.J.: Transaction Books.

THELNETHAM. Thelnetham was a community established on the border of Norfolk and Suffolk by John Murry (1889–1957) on 183 acres, October 1941 at Lodge Farm. Investing all his savings in the venture, Murry bought it for £3,325 in 1942. Profits were to be shared and applied to the purchase of the farm from him, at 4.5 percent interest. It was known as Lodge Farm Community. At the center was a roomy old farmhouse. Stock was bought from the Adelphi Center. The venture failed due to poor harvests and bad publicity. The members were condemned as cranks who were frustrated and sexually unfulfilled. The community survived until 1948.

See Also Murry, John Middleton

Source:

Armytage, Walter H. Green. 1961. *Heavens Below: Utopian Experiments in England 1560–1950*. London: Routledge and Kegan Paul.

THEOSOPHICAL SOCIETY. In the United States the Theosophical Society was formed in New York in 1875 after Helena Petrovna Hahn Blavatsky (1831–1891) met Henry Steel Olcott (1832–1907). She had arrived two years before and displayed evidence of spiritualistic powers after her travels in the Orient. Together they formed the group that would later become the Theosophical Society. The society's objectives were to establish the nucleus of a Universal Brotherhood of humanity, unaffected by differences in race, creed, sex, caste, or color. The society would promote the study of Aryan and other Eastern literature, religion, and science and investigate the hidden mysteries of nature and humankind's latent psychical powers. With such knowledge they would make the world a far better place.

See Also Blavatsky, Helena Petrovna Hahn

Source:

Hine, Robert V. 1953. *California's Utopian Colonies.* 1983 ed. Berkeley: University of California Press.

THOMPSON, ELIZABETH ROWELL. Elizabeth Rowell Thompson (1821–1899) was born in New England and employed as a housemaid until she married a patron of the arts, Thomas Thompson (1843). They lived in Boston until 1860, moved to New York City, and became known for their philanthropic work. When Thomas died, his wife was left $50,000 a year, which she used partly to further woman suffrage and the temperance movement. Influenced by the ideas of Robert Owen (1771–1858), in 1871 she provided funds for the Co-operative Colony Aid Association. The association's main aim was to relieve urban unemployment and provoke a return to agricultural work as a natural, self-supporting, self-providing, self-directing activity. The Chicago-Colorado Company at Longmont in the early 1870s and Thompson Colony (1879–1880) were the result of her support for this view. To further her understanding of cooperation, she sailed to Britain and studied cooperative societies that were working to overcome urban poverty in England. Her views on alcohol appeared in *The Figures of Hell, and the Temple of Bacchus Dedicated to License and Manufacture of Beer and Whisky* (1882). Also she was much concerned with the future education of children. In 1873 she published her *Kindergarten Homes*, which envisaged a better future through educating children—the present is too late for adults—to prevent poverty and crime. In her "homes," children would live with loving houseparents in the fresh air, playing on verandas, learning, first, domestic skills and, later, working trades and crafts, and ultimately becoming self-supporting. Her theory was applied by John Newbrough (1827–1891) at the children's colony, Shalam, at Dona Ana in New Mexico on 1,490 acres near the Rio Grande. She also supported scientific research, was the first patron of the American Association for the Advancement of Science, and supported the ideas of Stephen Pearl Andrews (1812–1886).

See Also: Andrews, Stephen Pearl; Newbrough, John Ballou; Owen, Robert; Shalam Colony; Thompson Colony

Sources:

Fogarty, Robert. 1990. *All Things New: American Communes and Utopian Movements 1860–1914.* Chicago: University of Chicago Press.

James, Edward T. 1971. *Notable American Women 1607–1950*. Cambridge: Harvard
  University Press, Belknap Press.

THOMPSON, WILLIAM IRWIN. William Irwin Thompson (b. 1938) was
born in Chicago and educated at Pomona College (B.A., 1962) and Cornell
University (M.A., 1964; Ph.D., 1966). He taught at MIT, and York University,
(1965–1972). Among his awards were a Woodrow Wilson Fellowship (1962)
and Old Dominion Fellowship (1967). His first book was *The Imagination of
an Insurrection: Dublin, Easter 1916* (1967). In 1972 his *At the Edge of History*
(1971) was nominated for the U.S. National Book Award. He founded the Lindisfarne Association in December 1972. Its first activities began in Southampton,
Long Island, August 1973. Resident staff of the association lived communally
on thirteen acres and provided educational services for Greater New York, 1973–
1979. The work of the society appears in *Earth's Answer: Explorations of Planetary Culture at the Lindisfarne Conferences* (1977). Thompson wrote *Passages
about Earth: An Exploration of the New Planetary Culture* (1974), *From Nation
to Emanation: Planetary Culture and World Governance* (1982), *A Way of
Knowing* (1987), and *Worlds Interpenetrating and Apart* (1996), among others.
  See Also Lindisfarne Association

Source:

Who's Who in America. 1986–1991. Providence, N.J.: Marquis.

THOMPSON COLONY. Thompson Colony was a communal farming settlement, Salina, Kansas, established in principle in November 1879 with funds
from Elizabeth Rowell Thompson (1821–1899), a philanthropist, and formed by
the Co-operative Colony Aid Association of New York City. Colonists had a
home and land allotted to them, large tracts were worked cooperatively, time
was allocated to the colony work and maintenance, and the profits were distributed on a pro rata basis. The general aim was to show the value of cooperation
over competition. The members worked fields in common, shared the use of
tools and machinery, and were expected to repay the money borrowed in annual
installments. They lived in separate homes and tended their own gardens. The
ideal number for a colony was to be twenty-five families. Once established, it
was thought that members could choose to continue a communal life or turn to
individual farming ventures. The Thompson Colony ended in the drought of
1880.
  See Also Thompson, Elizabeth Rowell

Sources:

Fogarty, Robert S. 1980. *Dictionary of American Communal History*. Westport, Conn.:
  Greenwood Press.
———. 1990. *All Things New: American Communes and Utopian Movements 1860–
  1914*. Chicago: University of Chicago Press.

THOREAU, HENRY DAVID. Henry David Thoreau (1817–1862) was born in Concord, Massachusetts, and educated at Harvard University (1837) and became a teacher for a short time in his hometown. He worked with his father, a pencil maker, and grew to like walking and studying nature. In 1835 he began to keep a diary of his walks and observations; it became a lifetime activity. He published *A Week on the Concord and Merrimack Rivers* (1849); during the 1840s he befriended and briefly lived with Ralph Waldo Emerson (1803–1882), the noted U.S. poet and essayist. In 1845 he built a hermit's shack for himself in woods by Walden Pond, lived there for two years, and in 1854 published *Walden, or, Life in the Woods*, an American literary classic that influenced many utopian practitioners who revered the outdoor life and modern thinkers, for example, B. F. Skinner, who wrote *Walden Two* (1948). Thoreau attracted the soubriquet "hermit of Walden," and Walden became an ideal, utopian place of natural harmony and inner peace. He lived by writing and doing odd jobs, publishing essays and short pieces based on his memoirs and diary. He is noted for his *Civil Disobedience* (1849), written in response to the U.S. involvement in war with Mexico.

See Also Skinner, B. F.; *Walden, or, Life in the Woods*; *Walden Two*

Sources:

Magnussen, Magnus, and Rosemary Goring, eds. 1990. *Chambers Biographical Dictionary*. 5th ed. Edinburgh: Chambers.

Myerson, Joel, ed. 1995. *The Cambridge Companion to Henry David Thoreau*. Cambridge: Cambridge University Press.

Richardson, Robert D., Jr. 1986. *Henry Thoreau: A Life of the Mind*. Berkeley: University of California Press.

Schneider, Richard J. 1987. *Henry David Thoreau*. Boston: Twayne.

Wagenknecht, Edward. 1981. *Henry David Thoreau: What Manner of Man?* Amherst: University of Massachusetts Press.

TILDEN, JAN. Jan Tilden (born c. 1953) was raised in Brisbane, Queensland, Australia. As a child she wanted to run away to sea but decided against it in adolescence. She became interested in scientific observation and realized time was an artifact of human awareness. This led her to study science at the University of Queensland. At the university sex and politics intrigued her as much as zoology; she became an active feminist with a preference for the company of men over women. After graduation she spent time at Maleny, inland from Queensland's Sunshine Coast, where suddenly she realized she was free to do whatever she wanted with her life. After having different jobs, she decided to pursue a Ph.D. in psychology. She gave up her man partner, befriended Jill Jordan, took up a serious interest in a commune at Frogs' Hollow near Maleny, and with two more women established a small community. They did not plan it to be single-sex community; in time the group grew into a mixed-sex community and faced many physical, emotional, and intellectual challenges in its establishment phase. Jan's interests turned to sociology, and she studied women in intentional communities for her Ph.D. For several years she worked at her thesis and helped the commune resolve problems and manage conflicts with outside authorities, for example, building a dam on the community's border. After seventeen years Jan identified the conditions she thought contributed to the success of their community: an agreed reason for being together; a belief that although isolation may contribute to internal conflicts, it is preferable to life in suburbia; avoidance of overly comprehensive, long-term planning; using the opportunity to move away from others in the commune rather than to quit the commune altogether when problems arose; continuous clarification of community goals; a leadership style based on collaboration, the reinforcement of self-worth, and valuing initiatives for all rather than competitive careerism; regular sharing of the community's history.

See Also Frogs' Hollow/Manduka

Source:

Tilden, Jan. 1995. "From Academic Exercises to Jumping Spiders." In Bill Metcalf, ed., *From Utopian Dreaming to Communal Reality: Cooperative Life Styles in Australia*, pp. 57–73. Sydney: University of New South Wales Press.

TIME STORE. Time Store was a libertarian community (1827–1830) where Josiah Warren (1798–1874) put his labor theory of value into practice. The Time Store was an "equity" or "time" store opened by Warren in Cincinnati two years after Warren's experiences in the Owenite community New Harmony, 1825. Labor notes that promised a specific number of hours of work were exchanged for goods at the store.

See Also Warren, Josiah

Sources:

Fogarty, Robert S. 1980. *Dictionary of American Communal History*. Westport, Conn.: Greenwood Press.
Veysey, Laurence. 1973. *The Communal Experience: Anarchist and Mystical Countercultures in America*. New York: Harper and Row.

TINGLEY, KATHERINE AUGUSTA WESTCOTT. Katherine Augusta Westcott Tingley (1847–1929) was born in Newburyport, Massachusetts. Her father was a shipwright who became an officer in the Civil War (1861–1865) and later owner of a hotel in Newburyport. She was descended from Stukely Westcott, one of the associates in the founding of Providence Plantations. Little is known of her early life. Some accounts say she had religious visions in childhood. Educated in public schools and by private tutors, she might have spent two years in a convent in Montreal. While a young woman, she married three times, her last husband being an inventor, Philo B. Tingley. She lived in obscurity until a little over forty, when she emerged in New York City as a spiritualist medium and philanthropist in a mission on the East Side. She combined two major interests, philanthropy and occultism. She established the Society of Mercy

(1887), the Martha Washington Home for the Aged (1889), and the DO-good Mission. She helped organize two children's homes, and during the Spanish-American War (1898) she set up an emergency hospital for wounded and sick soldiers. She was converted to theosophy and rose to authority in the Theosophical Society in the mid-1890s. She wanted its name changed in keeping with her strong feelings for brotherhood. It became the Universal Brotherhood and Theosophical Society. She led theosophists away from their psychic interests to more utopian and brotherly ventures. In 1896 she became the leader of the theosophists and had land bought at Point Loma, San Diego, for the International Headquarters of the Universal Brotherhood. In 1898 she invited theosophists to help build a community at Point Loma by 1900. For twenty-seven years she ruled Point Loma, a religious utopia. In 1904 she led a theosophical crusade around the world and established a home for orphan children and built a children's summer home at Spring Valley, New York. She also built a Theosophical Institute at Newburyport in Massachusetts and established three schools in Cuba and theosophical centers elsewhere. At the end of her life she lived in Europe, where she lectured annually in Paris and Berlin. She suffered serious injuries in a car accident in June 1929 in Berlin and died soon after.

See Also Point Loma

Sources:

Fogarty, Robert S. 1990. *All Things New: American Communes and Utopian Movements 1860–1914*. Chicago: University of Chicago Press.

Hine, Robert V. 1953. *California's Utopian Colonies*. 1983 ed. Berkeley: University of California Press.

Malone, Dumas, ed. 1935. *Dictionary of American Biography*. Vol. 9. New York: Charles Scribner's Sons.

TOLSTOY, LEO. Leo Nikolayevich Tolstoy (1828–1910) was born at Yasnaya Polyana, Russia, into a notable family among the landed gentry. His parents were dead when he was nine, and his aunt raised him and educated him privately. He studied literature and law at Kazan University and attended Petersburg University briefly but did not complete any degree. He began writing and returned to his hometown before going to the Caucasus where he was made an army officer, and in 1854 he was assigned to the war front in the Crimea. His war experiences appear in the psychological *Tales of Sebastopol* (1855). He married in 1862, and his writing brought him great fame. His masterpieces were *War and Peace* (1865–1868) and *Anna Karenina* (1878). He suffered a crisis of faith, rejected orthodox Christianity, and searched for a new personal philosophy. In this he was greatly influenced by Prugavin Syntayev, a peasant mystic (1881) who explained his beliefs on communal ownership of all property; bans on commerce, courts, the militia, and taxes; working for unity among humankind through the heart; and never punishing or hurting a person or animal. In 1882 Tolstoy wrote his *What Then Must We Do?*, which embodies the principles of his Christian communitarianism. When his close supporters were exiled to England, he sent his social reform essays and letters to be published in England. While his ideas were banned in Russia, they attracted an international following. Visitors came to him from around the world every summer, and among them were leading socialists, pacifists, artists, writers, and social reformers. He lived an ascetic life; he ate vegetables and porridge, drank water only, chopped his own wood, and quit fashionable society. He stated principles for utopian villages and housing, and was willing to share his income with those who worked his land. He had an enormous following, largely due to his fame as a writer and his willingness to give a view on any topic. He loathed the modern state's attempts to regulate people's lives because it turned attention away from humankind's needs and sought action largely based on physical coercion and often violence. He wanted a new Christian organic society, self-governing, composed of cooperative units in a federation. Such units would be small communities, each with a close link to nature, motivated by Christianity without its dogma, institutions, and mysticism but instead with joy and bliss in spirit and directed to the unification of human kind. He denounced war, and his nonresistance policy attracted such followers as Gandhi (1869–1948) and Martin Luther King, Jr. (1929–1968). He helped the Doukhobors—Russian pacifists—to emigrate to Canada. Also he linked Christian pacifism with anarchism. He attacked such modern devices as electricity, the telegraph, and the railways, saying machines themselves produced nothing; the telegraph sent worthless dispatches; books spread pointless news; and the railways took whomever on directionless travels. He saw in the modern world people gather aimlessly in a horde before a dominating leader. Many later writings were religious or philosophical, excepting *Resurrection* (1900). Among them were *A Confession* (1879), *What I Believe In* (1882), *The Death of Ivan Ilyich* (1884), the drama *The Power of Darkness* (1886), *The Kreutzer Sonata* (1889), and his aesthetic study *What Is Art?* (1987).

See Also Doukhobors; Tolstoyan communities

Sources:

Armytage, Walter H. Green. 1961. *Heavens Below: Utopian Experiments in England 1560–1950.* London: Routledge and Kegan Paul.
Berlin, Isaiah. 1953. *The Hedgehog and the Fox: An Essay on Tolstoy's View of History.* London: Weidenfeld and Nicolson.
Maude, Almyer. 1930. *The Life of Tolstoy.* Revised ed. London: Oxford University Press.
Rowe, William Woodin. 1986. *Tolstoy.* Boston: Twayne.
Troyat, Henri. 1965. *Tolstoy.* 1970 ed. Harmondsworth: Penguin Books.
Wilson, Angus N. 1988. *Tolstoy: A Biography.* London: Hamilton.

TOLSTOYAN COMMUNITIES. To Tolstoy an ideal society would be based on the renunciation of the modern industrial system and return to self-supportive manual labor, bread labor. Accordingly, it would be humankind's first duty to produce food, shelter, and clothing—all of which would come from the land— and do so in comradeship, honesty, and nonviolence and following noncoercive principles. Because all production would come from the land, it should be free for everyone to use. People would live without laws, taxes, money, or legal marriage. No one would vote, and everyone would live a sexually chaste life and never actively object to the behavior of others. Change would come to the community not through external pressures and law but through changes to individuals when they entered new relationships and became aware of a new consciousness within themselves. Such changes would emerge when social and economic structures were not elaborate, and the basic activities of production and community life were simple and clear. Wasteful activity and oppressive controls would evaporate as individuals regained their lost natural state.

See Also Purleigh Colony; Tolstoy, Leo

Sources:

Armytage, Walter H. Green. 1961. *Heavens Below: Utopian Experiments in England 1560–1950*. London: Routledge and Kegan Paul.
Marsh, Jan. 1982. *Back to the Land: The Pastoral Impulse in England, from 1880 to 1914*. London: Quartet.
Tolstoy, Leo N. 1882. *What Then Must We Do?* Reprinted, 1925. London: Oxford University Press.
———. 1884. *The Kingdom of God Is Within You*. New York: Cassell. Translated by Constance Garnett. Lincoln: University of Nebraska Press.

TOPOLOBAMPO COLONY. Topolobampo Colony was a utopian community established on the Pacific coast of Mexico in the early 1870s by Albert Kimsey Owen (1847–1916). He had similar ideas to those of Henry George (1939–1897) and worked for a prominent developer of towns and railroads in the 1870s and 1880s. He believed a railroad should be built across the United States from Virginia to a port on the Pacific coast of Mexico; having the Pacific terminus at the Mexican port of Topolobampo would cut 400–600 miles from the journey across North America and attract shippers with an eye on trade with the Orient. In 1872 he explored Topolobampo Bay and proposed that a commune be developed along with the railroad and was the chief publicist for the colony. It aimed first to provide a home for all those who sought to organize cooperative industries, pursue equity, and protect home industries. It was to be Pacific City. Work on the railroad began in the 1880s, and by 1886 permanent settlement at the bay had begun. Owen left in 1893 amid many factious conflicts in the scheme. By 1894, 1,189 people were reported to have arrived, although the population was never that high at any one time. The railroad was never finished; meanwhile, two factions developed amid disputes over land and water rights, among other subjects. Also there was some thought given to the adoption of Herzka's ideas from his *Freeland* (1889). Litigation led to evictions and dispossession from land. Some of the Americans married Mexicans and remained there, but most returned home shortly after 1894.

See Also George, Henry; Hertzka, Theodor; Owen, Albert Kimsey

Sources:

Buder, Stanley. 1990. *Visionaries and Planner*. New York: Oxford University Press.

Fogarty, Robert S. 1990. *All Things New: American Communes and Utopian Movements 1860–1914*. Chicago: University of Chicago Press.

Kerr, John L. 1968. *Destination Topolobampo: The Kansas City Mexican and Orient Railway*. San Marino, Calif.: Golden West Books.

Miller, Timothy. 1990. *American Communes 1860–1960*. New York: Garland.

Reynolds, Ray. 1971. *Cats Paw Utopia*. Rev. ed. San Bernardino, Calif.: Borgo Press.

Spann, Edward K. 1989. *Brotherly Tomorrows: Movements for a Cooperative Society in America 1820–1920*. New York: Columbia University Press.

TOWNER, JAMES WILLIAM. James William Towner (1823–1913) was born in Willsboro, Essex County, New York, and at thirty-three went to Cleveland, Ohio, to practice as a Universalist minister (1845). After he married (1851), he lived in Westfield, Ohio, and continued preaching for three years. He wrote articles for the *Social Revolutionist*, a magazine of the Berlin Heights Society, a small communal group near Sandusky, Ohio. In West Union, Iowa, he established a law practice (1859) and in 1861 joined the Union army, lost an eye in battle at Pea Ridge, and was given a commission in the Invalid Cavalry Corps. He lived at Berlin Heights Community, a loose group of families whose members practiced free love, switching partners in unbridled sensuality, quite unregulated by God. In 1866 Towner repented his sins of the flesh and applied for membership in Oneida. Oneida declined to admit him. He applied again in 1874, after the Berlin Heights Community had disbanded. Towner and eleven others went to the Oneida Community and brought with them $14,000. At the time the colony was greatly conflicted over the stirpiculture plan and the leadership of the son of the founder of the Oneida Community. Towner took a central role in opposing the founder of Oneida, John Humphrey Noyes (1811–1886), and the failure of the colony was accelerated by the formation of a group of "Townerites." After the decline of the Oneida Community, he traveled to California (1882) and helped form the town of Santa Ana; also he assisted in the organization of Orange County in 1885 and became a judge; in 1897 he retired. He died in Santa Ana.

See Also Noyes, John Humphrey; Oneida community

Sources:

Fogarty, Robert S. 1980. *Dictionary of American Communal History*. Westport, Conn.: Greenwood Press.

Klaw, Spencer. 1993. *Without Sin; The Life and Death of the Oneida Community*. New York: Penguin.

Oved, Yaacov. 1987. *Two Hundred Years of American Communes*. New Brunswick, N.J.: Transaction Books.

TOYNBEE, ARNOLD. Arnold Toynbee (1852–1883) was born in Saville Row, London. Although when his father died, Arnold was only fourteen, the father inspired his son with a love of literature and helped plant the social ideals that were later the main interests of Toynbee's life. After his education at preparatory school, Black Heath, he developed a deep interest in poetry, history, and philosophy. Gradually, he turned his mind from the military career others had chosen for him to more philosophical interests. In January 1873 at Pembroke College, Oxford, he studied philosophy and religion. He had a strong desire to assist in raising material and moral conditions of the poor in England. It became an absorbing passion, and he devoted great energy to the study of economics, graduated (1878), and was appointed tutor at Balliol College. In the next four and a half years his influence spread not only at Oxford but also among those interested in the social and industrial problems of the industrial age. He taught at workers' adult education classes and with Samuel Barnett (1844–1913) did much social work in London's East End. In his memory Toynbee Hall was established. His most notable work was *The Industrial Revolution in England* (1884). He coined the term "industrial revolution." He was the uncle of the notable historian Arnold Joseph Toynbee (1889–1975), who wrote a ten-volume history of the world.

See also Barnett, Samuel Augustus; Toynbee Hall

Sources:

Jones, Barry. 1989. *The Macmillan Dictionary of Biography*. Melbourne: Macmillan.
Kadish, Alon. 1986. *Apostle Arnold: The Life and Death of Arnold Toynbee, 1852–1883*. Durham, N.C.: Duke University Press.
Magnussen, Magnus, and Rosemary Goring, eds. 1990. *Chambers Biographical Dictionary*. 5th ed. Edinburgh: Chambers.
Stephen, Leslie, and Sydney Lee, eds. 1917. *The Dictionary of National Biography*. London: Oxford University Press.

TOYNBEE HALL. Toynbee Hall opened Christmas Eve 1884 in Commercial Street, Whitechapel, London. It was a residential community, sometimes referred to as a social workshop, in one of the city's poor areas and promoted free advice on the law, the Workers' Educational Association, and the Whitechapel Art Gallery. Moves to establish Toynbee Hall began in 1883, and the formal opening was January 1885. The institute was named after a young history scholar from Oxford, Arnold Toynbee (1852–1883), whose death was accompanied in Britain by a growing interest in a sociological appreciation of the expanding hunger, squalor, poor housing, and widespread misfortune among the poor and an awareness that current political ideas and economic policies did not serve Britain well. The electorate was expanding, and the obligations of the wealthy to the poor— who now had the vote—were becoming clearer. Toynbee Hall was established after the anonymous publication of a most influential pamphlet *The Bitter Cry of Outcast London* and its publicity in the *Pall Mall Gazette* and the *Daily News*. The pamphlet identified in London considerable moral corruption, heartbreaking misery, godlessness, and dark regions of poverty, misery, squalor, and immorality. A leader was sought for a crusade against the social evils. The first to preach this was the headmaster of Harrow, and he was followed by Rev. Samuel Augustus Barnett (1844–1913), vicar of St. Jude's, Whitechapel. On the subject of the settlement of "university men in great towns," speakers invited academics to visit London and see what they might do. In time Toynbee Hall was established. After its foundation many people enrolled in extension lectures, and the numbers rose from 300 to 600 between 1883 and 1886; 130 courses were offered in the 1890s, when enrollments reached close to 1,000. Toward the end of the 1890s interest in such education declined; nevertheless, over its 100 years of work its main principles have been followed, and its primary aims have been achieved. Today Toynbee Hall continues to pursue its original goals. Many notables have made contributions to them, including William Beveridge (1879–1963), Richard Henry Tawney (1880–1962), Clement Attlee (1883–1967), Graham Wallas (1858–1932), Harold J. Laski (1893–1950), J. Ramsay MacDonald (1866–1937), B. Seebohm Rowntree (1871–1954), Norman Angell (1872–1967), Viscount Astor (1886–1971), and George Bernard Shaw (1856–1950). Toynbee Hall has its own theater, music room, a roofed playground, a library, and warden's lodgings. Each year Toynbee Hall holds the Barnett Lecture and the Attlee Foundation Lecture. Occasionally, royalty attend fund-raising events. Toynbee Hall helped establish the British Dance Theatre (1950), and it is the center of Stepney Children's Fund. Among its recent undergraduates it claims the authoritative biographer Lady Antonia Fraser (b. 1932) and Benazir Bhutto (b. 1953). Since 1982 John Profumo (b. 1915) has been administrator of Toynbee Hall.

See Also Barnett, Samuel Augustus; Toynbee, Arnold

Source:

Briggs, Asa, and Anne Macartney. 1984. *Toynbee Hall: The First Hundred Years.* London: Routledge and Kegan Paul.

TRANSCENDENT SOCIETY. The Transcendent Society is a postmodern utopia at the center of reports of near-death experiences. They are positive reports of a society beyond death, a world of beautiful skies and lush vegetation crisscrossed by streams, dotted by lakes and a few forests, lawns, parks, and gardens of flowers of unique and unprecedented beauty. People here are more capable in seeing, thinking, and moving about; the environment is idyllic and rural, but occasionally there are cities with halls, houses, temples, libraries, and places of high learning. People are content and happy. Life is orderly and harmonious, with no disorder or confusion. People work in some kind of service industry; relations are cooperative, and there are a few sanctions for the control of deviance. Moral lines determine stratification; the society comprises different communities and levels of moral action based on different degrees of moral progress. Problem groups are isolated so as not to affect the smooth operation of the society. The Transcendent Society is attractive to a broad array of various groups and has elements of the Land of Cockaygne, a mythical utopia in mock-serious poems of the thirteenth century. It shows some restraints; has a few millenarian elements, and forms a pastiche of earlier ideal societies. Like some utopias and utopian ventures it is critical of some modern values—competition and materialism—and prefers humanism and spiritualism. Also it is eclectic and manages criticism and paradoxes well. As a utopia the Transcendent Society has little of the social programs and policies that characterize many utopias.

Sources:

Gallup, George, Jr., and William Proctor. 1982. *Adventures in Immortality: A Look beyond the Threshold of Death.* New York: McGraw-Hill.
Kellehear, Allan. 1995. "Near-Death Experiences and the Pursuit of the Ideal Society." *Journal of Near-Death Studies* 10: 79–95.
Moody, Raymond A., and Paul Perry. 1988. *The Light Beyond.* London: Macmillan.
Zaleski, Carol. 1987. *Otherworld Journeys: Accounts of Near-Death Experiences in Medieval and Modern Times.* New York: Oxford University Press.

TRIAL, THE. *The Trial* (1925) is one of two influential dystopian novels by Franz Kafka (1883–1924). Suddenly and for no reason, Joseph K., a bank assessor, is arrested for a crime he is not aware of. He cannot discover the charges leveled at him or the authority of the secret law court that condemned him. The court is in a poor tenement area of a German city and meets in a ramshackle building. In panic Joseph K. tries to defend himself and seeks help from anyone who he thinks might be influential. A small servant, Leni, gets Joseph an interview with Titorelli, his advocate, but this is of no help. Leni suggests to Joseph K. that he confess and beg mercy from the court. He is already guilty, so there are only two avenues open to him: have the case postponed indefinitely or gain a temporary release, which itself may lead to being arrested again. Joseph K. cannot win either way, largely because he resists the authority of the court. An unknown organization commissions two agents to catch Joseph K., and he is murdered. *The Trial*, like *The Castle*, (1926), concerns humankind's relations with a dystopian authority that is inefficient, tyrannical, brutal, insanely unreasonable, and, perceived this way, such authority reflects humankind itself. In the reflection can be seen our failure to grasp God's revealed laws, for which our flaws of understanding are entirely responsible. Humankind's fate is certain because it wants to follow its impaired thought processes in the face of divine retribution. The lesson is that, first, in this world people who feel secure are among the lower orders because they voluntarily obey and never question any directives; second, people who think, reflect, ask questions, study alternatives, wish to learn more about everyday processes, and have standards of their own will find life utterly frustrating, filled with despair, and, as they struggle to understand life, will face nothing but punishment from official bureaucracies.

The struggle against the unintelligible power of these bureaucracies is a nightmare that many people can recall having as they ponder over, and attempt, unrealizable goals.

See Also Castle, The; Dystopia; Kafka, Franz

Sources:

Booker, M. Keith. 1994. *Dystopian Literature: A Theory and Research Guide*. Westport, Conn.: Greenwood Press.
Hawkins, Joyce M., ed. 1986. *The Oxford Reference Dictionary*. Oxford: Clarendon.

TRIST, ERIC LANSDOWN. Eric Lansdown Trist (1909–1993) was born in Dover, England, into a maritime family and educated at Dover County Boys' School and Pembroke College, Cambridge, where he studied English and psychology. He graduated with distinction and studied at Yale University as a fellow with the Commonwealth Fund. He married and on returning to England worked on social and economic problems of unemployment in Dundee, Scotland. He was a psychologist in World War II and helped devise the War Office Selection Board methods and later the Civil Resettlement Units for returning prisoners of war. Supported by the Rockefeller Foundation, he helped establish the Tavistock Institute of Human Relations, London, founded the journal *Human Relations*, and with his Australian colleague Fred Emery (1925–1997) wrote *The Causal Texture of Organizational Environments*, a widely read revision of how to study the environments of human organizations (1965). He and Emery researched the sociotechnical system theory of organizations (1946–1963), and in 1959–1960 they devised the Search Conference to change organizations and small working groups. He researched the quality of working life and social ecology. After his wife's death he remarried, and in 1966 he taught and did research at the University of California at Los Angeles (1966–1969), the Wharton School of Business (1969–1978), and York University. He was honored by the International Academy of Management (1983) and made doctor of laws (1989) at York University for notable and outstanding achievements in research and teaching for the practice of management. He died in Carmel, California, while preparing a three-volume anthology of the work done by scholars and practitioners at the Tavistock Institute, *The Social Engagement of Social Science* (1990–1997).

See Also Emery, Frederick E.; Search Conference

Sources:

Trahair, Richard C. S. 1996. "Trist, Eric Lansdown." In Malcolm Warner, ed., *International Encyclopedia of Business and Management*, pp. 4974–4978. London: Thomson Press.
Trist, Eric L. 1993. "Guilty of Enthusiasm." In Arthur G. Bedeian, ed., *Management Laureates: A Collection of Autobiographical Essays*, vol. 3, pp. 191–221. Greenwich, Conn.: JAI Press.

TROTSKY, LEON. Leon Trotsky, pseudonym for Lev Davidovich Bronstein (1879–1940), was the son of a prosperous Jew in the Ukraine. As a student he was influenced by the revolutionary movement in Russia and in 1898 was arrested for political agitation and exiled to Siberia. There he joined the new Russian Social Democratic Worker's Party and in 1902 escaped to join the party's leaders in Switzerland. During the revolution of 1905 he returned to Russia, was arrested when the revolution failed, and was again exiled to Siberia but again managed to escape abroad. After the 1917 revolution Trotsky returned to Russia, joined the Bolsheviks, and quickly became Lenin's second-in-command. During the civil war of 1918–1920 Trotsky was in charge of military operations and distinguished himself with energetic leadership. His actions aroused the hostility of other communist leaders, particularly Stalin (1879–1953). In 1924 Trotsky was publicly attacked for the heresy of worldwide revolution, or "Trotskyism," and in 1928 exiled to Soviet Central Asia. In 1937 he settled in Mexico and was murdered by a communist agent in 1940.

See Also Bolshevism; Stalin, Joseph

Sources:

Beilharz, Peter. 1987. *The Social and Political Thought of Leon Trotsky*. Oxford: Clarendon Press.
Brone, Pierre. 1988. *Trotsky*. Paris: Fayard.
Callinicos, Alex. 1991. *Trotskyism*. Buckingham: Open University Press.
Carmichael, Joel. 1975. *Trotsky: An Appreciation of His Life*. London: Hodder and Stoughton.
Devine, Elisabeth, Michael Held, James Vison, and George Walsh, eds. 1983. *Thinkers of the Twentieth Century: A Biographical, Bibliographical and Critical Dictionary*. London: Macmillan.
Howe, Irving. 1978. *Trotsky*. Hassocks: Harvester Press.
Mandel, Ernest. 1979. *Revolutionary Marxism Today*. London: New Left Books.
Sinclair, Louis. 1989. *Trotsky: A Bibliography*. Brookfield, Vt.: Scolar.
Trotsky, Leon. 1930. *My Life*. 1975 ed. Harmondsworth: Penguin.

TRUTH, SOJOURNER. Sojourner Truth (1799–1883) was born a slave in Ulster County, New York. Little is known about her early life. She spoke Dutch and served in a New Paltz house in New York (1810–1827), had five children, and was named Isabella. In 1827 she escaped slavery and worked for a Dutch family whose surname she adopted. Influenced by Quaker ideas, she attended Methodist camp meetings. In 1829 she moved to New York City, joined black and white reform groups, and worked for Elijah Pierson's (d. 1834) house, a community that ministered to prostitutes on Bowery Hill and that became known as the Kingdom. When Robert Matthews (Matthias) was charged with murdering Pierson, she was charged with conspiring with him. They were found not guilty. In 1843, at God's call, she changed her name to Sojourner Truth, took up mysticism, and traveled as a preacher and reformer. She participated in the Northampton Association of Education and Industry, Florence, Massachusetts;

in 1856 she was in Battle Creek, Michigan, and stayed also at the spiritualist Quaker settlement of Harmonia. She would lecture on abolition of slavery and woman's rights and attract great crowds. She became known nationally and was a heroine to many. In 1863 Harriet Beecher Stowe (1811–1896) wrote an article about Sojourner Truth for the *Atlantic Monthly*, extolling her piety, religiosity, and mysticism. During the Civil War (1861–1865), Truth was invited to the White House to meet Abraham Lincoln (1809–1865). She helped establish the Freedmen's Village in Arlington, Virginia. She worked there as a counselor, appointed by Lincoln. It was a model camp for escaped slaves. For the feminist movement Truth was a bold, fighting visionary and worked unceasingly to get a state in the West for the United States' former slaves.

See Also Harmonia; Matthias, Robert

Sources:

Bernard, Jacqueline. 1967. *Journey toward Freedom—the Story of Sojourner Truth*. New York: Norton.
Chmielewski, Wendy E. 1993. "Sojourner Truth: Utopian Vision and Search for Community, 1797–1883." In Wendy E. Chmielewski, Louis J. Kern, and Marilyn Klee Hartzell eds. *Women in Spiritual and Communitarian Societies in the U.S.*, pp. 21–37. Syracuse, N.Y.: Syracuse University Press.
Fitch, Suzanne P., and Roseann M. Mandziuk, 1997. *Sojourner Truth as Orator*. Westport, Conn.: Greenwood Press.
Fogarty, Robert S. 1980. *Dictionary of American Communal History*. Westport, Conn.: Greenwood Press.
Magnussen, Magnus, and Rosemary Goring, eds. 1990. *Chambers Biographical Dictionary*. 5th ed. Edinburgh: Chambers.
Pauli, Hertha. 1962. *Her Name Was Sojourner Truth*. New York: Appleton-Century-Crofts.
Titus, Frances. 1878. *Narrative of Sojourner Truth, a Bondswoman of Olden Time and Her Book of Life*. Reprinted, 1990. Salem, N.H.: Ayer.

TUCKER, HORACE FINN. Rev. Horace Finn Tucker (1849–1911) was born in Cambridge, England, son of a clergyman, agent of the British and Foreign Bible Society. The family arrived in Australia in 1861. Horace was educated in New South Wales at the Theological College and ordained in 1874. He married in Melbourne, Victoria, and was promoted to the prosperous parish of South Yarra (1880). He founded three mission churches and a grammar school. In the 1890s depression he promoted the settlement of the unemployed in Gippsland and central Victoria by founding the Village Settlement Association in 1892. Tucker was a utopian socialist and until 1896 put into practice the ideals of his *The New Arcadia: Australian Story* (1894). In 1894 he was elected canon of St. Paul's Cathedral in Melbourne and after retiring in 1908 continued parish work until he died.

See Also Tucker Village Settlements

Sources:

Metcalf, Bill, ed. 1995. *From Utopian Dreaming to Communal Reality: Cooperative Life Styles in Australia.* Sydney: University of New South Wales Press.
Pike, Douglas, et al. 1966–1990. *Australian Dictionary of Biography.* Carlton, Victoria: University of Melbourne Press.

TUCKER VILLAGE SETTLEMENTS. Tucker Village Settlements were the work of Rev. Horace Tucker (1849–1911). In 1892 he established the Village Settlement Association and cooperative communities in the colony of Victoria at Croydon, Jindivick, Moora, Red Hill, Horsham, and Kilfera. By 1894 these communities had 700 families and seemed to prosper. However, as the depression deepened, the scheme became handicapped by a lack of capital, poor management, Tucker's inadequate leadership, poor quality of the land, and a lack of irrigation. The government passed the Settlement of Lands Act (1893) to help future settlements. Residents began to leave because they could get better support financially if they took part in government-sponsored settlements. In 1896 Tucker's communal experiment ended.

See Also Leongatha Labor Colony; Tucker, Horace Finn

Sources:

Blake, L. J. 1964. "Village Settlements." *The Educational Magazine* 21: 425–432, 463–468, 496–501.
———. 1966. "Village Settlements." *The Victorian Historical Magazine* 37: 189–201.
Metcalf, Bill, ed. 1995. *From Utopian Dreaming to Communal Reality: Cooperative Life Styles in Australia.* Sydney: University of New South Wales Press.

TUNTABLE FALLS CO-ORDINATION CO-OPERATIVE. Tuntable Falls Co-ordination Co-operative is the largest surviving alternative community in Australia. It evolved from the 1973 Alternative Lifestyle Festival in the United States. At Nimbin 10,000 people gathered for the Aquarius Festival; the experience affected many, and some stayed to establish an alternative style of life in communal living. To a few it was an escape from the misery of capitalism, and to others it was an opportunity to shape a new, if nebulous, future. Small communes flourished around the countryside. Larger communities found it hard to establish themselves because land had to be bought, and the turnover of members was high. A few devoted members bought 1,200 acres with a $110,000 mortgage and created the Tuntable Falls Land Co-operative Proprietary Limited. Shares entitled the owner and family access to the whole property. No one can own a specific piece of land. With 500 members the company paid off its mortgage. In 1976 about 40 to 100 people were residents, depending on the season. At first all residents lived under one roof, the White House, sharing what little they had and tolerating much inconvenience. Gradually, the sense of community gave over to one of settlement. One group established a shop to sell bread, another sold garden produce, and another sold craft work in local towns.

By printing cardboard coins an attempt was made to establish a form of social credit. After debates over how to educate the children born in the cooperative, a minimal school was established; a group of the original settlers formed a committee to set rules for everyday life, for example, no soap in the creek, no dogs or cats, no motor vehicles, limits on the number of visitors. Soon it appeared the settlement structure gave over quickly to a rational and legal society dominated by a cooperative that valued private land. Today elected coordinators are supported by monthly members' meetings in managing the community. They have established a preschool, a primary school, and Rainbow Cafe in Nimbin, along with a LETS and other communal and employment-creating projects, including services for the disabled.

See Also LETS; Nimbin

Sources:

Cock, Peter. 1979. *Alternative Australia: Communities of the Future?* Melbourne: Quartet Books.

Constaine, Gloria. 1995. ''From a London Slum to Nimbin's Magic.'' In Bill Metcalf, ed., *From Utopian Dreaming to Communal Reality: Cooperative Life Styles in Australia*, pp. 74–83. Sydney: University of New South Wales Press.

TUPAMAROS. Tupamaros was a band of up to 10,000 left-wing urban guerrillas, founded about 1963 and led by Raúl Sendic (d. 1989), a labor organizer in Uruguay. They aimed for a utopian Uruguay through Marxist revolution and followed the same practices as England's legendary Robin Hood (fl. c. 1250–c.1350) to get their resources; that is, in 1969 they robbed banks, blew up radio stations, raided government arms supplies, and abducted, kidnapped, and held to ransom notable foreigners in Uruguay. In 1972 police right-wing, paramilitary groups began to crush the Tupamaros, and they were beaten by 1974. They based their name on Túpac Amarú II, an eighteenth-century Inca leader who led a revolt against the Spaniards. The name was assumed by José Gabriel Condorcanqui (1742–1781), who was born at Tinta, near Cuzco in Peru. Unlike the modern Tupamaros, his aim was to improve the lot of Indians rather than topple their oppressive Spanish overlords. But like the modern Tupamaros he failed and eventually was forced to lead a violent rebellion; finally, he, too, was caught and tortured to death. Raúl Sendic was imprisoned for thirteen years.

Sources:

Cook, Chris. 1983. *Macmillan Dictionary of Historical Terms*. London: Macmillan.

Dudley, Lavinia P. 1963. *The Encyclopedia Americana*. International ed. New York: Americana Corporation.

Howatt, Gerald M. D. 1973. *Dictionary of World History*. London: Nelson.

McHenry, Robert, ed. 1992. *The New Encyclopedia Britannica*. Chicago: Encyclopedia Britannica.

TUSCARAWAS. Tuscarawas was a community founded by Josiah Warren (1798–1874) on 400 acres in Tuscarawas County, Ohio, in Tuscarawas River

Valley (1831). It was the first U.S. anarchist community. Members invested their capital voluntarily in a steam sawmill, with no return on interest and the freedom to withdraw their investment at any time. Disease rather than an unstable economy destroyed the community (1833–1835). It had been established in a low-lying area where malaria was common, and at the end of the first summer over half the adults were ill; further disaster followed in the next year, and by the winter of 1834 many died of influenza. In 1835 most inhabitants abandoned the village, including Josiah Warren. A few stayed until 1837. The place was also called Equity, named after Warren's time-labor system. The financial loss was great because most investment had been in land and buildings. Nevertheless, Tuscarawas inspired its founder to build communities based on individuals' voluntary agreements rather than majority rule of members.

See Also Anarchist Utopias; Equity Colony; Warren, Josiah

Sources:

Fogarty, Robert S. 1980. *Dictionary of American Communal History*. Westport, Conn.: Greenwood Press.

Martin, James J. 1953. *Men against the State: The Expositors of Individual Anarchism in America, 1827–1908*. Dekalb, Ill.: Adrian Allen Associates.

Oved, Yaacov. 1987. *Two Hundred Years of American Communes*. New Brunswick, N.J.: Transaction Books.

Schuster, Eunice M. 1931–1932. "Native American Anarchism." *Smith College Studies in History* 17: 1–4.

TWIN OAKS. Twin Oaks Community, comprising forty members in 1973, was based partly on B. F. Skinner's (1904–1990) *Walden Two*. It was established in Louisa, Virginia, and upholds egalitarian relations, justice, a belief in progress and efficiency, and the use of effective management and technology. Work was organized under a labor credit system. The labor credits were eventually abandoned from want of a means to measure the variable acceptance of different tasks. Much time is now given over to the quota of work done for this community and the process of decision making; however much time this takes, the community efforts flourish in drama, painting, writing, sculpture, and music, for which no labor credits are given. Membership rights and responsibilities are governed by a growing set of policies. Charismatic leadership is not accepted as a method of establishing policy at Twin Oaks. Twin Oaks depends on the external market economy to sell rope hammocks. Currently, it has eighty-five adults and twelve children. The guiding principles of Twin Oaks are a private room and a public life, following Skinner's belief that one does not sacrifice privacy because one chooses community life. Everyone has a room of his or her own, and private time is achieved by the sharing of housework and child care.

See Also Federation of Egalitarian Communities; Skinner, B. F.; *Walden Two*

Sources:

Goldenberg, Zena. 1993. "The Power of Feminism at Twin Oaks Community." In Wendy E. Chmielewski, Louis J. Kern, and Marlyn Klee-Hartzell, eds., *Women* in *Spiritual and Communitarian Societies in the U.S.*, pp. 256–266. Syracuse, N.Y.: Syracuse University Press.

Hall, John R. 1978. *The Ways Out: Utopian Communal Groups in an Age of Babylon.* London: Routledge and Kegan Paul.

Kincade, Kathleen. 1973. *A Walden Two Experiment: The First Five Years of the Twin Oaks Community.* Foreword by B. F. Skinner. New York: Morrow.

———. 1994. *Is It Utopia Yet?* Louisa, Vir.: Twin Oaks Community Press.

Komar, Ingrid. 1983. *Living a Dream: A Documentary Study of the Twin Oaks Community 1979–1983.* Norwood, Pa.: Norwood.

Weinbaum, Batya. 1984. ''Twin Oaks: A Feminist Looks at Indigenous Socialism in the United States.'' In Ruby Rohrlich and Elaine Hoffman Baruch, eds., *Women in Search of Utopia: Mavericks and Myth Makers*, pp. 157–167. New York: Schocken Books.

TYTHERLY. Tytherly, also known as Queenwood or Harmony Hall, was an Owenite utopian venture in East Tytherly, Hampshire, where fifty-seven Owenites organized themselves into the Home Colonisation Society and took a property, October 1839, to develop their colony. It was named Tytherly after the principal farm on the estate, and the community was called Harmony Hall. Robert Owen (1771–1858) leased three adjoining farms to increase the total acreage to 1,000. Members subscribed for £50 and received food and accommodations, but no wages. Most were artisans from northern industrial towns. They would rise at 5 A.M., study mathematics, labor all day, and study fine arts in the evenings. They built a dining hall and bedrooms, but the accommodations were too small, and by the summer of 1840 many had left, and the membership of the colony fell to twelve impoverished adults and seven children. In February 1841, when Manea Fen failed, great effort was made to enlarge Tytherly. Funds were collected, and a fine brick building was erected for the residents following the design of architect Joseph Hansom (1803–1882), the cab inventor. A school was planned for 500 children. It was to be an industrial school, and it was started by Robert Owen. It would take the children at birth, educate them, and lead them into marriage and high social responsibility for the community. The community raised its membership to 300, and Owen issued a prospectus for £25,000 from the public. He could raise only £1,900. The local community ridiculed the venture in communism by pointing out that wives and children were being shared in the colony, and this put the paternity of the children in doubt; and the economic exchange in the community was based on barter and therefore was very confusing. Sufficient funds were never found. In 1844 Tytherly came to an end, Owen resigned, and the enterprise was wound up in August 1845.

See Also Manea Fen; Owenism

Sources:

Armytage, Walter Henry Green. 1961. *Heavens Below: Utopian Experiments in England 1560–1950.* London: Routledge and Kegan Paul.

Harrison, John F. C. 1969. *Robert Owen and the Owenites in Britain and America: Quest for the New Moral World*. New York: Charles Scribner's Sons.

Pollard, Sidney and John Salt, eds. 1971. *Robert Owen: Prophet of the Poor*. Lewisburg, Pa.: Bucknell University Press.

U

UNION COLONY. Union Colony was organized in New York City December 1869 by Nathaniel Cook Meeker (1817–1879), the agriculture editor of the *New York Tribune*. Its aim was to establish a settlement in Colorado. There were 442 members; each paid $150. Two-thirds of the membership were from New York, Ohio, and Pennsylvania, were nonsectarian, and practiced temperance. On the site chosen in the Cache La Poudre Valley northeast of Denver, the town of Greeley was founded in 1870, named after Horace Greeley (1811–1872) who was the editor of the *New York Tribune*. In return for fees varying between $50 and $200, members received farmland and the right to buy lots in the colony town. In the Union Colony saloons and billiard halls were not tolerated. Immediately, a school was opened, a library was begun, and a lyceum was founded. The inhabitants of Colorado thought that the colonists were foolish and that Meeker a tall, awkward, slow-speaking man, was a tactless crank. The colonists changed their communal institution into a township indistinguishable from others nearby. Later, a dozen families joined the Puget Sound Cooperative Colony in Washington state.

See Also Greeley, Horace; Meeker, Nathaniel Cook

Sources:

Fogarty, Robert S. 1980. *Dictionary of American Communal History*. Westport, Conn.: Greenwood Press.
James, Truslow Adams, ed. 1940. *Dictionary of American History*. New York: Charles Scribner's Sons.
Malone, Dumas, ed. 1933. *Dictionary of American Biography*. Vol. 6. New York: Charles Scribner's Sons.

UNITED STATES AS UTOPIA. The nineteenth-century United States has been seen as a utopia by social theorists and those who came to the United

States to lead a better life. The country was expansive, open, and new, lacked preexisting government systems, and inspired settlers who were looking for a better world. There people felt they could quit the problems of the past in the Old World and start afresh in the New World. When the continent was discovered, the United States was given many features of a utopia. Its native inhabitants seemed to live without an old and oppressive government, and its communities owned the land and the goods they made. Later, the Puritans could see that the country gave them a choice to live their own way in a new and apparently holy place. The wilderness was theirs to conquer, and the land was theirs to take, and they could create and control a better world for themselves in the United States. Protestant reformers considered the New World as the place where the Antichrist would be defeated, the Reformation could be completed, and religious movements would find or could establish their holy city. As the United States industrialized work, the nation became secularized, and utopian movements and ventures took a secular form. Radical social democracy emerged, rational government became possible, and it seemed that the United States, the New World, could create new political structures that had never been possible in the Old World. As commerce grew, and industrialization sped on, the country became a place of antiutopias, where, as personal opportunities and freedom grew, corruption and mass poverty expanded. Consequently, some observers argue that the United States, like the USSR, is an enormous, failed utopia. Similar ideas are examined in a history and criticism of the United States as a utopia in fiction (Roemer, 1981).

See Also Russia as Utopia

Sources:

Holloway, M. 1951. *Heavens on Earth: Utopian Communities in America: 1680–1880*. New York: Dover.

Holstun, James. 1987. *A Rational Millennium: Puritan Utopias of Seventeenth-Century England and America*. New York: Oxford University Press.

Kumar, Krishan. 1987. *Utopia and Anti-Utopia in Modern Times*. Oxford: Basil Blackwell.

———. 1991. *Utopianism*. Milton Keynes, U.K.: Open University Press.

Roemer, Kenneth M., ed. 1981. *America as Utopia*. New York: B. Franklin.

UNITY HOUSE. Unity House, in New York City, was a cooperative household where Stephen Pearl Andrews (1812–1886) headed a spiritual order that attracted a few followers, including Marie Howland (1835–1921). It was one of the few U.S. utopian ventures located within a metropolis.

See Also Andrews, Stephen Pearl; Howland, Marie Stevens

Source:

Fogarty, Robert S. 1990. *All Things New: American Communes and Utopian Movements 1860–1914*. Chicago: University of Chicago Press.

UNIVERSAL BROTHERHOOD. The Universal Brotherhood is at the isolated township of Balingup, 150 miles (240 km) from Perth, Western Australia, on 317 acres. The climate is mild to warm, and the area is well watered and has a soil rich in loam, altogether making the area amenable to growing wheat, rye, oats, barley, vegetables, herbs, apples, nectarines, and peaches. The community maintains bees, hens, goats, cows, and 200 sheep; the wool and surplus agricultural goods are sold in Perth. The main source of income comes from a weekly charge to each resident to cover board and participation. All personal possessions are retained by members, who are not required to donate their capital to the community. Members pool their labor, and the community is governed by a hierarchy of twenty-two policymakers from the more stable and senior members; their policies are executed by a management committee of nine of the policymakers. Possibly the oldest and largest of Australia's New Age communities, it comprises mainly young people who strongly oppose unmarried sex, nudity, and drugs. They assume that the future lies in the hands of extraterrestrial "elder brothers" who, from their flying saucers, assist humankind to expand consciousness and thereby become ever more aware of its responsibility to the planet earth and its role in the universe. Although the local community does not share their beliefs, the members of the brotherhood enjoy friendly relationships with immediate outsiders. The community was founded by Fred Robinson (c.1891–1983); he did not run the community while he was alive but was often away visiting friends and lecturing. The community was registered as the Universal Brotherhood when its constitution was drawn up in 1974. The government recognizes it as a religious denomination. Its constitution states that it was formed to assist in the gathering together in communities of people of like mind adhering to the spiritual principles of universal brotherhood, to encourage persons to manifest the living principles of Christ within them, so as to create an environment for living a pure life in harmony with both nature and God. They uphold nonviolence, obey the Ten Commandments, and aim for an ecological balance with the environment, for example, soil conservation, organic gardening, and recycling.

See Also Robinson, Fred

Source:

Popenoe, Cris, and Oliver Popenoe. 1984. *Seeds of Tomorrow.* San Francisco: Harper and Row.

UNWIN, RAYMOND. Raymond Unwin (1863–1940) was an architect born at Rotherham, Yorkshire. He was the youngest son of an Oxford private coach, was educated at Magdalen School, and afterward trained as an engineer and architect. A founding father of urban communities in Britain, his mentors were John Ruskin (1819–1900) and William Morris (1834–1896). He was a member of the Fabian Society and the Socialist League. He began practicing architecture in 1896 with Richard Barry Parker (1867–1947). In 1904 he planned New Earswick, a model village near York. They designed the first Garden City at Letch-worth (1904) under the direction of Ebenezer Howard (1850–1928). In 1907 they worked on the Hampstead Garden suburb. He became increasingly inter-ested in town planning, in 1909 published *Town Planning in Practice*, and in 1910 organized the Town Planning Conference of the Royal Institute of British Architects. He designed such towns as Gretna Green around the munitions fac-tories of World War I. After the war he took charge of town and building planning at the Ministry of Health and sat on the committee of the League of Nations Union. He maintained several positions in town and country planning after he retired from the civil service in 1928. He was knighted in 1932 and in 1936 took up an academic appointment at Columbia University, New York, as a professor of town planning. He was awarded a gold medal for his contributions to architecture in 1937 by the Royal Institute of British Architects. He died in Lyme, Connecticut.

See Also Fabians; Garden City; Hampstead Garden Suburb; Howard, Ebe-nezer; Letchworth; Morris, William; Parker, Richard Barry; Ruskin, John

Sources:

Creese, Walter L. 1967. *The Legacy of Raymond Unwin: A Human Pattern for Planning.* Cambridge: MIT Press.

Gill, Roger. 1984. "In England's Green and Pleasant Land." In Peter Alexander and Roger Gill, eds., *Utopias*, pp. 109–117. London: Duckworth.

Jackson, Frank. 1985. *Sir Raymond Unwin: Architect, Planner and Visionary.* London: Zwemmer.

Marsh, Jan. 1982. *Back to the Land: The Pastoral Impulse in England, from 1880 to 1914.* London: Quartet.

Miller, Mervyn. 1992. *Raymond Unwin: Garden Cities and Town Planning.* Leicester: Leicester University Press.

USONIA. Usonia, an acronym for "United States of North America," was Frank Lloyd Wright's (1867–1959) architectural utopia for the United States. In his utopia, which was conceived in the 1920s and 1930s and which he later designed, each family would own and live on one acre in the countryside. All homes would fit in the agricultural landscape and be grouped or clustered evenly across the nation, and around them would be built small factories and farms, groups of schools, government buildings, and offices. This vision was built as a 144-square-foot model named Broadacre City (1934). It covered four square miles and could be easily replicated over thousands of acres.

See Also Wright, Frank Lloyd

Source:

Rosenbaum, Alvin. 1993. *Usonia: Frank Lloyd Wright's Design for America.* Washing-ton, D.C.: Preservation, National Trust for Historic Preservation.

UTOPIA. Utopia was one of the three anarchist communities—Equity and Modern Times were the others—established between 1834 and 1850 by Josiah

Warren (1798–1874) in Ohio. Utopia was planned to flourish with no leader or institutions, and it did for about two decades. By 1865 it had gone. After 1880, as immigration increased from Germany and Russia, the U.S. anarchist movement turned from free love and the labor theory of value to the conventional ideas and practices of international socialism. Thereafter, anarchist communities became less attractive to new members and dissolved.

See Also Anarchist Utopias; Equity Colony; Modern Times; Time Store; Warren, Josiah

Sources:

Fogarty, Robert S. 1980. *Dictionary of American Communal History*. Westport, Conn.: Greenwood Press.
Oved, Yaacov. 1987. *Two Hundred Years of American Communes*. New Brunswick, N.J.: Transaction Books.

UTOPIA. *Utopia* (1516) by Thomas More (1478–1535) was written in Latin and translated into English in 1551. The narrative about Utopia—Greek for "nowhere"—is presented by Raphael Hythloday—again Greek for "talker of nonsense"—who might have traveled with Amerigo Vespucci (1451–1512). Many of the practices in Utopia match those of the Incas of Peru. In Book I the evils of the world are cataloged; Book II sets down the features of an ideal place, Utopia. It is isolated, self-contained, and immune from outside forces; private ownership is banished; residents work for only six hours per day; city dwellers and farmers alternate functions; all lend a hand at harvest time. Throughout the land vast storehouses hold the produce. Everything is held in common; all houses are the same, and none have locks. Government is both paternalistic and democratic; special arrangements are made to educate gifted children. Social practices include inspection of men and women in the nude before marriage lest there be concealed defects; cosmetics are banned; euthanasia is normal; there is no conflict between religious sects; material rewards are given for virtue, and for crimes the punishment is slavery. In a recent discussion of the origins of the work, the argument is put that More's book was an account of idealized Mayan civilization in the Yucatan, Central America (Stobbart, 1992). Written in a literary, urbane, colloquial Latin, primarily for educated humanists of Western Europe (McCutcheon, 1992, p. 103) this political speculation appeared in four editions between 1516 and 1518 and may be based on Amerigo Vespucci's (1451–1512) *Four Voyages* (1507). First it offers a criticism of English social life in the early sixteenth century, where private property is misused, and corruptive tyranny is central to politics. The church and other corporate bodies control the nation's wealth, the poor are dispossessed, unemployment is rife, crime spreads, and oppressive laws dominate. Second, on an imaginary island, "Nowhere Land," tyranny is gone, private property is banished, manual labor is highly valued, and luxury is absent. Once thought to be an adaptation of Plato's *Republic* and Saint Augustine's *De Civitate Dei*,

More's work is recognized for its valuable approach to social issues in politics and economics and appreciated for its philosophical and satirical style. It is often taken as a reformer's world and thought to be inconsistent as well as a precursor to Marxist communism; but nowadays More's inconsistencies are allowed because his world is an ideal, not a blueprint; and he was much opposed to the misuse, rather than the abolition, of private property.

See Also More, Thomas

Sources:

McCutcheon, Elizabeth. 1992. "Review Essay: Ten English Translations/Editions of Thomas More's *Utopia.*" *Utopian Studies* 3, no. 2: 103–120.

More, Thomas. 1516. *Utopia.* 1966 ed. Leeds, England: Scolar Press.

Snodgrass, Mary Ellen. 1995. *Encyclopedia of Utopian Literature.* Santa Barbara, Calif.: ABC-CLIO.

Stobbart, Lorraine. 1992. *Utopia, Fact or Fiction: The Evidence from the Americas.* London: Alan Sutton.

V

VALLEY FORGE. The Friendly Association for Mutual Interests established a community in Valley Forge, Chester County, Pennsylvania. It was founded by Owenites from Philadelphia and Wilmington, Ohio, who were seeking to live in villages that were self-supporting and cooperative in January 1826. Friction arose between the community and local residents, and the community disbanded in the following September. Fifty of its members joined the Shaker community at New Lebanon.

See Also Owen, Robert; Owenite communities

Sources:

Fogarty, Robert S. 1980. *Dictionary of American Communal History*. Westport, Conn.: Greenwood Press.

Harrison, John F. C. 1969. *Robert Owen and the Owenites in Britain and America: Quest for the New Moral World*. New York: Charles Scribner's Sons.

Pitzer, Donald E. 1971. *Robert Owen's American Legacy*. Indianapolis: Indiana Historical Society.

VASTO, LANZA DEL. Lanza del Vasto (1901–1981) was born into a Catholic family among the nobility of Sicily and in his thirties wandered through Europe on a spiritual adventure until Italy invaded and occupied Ethiopia/Abyssinia (1935–1941). Fearing a European war, he went to India (1936), where he visited Mahatma Gandhi (1869–1948) at his village, Wardha, and trained in the principles of nonviolent politics, that is, integration of spiritual and manual work, life of minimum need gratification, self-sufficiency, self-reliance, humane work employing simple procedures. Lanza received the spiritual name Shantidas (''servant of peace'') and made the obligatory pilgrimage of truly devout Hindus to the source of the Ganges River. On the pilgrimage he integrated his Hindu faith with his Catholic beliefs and found within himself a message instructing him to return to the West and establish a nonviolent and self-reliant community that would thrive on poverty and hard manual work and set an example to Westerners of the proper way to peace. This was achieved in 1945 with small weekly meetings in Paris and later, after some disputes, in 1955, when he and his wife founded the Community of the Ark in the rural home of his wife's family. The community grew, and by 1963 it occupied la Borie Noble ("the noble borough") on 1,200 acres in the Languedoc region of southern France.

See Also Community of the Ark; Gandhi, Mohandas K.

Sources:

Popenoe, Cris, and Oliver Popenoe. 1984. *Seeds of Tomorrow*. San Francisco: Harper and Row.

Vasto, Lanza del. 1968. *Return to the Source*. New York: Schocken Books.

VERIGIN, PETER VASIL'EVICH. Peter Vasil'evich Verigin (1859–1924) was one of seven sons in a noble Russian family among the Doukhobors. He was educated privately. Robust and moody, he immersed himself in Doukhobor tradition. At age twenty years he married, but the marriage was annulled by Luker'ia Kalmykova, an influential widow of a local Doukhobor leader, even though the bride was pregnant. He left her and their newborn son, Peter. Kept by Luker'ia Kalmykova at the Doukhobors' palace, oddly named the Orphan House, Peter was groomed for leadership of the Doukhobors. In 1886, on the death of the widow, conflict emerged within the Doukhobor community and was partly resolved when Peter secured the leadership through claims to working miracles and divine intervention. He became "Peter the Lordly." The split in the community remained until the Doukhobors emigrated from Russia at the turn of the century. Peter and his community were subject to unrelenting persecution and exile to villages in Russia's cold north. In exile he studied Tolstoy's (1828–1910) doctrines, reorganized his community to promote generosity, sharing, and charity for their impoverished members, promoted vegetarianism, banned alcohol and tobacco, practiced anarchy, and advocated a Christian communist utopia, civil disobedience, and pacifism. Doukhobors were persecuted cruelly under the militarism of Nicholas II after 1894. By 1896 his community was the Christian Community of Universal Brotherhood, having adopted some ideas of John Coleman Kenworthy (1861–c.1934), the English publicist and supporter of Tolstoy. In the mid-1890s the Doukhobors were supported in their pacifism worldwide and allowed to emigrate to Canada. In 1903 Peter followed them, and his anarchic policies were applied in Canada. His followers were not permitted to take the oath of allegiance that was required if they were to receive Canadian government land grants. They acquired farms in the Kootenay areas of British Columbia and established self-supporting and self-governing communes. Peter organized the communities capably but refused to have his followers subject to compulsory education. In his view education and manual labor were intertwined. He died in a mysterious train explosion of unknown origin.

His community fell into disarray, but otherwise members maintained themselves as a sect of Christian pacifists. He was an ideal messianic-charismatic leader, typical of millenarian movements. His son, Peter, would later become a leader of Doukhobors in Canada, known as Peter the Purger.

See Also Doukhobors; Kenworthy, John Coleman; Tolstoy, Leo

Sources:

Marsh, James H., ed. 1988. *The Canadian Encyclopedia*. 2d ed. Edmonton: Hurtig.

Rasporich, Anthony W. 1992. "Utopian Ideals and Community Settlements in Western Canada 1880–1914." In R. Douglas Francis and Howard Palmer, eds., *The Prairie West: Historical Readings*, 2d ed., pp. 338–361. Edmonton, Alberta: Pica Pica Press.

Woodcock, George, and Ivan Avakumovic. 1968. *The Doukhobors*. London: Faber and Faber.

VILLAGE SETTLEMENTS OF SOUTH AUSTRALIA. Village Settlements of South Australia were founded by an act of Parliament (1893). Three communal settlements of 17,700 members were established, but not all relied on government funds. Two were known as utopian experiments, Murtho and Lyrup. Murtho was modeled on New Australia, the Paraguayan utopia. People in those utopias often exchanged letters. Harry Taylor (1873–1932), a notable South Australian socialist, left Cosme, the splinter group in Paraguay, to return to Murtho. In Lyrup rules were established for the other communities, and members shared property and avoided monetary exchange between themselves. Managers were elected, but only two of the thirteen, Murtho and Mount Remarkable, allowed women to vote. All members had to be English-speaking, and no Asians were admitted. Members were formally married or strictly single; alcohol was permitted but only for medicinal purposes. In time, sharing ceased, and private property and individual determination prevailed, along with prohibitive indebtedness. These settlements were not regarded as experiments in communism. The land they farmed was too poor and not easily irrigated, and the settlers were inexperienced in farming. However, when the land was turned over to private property as small farms, fruit growing especially was a success. Lyrup Village Association remains today and provides local irrigation.

See Also Murtho; New Australia; Taylor, Harry Samuel

Sources:

Jones, A. 1994. *Lyrup Village: A Century Association*. Lyrup: Lyrup Village Centenary Committee.

Metcalf, Bill, ed. 1995. *From Utopian Dreaming to Communal Reality: Cooperative Life Styles in Australia*. Sydney: University of New South Wales Press.

W

WAKEFIELD, EDWARD GIBBON. Edward Gibbon Wakefield (1796–1862) was born into a large family in London, educated at Westminster School and Edinburgh High School, and admitted to Gray's Inn. In 1816 he eloped with a ward of chancery, had the marriage approved by Parliament, and fathered two children before his young wife died in 1820, leaving him a comfortable income. In 1826 he abducted a young heiress, was caught and tried, and while in jail (1827) studied and published on crime, emigration, and colonization. He wrote *A Letter from Sydney* (1829), stating his ideas on colonization, which he hoped would replace transportation of convicts with the sale of small landholdings to approved purchasers. These ideas were extended in *England and America* (1833) and *A View of the Art of Colonization* (1849). He argued that from the proper sale of colonial lands sufficient funds could be raised to encourage young people to emigrate to Australia and thereby relieve the pressure of population in Britain and expand the British empire with productive colonies. Land prices should be set high enough to dissuade laborers from purchasing land they could not effectively use and encourage those with capital to buy land and on it employ the young colonists as laborers. In 1834 he helped form the South Australian Association, which led to the founding of South Australia two years later and afterward the establishment of the city of Adelaide. His ideas also influenced the colonization of Western Australia. In 1837 he established the New Zealand Association and, to prevent the designs of the French diplomats, sent colonists to New Zealand to force Britain to recognize the colony. In 1838, as secretary to Lord Durham, Wakefield's ideas influenced the Durham report on Canada. Also, in New Zealand he formed the Anglican Colony of Canterbury and settled there in 1853 and was elected to the first New Zealand General Assembly. His criminal record prevented him from holding significant political posts and forced him to be a promoter rather than an administrator of colonial policy.

Sources:

Bloomfield, Paul. 1961. *Edward Gibbon Wakefield, Builder of the British Common-wealth*. London: Longmans.
Garnett, Richard. 1898. *Edward Gibbon Wakefield, the Colonization of South Australia and New Zealand*. 1908 ed. London: Fisher Unwin.
Pike, Douglas, et al. 1966–1990. *Australian Dictionary of Biography*. 12 vols. Carlton, Victoria: Melbourne University Press.

WAKEFIELD SYSTEM. The Wakefield System was a utopian scheme for colonization to extend the British empire in the nineteenth century by advocating that colonial Crown land should be sold at a fixed price, and the money used to encourage emigration to the colony. It was assumed the colony's economy would develop, and investors in its industry would prosper. Land prices should be set high enough to dissuade laborers from purchasing land and encourage capitalists to buy land and employ young colonists as laborers. The scheme was devised by Edward Gibbon Wakefield (1796–1862), a British writer, politician, and radical colonialist who believed that systematic British colonial settlement would solve many domestic tensions and create healthy new societies. His ideas affected the development of Western Australia, South Australia, Canada, and New Zealand.

See Also Wakefield, Edward Gibbon

Sources:

Gill, Roger. 1984. "In England's Green and Pleasant Land." In Peter Alexander and Roger Gill, eds., *Utopias*, pp. 109–117. London: Duckworth.
Harrop, Angus J. 1928. *The Amazing Career of Edward Gibbon Wakefield*. London: Allen and Unwin.
Preece, Warren E., ed. 1965. *Encyclopedia Britannica*. Chicago: Encyclopedia Britannica.
Stephen, Leslie, and Sydney Lee, eds. 1917. *The Dictionary of National Biography*. London: Oxford University Press.

WALD, LILLIAN. Lillian Wald (1869–1940) was born in Cincinnati, Ohio. Her grandparents had come to the United States after the 1848 revolutions in Poland and Germany to establish themselves in business and enjoy political freedom not available in Europe. In Rochester, Lillian attended an English-French boarding school, trained to be a nurse and graduated in 1891, and enrolled in the Women's Medical College, New York. In 1893 she helped organize home nursing education for immigrant families in the poor district of New York City. She moved to the East Side on Manhattan, unaware of the pioneering work in Chicago by Jane Addams (1860–1935). With financial support from the banker Jacob H. Schiff (1847–1920) she founded the Nurses' Settlement. Members were to live in the local community, accept it as their own, and be social workers and citizens as well as nurses. The Nurses' Home became the Henry Street Settlement, a neighborhood house for civic programs, education, and a focus for philanthropic contributions to society. Her social work and her nursing were of equal influence. She aimed to eradicate tuberculosis, improve accommodations for poor folk, and establish playgrounds and parks.

See Also Addams, Jane; Settlement House of Henry Street, Hull House

Source:

James, Edward T., ed. 1974. *Notable American Women, 1607–1956.* Cambridge: Harvard University Press, Belknap Press.

WALDEN, OR, LIFE IN THE WOODS. *Walden, or, Life in the Woods* is a spiritual biography of a man who objects to the machine age and chooses to follow a practical alternative rather than descend into mysticism. The author, David Henry Thoreau (1817–1862), left his occupation as a pencil manufacturer and established himself at Walden Pond outside Concord in Massachusetts. He wanted to show that humankind can live with little and find contentment. Elegant simplicity was the way of life at Walden. He was a carpenter, mason, surveyor, and mechanic for two years at his haven from the world of advancing technology. In eighteen essays he records his life and views on the troubles of the world and makes careful observations of the natural environs. At the same time the author wrote *A Week on the Concord and Merrimack Rivers* (1849). It is a book that extols U.S. virtues of self-reliance and the great and wholesome outdoors. In 1849 he wrote *Civil Disobedience*, a criticism of the United States' imperialist policies in the war against Mexico, the institution of slavery, and treatment of Native Americans.

See Also Thoreau, Henry David

Sources:

Francis, Richard. 1997. *Transcendental Utopias: Individual and Community at Brook Farm, Fruitlands and Walden.* Ithaca, N. Y.: Cornell University Press.

Thomas, Owen, and William Rossi, eds. 1991. *Walden and Resistance to Civil Government.* 2d ed. New York: Norton.

Thoreau, Henry David. 1854. *Walden.* Edited by J. Lyndon Shanley. Introduction by Joyce C. Oates. 1971 ed. Princeton: Princeton University Press.

WALDEN TWO. *Walden Two* is a novel by B. F. Skinner (1904–1990) about a tour through a contemporary U.S. community. The founders of Walden Two are adults who assume that traditional adult attitudes are established at an unexpectedly early age. Therefore, to produce happy citizens, child raising must be wisely conducted from birth so that at adulthood humankind's beliefs are cognate with those of the community, bad feelings are curbed, and cooperation is enhanced. The first main point of the novel is that techniques are available to modernize child raising and to reach that point of civilized development where deep, unpleasant feelings are banished, and cooperative social relations are upheld securely. Second, great respect is given to science as the grounds for reliable knowledge, while efficiency is highly valued and attaches to education and the economy as well as child raising. The society is not competitive, and members grow doing only what is good for themselves and the community. The advantage of education of children through scientific conditioning is that it is systematic rather than scatterbrained, follows known principles rather than old ideas, and can be readily altered for the next generation in the interests of progress. The community is run by appointed planners and managers according to a code of behavior. Some objections are that scientifically based knowledge is achieved at the expense of insight, understanding, and creativity; rejecting futurism and history is hardly acceptable; speedy social change is unlikely because all learning has been done with positive sanctions, and coercive learning has been replaced with persuasive argument and the rewarding, but false, feeling that individuals have shared in their development; the practice of democracy is illusory; community members have the right of appeal over the community's code of behavior but no right to consultation or meeting to discuss policy; tyrants may claim special knowledge and rule for private motives; cooperation is made an alternative to competition rather than a realistic adjunct to it. The novel has been discussed for many years and used as a model for community life at Twin Oaks with success. Because of the controversy about the novel it is sometimes used to illustrate the distinction between dystopian and ideal societies. To some critics *Walden Two* is a psychological nightmare where humans are raised to become machines. For this reason it is read in conjunction with the utopian literature of Edward Bellamy (1850–1898), Aldous Huxley (1894–1963), Thomas More (1478–1535), William Morris (1834–1896), and H. G. Wells (1866–1946).

See Also Skinner, B. F.

Sources:

Booker, M. Keith. 1994. *Dystopian Literature: A Theory and Research Guide.* Westport, Conn.: Greenwood Press.
Skinner, B. F. 1948. *Walden Two.* New York: Macmillan.

WALDENSES. Waldenses were austere Christians, a brotherhood that sought a better life in apostolic poverty and a simple interpretation of the gospel. Pope Alexander III (c.1105–c.1181) tolerated their founder, Peter Waldo (fl. 1170–1217), but in 1179 the Third Lateran Council condemned his "Poor men of Lyon," as the brotherhood was known. Forbidden to preach by Pope Lucius III and later excommunicated for their disobedience (1184), the Waldenses formed a separate church and allied themselves with other dissident groups. During the thirteenth century they established themselves in the mountain valleys of southeastern France and Piedmont. The modern Waldensian church belongs to the alliance of Presbyterian churches.

See Also Waldo, Peter

Sources:

Cross, Frank L. 1974. *The Oxford Dictionary of the Christian Church.* 2d ed. New York: Oxford University Press.

Douglas, James D., ed. 1974. *The New International Dictionary of the Christian Church*. Exeter: Paternoster Press.
Douglas, James D., Walter A. Elwell, and Peter Toon. 989. *The Concise Dictionary of Christian Tradition*. London: Marshall Pickering.
Eliade, Mircea, ed. 1987. *Encyclopedia of Religion*. New York: Macmillan.
Ferguson, Sinclair B., and David F. Wright. 1988. *New Dictionary of Theology*. Leicester, U.K.: Inter-Varsity Press.
McDonald, William J., ed. 1967. *New Catholic Encyclopedia*. New York: McGraw-Hill.

WALDO, PETER. Peter Waldo (fl. 1170–1218) was born in Lyon and became a wealthy trader. He was originally known as Valdes. In c.1170–1173 Waldo heard the call to Christ's teaching. He gave away his fortune to the poor, gave an income to his wife, and put his daughter in an abbey at Fontevrault. He followed the call and began to preach in the streets, and a brotherhood grew around him. In time his followers became known as ''Poor men of Lyon'' and ''the Holy Paupers.'' About 1182–1183 he and his followers broke a church ban on unofficial preaching and were excommunicated and banished from Lyon (1184). A modern version of his beliefs is part of Presbyterian theology.

See Also Waldenses

Sources:

Cross, Frank L. 1974. *The Oxford Dictionary of the Christian Church*. 2d ed. New York: Oxford University Press.
Douglas, James D., ed. 1974. *The New International Dictionary of the Christian Church*. Exeter: Paternoster Press.
Magnussen, Magnus, and Rosemary Goring, eds. 1990. *Chambers Biographical Dictionary*. 5th ed. Edinburgh: Chambers.

WALHACHIN. Walhachin was an aristocratic utopia based upon social escape and pastoral ideals. It was founded between Kamlogos and Lytton, New Brunswick, Canada (1910–c. 1915) and, like Cannington Manor, comprised aristocratic bachelors—some 200 ex-public school and ex-army remittance men—who based their economy on producing apples and bourgeois pleasure. Concentrating on one crop and using an expensive irrigation system, their experimental community began failing financially when World War I called members away to administrative or military posts, and a change in government disheartened the largest landowner, the marquis of Anglesy.

See Also Cannington Manor

Sources:

Munro, Kathleen. 1955. ''The Tragedy of Walhachin.'' *Canadian Cattleman* 18: 7–31.
Rasporich, Anthony W. 1992. ''Utopian Ideals and Community Settlements in Western Canada 1880–1914.'' In R. Francis and R. Douglas, eds., *The Prairie West: Historical Readings*, 2d ed., pp. 338–361. Edmonton, Alberta: Pica Pica Press.
Riis, Nelson A. 1972. ''Settlement Abandonment: A Case Study of Walhachin, B. C.'' *Urban History Review* 2: 19–21.

WALLAS, GRAHAM. Graham Wallas (1858–1932) was born in Monkwearmouth, Sunderland, in the northeast of England, was educated at Shrewsbury, and studied at Oxford University. He was lecturer at the London School of Economics and joined the Fabian Society (1886–1904). He became involved in local politics and was a socialist on the London County Council (1904–1907). He was one of the early British scholars in social psychology and concentrated on the application of social psychology to politics. He published *Human Nature in Politics* (1908) and *The Great Society* (1914) and identified the irrational factors that contribute to political attitudes and public opinion. He was much interested in the role of fear, pain, pleasure, and hatred in the psychology of the crowd. He argued that the great society—the utopian civilization—would need to have three elements of organization: property and its relation to individuals, the democratic state and its relation to socialism, and the nonlocal association and its relation to syndicalism. Each would need to be reconsidered and developed for the great society to emerge. A similar approach he thought would be needed for the establishment of an international organization to effect peace and understanding. He was made professor of political science at the University of London (1914–1923).

See Also Cole, George Douglas Howard; Fabians; Shaw, George Bernard; Webb, Beatrice Martha; Webb, Sidney James; Wells, H. G.

Sources:

Magnussen, Magnus, and Rosemary Goring, eds. 1990. *Chambers Biographical Dictionary*. 5th ed. Edinburgh: Chambers.
Wallas, Graham. 1914. *The Great Society*. New York: Macmillan.

WARDLEY, JANE AND JAMES. Jane and James Wardley (fl. 1747–1774) were adherents of the French prophets the Camisards, who had fled oppression in France to refuge in Britain after the revocation of the Edict of Nantes (1685) by Louis XIV, which had guaranteed liberty of conscience to Protestants. The Wardleys were Quaker tailors in Bolton-on-the Moors, north of Manchester, England. In about 1747 they joined the Camisards, radical Calvinists from the Cevennes who held secret meetings throughout Britain. Their leader at the time had settled in London (1738). The Wardleys belonged to the Quakers, the Friends, but after they considered the experiences of the Camisards, they were much drawn to their extreme beliefs and practices, for example, fasting, trances, shaking of the limbs, calling for repentance, the Second Coming, miracles, and signs of the presence of a spirit, like lights in the sky and voices. The Wardleys established their own society and at meetings would follow the Quaker practice of meditation at first; then, using a form of trembling to indicate God's disgust with sin, they would shake, sing, shout, walk about in agitation, and claim to be acting under spiritual guidance according to supernatural forces. These Shaking Quakers—later to be called simply ''Shakers''—had no ideology other than to claim to understand, intuitively, great millenarian and apocalyptic forces.

Jane—later to become "Mother Jane"—would demand immediate repentance from all members, for fear of what might happen to the sinful at the moment of the imminent Second Coming. After joining the group for four years and declaring outrageous and spellbinding heresies, Ann Lee (c. 1736–1784), a young member, was imprisoned. Imprisonment made a martyr of her, and on her release she became leader of the Shakers, emigrated to the United States, and founded her own sect (1774). Left with the rump of their society the Wardleys quit the group, perhaps in protest at its new radical turn under Ann Lee, and took refuge in a poorhouse, only to see their remaining followers disperse.

See Also Camisards; Lee, Ann; Shakers, Shaking Quakers

Sources:

Andrews, Edward Deeming. 1953. *The People Called Shakers: A Search for the Perfect Society.* 1963 ed. New York: Dover.

Whitworth, John McKelvie. 1975. *God's Blueprints: A Sociological Study of Three Utopian Sects.* London: Routledge and Kegan Paul.

WARREN, FISKE. Fiske Warren (1862–1937) was born at Waltham, Massachusetts, and studied at Harvard (B.A., 1874). Also he studied law at Oxford in England (1906–1907). He manufactured paper. He won the amateur tennis championship of the United States at the court of the Boston Athletic Association in 1893 and toured the world in 1897, 1901, 1905, 1907, and finally in 1931. He founded several single-tax communities: Tahanto in Massachusetts (the first) (1909–1934); Halidon, Westbrook, Maine (1911); and Santa Jordi in Santa Coloma in the Republic of Andorra (1918). For the promotion of the single-tax principles he founded the Georgian Trust (1920). He was director of the American Peace Society and an occasional writer of articles on single-tax principles. The single-tax colonies were the result of the ideas of Henry George (1862–1916), a political economist whose *Progress and Poverty* (1879) was widely read. Warren was also influenced by William E. Smythe (1861–1922), who proclaimed that the increased value of land should accrue to the community as a whole.

See Also Henry George League; Smythe, William Ellsworth

Sources:

Fogarty, Robert S. 1980. *Dictionary of American Communal History.* Westport, Conn.: Greenwood Press.

Who Was Who in America 1897–1942. 1966. Vol. 2. Chicago: Marquis, Who's Who.

WARREN, JOSIAH. Josiah Warren (1798–1874) was born in Massachusetts and became a writer, community planner, notable anarchist, and libertarian. At age twenty he married, settled in Cincinnati, established a lamp factory, taught music, and led an orchestra. In 1825, after hearing Robert Owen (1771–1858) lecture, Warren's interest turned to cooperative societies. He sold his lamp factory and settled at New Harmony, the Owenite community, but found he was more interested in anarchist ideology. He developed a great distrust of power; loathed monopolies; preferred summary justice, decentralized power, and free expression; and upheld the sovereignty of the individual, respect of individual conscience, and the labor theory of value. After two years, he returned to Cincinnati, where he opened Time Store, a labor exchange, where people left labor notes that promised so many hours of work in return for goods from the store. Time Store closed in 1830. That year he founded a communal school for orphans, Spring Hill, in Ohio, where he experimented with vocational training and techniques of self-sufficiency. Warren established *The Peaceful Revolutionist*, an anarchist journal that folded in 1835. He helped found Equity, a community in Tuscarawas County, Ohio (1831–1837), Utopia, and Modern Times. Warren turned to printing, invented some printing devices, and worked at the trade for fifteen years. In 1841 he published the *Herald of Equity*; in 1847 he published *Equitable Commerce*, which discussed the value of labor, individual freedom, and personal property and its security. In 1849 he lived at Utopia, whose members by 1852 were using the exchange of labor principle of the Time Store and had attracted 100 residents. He also helped Stephen Pearl Andrews (1812–1886) to found Modern Times on Long Island, where anarchists preached and practiced free love. Utopia and Modern Times lasted for about twenty years before becoming conventional communities. After the forcefulness of his leadership came into question, in 1860 Warren returned to Boston and reverted to his early interest in music.

See Also Andrews, Stephen Pearl; Modern Times; New Harmony Community; Owen, Robert; Time Store; Tuscarawas; Utopia

Sources:

Bailie, William. 1906. *Josiah Warren: The First American Anarchist*. Boston: Smal, Maynard.

Fogarty, Robert S. 1980. *Dictionary of American Communal History*. Westport, Conn.: Greenwood Press.

Martin, James J. 1953. *Men against the State: The Expositors of Individual Anarchism in America, 1827–1908*. Dekalb, Ill.: Adrian Allen Associates.

Oved, Yaacov. 1987. *Two Hundred Years of American Communes*. New Brunswick, N.J.: Transaction Books.

Veysey, Laurence. 1973. *The Communal Experience: Anarchist and Mystical Counter-cultures in America*. New York: Harper and Row.

WAYLAND, JULIUS A. Julius A. Wayland (1854–1912) was born into a poor family at Versailles, Indiana. As a young man he entered local politics and became involved in the publication of the local newspaper, the *Versailles Gazette* (1877). He moved to Harrisonville, Missouri, where he published *Cass News*; an ardent Republican, his work raised great controversies among his readers. In 1882 he moved to Pueblo, Colorado, where he made his fortune in real estate. In the 1890s he changed from being a radical and aggressive capitalist to a militant socialist; his socialist activities centered on the local community whose paper he edited. At the same time he read widely in socialist literature, for example, Edward Bellamy (1850–1898), Laurence Gronlund (1846–1899), and other U.S. utopian thinkers. During the 1890s recession, when many Americans endured social hardship, Wayland sold his property and published *The Coming Nation*, a socialist weekly that affected ideas on communal settlement in the United States. He was a main contributor to the establishment of Ruskin Colony, west of Nashville, Tennessee (1894–1899). However, when factions developed in the community, Wayland became disillusioned at its lack of unity and abandoned the colony, leaving with it the newspaper he had founded.

See Also Bellamy, Edward; Gronlund, Laurence; Ruskin Colony

Sources:

Fogarty, Robert S. 1980. *Dictionary of American Communal History*. Westport, Conn.: Greenwood Press.
Oved, Yaacov. 1987. *Two Hundred Years of American Communes*. New Brunswick, N.J.: Transaction Books.

WE. *We* (1920–1921), an antiutopian novel by Evgeny Ivanovich Zamyatin (1884–1937), is set in One State and owes much to *When the Sleeper Wakes* (1899) by H. G. Wells (1866–1946). One State emerged after a 200-year war that destroyed human civilization 1,000 years ago. Benefactor and the Guardians rule One State autocratically. It is hemmed in by an impenetrable Glass Wall that protects it from a rampant wilderness. All its institutions are driven by reason and science, its activities are highly mechanized, and relations between citizens are officially harmonious. Citizens are ciphers without names; rulers use mathematics to overbear all thought and resolve all problems—subjective or objective—by the application of the principles of time and motion engineering established by the ''father of scientific management,'' Frederick Winslow Taylor (1856–1915), a venerated prophet who conceived One State. Privacy is abolished, as citizens live in glassed rooms and may draw blinds for only two hours a day; sex is clearly separated from love and reproduction, while sexual relief is achieved by matching citizens with the same level of desire; childbirth is controlled by eugenic principles; deep feeling is buried, so tragedy is absent, and harmony rules all interpersonal relations. In *We*, D-503, a noted engineer, falls in love with I-330, a rebellious and seductive woman associated with the Memphi, a secret band of revolutionaries with connections among animals in the uncontrollable wilderness outside. The Memphi adherents break through part of the Glass Wall, and the invading animals create a great disturbance for One State. On oppressing this outrage, Benefactor and associates capture D-503, remove his imagination surgically, and indoctrinate him with totalitarian rationalizations; he readily betrays his Memphi associates, including his ex-lover, all of whom are executed by being placed in a vacuum. At the end of the book the revolution is being maintained, and doubts arise about its outcome that engender some degree of hope that citizens will wake from their dystopian nightmare. The novel falls between the writing of Wells and that of Aldous Huxley (1894–1963) and George Orwell (1903–1950). Because *We* is so pessimistic about the misuse of science and technology and celebrates the end of social change and the depersonalization of human relations to eliminate conflict, the work is now considered a dystopic warning that a socialist state may become a nightmare after the Bolshevik revolution.

See Also Brave New World; Dystopia; Huxley, Aldous; *Nineteen Eighty-Four*; Orwell, George; Wells, H. G.; Zamyatin, Evgeny Ivanovich

Sources:

Booker, M. Keith. 1994. *Dystopian Literature: A Theory and Research Guide*. Westport, Conn.: Greenwood Press.

Kumar, Krishan. 1987. *Utopia and Anti-Utopia in Modern Times*. Oxford: Basil Blackwell.

Snodgrass, Mary Ellen. 1995. *Encyclopedia of Utopian Literature*. Santa Barbara, Calif.: ABC-CLIO.

Wegner, Phillip. 1993. "On Zamyatin's *We*: A Critical Map of Utopia's 'Possible Worlds.' " *Utopian Studies* 4, no. 2: 94–116.

WEBB, BEATRICE MARTHA. Beatrice Martha Webb, née Potter (1858–1943), was born near Gloucester, the eighth of nine children of a railway and industrial magnate. Governesses educated Beatrice at home; she read and traveled widely. In 1882, following her mother's death, Beatrice became a close associate of her father in his business affairs, helped manage them, and often traveled with him. In 1883 she managed the rent collection from her father's properties. This activity led to the investigation of life and work in London (*Life and Labour of the People of London*). Some findings were published in *Nineteenth Century* (October 1887); other articles followed, and one in particular on sweated labor brought her before an inquiry by the House of Lords to give evidence (1888). Later, she published *The Co-Operative Movement in Great Britain* (1891). After her marriage to Sidney Webb (1892), they established themselves at "Millbank." Their social research contributed much to socialist thought in Britain. In 1923 they acquired Passfield Corner, Liphook, in Hampshire, where they intended to continue their work and to write. After a tour of Russia (1932) and a meeting with the exiled Leon Trotsky (1879–1940), who impressed them deeply, they wrote *Soviet Communism: A New Civilisation?* (1935). It was not welcomed by Fabians, who held to the principle of gradualism in social change. From the mid-1930s she was greatly interested in events in Russia.

See Also Cole, George Douglas Howard; Fabians; Shaw, George Bernard; Webb, Sidney James

Sources:

Legg, Leopold G. W., and E. T. Williams, eds. 1959. *Dictionary of National Biography 1941–1950*. London: Oxford University Press.

McKenzie, Jeanne. 1979. *A Victorian Courtship: The Story of Beatrice Potter and Sidney Webb*. London: Weidenfeld and Nicolson.

Muggeridge, Kitty, and Ruth Adam. 1967. *Beatrice Webb: A Life, 1858–1943*. London: Secker and Warburg.

Seymour-Jones, Carol. 1992. *Beatrice Webb: Woman of Conflicts*. London: Allison and Busby.

Webb, Beatrice. 1926. *My Apprenticeship*. Reprinted 1975. London: Longmans Green.

———. 1948. *Our Partnership*. New York: Longmans, Green.

WEBB, SIDNEY JAMES. Sidney James Webb (1859–1947) was born in London, the younger son of an accountant, and was educated in Switzerland, Mecklenburg-Schwerin, Birkbeck Institute in London, and the City of London College. He loved reading. In 1885 he entered Gray's Inn, and in 1886 London University awarded him an LL.B. In 1879 he had befriended Bernard Shaw (1856–1950), who, in 1885, introduced Webb to the Fabian Society. His great knowledge and administrative ability helped put the new society on a sound base. He wrote Fabian tracts, for example, *Facts for Socialists* (1887), and *Facts for Londoners* (1889), and contributed one of the best essays on socialism to the *Fabian Essays on Socialism* (1889). His contribution was greatly admired by Beatrice Martha Potter (1858–1943). They married and in a well-planned life together made a significant contribution to British social thinking. Notwithstanding, they came under attack within the Fabian Society. Herbert G. Wells (1866–1946) resigned (1908) and attacked them in his *The New Machiavelli* (1911); G.D.H. Cole (1889–1959) opposed their bureaucratic methods. They continued with their work. He helped establish the London School of Economics and Political Science (1895) and was its professor of public administration (1912–1927). In 1918, as a Fabian socialist, he drafted Clause IV of the British Labor Party's constitution that committed members to public ownership of key industries, the "common ownership of the means of production, distribution and exchange." The utopian phrases of the clause became a symbol for a broad agenda of radical social change among those who wanted nationalization of the economy and strong links between the party and the trade unions. It stood until 1995, when revised due to the influence of Britain's present prime minister. Webb's essays are still regarded as valuable contributions to British socialism. He became a member of Parliament (1922) and in 1924 in the first labor government was the president of the Board of Trade. He remained in Parliament, filling several administrative positions, until 1931. After careful preparation for their visit to Russia in 1932 they returned greatly impressed and published *Soviet Communism: A New Civilisation?* (1935). Fabians were shocked by its abandonment of gradualism, the central feature of their position on social change.

See Also Cole, George Douglas Howard; Fabians; Shaw, George Bernard; Webb, Beatrice Martha; Wells, H. G.

Sources:

Crystal, David. 1994. *The Cambridge Biographical Encyclopedia*. New York: Cambridge University Press.

Legg, Leopold G. W., and E. T. Williams, eds. 1959. *Dictionary of National Biography 1941–1950*. London: Oxford University Press.
McKenzie, Jeanne. 1979. *A Victorian Courtship: The Story of Beatrice Potter and Sidney Webb*. London: Weidenfeld and Nicolson.

WEIMAR REPUBLIC. The Weimar Republic was a utopian attempt to secure a democratic republic in Germany after World War I. Nine months after Kaiser Wilhelm II (1859–1941) abdicated, the Weimar Republic was established, August 1919. It was based on a constitution that declared that the people were sovereign—"political power emanates from the people"; men and women were given the vote at twenty; all Germans were equal before the law; personal liberty was inviolable; every German had the right to express an opinion freely and to form associations and societies; and all Germans had the right to enjoy complete liberty of belief and conscience. In the whole world, no person would be more free than a German citizen, and no government would be more liberal or democratic than the government of Germany. The republic faltered until the 1930s depression. It did not get popular and undivided support in Germany and was much resented by devoted monarchists. On one hand, German conservatives blamed the republic for allowing the disgrace of the nation by the strict terms of the Treaty of Versailles (7 May, 1919); on the other hand, left-wing radicals abused the Weimar Republic for helping to stage a national upheaval in Germany and international revolution in world politics. The unforgiving foreign policy of the French also played a powerful role in the collapse of the republic. Weimar is used to symbolize the failure of Germans to accept the utopian ideal of democracy. Notwithstanding, in the 1920s, there were important cultural advances in art, theater, and music, and, particularly, advances in movie making that later were seen in British, Soviet, and U.S. cinema. Leaders of the republic were Friedrich Ebert (1919–1925) and von Hindenburg (1925–1934). The Weimar Republic vanished when Adolf Hitler (1889–1945) became chancellor (1933) and began instituting the Third Reich—itself a totalitarian utopia-cum-dystopia—by passing the Enabling Act (1933), which was used to overthrow Germany's constitutional government after Hindenburg, its president, had died and to replace democratic government with personal dictatorship.

See Also Ebert, Friedrich; Hindenburg, Paul von

Sources:

Cerci, Ian, ed. 1990. *Weimar: Why Did German Democracy Fail?* New York: St. Martin's.
Fisher, Peter S. 1991. *Fantasy and Politics: Visions of the Future in the Weimar Republic*. Madison: University of Wisconsin Press.
Gay, Peter. 1969. *Weimar Culture: The Outsider as Insider*. London: Secker and Warburg.
Laqueur, Walter. 1974. *Weimar: A Cultural History, 1918–1933*. London: Weidenfeld and Nicolson.

Vincent, C. Paul. 1997. *A Historical Dictionary of Germany's Weimar Republic, 1918–1933*. Westport, Conn.: Greenwood Press.

WELLS, H. G. Herbert George Wells (1866–1946) was born in Bromley, Kent, England, son of a shopkeeper. At eighteen he left his job to further his education and studied biology (B.Sc., 1890) under Thomas Henry Huxley (1825–1895). He had a great influence on Wells and the variety of utopia that he wanted, that is, a complex society run by an intelligent and otherwise superior scientific elite. At first Wells taught for the Universal Tutorial College. He loved writing, and later, when his short stories were so successful, he chose to live by his pen. He did this by entering into many social issues, for example, free love, progressive education, world government, human rights, use of science and technology, and modern socialism. He joined the Fabian Society. He married often and worked hard, wrote countless articles and over 100 books, and achieved great fame and notoriety. However, his fame had all but evaporated at the time he died. He contributed to utopian thought through science fiction and in his *Time Machine* (1895) described a future society of two classes. His *The Island of Dr. Moreau* (1896) and *The War of the Worlds* (1898) established him securely as a science fiction writer with a strong utopian theme, more generally so in his *A Modern Utopia* (1905). He was a Fabian, but, eternally restless, he argued with George Bernard Shaw (1856–1950) and Sidney Webb (1859–1947) and Beatrice Webb (1858–1943). He was not keen on the rational administrative procedures used by members of the socialist movement to curb the growth of injustices during the emergence of representative democracy in Britain. In 1911 he published *The New Machiavelli* about a politician embroiled in a sex scandal, which was seen as a personal criticism of his erstwhile Fabian colleagues, the Webbs. Wells was a strong advocate of the League of Nations. His ideal society appears in *A Modern Utopia*. It relies on advanced technology and depicts the world as one state. It is ruled by a benevolent elite, reincarnations of the Guardians in Plato's *Republic*, who serve their society, live ascetically, and do not use power to advance themselves. In this world technological advances we enjoy today are commonplace; the people are educated in social and artistic skills as well as technical skills; parenthood is planned, welfare is guaranteed, and government is good. In principle utopia is extended forever by constantly changing for the good all that can be changed.

See Also Cole, George Douglas Howard; Fabians; Shaw, George Bernard; Wallas, Graham; Webb, Beatrice Martha; Webb, Sidney James

Sources:

Booker, M. Keith. 1994. *Dystopian Literature: A Theory and Research Guide*. Westport, Conn.: Greenwood Press.

Brome, Vincent. 1951. *H. G. Wells*. Reprinted 1970. Westport, Conn.: Greenwood Press.

Foot, Michael. 1995. *H. G.: The History of Mr. Wells*. Washington, D.C.: Counterpoint.

Hammond, John R. 1991. *H. G. Wells and Rebecca West*. New York: Harvester Wheatsheaf.

Magnussen, Magnus, and Rosemary Goring, eds. 1990. *Chambers Biographical Dictionary*. 5th ed. Edinburgh: Chambers.
Snodgrass, Mary Ellen. 1995. *Encyclopedia of Utopian Literature*. Santa Barbara, Calif.: ABC-CLIO.

WHITE CITY. White City, a preacher's vision of heaven, like The Celestial City in *The Pilgrim's Progress* (1678, 1684), was built outside Chicago for the World's Columbian Exposition, 1893. The exposition marked the 400 years since Christopher Columbus (1451–1506) discovered the New World; also it marked the United States as a great civilization. White City, as it became known, lay at the end of a dirt road and a sooty railroad. The architecture of White City was threaded with themes of classical Greek grandeur, the greatness of fine European buildings, the mysteries of Asia, all centered in the Great Basin with a laurel-wreathed statue that symbolized the U.S. republic. On 633 acres were constructed 200 white buildings like department stores. A bright courtyard surrounded a lagoon, and the great white buildings housed astounding achievements in electrification, telecommunication, the phonograph, and the automobile. The Emerald City in L. Frank Baum's (1856–1919) *The Wonderful Wizard of Oz* was modeled on, and inspired by, White City.

Sources:

Appelbaum, Stanley. 1980. *The Chicago World's Fair of 1893: A Photographic Record*. New York: Dover.
Burg, David. 1976. *Chicago's White City of 1893*. Lexington: University of Kentucky Press.
Gilbert, James. 1991. *Perfect Cities: Chicago's Utopias of 1893*. Chicago: University of Chicago Press.
Grosso, Robert M. 1993. *Celebrating the New World: Chicago's Columbian Exposition of 1893*. Chicago: Ivan R. Dee.
Patton, Phil. 1993. "Sell the Cookstove If Necessary, but Come to the Fair." *Smithsonian* 24, no. 3: 38–50.

WHITE OAK. White Oak was a branch of the Shaker Community on 4,000 acres at White Oak, in southeastern Georgia, 1898. It comprised a small colony of Shakers from the Union Village Community. This was probably the last Shaker colony and was much smaller than other Shaker groups. They attempted to settle in 1897 near Brunswick, Georgia, on some 7,000 acres. In 1902 the Georgia Shakers sold out and went back to Ohio.

See Also Shakers, Shaking Quakers

Sources:

Andrews, Edward Deeming. 1953. *The People Called Shakers: A Search for the Perfect Society*. 1963 ed. New York: Dover.
Desroche, Henri. 1971. *The American Shakers*. Amherst: University of Massachusetts Press.

Fogarty, Robert S. 1980. *Dictionary of American Communal History.* Westport, Conn.: Greenwood Press.

WHITLEY, JOHN HENRY. John Henry Whitley (1866–1935) was born in Halifax and educated at Clifton and London University. He worked for his father, a cotton spinner of Halifax and, with a strong interest in planning, architecture, youth, and social work, became a member of the local town council (1893–1900). Elected a Liberal member of Parliament (MP) for Halifax (1900–1928), he was chosen to be Liberal whip (1907–1910) and chairman of ways and means. In the difficult industrial relations climate following the World War I reconstruction of British industry, Whitley's name attached to the joint consultation machinery (national joint councils, district councils, works committees) that was recommended by the committee of inquiry that he had chaired (1917, 1918). The reports aimed for conciliation and cooperation in industrial relations, and its ideas gained wide support at the time. He made speeches on education and was elected speaker (1921–1928), having been deputy speaker for ten years. As speaker he witnessed the conflicts in industry that culminated in the General Strike (1926). Whitley was also chairman of a royal commission on labor in India (1929–1931), and he was appointed to chair the board of governors of the British Broadcasting Corporation (1930).

See Also Whitley Councils

Source:

Legg, Leopold G. W., ed. 1949. *Dictionary of National Biography 1931–1940.* London: Oxford University Press.

WHITLEY COUNCILS. Whitely Councils were groups of industrial workers and their employers and managers that reached for the utopian aim of resolving conflict at work through discussion, negotiation, bargaining, mediation, and conciliation instead of lockouts, strikes, and other forms of industrial violence common in Britain before and during World War I. Each council was a joint standing industrial council and functioned at a national or local level of industry; they were composed of representatives of employers and workers in an organized trade, and they considered and settled conditions of employment. They were recommended in the report by the British Reconstruction Subcommittee (1917, 1918). Although they did not eliminate industrial action in British industry in the 1920s, they were recognized as a peaceful alternative that had great value in getting each side to an industrial dispute to recognize some bases of their differences and, in some small degree, helped introduce the recognition much later of participatory or democratic decision making in the workplace.

See Also Whitley, John Henry

Sources:

Marsh, Arthur. 1979. *Concise Encyclopedia of Industrial Relations.* Westmead, Farnborough, Hants: Gower.

McHenry, Robert, ed. 1992. *The New Encyclopedia Britannica*. Chicago: Encyclopedia Britannica.

WILKINSON, JEMIMA. Jemima Wilkinson (c. 1753–1819) was born in Rhode Island and raised a Quaker. At twenty she was pronounced dead from fever by her physicians. As her friends assembled for the last rites, she rose from her coffin. She believed this was evidence that her former self had died and passed to the land of the spirit and that her present self was her resurrection and spiritual body. She announced that her body and spirit had been commissioned by the Holy One with the power of Jesus Christ until his Second Coming. With this power she could judge the world, perform miracles, and had the authority to establish a holy church on earth. Persuasive and shrewd, she attracted many followers and by 1789 had established Jerusalem, a utopian community on 1,400 acres in Yates County, New York. She took the name "Public Universal Friend," and two "witnesses" accompanied her, Sarah Richards and Rachael Miller. They insisted on the Shaker doctrine of celibacy. She followed Shakers' practices at religious meetings and would stand in her bedroom doorway, wearing a waistcoat, stockings, and white silk cravat when she preached. Although she supported poverty, her methods of persuasion allowed her to live in considerable comfort, and she owned and had the use of land purchased in the name of Rachael Miller. Her sect dispersed when she died.

See Also Jerusalem

Sources:

Hinds, William Alfred. 1878. *From American Communities and Co-Operative Colonies*. 2d. rev. ed. Philadelphia: Porcupine Press.
Hinds, William A. 1973. "Benign Charisma—Jemima Wilkinson and Her Jerusalem." In Rosabeth Moss Kanter, *Communes: Creating and Managing the Collective Life*, pp. 206–208. New York: Harper and Row.
Malone, Dumas, ed. 1936. *Dictionary of American Biography*. Vol. 10. New York: Charles Scribner's Sons.
Oved, Yaacov. 1987. *Two Hundred Years of American Communes*. New Brunswick, N.J.: Transaction Books.
Wilson, James, and John Fiske, eds. 1889. *Appleton's Cyclopaedia of American Biography*. New York: P. Appleton.

WILLARD, CYRUS FIELD. Cyrus Field Willard (1858–1935) was born in Lynn, Massachusetts, into a family of six children that moved to South Boston in 1866, where he attended the Bigelow Grammar School. He worked as a reporter on the *Boston Globe* and in 1888 played a major role in forming the first Nationalist Clubs, whose members followed Bellamy's *Looking Backward* (1888). Later, he wrote a regular column for the *Nationalist* (1889–1891). He was a theosophist and integrated those interests with his belief in nationalism. In 1897 he became involved with Eugene Debs' (1855–1926) Social Democracy Party and was the secretary to the colonization committee that searched for land for a socialist colony in the western United States. In 1898 the social democracy convention at Chicago was split on the colonization question, and at the conference Willard argued unsuccessfully for the colonization plan. Later, he joined others in purchasing land at what became known as the Burley Colony, where he stayed for two years. After leaving Burley Colony, he worked for the Theosophical Society until he died in Los Angeles.

See Also Burley Colony

Sources:

Fogarty, Robert S. 1980. *Dictionary of American Communal History.* Westport, Conn.: Greenwood Press.
Oved, Yaacov. 1987. *Two Hundred Years of American Communes.* New Brunswick, N.J.: Transaction Books.

WOLERY, THE. The Wolery was founded in 1977 close to Albany, Western Australia. Several members of the Humanist Society purchased jointly 160 acres (sixty-five hectares) for their settlement. At first local opinion was firmly against their putting several dwellings on the property, but at state level an appeal forced the local council to allow the settlement. Twenty-five members are there today. Members have made equal financial contributions and donate their money and labor on communal projects. The community is administered by a monthly or more frequent meeting, where consensus is the ideal. A 75 percent majority is accepted for decision making. New members are selected with much caution, as the constitution contains no expulsion clauses. Residents share tolerant social attitudes and a respect for beauty in the environment. The Wolery takes its name from the home of Owl, referred to as ''Wol,'' in the British children's classic *Winnie the Pooh* (1926) by A. A. Milne (1882–1956).

Sources:

Conochie, Enid. 1995. ''From Communism to Communalism.'' In Bill Metcalf, ed., *From Utopian Dreaming to Communal Reality: Cooperative Life Styles in Australia,* pp. 170–185. Sydney: University of New South Wales Press.

WOMAN IN THE WILDERNESS COMMUNITY. Woman in the Wilderness Community consisted of Pietists—all men—who emigrated to the United States in the seventeenth century to avoid religious persecution in Europe. Expecting that the Kingdom of Heaven was imminent in 1694, forty Pietists, mainly students and university graduates who felt persecuted in their homeland, sailed from Germany to the United States to greet the anticipated millennium. The group landed near Bohemia Manor, Chesapeake Bay, a commune already established in 1683 by the Labadists from Holland and other Northwestern European countries. Their leader was Johann Kelpius (1673–1708), age twenty, a mathematician who had graduated from Altdorf University and become a mystic and a millenarian. Immediately, the group headed for Germantown, Philadelphia, bought 175 acres, and on a hill built a tabernacle, their central residence. Because forty was their symbolic number, the tabernacle was of forty square feet. It housed studies, a cell for each member, and an assembly hall, with an observation tower erected on the roof. Surrounding the tabernacle was a vegetable and herb garden, and from the observation tower the members expected to see evidence of the heavenly bodies that announced the millennium. They named the acreage ''Woman in the Wilderness'' because of their felt isolation while waiting for the Kingdom of Heaven. Curiously enough, the group included no women, and the settlement was not in the wilderness but on a wooded hill close to a populated neighborhood. They did not despair when, at the end of the year, no kingdom appeared. Kelpius helped maintain the belief in the Kingdom of Heaven by regularly postponing the millennium. After his death in 1708 the group began to disperse.

See Also Kelpius, Johann; Labadists

Sources:

Fogarty, Robert S. 1980. *Dictionary of American Communal History.* Westport, Conn.: Greenwood Press.
Oved, Yaacov. 1987. *Two Hundred Years of American Communes.* New Brunswick, N.J.: Transaction Books.

WOMEN'S COMMONWEALTH (SANCTIFICATIONISTS). Martha Mc-Whirter's (1827–1904) Women's Commonwealth began in 1874 with Bible readings in Belton, Texas, and concluded with a celibate community of Sanctified Sisters living in a mansionlike boardinghouse in the District of Columbia and on a farm in Maryland. The group's term for pentecostal vision was ''sanctification'' and took its origin from prayer meetings under the leadership of Martha McWhirter. In 1874, besides the thirty-two original women, there were four unmarried men. Most members were married women of well-to-do families with young children. Their communal tendencies developed gradually as they rebelled against the authoritarianism of their local churches and asserted financial and sexual independence from their spouses. The Sanctified Sisters achieved their aim of financial independence in 1879. They began to live communally, shared work, sold dairy goods, and did laundry. By 1883 they had opened a hotel established at a house inherited by one sister on her husband's death. All members went to New York City in 1890 and that year started Belton's first public library. Membership reached thirty-one in 1891, and their hotel was incorporated as the Central Hotel Company. By 1898 they had leased two more hotels, one in Waco. That year the community moved to Mount Pleasant, Washington, D.C. They lived mainly off their own savings and occasionally took in boarders. In 1903 they bought 120 acres in Maryland. During the life of this group Martha McWhirter was the leader and spiritual guide, and when she died, the colony began to disintegrate. In 1914 the remaining sisters moved to the Maryland farm, and the community lasted a few more years. The commonwealth flourished due to the force of women's moral reform societies and voluntary associations that formed private networks of women, such as Bible study groups and prayer meetings, all making for solidarity among women. This was helped by the strong social reformist and evangelical characteristics of the anti-Calvinist Methodism, as well as the many examples of utopian commitment in nineteenth-century United States that centered on women's economic assets.

See Also McWhirter, Martha White

Sources:

Andreadis, A. Harriette. 1984. "The Women's Commonwealth: Utopia in Nineteenth-Century Texas." In Ruby Rohrlich and Elaine Hoffman Baruch, eds., *Women in Search of Utopia: Mavericks and Mythmakers*, pp. 86–96. New York: Schocken Books.

Chmielewski, Wendy E. 1993. "Heaven on Earth: The Women's Commonwealth, 1867–1983." In Wendy E. Chmielewski, Louis J. Kern, and Marlyn Klee-Hartzell, eds., *Women in Spiritual and Communitarian Societies in the U.S.*, pp. 52–67. Syracuse, N.Y.: Syracuse University Press.

Fogarty, Robert S. 1980. *Dictionary of American Communal History*. Westport, Conn.: Greenwood Press.

Kitch, Sally. 1989. *Chaste Liberation: Celibacy and Female Cultural Staus*. Urbana: University of Illinois Press.

Wright, Gwendolin. 1981. "The Women's Commonwealth: A Nineteenth Century Experiment." *Heresies* 11: 24–27.

WOODCLIFF COMMUNITY. Woodcliff Community, also known as "Lord's Farm," comprised vegetarian celibates who lived on twenty-three acres under the leadership of Paul Blandin Mason (also known as "Mnason") and Mason T. Huntsman. The community flourished in New Jersey, 1889–1907, and by 1906 among its members were about twenty-seven men, eight women, and five children. Many socialists and anarchists visited the community.

See Also Huntsman, Mason T.

Source:

Fogarty, Robert S. 1980. *Dictionary of American Communal History*. Westport, Conn.: Greenwood Press.

WRIGHT, FRANCES. Frances Wright (1795–1852) was born in Dundee, Scotland. She was the heiress to a large fortune and she was a very difficult and rebellious child. At age eighteen she wrote a work that contained the philosophy she followed for life. It was published in 1822 as *A Few Days in Athens*. In 1818 she emigrated to New York City, visited two of the northern and eastern states of the United States, and returned to England in 1820 and composed her *Views of Society and Manners in America* (1821), an unusual appreciation of the United States. In 1824 she returned to the United States with the Marquis de Lafayette (1757–1834) and visited Thomas Jefferson (1743–1826) and James Madison (1751–1836). They approved of her plan of emancipation for Negro slaves. In western Tennessee she invested a large portion of her inheritance in land called Nashoba and tried to give practical advice on her emancipation theory. Within the colony, however, socialist associates introduced the idea of free love in opposition to marriage, and this view wrongfully attached itself to Frances Wright herself. With Robert Dale Owen (1801–1877) of the *New Harmony Gazette*, she appeared as a lecturer attacking religion, the present system of education, the marriage laws, and the subjugation of women. Between 1830 and 1835 she traveled abroad and returned to the United States to continue her writing and lecturing, taking up such issues as birth control and the equal distribution of property between men and women. During her last year she gave much effort to propaganda for the abolition of the banking system.

See Also Nashoba; Owen, Robert Dale and brothers

Sources:

Bensoman, Marilyn. 1984. ''Francis Wright: Utopian Feminist.'' In Ruby Rohrlich and Elaine Hoffman Baruch, eds., *Women in Search of Utopia: Mavericks and Mythmakers*, pp. 62–69. New York: Schocken Books.

Eckhardt, Celia Morris. 1984. *Fanny Wright: Rebel in America*. Cambridge: Harvard University Press.

Egerton, John. 1977. *Visions of Utopia*. Knoxville: University of Tennessee Press.

Kolmerten, Carol A. 1990. *Women in Utopia*. Bloomington: Indiana University Press.

Oved, Yaacov. 1987. *Two Hundred Years of American Communes*. New Brunswick, N.J.: Transaction Books.

Perkins, Alice J. G., and Theresa Wolfson. 1939. *Frances Wright, Free Enquirer: The Study of Temperament*. 1972 ed. Philadelphia: Porcupine Press.

Wright, Frances. 1987. *Fanny Wright Unmasked by Her Own Pen*. Microform. Alexandria, Va.: Chadwyck-Healey.

WRIGHT, FRANK LLOYD. Frank Lloyd Wright (1867–1959) was born and raised in Richmond Center, Wisconsin, and studied civil engineering at the University of Wisconsin. After seeing the collapse of a state building, he sought to integrate the principles of engineering with the art of building. He became the United States' most important architect with his low-built, prairiestyle domestic architecture, timeless furniture designs, and unconventional public buildings. He was introduced to the progressive style of politics by Wisconsin's governor and later took up the ideals of the Progressive Party, for example, conservation, scientific agriculture, hydroelectric power, and a strong rural economy. Wright was greatly influenced by Henry Ford (1863–1947), who saw the automobile as the means for easy access by rural workers to urban markets and offices. Wright was also influenced by the Tennessee Valley Authority project. Usonia was an expression of Wright's antiurban philosophy, on which he lectured at Princeton University in 1930 and insisted that, helped by the automobile and water-powered utilities, people would readily move out of congested cities to a superior and healthy life in the countryside. Wright's Usonian house made this vision a possibility for Americans. His parents' home—like the Usonian home— was a prototype of the all-American residence, inexpensive and mass-producible.

His best-known buildings are the Imperial Hotel in Tokyo (1916–1920); a home, Falling Water, Ohio (1936); Johnson Wax Office, Wisconsin (1936); and New York's Guggenheim Museum (1959).

See Also Usonia

Sources:

Gill, Brendan. 1987. *Many Masks: A Life of Frank Lloyd Wright.* New York: Putnam.

Rosenbaum, Alvin. 1993. *Usonia: Frank Lloyd Wright's Design for America.* Washington, D.C.: Preservation, National Trust for Historic Preservation.

Secrest, Meryle. 1992. *Frank Lloyd Wright.* New York: Alfred A. Knopf.

Twombly, Robert C. 1979. *Frank Lloyd Wright: His Life and Architecture.* New York: Wiley.

Wright, Frank Lloyd. 1932. *An Autobiography.* New York: Longmans, Green.

———. 1941. *On Architecture.* New York: Duell, Sloan, and Pearce.

Y

YAMAGISHI-KAI. Yamagishi-Kai is a Japanese association of kibbutzlike communes. "Kai" means "association," and the name comes from that of Miyoco Yamagishi (fl. 1922–1961). He was a chicken farmer who developed a philosophy of personal development and a theory of social relations (1922). He established a movement comprising over 1,500 members living in communes and 30,000 supporters in Japan. Yamagishi studied Chinese philosophy, nonviolence, Zen Buddhism, Marxism, and anarchism and integrated them. He spread his philosophy by calling together peasant farmers to learn new methods of chicken raising; when the farmers appeared, he had them discuss both chicken raising and his ideas. Results were good, and the movement began in 1953. Three years later Yamagishi promoted seminars to train his followers in the principles of "Kensan," his philosophy, which centered attention on the material and the spiritual, anger management, unity of society, the individual's spirit and body, property and sharing, and how to put his ideas into practice. In 1958 a Yamagishi-Kai Centre was begun at the opening of a large chicken-farming commune at Kasuga. In time other communes were started. In 1961 Yamagishi died. For six weeks his followers argued about how to interpret his philosophy and establish their communal policy in the future. In the conflict many members left; a core group remained, and the original population of 300 was restored with new members. The largest of the Yamagishi-Kai communities is Toyosato (meaning "rich village"). It began on 110 acres in 1970 and has a large dining hall and bathhouses for men and women, the elderly and infirm. Members have a communal house for residents and children to the age of six. At that age the children have their own house. Members are grouped into large, heterogeneous, self-governing "families." Work is run by operating departments related to various farming activities; two members from each department are elected to the governing body. Problems and attitudes toward them are explored and resolved in discussion. In October 1994, 4,808 members lived in thirty-five Yamagishism communes in Japan. Toyosato has 1,613 members. Outside Japan are seven communes, one each in Australia, Brazil, Germany, Thailand, South Korea, Switzerland, and the United States.

Sources:

Fairfield, Richard. 1972. *The Modern Utopian Communes, Japan.* San Francisco: Alternatives Foundation.
Niijima, Atsuyoshi. 1996. "In Pursuit of an Ideal Society—Yamagishi Toyosato." In Bill Metcalf, ed., *Shared Visions, Shared Lives: Communal Living around the Globe.* Forres, Scotland: Findhorn Press.
Popenoe, Cris, and Oliver Popenoe. 1984. *Seeds of Tomorrow.* San Francisco: Harper and Row.

YAMATOYAMA. Yamatoyama is one of the largest intentional communities. In the mid-1980s it had 60,000 Japanese members on 5,000 acres in a valley in the traditional far north of Honshu. It began in 1946, when Seishiro Tazawa (1884–1966) and his son established a Shintoist religious community by originally leasing a tiny region in Aomori. By the late 1960s, with help from the local government, the land managed by the community expanded to 5,000 acres. The community reafforested some land and farmed other areas. It has a construction and real estate company, an organic fertilizer plant, and a bonsai business and offers education in a renowned boarding school to students from all over Japan. The spiritual, environmental, and pacifist religion of the Tazawas gained followers outside the community itself from visitors. The community's publicity includes impressive illustrated books and films.

See Also Tazawa, Seishiro

Sources:

Popenoe, Cris, and Oliver Popenoe. 1984. *Seeds of Tomorrow.* San Francisco: Harper and Row.
Yasusaburo, Tazawa. 1980. *My Response to the Challenge of Peace.* Aomori, Japan: Yamatoyama.

YELLOW SPRINGS COMMUNITY. Yellow Springs was a short-lived Owenite community in Yellow Springs, Ohio. Daniel Rowe (fl. 1820s), a Swedenborgian minister from Cincinnati, founded the community. In 1822 Rowe's congregation in Cincinnati split over their religious practices; two years later, after he met Robert Owen (1771–1858), Rowe turned from anticlericalism to socialism. The community was modeled on New Harmony and was expected to thrive on the basis of a community of interests. They agreed that all additional property they might later acquire would be added to the common trust for the benefit of all. The community soon disbanded because of factions. According to its leaders, a community of social equality had become impossible. The women were dissatisfied with the extraordinary amount of work they had to do and found that the life of equality proposed by Owenites was quite dysfunctional. Little time had been given to the question of who should perform the ceaseless domestic tasks necessary to communal survival. If women were to insist on real equality, the community could not run smoothly. By 1826 only nine members remained on the property; others had established a hotel at Yellow Springs and did not wish to share their profits. In January 1827 the property was returned to the original owners. It was the original Owenite colony in the United States.

See Also Owen, Robert

Sources:

Block, Marguerite Beck. 1932. *The New Church in the New World: A Study of Sweden-borgianism in America.* New York: Holt. 1968 ed., New York: Octagon.

Fogarty, Robert S. 1980. *Dictionary of American Communal History.* Westport, Conn.: Greenwood Press.

Harrison, John F. C. 1969. *Robert Owen and the Owenites in Britain and America: Quest for the New Moral World.* New York: Charles Scribner's Sons.

Kolmerten, Carol A. 1990. *Women in Utopia.* Bloomington: Indiana University Press.

Oved, Yaacov. 1987. *Two Hundred Years of American Communes.* New Brunswick, N.J.: Transaction Books.

Pitzer, Donald E., ed. 1971. *Robert Owen's American Legacy.* Indianapolis: Indiana Historical Society.

YODFAT. Yodfat is an idealistic kibbutz in Israel. Besides Israel's kibbutz movement emerged the moshav, an idealistic society or cooperative. Two types of moshavim arose—*shitufi* and *ovdim.* The *moshav* shitufi has an economy much like the kibbutzim. Yodfat is a moshav shitufi in rocky and hilly Galilee, where cultivation is difficult. Yodfat began in 1952, when twenty high school students who were studying idealistic views of civilization decided to form their own community outside the kibbutz system. They sought government support but were granted none. Unlike other settlements they wanted to establish the proper relation between humankind and God, naturally, humanly, and divinely. Following God's direction, they worked closely on their spiritual mission, refusing to join other settlements. They preferred brotherhood, participation, and a balanced family life to political ideologies like socialism. Also they practiced organic farming. After eight years they were recognized and given 900 acres for reafforestation (1960). Yodfat was firmly established. Except for household items all property is communal, and children live at home and are educated both locally and at a distance. At age six they attend outside school and are given significant responsibilities and helped to develop open, natural relationships. Families pool half their income and follow a policy that each family is basically catered to. Although the economy is primarily agrarian, some income is derived from professional work outside. All members vote for community leaders, who themselves serve, in turn, for limited periods. Meetings are open, and consensus is preferred for decision making. Most members are born in Israel, and others come from the United States, the U.K., and Canada. Yodfat concentrates on spiritual development and practices it in personal life, interpersonal relations, and daily work. It aims for productive and peaceful relations with surrounding Arabs and has successfully integrated spiritual and material worlds.

See Also Kibbutz

Source:

Popenoe, Cris, and Oliver Popenoe. 1984. *Seeds of Tomorrow*, Chapter 15. San Francisco: Harper and Row.

YOUNG, BRIGHAM. Brigham Young (1801–1877) was born in Whitingham, Vermont, and became a carpenter, painter, and glazier in Mendon, New York. In 1830 he saw the *Book of the Mormon* and in 1832 converted to Mormonism through a brother of Joseph Smith (1805–1844), was baptized, and began to preach near Mendon. He was made an elder and preached also in Canada (1832–1833) and in 1835 was appointed to serve the Twelve Apostles of the Church. Between 1839 and 1842 he gained 2,000 followers while visiting England. He directed the Mormon settlement at Nauvoo, Illinois, and in 1844, after Joseph Smith died, he became president. When the Mormons were driven from Nauvoo, he led them to Utah in 1847. In 1847 most Mormons went to Utah and founded Salt Lake City; in 1850 Brigham Young was appointed governor of Utah territory. There was much public controversy over the Mormon practice of polygamy, and in 1857 a new governor was sent with troops to suppress the practice. In 1869, when another governor was appointed, he much reduced Young's authority. Young was a farsighted administrator, was highly practical, encouraged agriculture, manufactures, and the building of roads and bridges, and saw a contract through for 100 miles of the Union Pacific Railroad. When he died, he left $2.5 million to his seventeen wives and fifty-six children.

See Also Mormons; Smith, Joseph

Sources:

Arrington, Leonard. 1985. *Brigham Young: American Moses*. New York: A. A. Knopf.
Bringhurst, Newell. 1986. *Brigham Young*. Edited by Oscar Handlin. Boston: Little, Brown.
Magnussen, Magnus, and Rosemary Goring, eds. 1990. *Chambers Biographical Dictionary*. 5th ed. Edinburgh: Chambers.
Palmer, Richard F., and Karl D. Butler. 1982. *Brigham Young: The New York Years*. Salt Lake City, Utah: Charles Redd Center for Western Studies.
Stott, Clifford L. 1984. *Search for Sanctuary*. Salt Lake City: University of Utah Press.
Werner, Morris R. 1925. *Brigham Young*. New York: Harcourt, Brace.

YUNUS, MUHAMMAD. Muhammad Yunus (b. 1940) was born in Bangladesh. His father was a gold trader. Yunus was an outstanding pupil in high school, became a Boy Scout, at twelve visited West Pakistan and India, and at fifteen participated in the World Jamboree in Canada. He came home to Chittagong via New York, Washington, D.C., England, and Iraq and through many Indian cities. After high school he studied arts and considered becoming a barrister like Gandhi (1869–1948). Yunus studied economics and for his class project started a packaging business. He won a Fulbright Scholarship to a university in Nashville, Tennessee (1965), where he learned the value of having a choice. Yunus completed his Ph.D. at Vanderbilt University and taught at Tennessee State University and in Colorado and Washington, D.C., where he lobbied to stop military aid to Pakistan (1971). He married and returned to Bangladesh in 1972 after independence. A senior economist with a new government, he resigned because of the corrupt, inefficient bureaucracy. After becoming head of the Economics Department of Chittagong University, he introduced democratic staff–student relations and with a Ford Foundation grant established a Rural Economic Program and became well known in the local village. In response to local poverty, he and his students worked for socioeconomic change in the villages by raising the education level of inhabitants. Early plans were moderately effective. Economic development theories did not solve the poverty problems of the landless—half the population—who had to beg and steal to live. In 1976 he advocated a self-reliant approach to poverty in villages. Opponents disagreed that real power would reach the poor through village politics because the rich would always take control. That year he found a solution: lend the poor women money to purchase material for making the products that they could sell. The women repaid the tiny loans. Because no bank would lend the women money, he decided to form a village bank, a "Grameen" bank. In time similar banks appeared in Malaysia, Malawi, Philippines, Africa, and South and North America. Conventional banks held that credit is appropriate for only fortunate people. Yunus showed that by changing the environment of impoverished villages, capable, intelligent residents can prosper sufficiently to escape poverty. The Grameen bank began to insist its borrowers save for emergencies, to provide for death benefits, and to establish a village medical support system. By 1994 the bank revolved its loan capital five times and helped millions move from two to three meals daily, pay for their children's education, build houses, buy medicine, save for old age, and pay for their daughters' weddings. Yunus now lectures on the bank.

See Also: Grameen Bank

Sources:

Bornstein, David. 1996. *The Price of a Dream*. Dhaka, Bangladesh: University Press; New York: Simon and Schuster.

Yunus, Muhammad, ed. 1991 *Jorimon and Others; Faces of poverty*. Translated by Syed Manzourul Islam, and Arifa Raman. Dhaka: University Press.

Z

ZAMENHOF, LAZARUS LUDWIG. Dr. Lazarus Ludwig Zamenhof (1859–1917), the eldest son in a Jewish family, was born in Bialystok, in Russian Poland. His father taught languages in an effort to integrate Jews and Gentiles in a community of Russians, Poles, and Germans. Lazarus was much impressed by the hostility he saw in Bialystok between the main ethnic groups. He was also impressed by the tale in the Bible about the Tower of Babel and at age ten wrote a five-act tragedy on the theme of conflict and set the scene in his hometown. He began to see that mutual understanding was necessary between the ethnic groups if tensions between them were to dissipate. The family moved to Warsaw, where Lazarus studied languages and sciences and took a medical degree (1885). He studied ophthalmology in Vienna (1886). Feeling unsuited to general practice, Lazarus returned to his youthful interest in ethnic conflicts and the belief that national and racial tensions were exacerbated by language differences. He concluded that a language of the world would help promote understanding and peace. With high hopes he devised Esperanto and advocated his system in 1887 with the publication in Russian of *Lingvo Internacia de la Doktoro Esperanto* (An International Language by Doctor Esperanto).

See Also Esperanto

Source:

Boulton, Marjorie. 1960. *Zamenhof, Creator of Esperanto*. London: Routledge and Kegan Paul.

ZAMYATIN, EVGENY IVANOVICH. Evgeny Ivanovich Zamyatin (1884–1937) was born in central Russia and studied in St. Petersburg; he joined and later abandoned the Bolshevik Party and was arrested and exiled (1905). He began to write in 1908 and supported himself as a lecturer in naval architecture at the St. Petersburg Polytechnic Institute. He went to England during World

War I and at Newcastle upon Tyne supervised the building of a Russian ice-breaker (1995–1916). At the time he was writing stories that criticized life in Britain, much of it being drawn from observing work on the docks. He became known for his love of the good things of England, especially English literature, and after the Russian revolution (1917) he edited collections of works by writers of English. He favored the writings of Jonathan Swift (1667–1745), George Bernard Shaw (1856–1950), and Herbert George Wells (1866–1946); and edited collections of work by Wells, Shaw, and Jack London (1876–1916). In 1920–1921 he published an antiutopian satire, *We*. When it appeared abroad (1924), it so badly affected his reputation in Russia that he emigrated to Paris (1931). His novel owes much to Wells' *When the Sleeper Wakes* (1899) and his ideas on a two-tiered society in *The Time Machine* (1895); Zamyatin thought Wells' utopian novel to be antiutopian, that is, not about ideal societies but rather about exposing the flaws in the social order through the use of dynamic conflicts in the plot. Today this antiutopian theme is a prime element of dystopian literature; consequently, many commentators consider *We* to have greatly influenced Aldous Leonard Huxley (1894–1963) in writing his *Brave New World* (1932)—an assertion Huxley denied—and George Orwell (1903–1950) in his *Nineteen Eighty-Four* (1949).

See Also *Brave New World*; Dystopia; Huxley, Aldous; *Nineteen Eighty-Four;* *We*; Wells, H. G.

Sources:

Booker, M. Keith. 1994. *Dystopian Literature: A Theory and Research Guide*. Westport, Conn.: Greenwood Press.

Kumar, Krishan. 1987. *Utopia and Anti-Utopia in Modern Times*. Oxford: Basil Blackwell.

Snodgrass, Mary Ellen. 1995. *Encyclopedia of Utopian Literature*. Santa Barbara, Calif.: ABC-CLIO.

ZINZENDORF, COUNT NIKOLAUS LUDWIG, GRAF VON. Count Nikolaus Ludwig Graf von Zinzendorf (1700–1760) organized and led the Moravian Brethren. He was born in Dresden, and his family and education taught him Pietism. He studied law at Wittenberg and in 1721 accepted a post in Dresden until he turned to the concerns of his tenants on the Berthelsdorf estate in upper Lusatia. He was mainly interested in a group of refugees from Austria, Bohemia, and Moravia. Many of them had descended from Bohemian Brethren. He supported them as they developed their own Moravian church and in time was ever more involved in their beliefs, eventually becoming convinced that to survive, all communities required Christianity. The church members gathered to sing in choirs, and these provided the basis for communal living and the provision of employment and exchange of food and clothing. In this way he hoped to transform the world through the Gospels and communal life. At first he sponsored the immigrants and was their patron, but later he became their leader by establishing their constitution (1727). He worked to engender a deep love of Christ and a devout common life among the Moravians and worked with great missionary enthusiasm to inspire them as founders of Protestant missionary work abroad. He was ordained as a Lutheran priest in 1734 and later as a bishop of the Unitas Fratrum. Banished from his estate in 1734, he started to establish Moravian settlements abroad. He sailed to the United States (1741–1743) and in New York and Pennsylvania established congregations. His attempts to unite various German Protestant churches met with little success. In 1749 the Church of Unity was recognized in Germany. Nevertheless, he had many enemies who opposed his vision of a worldwide Christian community.

See Also Moravian Bethlehem

Sources:

Magnussen, Magnus, Rosemary Goring, and John O. Thorn, eds. 1990. *Chambers Biographical Dictionary*. Edinburgh: Chambers.

McHenry, Robert, ed. 1992. *The New Encyclopedia Britannica*. Chicago: Encyclopedia Britannica.

Oved, Yaacov. 1987. *Two Hundred Years of American Communes*. New Brunswick, N.J.: Transaction Books.

ZION CITY. Zion City, the short name of the Christian, Catholic, Apostolic Church in Zion, flourished at Zion, Illinois (1901–1906). In 1896 it was organized by John Alexander Dowie (1847–1907), a successful Scottish faith healer. Although Dowie chose Zion City on Lake Michigan (1896) to ensure his followers lived in isolation, it was not meant to be a total withdrawal from the world. Zion's political wing, the Theocratic Party, which would form in 1902, was intended to change the United States' political system. Dowie was an autocrat under whose rule Zion City's population of 8,000 grew rapidly. Although the community was self-contained, the Dowieites did not promote the communal housing and dining often found in utopian ventures. Like an autocratic king Dowie owned all businesses: Zion City Bank, general stores, factories, and fresh fruit supply. His kingdom revolted against him in 1906, and he fell from power largely because finances became unstable. After his fall Dowie's name was dropped from Zion literature, and ''Apostolic'' was extirpated from the organization's title.

See Also Dowie, John Alexander

Sources:

Cook, Philip. 1995. *Zion City, Illinois: Twentieth-Century Utopia. Utopianism and Communitarianism*. Syracuse, N.Y.: Syracuse University Press.

Fogarty, Robert S. 1980. *Dictionary of American Communal History*. Westport, Conn.: Greenwood Press.

ZIONISM. Zionism was a movement that sought to establish the Jewish sovereign nation-state in Palestine. When an independent state of Israel was established in 1748, Zionism was dedicated to sponsoring Jewish immigration to Israel, the Promised Land, to reconstruct Jewish society. In the late nineteenth century the movement gathered pace and owed much to Theodore Herzl. Many utopian ventures of Zionist character established themselves in Palestine, especially when the modern state of Israel was created after World War II. Elsewhere similar and sometimes bizarre schemes were mooted, but failed to take hold, for example, Poynduk.

See Also Altneuland; Herzl, Theodor; Kibbutz; Poynduk; Yodfat

Source:

Roth, Cecil E., ed. 1971. *Encyclopedia Judaica.* New York: Macmillan.

ZOARITES. Zoarites are members of the Society of Separatists of Zoar from Würtemberg, Bavaria, and Baden who came to the United States from Hamburg (1817–1898). Joseph Michael Bimeler (Bäumler) (1778–1853) became their caring leader. They landed in Philadelphia, 14 August 1817. They were received and cared for by members of the Society of Friends who helped them to buy 5,500 acres of upland, well provided with forest, in Tuscarawas County, Ohio. With a few others Bimeler led the main party, cleared the ground for crops, built a cabin, and set out the village of Zoar, which was named for the small city to which Lot had fled from Sodom and Gomorrah. To support the colony, members had to pay for their land: to achieve this they agreed that no one was to marry and that husbands were to live away from their wives; and although it was against Bimeler's own judgment, members adopted a community of goods. The colony became prosperous. The land was paid for, and marriage was reintroduced. Bimeler married. Zoar established a brewery, flour mill, and woolen and linen manufacturing. Although the ironworks did not prosper, Bimeler kept the plant in operation so outsiders employed in it could retain their living. With the establishment of a sound economic base under the community's spiritual life, Zoar became successful; for example, there were no criminals in the community, and the village jail was used for visitors. Bimeler enjoyed some extra comforts himself, and in response a few malcontents took legal action against him and even took their suit to have the property partitioned before the U.S. Supreme Court. The Court upheld the society, vindicated Bimeler's administration, and regarded him as well above reproach, a man of great energy and capacity for business. Shortly after Bimeler died, the colony lost its vigor, and after the Civil War (1861–1865) the community declined economically, and in 1898 the remaining 222 members divided the property.

See Also Bimeler, Joseph Michael

Sources:

Berry, Brian J. 1992. *America's Utopian Experiments: Communal Havens from Long-Wave Crises.* Hanover, N.H.: University Press of New England.
Fogarty, Robert S. 1980. *Dictionary of American Communal History.* Westport, Conn.: Greenwood Press.

Nordhoff, Charles. 1875. *The Communistic Societies of the U.S.* Reprinted, 1960. New York: Hillary House.

Nixon, Edgar B. 1973. ''Applicants for Membership in Zoar.'' In Rosabeth Moss Kanter, *Communes: Creating and Managing the Collective Life*, pp. 88–96. New York: Harper and Row.

Oved, Yaacov. 1987. *Two Hundred Years of American Communes*. New Brunswick, N.J.: Transaction Books.

SELECTED READINGS

The most valuable source for modern discussions and book reviews of utopia and utopians is the journal *Utopian Studies*, published by the Society for Utopian Studies. Following appears a select list of utopian works. Readers who want a dictionary of utopian Literature should turn to Mary Ellen Snodgrass, 1995, *Encyclopedia of Utopian Literature* (Santa Barbara, Calif.: ABC-CLIO). Those who want a comprehensive catalog and recent critical review of the concept should turn to Lyman Tower Sargent, 1988, *British and American Utopian Literature: 1516–1985. An Annotated Chronological Bibliography* (New York: Garland); and Lyman Tower Sargent, 1994, ''The Three Faces of Utopianism Revisited,''*Utopian Studies* 5, no. 1: 1–37. For an introduction to dystopian writing see M. Keith Booker, 1994, *Dystopian Literature: A Theory and Research Guide* (Westport, Conn.: Greenwood).

Armytage, Walter H. Green. 1961. *Heavens Below: Utopian Experiments in England 1560–1950.* London: Routledge and Kegan Paul.

Baker, Robert S. 1990. *Brave New World: History, Science, and Dystopia.* Boston: Twayne.

Bammer, Angelika. 1991. *Partial Visions: Feminism and Utopianism in the 1970s.* London: Routledge.

Beecher, Jonathan, and Richard Bienvenu, eds. 1972. *The Utopian Vision of Charles Fourier: Selected Papers on Work, Love and Passionate Attraction.* London: Cape.

Beilharz, Peter. 1992. *Labour's Utopias: Bolshevism, Fabianism, Social Democracy.* London: Routledge.

Bellamy, Edward. 1888. *Looking Backward: 2000–1887.* Boston: Ticknor (later, Houghton Mifflin). Edited with introduction by Daniel H. Borus, 1995, St. Martin's Press, Bedford Books.

Bestor, Arthur, Jr. 1950. *Backwoods Utopias: The Sectarian and Owenite Phases of Communitarian Socialism in America, 1663–1829.* Philadelphia: University of Pennsylvania Press.

Bloch, Ernst. 1988. *The Utopian Function of Art and Literature: Selected Essays*. Cambridge Mass.: MIT Press.

Bowman, Sylvia E., et al. 1962. *Edward Bellamy Abroad: An American Prophet's Influence*. New York: Twayne.

Brian, Joe Lobley. 1992. *America's Utopian Experiments: Communal Havens from Long-Wave Crises*. Hanover, N.H.: University Press of New England.

Chmielewski, Wendy E., J. Louis Kern, and Marlyn Klee-Hartzell, eds. 1993. *Women in Spiritual and Communitarian Societies in the U.S.* Syracuse, N.Y.: Syracuse University Press.

Claeys, Gregory, ed. 1994. *Utopias of the British Enlightenment*. New York: Cambridge University Press.

———. 1997. *Modern British Utopias, 1700–1850*. 8 vols. London: Pickering and Chatto.

Cock, Peter. 1979. *Alternative Australia: Communities of the Future?* Melbourne: Quartet Books.

Conway, Ronald. 1992. *The Rage for Utopia*. Sydney: Allen and Unwin.

Dare, Philip N. 1990. *American Communes to 1860: A Bibliography*. New York: Garland.

Davis, J. C. 1981. *Utopia and the Ideal Society: A Study of English Utopian Writing*. Cambridge: Cambridge University Press.

Egerton, John. 1977. *Visions of Utopia: Nashoba, Rugby, Ruskin and the "New Communities" in Tennessee's Past*. Knoxville: University of Tennessee Press.

Eliav-Feldon, Miriam. 1982. *Realistic Utopias: The Ideal Imaginary Societies of the Renaissance, 1516–1630*. Oxford: Clarendon Press.

Erasmus, Charles. 1977. *In Search of the Common Good: Utopian Experiments Past and Future*. New York: Free Press.

Ferguson, John. 1975. *Utopias of the Classical World*. Ithaca, N.Y.: Cornell University Press.

Fogarty, Robert S. 1972. *American Utopianism*. Itasca, Ill.: F. E. Peacock.

———. 1980. *Dictionary of American Communal History*. Westport, Conn.: Greenwood Press.

———. 1990. *All Things New: American Communes and Utopian Movements 1860–1914*. Chicago: University of Chicago Press.

Fox, Richard G. 1989. *Gandhian Utopia: Experiment with Culture*. Boston: Beacon Press.

Franklin, B. 1981. *America as Utopia*. New York: B. Franklin.

Gilbert, James B. 1991. *Perfect Cities: Chicago's Utopias of 1893*. Chicago: University of Chicago Press.

Gill, Roger. 1984. "In England's Green and Pleasant Land." In Peter Alexander and Roger Gill, eds., *Utopias*, pp. 109–117. London: Duckworth.

Golffing, Francis. 1990. *Possibility: An Essay in Utopian Vision*. New York: P. Lang.

Goodwin, Barbara. 1982. *The Politics of Utopia: Study in Theory and Practice*. New York: St. Martin's Press.

Hall, John R. 1978. *The Ways Out: Utopian Communal Groups in an Age of Babylon*. London: Routledge and Kegan Paul.

Harrison, John F. C. 1969. *Robert Owen and the Owenites in Britain and America: Quest for the New Moral World*. New York: Charles Scribner's Sons.

Hine, Robert V. 1953. *California's Utopian Colonies*. 1983 ed. Berkeley: University of California Press.

Holloway, M. 1951. *Heavens on Earth: Utopian Communities in America: 1680–1880*. New York: Dover.

Jones, Libby F. and Sarah W. Goodwin, eds. 1990. *Feminism, Utopia and Narrative*. Knoxville: University of Tennessee Press.

Kanter, Rosabeth Moss. 1972. *Communes: Creating and Managing the Collective Life*. Cambridge, Mass.: Harvard University Press.

———. 1973. *Communes: Creating and Managing the Collective Life*. New York: Harper and Row.

Kesten, Seymour 1993. *Utopian Episodes: Daily Life in Experimental Colonies Dedicated to Changing the World*. Syracuse, N.Y. Syracuse University Press.

Klaw, Spencer. 1993. *Without Sin: The Life and Death of the Oneida Community*. New York: Penguin Books.

Knapp, Jeffrey. 1992. *An Empire Nowhere: England, America, and Literature from Utopia to The Tempest*. Berkeley: University of California Press.

Kumar, Krishan. 1987. *Utopia and Anti-Utopia in Modern Times*. Oxford: Basil Blackwell.

———. 1991. *Utopianism*. Milton Keynes: Open University Press.

Levin, Bernard. 1994. *A World Elsewhere*. London: Cape.

Levitas, Ruth. 1990. *The Concept of Utopia*. London: Philip Allon.

LeWarne, Charles Pierce. 1975. *Utopias on Puget Sound, 1885–1915*. Seattle: University of Washington Press.

Lukashevich, Stephen. 1977. *N. F. Fedorov (1828–1903): A Study of Russian Eupsychian and Utopian Thought*. Newark: University of Delaware Press.

Manuel, Frank Edward. 1966. *French Utopias: An Anthology of Ideal Societies*. New York: Free Press.

———, ed. 1966. *Utopias and Utopian Thought*. Boston: Houghton Mifflin.

Manuel, Frank Edward, and Fritzie P. Manuel. 1979. *Utopian Thought in the Western World*. Cambridge, Mass.: Harvard University, Belknap Press.

Marsh, Jan. 1982. *Back to the Land: The Pastoral Impulse in England, from 1880 to 1914*. London: Quartet.

McCord, William. 1989. *Voyages to Utopia: From Monastery to Commune, the Search for the Perfect Society in Modern Times*. New York: W. W. Norton.

McLaughlin, Corinne. 1985. *Builders of the Dawn: Community Lifestyles in a Changing World*. Walpole, N.H.: Stillpoint.

Metcalf, Bill, ed. 1995. *From Utopian Dreaming to Communal Reality: Cooperative Life Styles in Australia*. Sydney: University of New South Wales Press.

———. 1996. *Shared Visions, Shared Lives: Communal Living around the Globe*. Forres, Scotland: Findhorn Press.

Miller, Timothy. 1990. *American Communes 1860–1960*. New York: Garland.

Molner, Thomas S. 1990. *Utopia: The Perennial Heresy*. Lanham, Md.: University Press of America.

Moos, Rudolf H. 1977. *Environment and Utopia: A Synthesis*. New York: Plenum Press.

Morely, Henry, ed. 1968. *Ideal Commonwealth: Comprising More's Utopia, Bacon's New Atlantis, Campanella's City of the Sun and Harrington's Oceana*. Port Washington, N.Y.: Kennikat Press.

Mumford, Lewis. 1922. *The Story of Utopias*. 1962 ed. New York: Viking.

Negley, Glenn R., and J. Max Patrick, eds. 1953. *The Quest for Utopia: An Anthology of Imaginary Societies*. 1971 ed. College Park, Md.: McGrath.

Negley, Glenn Roberts. 1977. *Utopian Literature: A Bibliography with a Supplementary Listing of Works Influential in Utopian Thought.* Lawrence: Regents Press of Kansas.

Nursey-Bray, Paul F., ed. 1992. *Anarchist Thinkers and Thought: An Annotated Bibliography.* Westport, Conn.: Greenwood Press.

Oved, Yaacov. 1987. *Two Hundred Years of American Communes.* New Brunswick, N.J.: Transaction Books.

Pitzer, Donald E. 1984. "Collectivism, Community and Commitment: America's Religious Communal Utopias from the Shakers to Jonestown." In Peter Alexander and Roger Gill, eds., *Utopias,* pp. 119–135. London: Duckworth.

Plottel, Martin G. 1972. *Utopian and Critical Thinking.* Pittsburgh: Duquesne University Press.

Popenoe, Cris, and Oliver Popenoe. 1984. *Seeds of Tomorrow.* San Francisco: Harper and Row.

Rasporich, Anthony W. 1992. "Utopian Ideals and Community Settlements in Western Canada 1880–1914." In R. Douglas Francis and Howard Palmer, eds., *The Prairie West: Historical Readings,* 2d ed., pp. 338–361. Edmonton, Alberta: Pica Pica Press.

Ricoeur, Paul. 1986. *Lectures on Ideology and Utopia.* New York: Columbia University Press.

Roberts, Leslie J. 1991. "Étienne Cabet and His *Voyage en Icarie* 1840." *Utopian Studies* 2, nos. 1, 2: 77–94.

Rohlich, Ruby, and Elaine Baruch, eds. 1984. *Women in Search of Utopia, Mavericks and Mythmakers.* New York: Schocken Books.

Sargent, Lyman Tower. 1967. "Three Faces of Utopianism." *Minnesota Review* 7, no. 3: 222–230.

———.1979. *British and American Utopian Literature: 1516–1975.* Boston: G. K. Hall.

———1988. *British and American Utopian Literature: 1516–1985. An Annotated Chronological Bibliography.* New York: Garland

———. 1994. "The Three Faces of Utopianism Revisited." *Utopian Studies* 5, no. 1: 1–37.

Shencker, Barry. 1986. *International Communities: Ideology and Alienation in Communal Societies.* London: Routledge and Kegan Paul.

Spann, Edward K. 1989. *Brotherly Tomorrows: Movements for a Cooperative Society in America 1820–1920.* New York: Columbia University Press.

Spiro, M. E. 1956. *Kibbutz: Venture into Utopia.* Boston: Harvard University Press; 1963 ed. New York: Schocken.

Stites, Richard. 1989. *Revolutionary Dreams: Utopian Vision and Experimental Life in the Russian Revolution.* New York: Oxford University Press.

Stobbart, Lorraine. 1992. *Utopia, Fact or Fiction?: The Evidence from the Americas.* London: Alan Sutton.

Taylor, Keith. 1981. *The Political Ideas of the Utopian Socialists.* London: Cass.

TeSelle, Sallie, ed. 1971. *The Family, Communes, and Utopian Societies.* New York: Harper and Row.

Thomas, John L. 1983. *Alternative America: Henry George, Edward Bellamy, Henry Demarest Lloyd, and the Adversary Tradition.* Cambridge, Mass: Harvard University Press, Belknap Press.

Tod, Ian, and Michael Wheeler. 1978. *Utopia.* New York: Harmony Books.

Tuveson, Ernest Lee. 1972. *Millennium and Utopia: A Study in the Background of the Idea of Progress*. Gloucester, Mass.: Peter Smith.

Veysey, Laurence. 1973. *The Communal Experience: Anarchist and Mystical Counter-cultures in America*. New York: Harper and Row.

Walters, Kerry S. 1988. *The Sane Society Ideal in Modern Utopianism*. Lewiston, Queenstown, and New York: Edwin Mellen Press.

Whitworth, John McKelvie. 1975. *God's Blueprints: A Sociological Study of Three Utopian Sects*. London: Routledge and Kegan Paul.

Zablocki, Ben David. 1980. *Alienation and Charisma: A Study of Contemporary American Communes*. New York: Free Press.

Zedek, Simon. 1993. *An Economics of Utopia: The Democratization of Scarcity*. London: New Economics Foundation.

INDEX

Page numbers in **bold type** refer to main entries in the dictionary.

About the Author

RICHARD C. S. TRAHAIR is Social Research Advisor and Consulting Psychologist in the School of Sociology, Politics, and Anthropology at La Trobe University-Australia. His previous books include *From Aristotelian to Reaganomics: A Dictionary of Eponyms with Biographies in the Social Sciences* (Greenwood, 1994).

ISBN 0-313-29465-8

EAN

90000>

9 780313 294655

HARDCOVER BAR CODE